SIR NICHOLAS HARRIS NICOLAS was born in 1799, and served in the Royal Navy in the Mediterranean from 1808 to 1816 under Admiral Duckworth and Lord Exmouth. Retired on half-pay at the end of the Napoleonic Wars, he turned to antiquarian and literary pursuits after a brief legal career, compiling and editing a large number of scholarly works. This seven-volume annotated compilation of Nelson's correspondence was originally published by Henry Colburn between 1844 and 1847, and was to be followed by his ambitious *A History of the British Navy, from the Earliest Times to the Wars of the French Revolution*, but when he died in France in 1848, only the first two volumes, covering up to the year 1422, had been completed.

THE

# DISPATCHES AND LETTERS

OF

VICE ADMIRAL

# LORD VISCOUNT NELSON

WITH NOTES BY

## SIR NICHOLAS HARRIS NICOLAS, G.C.M.G.

" The Nation expected, and was entitled to expect, that while Cities vied with each other
in consecrating Statues in marble and brass to the memory of our NELSON, a Literary Monument would be erected, which should record his deeds for the immortal honour of his own
Country, and the admiration of the rest of the World." — QUARTERLY REVIEW.

## THE THIRD VOLUME.

JANUARY 1798 TO AUGUST 1799.

CHATHAM PUBLISHING

LONDON

Published in 1997 by
Chatham Publishing,
1 & 2 Faulkner's Alley, Cowcross Street,
London EC1M 6DD

Chatham Publishing is an imprint of
Gerald Duckworth and Co Ltd

First Published in 1845
by Henry Colburn

ISBN 1 86176 050 7

A catalogue record for this book is available
from the British Library

Printed and bound in Great Britain by
Redwood Books, Trowbridge, Wiltshire

# PREFACE.

Though the Letters in the present Volume relate only to about one year and eight months (namely, from the 1st of January 1798, to the 31st of August 1799), they illustrate, perhaps, the most important as well as most interesting events of Nelson's Life,—the first of his brilliant Victories, and the only transactions in his professional career to which blame has ever been attached.

Having hoisted his Flag on board the Vanguard, in March 1798, and joined the Earl of St. Vincent's Fleet, off Cadiz, he was sent in May, with a Squadron of observation, up the Mediterranean. Early in June, he was re-inforced by ten Sail of the Line, when he proceeded in search of the French Fleet to Naples, and thence to Alexandria; but not finding it, he returned to Syracuse, from which place he again sailed for Egypt. His anxiety to discover the Enemy, and his disappointment at missing them, are the principal subjects of his Correspondence, until his exertions were at last rewarded by finding the French Fleet at anchor in Aboukir Bay, on the 1st of August 1798, when he achieved a greater Naval Victory than had ever adorned the British Annals.

His celebrated Dispatch after the Battle of the Nile, has been illustrated by the clear and modest Narrative of his Captain, Sir Edward Berry; by the Vanguard's Log; by Letters from some of his Captains, written immediately after the Action; and by the French Rear-Admiral Blanquet's official account of it. All the facts respecting the only two disputed points connected with that Event have also been collected. To these illustrations are added the Letters which were addressed to NELSON after his Victory, by Sir William Hamilton and Sir John Acton, describing the general joy at Naples, and the gratitude of the King, Queen, and Royal Family for his success; and those from the Earl and Countess Spencer—whose letter was worthy of a Roman matron—when the news reached England. An account of the Honours and Rewards conferred upon him by his Sovereign, by Parliament, by the Country, and by Foreign Monarchs, is likewise given, together with the Letters of congratulation from two of his old personal friends, Lady Parker and the Duke of Clarence, and from most of the great Naval Veterans of the day, Admirals Earl Howe, the Earl of St. Vincent, Viscount Hood, Goodall, and Roger Curtis, and from Captains Collingwood and Locker. The brief account of the Captains who commanded Ships in the Battle,—that " Band of Brothers," as NELSON so affectionately and so emphatically called them,—cannot be considered mis-placed.

Between the 1st and the 19th of August, when NELSON sailed from Aboukir Bay for Naples, his Letters were chiefly about the disposition of the Prizes, and the French Army in Egypt. He arrived at Naples on the 22nd of September, and remained there until the middle of October, refitting "the poor wretched Vanguard." His Correspondence at that time relates to the state of the Kingdom of Naples, to the French Armies in Italy, and to the blockade of Malta, to which Island he proceeded in October; but agreeably to a promise he had made to his Sicilian Majesty, he returned to Naples on the 5th of November. On the 17th of that month, he learnt that he had been created a Peer by the Title of "BARON NELSON of the Nile, and of Burnham Thorpe, in the County of Norfolk," — a reward certainly inadequate to his services; and, in common with almost every other person, he felt that he had not received the Honours to which he was justly entitled.

About that time, the Sicilian Squadron was placed under his orders, as the Portuguese had been im-mediately after the Battle of the Nile. Towards the end of November LORD NELSON went with a small Squadron to Leghorn, which surrendered on his appear-ance, and he immediately returned to Naples, where he continued until the 21st of December, when the ap-proach of the French Army compelled the King, Queen, and Royal Family, many of the principal persons of the Court, together with the British Minister, Sir William Hamilton, Lady Hamilton, and the other English in that City, to proceed to Palermo.

LORD NELSON, who was promoted to the rank of REAR-ADMIRAL OF THE RED, on the 14th of February 1799, continued at Palermo until May, during which period his Letters relate chiefly to the reduction of La Valetta, in Malta; to the appointment of Captain Sir Sidney Smith, the Joint-Minister at the Ottoman Porte, to, as he erroneously supposed, a separate command in Egypt; to the defence of Sicily; to the condition of Naples, (then in the hands of the French,) to which city he had sent several Ships under Captain Troubridge ; and to the conduct of the Barbary States.

Intelligence having arrived on the 13th of May, that the French Fleet had passed the Straits of Gibraltar and was expected in Sicily, LORD NELSON collected all his Squadron from Naples and Malta, and proceeded off Maritimo ; but he returned to Palermo on the 29th of May. In June, he quitted the Vanguard for the Foudroyant, which had been sent out for his Flag ; and, at the earnest request of the King of the Two Sicilies, he sailed on the 13th of that month for Naples, with the design of expelling the French forces and subduing the Neapolitan Republicans, having on board the Prince Royal, many Sicilian Officers, and a large body of Troops. The next day, however, LORD NELSON received information respecting the Enemy's Fleet, which induced him, for the moment, to abandon that expedition, and to repair with his whole Squadron off Maritimo, merely touching at Palermo to land the Sicilian Prince and his *suite*. But other intelligence on the 20th having enabled him to resume that design, he arrived at Palermo on the 21st; and after embarking Sir William and Lady Hamilton, sailed with his Squadron of eighteen Ships of the Line to Naples, where he arrived in the afternoon of the 24th of June.

LORD NELSON'S proceedings after his arrival at Naples are among the most important, and have been generally considered as the only unfortunate part of his public life. As the duties of an Editor are distinct from those of a Biographer, he might without impropriety have contented himself with collecting, and placing before the world all the documents that he could discover on the subject ; but he trusts that he shall, under the peculiar circumstances of the case, be excused for attempting more.

Finding that the heaviest accusations with which it is possible to charge an Officer, or a Man, have been brought against LORD NELSON, by Authors of every degree of literary reputation, and that the latest among those Writers, who to high intellectual powers unites eminent station, has said of NELSON—that " seduced by the " profligate arts of one woman, and the perilous fasci- " nations of another, he lent himself to a proceeding " deformed by the blackest colours of treachery and " murder," it seemed imperative upon the Editor to investigate those transactions, to be the relater of every fact, and without becoming the advocate to be at least

the expounder of what fairly appear to have been
NELSON'S conscientious motives and opinions, in the
arduous situation in which he was placed.

After inserting in their proper places all the Letters and
other Documents written by LORD NELSON respecting the
Capitulation of Castel Nuovo and Castel del Uovo, and
the trial and execution of Caraccioli, the Editor has
placed in the APPENDIX *every* other Document he could
discover in all the repositories to which he has had
access. He has withheld nothing which can, in any
way, throw light upon those affairs, while his anxiety
to collect information is shown by the numerous sources
from which papers and facts on the subject have been
obtained.

He will not anticipate the judgment of LORD NELSON'S
conduct, which these new facts, and the exposure of the
ignorance, prejudice, and falsehoods that more or less
pervade every statement on the subject, may induce his
countrymen to form. It may still be the opinion of some,
notwithstanding the authorities referred to, that NELSON
was mistaken in thinking that the disobedience of Cardinal Ruffo to his Sovereign's order not to treat with
Rebels, and his arrival *before* the Capitulation was
begun to be carried into execution, justified him in
reserving it for the determination of the King of the Two
Sicilies; but it must be admitted that these were questions which fairly presented themselves to his mind; that
his right to suspend the execution of the Capitulation is
supported by the opinions of eminent writers, and by

the usage of Nations; and that even an erroneous decision might have been formed upon them, conscientiously and honestly. It may also be thought by some that the execution of Caraccioli was an act of unnecessary severity; but no candid mind will discover, in these transactions, aught that is inconsistent with the belief that NELSON acted only from the spontaneous and genuine dictates of his own judgment, and in obedience to a scrupulous sense of duty.

However harsh LORD NELSON may be considered for having ordered the execution of Caraccioli, it is certain that he had full authority for the purpose, that the sufferer was not in any degree protected by the Capitulation of Uovo and Nuovo, and that he merited whatever may be deemed the proper punishment due to an Officer of high rank, who, in the command of an armed Force, fires upon a Ship bearing the colours of his own Sovereign.

Death, it has been said, " canonizes and sanctifies a great character;"—but neither a death the most glorious, nor a life the most honourable has prevented NELSON'S integrity and motives from being suspected and aspersed, chiefly, it is painful to remark, by men of his own profession. It has been found necessary to advert freely in this Volume to the conduct of the late Vice-Admiral Sir Edward James Foote, K.C.B., who signed the Capitulation of Uovo and Nuovo, as well on the occasion of that Capitulation, as in assailing LORD NELSON'S character after his death. That Officer is unfortu-

nately no more; but as the death of NELSON did not
restrain him from severely arraigning his Admiral's share
in those transactions, his own death must not now be
allowed to stop the inquiry, whether the conduct which
he himself adopted at the time was such as to entitle
him (of all men in the world) to stand forth as the
accuser of NELSON.

Little more need be said in this place respecting
matters, upon which, for the first time, all the evidence
has been brought together, except to add the important
fact, recently ascertained, that while historians and biographers have found nothing in LORD NELSON's conduct but weakness, cruelty, and treachery, and while
scarcely one of them even allows him the merit of having acted from an honest sense of duty, yet in the
opinion of Earl Spencer, then First Lord of the Admiralty—a Statesman of the highest honour, and of
singular humanity of character—written soon after, and
evidently with reference to his proceedings at Na les,
" the intentions and motives by which all his measures
" had been governed, had been as pure and good as their
" success had been complete." [1]

As soon as LORD NELSON obtained possession of the
Castles of Uovo and Nuovo, he took measures for investing that of St. Elmo, by landing the Seamen and Marines
of his Squadron under Captain Troubridge, which Fortress
soon surrendered. That gallant Officer shortly afterwards
succeeded in taking Gaeta and Capua, and these pro-

[1] Vide p. 509.

ceedings form the subject of many of LORD NELSON'S Letters in this Volume.

On the 10th of July 1799, the King of the Two Sicilies arrived at Naples; but he was not, as has generally been said, accompanied by the Queen—a fact of some importance, because it proves that the presence of her Majesty could not, as has been asserted, have influenced LORD NELSON's conduct there. The King remained on board the Foudroyant, in Naples Bay, until the French were expelled from his Dominions, and the Neapolitan Republicans reduced to obedience. His Sicilian Majesty then returned to Palermo in the Foudroyant; and on the 13th of August, LORD NELSON was created DUKE OF BRONTE, the feudal estate of Bronté, in Sicily, being annexed to the Title. Shortly before he received that Dignity, the East India Company had marked its sense of his services at the Nile, by voting him ten thousand pounds; and the Letters in which he directed a large part of that sum to be given to his family, and informed his father that he had appropriated a portion of the revenue of the Bronté estate to his use, display the kindness and generosity of his heart.

About that time, LORD NELSON ventured to disobey the orders of his Commander-in-Chief, Lord Keith, who had directed him to send his Squadron for the protection of Minorca, for which disobedience he was censured by the Admiralty. His Letters on the subject are of much professional value, as they prove that though he did not hesitate to risk his Commission, by taking upon him the greatest responsibility an Officer can incur, yet, with a proper sense of discipline, he submitted, without remonstrance, to the reproof of his Superiors.

Since the publication of the second Volume of this Work, the Editor has obtained additional materials of great value. It will be perceived that the authority for most of the Documents now printed, is LORD NELSON'S "Letter-Book," or "Order-Book,"—manuscript volumes, containing a full copy of all his public, and of many of his private Letters, and of every Order issued by him. These important Manuscripts, together with a very large collection of Letters and other Papers, (of a similar kind to those entrusted to the Editor by Lord Bridport, and referred to as "the Nelson Papers,") are in the possession of the Right Honourable John Wilson Croker; and he not only begs leave to offer Mr. Croker his warmest thanks for the service which he has conferred upon the Public, by placing those Documents at the Editor's disposal, but he desires to express his deep sense of the frankness and kindness with which the favour was conferred, and his gratitude for many valuable suggestions.

Another important accession is a collection of very interesting Letters from LORD NELSON to the late Right Honourable Hugh Elliot, when Minister at the Court of Sicily, for which he is indebted to his son, the Reverend Gilbert Elliot.

To Lady Egerton, wife of Lieutenant-General Sir Charles Bulkeley Egerton, G.C.M.G., and daughter of

the most esteemed and most loved of all NELSON'S
Companions—the late Rear-Admiral Sir Thomas Troubridge, Bart.,—the Editor is under much obligation for
permission to make extracts from the Journal of the
late Miss Knight, daughter of Rear-Admiral Sir Joseph
Knight.  Miss Knight, whose literary works are well-
known, and who was afterwards Preceptress to Her
Royal Highness the Princess Charlotte of Wales, lived
many years at Naples and Palermo, when LORD NELSON
was there, and came to England with him and Sir William
and Lady Hamilton, in 1800.  Her Journal contains
many anecdotes which she heard of him, as well as what
she herself either knew, or was told, of passing events.

He likewise begs leave to offer his best acknowledg-
ments to Admiral Sir Edward Codrington, G.C.B., to
Rear-Admiral Browne, to Rear-Admiral Sir Charles
Malcolm, to Rear-Admiral Thomas, and to his friend
Peter Smith, Esq., for Letters or information, communi-
cated in the most obliging manner.

*Torrington Square, June 6th, 1845.*

*Outer Shoal*

# Plan of Attack
### of the
## BATTLE OF THE NILE
### About ½ Past 7 O'Clock P.M.
### 1st August, 1798.

*Aboukir or Nelson's I.*

*Breakers*

FORT

*Scale of Miles*

½          1

*Sandy*

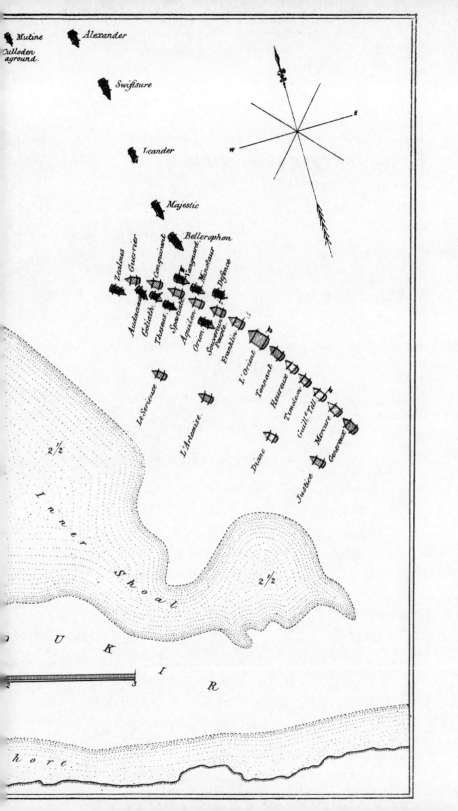

# CONTENTS.

## LETTERS.

### 1798.

## 1798, *continued.*

1798, *continued.*

## 1798, *continued.*

## 1798, *continued.*

1798, *continued.*

1798, *continued.*

1798, *continued.*

# 1799.

1799, *continued.*

1799, *continued.*

1799, *continued.*

1799, *continued.*

## 1799, *continued.*

## 1799, *continued.*

## 1799, *continued.*

1799, *continued.*

# APPENDIX.

------

## ERRATUM.

Page 384, *dele* "The Hereditary Prince." See p. 492.

# ANALYSIS

#### OF THE

# LIFE OF NELSON,

## FROM JANUARY 1798 TO AUGUST 1799.

---

| YEAR. | MONTH. | FACTS. |
|---|---|---|
| 1798. | | REAR-ADMIRAL OF THE BLUE. |
| — | January 1st to 29th | }...At Bath. |
| — | March 28th | .........In London. |
| — | — 29th | .........Hoisted his Flag, as Rear-Admiral of the Blue, on board the *Vanguard* at Spithead. |
| — | April 1st to 9th | }...At St. Helen's. |
| — | — 10th | ............Sailed for Lisbon with a Convoy. |
| — | — 23rd | ............Arrived at Lisbon. |
| — | — 30th | ............Joined the Earl of St. Vincent's Fleet off Cadiz. |
| — | May 2nd | ...............Ordered to Gibraltar, and thence with a Squadron of Observation up the Mediterranean. |
| — | — 8th | ...............Sailed from Gibraltar with a small Squadron. |
| — | — 17th | ...............Off Cape Sicie. |
| — | — 20th | ...............The Vanguard disabled and partially dismasted in the Gulf of Lyons. |
| — | — 24th | ...............At St. Pierre's, in Sardinia, to which place the *Vanguard* proceeded to repair damages. |
| — | — 27th | ...............Sailed from St. Pierre. |
| — | June 7th | ...............Joined by a Squadron of ten Sail of the Line, and the *Leander* 50, under Captain Troubridge, off Toulon, and proceeded in search of the French Fleet, which had sailed from Toulon on the 20th of May. |

| YEAR. | MONTH. | FACTS. |
|---|---|---|

1796, *continued* .............. REAR-ADMIRAL OF THE BLUE, with his Flag in the *Vanguard.*

— June 12th ..............Off Elba.

— — 13th ⎫
— — 14th ⎬ ...Off Cività Vecchia.

— — 15th ..............Off the Ponza Islands.

— — 17th ..............In Naples Bay.

— — 20th ..............Off Messina.

— — 21st ..............Off Syracuse.

— — 22nd..............Near Cape Passaro in Sicily. Proceeded to Alexandria.

— — 28th..............Off Alexandria.

— July 12th..............Off Candia.

— — 20th..............Returned with the Squadron to Syracuse.

— to ⎫
— — 22nd ⎬ ...At Syracuse.

— — 23rd..............Sailed from Syracuse for Egypt.

— August 1st..............Off Alexandria. Discovered the French Fleet.

BATTLE OF THE NILE.

— — 2nd ⎫
— to ⎬ ...In Aboukir Bay, (or Bequieres Roads.)
— — 18th ⎭

— — 19th ............Sailed, in company with the *Culloden, Alexander,* and *Bonne Citoyenne,* for Naples.

— — 27th ........ ...Off Rhodes.

— September 1st .........Off Candia.

— — 15th ......Off Stromboli.

— — 22nd ......Arrived at Naples.

— to ⎫
— October 14th ⎬ ...At Naples.

— — 15th .........Sailed for Malta with four Sail of the Line.

— — 24th ⎫
— to ⎬ ...Off Malta.
— — 30th ⎭

— — 31st .........Sailed for Naples with the *Minotaur.*

— November 5th .........Arrived at Naples.

— to ⎫
— — 21st ⎬ ...At Naples.

— — 22nd ......Sailed with a small Squadron and Troops against Leghorn, which surrendered on the 28th.

— — 28th ⎫
— — 29th ⎬ ...Off Leghorn.

— — 30th ......Sailed for Naples.

— December 5th ⎫ At Naples. On the 21st the King and Royal
— to ⎬ Family embarked for Palermo, and sailed
— — 23rd ⎭ on the 23rd.

— — 26th ......Arrived at Palermo.

| YEAR. | MONTH. | FACTS. |
|---|---|---|

1798, *continued* .............. REAR-ADMIRAL OF THE RED.

— December 26th
to
1799. May 19th

{ At Palermo. On the 1st of February 1799, he shifted his Flag to the *Bellerophon*; it was re-hoisted in the *Vanguard* on the 12th. On the 14th, Lord Nelson was promoted to be a REAR-ADMIRAL OF THE RED. On the 23rd of March, his Flag was transferred to the *Culloden*. On the 31st it was removed to a Transport, but was rehoisted in the *Vanguard*, on her return, on the 2nd of April. On the 5th, Lord Nelson heard of his promotion, when the Flag was changed from Blue to Red.

— — 20th ............Sailed with the Squadron for Maritimo.

— — 21st
to
— — 28th
} ...Off Maritimo.

— — 29th ............Arrived at Palermo.

to
— June 12th

{ At Palermo. On the 8th of June Lord Nelson removed to the *Foudroyant* with Captain Hardy and his other Officers.

— — 13th...............Embarked the Hereditary Prince, &c., and Sailed for Naples; but on receiving intelligence from Lord Keith of the French Fleet,

— — 15th...............Returned to Palermo, landed the Prince, and proceeded with the Squadron off Maritimo.

— June 16th
to
— — 20th
} ...Off Maritimo.

— — 21st...............Arrived at Palermo, embarked Sir William and Lady Hamilton, and proceeded with the Squadron to Naples.

— — 24th ............Off Ischia. He heard of the Capitulation for the surrender of the Castles of Uovo and Nuovo. Arrived in Naples Bay, and annulled the signal of Truce then flying on the Castles and on board the *Seahorse*.

— — 25th
to
— August 4th

{ At Naples. On the 25th Cardinal Ruffo came on board the *Foudroyant*. Lord Nelson intimated to the Neapolitan Rebels that they must submit to the mercy of their Sovereign, and refused to ratify the Capitulation for the surrender of Uovo and Nuovo, without the consent of the King of Naples, of which Castles he took possession

YEAR.    MONTH.                 FACTS.

1799, *continued* .............. REAR-ADMIRAL OF THE RED.

— June 25th
     to
— August 4th

in the evening. Summoned Fort St. Elmo to surrender. On the 29th he issued a proclamation requiring all who had served the Republic to give themselves up : Carracioli was brought on board the *Foudroyant,* tried there by Sicilian Officers, and executed on board the Sicilian Frigate *La Minerva.* On the 8th of July the King of Naples arrived, and on the 10th came on board the *Foudroyant,* where he remained. On the 13th Lord Nelson received Lord Keith's orders to send Ships to Minorca, with which he declined to comply. On the 31st, Capua and Gaeta surrendered to Captain Troubridge.

— — 5th ............Sailed from Naples for Palermo with the King of Naples

— — 8th ........ ...Arrived at Palermo, and landed the King.

     to
    31st

At Palermo. On the 13th of August he was created DUKE OF BRONTE; and his Flag was on that day transferred to the Samuel and Jane Transport.

# LETTERS

# LETTERS.

## 1798—ÆT. 39.

### TO WILLIAM SUCKLING, ESQ.

[Autograph, in the possession of Captain Montagu Montagu, R.N.]

My dear Sir,                                     Bath, January 3rd, 1798.

I most heartily congratulate you on the attainment of your wishes for the Major, and it gave me real pleasure to read his promotion in the Gazette as Lieut.-Colonel.[1] He has been a most fortunate man to rise to the top in one Regiment: it is what can rarely be obtained by any interest or money. I have the pleasure to tell you that I never have of late years seen my father so well. He joins with Lady Nelson and myself in wishing you, Mrs. Suckling, Mr. Rumsey, and all your family, very many happy returns of this season; and believe me, my dear Sir, your most obliged and affectionate,

HORATIO NELSON.

You must excuse short letters from me.

---

### TO CAPTAIN ALBEMARLE BERTIE, H. M. SHIP ARDENT.

[From the "Naval Chronicle," vol. xxvi. p. 10.]

My dear Bertie,                                  Bath, January 4th, 1798.

I thank you very much for your early notice of the event of Captain W.'s[2] long trial. The Court has been a most patient, and

[1] Mr. Suckling's natural son, Major William Suckling, was promoted to be Lieutenant-Colonel of the Third Regiment of Dragoon Guards, on the 21st of December, 1797.

[2] Captain Williamson, who had misconducted himself in command of the Agincourt, in the battle of Camperdown. Vide vol. ii. p. 458. He died suddenly on the 6th of November, 1798.

certainly a most lenient one. As to myself, upon the general
question, that if a man does not do his utmost in time of
Action, I think but one punishment ought to be inflicted.
Not that I take a man's merit from his list of killed and
wounded, for but little may be in his power; and if he does
his utmost in the station he is placed, he has equal merit to
the man who may have his Ship beat to pieces, but not his
good fortune. I dare say there were some favourable circumstances on W.'s trial, and it is a virtue to lean on the
side of mercy; and I have only to hope it will have its effect
upon Officers going into Action. I would have every man
believe, I shall only take my chance of being shot by the
Enemy, but if I do not take that chance, I am certain of being
shot by my Friends. I shall finish my observations in wishing
you joy of its being over.

Sheerness is a miserable place. When I was at Chatham,
I went on board the Ardent, and I think her the finest man-
of-war upon her decks that ever I saw. I hope by this time
you are known to Captain Berry. I can assure you that
he is a perfect gentleman in all his ideas, and one of the best
and most gallant Officers in our service. Pray tell Berry I
thank him for his letter, and will write to him in a day or two.
Remember me to Mr. Proby,[3] and all my friends about you;
and believe me, my dear Bertie,

Your most obliged and sincere friend,

HORATIO NELSON.

---

TO WILLIAM MARSDEN, ESQ., SECRETARY TO THE ADMIRALTY.

[Original, in the Admiralty.]

Bath, January 7th, 1798.

My dear Sir,

I am much obliged by your note, and memorandum about
the Flag Lieutenant. There is also another little alteration I wish for; and if I knew the particular Lord of the
Admiralty that managed this business, I would take the
liberty of writing to him.

[3] Captain Charles Proby, brother of John, first Lord Carysfort, Commissioner of
the Navy at Chatham Dockyard.

Lieutenant Irwine was recommended to me; I gave to you the name of Thomas Irwine, who I knew nothing about, instead of the Officer recommended to me, who being since commissioned for the Ganges, desires to remain where he is. I have, therefore, to request that the name of Thomas Irwine may be erased from the Commission for the Vanguard, and that it may be open till I send you another name.

I am, dear Sir, &c.

HORATIO NELSON.

————————

TO THE EARL OF ST. VINCENT.

[From Clarke and M'Arthur, vol. ii. p. 48, who state that he had informed the Earl, in a former part of this Letter, that the Vanguard was rigged, had her groundtier on board, and nearly 400 men.]

Bath, 10th January, 1798.

I hope to be with you early in March, for to you I trust I am going, unless you are destined for the Channel. I have been much flattered by the kind notice of Lord Lansdowne,[4] who speaks of you in the manner you always ought to be spoken of. I have no wishes to convey, but that my son-in-law, Josiah, may merit your good opinion, and that health and every blessing may attend you, in all which Lady Nelson most cordially joins. I am, &c.

HORATIO NELSON.

————————

TO THE REVEREND MR. WEATHERHEAD, SEDGEFORD, NORFOLK.

[Autograph.]

Bath, January 27th, 1798.

My dear Sir,

Your letter, of January 18th, only came to me yesterday. I have this day wrote to Captain Berry to endeavour to get Thomas Meek[5] from the Nore on board the Vanguard; but I am sure you will agree with me, that there ought to be the

---

[4] William, first Marquis of Lansdowne, and second Earl of Shelburne, K.G., who died 7th May, 1805.

[5] He appears to have been made a Midshipman of the Vanguard, and to have been killed by accident in May following. Vide p. 18, post.

B 2

greatest difference made between a forced man and the man who voluntarily offers his life to preserve his Country. However, you may be assured I will do everything which is right to serve the young man as he merits, if he can be got from the Zealand at the Nore; but being an impressed man, that is not certain.

I am very sorry that good Captain Miller should have awakened your feelings for the loss of your gallant son.[6] I think I informed you that he was shot by my side at the Mole of Santa Cruz, and that he survived the wound four days, when he left this world, to the regret of all who knew his worth; and what must ever give consolation to his surviving friends, that he fell in the service of his Country.

With every kind wish towards you and your family, believe me, dear Sir, &c.

HORATIO NELSON.

---

TO THOMASLLOYD, ESQ., MAY'S BUILDINGS, LONDON.

[From a Fac-simile.]

Bath, January 29th, 1798.

My dear Lloyd,

There is nothing you can desire me to do that I shall not have the greatest pleasure in complying with, for I am sure you can never possess a thought that is not most strictly honourable. I was much flattered by the Marquis's[7] kind notice of me, and I beg you will make my respects acceptable to him. Tell him that I possess his place in Mr. Palmer's box; but his Lordship did not tell me all its charms, that generally some of the handsomest ladies in Bath are partakers in the box, and was I a bachelor I would not answer for being tempted; but as I am possessed of everything which is valuable in a wife, I have no occasion to think beyond a pretty face. I am sorry the King is so poor. Had he been worth what those vile dogs of Opposition think, what a vast sum would have been given to the Nation; but I now hope all the Nation

---

[6] Vide vol. ii. p. 451.     [7] Of Lansdowne.

will subscribe liberally.[8]　You will believe that I do not urge others to give, and to withhold myself; but my mode of subscribing will be novel in its manner, and by doing it, I mean to debar myself of many comforts to serve my Country, and I expect great consolation every time I cut a slice of salt beef instead of mutton.　The Vanguard will be at Sheerness, Saturday, and, if this wind holds, she will be at Portsmouth before Thompson[9] quits the Channel.　I only pray that the French may not be ready to leave Brest.　I have been in a fever ever since the Boadicea's return with the account of their being ready for sea.　Lady Nelson and my father thank you for your kind remembrance of them, and believe me, my dear Lloyd,

Your most affectionate<br>HORATIO NELSON.

---

TO LADY COLLIER.[1]

[Autograph, in the possession of Commodore Sir Francis Augustus Collier, C.B., K.C.H.]

March, 1798.

Dear Madam,

From twelve till one this day I shall be at home, and if Lady Collier does not find it convenient to come to Bond Street at that time, Sir H. will call on Lady Collier after he comes from the Levee about $\frac{1}{2}$ past two.　I shall have much pleasure in having so very fine a lad under my wing; and indeed it is our duty to be useful to the children of our brethren.

Believe me, Madam, &c.<br>HORATIO NELSON.

Wednesday Morning.

I shall be at home at $\frac{1}{4}$ past two from the Levee.

---

[8] A voluntary subscription for the support of the War.

[9] Vice-Admiral Sir Charles Thompson, Bart., third in command of the Channel Fleet, under Lord Bridport.

[1] Widow of Vice-Admiral Sir George Collier, of whom a Memoir is given in the "Naval Chronicle," vol. xxxii., p. 265. The "fine lad" was her second son, the present Commodore Sir Francis Augustus Collier, C.B.

## TO MRS. COLLINGWOOD.

[Autograph, in the possession of the Honourable Mrs. Newnham Collingwood.]

96, Bond Street, March 12th, 1798.

Dear Madam,

As I am going to Lisbon in a few days, if you have any parcels to send to my old and dear friend Collingwood, I beg I may be honoured with them. Hoping some future day to be known to you, believe me,

Your most affectionate, humble servant,

HORATIO NELSON.

## TO THE REVEREND EDMUND NELSON, BATH.

[From Clarke and M'Arthur, vol. ii. p. 49.]

London, 14th March, 1798.

My dear Father,

I thank you for your affectionate letter, as indeed yours always are; and I hope in a few months to return with the olive branch, and to find you in as good a state as when we parted. I have this day taken leave of the King; and on Saturday I expect to be ordered to leave Town for Portsmouth, where I hope I shall not remain forty-eight hours, but my movements now depend on Lord Spencer. Lady Nelson intends setting out for Bath the same moment I do for Portsmouth. At all times, and in all places, believe me ever, with the truest filial affection, your dutiful Son,

HORATIO NELSON.

## MEMORANDUM.

[Original, in the Admiralty.]

To discharge from the Vanguard into the Royal William such men as are at the Hospital, and to have the Vanguard's complement completed before she proceeds to sea.—March 27th.                                   HORATIO NELSON.

## TO EVAN NEPEAN, ESQ., SECRETARY TO THE ADMIRALTY.

[Original, in the Admiralty. At 8 P.M. on the 29th of March, Rear-Admiral Sir Horatio Nelson hoisted his Flag, Blue at the Mizen, on board the Vanguard,[2] at Spithead. After remaining some days at St. Helen's, she quitted England, on the 10th of April, with the Portugal, Gibraltar, and Mediterranean convoy, to join Lord St. Vincent's Fleet at Lisbon.]

Sir,        Vanguard, Spithead, 29th March, 1798.   Wind N.N.E.

There being twenty-five men at the Hospital, who cannot return to the Ship before she proceeds to sea, nor can they be 'DSQ,'[3] they not having been twenty-eight days at the Hospital, and also five or six men absent without leave, who cannot be 'Run' on the Ship's Books, not having been absent three musters; therefore I beg leave to observe that after the Ship has been a few days at sea she will be considerably short of complement. I have therefore to request that their Lordships will be pleased to order the same number of men as will be left on shore, in order that she may sail with her numbers complete.

I am, Sir, &c.

HORATIO NELSON.

---

## TO THE REVEREND MR. NELSON, HILBOROUGH.

[Autograph in the Nelson Papers.]

Portsmouth, March 31st, 1798.

My dear Brother,

You will not, I hope, attribute my not answering your two letters to any other cause than that of really being hurried by my approaching departure. I participate in your sorrow at G. Thurlow's deficiency of rent, and his determination to give up the farm, but all landlords are at times plagued with their tenants. In short, the times are big with events, and before the year gets round we shall either have a good Peace, or what I dread to think on. But God's will be done. The

---

[2] The Officers of the Vanguard were, Captain Edward Berry; Lieutenants, Edward Galwey, Nathaniel Vassal, William Standwaye Parkinson, Henry Compton, John Miller Adye, the Honourable Thomas Bladen Capel; Captain of Marines, William Faddy; Lieutenants of Marines, Christopher Noble, Thomas Young, and Ivey Hare; Master, Wales Clod; Chaplain, Reverend Mr. Comyn; Purser, Alexander Sheppard; Surgeon, Michael Jefferson; and Admiral's Secretary, J. Campbell.

[3] Discharged to Sick Quarters.

wind is fair: in two hours I shall be on board, and with the
lark I shall be off to-morrow morning; therefore I have only
time to say God bless you and yours, and ever believe me,

> Yours most affectionately,
> HORATIO NELSON.

---

### TO LADY COLLIER.

[Autograph, in the possession of Commodore Sir Francis Augustus Collier, C.B.]

Vanguard, St. Helen's, April 8th, 1798.

Dear Madam,

I am only this moment favoured with your letter of the 2nd,
the weather having prevented our communicating with the
shore. You may rely that your son shall spend as little as
possible, for he will be a very lucky fellow if he gets on shore
twice in a year. With every sentiment of respect, believe me,

> Your Ladyship's most obedient servant,
> HORATIO NELSON.

I beg my best respects to Mrs. Mills: desire her to remember
my advice; it may do good, and cannot be hurtful. The
more I see, the more necessary to follow my advice.

---

### TO JOHN LOCKER, ESQ.

[From a Copy in the possession of Edward Hawke Locker, Esq.]

St. Helen's, 8th April, 1798.

My dear Sir,

It was only last night that I was favoured with your letter
of the 4th, it having blown so strong as to prevent all inter-
course with the shore.

Captain Faddy[3] is embarked in the Ship, and assure your
good father of my attention to whoever he recommends.
Captain F. appears a very good kind of man. Captain Berry
has taken his son on board.

I am sorry to hear that your father's head yet troubles
him, but I hope that he and you will very soon recover. I

---

[3] Of the Marines: he was killed at the Battle of the Nile, and Nelson took much
interest in the welfare of his family.

am fast tied with the wind at S. W., and likely to continue. I beg my kindest remembrances to your good father, sister, and brothers, and believe me ever yours most affectionately,

HORATIO NELSON.

---

### TO WILLIAM SUCKLING, ESQ.

[Autograph, in the Royal Navy Club.]

My dear Sir,  St. Helen's, April 9, 1798.

I cannot quit England without thanking you and Mrs. Suckling for the great kindness you both have shewn to my dear wife and myself; and, [from] my heart, I wish you health and every other blessing; and I hope soon to meet you in Peace. With my kindest respects to Mrs. Suckling and all your family, believe me,

Your most obliged and affectionate Nephew,

HORATIO NELSON.

---

### TO EVAN NEPEAN, ESQ., ADMIRALTY.

[Original, in the Admiralty. The Vanguard arrived at Lisbon on the 23rd of April, and sailed on the 27th for Earl St.Vincent's Fleet, off Cadiz, which she joined on the 30th of that month. The Fleet consisted of eighteen Sail of the Line, two Frigates, and a Brig.]

His Majesty's Ship Vanguard, Lisbon, 23rd April, 1798.

Sir,

I have to request you will inform the Lords Commissioners of the Admiralty, that I arrived here this day with H. M. Ship Vanguard and the Convoy for Lisbon, &c., a List of which I send herewith, together with remarks annexed thereto tfor heir Lordships' information. I am, &c.,

HORATIO NELSON.

---

### TO LADY NELSON.

[From Clarke and M'Arthur, vol. ii. p. 50.]

Lisbon, 24th April, 1798.

We arrived here yesterday, in fourteen days from St. Helen's. Lord St. Vincent is at sea off Cadiz, having wished to prevent some Spanish Ships from getting out, but without

effect; for one Ship of the Line, the Monarca, and two
Frigates, escaped on the 12th; the Neptuno 84, and two
more Frigates, are also on the wing, but I hope they will not
escape his vigilance. The Dolphin is here, and her Captain,
Josiah is very well.[4] If possible, I shall sail to-morrow to join
the Fleet. I can hardly describe to you the miserable appearance of this place after seeing England. I pray fervently
for Peace. Yours, &c.,

HORATIO NELSON.

## TO HIS ROYAL HIGHNESS THE DUKE OF CLARENCE.

[From Clarke and M'Arthur, vol. ii. p. 50.]

April 24th, 1798.

The new Viceroy of Mexico has got off. By their De-
tachments, it does not appear probable that the Spanish
Fleet will put to sea for the sake of fighting; therefore, I
fear we shall have a dull campaign off Cadiz; and the Earl's
force will not, I apprehend, admit of his detaching me up the
Mediterranean, to endeavour to get hold of the French
Squadron, now masters of that sea. I am, &c.

HORATIO NELSON.[5]

[4] His step-son, Captain Josiah Nisbet, then commanded the Dolphin, of 24 guns.

[5] His Royal Highness replied to this Letter on the 1st of June :—"Dear Sir,
I am to acknowledge the receipt of yours of 24th April, from Lisbon. I trust
the Campaign not only will be less dull than you imagine, but that you are by this
time up the Mediterranean with a sufficient Force to employ the Toulon Fleet
whilst the Earl watches the Spaniards off Cadiz. I differ with you entirely about
Portugal. I do not believe the Directory have that weight at Lisbon that you
imagine; on the contrary, they have plenty on their hands. Austria, Prussia,
Russia, and even America, are by no means satisfied; and there is every reason
to believe the War on the Continent will break out again. Denmark and
Sweden seem inclined to take up arms for the Empire, and the Congress at
Radstadt most likely will be dissolved without accomplishing Peace. The Spaniard
even has had, we are told, spirit enough to insist on a change of Minister from
France. I am in hopes the Directory, and that accursed Nation, have seen their
best day, and their fall has begun. As for Invasion here, it is absurd, and
without the most scandalous inattention, the French cannot effect a landing in
Ireland. I therefore consider that Country as safe, if Government pursue vigorous
measures there, and keep up a proper Naval Force. The Directory and the French
Army will consequently be reduced to inactivity, which must produce to them ill effect,
unless War begins again on the Continent, in which case the Swiss will certainly

## TO LADY NELSON.

[From Clarke and M'Arthur, vol. ii. p. 53.]

Lisbon, [1st May, 1798.]

I joined the Fleet yesterday, and found Lord St. Vincent everything I wished him;[6] and his friends in England have done me justice for my zeal and affection towards him. I have my fears that he will not be much longer in this Command, for I believe he has written to be superseded, which I am sincerely sorry for. It will considerably take from my pleasure in serving here; but I will hope for the best. The Dons have, I find, long expected my return with Bomb-vessels, Gun-boats, and every proper implement for the destruction of Cadiz and their Fleet. They have prepared three floating batteries to lie outside their walls, to prevent the fancied attack; and, lo, the mountain has brought forth a mouse:—I am arrived with a single Ship, and without the means of annoying them. The Admiral probably is going to detach me with a small Squadron; not on any fighting expedition, therefore do not be surprised if it should be some little time before you hear from me again. I direct this to our

rise. This brings me to that part of your Letter relative to Peace. Perhaps we may have it sooner than we expect; for France is certainly not the formidable Power she was. You cannot more ardently wish for an *honourable* Peace than I do, and nothing but the preparation to continue the War, if requisite, can effect so desirable an object. Adieu for the present: write frequently, and ever believe me, dear Sir, yours sincerely, WILLIAM."—*Autograph*, in the Nelson Papers.

[6] On placing Nelson again under Lord St. Vincent's command, Lord Spencer wrote to his Lordship, on the 30th of March, 1798—" I am very happy to send you Sir Horatio Nelson again, not only because I believe I cannot send you a more zealous, active, and approved Officer, but because I have reason to believe that his being under your command will be agreeable to your wishes. If your Lordship is as desirous to have him with you as he is to be with you, I am sure the arrangement must be perfectly satisfactory." Lord St. Vincent wrote in reply, on the 1st of May,—" I do assure your Lordship that the arrival of Admiral Nelson has given me new life: you could not have gratified me more than in sending him; his presence in the Mediterranean is so very essential, that I mean to put the Orion and Alexander under his command, with the addition of three or four Frigates, and to send him away the moment the Vanguard has delivered her water to the in-shore Squadron, to endeavour to ascertain the real object of the preparations making by the French."—*Clarke and M'Arthur*, vol. ii. p. 53.

Cottage,[8] where I hope you will fix yourself in comfort, and I
pray that it may very soon please God to give us Peace.
England will not be invaded this summer. Buonaparte is
gone back to Italy, where 80,000 men are embarking for
some expedition. With every kind wish that a fond heart
can frame, believe me, as ever, your most affectionate
husband.

HORATIO NELSON.

TO LADY NELSON.

[From Clarke and M'Arthur, vol. ii. p. 54. On the 2nd of May, Sir Horatio
Nelson received a "Most Secret" order from Lord St. Vincent, which, after reciting
that he had received intelligence that a considerable Armament was preparing at
Toulon, and a number of Transports collecting at Marseilles and Genoa, for an
embarkation of troops, directed him to proceed with such of the Squadron as
might be at Gibraltar, up the Mediterranean, and to endeavour to ascertain,
either on the coast of Provence or Genoa, the destination of that Expedition,
which, according to some reports, was Sicily and Corfu, and according to others,
Portugal or Ireland. If he found that the Enemy intended to join a Squadron
of Spanish Ships said to be equipping at Carthagena, to which he was also to
give his attention, he was to dispatch the Bonne Citoyenne or Terpsichore with
the information to Lord St. Vincent, and to continue, with the rest of the
Squadron, on that service as long as he might think it necessary. If the Enemy's
Armament was coming down the Mediterranean, he was to take special care not to
suffer it to pass the Straits before him, so as to impede his joining Lord St. Vincent
in time to prevent a union between it and the Spanish Fleet in Cadiz Bay.—*Original* in the Nelson Papers. The Vanguard arrived at Gibraltar on the 4th of May,
where she found the Princess Royal, with the Flag of Rear-Admiral Sir John Orde,
Bart., the Orion, Majestic, Hector, and Alexander, seventy-fours, and several
Frigates.]

Gibraltar, 4th May, 1798.

I have no turn for such things,[9] when we had better be
alongside a Spaniard. Apropos—my Frigate, the Sabina,[1] is
at Algesiras, about five miles from this place; she looks well,
and if I catch her at sea, I shall certainly make free to take

---

[8] Before Nelson quitted England, he obtained the object he had so long desired
by purchasing a "*Cottage*" and a few acres of land, called Round-Wood, near
Ipswich; and on the 28th of May, Lady Nelson wrote to him:—" On Sunday, the 20th
of May, we arrived at Round-Wood. The satisfaction I felt was very great on being
under your own roof. No thanks to any earthly being. Our Father was for staying,
although the house had little or no accommodation. He viewed everything atten-
tively, and I never saw him so thoroughly satisfied as he was, and says the more he
examines everything the better he is pleased. The house is quite large enough."

[9] Fêtes given by the garrison of Gibraltar.

[1] Vide vol. ii. p. 313.

my property. The folks here are certainly very civil, but merry; and where we had better be filling water, and getting quickly to our excellent Commander-in-Chief. Yours, &c.,

　　　　　　　　　　　　　　　HORATIO NELSON.

---

### TO THE EARL OF ST. VINCENT.

[From Clarke and M'Arthur, vol. ii. p. 55.]

　　　　　　　　　　　　　　　　　　6th May, 1798.

I have ordered the Ships[2] to weigh with me on Tuesday morning. Thompson[3] regrets not going with me; he is an active young man. Sir John Orde will know by his eye what Ships go with me, therefore I shall show him the list. I do not believe any person guesses my destination. It shall go hard but I will present you at least with some Frigates, and I hope something better. I shall pick up Caroline off Cape Palos, round Minorca, stand in sight of the Coast towards Barcelona, and get in the straight line between Cape St. Sebastian's and Toulon, there I shall procure information enough to regulate my further proceedings; and as I take Frigates, shall send one to have charge of each, keeping the large Ships complete, to fight, I hope, larger ones. God bless you.

　　　　　　　　　　　　　　　I am, &c.,

　　　　　　　　　　　　　　　HORATIO NELSON.

---

### TO THE RESPECTIVE CAPTAINS OF HIS MAJESTY'S SHIPS ORION, ALEXANDER, AND VANGUARD.

[Order-Book.]

　　　　　　　　　　　　　　Gibraltar Bay, 7th May, 1798.

It being of the very greatest importance that the Squadron should not be separated, it is my positive orders that no tempta-

Among the Nelson Papers are several Journals and Logs from March 1798, to October 1805, some of which, though not in Nelson's hand, are written in the *first* person: " Wednesday, 9th May, 1798, at $\frac{1}{2}$ past 3 P.M. issued orders, dated the 7th, to the Captains of H.M. Ships following to put themselves under my command—viz., Orion, Alexander, Vanguard, Caroline, Flora, Emerald, Terpsichore, and Bonne Citoyenne, as also several other orders."—*Journal.*

Captain, (afterwards Vice-Admiral Sir) Thomas Boulden Thompson, of the Leander, who arrived at Gibraltar a few days before. The Leander did afterwards join the Squadron, and distinguished herself greatly at the Nile.

tion is to induce a Line-of-Battle Ship to separate from me, except the almost certainty of bringing a Line-of-Battle Ship of the Enemy to Action; but in common chaces, if the weather is such as to risk separation, or the approach of night, it is my directions you leave off chace, and rejoin me, even without waiting the signal of Recall, unless I make the signal to continue the pursuit, by No. 104, page 30, S.B.

HORATIO NELSON.

---

TO WILLIAM LUKE, ESQ., CAPTAIN OF HIS MAJESTY'S SHIP CAROLINE, AND R. G. MIDDLETON, ESQ., CAPTAIN OF HIS MAJESTY'S SHIP FLORA.

[Order-Book.]

Vanguard, Gibraltar Bay, 7th May, 1798.

It being of very great importance to obtain correct information of the destination of the large Fleet of the Enemy, and of the Fleet of Transports with troops, which is said to accompany them, reports making it probable they are bound down the Mediterranean, in order to pass the Straits of Gibraltar, other reports inducing a belief they are destined for Naples,—you are therefore hereby directed to proceed to the Eastward, looking with proper caution into Barcelona, and from thence taking your station in a direct line between Saint Sebastian's and Toulon, endeavouring, by speaking of Vessels, to obtain the desired information, which, when got, you are to make all possible dispatch to the Commander-in-Chief off Cadiz, especially if you have reason to believe the Enemy's Fleet are bound down the Mediterranean, in order that he may be enabled to take a proper position for intercepting them; and I also recommend that, if it can be done without any delay, that you communicate, in your passage through the Straits, in confidence, your information to the Governor of Gibraltar, and the commanding Sea-Officer in the Bay. You are not to remain longer than ten days on the Station between St. Sebastian's and Toulon, when, not getting any information or farther directions from me, you will return to Gibraltar Bay, where you will receive orders for your further proceedings.

HORATIO NELSON.

## TO ADMIRAL THE EARL OF ST. VINCENT, K.B.

[From Clarke and M'Arthur, vol. ii. p. 57.]

8th May, 1798.

I shall not make sail to the Eastward until dark, and it will be late before all are clear of Europa Point. My first Lieutenant, Galwey,[4] has no friends, and is one of the best Officers in my Ship. I am, &c.

HORATIO NELSON,

---

## TO THE EARL OF ST. VINCENT.

[Letter-Book. The Squadron sailed from Gibraltar on the 8th of May. On the 11th of that month, Lord St. Vincent issued another Order to Sir Horatio Nelson, which stated that the Admiralty having directed that the whole Naval force under his (Lord St. Vincent's) command should be collected " to prepare for a service of very great importance," he was, after ranging the coast of Provence and the Western Riviera of Genoa, or before, if he discovered that the preparations on the Coast were in forwardness, to make the best of his way to Gibraltar, with his Line-of-Battle Ships and worst sailing Frigates, and on his arrival there, to use all dispatch in completing the water and provisions of the Squadron, and to join his Lordship off Cadiz. This Order was accompanied by a private Letter, also dated on the 11th of May, in which Lord St. Vincent said, " The Admiralty had at last discovered that it is necessary to provide a force to look after the French in the Mediterranean," and that some Ships were expected from England, and added, " You, and you only, can command the important service in contemplation; therefore make the best of your way down to me, or the first division from England will be here before you. I shall bring Murray[5] from Lisbon, for the Colossus is now most powerfully manned, and he is too good a fellow to be left there when so much is to be done. You shall also have some choice Fellows of the in-shore Squadron."—*Originals* in the Nelson Papers.]

My Lord,        Vanguard, off Cape Sicie, May 17th, 1798.

This morning, the Terpsichore captured a small French Corvette,[6] of six guns and sixty-five men, which came out of Toulon at 11 o'clock, last night. From the general report of Vessels spoke, you will observe the uniformity of the reports —viz., that an expedition is preparing to sail from Toulon. We have separately examined the crew of this Corvette, and, from the whole, I believe the following may be depended on as near the truth—that Buonaparte arrived at Toulon last Fri-

---

[4] Afterwards a Rear-Admiral. Vide vol. ii. p. 453.

[5] Captain George Murray, of the Colossus: he died a Vice-Admiral and K.C.B., in February 1819.

[6] Le Pierre, a French National polacre Corvette, mounting six guns and two swivels, with sixty-five men.—Vanguard's *Log.*

day, and has examined the troops which are daily embarking in the numerous Transports; that Vessels with troops frequently arrive from Marseilles; it is not generally believed that Buonaparte is to embark, but no one knows to what place the Armament is destined. Fifteen Sail of the Line are apparently ready for sea, but nineteen are in the harbour, and yet it is said only six Sail of the Line are to sail with the Transports now ready; that about 12,000 men are embarked; their cavalry arrived at Toulon, but I cannot learn that any are yet embarked. Reports say they are to sail in a few days, and others that they will not sail for a fortnight. This Corvette was bound to the westward, I believe, with dispatches, but the Commander denies it.

The Admiral Brueys has his Flag in L'Orient, 120 guns; Le Formidable and Spartanade, of 80 guns, are also Flag-ships. The Venetian Ships are considered as very bad in every respect, but I do not learn that the Fleet is deficient in either men or stores. All this information is but little more than you knew when I left you, but, still, knowing that late information of the state of the Enemy's Fleet is very desirable, I send an intelligent young man, Mr. Charles Harford,[7] who has just served his Time, with this letter, and I beg leave to recommend him to your notice. You may rely, my Lord, that I shall act as occasions may offer, to the best of my abilities, in following up your ideas for the honour of His Majesty's Arms, and the advantage of our Country, and believe me, your Lordship's obedient Servant,

HORATIO NELSON.

I saw three French Frigates this afternoon, but as they did not see the Squadron, I am in hopes of getting near them. The Squadron is as I wish them.

---

TO ADMIRAL THE EARL OF ST. VINCENT, K.B.

[From Tucker's " Memoirs of the Earl of St. Vincent," vol. i. p. 444.]

My dear Lord,                                   May 18th, 1798.

I have, in fact, no farther particulars to tell you, than are in my public letter. They order their matters so well in

[7] In command of the Prize Corvette. On the 21st of May, the Squadron captured a French Brig from Smyrna going to Marseilles, laden with cotton.—*Journal.*

France, that all is secret. The bearer is the young man recommended by our friend Lloyd.[8] We are all healthy, and
in good humour. I sincerely hope this will find you fixed to
remain our Chief. Without a compliment, none will be found
that has so much the confidence of his Fleet. As to what
may become of us to-morrow, who can say? but rest assured
of my zealous endeavours to meet your wishes. Pray have
the goodness to forward the enclosed, and ever believe me
your most obliged and affectionate

HORATIO NELSON.

9 A.M.

You will see by Sir James Saumarez's account, that Cavalry
are embarked. Having all we know, you will form your own
conjectures.

---

TO LADY NELSON.

[From a Copy in the possession of Mrs. Conway, and another Copy in the Nelson
Papers. This beautiful Letter is printed in most of the "Lives of Nelson," and also
in the "Gentleman's Magazine" for 1799, vol. lxix. p. 344, in p. 392 of which work a
suspicion is, however, expressed that it is not genuine; but there are no grounds for
doubting its authenticity. The storm and its effects are admirably described in a
letter from Captain Berry, of the Vanguard,[9] who, when alluding to this circumstance in his "Narrative of the Battle of the Nile," says that, "at the moment
when the misfortune befell the Vanguard, the British Squadron was not many leagues
distant from the French Fleet under Buonaparte, which had on that very day set
sail from Toulon."]

Vanguard, Island of St. Peter's, in Sardinia, May 24, 1798.

My dearest Fanny,

I ought not to call what has happened to the Vanguard by
the cold name of accident: I believe firmly, that it was the
Almighty's goodness, to check my consummate vanity. I

---

[8] Thomas Lloyd, Esq., vide p. 4, ante. He was a Superannuated Captain, and
commanded the Glasgow, in 1779, when she was burnt. (Vide vol. i. p. 29.) Captain Lloyd died about 1801. "The young man" was Mr. Harford: he was made a
Lieutenant in 1799.

[9] CAPTAIN BERRY, TO HIS FATHER IN-LAW, THE REVEREND DR. FOSTER.

"Vanguard, at Sea, off Sardinia, 29th May, 1798.

"After arriving at the height of our wishes at sea, and elated beyond description
at being so fortunate as to be the detached Squadron in the Mediterranean, and surrounded by Enemies, and but little chance of seeing anything else on these seas—
our Squadron though small being very choice—the passage from Gibraltar to the
Gulf of Lyons being favourable in all respects, fine weather, and not discovered by

hope it has made me a better Officer, as I feel confident it has
made me a better Man.   I kiss with all humility the rod.
Figure to yourself a vain man, on Sunday evening at sun-set,
walking in his cabin with a Squadron about him, who looked
up to their Chief to lead them to glory, and in whom this Chief
placed the firmest reliance, that the proudest Ships, in equal
numbers, belonging to France, would have bowed their Flags;
and with a very rich Prize lying by him.   Figure to yourself
this proud, conceited man, when the sun rose on Monday
morning, his Ship dismasted, his Fleet dispersed, and himself
in such distress, that the meanest Frigate out of France would
have been a very unwelcome guest.   But it has pleased Almighty God to bring us into a safe Port, where, although we

the Enemy, though close to their ports, we thought ourselves in the height of our
glory : what more could we wish for ?   But, alas! how liable to a reverse, and how it
was verified !   Sunday, the 20th of May, being exactly in the situation for intercepting the Enemy's Ships bound into Marseilles, Toulon, &c., and that afternoon
having captured a tolerably rich Prize, we stood in towards Cape Sicie, off Toulon,
with a moderate breeze : towards sunset the weather did not appear so promising;
we consequently got down our top-gallant yards &c.; before 12 at night, the gale
came on, and increased with rapid violence, which obliged us to furl all the sails,
and try under a main storm-staysail.   At about two, the main-topmast went over
the side, with the top-sail yard full of men.   I dreaded the inquiry of who were
killed and drowned; fortunately only one man fell overboard, and one fell on the
booms, and was killed on the spot.   At half-past two the mizen-topmast went over
the side; the fore-mast gave an alarming crack, and at a quarter past three went by
the board with a most tremendous crash, and, what was very extraordinary, it fell in
two pieces across the forecastle.   Our situation was really alarming : the wreck of
the fore-topmast and foremast hanging over the side, and beating against the Ship's
bottom; the best bower-anchor was flung out of its place, and was also thumping
the bottom; the wreck of the main topmast swinging violently against the main-
rigging, every roll endangering the loss of the mainmast, which we expected to fall
every moment :—thus circumstanced, we endeavoured, though with but little hopes
of success, to wear, having no head-sail, and knowing we were driving on an Enemy's
shore.   Fortunately there was a small rag of the sprit-sail left, and by watching a
favourable moment, we got her on the other tack.   The bowsprit did not go, though
it was sprung in three different places.   The Ship rolled and laboured dreadfully, but
did not make any water, more than we shipped over all.   We cut the anchor from the
bows, and got clear of the wreck, with the loss of a boat and topsail-yard, &c., and
were not apprehensive of our bottom being damaged.   The gale did not abate in the
smallest degree, and the main-rigging, from being new, stretched to that degree,
that it was no support to the mast; we struck the main-yard, which eased it greatly,
and secured the rigging as well as laid in our power.   We shipped so much water,
that it was necessary to scuttle the lower deck, still we were consoled that she did
not leak.   Here I have to lament the loss of a most active young man, a Midshipman of the name of Meek, recommended by Mr. Coke, of Norfolk.   He showed
himself so particularly active at the time everybody admired him : by accident

are refused the rights of humanity, yet the Vanguard will in two days get to sea again, as an English Man-of-War.

The exertions of Sir James Saumarez, in the Orion, and Captain A. Ball, in the Alexander, have been wonderful ; if the Ship had been in England, months would have been taken to send her to sea : here, my operations will not be delayed four days, and I shall join the rest of my Fleet on the rendezvous.

If this letter gets to you, be so good as to write a line to Lord Spencer, telling him that the Vanguard is fitted tolerably for sea, and that what has happened will not retard my operations. We are all health and good humour : tell Lady Saumarez Sir James never was in better health. With kind love to my Father, believe me ever your affectionate husband,

HORATIO NELSON.

he was suddenly killed. For want of masts we rolled dreadfully. The storm did not abate till Tuesday afternoon, which enabled the Alexander to take us in tow. Our situation on Tuesday night was the most alarming I ever experienced : we stood in for the Island of Sardinia, and approached the S.W. side of the Island, intending to go into Oristan Bay, which we were not acquainted with, but it was absolutely necessary to go somewhere. Finding we could not fetch Oristan, the Admiral determined to try for St. Pierre's, which we could have fetched had the breeze continued, but unfortunately it fell light airs, and at times almost calm ; so much so, that we had determined to order the Alexander to cast off the hawser, and desire her to shift for herself—trust to our own fate, but not involve any other Ship in our difficulties. All this time there was a heavy western swell driving in towards the shore, so that at midnight we were completely embayed. You may easily figure to yourself our situation, and the feelings of those who *knew the danger*, when I tell you I could easily distinguish the surf breaking on the rocky shore ; still there was hope anchorage might be found, though we knew of none. We therefore bent our cables and prepared for the worst, anxiously wishing for daybreak, which at length arrived, and we found ourselves about five miles from the shore, the western swell still continuing to drive us in, and no wind to enable us to get off. Indeed, the Vanguard was a perfect wreck, but the Alexander still had us in tow. Fortunately, at about six o'clock on Wednesday, the 23rd of May, a breeze sprang up, the Alexander's sails filled, we weathered the rocks to windward of the Island of St. Pierre's, and before 12 we anchored in six fathoms, and fine smooth water—a luxury to us scarcely to be equalled, and if ever there was a satisfaction at being in distress, we felt it. The ready assistance of our friends Sir James Saumarez, Captain of the Orion, 74, and Captain Alexander John Ball, of the Alexander, 74, by their united efforts, and the greatest exertion we all used, the Vanguard was equipped in four days, and actually at sea, not bound (I would have you observe) to Gibraltar or any English port to be refitted, but again cruizing after the enemy on their own coast ! with a main top-mast for a fore-mast, and a topgallant-mast for a top-mast, consequently everything else reduced in proportion. By our superiority of sailing with other ships, we find the loss trifling to what it would have been to the generality of ships. With such perseverance you will say we deserve success."—*Original*, in the possession of Lady Berry.

I have wrote to Lord S. by another, but I still wish you to write a line to say we are all well, for yours may arrive and his Lordship's miscarry.

P.S.—Mr. Thomas Meek, who was recommended by Mr. Hussey and my brother Suckling, was killed, and several seamen were wounded.

---

### TO ADMIRAL THE EARL OF ST. VINCENT, K.B.

[Letter-Book.]

Vanguard, Island of St. Peter's, in Sardinia, May 24th, 1798.

My Lord,

I am sorry to be obliged to inform you of the accidents which have happened to the Vanguard. On Saturday, May the 19th, it blew strong from the N.W. On Sunday it moderated so much, as to enable us to get our top-gallant masts and yards aloft. After dark it began to blow strong; but as the Ship was prepared for a gale, my mind was easy. At half-past one A.M. on Monday, the main-top-mast went over the side, as did soon afterwards the mizen-mast. As it was impossible for any night-signal to be seen, I had hopes we should be quiet till day-light, when I determined to wear, and scud before the gale; but about half-past three the fore-mast went in three pieces, and the bowsprit was found to be sprung in three places. When the day broke, we were for-tunately enabled to wear the Ship with a remnant of the sprit-sail. The Orion, Alexander, and Emerald wore with us; but the Terpsichore, Bonne Citoyenne, and a French Smyrna ship, continued to lay to under bare poles. Our situa-tion was 25 leagues south of the Islands of Hieres; and as we were laying with our head to the N.E., had we not wore, which was hardly to be expected, the Ship must have drifted to Corsica. The gale blew very hard all the day, and the Ship laboured most exceedingly. In the evening, being in lati-tude 40° 50′ N., I determined to steer for Oristan Bay, in the Island of Sardinia: during the night, the Emerald parted company, for what reason I am at present unacquainted with. Being unable to get into Oristan, the Alexander took us in tow, and by Captain Ball's unremitting attention to our distress,[1] and by Sir James Saumarez's exertions and ability in finding out the Island of St. Peter's, and the proper anchorage, the Vanguard was, on May the 23rd, at noon, brought safely to an anchor into the harbour of St. Peter's.

　　　　　　I have the honour to be, &c.

　　　　　　　　　　　　HORATIO NELSON.

---

## TO HIS EXCELLENCY THE VICE-ROY OF SARDINIA.

[Letter-Book.]

His Britannic Majesty's Ship Vanguard,
At Anchor, off the Island of St. Peter, 26th May, 1798.

Sir,

Having, by a gale of wind sustained some trifling damage, I anchored a small part of his Majesty's Fleet, under my orders, off this Island, and was surprised to hear, by an Officer sent by the Governor, that admittance was to be refused to the Flag of his Britannic Majesty into this Port. When I reflect that my most gracious Sovereign is the oldest, (I believe,) and certainly the most faithful, Ally which his Majesty of Sardinia ever had, I could feel the sorrow which it must have been to his Majesty to have given such an order, and also for your Excellency, who has to direct its execution. I cannot

---

[1] In 1783, Captain Ball became slightly known to Nelson at St. Omer's, (Vol. i. p. 88,) when they seem to have conceived a strong prejudice against each other, and they never met again until the Alexander was placed under his orders. For the following anecdote, the Editor is indebted to the Reverend Francis Laing, who heard it from Sir Alexander Ball himself. On joining the Vanguard, Captain Ball went on board her to pay his respects to the Rear-Admiral; but the reception he met with was not flattering: "What," said the Admiral, "are you come to have your bones broken?" Captain Ball, who was remarkable for command of temper, quietly replied, that he certainly had no wish to have his bones broken, unless his duty to his King and Country required such a sacrifice, and then they should not be spared. Soon after the Vanguard was taken in tow by the Alexander, Sir Horatio Nelson fearing, from the state of the weather, that *both* Ships would go down, peremptorily desired that the Vanguard should be abandoned to her fate. Captain Ball, however, resolved to persevere, under the conviction that his endeavours to save the Vanguard would be successful. When the Ships arrived at St. Pierre's, Sir Horatio lost no time in going on board the Alexander to express his gratitude, and cordially embracing Captain Ball, exclaimed, "A friend in need is a friend indeed!" From that moment their friendship commenced; Nelson soon discovered the injustice he had done to Ball's character and abilities; and numerous Letters to him in this Collection prove how highly he afterwards esteemed him.

but look at Afric's shore, where the followers of Mahomet
are performing the part of the good Samaritan, which I look
for in vain at St. Peter's, where it is said the Christian Religion
is professed. May I request the favour of your Excellency
to forward one Letter for his Britannic Majesty's Minister at
Turin, and the other for his Britannic Majesty's Consul at
Leghorn. May God Almighty bless your Excellency is the
sincere wish of your most obedient servant,

                                          HORATIO NELSON.

---

### TO ADMIRAL THE EARL OF ST. VINCENT, K.B.

[Letter-Book. The Vanguard having rigged a jury Fore-mast, and otherwise
repaired as far as possible her damages, sailed from St. Pierre's in company with her
consorts, the Alexander and Orion, on the 27th of May. Captain Berry justly
observes that many Admirals, under such circumstances, would have shifted their
Flag to a more effective Ship ; but Nelson never expressed the smallest intention
of doing so.—*Narrative of the Battle of the Nile.* They captured a Spanish Snow
on the 28th, and proceeded to Toulon.]

                                  Vanguard, at Sea, May 28th, 1798.
  My Lord,
    In my last Letters of May 24th, I acquainted you of our
arrival at St. Peter's, and I have now the pleasure to inform
you that, by the indefatigable exertions of the Captains of
the Orion, Alexander, and Vanguard, and the great ability of
Mr. James Morrison, Carpenter of the Alexander, the Vanguard was completed for sea on the 26th at night, and that I
sailed on the 27th, at daylight, to proceed on the service you
were pleased to intrust to my direction. As your Lordship will
observe the state of the Vanguard on her arrival at St. Peter's,
the exertions of all classes will strike forcibly ; therefore it
is only necessary to observe, that the Ship was fitted under
the advice of the Carpenter of the Alexander, an old and
faithful servant of the Crown, and who has been near thirty
years a warranted Carpenter ; and I beg most earnestly, that
your Lordship will have the goodness to recommend Mr.
Morrison to the particular notice of the Board of Admiralty.
          I have the honour to remain, &c.
                                          HORATIO NELSON.

TO ADMIRAL THE EARL OF ST. VINCENT, K.B.

[From Clarke and M'Arthur, vol. ii. p. 60.]

My dear Lord,　　　　　　　　31st May, 1798.

My pride was too great for man; but I trust my friends will think that I bore my chastisement like a man. It has pleased God to assist us with his favour, and here I am again off Toulon. I am, &c.,

HORATIO NELSON.

ORDER OF BATTLE AND SAILING.

[Order-Book.]

| No. | Ships. | Captains. | Guns. | Men. |
|---|---|---|---|---|
| 1 | Culloden | T. Troubridge | 74 | 590 |
| 2 | Theseus | R. W. Miller | 74 | 590 |
| 3 | Alexander | Alexander J. Ball | 74 | 590 |
| 4 | Vanguard | Edward Berry | 74 | 595 |
| 5 | Minotaur | Thomas Louis | 74 | 640 |
| 6 | Swiftsure | Benjamin Hallowell | 74 | 590 |
| 7 | Audacious | Davidge Gould | 74 | 590 |
| 8 | | | | |
| 9 | Defence | John Peyton | 74 | 590 |
| 10 | Zealous | Samuel Hood | 74 | 590 |
| 11 | Orion | Sir James Saumarez | 74 | 590 |
| 12 | Goliath | Thomas Foley | 74 | 590 |
| 13 | Majestic | George B. Westcott | 74 | 590 |
| 14 | Bellerophon | Henry D'E. Darby | 74 | 590 |

Vanguard 2 Points.
Order of Sailing.

All Frigates to repeat.

Leander

Starboard Squadron.

Larboard Squadron.

All Frigates to repeat.

Rear Admiral Sir Horatio Nelson, K.B., &c.

Given on board his Majesty's Ship Vanguard, at Sea, 7th June, 1798.

HORATIO NELSON.

A Copy of this delivered to each of the Captains of the Line-of-Battle Ships;—Captain Thompson, of the Leander.

TO CAPTAIN T. B. THOMPSON, OF HIS MAJESTY'S SHIP LEANDER.

[Order-Book.]

Vanguard, at Sea, 7 P.M., 8th June, 1798.

The Leander to remain where I am at this instant, to acquaint Sir James Saumarez and Captain Ball, of the Alexander, that I am steering a straight course for Cape

Corse, E. by S., and shall remain there twenty-four hours;
from thence to the southward, towards Naples.   Not finding
the Alexander or Orion in eight and forty hours, the Leander
to join me with all possible dispatch.   To fire a gun every
half-hour during the night, and carry a light at each mast-
head.   The Leander to show a top and stern light during
this night.
                                          HORATIO NELSON.

-----

### TO ADMIRAL THE EARL OF ST. VINCENT, K.B.

[From Clarke and M'Arthur, vol. ii. p. 60.   On the 19th of May, 1798, Lord St.
Vincent received most secret Instructions from the Admiralty, dated on the 2nd
of that month, which, after stating that " the state of affairs rendered it absolutely
necessary that the Fleet and Armament fitting at Toulon should be prevented from
accomplishing its object," and that their Lordships had in consequence reinforced
his Fleet with eight Sail of the Line and two Fire Ships, under Rear-Admiral Sir
Roger Curtis, proceeded thus :—
    " Having been joined by the Rear-Admiral, and the Ships above-mentioned, your
Lordship is to lose no time in detaching from your Fleet a Squadron, consisting of
twelve Sail of the Line, and a competent number of Frigates, under the command of
some discreet Flag-Officer, into the Mediterranean, with instructions to him to
proceed in quest of the said Armament ; and on falling in with it, or any other
Force belonging to the Enemy, to take or destroy it.   Your Lordship is to direct
the Commanding-Officer of the above-mentioned Squadron, to remain upon this
service so long as the provisions of the said Squadron will last, or as long as he
may be enabled to obtain supplies from any of the ports in the Mediterranean, and
when, from the want of provisions, or any other circumstance, he shall be no
longer able to remain within the Straits, to lose no time in rejoining you."—
Original, in the Nelson Papers.   These Instructions were accompanied by a
private and confidential Letter from Lord Spencer, dated on the 29th of April 1798,
of which Clarke and M'Arthur give the following abstract: " It dwells at considerable length on the late proceedings of the Cabinet, the state of the Continent,
and the probable intentions of the French armament at Toulon.   The appearance of a British Squadron in the Mediterranean, was declared to be a condition
on which the fate of Europe at that moment depended ; every nerve was to be
strained, and considerable hazard incurred, in effecting it : yet Government entirely left it to Lord St. Vincent's determination, either to make a Detachment from
his Fleet, or to take his whole force into the Mediterranean ; and the defeat of
the purpose of the Toulon armament, whatever it might be, was to have a preference to the great advantages which had hitherto been obtained, from the constant check which the noble Admiral had kept on the Spanish Fleet in Cadiz.
This check, however, was if possible to be continued ; and it was hoped that
it might be found practicable to send a Detachment from the Fleet into the
Mediterranean sufficiently strong to attain the end proposed.   'If you determine,'
adds Lord Spencer, ' to send a Detachment, I think it almost unnecessary to
suggest to you the propriety of putting it under the command of Sir H. Nelson,
whose acquaintance with that part of the world, as well as his activity and disposition seem to qualify him in a peculiar manner for that service.   We shall

take care to send you out Ships which are the best suited for Foreign service of any that we have to dispose of: in order to make your Fleet as effective as possible' . . . . . . 'I have thought it necessary,' concluded the noble Lord, 'to enter into this reasoning, to impress your Lordship with the great urgency and importance of the measure which has now been determined upon, and to justify our calling upon you to place yourself, at least for a short time, in a situation of more difficulty than any less pressing emergency would warrant us in doing.'"—Vol. ii. p. 56.

The selection of so young a Rear-Admiral as Nelson, in preference to his seniors in Lord St. Vincent's Fleet—viz., Sir William Parker and Sir John Orde, naturally gave great offence to those Officers. Writing to Nelson, on the 22nd of June, Lord St. Vincent said—" Sir William Parker and Sir John Orde have written strong remonstrances against your commanding the detached Squadron, instead of them. I did all I could to prevent it consistently with my situation ; but there is a faction fraught with all manner of ill will to you, that, unfortunately for the two Baronets, domin'd over any argument or influence I could use. They will both be ordered home the moment their letters arrive." The Correspondence between Lord St. Vincent and Sir John Orde was printed, and the proceedings on the subject are well known. It has been doubted by whom the selection of Nelson for that important service was actually made. The Instructions of the 3rd of May, to Lord St. Vincent, would seem to have left the matter entirely in his hands ; but Lord Spencer's private Letter appears, in fact, to have allowed St. Vincent little discretion, as he was all but ordered to appoint Nelson. The King himself, however, claimed the whole merit of the transaction : " The Duke of Clarence," says Sir Edward Berry, in a letter to Lord Nelson, dated London, December 30th, 1798, " desired I would tell you from him that it was the *King that sent you* with the Squadron up the Mediterranean, and formed the whole plan. *I believe it seriously.*" —*Autograph*, in the Nelson Papers.

It would be unjust to Nelson's zealous friend, Sir Gilbert Elliot, then Lord Minto, not to refer to a Letter from that distinguished Nobleman to him, dated on the 25th of April 1798, in which he informed Nelson that he had, on the previous day, called on Lord Spencer, and told him, that Nelson was "the fittest man in the world for the command" of the Squadron, which was to be sent into the Mediterranean, and pointed out his various qualifications for that service. Lord Spencer said, in reply, that, "if the measure I attended [alluded] to were taken, he might venture to assure me there was no chance of any other person being thought of for the command, and that your [Nelson's] name would certainly have been the first that would have occurred to himself. That there could be the less doubt of your being appointed, as it would naturally be left to Lord St. Vincent to name the Officer, and that I knew his high opinion of you. He added, however, that in writing to Lord St. Vincent on the subject, while he left the nomination to him, he should express his own opinion, and that of Government, that you are the proper man. Our conversation ran into greater length than I need relate : what I have already said was the most material." . . . " Whether twelve Ships will enable you to keep them at home, or to find work for them there, you are a better judge than me. In the meanwhile, I own I wish most anxiously to see the twelve Ships fairly under your command. Lord Spencer, at the close of the conversation, thanked me for mentioning this subject, though his opinion was already exactly the same with mine, (I mean in what relates to you,) and said he should be very glad to receive any other suggestion I might think useful on a matter on which he supposed me likely to be well informed."—*Tucker's Memoirs of Earl St. Vincent*, vol. i. p. 349. The following Orders from Lord St. Vincent to Nelson, dated on the 21st of May, 1798, were brought by Captain Troubridge, in the Cul-

loden:—" In pursuance of instructions I have received from the Lords Commissioners of the Admiralty, to employ a Squadron of his Majesty's Ships
within the Mediterranean, under the command of a discreet Officer, (copies of
which are enclosed and of other papers necessary for your guidance) in conformity thereto, I do hereby authorize and require You, on being joined by the Ships
named in the margin, [viz., Culloden, Goliath, Minotaur, Defence, Bellerophon,
Majestic, Audacious, Zealous, Swiftsure, Theseus,] to take them and their Captains under your command, in addition to those already with you, and to proceed with them in quest of the Armament preparing by the Enemy at Toulon
and Genoa, the object whereof appears to be, either an attack upon Naples and
Sicily, the conveyance of an Army to some part of the Coast of Spain, for the purpose of marching towards Portugal, or to pass through the Straits, with the view
of proceeding to Ireland. On falling in with the said Armament, or any part thereof,
you are to use your utmost endeavours to take, sink, burn, or destroy it. Should it
appear to you, from good authority, on your arrival up the Mediterranean, that the
Enemy's force capable of being sent to sea, should be inferior to what is reported
by the intelligence herewith transmitted, you are in this case to direct such Ships to
rejoin me as may not absolutely be required to insure your superiority the moment you shall find yourself in a situation so to do. You are to remain upon this
Service so long as the provisions of your Squadron will last, or as long as you may
be enabled to obtain supplies from any of the Ports in the Mediterranean, and when,
from the want of provisions or any other circumstance, you shall be no longer able
to remain within the Straits, or that the Enemy's armament should escape to the
westward of you, which you will take especial care to prevent, you are to lose no
time in rejoining me, wherever I may be. On the subject of supplies, I enclose also
a copy of their Lordships' order to me, and do require you strictly to comply with
the spirit of it, by considering and treating as hostile any Ports within the Mediterranean, (those of Sardinia excepted,) where provisions or other articles you may be in
want of, and which they are enabled to furnish, shall be refused ; and you are to treat
in like manner, and capture the Ships and Vessels of Powers or States adhering to
his Majesty's Enemies, or under other circumstances enumerated in the said order,
determining to the best of your judgment upon the several cases under this head,
that may occur during your command." The following " Additional Instructions"
were also dated on the 21st of May :—" From the tenor of the instructions from
the Lords Commissioners of the Admiralty which you will receive with this, it
appears that their Lordships expect favourable neutrality from Tuscany and the
Two Sicilies. In any event, you are to exact supplies of whatever you may
be in want of from the territories of the Grand Duke of Tuscany, the King of
the Two Sicilies, the Ottoman Territory, Malta, and ci-devant Venetian Dominions now belonging to the Emperor of Germany. You will also perceive by
an extract of a letter from Mr. Master, his Majesty's Consul for Algiers, that the
Dey is extremely well-disposed towards us. The Bey of Tunis, by the report of
Captain Thompson of his Majesty's Ship the Leander is also perfectly neutral and
good-humoured. From the Bashaw of Tripoli, I have every reason to believe,
any Ships of your Squadron having occasion to touch there will be received in the
most friendly manner. In a private letter from Lord Spencer, I am led to believe,
that you are perfectly justifiable in pursuing the French Squadron to any part of the
Mediterranean, Adriatic, Morea, Archipelago, or even into the Black Sea, should its
destination be to any of those parts ; and thoroughly sensible of your zeal, enterprise,
and capacity, at the head of a Squadron of Ships so well appointed, manned, and
commanded, I have the utmost confidence in the success of your operations. I
send Mr. Littledale to you as an aid in the Victualling branch, Mr. Heatly having

been well satisfied with the conduct of the house to which he belongs at Leghorn. Their former contracts for the supply of the Fleet will serve as a guide to you. If a plan I have directed Mr. Heatly to make, does not arrive in time to go by Captain Troubridge, I will send it by the first good conveyance. It is hardly necessary to instruct you to open a correspondence with his Majesty's Ministers at every Court in Italy, at Vienna, and Constantinople, and the different Consuls on the Coasts of the seas you are to operate in. Those of Algier and Tunis are absent from their Posts, and not likely to resume them. You will see the necessity of my being informed of your movements from time to time. A good Sparonara or Felucca with faithful people on board, if to be found, will serve for an Advice-boat during the summer months. When I have a Cutter to spare, you shall have her.—St. Vincent. Provisions and stores for the service of your Squadron will be lodged at Gibraltar."—*Original*, in the Nelson Papers.]

June 11th.

The Mutine, Captain Hardy, joined me on the 5th, at day-light, with the flattering account of the honour you intended me of commanding such a Fleet.[4] Mutine fell in with Alcmene, off Barcelona on the 2nd. Hope[5] had taken all my Frigates off the rendezvous, on the presumption that the Vanguard, from her disabled state, must return to an arsenal. I joined dear Troubridge with the reinforcement of ten Sail of the Line, and the Leander on the 7th in the evening:[6] it has been nearly calm ever since, which grieves me sorely. The French have a long start,[7] but I hope they will rendezvous in Telamon bay, for the 12,000 men from Genoa in 100 Sail of Vessels, escorted by a Frigate, had not put to sea on the 2nd,

[4] " Tuesday, 5th June, H.M. Brig La Mutine joined the Squadron, when Captain Hardy came on board with orders for me, and to acquaint me that Captain Troubridge, with ten Sail of the Line, was coming to join me, and that Captain Hope had taken my Frigates off the rendezvous."—*Journal*. " This intelligence was received," says Captain Berry, " with universal joy throughout our little Squadron, and the Admiral observed to him, that he would then be a match for any hostile Fleet in the Mediterranean, and his own desire would be to encounter one."—*Narrative*.

[5] Captain George Hope, of the Alcmene, who will be frequently mentioned.

[6] " 7th June.—At 10 m. past 1, discovered a strange Fleet, E. by N., which I supposed to be the Squadron under Captain Troubridge. After I made the Private Signal, I observed it was answered by the Culloden shewing her distinguishing Pendants, by which I was satisfied the Ships in sight were the Squadron sent to join me. 30 m. past 6, the under-mentioned Ships having joined me, I hove-to the Fleet."—*Log*. The Ships were the Culloden, Bellerophon, Minotaur, Defence, Zealous, Audacious, Goliath, Majestic, Swiftsure, Theseus, Leander; and the *Log* gives the names of their Captains, force, and guns, but as these will appear in the account of the Battle of the Nile, it is unnecessary to insert them here.

[7] The French Fleet sailed from Toulon on the 20th of May; and on the 14th of June, Nelson learnt, from a Vessel spoken by the Leander, that on the 4th of that month, the Enemy's Fleet were seen off Trapani in Sicily, steering to the eastward.—*Log*.

nor were all the troops embarked. You may be assured I will fight them the moment I can reach their Fleet, be they at anchor, or under sail. I am, &c.,

HORATIO NELSON.

---

TO HIS EXCELLENCY SIR WILLIAM HAMILTON, K.B.

[Letter Book.]

Vanguard, off Elba, June 12th, 1798.

My dear Sir,

If the Transfer Sloop of War has arrived at Naples, you will know that the British Fleet is in the Mediterranean, and that I have the honour of commanding it. It has been a misfortune that a Fleet was not ordered a fortnight sooner; but, no blame attaches itself anywhere, and from Sir Roger Curtis' junction with Lord St. Vincent, we are much sooner on the Coast of Italy than could have been expected. But I hope we are in good time to save Naples or Sicily from falling into the hands of the Enemy. I beg you will assure the King and Queen of Naples that I will not lose one moment in fighting the French Fleet, and that no person can have a more ardent desire of serving them and of fulfilling the orders of the good and great King our Master. As I am not quite clear, from General Acton's Letters to you of April 3rd and 9th, what co-operation is intended by the Court of Naples, I wish to know perfectly what is to be expected, that I may regulate my movements accordingly, and beg clear answers to the following questions and requisitions:—

Are the Ports of Naples and Sicily open to his Majesty's Fleet? Have the Governors orders for our free admission? and for us to be supplied with whatever we may want?

If it is *convenient*, I much wish for some Frigates and other fast-sailing Vessels, for, by a fatality,[8] all mine have left me. I want information of the French Fleet; for I hope they have passed Naples. I want good Pilots—say six or eight, for the Coast of Sicily, the Adriatic, or for whatever place the Enemy's Fleet may be at; for I mean to follow them if

[8] See p. 25, ante.

they go to the Black Sea.  As the 12,000 men had not sailed
from Genoa on the 2nd of June, nor, indeed, were they all
embarked, I trust, if the French are landed in the Neapolitan
territory, that the Kingdom will not be lost in a few days,
for I again repeat, that when it is considered that the orders
for a Fleet to go into the Mediterranean were only dated
May 2nd, and that Sir R. Curtis only came in sight of Lord
St. Vincent on May the 24th, on which moment Captain
Troubridge was sent away with the Detachment to join me
off Cape Sicie, that the British Fleet is much sooner on the
Coast of Italy than could have been expected at this season of
the year.

I trust to your Excellency's goodness in impressing General
Acton with a favourable opinion of my zeal in our Master's
service, and although, I most readily admit that many more
able Sea-Officers might have been selected for this service,
yet one more anxious to approve himself a faithful servant to
his King is not to be met with, than your Excellency's most
obedient Servant,

HORATIO NELSON.

---

TO ADMIRAL THE EARL OF ST. VINCENT, K.B.

[From Clarke and M'Arthur, vol. ii. p. 62.]

12th of June, 1798.

As I see no immediate prospect of a Letter, I shall continue
my private one in form of a Diary, which may not be unpleasant to refer to : therefore to begin.  Being so close to the
Enemy, I take the liberty of keeping Orion for a few days.
Owing to want of wind, I did not pass Cape Corse until this
morning; at four we were becalmed.  The moment we had
passed, I sent the Mutine to look into Telamon Bay, which, as
all the French troops had not left Genoa on the 6th, I thought
a probable place for the rendezvous of a large Fleet; and went
with the Squadron between Monte Christi, and Giulio, keeping
the Continent close on board.

13th of June.—Mutine joined; nothing in Telamon Bay.
I then ran the Fleet between Plenosa and Elba, and Monte
Christi; and on the 14th at noon, am now off Civita Vecchia;
spoke a Tunisian cruiser, who reported he had spoke a Greek, on

the 10th, who told him, that on the 4th, he had passed through the French Fleet, of about 200 Sail, as he thought, off the N.W. end of Sicily, steering to the eastward. Am in anxious expectation of meeting with Dispatch-boats, Neapolitan cruisers, &c., with letters for me from Naples giving me information. 15th of June.—Off the Ponza Islands ; my hopes of information were vain. Not finding a Cruiser, I shall send Troubridge into Naples, in the Mutine, to talk with Sir William Hamilton and General Acton. Troubridge possesses my full confidence, and has been my honoured acquaintance of twenty-five years' standing. I only beg that your Lordship will believe, I shall endeavour to prove myself worthy of your selection of me for this highly honourable Command. Not a moment shall be lost in pursuing the Enemy. I am, &c.,

HORATIO NELSON.

---

TO THE RIGHT HONOURABLE SIR WILLIAM HAMILTON, K.B.

[Letter-Book.]

Vanguard, off Civita Vecchia, 14th June, 1798.

My dear Sir,

I have heard by a Vessel just spoke with, that the French Fleet were seen off the north End of Sicily, steering to the eastward, on the 4th of June. If they mean an attack on Sicily, I hope by this time they have barely made a landing, for if their Fleet is not moored in as strong a Port as Toulon, nothing shall hinder me from attacking them ; and, with the blessing of Almighty God, I hope for a most glorious victory. I send Captain Troubridge to communicate with your Excellency, and, as Captain Troubridge is in full possession of my confidence, I beg that whatever he says may be considered as coming from me. Captain Troubridge is my honoured acquaintance of twenty-five years, and the very best Sea-Officer in His Majesty's Service. I hope, Pilots will be with us in a few hours ; for I will not lose one moment after the Brig's return, to wait for anything. Believe me your Excellency's most obedient servant,

HORATIO NELSON.

TO EARL SPENCER.

[Letter-Book.]

Vanguard, off the Island of Ponza, [15th June, 1798.]

My Lord,

Not having received orders from my Commander-in-Chief
to correspond with the Secretary of the Admiralty, I do not
feel myself at perfect liberty to do it, unless on extraordinary
occasions, when I shall send copies of my Letters to Lord St.
Vincent; but as your Lordships must be anxious to hear of us,
I take the liberty of acquainting you that Captain Troubridge
joined on the 7th, but it was the 12th before we passed Cape
Corse. The last account I had of the French Fleet, was from
a Tunisian Cruizer, who saw them on the 4th, off Trapani, in
Sicily, steering to the eastward. If they pass Sicily, I shall
believe they are going on their scheme of possessing Alexandria, and getting troops to India—a plan concerted with
Tippoo Saib, by no means so difficult as might at first view
be imagined; but be they bound to the Antipodes, your
Lordship may rely that I will not lose a moment in bringing
them to Action, and endeavour to destroy their Transports.
I shall send Captain Troubridge on shore to talk with General
Acton, and I hope the King of Naples will send me some Frigates; for mine parted company on the 20th of May, and have
not joined me since. The whole Squadron is remarkably
healthy, and perfectly equal to meet the French Fleet. As I
send this before I receive accounts from Naples, it is not in
my power to say anything more of the Enemy, for I shall
make sail and pass the Faro of Messina the moment Captain
Troubridge returns.

Highly honoured as I feel with this very important command, I beg you will believe that I shall endeavour to approve
myself worthy of it, and that I am, with the highest respect,

Your Lordship's most obedient servant,

HORATIO NELSON.

I have taken the liberty of enclosing a letter for Lady
Nelson, which I beg your Lordship will have the goodness
to order to be sent to her.

## TO ADMIRAL THE EARL OF ST. VINCENT, K.B.

[Letter-Book.]

Vanguard, off the Islands of Ponza, June 15th, 1798.

My Lord,

I have the honour to acquaint you of my arrival here with the whole Line-of-Battle Ships, the Fifty, and Brig, all in the most perfect health. I am sending Captain Troubridge in the Mutine to see Sir William Hamilton and General Acton, and to get accounts of the French Fleet. I shall lay with the Squadron off Ischia till Captain Troubridge's return, when not a moment shall be lost in pursuing the Enemy, and bringing them to Action. With the highest respect, believe me, your Lordship's most obedient servant,

HORATIO NELSON.

---

## TO ADMIRAL THE EARL OF ST. VINCENT, K.B.

[Autograph draught, in the Nelson Papers and "Letter-Book."]

Vanguard, off Naples, 17th June, 1798.

My Lord,

I have only to assure you, I will bring the French Fleet to Action the moment I can lay my hands on them. Till then, Adieu. Believe me, &c.

HORATIO NELSON.

---

## TO THE RIGHT HONOURABLE SIR WILLIAM HAMILTON, K.B.

[Letter-Book. " Sunday, 17th June.—At 8 A.M. hove-to in the Bay of Naples. At 11, received a Letter from Sir William Hamilton, by a boat from Naples; returned an answer by the same boat. Fleet in Company."—*Journal.*]

Vanguard, Naples Bay, eleven o'clock, 17th June.

My dear Sir,

Your Letter by the Boat yesterday did not come to me, but I am just favoured with yours of yesterday. Captain Troubridge will say everything I could put in a ream of paper. I have only to observe, in my present state, if I meet the Enemy at Sea, the Convoy will get off, for want of Frigates. I submit this to you, to urge General Acton upon.

If the Enemy have Malta, it is only as a safe harbour for
their Fleet, and Sicily will fall the moment the King's Fleet
withdraws from the Coast of Sicily; therefore we must have
free use of Sicily, to enable us to starve the French in Malta.
I need not say more on this very important subject. The
King of Naples may now have part of the glory in destroying
these pests of the human race; and the opportunity, once
lost, may never be regained. God bless you. Depend on
my exertions.

I am, &c.

HORATIO NELSON.

---

TO THE RIGHT HONOURABLE SIR WILLIAM HAMILTON, K.B.

[Letter-Book. Captain Troubridge returned on the 18th of June, with a *report* that
the Enemy had gone towards Malta, and the Fleet immediately made sail for the Faro
of Messina, and thence, on the 20th, for Malta. On Friday, the 22nd, being near Cape
Passaro, in Sicily, Captain Hardy, of the Mutine, learnt from the master of a Vessel,
that the French had taken Malta on the 15th, and that their Fleet had sailed from
that Island on the 18th, with a fresh gale at N.W., but he could give no information
respecting its destination. The Squadron immediately made sail for Alexandria.]

Private.

My dear Sir,　　　　　　Vanguard, at Sea, 18th June, 1798.
　　I would not lose one moment of the breeze, in answering
your Letter. The best sight (as an Irishman would say)
was to see me out of sight; especially, as I had not time to
examine the Marquis de Gallo's note to you. I send you an
extract of the Admiralty orders to Earl St. Vincent, by
which it would appear as determined by the Cabinet, to keep
a superior Fleet to the Enemy in the Mediterranean; for
the Admiralty, you know, can give no such orders, but by
an order from the Secretary of State. As for what depends
on me, I beg, if you think it proper, to tell their Sicilian
Majesties, and General Acton, that they may rest assured that
I shall not withdraw the King's Fleet, but by positive orders,
or the impossibility of *procuring supplies*. I wish them to
depend upon me, and they shall not be disappointed. God
forbid it should so happen, that the Enemy escape me, and
get into any Port. You may rely if I am properly supplied,
that there they shall remain, a useless body, for this summer.

But, if I have Gun and Mortar Boats, with Fire-Ships, it is most probable they may be got at: for, although I hope the best, yet it is proper to be prepared for the worst, (which, I am sure, all this Fleet would feel,) the escape of the Enemy into Port. My distress for Frigates is extreme; but I cannot help myself, and no one will help me. But, thank God, I am not apt to feel difficulties. Pray, present my best respects to Lady Hamilton. Tell her, I hope to be presented to her crowned with laurel or cypress. But God is good, and to Him do I commit myself and our Cause. Ever believe me, my dear Sir, your obliged and faithful

HORATIO NELSON.

---

TO THE MOST ILLUSTRIOUS THE GRAND MASTER OF MALTA.

[Letter-Book.]

His Britannic Majesty's Ship Vanguard, off Messina, 20th June, 1798.

Most Illustrious Sir,

It is with particular satisfaction I have the honour to acquaint you I am making all possible dispatch with the Squadron of his Britannic Majesty under my command towards Malta, with a full determination to prevent your Island from falling into the hands of the common Enemy. I therefore trust you will be pleased to give directions to assemble all your Ships of War, Fire-ships, Bombs, Galleys, &c., immediately, to form a speedy junction with me the moment I appear off Malta (which I expect will be on Friday next) for the better insurance of success, as no time must be lost in destroying the French Fleet. I have the honour to be, &c.,

HORATIO NELSON.

---

TO HIS EXCELLENCY THE RIGHT HONOURABLE SIR WILLIAM HAMILTON, K.B.

[Letter-Book.]

Vanguard, off the Faro of Messina, June 20th, 1798.

My dear Sir,

I have thought so much, and heard so much, of the French, since I left Naples, that I should feel culpable, was I for a

moment to delay expressing my sentiments on the present
situation of the Kingdom of the Two Sicilies. I trust it will
be received as I mean it—as a proof of the lively interest I
take in the fate of their Sicilian Majesties. I shall begin by
supposing myself commanding a Fleet attending an Army
which is to invade Sicily. If the General asked if Malta
would not be a most useful place for the depôt of stores, &c.,
&c., my answer would be, if you can take Malta, it secures
the safety of the Fleet, Transports, stores, &c., and insures
your safe retreat should that be necessary; for if even a
superior Fleet of the Enemy should arrive, before one week
passes, they will be blown to leeward, and you may pass with
safety. This would be my opinion. There can be no doubt
but the French know as well as you and I do, that their
Sicilian Majesties called for our help to save them, (even this
is crime enough with the French.) Here we are, and are
ready, and will shed our blood in preventing the French from
ill-treating them. On the arrival of the King's Fleet I find
plenty of good will towards us, with every hatred towards the
French; but no assistance for us—no hostility to the French.
On the contrary, the French Minister is allowed to send off
Vessels to inform the Fleet of my arrival, force, and destination, that instead of my surprising them, they may be prepared for resistance. But this being past, I shall endeavour
briefly to state what in my opinion is now best to be done,
and what Naples ought to do, if it is earnestly wished to save
Sicily. I shall suppose the French not advanced since the
last accounts, but still on Gozo and Comino, the Fleet anchored
between them. By the communication from Naples, they
will be formed in the strongest position, with Batteries and
Gun-boats to flank them. We shall doubtless injure them,
but our loss must be great; and I do not expect to force them
from the anchorage, without Fire-ships, Bomb-vessels, and
Gun-boats, when one hour would either destroy or drive them
out. If our Fleet is crippled, the blockade ends; if not, it will
be continued, by attention, and sending two Ships at a time to
Sicily to get refreshments, for the summer, at least; but whenever this Fleet may be drawn away, and the Ministry find
what has passed at Naples—*no co-operation*, although we are
come to their assistance—who can say that the Fleet will be

kept in these seas? I have said and repeat it, *Malta is the
direct road to Sicily.* It has been, and may be yet in the King
of Naples' power, by giving me help of every kind, directly
to destroy this Armament, and force the Army to unconditional submission. Naples must soon find us masts, yards,
stores, ammunition, &c., &c. Will not this be a declaration of War against the French?—therefore why delay sending help, if it is only six Gun-boats at a time. But not a
moment must be lost—it can never be regained. I recollect
General Acton, in his letter to you calling for our help, says,
' Will the King and Ministry wish to see these fine Countries in
the hands of the French?' The answer is, No ; and we have
sent the means of preventing it. It may now be asked—will
the Ministry of their Sicilian Majesties permit these fine
Countries to fall into the hands of the French? This will
assuredly happen if they do not co-operate with us. If I have
wrote my mind too freely, I trust it will be excused. The
importance of the subject called for my opinion. I have given
it like an honest man, and shall wish to stand or fall with it.

I am, dear Sir, with the highest respect, &c.

HORATIO NELSON.

---

TO GEORGE BALDWIN, ESQ., CONSUL AT ALEXANDRIA.

[Letter-Book.]

(Private.)                                    June 24th, 1798.
Dear Sir,

I am so persuaded of the intention of the French to attempt
driving us from India, in concert with Tippoo Saib, that I
shall never feel secure till Mangalore, and all Tippoo's Sea-
Coast, is in our possession. We ought to get hold of the
Coast, even at the certainty of a War with him. Had I been
his Peace-Maker, he should have had my head before Mangalore, or one foot of Coast. I send you some Reviews and
Magazines—they may be pleasant, although old ; and if I can
get near you with the Fleet, and am favoured with five
minutes' conversation, I shall have great pleasure in supplying you with anything in my power; for believe me, dear
Sir, your most obedient servant,

HORATIO NELSON.

Pray do not detain the Mutine, for I am in a fever at not finding the French. At Naples they have English news to the 16th of May. No fears of an Invasion: Pitt stronger than ever.

---

TO GEORGE BALDWIN, ESQ., CONSUL AT ALEXANDRIA.

[Letter-Book. On the 26th, Alexandria bearing at Noon S 68 E. 233 miles. "At 9 A.M. Captain Hardy, of the Mutine, came on board, per signal. I gave him orders to proceed to Alexandria, and endeavour to procure intelligence of the French Fleet, then to join me, immediately after having delivered my Dispatches to the British Consul, which I committed to his charge."—*Journal.*]

Vanguard, at Sea, 26th June, 1798.

Sir,

The French having possessed themselves of Malta, on Friday, the 15th of this month, the next day, the whole Fleet, consisting of sixteen Sail of the Line, Frigates, Bomb-vessels, &c., and near three hundred Transports, left the Island. I only heard this unpleasant news on the 22nd, off Cape Passaro. As Sicily was not their object, and the wind blew fresh from the westward, from the time they sailed, it was clear that their destination was to the eastward; and I think their object is, to possess themselves of some Port in Egypt, and to fix themselves at the head of the Red Sea, in order to get a formidable Army into India; and, in concert with Tippoo Saib, to drive us, if possible, from India. But I have reason to believe, from not seeing a Vessel, that they have heard of my coming up the Mediterranean, and are got safe into Corfu. But still I am most exceedingly anxious to know from you if any reports or preparations have been made in Egypt for them; or any Vessels prepared in the Red Sea, to carry them to India, where, from the prevailing winds at this season, they would soon arrive; or any other information you would be good enough to give me, I shall hold myself much obliged.

I am, Sir, &c.,

HORATIO NELSON.

TO ADMIRAL THE EARL OF ST. VINCENT, K.B.

[Letter-Book. On Friday, the 29th of June, off Pharos Tower, Alexandria, the Mutine rejoined, and Captain Hardy reported, that he could not obtain any intelligence of the French Fleet.]

Vanguard, at Sea, June 29th, 1798.

My Lord,

Although, I rest confident, that my intentions will always with you have the most favourable interpretations, yet where success does not crown an Officer's plan, it is absolutely necessary that he should explain the motives which actuate his conduct, and therefore, I shall state them as briefly as possible.

Captain Troubridge joined me on the 7th of June. From calms it was the 12th before I got round Cape Corse; (I must here state, that I had nothing in the shape of a Frigate except the Mutine Brig). I then sent the Mutine to look into Telamon Bay, which, as all the French troops had not left Genoa on the 6th, I thought a probable place for the rendezvous of a large Fleet, for, completely ignorant as I was of the destination of the Enemy, I felt it my duty to take every precaution not to pass them. On the 13th, the Mutine looked into Telamon Bay, but found nothing there. I ran the Fleet between Planosa, Elba, and Monte Christi, and on the 14th, at noon, was off Civita Vecchia, when we spoke a Tunisian cruiser, who reported that he had spoken a Greek on the 10th, who told him that on the 4th, he had passed through the French Fleet off the N.W. end of Sicily, steering to the eastward. From this moment, I was in anxious expectation of meeting with Dispatch-boats, Neapolitan Cruisers, &c., with letters for me from Naples, giving me every information I could desire, (but my hopes were vain.) On the 15th, I made the Ponza Islands, where not finding a Cruiser, I sent Captain Troubridge in the Mutine to talk with Sir William Hamilton and General Acton, and to state my distress for Frigates.

On the 17th, in the Bay of Naples, I received my first letter from Sir William Hamilton, and in two hours Captain Troubridge returned with information, that the French Fleet were off Malta on the 8th, going to attack it, that Naples was at

Peace with the French Republic, therefore, could afford us
no assistance in Ships, but that, under the rose, they would
give us the use of their Ports, and sincerely wished us well,
but did not give me the smallest information of what was, or
likely to be, the future destination of the French armament.
With this comfortable account, I pushed for the Faro [of]
Messina. On my way I heard of the French landing in
Malta, and that on Tuesday the 12th they had taken the old
City : that the Fleet was anchored between Gozo and Malta.
On the 20th, off Messina, the English Consul came on board
to tell me that Malta had surrendered on the 15th, the
Russian Minister having arrived the day before from Malta,
when the intelligence came over, but I received not the
smallest information or notice from the Sicilian Government.
Keeping the Sicilian shore on board, on the 21st, I was close
off Syracuse and hoisted our colours. A boat in the evening
rowed out about a mile, but although I brought to and sent
the Mutine in shore, she rowed back again. On the 22nd,
in the morning, being off Cape Passaro, the Mutine spoke a
Brig which sailed from Malta the day before. The Master
reported that Malta surrendered on Friday the 15th of June,
and that on Saturday, the 16th, the whole French Fleet left it,
as was supposed, for Sicily : that a French garrison was left in
the Town, and French colours flying. The wind at this time was
blowing strong from the W.N.W. the Vessel had been spoken
three hours before, and was gone out of my reach. I could
not get to Malta till it moderated, and then I might get no
better information. Thus situated I had to make use of my
judgment. With information from Naples, that they were at
peace with the French Republic, that General Buonaparte
had sent on shore to Sicily, that the King of Naples need not
be alarmed at the French armament, for it had not Sicily
for its object. It was also certain the Sicilian Government
were not alarmed or they would have sent off to me. I recalled all the circumstances of this Armament before me,
40,000 troops in 280 Transports, many hundred pieces of
artillery, waggons, draught-horses, cavalry, artificers, na-
turalists, astronomers, mathematicians, &c. The first rendezvous in case of separation was Bastia, the second, Malta,—
this Armament could not be necessary for taking possession of

Malta. The Neapolitan Ministers considered Naples and Sicily
as safe; Spain, after Malta, or indeed any place to the westward, I could not think their destination, for at this season
the westerly winds so strongly prevail between Sicily and
the Coast of Barbary, that I conceive it almost impossible
to get a Fleet of Transports to the westward. It then
became the serious question, where are they gone? (Here I
had deeply to regret my want of Frigates, and I desire it may
be understood, that if one-half the Frigates your Lordship had
ordered under my command had been with me, that I could
not have wanted information of the French Fleet.) If to
Corfu, in consequence of my approach (which they knew
from Naples on the 12th or 13th) they were arrived by this
time, the 22nd.

Upon their whole proceedings, together with such information as I have been able to collect, it appeared clear to
me, that either they were destined to assist the rebel Pacha
and to overthrow the present Government of Turkey, or to
settle a Colony in Egypt, and to open a trade to India by
way of the Red Sea; for, strange as it may appear at first
sight, an enterprising Enemy, if they have the force or consent of the Pacha of Egypt, may with great ease get an
Army to the Red Sea, and if they have concerted a plan with
Tippoo Saib, to have Vessels at Suez, three weeks, at this season, is a common passage to the Malabar Coast, when our
India possessions would be in great danger.

I therefore determined, with the opinion of those Captains
in whom I place great confidence,[4] to go to Alexandria; and
if that place, or any other part of Egypt was their destination,
I hoped to arrive time enough to frustrate their plans. The
only objection I can fancy to be started is, ' you should not
have gone such a long voyage without more certain information of the Enemy's destination:' my answer is ready—who
was I to get it from? The Governments of Naples and
Sicily either knew not, or chose to keep me in ignorance. Was
I to wait patiently till I heard certain accounts? If Egypt
was their object, before I could hear of them they would

---

[4] Namely, Sir James Saumarez, Troubridge, Ball, and Darby, who were signalled
to come on board the Vanguard, immediately after La Mutine had spoken the Vessel
on the 22nd of June.—*Vanguard's Log.*

have been in India. To do nothing, I felt, was disgraceful: therefore I made use of my understanding, and by it I ought to stand or fall. I am before your Lordship's judgment, (which in the present case I feel is the Tribunal of my Country,) and if, under all circumstances, it is decided that I am wrong, I ought, for the sake of our Country, to be superseded; for, at this moment, when I know the French are not in Alexandria, I hold the same opinion as off Cape Passaro—viz., that under all circumstances, I was right in steering for Alexandria, and by that opinion I must stand or fall. However erroneous my judgment may be, I feel conscious of my honest intentions, which I hope will bear me up under the greatest misfortune that could happen to me as an Officer—that of your Lordship's thinking me wrong. I have the honour to be, with the highest respect,

Your Lordship's most obedient Servant,

HORATIO NELSON.[5]

------

TO ADMIRAL THE EARL OF ST. VINCENT, K.B.

[Letter-Book.]

Vanguard, 12 Leagues West of Candia, 12th July, 1798.

My Lord,
By my Letter of the 29th of June, your Lordship will know why I thought it right to steer for Alexandria. I have now

------

[5] Nelson having shewn this Dispatch to Captain Ball, that Officer wrote him a very able Letter to dissuade him from sending it; urging similar advice to that given by King Charles the First to Lord Strafford, not to defend himself before he was accused:—" I was particularly struck," Captain Ball said, " with the clear and accurate style, as well as with the candour of the statement in your Letter; but I felt a regret, that your too anxious zeal should make you start an idea, that your judgment was impeachable, because you have not yet fallen in with the French Fleet, as it implicates a doubt, and may induce a suspicion, that you are not perfectly satisfied with your own conduct. I should recommend a friend, never to begin a defence of his conduct before he is accused of error: he may give the fullest reasons for what he has done, expressed in such terms as will evince that he acted from the strongest conviction of being right; and, of course, he must expect that the public will view it in the same light. The great Lord Chatham, when speaking in the House of Lords of the failure of a General Officer, said, ' I will not condemn Ministers; they might have instructed him wisely, he might have executed his instructions faithfully and judiciously, and yet he might have miscarried. There are many events which the greatest human foresight cannot provide against.' "— *Autograph* in the Nelson Papers, printed at length in Clarke and M'Arthur, vol. ii. p. 60.

the honour to acquaint you that I arrived off Alexandria on the 28th ultimo, and found lying there one Turkish Ship of the Line, four Frigates, about twelve other Turkish vessels in the old Port, and about fifty Sail of different Nations' vessels, in the Franks' Port. I directed Captain Hardy, of the Mutine, to run close in, and to send an Officer on shore with my letter to Mr. Baldwin, and to get all the information in his power. Herewith I send you the Officer's report. Mr. Baldwin had left Alexandria near three months. We observed the Line-of-Battle Ship to be landing her guns, and that the place was filling with armed people. After receiving this information, I stretched the Fleet over to the Coast of Asia, and have passed close to the southern side of Candia, but without seeing one Vessel in our route; therefore to this day I am without the smallest information of the French Fleet since their leaving Malta. I own I fully expected to have found Dispatches off this end of Candia; for both Sir William Hamilton and General Acton, *I now know*, said they believed Egypt was their object; for that when the French Minister at Naples was pressed, on the Armament appearing off Sicily, he declared that Egypt was their object. I have again to deeply regret my want of Frigates, to which I shall ever attribute my ignorance of the situation of the French Fleet. I shall endeavour to keep in the opening of the Archipelago in Lat. between 36° and 37° N., steering with all sail to the westward, and hope soon to gain information from some Merchant-vessel. I have the honour to be, &c.,

HORATIO NELSON.

---

TO HIS EXCELLENCY SIR WILLIAM HAMILTON, K.B., NAPLES.

[Original, in the State Paper Office. On the 30th of June, the Squadron took a Prize, which was set on fire the next day, and then proceeded for the coast of Caramania, steering along the south side of Candia, and thence back to Sicily, and anchored at Syracuse on the 20th of July, where the Squadron, consisting of thirteen Sail of the Line, and the Leander, of 50 guns, watered and obtained fresh provisions, &c.]

Vanguard, Syracuse, July 20th, 1798.

My dear Sir,

It is an old saying, ' the Devil's children have the Devil's luck.' I cannot find, or to this moment learn, beyond vague

conjecture where the French Fleet are gone to. All my ill
fortune, hitherto, has proceeded from want of Frigates. Off
Cape Passaro, on the 22nd of June, at day-light, I saw two
Frigates, which were supposed to be French, and it has been
said since that a Line of Battle Ship was to leeward of them,[6]
with the riches of Malta on board, but it was the destruction
of the Enemy, not riches for myself, that I was seeking.
These would have fallen to me if I had had Frigates, but
except the Ship of the Line, I regard not all the riches in this
world. From every information off Malta I believed they
were gone to Egypt. Therefore, on the 28th, I was communicating with Alexandria in Egypt, where I found the
Turks preparing to resist them, but know nothing beyond
report. From thence I stretched over to the Coast of Caramania, where not meeting a Vessel that could give me information, I became distressed for the Kingdom of the Two
Sicilies, and having gone a round of 600 leagues at this
season of the year (with a single Ship[7]) with an expedition incredible, here I am as ignorant of the situation of the Enemy
as I was twenty-seven days ago. I sincerely hope, that the
Dispatches which I understand are at Cape Passaro, will give
me full information. I shall be able for nine or ten weeks
longer to keep the Fleet on active service, when we shall want
provisions and stores. I send a paper on that subject herewith. Mr. Littledale is, I suppose, sent up by the Admiral
to victual us, and I hope he will do it cheaper than any other
person ; but if I find out that he charges more than the fair
price, and has not the provisions of the very best quality, I
will not take them ; for, as no Fleet has more fag than this,
nothing but the best food and greatest attention can keep
them healthy. At this moment, we have not one sick man in
the Fleet. In about six days I shall sail from hence, and if I
hear nothing more from the French, I shall go to the Archipelago, where if they are gone towards Constantinople I shall
hear of them. I shall go to Cyprus, and if they are gone to

[6] It appears from the Vanguard's *Log*, that the Leander chased those Ships, but
that on obtaining the information about the French Fleet from La Mutine, Nelson
recalled her, and made all sail for Egypt.

[7] *Sic.* Query, " without *seeing* a single Ship," or, " with a *crippled* Ship" ?

Alexandretta, or any other part of Syria or Egypt, I shall get information. You will, I am sure, and so will our Country, easily conceive what has passed in my anxious mind, but I have this comfort, that I have no fault to accuse myself of. This bears me up, and this only. I send you a Paper, in which a letter is fixed for different places, which I may leave at any place, and except those who have the key, none can tell where I am gone to.

July 21st.—The Messenger has returned from Cape Passaro, and says, that your letters for me are returned to Naples. What a situation am I placed in! As yet, I can learn nothing of the Enemy; therefore I have no conjecture but that they are gone to Syria, and at Cyprus I hope to hear of them. If they were gone to the westward, I rely that every place in Sicily would have information for us, for it is news too important to leave me one moment in doubt about. I have no Frigate, nor a sign of one. The masts, yards, &c. for the Vanguard will, I hope, be prepared directly; for should the French be so strongly secured in Port that I cannot get at them, I shall immediately shift my Flag into some other Ship, and send the Vanguard to Naples to be refitted; for hardly any other person but myself would have continued on service so long in such a wretched state.[7] I want to send a great number of Papers to Lord St. Vincent, but I dare not trust any person here to carry them even to Naples. Pray send a copy of my letter to Lord Spencer. He must be very anxious to hear of this Fleet. I have taken the liberty to trouble your Excellency with a letter for Lady Nelson. Pray forward it for me, and believe me, with the greatest respect, your most obedient Servant,

HORATIO NELSON.

---

TO LADY NELSON.

[From Clarke and M'Arthur, vol. i. p. 71.]

Syracuse, July 20th, 1798.

I have not been able to find the French Fleet, to my great mortification, or the event I can scarcely doubt. We have been off Malta, to Alexandria in Egypt, Syria, into Asia, and

[7] From the effect of the storm on the 21st of May, having only a Jury Foremast.

are returned here without success: however, no person will
say that it has been for want of activity.   I yet live in hopes
of meeting these fellows; but it would have been my delight
to have tried Buonaparte on a wind, for he commands the
Fleet, as well as the Army.   Glory is my object, and that
alone.   God Almighty bless you.

HORATIO NELSON.

TO ADMIRAL THE EARL OF ST. VINCENT, K.B.

[Letter-Book.]

Vanguard, Syracuse, 20th July, 1798.

My Lord,

From my Letter of the 12th, you will be informed of my
conduct to that time.   I have now to acquaint you that
having spoke several vessels from the westward, and one from
Corfu, I know, as far as their reports, that the French are
neither to the Westward of Sicily nor at Corfu.   Yesterday I arrived here, where I can learn no more than vague
conjecture that the French are gone to the eastward.   Every
moment I have to regret the Frigates having left me, to which
must be attributed my ignorance of the movements of the
Enemy.   Your Lordship deprived yourself of Frigates to
make mine certainly the first Squadron in the world, and I
feel that I have zeal and activity to do credit to your appointment, and yet to be unsuccessful hurts me most sensibly.   But
if they are above water, I will find them out, and if possible
bring them to Battle.   You have done your part in giving me
so fine a Fleet, and I hope to do mine in making use of them.
We are watering, and getting such refreshments as the place
affords, and shall get to sea by the 25th.   It is my intention
to get into the Mouth of the Archipelago, where, if the
Enemy are gone towards Constantinople, we shall hear of
them directly: if I get no information there, to go to Cyprus,
when, if they are in Syria or Egypt, I must hear of them.
Seventeen Sail of the Line, eight Frigates, &c. of War, went
from Malta with them.   We have a report that on the 1st of
July, the French were seen off Candia, but near what part
of the Island I cannot learn.   I have the honour to remain, &c.

HORATIO NELSON.

TO THE COMMANDERS OF ANY OF HIS MAJESTY'S SHIPS.

[Letter-Book.]

Sir,                    Vanguard, Syracuse, 22nd July, 1798.

Resting with the greatest confidence that had the French
Fleet proceeded to the westward from Malta, that his
Majesty's Minister at Naples would have taken care to have
lodged information for me in every Port in Sicily, knowing I
was gone to the eastward, I now acquaint you that I shall
steer direct for the Island of Cyprus, and hope in Syria to
find the French Fleet.  I am, &c.

HORATIO NELSON.

Having received some vague information of the Enemy,
I shall steer to the north of Candia, and probably send a
Ship to Milo, and if the Enemy are not in those seas, I shall
pass on for Cyprus, Syria, and Egypt.[8]

[8] At the end of the Copy of this Letter in the "Letter Book," which Book was
long in Lady Hamilton's possession, she wrote:—"The Queen's Letter, privately
got by me, got him and his Fleet victualled and watered in a few days.—EMMA
HAMILTON." It appears from the Letters to Sir William Hamilton, of the 22nd
and 23rd of July (pp. 47 and 48) that Nelson was not aware that any private order
for supplying his Squadron had been issued; and as those Letters (which are
unquestionably authentic) do not agree with the other Letter in p. 47, to Sir William and Lady Hamilton, a suspicion arises as to its genuineness, which is strengthened by the facts that Harrison was then endeavouring to support Lady Hamilton's
claim to a pension, founded mainly on her having obtained an order for victualling Nelson's Squadron; that the classical allusion is not in Nelson's style; and
that the conclusion is in nearly the same words as occur in the Letter in p. 34.  If
the Letter, which Harrison calls "a secret epistle," was a forgery, it was a clumsy
one, as he also printed the Letter to Sir William Hamilton, in p. 47.

The Supplies, however obtained, were made the subject of a spirited protest from
Monsieur La Cheze, Chargé des Affaires of the French Republic at Naples, in a
Letter to the Marquis de Gallo, dated, "Naples, 17 Thermidor, An. 6," (August 4,
1798.)  On the same day, he also called the Marquis's attention to the fact, that
the Portuguese Squadron, as well as our Ships "Le Lion de 64 canons, Le George
Thomson de 18, la Fregate la Dorothée de 40, prise faite par le même vaisseau le Lion," were also at that moment moored in the Road of Naples, contrary to
the third Article of the Treaty of Peace, which provided, that no more than four
Ships of the Line of any Enemy of the Republic should be there at one time.

TO THE RIGHT HON. SIR WILLIAM HAMILTON, K.B.

[From Copies in the State Paper Office, Admiralty, and Letter-Book.]

Vanguard, Syracuse, July 22, 1798.

My dear Sir,

I have had so much said about the King of Naples' orders only to admit three or four of the Ships of our Fleet into his Ports, that I am astonished. I understood that private orders, at least, would have been given for our free admission. If we are to be refused supplies, pray send me by many Vessels an account, that I may in good time take the King's Fleet to Gibraltar. Our treatment is scandalous for a great Nation to put up with, and the King's Flag is insulted at every Friendly Port we look at. I am, with the greatest respect, &c.,

HORATIO NELSON.

You will observe that I feel as a Public man, and write as such. I have no complaint to make of private attention, quite the contrary. Every body of persons have been on board to offer me civilities.

---

TO SIR WILLIAM AND LADY HAMILTON.

[From Harrison's " Life of Nelson," vol. i. p. 256.]

22nd July, 1798.

My dear Friends,

Thanks to your exertions, we have victualled and watered: and surely watering at the Fountain of Arethusa, we must have victory. We shall sail with the first breeze, and be assured I will return either crowned with laurel, or covered with cypress.

---

TO THE RIGHT HONOURABLE SIR WILLIAM HAMILTON, K.B.

[From a Copy in the Admiralty.]

Vanguard, Syracuse, 23rd July, 1798.

My dear Sir,

The Fleet is unmoored, and the moment the wind comes off the land, shall go out of this delightful harbour, where our present wants have been most amply supplied, and where every attention has been paid to us ; but I have been tormented by no private orders being given to the Governor for our admission. I have only to hope that I shall still find the French Fleet, and be able to get at them: the event then will be in the hands of Providence, of whose goodness none can doubt. I beg my best respects to Lady Hamilton, and believe me ever your faithful

HORATIO NELSON.

*No Frigates!*—to which has been, and may again, be attributed the loss of the French Fleet.

---

### BATTLE OF THE NILE.

As Nelson's Dispatch states the result rather than describes, the BATTLE OF THE NILE, it is desirable to prefix to his Official Letter the Narrative of the Battle written by his Captain, Sir Edward Berry, and published, with a Plan, immediately after the Event, entitled, "An authentic Narrative[2] of the proceedings of His Majesty's Squadron under the Command of Rear-Admiral Sir Horatio Nelson, from its sailing from Gibraltar to the conclusion of the glorious Battle of the Nile, drawn up from the Minutes of an Officer of Rank in the Squadron," 8vo. 1798, in the "Advertisement" to which, it is justly remarked, that "the account of the general result of this Action, even the best historians that shall hereafter record it, will be proud to borrow from the unaffected and eloquent Letter of the Admiral himself; but in every transaction of the kind, after the first tumult of National exultation shall have in some degree subsided, a thousand circumstances remain to be supplied for the satisfaction of the inquiring mind, and which are essential to gain a just and perfect impression of the actual merit of the great services which have been performed." To that Narrative some particulars will be added from other sources.

"From Syracuse the Squadron proceeded with all expedition to the Morea, and nothing particular occurred on the passage except that, on the 28th of July, being near the Morea, the Culloden was sent into the Gulf of Coron for intelligence, and on her return, the next day, she brought with her a French brig, a prize, and information that the Enemy's Fleet had been seen steering to the S.E. from Candia about four weeks before. The Alexander, Captain Ball, on the same day obtained similar intelligence from a Vessel passing close to the Fleet, and Nelson immediately bore up, under all sail, for Alexandria. At seven in the evening, of the 31st of July, the

---

[2] Sir Edward Berry, having sent a Copy of the Narrative to the Duke of Clarence, he received the following note from his Royal Highness: "Dear Sir—I am to return you many thanks for having sent me the Narrative. I showed it to the King who has taken it: the Queen is desirous of having one. I must, therefore, request you will enclose to me half-a-dozen more copies. I have wrote to Lord Nelson a very long Letter which, I hope and believe, will be satisfactory to both parties. I shall be anxious to see you before you return to his Lordship, and must desire you will then take charge of a Letter for the Hero of the Nile. I am, dear Sir, yours sincerely, WILLIAM."—*Autograph* in the possession of Lady Berry.

Admiral made the signal for the Fleet to close, and early in the morning of the 1st of August, the Alexander and Swiftsure were sent ahead to look out, and " at 10 A.M. the Alexander made a signal supposed for the land, all the Fleet in company. At 1 P.M. saw Alexander bearing S.E. ½ S. seven or eight leagues. At ¼ past 2, recalled the Alexander and Swiftsure. At ½ past 2, hauled our wind, unbent the best bower cable, took it out of the stern port and bent it again. At 4, Pharos Tower S.S.W. distant four or five leagues, the Zealous made the signal for the French Fleet, sixteen Sail of the Line. At 5, bore up for the French Fleet."—*Vanguard's Journal*.

" The utmost joy," says Captain Berry, " seemed to animate every breast on board the Squadron, at sight of the Enemy; and the pleasure which the Admiral himself felt, was perhaps more heightened than that of any other man, as he had now a certainty by which he could regulate his future operations. The Admiral had, and it appeared most justly, the highst opinion of, and placed the firmest reliance on, the valour and conduct of every Captain in his Squadron. It had been his practice during the whole of the cruize, whenever the weather and circumstances would permit, to have his Captains on board the Vanguard, where he would fully develop to them his own ideas of the different and best modes of attack, and such plans as he proposed to execute upon falling in with the Enemy, whatever their position or situation might be, by day or by night. There was no possible position in which they could be found, that he did not take into his calculation, and for the most advantageous attack of which he had not digested and arranged the best possible disposition of the force which he commanded. With the masterly ideas of their Admiral, therefore, on the subject of Naval tactics, every one of the Captains of his Squadron was most thoroughly acquainted; and upon surveying the situation of the Enemy, they could ascertain with precision what were the ideas and intentions of their Commander, without the aid of any further instructions; by which means signals became almost unnecessary, much time was saved, and the attention of every Captain could almost undistractedly be paid to the conduct of his own particular Ship, a circumstance from which, upon this occasion, the advantages to the general service were almost incalculable. It cannot here be thought irrelevant, to give some idea of what were the plans which Admiral Nelson had formed, and which he explained to his Captains with such perspicuity, as to render his ideas completely their own. To the Naval service, at least, they must prove not only interesting, but useful. Had he fallen in with the French Fleet at sea, that he might make the best impression upon any part of it that should appear the most vulnerable, or the most eligible for attack, he divided his force into three Sub-squadrons, viz.—

| | | |
|---|---|---|
| Vanguard, | Orion, | Culloden, |
| Minotaur, | Goliath, | Theseus, |
| Leander, | Majestic, | Alexander, |
| Audacious, | Bellerophon, | Swiftsure. |
| Defence, | | |
| Zealous, | | |

Two of these Sub-squadrons were to attack the Ships of War, while the third was to pursue the Transports, and to sink and destroy as many as it could. The destination of the French armament was involved in doubt and uncertainty; but it forcibly struck the Admiral, that, as it was commanded by the man whom the French had dignified with the title of the Conqueror of Italy, and as he had with him a very large body of troops, an expedition had been planned which the land force might execute without the aid of their Fleet, should the Transports be permitted to make their escape, and reach in safety their place of rendezvous; it therefore became a material consideration with the Admiral so to arrange his force as at once to engage the whole attention of their Ships of War, and at the same time materially to annoy and injure their convoy. It will be fully admitted, from the subsequent information which has been received upon the subject, that the ideas of the Admiral upon this occasion were perfectly just, and that the plan which he had arranged was the most likely to frustrate the designs of the Enemy. It is almost unnecessary to explain his projected mode of attack at anchor, as that was minutely and precisely executed in the Action which we now come to describe. These plans, however, were formed two months before an opportunity presented itself of executing any of them, and the advantage now was, that they were familiar to the understanding of every Captain in the Fleet.

" We saw the Pharos of Alexandria at noon on the first of August. The Alexander and Swiftsure had been detached a-head on the preceding evening, to reconnoitre the Ports of Alexandria, while the main body of the Squadron kept in the offing. The Enemy's Fleet was first discovered by the Zealous, Captain Hood, who immediately communicated, by signal, the number of Ships, sixteen, laying at anchor in Line of Battle, in a Bay upon the larboard bow, which we afterwards found to be Aboukir Bay. The Admiral hauled his wind that instant, a movement which was immediately observed and followed by the whole Squadron; and at the same time he recalled the Alexander and Swiftsure. The wind was at this time N.N.W., and blew what seamen call a top-gallant breeze. It was necessary to take in the royals when we hauled upon a wind. The Admiral made the signal to prepare for battle, and that it was his intention to attack the Enemy's van and centre, as they lay at anchor, and according to the plan before developed. His idea, in this disposition of his force was, first to secure the victory, and then to make the most of it according to future circumstances. A bower cable of each Ship was immediately got out abaft, and bent forward. We continued carrying sail, and standing in for the Enemy's Fleet in a close Line of Battle. As all the officers of our Squadron were totally unacquainted with Aboukir Bay, each Ship kept sounding as she stood in. The Enemy appeared to be moored in a strong and compact Line of Battle, close in with the shore, their line describing an obtuse angle in its form, flanked by numerous Gun-boats, four Frigates, and a battery of guns and mortars, on an Island in their Van. This situation of the Enemy seemed to secure to them the most decided advantages, as they had nothing to attend to but their artillery, in their superior skill in the use of which the French so much pride themselves, and to which indeed their splendid series of land victories are in a great measure to be imputed.

" The position of the Enemy presented the most formidable obstacles ; but the Admiral viewed these with the eye of a seaman determined on attack, and it instantly struck his eager and penetrating mind, *that where there was room for an Enemy's Ship to swing, there was room for one of ours to anchor.* No further signal was necessary than those which had already been made. The Admiral's designs were as fully known to his whole Squadron, as was his determination to conquer, or perish in the attempt. The Goliath and Zealous had the honour to lead inside, and to receive the first fire from the Van ships of the Enemy, as well as from the Batteries and Gun-boats with which their van was strengthened. These two Ships, with the Orion, Audacious, and Theseus, took their stations inside of the Enemy's Line, and were immediately in close action. The Vanguard anchored the first on the outer side of the Enemy, and was opposed within half pistol-shot to Le Spartiate, the third in the Enemy's Line. In standing in, our leading Ships were unavoidably obliged to receive into their bows the whole fire of the broadsides of the French line, until they could take their respective stations; and it is but justice to observe, that the Enemy received us with great firmness and deliberation, no colours having been hoisted on either side, nor a gun fired, till our Van ships were within half gun shot. At this time the necessary number of our men were employed aloft in furling sails, and on deck, in hauling the braces, &c. preparatory to our casting anchor. As soon as this took place, a most animated fire was opened from the Vanguard, which Ship covered the approach of those in the rear, which were following in a close line. The Minotaur, Defence, Bellerophon, Majestic, Swiftsure, and Alexander, came up in succession, and passing within hail of the Vanguard, took their respective stations opposed to the Enemy's line. All our Ships anchored by the stern, by which means the British line became inverted from van to rear. Captain Thompson, of the Leander, of 50 guns, with a degree of skill and intrepidity highly honourable to his professional character, advanced towards the Enemy's line on the outside, and most judiciously dropped his anchor athwart hause of Le Franklin, raking her with great success, the shot from the Leander's broadside which passed that Ship all striking L'Orient, the Flag Ship of the French Commander in-Chief.

" The action commenced at sun-set, which was at thirty-one minutes past six P.M., with an ardour and vigour which it is impossible to describe. At about seven o'clock total darkness had come on, but the whole hemisphere was, with intervals, illuminated by the fire of the hostile Fleets. Our Ships, when darkness came on, had all hoisted their distinguishing lights, by a signal from the Admiral. The Van ship of the Enemy, Le Guerrier, was dismasted in less than twelve minutes, and, in ten minutes after, the second ship, Le Conquérant, and the third, Le Spartiate, very nearly at the same moment were almost dismasted. L'Aquilon and Le Souverain Peuple, the fourth and fifth Ships of the Enemy's line, were taken possession of by the British at half-past eight in the evening. Captain Berry, at that hour, sent Lieutenant Galwey, of the Vanguard, with a party of marines, to take possession of Le Spartiate, and that officer returned by the boat, the French Captain's sword, which Captain Berry immediately delivered to the Admiral, who was then below, in consequence of the severe wound which he had received in the head during the heat of the attack. At this time it appeared that victory had already declared itself in our favour, for although L'Orient, L'Heureux, and Tonnant were not taken possession of, they were considered as completely in our power, which pleasing intelligence Captain Berry had likewise the satisfaction of communicating in person to the Admiral. At ten minutes after nine, a fire was observed on board L'Orient, the French Admiral's Ship, which seemed to proceed from the after part of the cabin, and which increased with great rapidity, presently involving the whole of the after part of the Ship in flames. This circumstance Captain Berry immediately communicated to the Admiral, who, though suffering severely from his wound, came up upon deck, where the first consideration that struck his mind was concern for the danger of so many lives, to save as many as possible of whom he ordered Captain Berry to make every practicable exertion. A boat, the only one that could swim, was instantly dispatched from the Vanguard, and other Ships that were in a condition to do so, immediately followed the example; by which means, from the best possible information, the lives of about seventy Frenchmen were saved. The light thrown by the fire of L'Orient upon the surrounding objects, enabled us to perceive with more certainty the situation of the two Fleets, the colours of both being clearly distinguishable. The cannonading was partially kept up to leeward of the Centre till about ten o'clock, when L'Orient blew up with a most tremendous explosion. An awful pause and death-like silence for about three minutes ensued, when the wreck of the masts, yards, &c. which had been carried to a vast height, fell down into the water, and on board the surrounding Ships. A port fire from L'Orient fell into the main royal of the Alexander, the fire occasioned by which was, however, extinguished in about two minutes, by the active exertions of Captain Ball.

" After this awful scene, the firing was recommenced with the Ships to leeward of the Centre, till twenty minutes past ten, when there was a total cessation of firing for about ten minutes; after which it was revived till about three in the morning, when it again ceased. After the victory had been secured in the Van, such British ships as were in a condition to move, had gone down upon the fresh Ships of the Enemy, which occasioned these renewals of the fight, all of which terminated with the same happy success in favour of our Flag. At five minutes past five in the morning, the two Rear ships of the Enemy, Le Guillaume Tell and Le Généreux, were the only French ships of the Line that had their colours flying. At fifty-four minutes past five, a French frigate, L'Artemise, fired a broadside and struck her colours; but such was the unwarrantable and infamous conduct of the French Captain, that after having thus surrendered, he set fire to his Ship, and with part of his crew, made his escape on shore. Another of the French frigates, La Sérieuse, had been sunk by the fire from some of our Ships; but as her poop remained above water, her men were saved upon it, and were taken off by our boats in the morning. The Bellerophon, whose masts and cables had been entirely shot away, could not retain her situation abreast of L'Orient, but had drifted out of the line to the lee side of the Bay, a little before that Ship blew up. The Audacious was in the morning detached to her assistance. At eleven o'clock, Le Généreux and Guillaume Tell, with the two Frigates, La Justice and La Diane, cut their cables and stood out to sea, pursued by the Zealous, Captain Hood, who, as the Admiral himself has stated, handsomely endeavoured to prevent their escape: but as there was no other Ship in a condition to support the Zealous, she was recalled. The whole day of the 2nd was employed in securing the French ships that had struck, and which were now all completely in our possession, Le Tonnant and Timoléon excepted; as these were both dismasted, and consequently could not escape, they were naturally the last of which we thought of taking possession. On the morning of the third, the Timoleon was set fire to, and Le Tonnant had cut her cable and drifted on shore, but that active officer, Captain Miller, of the Theseus, soon got her off again, and secured her in the British line. The British force engaged consisted of twelve Ships of 74 guns, and the Leander, of 50.

" From the over anxiety and zeal of Captain Troubridge to get into action, his Ship, the Culloden, in standing in for the Van of the Enemy's line, unfortunately grounded upon the tail of a shoal running off from the Island, on which were the mortar and gun batteries of the Enemy; and notwithstanding all the exertions of that able officer and his Ship's company, she could not be got off. This unfortunate circumstance was severely felt at the moment by the Admiral and all the officers of the Squadron, but their feelings were nothing compared to the anxiety and even anguish of mind which the Captain of the Culloden himself experienced, for so many eventful hours. There was but one consolation that could offer itself to him in the midst of the distresses of his situation, a feeble one it is true—that his ship served as a beacon for three other Ships, viz., the Alexander, Theseus, and Leander, which were advancing with all possible sail set close in his rear, and which otherwise might have experienced a similar misfortune, and thus in a greater proportion still have weakened our force. It was not till the morning of the second, that the Culloden could be got off, and it was found she had suffered very considerable damage in her bottom, that her rudder was beat off, and the crew could scarcely keep her afloat with all pumps going. The resources of Captain Troubridge's mind availed him much, and were admirably exerted upon this trying occasion. In four days he had a new rudder made upon his own deck, which was immediately shipped; and the Culloden was again in a state for actual service, though still very leaky.

" The Admiral, knowing that the wounded of his own Ships had been well taken care of, bent his first attention to those of the Enemy. He established a truce with the Commandant of Aboukir, and through him made a communication to the Commandant of Alexandria, that it was his intention to allow all the wounded Frenchmen to be taken ashore to proper hospitals, with their own surgeons to attend them—a proposal which was assented to by the French, and which was carried into effect on the following day. The activity and generous consideration of Captain Troubridge were again exerted at this time for the general good. He communicated with the shore, and had the address to procure a supply of fresh provisions, onions, &c. which were served out to the sick and wounded, and which proved of essential utility. On the 2nd [of August], the Arabs and Mamelukes, who during the Battle had lined the shores of the Bay, saw with transport that the victory was decisively ours, an event in which they participated with an exultation almost equal to our own; and on that and the two following nights, the whole coast and country were illuminated as far as we could see, in celebration of our victory. This had a great effect upon the minds of our prisoners, as they conceived that this illumination was the consequence, not entirely of our success, but of some signal advantage obtained by the Arabs and Mamelukes over Buonaparte. Although it is natural to suppose that the time and attention of the Admiral, and all the officers of his Squadron, were very fully employed in repairing the damages sustained by their own Ships, and in securing those of the Enemy, which their valour had subdued, yet the mind of that great and good man felt the strongest emotions of the most pious gratitude to the Supreme Being for the signal success, which, by his Divine favour, had crowned his endeavours in the cause of his Country, and, in consequence, on the morning of the second, he issued the following Memorandum to the different Captains of his Squadron. [See p. 61.] At two o'clock accordingly on that day, public service was performed on the quarter-deck of the Vanguard by the Rev. Mr. Comyn, the other Ships following the example of the Admiral, though perhaps not all at the same time. This solemn act of gratitude to Heaven seemed to make a very deep impression upon several of the prisoners, both officers and men, some of the former of whom remarked, ' that it was no wonder we could preserve such order and discipline, when we could impress the minds of our men with such sentiments after a victory so great, and at a moment of such seeming confusion.' On the same day, the following Memorandum was issued to all the Ships, expressive of the Admiral's sentiments of the noble exertions of the different officers and men of his squadron." [Vide p. 61.]

The Battle is thus described in the Log of the Vanguard :—

" Moderate Breezes and clear weather. At 1, saw Alexandria bearing S.E. $\frac{1}{2}$ S. 7 or 8 Leagues. At $\frac{1}{4}$ past 2, recalled the Alexander and Swiftsure; $\frac{1}{2}$ past, hauled our wind, unbent the best bower cable, took it out of the Stern-port, and bent it again. At 4, Pharos Tower S.S.W., distant 4 or 5 Leagues : the Zealous made the signal for the French Fleet—sixteen Sail of the Line. At 5, bore up for the French Fleet —sounding 15, 14, 13, 11, and 10 fathoms. At 28 minutes past 6, the French Fleet hoisted their Colours and opened their fire on our Van Ships : $\frac{1}{2}$ past 6, came-to, with the best bower in 8 fathoms, veered to half a cable. At 31 minutes past, opened our fire on the Spartiate, which was continued without intermission until $\frac{1}{2}$ past 8, when our opponent struck to us. Sent Lieutenant Galwey and a party of Marines to take possession of her. At 9, saw three others strike to the Zealous,

Audacious and Minotaur. At 55 minutes past 8, L'Orient took fire, the Ships ahead still keeping up a strong fire upon the Enemy. At 10, L'Orient blew up with a violent explosion, and the Enemy ceased their fire. 10 minutes past 10, perceived another Ship on fire, which was soon extinguished and a fresh cannonade began: 20 minutes past 10, a total cease of fire for 10 minutes, when it was again renewed. At 16 minutes past 12, Lieutenant Vassal with a party of Marines, went to take possession of a Prize: 15 minutes past 2, [A.M. of the 2nd of August] a Boat came from the Alexander: 55 minutes past 2, a total cease of firing. 28 minutes past 3, came a Boat from the Defence and Lieutenant Vassal returned, the Ship he went to having weighed before he could board her. Picked up three Frenchmen and brought on board. 5 minutes past 5, the Enemy to the Southward began firing: 54 minutes past 5, a French Frigate ahead fired a broadside and struck her Colours ; soon afterwards she took fire, and at 7, blew up. At 6, Goliath weighed and went to the Southward to the Enemy's ships which had not struck: 40 minutes past 6, she began firing: 50 minutes past six, one of the Enemy's Ships of the Line fired some guns and then struck her Colours, and was boarded. At 6, the Zealous weighed and went ahead. 57 minutes past ten, the English Ships began firing at a Frigate, gave her two broadsides and then ceased. ½ past 11, two French Ships of the Line and two Frigates got under weigh and stood out to Sea. Killed—Captain Faddy of the Marines and two Midshipmen. Wounded— . . . . . .,[1] two Lieutenants, Boatswain, two Midshipmen and Secretary. Killed 27, Wounded 68—Total 105. Moderate Breezes and clear. Employed clearing the wreck, knotting, splicing, &c. At 45 minutes past 12, the Zealous fired at the two French Ships of the Line and two Frigates standing out of the Bay, which they returned. At 12 minutes past 10, A.M., the Enemy set one of their Line of Battle Ships on fire, and at 47 minutes past 11, she blew up."

The Names and Force of the French Squadron, with the fate of each Ship, are given in p. 58, post, and a minute and impartial account of the Battle will be found in James' Naval History, Ed. Chamier, vol. ii. pp. 152-182. The following Returns (Clarke and M'Arthur's, vol. ii. p. 473) exhibit the comparative force of the two Squadrons :

| English. | Guns. | Number of Men. | Killed. | Wounded. | French. | Number of Guns. | Men. | How disposed of. |
|---|---|---|---|---|---|---|---|---|
| Vanguard | 74 | 595 | 30 | 75 | L'Orient | 120 | 1010 | Burnt |
| Orion | 74 | 590 | 13 | 29 | Le Franklin | 80 | 800 | Taken |
| Culloden | 74 | 590 | 0 | 0 | Le Tonnant | 80 | 800 | Do. |
| Bellerophon | 74 | 590 | 49 | 148 | Le Guerrier | 74 | 700 | Do. |
| Defence | 74 | 590 | 4 | 11 | Le Conquérant | 74 | 700 | Do. |
| Minotaur | 74 | 640 | 23 | 64 | Le Spartiate | 74 | 700 | Do. |
| Alexander | 74 | 590 | 14 | 58 | Le Timoléon | 74 | 700 | Burnt |
| Audacious | 74 | 590 | 1 | 35 | Le Souverain Peuple | 74 | 700 | Taken |
| Zealous | 74 | 590 | 1 | 7 | L'Heureux | 74 | 700 | Do. |
| Swiftsure | 74 | 590 | 7 | 22 | Le Mercure | 74 | 700 | Do. |
| Majestic | 74 | 590 | 50 | 143 | L'Artemise | 36 | 300 | Burnt |
| Goliath | 74 | 590 | 21 | 41 | L'Aquilon | 74 | 700 | Taken |
| Theseus | 74 | 590 | 5 | 30 | La Sérieuse | 36 | 300 | Sunk |
| Leander | 50 | 343 | 0 | 14 | L'Hercule (Bomb) | | 50 | Burnt |
| | | | | | La Fortune | 18 | 70 | Taken |
| | | | | | Le Guillaume Tell | 80 | 800 | Escaped |
| | | | | | Le Généreux | 74 | 700 | Do. |
| | | | | | La Justice | 40 | 400 | Do. |
| | | | | | La Diane | 40 | 400 | Do. |
| | 1012 | 8068 | 218 | 677 | | 1196 | 11,230 | |

[1] *Sic.* The name omitted was, apparently, that of Nelson.

Complement of Men on board the French Ships burnt, taken, and ⎫
   sunk at the Battle of the Nile, as by certificates from the Com- ⎬ . . .  8930
   missaries and Officers of the different Ships . . . . . . ⎭
Sent on Shore by cartel, including the Wounded, as by certificates ⎱
   from Captain Barré of L'Alceste . . . . . . . . . ⎰ . . 3105
Escaped from the Timoléon . . . . . . . . . . . . . . 350
Escaped from L'Hercule (Bomb) . . . . . . . . . . . . 50
Officers, Carpenters, and Caulkers, Prisoners on board the Fleet . . . 200
                                              —— 3705

                   Taken, drowned, burnt, and missing . . . . 5225

                                 HORATIO NELSON.

As Sir Horatio Nelson was a Rear-Admiral of the *Blue*, the *Blue* Ensign was the proper Colours of his Squadron. Pursuant, however, to an order from the Earl of St. Vincent, the *White*, or *Saint George's* Ensign was used in the Battle, because it was more distinct from the French Flag (the tri-colour, blue, white, and red, vertically) than either a Blue or a Red Ensign; and thus the Red Cross of Saint George, the ancient Banner of England, witnessed that glorious Victory:

      "And Egypt saw Britannia's Flag unfurl'd,
        Wave high its Victor Cross, deliverer of the world."

Besides their usual Colours, the Squadron displayed the Union Jack and Ensigns from various parts of their rigging. After sunset, each British ship was distinguished by four horizontal lights at the mizen peak.

Of NELSON himself, during this great event, little has yet been said. According to Clarke and M'Arthur—" Sir Horatio, for many preceding days, had hardly eaten or slept; but now, with a coolness peculiar to our Naval character, he ordered his dinner to be served, during which the dreadful preparation for battle was made throughout the Vanguard. On his Officers rising from table and repairing to their separate stations, he exclaimed—' Before this time to-morrow, I shall have gained a Peerage, or Westminster Abbey.' It is nowhere stated at what precise time Nelson was wounded; but Captain Berry's Narrative, compared with the Vanguard's Log, proves that it was before half-past eight in the evening; and his biographers say, he was at the moment looking over a rough sketch of the Bay of Aboukir, which had been taken out of a French Ship by Captain Hallowell, a few days before the action, and given by him to the Admiral.[2] He was struck in the forehead by a langridge shot, or a piece of iron, and the skin being cut by it at right angles, it hung down over his face, and as it covered his eye, he was rendered perfectly blind. Captain Berry, standing near him, caught him in his arms, and he exclaimed, " I am killed; remember me to my wife."[3] " On being carried below to the Cockpit, Mr. Jefferson, the Surgeon, immediately attended him, but he said, ' No, I will take my turn with my brave followers!' The pain was intense, and Nelson felt convinced that his wound was mortal. Mr. Jefferson assured him, on probing the wound, that there was no immediate danger. He would not, however, indulge any hope; and having desired Mr. Comyn, his Chaplain, to convey his

---

    [2] " The sketch was," add Clarke and M'Arthur, " stained with his blood; and he afterwards told one of his Captains that he had sent it, as that Officer thinks, to the British Museum;" but it certainly is not in the British Museum.
    [3] From the information of Lady Berry.

dying remembrance to Lady Nelson, he ordered the Minotaur to be hailed, that he might thank her brave and gallant Captain, Louis, for coming up so nobly to the support of the Vanguard:[4] the interview affected all who beheld it. Mr. Jefferson having bound up and dressed the wound, requested the Admiral to remain quiet in the bread-room; but nothing could repress his anxious and enthusiastic disposition. He immediately ordered his Secretary, Mr. Campbell, to attend him in the bread-room, that no time might be lost in writing to the Admiralty. This gentleman, who died soon after,[5] had been himself wounded; and beholding the blind and suffering state of the Admiral, became so much affected, that he could not write. The Chaplain was then summoned; but the eagerness and impatience of Nelson increasing, he took the pen himself, and contrived to trace some words which marked at that awful moment his devout sense of the success he had then obtained." It is then said, " He was after this left alone : when, suddenly, the news of the French Admiral's Ship, L'Orient, being on fire, re-echoed throughout the decks of the Vanguard. Unassisted and unnoticed amidst the general confusion, Nelson contrived to find his way up the ladders, and to the astonishment of every one, appeared again on the quarter-deck." This, however, is not true. On L'Orient's taking fire, Captain Berry went below, to acquaint the Admiral with the circumstance, and he led him upon deck to witness the conflagration.[6] " He immediately" (proceed his Biographers) " gave orders that his First-Lieutenant, Galwey, should be sent in the only boat which the Vanguard had saved, with others from his Squadron, to the relief of the Enemy. After the dreadful explosion of L'Orient, he was persuaded, though with some difficulty, to go to bed; but still continuing restless, he got up, and signed Captain T. M. Hardy's commission for the Vanguard, as Captain Berry was to go home with the dispatches, and Captain [Mr.] Capel's for the Mutine."—*Clarke and M'Arthur*, vol. ii. p. 83. Though Nelson was obliged, in his Dispatch, to mention that he was wounded, he did not allow his name to be inserted in the official Returns.

---

TO ADMIRAL THE EARL OF ST. VINCENT, K.B.,
COMMANDER-IN-CHIEF.

[From the " Letter-Book" and " London Gazette Extraordinary " of October 2nd, 1798.]

Vanguard, off the Mouth of the Nile, 3rd August, 1798.

My Lord,

Almighty God has blessed his Majesty's Arms in the late Battle, by a great Victory over the Fleet of the Enemy, who I attacked at sunset on the 1st of August, off the Mouth of the Nile. The Enemy were moored in a strong Line of Battle for defending the entrance of the Bay, (of Shoals,) flanked by

---

[4] It is said in the "Memoir of Nelson," in the *Naval Chronicle*, vol. iii. p. 183, that Captain Louis came on board the Vanguard at his desire; and the interview is also stated to have occurred, in vol. i. p. 287 of that work, with many additional particulars. But there is no mention, in the Vanguard's Log, of any communication having taken place, during the Battle, with the Minotaur.

[5] Mr. John Campbell died on the 3rd of December, 1799, being then Purser of the Canopus.

[6] From the information of Lady Berry.

numerous Gun-boats, four Frigates, and a Battery of Guns and Mortars on an Island in their Van; but nothing could withstand the Squadron your Lordship did me the honour to place under my command. Their high state of discipline is well known to you, and with the judgment of the Captains, together with their valour, and that of the Officers and Men of every description, it was absolutely irresistible. Could anything from my pen add to the character of the Captains, I would write it with pleasure, but that is impossible.

I have to regret the loss of Captain Westcott of the Majestic, who was killed early in the Action; but the Ship was continued to be so well fought by her First Lieutenant, Mr. Cuthbert, that I have given him an order to command her till your Lordship's pleasure is known.

The Ships of the Enemy, all but their two rear Ships, are nearly dismasted: and those two, with two Frigates, I am sorry to say, made their escape; nor was it, I assure you, in my power to prevent them. Captain Hood most handsomely endeavoured to do it, but I had no Ship in a condition to support the Zealous, and I was obliged to call her in.

The support and assistance I have received from Captain Berry cannot be sufficiently expressed. I was wounded in the head, and obliged to be carried off the deck; but the service suffered no loss by that event: Captain Berry was fully equal to the important service then going on, and to him I must beg leave to refer you for every information relative to this Victory. He will present you with the Flag of the Second in Command, that of the Commander-in-Chief being burnt in L'Orient.

Herewith I transmit you Lists of the Killed and Wounded, and the Lines of Battle of ourselves and the French. I have the honour to be, my Lord, your Lordship's most obedient Servant,

HORATIO NELSON.

### LINE OF BATTLE.

1. Culloden.—T. Troubridge, Captain, 74 Guns, 590 Men.
2. Theseus.—R. W. Miller, Captain, 74 Guns, 590 Men.
3. Alexander.—Alex. John Ball, Captain, 74 Guns, 590 Men.

4. Vanguard.—Rear-Admiral Sir Horatio Nelson, K.B., Edward Berry, Captain, 74 Guns, 595 Men.
5. Minotaur.—Thomas Louis, Captain, 74 Guns, 640 Men.
6. Leander.—Thomas B. Thompson, Captain, 50 Guns, 343 Men.
7. Swiftsure.—B. Hallowell, Captain, 74 Guns, 590 Men.
8. Audacious.—Davidge Gould, Captain, 74 Guns, 590 Men
9. Defence.—John Peyton, Captain, 74 Guns, 590 Men.
10. Zealous.—Samuel Hood, Captain, 74 Guns, 590 Men.
11. Orion.—Sir James Saumarez, Captain, 74 Guns, 590 Men.
12. Goliath.—Thomas Foley, Captain, 74 Guns, 590 Men.
13. Majestic.—George B. Westcott, Captain, 74 Guns, 590 Men.
14. Bellerophon.—Henry D'E. Darby, Captain, 74 Guns, 590 Men.

La Mutine, Brig.          HORATIO NELSON.

Vanguard, off the Mouth of the Nile, August 3, 1798.

## FRENCH LINE OF BATTLE.

1. Le Guerrier, 74 Guns, 700 Men.—Taken.
2. Le Conquérant, 74 Guns, 700 Men.—Taken.
3. Le Spartiate, 74 Guns, 700 Men.—Taken.
4. L'Aquilon, 74 Guns, 700 Men.—Taken.
5. Le Souverain Peuple, 74 Guns, 700 Men.—Taken,
6. Le Franklin, Blanquet, First Contre Amiral, 80 Guns, 800 Men.—Taken.
7. L'Orient, Brueys, Admiral and Commander-in-Chief, 120 Guns, 1010 Men.—Burnt.
8. Le Tonnant, 80 Guns, 800 Men.—Taken.
9. L'Heureux, 74 Guns, 700 Men.—Taken.
10. Le Timoleon, 74 Guns, 700 Men.  Burnt.
11. Le Mercure, 74 Guns, 700 Men.—Taken.
12. Le Guillaume Tell, Villeneuve, Second Contre Amiral, 80 Guns, 800 Men.—Escaped.
13. Le Généreux, 74 Guns, 700 Men.—Escaped.

### Frigates.

14. La Diane, 48 Guns, 300 Men.—Escaped.
15. La Justice, 44 Guns, 300 Men.—Escaped.

16. L'Artemise, 36 Guns, 250 Men.—Burnt.
17. La Sèrieuse, 36 Guns, 250 Men.—Dismasted and Sunk

HORATIO NELSON.

Vanguard, off the Mouth of the Nile, 3rd August, 1798.

A RETURN OF THE KILLED AND WOUNDED IN HIS MAJESTY'S
SHIPS, UNDER THE COMMAND OF SIR HORATIO NELSON, K.B.,
REAR-ADMIRAL OF THE BLUE, ETC. IN ACTION WITH THE
FRENCH, AT ANCHOR, ON THE 1ST OF AUGUST, 1798, OFF
THE MOUTH OF THE NILE.

Theseus.—5 Seamen, killed; 1 Officer, 24 Seamen, 5 Marines, wounded.—Total 35.

Alexander.—1 Officer, 13 Seamen, killed; 5 Officers, 48 Seamen, 5 Marines, wounded.—Total 72.

Vanguard.—3 Officers, 20 Seamen, 7 Marines, killed; 7 Officers, 60 Seamen, 8 Marines, wounded.—Total 105.

Minotaur.—2 Officers, 18 Seamen, 3 Marines, killed; 4 Officers, 54 Seamen, 6 Marines, wounded.—Total 87.

Swiftsure.—7 Seamen killed; 1 Officer, 19 Seamen, 2 Marines, wounded.—Total 29.

Audacious.—1 Seaman killed; 2 Officers, 31 Seamen, 2 Marines, wounded.—Total 36.

Defence.—3 Seamen, 1 Marine, killed; 9 Seamen, 2 Marines, wounded.—Total 15.

Zealous.—1 Seaman killed; 7 Seamen wounded.—Total 8.

Orion.—1 Officer, 11 Seamen, 1 Marine, killed; 5 Officers, 18 Seamen, 6 Marines, wounded.—Total 42.

Goliath.—2 Officers, 12 Seamen, 7 Marines, killed; 4 Officers, 28 Seamen, 9 Marines, wounded.—Total 62.

Majestic.—3 Officers, 33 Seamen, 14 Marines, killed; 3 Officers, 124 Seamen, 16 Marines, wounded.—Total 193.

Bellerophon.—4 Officers, 32 Seamen, 13 Marines, killed; 5 Officers, 126 Seamen, 17 Marines, wounded.—Total 197.

Leander.—14 Seamen wounded.

Total.—16 Officers, 156 Seamen, 46 Marines, killed; 37 Officers, 562 Seamen, 78 Marines wounded.—Total, 895.

### OFFICERS KILLED.

Vanguard.—Captain William Faddy, Marines; Mr. Thomas Seymour, Mr. John G. Taylor, Midshipmen.

Alexander.—Mr. John Collins, Lieutenant.

Orion.—Mr. Baird, Captain's Clerk.

Goliath.—Mr. William Davies, Master's Mate; Mr. Andrew Brown, Midshipman.

Majestic.—George B. Westcott, Esq. Captain; Mr. Zebedee Ford, Midshipman; Mr. Andrew Gilmour, Boatswain.

Bellerophon.—Mr. Robert Savage Daniel, Mr. Philip Watson Launder, Mr. George Joliffe, Lieutenants; Mr. Thomas Ellison, Master's Mate.

Minotaur.—Lieutenant John S. Kirchner, Marines; Mr. Peter Walters, Master's Mate.

### OFFICERS WOUNDED.

Vanguard.—Mr. Nathaniel Vassal, Mr. John M. Adye, Lieutenants; Mr. John Campbell, Admiral's Secretary; Mr. Michael Austin, Boatswain; Mr. John Weatherstone, Mr. George Antrim, Midshipmen.

Theseus.—Lieutenant Hawkins.

Alexander.—Alexander J. Ball, Esq., Captain; Captain J. Cresswell, Marines; Mr. William Lawson, Master; Mr. George Bulley, Mr. Luke Anderson, Midshipmen.

Audacious.—Mr. John Jeans, Lieutenant; Mr. Christopher Font, Gunner.

Orion.—Sir James Saumarez, Captain; Mr. Peter Sadler, Boatswain; Mr. Philip Richardson, Mr. Charles Miell, Mr. Lanfesty, Midshipmen.

Goliath.—Mr. William Wilkinson, Lieutenant; Mr. Lawrence Graves, Midshipman; Mr. Peter Strachan, Schoolmaster; Mr. James Payne, Midshipman.

Majestic.—Mr. Charles Seward, Mr. Charles Royle, Midshipmen; Mr. Robert Overton, Captain's Clerk.

Bellerophon.—H. D'E. Darby, Esq., Captain; Mr. Edward Kirby, Master; Captain John Hopkins, Marines; Mr. Chapman, Boatswain; Mr. Nicholas Bettson, Midshipman.

Minotaur.—Mr. Thomas Irwin, Lieutenant; Mr. John Jewell, Lieutenant Marines; Mr. Thomas Foxten, 2nd Master; Mr. Martin Wills, Midshipman.

Swiftsure.—Mr. William Smith, Midshipman.

HORATIO NELSON.

## MEMORANDUM.

### TO THE RESPECTIVE CAPTAINS OF THE SQUADRON.

[From Captain Sir Edward Berry's " Narrative."]

Vanguard, off the Mouth of the Nile, 2nd August, 1798.

Almighty God having blessed His Majesty's Arms with Victory, the Admiral intends returning Public Thanksgiving for the same at two o'clock this day; and he recommends every Ship doing the same as soon as convenient.

HORATIO NELSON.

### TO THE CAPTAINS OF THE SHIPS OF THE SQUADRON.

[From Captain Sir Edward Berry's " Narrative."]

Vanguard, off the Mouth of the Nile, 2nd day of August, 1798.

The Admiral most heartily congratulates the Captains, Officers, Seamen, and Marines of the Squadron he has the honour to command, on the event of the late Action; and he desires they will accept his most sincere and cordial Thanks for their very gallant behaviour in this glorious Battle. It must strike forcibly every British Seaman, how superior their conduct is, when in discipline and good order, to the riotous behaviour of lawless Frenchmen.

The Squadron may be assured the Admiral will not fail, with his Dispatches, to represent their truly meritorious conduct in the strongest terms to the Commander-in-Chief.

HORATIO NELSON.

### TO LIEUTENANT ROBERT CUTHBERT, HEREBY APPOINTED TO COMMAND HIS MAJESTY'S SHIP MAJESTIC.

[From a Copy in the Admiralty.]

In consequence of your gallant conduct in commanding His Majesty's Ship Majestic, after the death of the brave Captain Westcott, you are therefore to act as Commander of the Majestic until further orders.

Given on board His Majesty's Ship the Vanguard, off the Mouth of the Nile, 2nd of August, 1798.

HORATIO NELSON.

### BATTLE OF THE NILE.

The only disputed Points relating to the Battle of the Nile of any importance are, 1st, Whether the attack on the Enemy's Fleet from the *inside* was part of Nelson's own Plan, and done in obedience to his orders, or whether it was the spontaneous and unauthorized act of Captain Foley of the Goliath, the leading Ship of the Squadron? and, 2ndly, Whether L'Orient, the French Admiral's Ship, actually surrendered before she blew up? Upon both these Points, all that has been ascertained will be stated. Of Nelson's precise Plan of Attack very little is known. James[6] says, "As far as can be gathered from the vague accounts on the subject, Sir Horatio intended, with his fourteen[7] Seventy-fours, to pass the French Line on its outer side, down to the seventh Ship, L'Orient, so that every French Ship of the seven might have a British Ship on her bow and quarter. With respect to the 50 gun-Ship, admitting that Captain Thompson could succeed in persuading the Admiral to overlook her comparatively weak powers in such a conflict, it is probable that the Leander, would have been ordered to assist two of the Seventy-fours in overpowering the three decker." James further observes, that the Goliath "crossed the head of the French Line, and pouring a raking broadside into the Guerrier, bore up for that Ship's inner bow, where Captain Foley intended to take his station; but the anchor not dropping in time, the Goliath ran past the Guerrier, and did not bring up until abreast of the inner, or larboard, quarter of the second Ship, the Conquérant. The Goliath then commenced a warm action with the latter, and occasionally fired a few distant shot from her foremost starboard guns at the Sérieuse frigate, and Hercule mortar-brig, lying within her. The Zealous, following the Goliath in her manœuvre, and dropping her anchor in five fathoms, brought up abreast of the inner or larboard bow of the Guerrier, which was precisely the position Captain Foley had intended to take." [8]

Captain Berry does not, in his *Narrative*, state what the Admiral's Plan actually was; but, after describing his Plan of attack, if the Enemy had been met at *Sea*, says: —"It is almost unnecessary to explain his projected mode of attack at Anchor, as that was minutely and precisely executed in the Action. These plans were formed two months before an opportunity presented itself of executing any of them, and the advantage now was, that they were familiar to the understanding of every Captain of the Fleet." . . . "The Admiral's designs were fully known to his whole Squadron." . . . "The Goliath and Zealous had the honour to lead inside, and to receive the first fire from the Van Ships of the Enemy, as well as from the batteries and gun-boats with which their Van was strengthened. These two Ships, with the Orion, Audacious, and Theseus, took their stations inside of the Enemy's Line, and were immediately in close action. The Vanguard anchored the first on the outer side of the Enemy," &c.[9] These passages admit of no other inference than that *everything* which took place *was consistent with the pre-conceived Plan;* and that it was part of that Plan, for some of the Ships to attack the Enemy from the *inside.*

A claim has, however, been made on behalf of Captain Foley, (afterwards Admiral Sir Thomas Foley, G.C.B.,) to the merit of having, on his own responsibility,

---

[6] *Naval History*, ed. 1837, vol. ii. p. 162.

[7] *Sic*, but evidently a typographical error, as there were only *thirteen* Seventy-fours, and the Leander of 50 Guns.

[8] *Naval History*, ed. 1837, vol. ii. p. 164.          [9] pp. 50, 51, ante.

deviated from the Admiral's plan and orders, by passing *inside* the Enemy, the four
other Ships having "followed the example." It does not exactly appear when this
claim was first brought forward; but it appeared in print for the first time (it is believed) in 1800, in a Note to the Volume of the "Annual Register" for the year 1798.
It was again mentioned, but with additions and variations, in a Note to the Memoir of
Sir Thomas Foley in "Marshall's Naval Biography,"[1] where it is said, "It had long
been a favourite idea with Captain Foley, which he had mentioned on the preceding
evening to Captains Troubridge and Hood, that a considerable advantage would arise,
if the Enemy's Fleet were moored in Line of Battle in with the land, to lead between
them and the shore, as the French guns on that side were not likely to be manned, or
to be ready for action. The original plan of attack which Sir Horatio Nelson had intended to have adopted, if Captain Foley had not judged it expedient to lead within the
French Line, was to have kept entirely on its outer side; and to have stationed his
Ships, as far as he was able, one on the outer bow and another on the outer quarter
of each of the Enemy." From this statement it would seem that, in consequence of
Captain Foley having communicated his idea to Captains Troubridge and Hood
*before* the Enemy were discovered, Nelson had been induced to alter his design in
conformity with Foley's suggestion.

The claim was again renewed, and in a form that gave it great weight, in August
1837, in a Letter, from Major-General Sir Charles James Napier, G.C.B., to the
Editor of the "United Service Journal," in consequence, he said, of his close
connexion[2] with Sir Thomas Foley's family. Adverting to a statement, in which
the merit of the Battle was mainly attributed to Nelson's having *doubled* upon
the Enemy's van and centre, Sir Charles Napier said:—"Lord Nelson was not
the man who proved the adventure; the exploit was achieved by Sir Thomas
Foley; the chivalrous commander of the Goliath began the Action—he it was
who, in this critical moment, saw that there was room to pass between the
shore and the Enemy's Fleet; and though the orders of Lord Nelson were to
attack the French Line on the *outward* side, Foley, against those orders, passed
*inside* between the Enemy's Ships and the shore, thus incurring all the responsibility attaching to so daring a deed—the accumulated responsibility of disobedience,
of getting aground, and of defeat—not only the defeat of his own Ship, but of the
whole Fleet, already inferior to the Enemy. Sir, the action was great in itself,
and would have been great, even in the great Nelson; but it was greater in the
subordinate than in the chief. Far be it from me to desire that any warlike deed
achieved by Nelson should be disputed; but his actions can acquire no splendour
by attributing to him the deeds of another man—a man who was both his friend,
and the companion of his glory. It is also known that Lord Nelson said, 'Had he
seen the manœuvre in time, he would have made the signal for Foley not to go
inside.' The Victor of the Nile was too great to feel envy, nor desired to deprive
Foley of the glory which attached to his intrepid conduct: on the contrary, Lord
Nelson made that conduct more glorious and more public by his approbation."

Without intending the slightest disrespect to the gallant General, it must be observed that his statements would have been more satisfactory had he cited his authority for them.

Much light is thrown on the question by a Letter from Captain Hood of the Zealous,
to Lord Bridport, written immediately after the Battle:—"As we advanced towards
the Enemy, we plainly made out 13 Sail of the Line and 4 Frigates, with several

---

[1] Vol. i. p. 365, 8vo, 1823.
[2] Sir Thomas Foley married a first cousin of Sir Charles Napier.

small armed Vessels, all at anchor in the Road of Bequier, or Aboukir, very *close in*, and in Order of Battle. The Admiral then made the signal to anchor, and for Battle, and to attack the Van and Centre of the Enemy; and soon after, for the Line-a-head as most convenient. As we got pretty near abreast of the Shoal at the entrance, being within hail of the Admiral, he asked me if I thought we were far enough to the eastward to bear up clear of this Shoal: I told him I was in eleven fathoms; that I had no chart of the Bay; but if he would allow me, I would bear up and sound with the lead, to which I would be very attentive, and carry him as close as I could with safety: he said he would be obliged to me. I immediately bore away and rounded the Shoal, the Goliath keeping upon my lee-bow, until I found we were advancing too far from the Admiral, and then shortened sail; and soon found the Admiral was waiting to speak to a Boat. Soon after he made the signal to proceed on, the Goliath leading; and as we approached the Enemy, shortened sail gradually; the Admiral allowing the Orion, &c., to pass ahead of the Vanguard. The Van ship of the Enemy being in five fathom, I expected the Goliath and Zealous to stick fast on the Shoal every moment, and did not imagine we should attempt to pass within her, as the Van, with the mortars, &c., from the Island fired regularly at us. Captain Foley intended anchoring abreast of the Van ship, but his sheet-anchor, the cable being out of the stern-port, not dropping the moment he wished it, he brought up abreast of the second Ship, having given the Van one his fire. I saw immediately he had failed of his intention, cut away the Zealous's sheet-anchor, and came to, in the exact situation Captain Foley meant to have taken." [3]

Brenton[4] states that, "Nelson having seen his five Van ships begin the action, ' to his heart's content,' now came himself to their support. It appears from the information of Lord de Saumarez, [the second in command,] that the plan of placing the Enemy between two fires was *not* preconcerted: that it originated with Nelson himself, and probably but a minute previous to its execution," which must mean either that it was left to each Captain to place his Ship on whichever side of the Enemy he thought proper, and that Nelson, on finding five had gone *inside* of them, anchored the Vanguard on the *outside*, and thus placed the Enemy's Van between two fires; or, that he originally intended the whole of his Squadron to go *inside*, but that, when five had gone *inside*, he suddenly altered his plan by placing his own Ship on the *outside* of Le Spartiate.

None of these statements is decisive of the question, and some of them can scarcely be reconciled with the others. From Captain Hood's remark, that, in consequence of the shallowness of the water where the Van Ship lay, he expected the Goliath and Zealous to stick on the Shoal, and that he "did not imagine we should attempt to pass within her," it would seem that it was their *intention* to pass *inside* of the Van Ship, but that, on reaching the Enemy, he thought the want of water would prevent their doing so, which would agree with Marshall's assertion, that Captain Foley had communicated *his* plan on the preceding evening to Hood; but it would also agree with the proceeding having been part of Nelson's own plan. Moreover, the fact that four Captains besides Foley also went *inside*, (one of them, the Audacious, having passed between Le Guerrier and Le Conquérant to the *inner* bow of the latter Ship,) and that Nelson himself *first* anchored on the *outside*, supports the idea, that it was Nelson's original plan of attack for the leading Ships, if not for all his Ships, to go *inside* the Enemy.

At the end of Captain Berry's Pamphlet, in 1798, some remarks on the Battle were introduced; and it is there said, that " An idea has gone abroad that the

---

[3] Ekin's Naval Battles, p. 248.          [4] Naval History, vol. i. p. 405.

attack in Aboukir Bay was directed by accident. No idea can be more unfounded, or more injurious to the professional character of the gallant Admiral. It is proved, from this Narrative, that his mode of attack was the result of deep and deliberate cogitation; and so clearly had he explained himself to those who were to bear their respective shares in the execution of his plans, that when they discovered the Enemy, little remained to be done but to commence the premeditated attack." It might be supposed that these strong observations were meant as an answer to the claim made for Captain Foley; but the Editor is informed by Lady Berry (to whose intelligence, and intimate knowledge, derived from her gallant husband, of every Action in which he participated, he is greatly indebted) that she never heard Sir Edward Berry even allude to Captain Foley's having acted from his own idea; and though she often heard the Battle spoken of, both by the late Lord de Saumarez and Sir Thomas Hardy, yet neither of them ever said, in her presence, that Nelson was ignorant of Captain Foley's intention.

Southey does not allude to the question, and Clarke and M'Arthur are also silent. Southey, however, seems to have understood *doubling* on the Enemy to have consisted not in placing a Ship on *each side*, but in having one Ship on the *outer* bow and another on the *outer* quarter of each of the Enemy's ships, which plan, he says, Nelson learnt from Lord Hood's intended attack of the French fleet in Gourjean Bay. Southey adds—"When Captain Berry comprehended the scope of the design, he exclaimed, with transport, ' If we succeed what will the world say ?' ' There is no *if* in the case,' replied the Admiral, ' that we shall succeed is certain : who may live to tell the story is a very different question.'" These words, however, were never spoken; and as Captain Berry had, from the first moment of discovering the Enemy, been fully as confident of success as his Admiral, the statement caused him much annoyance.[3]

*Secondly*, Did L'Orient surrender before she blew up ?

James,[4] referring to Lord Nelson's assertion in a letter to Mr. Wyndham, cited in Clarke and M'Arthur,[5] that L'Orient certainly struck her Colours, and had not fired a shot for a quarter of an hour before she took fire, says : " It has been stated, we are aware, that the Orient herself hauled down her Colours before she blew up, but no such occurrence happened. The Orient's flag at the main was, by several of the British ships, seen in its place when the masts were thrown into the air; and until that flag was struck, there could have been no surrender. Moreover, the men fired from the Ship's lower deck battery, until they were driven from their quarters by the flames, and until some time after the Swiftsure and Alexander had ceased firing, to prepare for the explosion that ensued." Upon what authority James made these positive assertions nowhere appears. Captain Berry says, " At this time [apparently between half-past eight and nine o'clock], it appeared that victory had already declared itself in our favour, for although L'Orient, L'Heureux, and Tonnant were not taken possession of, they were considered as completely in our power, which pleasing intelligence he communicated in person to the Admiral. At 10 m. after 9, a fire was observed aboard L'Orient, &c."

That Nelson believed L'Orient to have struck her Colours is shown not only by his letter to Mr. Wyndham, but more strongly by his letter, hitherto unpublished, to Lord Minto, wherein he said : " It is no small regret that L'Orient is not in being

---

[3] From the information of Lady Berry.    [4] Naval History, vol. ii. p. 180.

[5] Life of Nelson, vol. ii. p. 81, 93. See the Letter, postea.

to grace our victory. She was completely beat, and I am sure had struck her Colours before she took fire ; for as she had lost her main and mizen masts, and on her Flag-staff which Hood cut from her wreck was no Flag, it must be true that the Flag was hauled down or it would have been entangled with the rigging, or some remnant remained at the mast-head."

The immense importance of the Victory of the Nile to the affairs of Europe, its unprecedented completeness, and the great event which it forms in the Life of Nelson, impart to it sô much general interest, that a few pages will doubtless be considered well occupied with some additional illustrations of the event, and more particularly, with those manifestations of Royal and National Gratitude, with which Nelson and his Companions were rewarded.

The following Letters to Nelson were written by Captains of Ships which particularly distinguished themselves : the first was from Captain Gould of the Audacious, and was written during the heat of the Battle :—

TO SIR HORATIO NELSON, K.B.

" Sir,                                          " Audacious, 1st August, 1798.

"I have the satisfaction to tell you the French Ship Le Conquérant has struck to the Audacious, and I have her in possession. The slaughter on board her is *dreadful :* her Captain is dying. We have but one killed, but a great many wounded. Our fore and main-mast are wounded, but I hope not very bad. They tell me the foremast is the worst. I give you joy. This is a glorious Victory. I am, with the utmost respect, yours in haste,          "D. GOULD."[6]

The following Letter was from Captain Foley of the Goliath :—

" My dear Sir Horatio,                          " 2nd August, 1798.

" After congratulating you on the most signal Victory possibly to be gained at sea, I take leave to inquire after your wound, which I trust will not be of serious consequence. I should not have waited the message you sent me to give assistance to the Theseus, could I have secured my main-mast sooner. The dread of losing it and the appearance of so little defence on the side of the Enemy this morning, induced me to be so late in heaving my anchor. The rigging more than the mast is the damaged part. I shall send a Boat to sound towards the Ships which still keep French colours up, and so soon as I can get the soundings I will endeavour to get nearer them. As far as I can at present collect, the killed on board the Goliath are seventeen, with thirty-three wounded. I have the honour to be, dear Sir, your faithful and obedient servant,          " TH. FOLEY."

The next two Letters are from Captain Berry (Nelson's Flag-Captain) to Captain Miller of the Theseus :

" My dear Miller,                          "Vanguard, 2nd August.

" There is but one heart and one soul in this glorious Victory ; your very handsome conduct we saw, and felt ; the Admiral is conscious of your doing right, and leaves it to you to order. He congratulates and thanks you,—hopes your wounds are of no consequence, as you say ; Sir Horatio, I believe, to be out of danger, though his wound is in the head, and he has been sick. Send a letter or a word to me for your wife as I may soon be off. God bless you, my dear friend. Ever yours most truly,

" E. BERRY."

" My dear Miller,                          " Vanguard, 3rd August.

" I am desired by Sir Horatio to say, you are to take the whole charge of the dismasted Prize you are near—He knows she is badly off for ground tackling, and

---

[6] *Autograph,* in the Nelson Papers.

knows you will do all you can.　He is now more easy than he was this morning, the *rage* being over.　Your getting under weigh pleased him much.　You know I am ever yours most truly,　　　　　　　　　　　　　　　　　　" E. BERRY."

On the 3rd of August, the Captains of the Squadron met on board of the Orion, Captain Sir James Saumarez, the senior Captain, and second in command in the Battle, and formed the resolution of testifying their admiration of their Chief:

" The Captains of the Squadron under the Orders of Rear-Admiral Sir Horatio Nelson, K.B., desirous of testifying the high sense they entertain of his prompt decision and intrepid conduct in the Attack of the French Fleet, in Bequier Road, off the Nile, the 1st of August, 1798, request his acceptance of a Sword ; and, as a further proof of their esteem and regard, hope that he will permit his Portrait to be taken, and hung up in the Room belonging to the Egyptian Club, now established in commemoration of that glorious day.

" Dated on board of His Majesty's Ship Orion, this 3rd of August, 1798.

| | |
|---|---|
| JAS. SAUMAREZ. | D. GOULD. |
| T. TROUBRIDGE. | TH. FOLEY. |
| H. D. DARBY. | R. WILLETT MILLER. |
| THO. LOUIS. | BEN. HALLOWELL. |
| IN⁰. PEYTON. | E. BERRY. |
| ALEX. JN⁰. BALL. | T. M. HARDY."[7] |
| SAM. HOOD. | |

Next in interest to the Victor's account of a Battle is the description given of it by the Vanquished.　The following " Translation of the French Rear-Admiral Blanquet's Account of the Battle of the Nile" is taken from a Copy in the Nelson Papers :

" The 1st of August, wind N.N.W., light breezes and fine weather.　The second division of the Fleet sent a party of men on shore, to dig wells.　Every Ship in the Fleet sent twenty-five men to protect the workmen from the continual attacks of the Bedouins and vagabonds of the Country.

" At two o'clock in the afternoon, the Heureux made the Signal for 12 Sail,W.N.W., which we could easily distinguish from the mast-head to be Ships of War.　The Signal was then made for all the boats, workmen, and guards to repair on board of their respective Ships, which was only obeyed by a small number.　At 3 o'clock, the Admiral not having any doubt but the Ships in sight were the Enemy, he ordered the hammocks to be stowed for Action, and directed the Alert and Railleur Brig, Sloops of War, to reconnoitre the Enemy, which we soon perceived were steering for Bequier Bay under a crowd of canvas, but without observing any order of sailing. At four o'clock, saw over the Fort of Aboukir, two Ships, apparently working to join the Squadron : without doubt they had been sent to look into the Ports at Alexandria.　We likewise saw a Brig with the 12 Ships.　In two hours there were 14 Ships of the Line in sight, and a Brig.

" The English Fleet was soon off the Island of Bequier.　The Brig Alert then began to put the Admiral's orders into execution—viz., to stand toward the Enemy until nearly within gun-shot, and then to manœuvre and endeavour to draw them toward the outer shoal lying off that Island.　But the English Admiral, without doubt, had experienced Pilots on board, as he did not pay any attention to the Brig's track, but allowed her to go away : he hauled well round all the dangers.　At

---

*Autograph*, in the Nelson Papers.　The name of Captain Thompson of the Leander was not affixed to this paper.

four o'clock, a small Country-boat dispatched from Alexandria to Rosetta, voluntarily bore down to the English Brig, which took possession of her, notwithstanding the repeated efforts of the Alert to prevent it, by firing a great many shot
at the Boat.    At five o'clock, the Enemy came to the wind in succession.    This
manœuvre convinced us that they intended attacking us that evening.    The Admiral
got the top-gallant-yards across, but soon after made the ¡signal that he intended
engaging the Enemy at anchor,—convinced, without doubt, that he had not seamen
enough to engage under sail; for he wanted at least 200 good seamen for each
Ship.    After this signal, each Ship ought to have sent a stream-cable to the Ship
astern of her, and to have made a hawser fast to the cable about twenty fathoms in
the water, and passed the opposite side to that intended as a spring.    This was not
generally executed.    Orders were then given to let go another bower-anchor, and
the broadsides of the Ships were brought to bear upon the Enemy.    Having the
Ships' heads S.E. from the Island of Bequier, forming a Line about 1300 fathoms
N.W. and S.E., distant from each other eighty fathoms, and in the position marked
Plan 1st,[8] each with an anchor out, in the S.S.E.    At a quarter past five, one of
the Enemy's Ships that was steering to get to windward of the headmost of her
Line, ran on the reef, E.N.E. of the Island.    She had immediate assistance from
the Brig, and got afloat in the morning.    The Battery on the Island opened a fire
on the Enemy, and the shells fell ahead of the second Ship in the Line.    At half-
past five, the headmost Ships of our Line, being within gun-shot of the English,
the Admiral made the signal to engage, which was not obeyed until the Enemy
were within pistol-shot and just doubling us.    The Action then became very warm.
The Conquerant began the fire—then Le Guerrier, Le Spartiate, L'Aquilon, Le
Peuple Souverain, and Le Franklin.    At 6 o'clock, the Sérieuse Frigate and the
Hercule bomb cut their cables, and got under weigh, to avoid the Enemy's fire.    They
got on shore.    The Sérieuse caught fire, and had part of her mast burnt.    The
Artemise was obliged to get under weigh and likewise got on shore.    These two
Frigates sent their Ships' companies on board of the different Line-of-Battle Ships.
The Sloops of War, two Bombs, and several Transports that were with the Fleet,
were more successful, as they got under weigh, and reached the anchorage under the
protection of the Fort of Aboukir.

    " All the Van were attacked on both sides by the Enemy, who ranged close along
our Line.    They had each an anchor out astern which facilitated their motions, and
enabled them to place themselves in the most advantageous position.    At a quarter
past 6, the Franklin opened her fire upon the Enemy from the starboard side : at
three-quarters past 6, she was engaged on both sides.    The L'Orient at the same
time began firing her starboard guns, and at 7 o'clock, the Tonnant opened her fire.
All the Ships, from the Guerrier to the Tonnant, were now engaged against a superior
force : this only redoubled the ardour of the French who kept up a very heavy and
regular fire.    At 8 o'clock at night, the Ship which was engaging L'Orient, on
the starboard quarter, notwithstanding her advantageous position, was dismasted
and so roughly treated, that she cut her cables, and drove rather far from the Line.
This event gave the Franklin hopes that L'Orient would now be able to assist her
by attacking one of the Ships opposed to her; but, at this very moment, the two Ships
that had been perceived astern of the Fleet, and were quite fresh, steered right for
the centre.    One of them anchored on L'Orient's starboard bow, and the other
cut the Line, astern of the L'Orient, and anchored on her larboard quarter.    The
Action in this part then became extremely warm.    Admiral de Brueys, who at this
time had been slightly wounded, in the head and arm, very soon received a shot in

---

[8] The Plans referred to are not attached to this Paper.

the belly, which almost cut him in two.  He desired not to be carried below, but to be left to die upon deck.  He only lived a quarter of an hour.  Rear-Admiral Blanquet, [who] as well as his Aide-de-camp, were unacquainted with this melancholy event, (until the Action was nearly over,) received a severe wound in the face which knocked him down.  He was carried off the deck, senseless.  At a quarter past 8, the Peuple Souverain drove to leeward of the Line, and anchored a cable's length abreast of L'Orient.  It was not known what unfortunate event occasioned it.  The vacant space she made placed the Franklin in a most unfortunate position, and it became very critical, by the manœuvre of one of the Enemy's fresh Ships, which had been to the assistance of the Ship on shore.  She anchored athwart the Franklin's bows, and commenced a very heavy raking fire.  Notwithstanding the dreadful situation of the Ships in the centre, they continually kept up a very heavy fire.  At half-past 8 o'clock, the Action was general, from the Guerrier to the Mercure, and the two Fleets engaged in the position indicated in Plan 2nd.

" The death of Admiral de Brueys, and the severe wounds of Rear-Admiral Blanquet, must have deeply affected the people who fought under them, but it added to their ardour for revenge, and the Action continued on both sides with great obstinacy.  At 9 o'clock the Ships in the Van slackened their fire, and soon after totally ceased ; and, with infinite sorrow, we supposed that they had surrendered.  They were dismasted very soon after the Action began, and so much damaged, that it is to be presumed that they could not hold out any longer against an Enemy so superior by her advantageous position, in placing several Ships against one.  At a quarter past 9 o'clock, L'Orient caught fire in the cabin ; it soon afterwards broke out upon the poop.  Every effort was made to extinguish it, but without effect, and very soon it was so considerable, that there were not any hopes of saving the Ship.

" At half-past 9, Citizen Gillet, Capitaine de Pavillon of the Franklin, was very severely wounded, and carried off the deck.  At three quarters past 9, the arm-chest, filled with musket-cartridges, blew up, and set fire to several places on the poop and quarter-deck, but was fortunately extinguished.  Her situation, however, was still very desperate ; surrounded by Enemies, and only eighty fathoms to windward of L'Orient, (entirely on fire,) there could not be any other expectation than falling a prey either to the Enemy or the flames.  At 10 o'clock, the main and mizen-masts fell, and all the guns on the main deck were dismounted.  At a quarter past 10, the Tonnant cut her cable, to avoid the fire from L'Orient.  The English Ship that was on L'Orient's larboard quarter, so soon as she had done firing at her, brought her broadside upon the Tonnant's bow, and kept up a very heavy raking fire.  The Heureux and Mercure conceived that they ought likewise to cut their cables.  This manœuvre created so much confusion among the Rear Ships, that they fired into each other, and did considerable damage.

" The Tonnant anchored ahead of the Guillaume Tell, Généreux, and Timoleon ; the other two Ships got on shore.  The Ship that had engaged the Tonnant on her bow, cut her cables ; all her rigging and sails were cut to pieces, and she drove down, and anchored astern of the English Ship that had been engaging the Heureux and Mercure, before they changed their position.  Those of the Etat Major and Ship's company of L'Orient who had escaped death, convinced of the impossibility of extinguishing the fire, (which had got down to the middle-gun deck,) endeavoured to save themselves.  Rear-Admiral Ganteaume saved himself in a boat, and went on board of the Salamine, and from thence to Aboukir and Alexandria.  The Adjutant-General Motard, although badly wounded, swam to the Ship nearest L'Orient, which proved to be English.  Commodore Casabianca and his son, only ten years old, who during the Action gave proofs of bravery and intelligence far above his age, were not so fortunate. They were in the water, upon the wreck of L'Orient's mast, (not being able to swim,) seeking each other, until three-quarters past 10, when the Ship blew up, and put an end to their hopes and fears. The explosion was dreadful, and spread the fire all round to a considerable distance. The Franklin's decks were with red-hot pincers, pieces of timber, and rope, on fire. She was on fire the fourth time, but luckily got it under. Immediately after the tremendous explosion, the Action ceased everywhere, and was succeeded by the most profound silence. The sky was obscured by thick clouds of black smoke, which seemed to threaten the destruction of the two Fleets. It was a quarter of an hour before the Ships' crews recovered from the kind of stupor they were thrown into. Towards 11 o'clock, the Franklin, anxious to preserve the trust confided to her, recommenced the Action with a few of her lower-deck guns; all the rest were dismounted, two-thirds of her Ship's company being killed or wounded, and those who remained much fatigued. She was surrounded by Enemy's Ships, some of which were within pistol-shot, and who mowed down the men every broadside. At half-past 11 o'clock, having only three lower-deck guns that could defend the honour of the Flag, it became necessary to put an end to so disproportioned a struggle; and Citizen Martinet, Captain of a Frigate, ordered the Colours to be struck.

" The Action in the Rear of the Fleet was very trifling, until three-quarters past 11 o'clock, when it became very warm. Three of the Enemy's Ships were engaging them, and two were very near, as may be seen in the Plan. The Tonnant, already badly treated, [which] was the nearest to the Ships engaged, returned a very brisk fire. About 3 o'clock in the morning, she was dismasted, and obliged to cut her cable a second time, and not having any more anchors left, she drove on shore. The Guillaume Tell, Le Généreux, and Le Timoleon, shifted their berth, and anchored further down, out of gun-shot. These Vessels were not much damaged. At half-past 3, o'clock the Action ceased throughout the Line. Early in the morning, the Frigate, La Justice, got under weigh, and made small tacks to keep near the Guillaume Tell, and at nine o'clock anchored, an English Ship having got under weigh, and making short tacks, to prevent her getting away. At 6 o'clock, two English Ships joined those which had been engaging the Rear, and began firing on the Heureux and Mercure, which were aground. The former soon struck, and the latter followed her example, as they could not bring their broadsides to bear upon the Enemy. (See the 4th Plan.) At a quarter past 7, the Ship's crew of the Artemise Frigate quitted her, and set her on fire. At 8 o'clock she blew up. The Enemy, without doubt, had received great damage in their masts and yards, as they did not get under weigh to attack the remains of the French Fleet. The French flag was flying on board of four Ships of the Line and two Frigates. This Division made the most of their time, and at three-quarters past 11, Le Guillaume Tell, Le Généreux, La Diane, and La Justice, were under weigh, and formed in Line of Battle. The English Ship that was under sail, stood towards her Fleet, fearing that she might be cut off; two other Enemy's Ships were immediately under weigh to assist her. At noon, the Timoleon, which probably was not in a state to put to sea, steered right for the shore, under her foresail, and as soon as she struck the ground, her foremast fell. The French Division joined the Enemy's Ships, which ranged along their Line, on opposite tacks, within pistol-shot, and received their broadsides, which she returned. They then each continued their route. The Division was in sight at Sunset.

" Nothing remarkable passed during the night of the 2nd.

" The 3rd of August.—In the morning the French colours were flying in the Tonnant and Timoleon. The English Admiral sent a Cartel to the former, to know

on being answered in the negative, he directed two Ships n they got within gun-shot of her, she struck, it being impo.... any longer. The Timoleon was aground, too near in for any Ship to approach .. r. In the night of the 2nd instant, they sent the greatest part of their Ship's company on shore, and at noon the next day they quitted her, and set her on fire.

" Thus ends the Journal of the 1st, 2nd, and 3rd days of August, which will ever be remembered with the deepest sorrow by those Frenchmen who possess good hearts, and by all those true Republicans who have survived this melancholy disaster."

Captain Berry, who was sent to England in the Leander with Nelson's dispatches, was captured off Candia, on the 18th of August, and Captain Capel proceeded with duplicates, overland, *via* Naples. Captain Capel reached Naples, in the Mutine, on the 4th of September, and as the Kingdom of the Two Sicilies was, perhaps, more than any other, affected by the defeat of the French Fleet, the intelligence was received with proportionate rapture by all ranks. Captain Capel, in his letter to Sir Horatio Nelson, announcing his arrival at Naples, dated on the 4th of September, 1798, said—

" I am totally unable to express the joy that appeared in everybody's countenance, and the bursts of applause and acclamations we received. The Queen and Lady Hamilton both fainted : in short, Sir, they all hail you as the Saviour of Europe. A courier sets off to morrow morning for Vienna, and I accompany him, so that I shall not lose an instant. I have every instruction and assistance from Sir William Hamilton and the other Foreign Ministers, who all are anxious to forward such glorious news."

The general joy at Naples was also shown by the following Letters to Nelson, from Sir William Hamilton, Sir John Acton, Prime Minister of the King, and from the Queen of Naples to the Marquis di Circello, Ambassador at the Court of London :

FROM SIR WILLIAM HAMILTON TO SIR HORATIO NELSON.

" Naples, September 8th, 1798.

" It is impossible, my dear Sir Horatio, for any words to express, in any degree, the joy that the account of the glorious and complete Victory you gained over the boasted French Fleet, at the Mouth of the Nile, on the first of August, occasioned at this Court, and in this City. Captain Capel arrived here on Monday last, about one o'clock in the afternoon, and was off the next day, with your Dispatches for our Government, and which I hope will be the first authentic account they will receive of the ever-memorable Battle of the Nile—a Battle, I believe, of the greatest importance that was ever fought, and the expected good consequences of which are incalculable. History, either ancient or modern, does not record an Action that does more honour to the Heroes that gained the Victory, than the late one of the first of August. You have now completely made yourself, my dear Nelson, *immortal*. God be praised, and may you live long to enjoy the sweet satisfaction of having added such glory to our Country, and most probably put an end to the confusion and misery in which all Europe would soon have been involved. This Country feels its immediate good effects ; and their Sicilian Majesties, their Ministry, and the Nation at large, are truly sensible of it, and loudly acknowledge eternal obligation to your undaunted courage, and steady perseverance. You may well conceive, my dear Sir, how happy Emma and I are, in the reflection that it is *you— Nelson—our bosom friend,* who has done such wondrous good, in having humbled these proud robbers and vain boasters. See, in the ' Malta Gazette' enclosed in the packet N., and read, if you can without laughing, the following words, at the bottom of page 5 :—' Une seule Nation—je me trompe, un seul Gouvernement est encore

l'ennemi de la France, et le votre.   Le cabinet de Londres conspire contre la paix, et l'humanité : mais reposez vous sur les guerriers François du soin de le soumettre, de punir, d'abaisser l'orgueil de l'Angleterre.   Elle apprendra bientôt que la victoire est fidele aux Francois, sur les deux élémens.   En vain ses vaisseaux fatigueront de leur poids les mers qui vous entourent.   Ses soldats n'oseront toucher le sol de votre Isle, ou s'ils paroissent, ils y trouveront comme à Ostende, le deshonneur, ou la mort.'  . . .
. . . "Captain Capel's arrival at Vienna with your glorious news, will, I hope, determine that wavering Government to take a firm and decided part.   The King of Naples has just raised 50,000 men more, and has ready 30,000 in tolerable discipline.   Italy might be cleared of these ragamuffins in a month's time.   They must learn of you.   You did not wait for daylight to attack the French Fleet on the first of August, nor for the arrival of your four Ships from Alexandria ; nor did the Culloden's being on shore prevent your falling on the Enemy directly, like a hawk on its prey.   That is the way to do business.   *Audendo agendoque respublica crescit, non iis consiliisquæ timidi cauta appellant.*   How proud I am of feeling myself an Englishman at this moment !   Great Britain alone has truly faced the Enemy in support of the good cause ; and Sir Horatio Nelson is the greatest Hero of that Great Britain.   Adieu, my dear and brave friend.   Your sincerely attached and humble servant,

"WILLIAM HAMILTON."[9]

FROM SIR JOHN ACTON TO SIR HORATIO NELSON.

"Sir,                                        "Naples, 9th September, 1798.

"The arrival in this Bay of Captain Capel, with the stupendous news of the total destruction of the French Naval Force, at the Mouth of the Nile, by the brave and most energetical exertions of the Squadron under your command, has filled their Sicilian Majesties, and all their faithful Subjects, with the most sensible joy, gratitude, and extensive admiration.   I have the honour to present you, by their Majesties' orders, with their best and sincere congratulations, and our full acknowledgment and conviction that you have saved Italy, and especially the Two Sicilies, from their ruin, by a meditated Invasion : we may even say Europe itself, as the projects of a democracy from the Coasts of Morea and Macedonia, for involving Poland and Hungary, was the intended meaning of the expensive Armament under Buonaparte, in order to destroy with an equal propagation of principles, Germany, and, at the same time, the rest of Italy.   Your presence, Sir, in these Seas, has forced another scheme, which, less obnoxious to Europe, will have the final end which we wish for.   You have saved us, Sir, by the most glorious Action, which, superior to many Battles fought at Sea since ages, has this singular and important consequence, of being to all Europe, I repeat it, of the highest advantage.   I hope, Sir, that you will live long to enjoy the true satisfaction of having produced so much benefit to all Nations, and the blessing of many Governments gratified by your courage, ability, and that of the brave Officers and people, who have, under your direction, so unanimously and admirably concurred to the most surprising Victory.   I hope, likewise, for the General Cause and support, that the Emperor will move, and by his and the Ottoman Porte's Declarations will put Malta and Corfu, with its Dependencies, very soon under a different Flag.   We are ready in what concerns ourselves for that purpose, and to join in the most sanguine manner with your future undertakings, as soon as Vienna answers to our repeated and warmest demands.   Your name, Sir, and co-operation, shall be a singular and sure omen for success.   I join with my warmest felicitations for your glory, and in the best wishes for your welfare.   Give me leave to assure you of my highest regard and attachment.   I have the honour to be, &c.,

JOHN ACTON, Bt."[1]

---

[9] *Autograph*, in the Nelson Papers.        [1] Ibid.

THE QUEEN OF NAPLES TO THE MARQUIS DI CIRCELLO.

" I write to you with the greatest joy. The brave and gallant Admiral Nelson has gained a most complete Victory. I wish I could give wings to the bearer of this news, and, at the same time, of our most sincere gratitude. Italy is saved on the part of the Sea, and that is only due to the gallant English. This Action, or better-named, total defeat of the regicide Fleet, is owing to the valour and courage of this brave Admiral, seconded by a Marine which is the terror of its Enemies. The Victory is so complete, that I can scarcely believe it, and if it was not the English Nation, which is accustomed to perform prodigies by sea, I could not persuade myself of it. This has produced a general enthusiasm. You would have been moved at seeing all my children, boys and girls, hanging on my neck, and crying for joy at the happy news, which has been doubled by the critical moment in which it arrived. Fear, avarice, and the malicious intrigues of the Republicans, have made all the cash disappear, and there is no one who has courage enough to propose a plan to put it in circulation; and this want of cash produces much discontent. We are distressed by the Republicans, with all those troubles which afflict this charming country, Italy. Many who thought things coming to a crisis, began to take off the mask; but this joyful news, the defeat of Buonaparte's Fleet, who, I hope, will perish with his Army in Egypt, makes them more timid, and does us great good. If the Emperor will move with activity, it is to be hoped that Italy may be saved. We are ready and eager to render ourselves worthy of being the friends and Allies of the brave defenders of the Seas. Present my respects to the King and Queen of England. Make my compliments to Lord Grenville, to Pitt, and to Lord Spencer, who has the honour to be at the head of this heroic Navy. Give them my thanks for sending the Fleet, and tell them that I rejoice in this event—as much for our own advantage, which is very great, as for their honour and glory. Assure them of my eternal gratitude. I hope that by the orders you have received by the last Courier, we shall be more secured, and that, by a good understanding, we shall be able to save Italy, and to afford to our Defenders advantages that will bind them to us for ever. The brave Nelson is wounded. He has the modesty never to speak of it. Recommend the Hero to his Master: he has made every Italian an enthusiast for the English Nation. Great hopes were entertained from his bravery, but no one could flatter themselves with so complete a destruction. All the world is mad with joy." [2]

Captain Capel reached London on the 2nd of October 1798, and it is only from reading the newspapers, and other periodical publications of the day, and the following letters and proceedings, that an adequate idea can be formed of the transcendent effect which the news of the Victory had on the Public mind. Nelson's failure in discovering the Enemy's Fleet had created much disappointment, and Government was censured for entrusting so important a command to a young Rear-Admiral, the heaviest part of the blame being, of course, attributed to the Admiralty. To this circumstance, the exuberant delight shewn in the noble Letter from Lady Spencer, wife of Earl Spencer, the First Lord of the Admiralty, may be ascribed.

A London Gazette Extraordinary announced the event to the Country on the 2nd of October, and on the same day, both Lord and Lady Spencer expressed their gratification to Nelson, in terms which manifestly proceeded from their hearts :—

FROM EARL SPENCER TO SIR HORATIO NELSON.

"Dear Sir Horatio,                    "Admiralty, 2nd October, 1798.

" Since my last Letter of the 30th ultimo, I have had the satisfaction of receiving your Letters by Captain Capel, and most sincerely and cordially do I congratulate

---

[2] *Copy*, in the Nelson Papers.

you on the very brilliant and signal Service you have performed to your Country in the glorious Action of the first of August last, which most certainly has not its parallel in Naval History. The Neapolitan Messenger, by whom this is to go, is to depart to-night, and I have only now time to say thus much. In my next, I shall have the pleasing task of acquainting you with the measures which will be taken by Government to mark their sense of the merits of yourself, and your gallant Officers, on this memorable occasion. I wrote immediately a line to Lady Nelson, to tell her you were safe, and what you had achieved. I was happy to hear from Capel that your wound was doing well. God bless you, my dear Sir Horatio, and continue to crown your Services with success, is the earnest and constant prayer of your ever faithful and obedient Servant, "SPENCER."[1]

FROM THE COUNTESS SPENCER TO SIR HORATIO NELSON.

"Admiralty, 2nd October, 1798.

"Captain Capel just arrived!

"Joy, joy, joy to you, brave, gallant, immortalized Nelson! May that great God, whose cause you so valiantly support, protect and bless you to the end of your brilliant career! Such a race surely never was run. My heart is absolutely bursting with different sensations of joy, of gratitude, of pride, of every emotion that ever warmed the bosom of a British woman, on hearing of her Country's glory—and all produced by you, my dear, my good friend. And what shall I say to you for your attention to me, in your behaviour to Captain Capel? All, all I *can* say must fall short of my wishes, of my sentiments about you. This moment the guns are firing, illuminations are preparing, your gallant name is echoed from street to street, and every Briton feels his obligations to you weighing him down. But if these strangers feel in this manner about you, who can express what *We* of this House feel about you? What incalculable service have you been of to my dear Lord Spencer! How gratefully, as First Lord of the Admiralty, does he place on *your* brow these laurels so gloriously won. In a public, in a private view, what does he not feel at this illustrious achievement of yours, my dear Sir Horatio, and your gallant Squadron's! What a fair and splendid page have you and your heroic companions added to the records of his administration of the Navy! And, as wife of this excellent man, what do *I* not feel for *you all*, as executors of *his* schemes and plans! But I am come to the end of my paper, luckily for you, or I should gallop on for ever at this rate. I am half mad, and I fear I have written a strange Letter, but you'll excuse it. Almighty God protect you! Adieu! How anxious we shall be to hear of your health! Lady Nelson has had an Express sent to her."[2]

On the 6th of October, the "London Gazette," announced the Creation of Nelson to the Dignity of a BARON, by the Style and Title of BARON NELSON OF THE NILE, AND OF BURNHAM THORPE, IN THE COUNTY OF NORFOLK, to hold to him and the heirs male of his body.[3]

Much dissatisfaction was felt by his friends, and surprise by the public, that a higher Dignity was not conferred upon him. It was borne in mind that Sir John Jervis had obtained an Earldom,[4] and Admiral Duncan a Viscountcy, being two steps in the Peerage to each, for the Battles of St. Vincent and Camperdown, neither of which was so complete in itself, nor so important to the Country and to Europe as that of the Nile. "Why not confer the same Honours on Nelson as they did on Duncan? is rung in my ears almost wherever I go," wrote Captain

---

[1] *Autograph*, in the Nelson Papers.  [2] *Copy*, in the Nelson Papers.
[3] See the Patent in the APPENDIX.  [4] Vide vol. ii. p. 337.

Berry.[5] An explanation of the circumstance is afforded by the annexed Letter from Lord Spencer; but who can hesitate a moment in denouncing, as paltry and ungenerous, the distinction drawn between the reward due to an Admiral commanding a Squadron of thirteen Sail of the Line, detached upwards of *two thousand miles* from the Commander-in-Chief, and what would be proper to have bestowed on such Commander-in-Chief had he achieved, even with the same number of Ships, the same Victory? The principle laid down must have been founded on this fallacy—that the Commander-in-Chief directed, or was responsible for the proceedings of the Squadron. Nelson was sent into the Mediterranean with merely general instructions,[6] to pursue and destroy the French Fleet, every operation and detail being left to his own judgment; and he did both without one single additional order. The pursuit, the discovery, and the destruction of the Enemy were his own acts: all the merit was confessedly his own. Why not, then, the full and unqualified reward? Had he failed, neither censure nor punishment could have fallen upon the Commander-in-Chief; and no man thought of rewarding that Chief for Nelson's success. Yet Nelson received less Honours than he would otherwise have done, simply because he had nominally a Superior, then two thousand miles from the scene of action, and a merit seems to have been made of granting him so much!

Nelson, for he was, as he says in one of his letters, " a man, and did feel," felt the injustice, as all minds of a magnanimous and sensitive nature feel injustice, deeply and scornfully; but it was one of the noble traits of his character, never to allow the slight of a Minister to lessen his ardour and devotion to his Country. It is true, as Mr. Pitt said, that " Nelson's glory did not depend on the rank to which he might be raised in the Peerage;" but the degree of rank was the measure of his Country's gratitude, and to bestow on one man, for a comparatively small service, that which is withheld from another for a greater achievement, is both a public injustice and an individual wrong.

FROM EARL SPENCER TO LORD NELSON.

" My dear Lord,       " Admiralty, 7th October, 1798.

"I have the greatest satisfaction in obeying His Majesty's commands, by acquainting you that His Majesty has been graciously pleased to testify his Royal approbation of your conduct in the signal and brilliant Victory you obtained over the French Fleet on the 1st of August, by conferring on you the Dignity of a Baron of Great Britain, by the name, style, and title of Baron Nelson of the Nile, and of Burnham Thorpe, in the County of Norfolk. In congratulating your Lordship on this high distinction, I have particular pleasure in remarking, that it is the highest honour that has ever been conferred on an Officer of your standing in the Service, and who was not a Commander-in-Chief; and the addition to the Title is meant more especially to mark the occasion on which it was granted, which, however, without any such precaution, is certainly of a nature never to be forgotten. His Majesty has also been pleased to signify his intention of accompanying this grant of Honour by a suitable Provision, which cannot, however, be completed till Parliament shall have met; and I am likewise commanded to take the necessary steps for presenting your Lordship and the Captains who served under your orders on that

---

[5] Letter to Nelson, dated London, 30th December, 1798. In this Letter Sir Edward Berry said, "*Lord Spencer did not ask me a question*, he invited me to dinner, where I took an opportunity of saying the Victory was decidedly ours, previous to the blowing up of the L'Orient. His Lordship acknowledged it was a circumstance he was before unacquainted with. *This was the case with the Nation.*"—*Autograph*, in the Nelson Papers.

[6] See the Instructions, pp. 25, 26, ante.

occasion, with gold Medals, similar to those which have been given in the other great Actions fought this War. The First-Lieutenants of the Ships engaged will also be distinguished by·Promotion, the necessary directions for which will be sent to Lord St. Vincent: and the Senior Marine Officer of the Squadron will be recommended to his Royal Highness the Commander-in-Chief, that he may have a step in Brevet rank conferred upon him. I have the honour to be, &c.,

"SPENCER."[7]

The City of London, with its usual patriotism, took the lead in acknowledging Nelson's services. On the 3rd of October, at a full Court of the Common Council of London, Lord Nelson's Letter, transmitting to the City of London the Sword of Admiral Blanquet, was read : it elicited a tumult of applause, and the Sword was ordered to be placed among the City regalia. The thanks of the Court were unanimously voted to him and to the Officers and Seamen under his command. Two days after, the Lord Mayor, sixteen Aldermen, and nearly two hundred Common Councilmen attended, and the Sword was directed to be placed in a glass case, in the most conspicuous part of the Council Room, with this inscription:—" The Sword of Monsieur Blanquet, the Commanding French Admiral in the glorious Victory off the Nile, on the first of August, 1798 ; presented to this Court by the Right Honourable Lord Nelson." The Court then resolved "that a Sword of the value of two hundred guineas should be presented to Rear-Admiral Lord Nelson, as a testimony of the high esteem they entertain of his public services to this City, and to the whole Empire ; that the Freedom of the City should be presented to Captain Berry, in a gold box of the value of one hundred guineas, as a testimony of the high esteem entertained of his gallant behaviour on the 1st of August last ; and that the thanks of the Court be given to the other Officers, Seamen, and Marines, for the undaunted bravery and steady conduct which they exhibited on that ever-memorable day." On the 24th of October, the Lord Mayor, Aldermen, and Common Council of London presented an Address to the King, offering His Majesty their "warmest congratulations on the very important Victory of the Nile—an event so glorious to this Nation, so splendid and decisive, unexampled in Naval History, and reflecting the highest honour on the courage and the abilities of the gallant Admiral and his Officers, and the discipline and irresistible bravery of British Seamen." His Majesty, in reply, expressed " peculiar satisfaction at receiving the Address on the late glorious Victory," and added—" I trust that the valour of my Fleets and Armies, the talents and conduct of my Officers, which were never more conspicuous than on this late occasion, the vigorous and united exertions of the whole body of my People, and, above all, the protection of Almighty God, will enable me to bring the war to a safe and honourable conclusion."

Prayer and Thanksgiving for the Victory were used in all Churches, on Sunday, the 21st of October, and repeated on the two following Sundays.

Parliament met on the 20th of November, and the King's Speech contained the following notice of the Battle of the Nile :—

" The unexampled series of our Naval Triumphs, has received fresh splendour from the memorable and decisive Action, in which a Detachment of my Fleet, under the command of Rear-Admiral Lord Nelson, attacked, and almost totally destroyed, a superior Force of the Enemy, strengthened by every advantage of situation. By this great and brilliant Victory, an enterprise of which the injustice, perfidy, and extravagance, had fixed the attention of the World, and which was peculiarly directed against some of the most valuable interests of the British Empire, has, in the first instance, been turned to the confusion of its authors ; and the blow thus given to

---

[7] *Autograph*, in the Nelson Papers.

the power and influence of France, has afforded an opening which, if improved by suitable exertions on the part of other Powers, may lead to the general deliverance of Europe."

A motion having been made in the House of Lords, by Earl Spencer, and seconded by Viscount Hood, on the 21st of November, to return the Thanks of the House to Lord Nelson and his Officers, Lord Minto, who never lost an opportunity of expressing his admiration of his friend, said, with great eloquence and feeling—

" I should not intrude on your Lordships, if it were possible to content myself with a silent vote on this occasion ; but I shall no doubt be excused, if a participation in the general exultation and enthusiasm excited by this extraordinary Action, enhanced I confess, by a warm affection for the man, urges me to add· my voice, however feeble, to that of the House ; and I feel no shame in seeking, perhaps, by these means, to gratify what will be thought the justifiable pride of such a friendship, especially when I can do so in unison with the acclamations of his Country, or rather with the full chorus of all Europe, and of the whole World. It is, however, by no means my intention to enlarge on this vast and fertile subject, and my purpose, I confess, will be fulfilled by expressing my joyful concurrence with this motion, rather on my legs than by my vote. To do more, indeed, if I had any pretensions to attempt it, would be much in vain. Neither my powers, which are inadequate to much smaller tasks, nor the powers of the most eloquent men of this or of any other Age or Country, are such as to exalt, by any possible flight of language, or imagination, or even numbers, this more than Epic Action. In truth, whoever would reach the height of this sublime subject, for such it is, would perhaps do well to abide by those few short words contained in that simple, modest, dignified, and, above all, pious account, which we possess under the hand of Lord Nelson himself. On this point I cannot refrain, (and I am sure the House will go along with me,) from contrasting the fervent and sincere piety of our Christian Conqueror, with the despicable and profane hypocrisy with which these French atheists, actuated, as they will say, by policy, but as I suspect by fear, were at that very moment pretending to worship Mahomet. Of the Action itself I would only say, that as it has done more to exalt the reputation of our Country, and added more to the ancient and already accumulated stock of British Naval glory, so it has contributed more essentially to the solid interests and security of this Empire, as well as to the salvation of the rest of the World, than perhaps any other single event recorded in History. Were I to indulge myself on the details of this memorable day, and in tracing all its beneficial consequences, I should quickly be drawn out of my own depth, and beyond the limits of your Lordships' time. I refrain therefore, content with having used the opportunity of rendering to this great man, and signal event, the homage at least, of an ardent and humble affection. I will, indeed, trust that the sentiments I profess towards my extraordinary Friend will not be deemed entirely of a private nature, and may be admitted into somewhat of a higher class ; since they were excited by a daily and hourly contemplation, for a considerable period of time, of the most unremitting exertions of zeal, ability, application, and courage in the service of his Country ; not on one occasion, but on all ; not in one branch of service, but in all ; in a long course of Naval vigilance, and perseverance, in Battles at sea, in Sieges on shore. That friendship, I say, is somewhat more than private, which was not indeed created, for it had an earlier date, but which was raised in my breast to the highest pitch of admiration and devotion by those exploits, which it is the singular felicity of my life to have witnessed with my own eyes on the ever-memorable St. Valentine's day ; I mean on the 14th of February, when the Spanish Fleet was defeated off Cadiz by the great and immortal St. Vincent. It was on that day my illustrious Friend performed those prodigies of valour and conduct never equalled,

I believe, before in the History of War, nor ever to be surpassed, if it be not, indeed, by this very Battle of Aboukir; for it is the peculiar privilege of my Friend, that, from the beginning of his life, there have been few of his actions which could be surpassed, unless it were by some other action of his own. There is one other point of excellence to which I must say a single word, because I am, perhaps, the man in the world who has had the best opportunity of being acquainted with it. The world knows that Lord Nelson can fight the Battles of his Country; but a constant and confidential correspondence with this great man, for a considerable portion of time, has taught me, that he is not less capable of providing for its political interests and honour, on occasions of great delicacy and embarrassment. In that new capacity I have witnessed a degree of ability, judgment, temper, and conciliation, not always allied to the sort of spirit which without an instant's hesitation can attack on one day the whole Spanish Line with his single Ship, and, on another, a superior French Fleet, moored and fortified within the Islands and shoals of an unknown Bay; what can I add to these two short facts? They are themselves a volume of praise, and must leave behind them all the common and vulgar forms of panegyric. It is enough for me to declare my hearty concurrence with this Vote."[8]

The Duke of Clarence also bore strong testimony to Nelson's merits.

The House Resolved, *Nemine dissentiente*, "That the Thanks of the House be given to Rear-Admiral Lord Nelson for his able and gallant conduct in the memorable and decisive Victory obtained over the French Fleet, near the Mouth of the Nile, on the 1st, 2nd, and 3rd of August last; and that the Lord Chancellor do communicate the same to his Lordship.

"That the Thanks of this House be given to the several Captains, and Officers in the Fleet, under the Command of Rear-Admiral Lord Nelson, on the 1st, 2nd, and 3rd of August last, who, by their bravery and good conduct, contributed to the glorious success of that day; and that Rear-Admiral Lord Nelson do signify the same to them.

"That this House doth highly approve of, and acknowledge the Services of the Seamen and Marines on board the Ships under the Command of Rear-Admiral Lord Nelson, in the late glorious Victory over the French Fleet near the Mouth of the Nile, and that the Officers commanding the several Ships, do signify the same to their respective Crews, and do thank them for their good behaviour."

The LORD CHANCELLOR transmitted these Resolutions, with the following Letter, to Lord Nelson:—

"My Lord,                                                "28th December, 1798.

"I am commanded by the House of Lords to communicate to your Lordship their unanimous Resolutions of Thanks for your able and gallant conduct in the memorable and decisive Victory obtained over the French Fleet, near the Mouth of the Nile, on the 1st, 2nd, and 3rd of August last, by a Detachment of his Majesty's Fleet under your command, and also to transmit to your Lordship, the Resolutions of Thanks to the Captains and Officers of the Squadron under your command for their bravery and good conduct, which contributed to the glorious success of that day; and of approbation and acknowledgment of the Services of the Seamen, Marines, and Soldiers, on board the Ships under your command in that memorable and decisive Action. No words can sufficiently express the satisfaction I feel in executing the Commands I have received, nor the admiration, respect, and esteem, with which I have the honour to be, &c.,—LOUGHBOROUGH, C."[9]

Similar Resolutions were voted on the same day by the House of Commons, on the motion of Mr. Secretary Dundas, together with a Resolution for an Address to

---

[8] *Copy*, in the Nelson Papers.          [9] *Autograph*, in the Nelson Papers.

the King, that he would give directions that a Monument be erected in St. Paul's to the memory of Captain George Blagdon Westcott, of the Majestic, "who fell glori ously in the Battle." The Parliament of Ireland had likewise voted their Thanks to Nelson, and the Officers and Crews, on the 5th of October; and those of the Irish House of Commons were accompanied by the following Letter from the Speaker, (Mr. Foster, afterwards Lord Oriel) :—

"TO SIR HORATIO NELSON, K.B.

"Sir,                                              "Dublin, October 6, 1798.

"I have the honour of sending the Thanks of the House of Commons of Ireland in the enclosed Resolution. I have often been honoured with transmitting the applause of this Nation for many glorious and important Victories, but never did I feel more pleasure and satisfaction than now, in conveying to you, and to your Officers and Men, the grateful sentiments of the People of Ireland. I beg leave to subscribe myself with the truest veneration and respect, &c.,—JOHN FOSTER, Speaker."[1]

On the 22nd of November, the following Message from the King was brought down to the House of Commons :—

"His Majesty having taken into his consideration the signal and meritorious Services performed by Rear-Admiral Lord Nelson, in the memorable and decisive Victory obtained over the French Fleet off the Mouth of the Nile, not only highly honourable to himself, but eminently beneficial to these Kingdoms, and his Majesty being desirous to confer upon him some considerable and lasting mark of his royal favour, in testimony of his approbation of his great Services, and therefore, to give and grant to the said Rear-Admiral Lord Nelson, and the two next heirs male, to whom the Title of Baron Nelson of the Nile, and Burnham Thorpe, in the County of Norfolk, shall descend, for their lives, the net sum of £2000 per annum: but his Majesty not having it in his power to grant any annuity to that amount, or for a period beyond his own life, his Majesty recommends it to his faithful Commons to consider the means of enabling his Majesty to extend and secure an annuity of £2000 per annum to Rear-Admiral Lord Nelson, and to the two next heirs male, on whom the Title of Baron Nelson of the Nile and Burnham Thorpe, in the County of Norfolk, shall descend, in such manner as shall be most advantageous for their interests."

On the Motion for going into Committee, to take the Message into consideration, MR. THOMAS TYRWHITT JONES, said—"It was not his intention to detain the House long; but so strong were his feelings of admiration at the brilliant and extensively-important Victory, the gallant achiever of which now occupied their attention, that he could not resist the opportunity of saying a few words on the subject. It was a Victory unexampled in point of glory, and singular beyond all recorded in ancient or modern history, for the almost instantaneous advantages which had resulted from it. Its ultimate consequences, indeed, depended on the manner in which it should be followed up by his Majesty's Ministers. But whatever its future influence on the state of this Country, and of Europe might be, he did not think it extravagant, when he regarded the impression which it had already made, to proclaim Lord Nelson the Saviour of the civilized portion of mankind."

The House having resolved itself into a Committee, MR. PITT said, that "from the mode in which the House had already manifested their feelings respecting the

---

[1] *Autograph*, in the Nelson Papers.

object of the Message, he was so satisfied of their unanimous concurrence in the Motion which he had now to make, that he should not detain them for one moment with any additional arguments in its support.  He should content himself with simply moving, that his Majesty be empowered to settle a Pension of 2000*l.* a year on Lord Nelson, and the next two heirs male of his body, who should inherit the title of Baron Nelson of the Nile, to commence from the 1st of August last."

GENERAL WALPOLE observed, that "he felt the highest admiration of the prowess, the skill, and the useful activity of Admiral Nelson.  Never was there achieved a more splendid and beneficial Victory than that of the 1st of August.  In saying this, he merely echoed the opinions of that House and of Europe; and so far was he from thinking any marks of distinction or favour which had been bestowed, or were now proposed to be bestowed, upon the gallant Hero who acquired it, too much, that he thought him entitled to still higher honours than those which had been conferred on him.  The argument that he commanded only a Detachment was absurd.  It was the same as to say, that in the distribution of reward, more attention should be paid to rank than to merit."

MR. PITT replied, that "he would not enter into the question, whether the rewards conferred on Lord Nelson were adequate to his merit.  He would only say, that his glory did not depend on the rank to which he might be raised in the Peerage; his Achievement would be perpetuated in the memory of his Countrymen and all Europe; nor did he think that it was the title of Baron, Viscount, or Earl, that could enhance his consideration with Englishmen.  His claim to their gratitude and admiration would always rest upon the intrinsic merits of his Victory, which they would ever regard as the most splendid and useful that has hitherto signalized the Naval annals of their Country.  The attention to the difference of rank in the distribution of Honours was not absurd.  That, however, was not a question for the consideration of the House, but should be reserved entirely for the determination of the Crown.  He would satisfy himself with stating, that in no instance within his recollection, where the merits of the achievements were equal, had an inferior Officer been distinguished by the same honour, as an Officer of higher rank."

The Resolution was carried *nem. con.*

Besides the Naval Medal, which was also conferred upon all the Captains commanding Ships of the Line, Lord Nelson received the following honourable Augmentation to his Arms; but the incongruity of these additions so greatly disfigured them—simplicity being the chief beauty of Heraldry—that they needed only the Supporters suggested by Admiral Goodall,—two *Crocodiles!* to have become if possible even a still more unfortunate specimen of modern Armory:

"The King has been graciously pleased to give and grant unto the Right Honourable Horatio Baron Nelson of the Nile and of Burnham Thorpe, in the County of Norfolk, Rear-Admiral of the Blue Squadron of his Majesty's Fleet, and K.B., in consideration of the great zeal, courage, and perseverance manifested by him upon divers occasions, and particularly of his able and gallant conduct in the glorious and decisive Victory obtained over the French Fleet near the Mouth of the Nile, on the 1st day of August last, his Royal licence and authority that he and his issue may bear the following honourable Augmentations to his Armorial ensigns; viz.:—*A Chief undulated argent, thereon waves of the Sea, from which a Palm tree, issuant between a disabled Ship on the dexter, and a ruinous Battery on the sinister, all proper;* and for his Crest, *on a Naval Crown, or, the Chelengk, or Plume of Triumph,* presented to him by the Grand Signior, as a mark of his high esteem, and of his sense of the gallant conduct of the said Horatio Baron Nelson in the said glorious and decisive Victory, with the Motto, " *Palmam qui meruit ferat;*" and to his Supporters, being a Sailor on the dexter, and a Lion on the sinister, the honourable Augmentations following—viz., *In the hand of the Sailor a palm branch, and another in the paw of the Lion, both proper, with the addition of a tri-coloured Flag and Staff in the mouth of the latter;* which augmentations to the Supporters to be borne by the said Horatio Baron Nelson, and by those to whom the said Dignity shall descend."

It appears, from Sir Isaac Heard's, (Garter King of Arms,) letter to Lord Nelson, dated on the 21st of December, 1798, that the idea of granting these Heraldic distinctions originated with the King; and Lady Nelson having, very naturally, asked what all these hieroglyphics meant, Sir Isaac gave her the following explanation, which may be as necessary to the reader as to her Ladyship:—" In cheerful obedience to the wishes of your Ladyship, communicated by Mr. Davison, for a particular explanation of the honourable Augmentations to the Armorial Ensigns of the highly distinguished Lord Nelson, I have the honour to state to your Ladyship, that, in consequence of his Majesty's gracious intention of granting honourable Augmentations to his Lordship's Armorial Ensigns, which was signified to me by his Grace the Duke of Portland, Secretary of State, sketches of the said Ensigns were submitted to the Sovereign, who was pleased to command that the Chelengk or Plume of Triumph, presented to Lord Nelson by the Grand Signior, should constitute part of a new Crest, and also to direct that the other honourable Augmentations should be granted in the manner described in the Royal Warrant, and illuminated in a painting thereunto annexed. A copy of the Royal Sign Manual is enclosed. I have the honour to submit to your Ladyship the following explanation of the respective augmentations. In the Chief of the Arms a *Palm Tree* (emblematic of Victory) between a *disabled Ship* and a *ruinous Battery*, form striking memorials of the glorious event of the 1st of August, in the Bay of Aboukir, near the Mouth of the Nile. In the Crest, the *Chelengk*, (a more minute description of which I had the pleasure of delivering to your Ladyship,) is an indication of the distinctions rendered to his Lordship's merits by the Grand Signior; and *the Naval Crown* may bear a striking allusion to his Lordship's victory in those Seas, where the *Corona Navalis*, was first conferred by the Romans on persons who had eminently distinguished themselves in Naval combats. *The Palm Branch* in the hand of the Sailor, and in the paw of the Lion, is a continuation of the emblem in the Chief of the Arms, as well as allusive to the Motto, ' *Palmam qui meruit ferat.*' The *tri-coloured Flag* of the subdued Enemy was added to, and involved with, the Colours in the mouth of the Lion, which had been granted to his Lordship in commemoration of his distinguished gallantry and services, on the 14th of February, 1797. With regard to your Ladyship's question—whether Lord Nelson is, in consequence of the Royal Warrant, precluded from the use of his Crest of the San Josef, I have no hesitation in giving my decided opinion, that he may bear it, *with his new Crest*, at his own pleasure."

It is said that the Motto also was suggested by the King; but Mr. Southey asserts that it was selected by Lord Grenville from an Ode by Dr. Jortin, in which it is proposed, to prevent bloodshed, that two Ships of equal size, instead of whole Fleets, should engage, and decide the National dispute :

> " Concurrant paribus cum ratibus rates,
> Spectent numina ponti, et
> *Palmam qui meruit ferat.*"

From FOREIGN SOVEREIGNS, Nelson received the most flattering compliments. The Emperor Paul of Russia sent him a gold box set with diamonds, and the following Letter:—

"Monsieur le Vice Amiral Nelson, Envisageant la cause de mes Alliés comme la mienne, je ne puis pas vous exprimer le plaisir que vos succès m'ont fait. La victoire complète que vous avez remportée sur l'ennemi commun, et la destruction de la flotte Françoise sont assurement des titres trop puissans pour ne pas vous attirer les suffrages de la saine partie de l'Europe. Pour vous donner un témoignage marquant de la justice que je rends à vos talens militaires, je joins à la presente une boete avec mon Portrait enrichi de brillans, et je desire qu'il vous soit garant de ma haute bienveillance. Sur ce je prie Dieu qu'il vous ait, Monsieur le Vice Amiral Nelson, en sa sainte et digne garde.

"St. Petersbourg, le 8 8bre, 1798."                    "PAUL.[1]

The Grand Signior immediately upon receiving the news of the Victory, directed a superb diamond Aigrette (called a Chelengk, or Plume of Triumph) taken from one of the Imperial turbans, to be sent to Lord Nelson, together with a piece of sable fur of the first quality. He directed also a purse of two thousand sequins to be distributed among the British Seamen wounded at the Battle of the Nile; and the following is a translation of the Note delivered to Mr. Spencer Smith, his Majesty's Plenipotentiary on the occasion:—

"It is but lately that by a written communication it has been made known how much the Sublime Porte rejoiced at the first advice received of the English Squadron in the White Sea, having defeated the French Squadron off Alexandria in Egypt. By recent accounts comprehending a specific detail of the Action, it appears now more positive, that his Britannic Majesty's Fleet has actually destroyed, by that Action, the best Ships the French had in their possession. This joyful event, therefore, laying this Empire under an obligation, and the service rendered by our much esteemed friend Admiral Nelson, on this occasion being of a nature to call for public acknowledgment, his Imperial Majesty, the powerful, formidable, and most magnificent Grand Signior, has destined as a present, in his Imperial name, to the said Admiral, a diamond Aigrette (Chelengk) and a sable fur, with broad sleeves; besides two thousand sequins to be distributed among the wounded of his crew. And as the English Minister is constantly zealous to contribute by his endeavours to the increase of friendship between the two Courts, it is hoped he will not fail to make known this circumstance to his Court, and to solicit the permission of the powerful and most august King of England, for the said Admiral to put on and wear the said Aigrette and Pelise."

The Mother of the Grand Signior also sent him a Box set with diamonds of the value of £1000.

The King of the Two Sicilies presented to Nelson the brilliant Sword which had been given to the King of Naples, with the following words, by Charles the Third, on his departure for Spain:—"With this Sword I conquered the Kingdom which I now resign to thee. It ought in future to be possessed by the first Defender of the same, or by him who restoreth it to thee, in case it should ever be lost."

By the King of Sardinia he was honoured with a Box set with diamonds; the Island of Zante sent him a gold-headed Cane; and the City of Palermo gave him, with the Freedom of that City, a gold Box and Chain;[2] and it will appear from his correspondence, that he afterwards received a gift of £10,000 from the East India Company, a piece of Plate from the Turkey Company, and £500 for a piece of

---

¹ *Autograph*, in the Nelson Papers.          ² Vide vol. i. p. 13.

Plate from the Patriotic Fund. The Freedom of numerous Corporations was voted to him, and his Countrymen seemed to vie with Foreigners in doing him honour.

But amidst this shower of Public Honours, nothing imparted more gratification to Nelson than the congratulations of his early friends, many of them Veterans of the Navy, who having themselves acquired high distinction could best appreciate the service he had rendered to his Country. From the numerous Letters of this description which he received, a selection will be made of those of the warm-hearted Lady Parker, wife of Admiral Sir Peter Parker, his oldest Patron;[3] H. R. H. the Duke of Clarence; Admiral Earl Howe, K.G.; Admiral the Earl of St. Vincent, K.B.; Admiral Viscount Hood, K.B.; Admiral Goodall, who was second in command with him,[4] in Lord Hotham's Action in 1795; of Rear-Admiral Sir Roger Curtis (because though his senior in rank, he betrayed no jealousy at his being preferred to him to command the Squadron); of Captain Collingwood; and of his old Captain, (Locker,) who told him "always to lay a Frenchman close and you would beat him." No Letter from Lady Nelson, nor from his Father, on the occasion, has been found.

FROM LADY PARKER.

" Admiralty House, Portsmouth, October 29th, 1798.

" My dear and immortal Nelson!

" I am very sure that you know what I feel upon your unparalleled Victory. Captain Cockburn will tell you that I am not yet come to my senses. Your conduct on the ever-memorable First of August was glorious and decisive. All Europe has cause to bless the day that you were born. I do most devoutly pray that you may return safe to your aged and worthy Father, and to your amiable Wife, and long live to enjoy the caresses of them and of your grateful Country, in defence of which you have so frequently and so successfully bled. I am very uneasy about the wound in your head, and would have you quit a situation that must retard your recovery. Quiet is the only remedy for a blow on the head, and it is impossible for you to enjoy a moment's rest while you remain in your present station. A few month's relaxation and a cold climate, will soon fit you for another enterprise, but should you continue in constant exertion of both body and mind, years, not months will be required for your recovery. Take this advice from one that always had your welfare at heart. Sir Peter and I ever regarded you as a Son, and are, of course, truly happy at your well earned Honours. Accept of the sincere congratulations of the whole of our family, and assure yourself of the everlasting regard of your affectionate

" MARGARET PARKER." [5]

FROM H. R. H. THE DUKE OF CLARENCE.

" My dear Lord,

" On Captain Capel's arrival with the news of your glorious Victory, I was both astonished and hurt at not receiving a line from my old friend. But being now assured that you had written by the Leander, I take up my pen to congratulate you on your Victory, of which no one thinks more highly than I do. My real friendship for you, and my love for the Navy, would not allow me to be silent in the House of Lords, and I hope I said what I ought; at least, it was what I felt. Lord Minto's speech was elegant, judicious, and well turned. Every body meant well, but were not so

---

[3] Vide vol. i. p. 5, and vol. ii. p. 377.          [4] Vide vol. ii. p. 18.
[5] *Autograph*, in the Nelson Papers.

G 2

able to express it as his Lordship. I most highly admire the disposition your
Lordship made of the King's Ships, and of your determination and instant decision
of going down at once to the attack of the Enemy. I admire and approve exceedingly your Lordship's having in so public a manner returned thanks to the Almighty,
for his gracious assistance afforded to His Majesty's Arms: I have frequently been
surprised it has not been practised in our Fleets oftener, and I trust every successful
Admiral will in future follow your Lordship's good example.

" You, my dear Nelson, I hope, well know my sentiments respecting the discipline of the Navy; I need not, therefore, say much relative to that order you issued,
in which you ascribed the honourable and meritorious exertions of the Seamen and
Marines to *obedience* and *good order;* for which the King and the Country are to
thank the invincible and immortal St. Vincent. Having said thus much, I suppose
you must be tired; I will, therefore, for the present, take my leave. Adieu, my dear
Lord; accept my most sincere wishes for your health and welfare, and ever believe
me your best friend,                                         " WILLIAM." [6]

FROM ADMIRAL EARL HOWE, K.G.

" Sir,                                   " Grafton Street, 3rd October, 1798.

" Tho' conscious how many letters of congratulation you are likely to receive
by the same conveyance, on the subject of your Dispatches by Captain Capel, I
trust you will forgive the additional trouble of my compliments on this singular
occasion; not less memorable for the *skill*, than cool judgment testified under the
considerable disadvantages in the superior force and situation of the Enemy, which
you had to surmount. I am, with great esteem, Sir, your most obedient servant,

" HOWE." [7]

Sir Edward Berry informed Lord Nelson that on meeting Lord Howe soon after
the Battle of the Nile, his Lordship said " it stood unparalleled, and singular in
this instance, that *every Captain* distinguished himself. He spoke very handsomely, in every respect, about it." [8]

FROM ADMIRAL THE EARL OF ST. VINCENT, K.B.

" Ville de Paris, before Cadiz, 27th September, 1798.

" My dear Admiral,

" God be praised, and you and your gallant band rewarded by a grateful Country,
for the greatest Achievement the history of the world can produce. I most sincerely lament the loss of Captain Westcott, and the number of brave Officers and
men who have fallen on this signal occasion. . . . . . The Leander not having yet
appeared, I cannot make out a Dispatch for the Admiralty. Capel will be Berry's
precursor, and receive all the incense and kisses of Lady Spencer and other heroines.
. . . . . Sir John Orde conducted himself in such a manner towards me, I was compelled to send him to England, and he sailed from the Tagus in the Blenheim,
accompanied by the Kingsfisher, with a Convoy of 80 or 90 Sail, on the 13th instant,
so indignant that he has applied for a Court-Martial, to try me for some offence, the
scene of which lay at Gibraltar when you was there with him, and for some expressions I am said to have made use of to Sir William Parker about the sentence of a
Court-Martial. But the original sin was, appointing you to command the detached
Squadron, the event of which has proved that my judgment was correct. At this
distance, I can give you no sense as to prospective events; in truth, you want

---

[6] Clarke and M'Arthur, vol. ii. 124.
[7] *Autograph*, in the Nelson Papers.
[8] *Autograph*, in the Nelson Papers, dated 4th June, 1799.

none, and will do much better by following your own impulse.  I think you had better keep the Alexander, if you can get her masted; for it is upon the cards, that the French will send the Squadron they have ready at Brest to the Mediterranean, when Lord Bridport is driven up Channel, or off his station, by the autumnal gales. . . . . Tell Lady Hamilton I rely on her to administer to your health at Naples, where I have no doubt it will soon be re-established.  For this, and every other blessing, you have the most fervent wishes of, my dear Admiral, yours very affectionately,

"St. Vincent. [9]

"Remember me kindly to Troubridge, and all your heroes."

FROM ADMIRAL VISCOUNT HOOD, K.B.

"My dear Lord,          "Royal College, Greenwich, October 15th, 1798.

"I have not words to express the real joy I felt from your Lordship's very affectionate Letter of the 10th of August, announcing the very signal and wonderful success of His Majesty's Arms under your command, upon which accept my most cordial congratulations, as well as those of Lady Hood, and every branch of our families.

"Your Victory, my dear Lord, is the most complete and splendid history records, and in its consequences must prove highly beneficial and important, not only to Great Britain, but to mankind; and it may be justly said that your Lordship has preserved from anarchy, distress, and misery, the greatest part of Europe.  No Officer, I will be bold to say, ever more highly merited the gracious notice of his Sovereign, and that of his Country.  I am, therefore, extremely disappointed that your well-earned Honours are not carried farther, particularly as Mr. Pitt told me, the day after Captain Capel arrived, that you would certainly be a Viscount, which I made known to Lady Nelson.  But it was objected to in a certain quarter, because your Lordship was not a Commander-in-Chief.  In my humble judgment, a more flimsy reason was never given.  All remunerations should be proportionate to the service done the public, let the Officer who does it be first, second, or third in command. But, in fact, your Lordship stood in the situation of Commander-in-Chief off the Mouth off the Nile, and could not possibly receive any advice or assistance, at the distance of near a thousand leagues from Earl St. Vincent, and conquered from your own personal zeal, ability, and judgment.  I do assure you, my dear and much-loved Lord, I am not singular in the sentiments I have stated.  They are in unison with the general voice of your grateful Country.  I long much for your Lordship's return to England, and hope you will not fail coming the moment you can, without doing violence to your active mind.

"I put this under cover to Sir William Hamilton, as the best chance of your getting it.  I fear the Leander is gone, but sincerely wish poor Berry may be safe. Lady Hood, Mrs. Hollwall, &c. &c., most cordially unite with me in all affectionate greetings to your Lordship, and I entreat you will believe me to be, with every sentiment of regard and esteem, my dear Lord, your very faithful, obliged, and affectionate friend,                                      "Hood." [1]

FROM ADMIRAL GOODALL.

"Exeter, October 3rd, 1798.

"With what pleasure, my dear Nelson, do I congratulate you on your glorious Victory!  I know not where to place the preference in my praises; whether to the boldness of the attempt, or the skill with which it was conducted, unrivalled in our Annals.  I have often been obliged to stand in the breach against the senseless criticisms of the noble and ignoble of this Country; you know them well—governed

---

[9] *Autograph*, in the Nelson Papers.          [1] Ibid.

by the tide of sure and immediate success.  Knowing my attachment to you, how
often have I been questioned, ' What is your favourite Hero about ?  The French fleet
has passed under his nose,' &c., &c.  To which I have ever answered, ' I know him
well; if fortune has not befriended his labours and anxieties in this event, yet
something capital will be done.  I know him, and most of his gallant companions
who are to support him in the day of battle.  You will not hear from him till he has
thundered in the storm, and directed the whirlwind that will overwhelm the Enemy.'
My presages have been happily confirmed.  You have by your gallantry silenced,
my dear friend, both jealousy and growing censure, and raised up to yourself, like
your namesake, the Roman Horace, a Name that will exist in futurity as long as
History or monumental inscription are preserved from the hand of Time; for with
*him* you may say—
> " Exegi monumentum ære perennius,
> Regalique situ Pyramidum altius."

Fortune, who turned her back upon you at Teneriffe, could not but admire the
greatness of the enterprise at the Nile, and give her countenance to the daring
attempt.  I rejoice, therefore, my dear friend, at your success.  You will be loaded
with deserved Honours, and your brave Brothers in Arms will be gratefully distinguished.  I am happy to learn your wound is slight—it will be an additional mark
of dignity.  God preserve you, and believe me to be, my little Hero, your sincere
friend and servant,                                   " J. GOODALL."

" P.S.—Remember me to Troubridge, whose feelings I sympathized with—to
Saumarez, Hallowell, Miller, &c., &c., and I would also have been happy to have
said to Westcott, but he sleeps in the bed of honour, and in all probability will be
immortalized among the heroes in the Abbey.. *Requiescat in pace.*  Never could
he have died more honourably.  I have him to lament among many deserving men
whom I have patronised, that have passed away, in the prime of their lives, by
disease or the sword.  This Letter has been writ these two days, and also the copy
of it, which I have sent by another Channel, and I have just learnt you are made an
English Baron, by what Title I know not; but 'tis not enough; as you are in the
range of Titles which your Brother-Officers availed themselves of, do you do the
same.  You have as just a claim.  Go as far as you can—Viscount, at least.  I
shall clamour for more, but shall not rest till I hail you Viscount.  This is an age
wherein Titles are not spared in the favourable moment.  You know Courtiers and
Ministers are profuse in the hour of success, but when the blaze has subsided
that flashed upon them—scanty, mean, and niggardly.  Take for your Supporters
the emblematical figures of the Nile—two Crocodiles, or an Egyptian Mameluke in
his dress for *one*, and a Crocodile for the other.  I do not like your present Supporters : they are too national, if I recollect right—one at least so.  You have now
an opportunity of changing them, and also your Motto, if you choose it, though it
is a very good and religious one.  Should you be so disposed, I have annexed a
string of them, any of which will suit your heroic actions."[2]

* FROM REAR-ADMIRAL SIR ROGER CURTIS.

" My dear Nelson,                    " Prince, off Cadiz, 28th October, 1798.

" I had much gratification in the receipt of your obliging Letter, dated the 29th
of the last month.  Of your unparalleled Victory I shall say very little.  The
general voice of all Europe does you and your brave companions justice, and my
individual voice is in unison with the universal sentiment expressed on the

---

[2] *Autograph*, in the Nelson Papers.

occasion. You speak of some uneasiness that your appointment to command the Mediterranean Squadron has occasioned. I know that you speak correctly when you say it was not solicited by you: and by whatever means the arrangement took place, you have certainly demonstrated that the important charge could not have been placed in abler hands. I sincerely felicitate you upon your success, and heartily wish you health very long to enjoy the high reputation you have acquired.* . . . . .
I am, &c.                                                    "ROGER CURTIS."[4]

### FROM CAPTAIN COLLINGWOOD.

"My dear Friend,          "Excellent, off Cadiz, September 27th, 1798.

"I cannot express how great my joy is for the complete and glorious Victory you have obtained over the French—the most decisive, and, in its consequences, perhaps the most important to Europe, that was ever won. And my heart flows with thankfulness to the Divine Providence for his protection of you through the great dangers which are ever attendant on services of such eminence. So total an overthrow of their Fleet, and the consequent deplorable situation of the Army they have in Africa, I hope will teach those tyrants in the Directory a lesson of humility, and dispose them to peace and dispose them to justice, that they may restore to those States they have ruined all that can be saved out of the wreck of a subverted Government and plundered people. I lament most sincerely the death of Captain Westcott, a good Officer and a worthy man: but if it was a part of our condition to choose a day to die on, where could he have found one so memorable, so eminently distinguished among great days? I have been here miserable enough all this summer, but I hope to go to England very soon. The Barfleur, Northumberland, and some other Ships are expected to relieve the old ones. Sir John Orde, you will have heard, went home in the Blenheim the beginning of this month. There were unhappily differences between him and the Admiral: I never knew what was the subject of them, or even that there was one. 'Trifles light as air served as confirmation of' deadly hatred. Such are the effects which for ever arise from inactive Armaments. Had we had more consequential business those animosities would not have arisen. Say to Lady Nelson when you write to her how much I congratulate her on the safety, the honours, and the services of her husband. Good God, what must be her feelings! how great her gratitude to Heaven for such mercies! Pray, my dear Sir, give my hearty congratulations to all my friends in your Fleet. I am glad to understand my worthy Ball and Darby are recovering well. May success ever attend you, my dear friend, is ever the prayer of, my dear Sir, your faithful and affectionate,

"CUTHBERT COLLINGWOOD."[5]

### FROM LIEUTENANT-GOVERNOR LOCKER.

"Royal Hospital, Sunday, 28th October, 1798.
"My dear, dear Lord,
"How happy you have made me, you can easier conceive than I describe, and indeed I believe the Nation. I am sure the worthy part of them at least. But enough of this, as I well know you don't love to be told of these matters. . . . . Believe me ever, my dear Lord, your most faithful and affectionate friend,

"J. LOCKER."[6]

To these Letters, it is right to add the congratulations of his old Correspondent, the Honourable William Frederick Wyndham, then Minister at Florence:
"Permit me with the sincerity of a grateful heart to congratulate you on your unexampled brilliant success, and on the high honours and respect you have

---

[4] *Autograph*, in the Nelson Papers.        [5] Ibid.        [6] Ibid.

gained from every individual of every Court of Europe. I have had the satisfaction of witnessing almost the beginning of your glory, and I have now that of seeing it attain its utmost summit; for it is impossible that any man can do more, or be greater in the eyes of all Europe than you now stand . . . . . I have the honour to be, &c.                                                "W. WYNDHAM."[7]

One of the most remarkable Letters to which the Battle of the Nile gave rise, was from a Polish Professor of Nelson's own name, a translation of which may amuse the reader:

"Warsaw, in Poland, 11th November, 1798.

"Your Excellence,.

"The fame of the most illustrious and great Victory, which your Excellence, through your high wisdom and great valour, hath obtained over the French, the Enemies of mankind, flies wide through every quarter of the world; it has been celebrated in fêtes of triumph, and "Long live the great, the valiant Victor, the English Admiral Nelson, Baron of the Nile, Burnham and Tarpes," resounds with heartfelt satisfaction through the States. Rich and poor rejoice in the most distant parts and every Monarch joins the chorus. Now, as we are brother Nelsons, we have taken the liberty of expressing our great satisfaction at the honour obtained for the Nelson's family by your Excellency's wisdom and valour. God Almighty strengthen the weapons of your Excellence against all the Enemies of Great Britain. Our grandfather Nelson left England in anno 1699, to go to Sweden as a Captain of Artillery and left some brothers in England. He resided afterwards in Stockholm as an Officer of Artillery. There our father, Ernest Nelson was born, who, after the death of his father, was in the service of the magnanimous King of Sweden, Charles the Twelfth, until that valiant Monarch lost his life at Fredericks-hall. After his death, our Father removed to Konigsberg, in Prussia, where myself and my brother were born. I, John Ernest Nelson, the writer of this letter, am the first-born and have the honour of paying my respects to your Excellence. I have studied Law and Physic. I was invested by her Imperial Majesty with the Order of the Golden Star, and also with the Portuguese Order of Christ. I reside at Warsaw in Poland. My brother Frederic Theodore Nelson belongs to the Queen of Prussia's Rechnungs-Rath, and resides at the Palace at Koningsberg. I have a son, named Charles Nelson, of the age of 15 years. I commit myself to your high protection, and remain during life with the profoundest veneration, &c.,

"JNO. ERNEST NELSON, Professor of Medicine, LL.D., &c."[8]

No present sent to Nelson after the Battle of the Nile was so extraordinary as that which he received from his gallant friend, Captain Hallowell of the Swift-sure; and the idea could have occurred only to a very original mind. After L'Orient blew up, part of her main-mast was taken on board of the Swiftsure; and in May 1799, Captain Hallowell, fearing the effect of all the praise and flattery lavished on his Chief, determined to remind him that he was mortal.[9] He therefore ordered a *Coffin* to be made out of part of L'Orient's mast, and was so careful that nothing whatever should be used in its construction that was not taken from it, that the staples were formed of the spikes drawn from the cheeks of the mast, which were driven into the edge of the Coffin, and when the lid was put on, toggles were put into the staples to keep it down, so as to prevent the necessity of using

---

[7] *Autograph*, in the Nelson Papers.

[8] *Autograph* and Translation, in the Nelson Papers.

[9] From the information of Rear-Admiral Inglefield, C.B., brother-in-law of Admiral Sir Benjamin Hallowell.

nails or screws for that purpose. The nails in the Coffin were likewise made from the spikes taken from the mast. A Paper was pasted on the bottom, containing the following Certificate:—"I do hereby certify that every part of this Coffin is made of the wood and iron of L'Orient, most of which was picked up by his Majesty's Ship, under my command, in the Bay of Aboukir. Swiftsure, May 23, 1799.— BEN. HALLOWELL."[1]

This singular present was accompanied by the following Letter, which is taken from the *original*, in the Nelson Papers, a fact it is necessary to state, because both Charnock and Harrison, not contented with destroying its simplicity, altered the address to "Sir," and changed the date to "August 1798," to make it appear that the Coffin was sent immediately after the Battle of the Nile. Though printed correctly by Clarke and M'Arthur, Southey followed the copy given by Charnock and Harrison. It is greatly to be regretted that Nelson's reply has not been found:

"THE RIGHT HON. LORD NELSON, K.B.

    "My Lord,
    "Herewith I send you a Coffin made of part of L'Orient's Main mast, that when you are tired of this Life you may be buried in one of your own Trophies—but may that period be far distant, is the sincere wish of your obedient and much obliged servant,
                                                    "BEN. HALLOWELL.[2]
    "Swiftsure, May 23rd, 1799."

The astonishment that prevailed among the Crew of the Vanguard, Lord Nelson's Flag-Ship, when they were convinced it was a *Coffin* which had been brought on board, will be long remembered by their Officers. "We shall have hot work of it indeed," said of one of the Seamen; "you see the Admiral intends to fight till he is killed, and there he is to be buried." Lord Nelson highly appreciated the present, and for some time had it placed upright, with the lid on, against the bulk-head of his cabin, behind the chair on which he sat at dinner. At length, by the entreaties of an old servant, he was prevailed on to allow it to be carried below. When his Lordship left the Vanguard, the Coffin was removed into the Foudroyant, where it remained for many days, on the gratings of the quarter-deck. While his Officers were one day looking at it, he came out of the cabin:— "You may look at it, Gentlemen," said he, "as long as you please: but, depend on it, none of you shall have it."[1] It is satisfactory to state that Nelson was actually buried in this Coffin.

The following brief notices of the "Heroes of the Nile," can scarcely fail to interest the public:—

CAPTAIN SIR JAMES SAUMAREZ, of the ORION, which Ship he commanded at the Battle of St. Vincent. He was created a Baronet, and received the Red Ribbon in June 1801; commanded at the Battle of Algesiras, in the July following; was appointed a Knight Grand Cross of the Order of the Sword of Sweden in 1813; and was elevated to the Peerage, by the title of Lord de Saumarez, in September, 1831. His Lordship died an Admiral of the Red, and General of Marines, in October 1836.

CAPTAIN THOMAS TROUBRIDGE, of the CULLODEN, which Ship he commanded at the Battle of St. Vincent. He received the Cross of Commander of the Order of St. Ferdinand and Merit, from the King of Naples; was created a Baronet in

---

[1] Marshall's Naval Biography, vol. i. p. 474.
[2] *Autograph*, in the Nelson Papers.

November 1799; became a Rear-Admiral of the Blue in 1804; and perished in the Blenheim, on her passage from the East Indies in 1805.

CAPTAIN HENRY D'ESTERRE DARBY, of the BELLEROPHON. He commanded the Spencer at Algesiras, in 1801; was made a Knight Commander of the Bath in 1820; and died an Admiral of the Blue, in March 1823.

CAPTAIN THOMAS LOUIS, of the MINOTAUR. He received the Orders of St. Ferdinand and Merit, and Maria Theresa; became a Rear-Admiral: was second in command, having his Flag in the Canopus, (previously Le Franklin, taken at the Nile,) in Sir John Duckworth's Action off San Domingo, in February, 1806, for which he was made a Baronet, when he adopted the very appropriate Motto—"In Canopo ut ad Canopum." He died on board the Canopus, in the Mediterranean, in May, 1807.

CAPTAIN JOHN PEYTON, of the DEFENCE. He died a Rear-Admiral of the Red, on the 2nd of August, 1809.

CAPTAIN ALEXANDER JOHN BALL, of the ALEXANDER. He was Governor of Malta after its surrender, received the Order of St. Ferdinand and Merit, and the Cross of Malta, and was created a Baronet in June 1801. He died at Malta, a Rear-Admiral of the Red, on the 25th of October, 1809.

CAPTAIN SAMUEL HOOD, of the ZEALOUS. He also received the Cross of Commander of the Order of St. Ferdinand and Merit, and the Cross of Maria Theresa; commanded the Venerable at the Battle of Algesiras, in 1801; obtained the Red Ribbon in 1804; lost his arm in Action with some French Frigates, in September 1806; and was created a Baronet in April, 1809. Sir Samuel became a Vice-Admiral of the Blue, and died at Madras in June 1815, being then Commander-in-Chief in the East Indies.

CAPTAIN DAVIDGE GOULD, of the AUDACIOUS, now an Admiral of the Red, and a Knight Grand Cross of the Bath. He is the sole survivor of all the Captains who were at the Nile.

CAPTAIN THOMAS FOLEY, of the GOLIATH. He was Captain of the Britannia, bearing the Flag of Sir Charles Thompson, at the Battle of St. Vincent, and commanded the Elephant, which bore Lord Nelson's Flag at Copenhagen, in 1801: in 1815 he was appointed a Knight Commander, and in 1820 a Knight Grand Cross of the Bath, and died an Admiral of the Blue, on the 13th of January, 1833.

CAPTAIN RALPH WILLETT MILLER, of the THESEUS, was accidentally blown up, on the 14th of May, 1799. (Vide vol. ii. p. 465.)

CAPTAIN GEORGE BLAGDON WESTCOTT, of the MAJESTIC, was killed in the Battle, and a Monument was erected to his memory in St. Paul's, at the Public expense.

CAPTAIN THOMAS BOULDEN THOMPSON, of the LEANDER, who again distinguished himself by his "gallant and almost unprecedented defence" of that Ship against Le Généreux of 74 Guns, on the 18th of August, 1799, when he was severely wounded and made prisoner. He was Knighted in February, 1799; lost a leg in command of the Bellona, 74, at Copenhagen, in 1801; was made a Baronet in December, 1806; a Knight Commander of the Bath in 1815, and a Knight Grand Cross in 1822; and died on the 3rd of March, 1828, being then a Vice-Admiral of the Red, and Treasurer of Greenwich Hospital.

CAPTAIN BENJAMIN HALLOWELL, of the SWIFTSURE, in which Ship he was captured by a French Squadron, in June, 1801, after a gallant defence. He received the Order of St. Ferdinand and Merit; was appointed a Knight Commander of the Bath in 1815, and a Knight Grand Cross in June, 1831. Sir Benjamin assumed the name of CAREW, and died an Admiral of the Blue, in September, 1834.

CAPTAIN EDWARD BERRY, of the VANGUARD. He was Knighted in December, 1798. Having commanded the Agamemnon at Trafalgar, and at the Battle of St. Domingo, in 1806, he had the rare and (except in the case of Lord Collingwood) the unprecedented distinction of wearing *three* Medals for General Actions. Sir Edward was made a Baronet in 1806, a Knight Commander of the Bath in 1815, and died in February, 1831, being then a Rear-Admiral of the White.

CAPTAIN THOMAS MASTERMAN HARDY, of the MUTINE BRIG. Though, from the insignificant size of his Vessel, Captain Hardy can scarcely be included in the list of Captains who commanded Ships in the Battle, yet, as he was the only other Captain present, he cannot properly be omitted. He was posted into the Vanguard, and was Nelson's Captain in the Victory, at Trafalgar, in consequence of which he was created a Baronet in 1806, a Knight Commander of the Bath in 1815, and a Knight Grand Cross in 1831. Sir Thomas Hardy died a Vice-Admiral of the Blue, and Governor of Greenwich Hospital, in September, 1839.

Thus, such were the subsequent distinguished services of those whom Nelson emphatically called his "Band of Brothers," that of the thirteen Captains who survived the Battle of the Nile, one was created a Knight of the Bath, a Baronet, and a Peer; four were made Baronets and Knights of the Bath; three obtained Baronetcies; and four received the Order of the Bath. Of the remaining two Captains, Miller lost his life in command of his Ship in the following year, and Peyton died in 1809, long before the close of the War.

---

TO CAPTAIN EDWARD BERRY,[4] OF H. M. SHIP VANGUARD.

[Order-Book.]

Vanguard, off the Mouth of the Nile, 2nd August, 1798.

Whereas I think it requisite that an Officer of your rank should have charge of my Dispatches to the Earl of St. Vincent, Commander-in-Chief, you are hereby required and directed to take charge of them, and go on board the Leander, Captain Thompson, who is ordered to carry you, without loss of time, to the Commander-in-Chief. After having delivered my Dispatches, you are to give him all further information relative to the late Victory over the French Fleet off the Mouth of the Nile.

HORATIO NELSON.

[4] Captain Berry proceeded with the Dispatches in the Leander, 50, (Captain Thompson,) pursuant to this order; but that Ship was captured after a very gallant resistance on the 18th of August, off Gozo, near Candia, by the Généreux, 74, which had effected her escape at the Nile. Captain Berry was wounded in the Action by a splinter, and suffered severely for many months. The Officers and crew of the Leander were taken into Corfu and thence sent to Trieste, where they were released on *parole;* and Captain Berry was Knighted on the 12th of December, 1798, immediately after his arrival in England.

TO THE CAPTAINS OF HIS MAJESTY'S SHIPS OFF THE NILE.[5]

[Autograph, in the possession of the Dowager Lady de Saumarez.]

Vanguard, August 3rd, 1798.

Gentlemen,

I feel most sensibly the very distinguished honour you have conferred upon me by your Address of this day. My prompt decision was the natural consequence of having such Captains under my command, and I thank God I can say, that in the Battle the conduct of every Officer was equal. I accept, as a particular mark of your esteem, the Sword you have done me the honour to offer, and will direct my Picture to be painted the first opportunity, for the purpose you mention.

I have the honour to [be], Gentlemen,

With the highest respect, your most obliged,

HORATIO NELSON.

---

TO THE CAPTAINS OF ANY FRIGATES CAPTAIN BERRY MAY MEET WITH.

[Order-Book.]

Vanguard, off the Mouth of the Nile, 5th August, 1798.

I expect to sail from this place the 19th instant, and shall steer for Candia, keep in shore on the south side of it, and proceed towards Cape Passaro, and down the Mediterranean. Sicily and Naples will be the most likely places to hear of me after my leaving Candia. I am, and have been, very much distressed for Frigates, and hope the Captains of them under my command, will use their utmost endeavours to join me, according to the above-mentioned expectations to find me.

HORATIO NELSON.

---

TO EVAN NEPEAN, ESQ., ADMIRALTY.

[Letter-Book, and "London Gazette," of October 2, 1798.]

Vanguard, Mouth of the Nile, August 7, 1798.

Sir,

Herewith, I have the honour to transmit you a Copy of my Letter to the Earl of St. Vincent, together with a Line-of-

[5] The Letter to which this was the Answer, is in p. 66, ante.

Battle of the English and French Squadrons, also a List of Killed and Wounded. I have the honour to inform you that eight of our Ships have already Top-gallant yards across, and ready for any service ; the others, with the Prizes, will soon be ready for sea. In an event of this importance, I have thought it right to send Captain Capel[6] with a Copy of my Letter (to the Commander-in-Chief) overland, which I hope their Lordships will approve ; and beg leave to refer them to Captain Capel, who is a most excellent Officer, and fully able to give every information ; and I beg leave to recommend him to their Lordships' notice.

I have the honour to be, &c.,

HORATIO NELSON.

P.S. The Island[7] I have taken possession of, and brought off the two thirteen-inch mortars, all the brass guns, and destroyed the iron ones.

---

TO THE RIGHT HONOURABLE SIR WILLIAM HAMILTON, K.B.[8]

[Letter-Book.]

Vanguard, Mouth of the Nile, 8th August, 1798.

My dear Sir,

Almighty God has made me the happy instrument in destroying the Enemy's Fleet, which I hope will be a blessing to Europe. You will have the goodness to communicate this

---

[6] The Honourable Thomas Bladen Capel, fifth son of William, fourth Earl of Essex, now a Vice-Admiral of the Red and a Knight Commander of the Order of the Bath. He was Signal-Lieutenant of the Vanguard in the Battle, and was promoted to command the Mutine, *vice* Captain Hardy, who was promoted to the Vanguard, *vice* Captain Berry, sent home with the Dispatches.

[7] Bequier Island, since known by the name of "Nelson's Island."

[8] It is remarkable that at the very time when the Action was being fought, Sir William Hamilton should have been writing to Nelson. His Letter is dated, "Naples, August 1, 1798, late at night," and after acknowledging the receipt of his packet of the 20th and 22nd of July from Syracuse, Sir William said : "You may judge of our disappointment, as, for ten days past, reports have been current of your having defeated the French Fleet in the Bay of Alexandretta, on the 30th of June, and taken Buonaparte prisoner ; but we must not repine ; you have done what man could do, and, as you say very well, 'the Devil's children have the Devil's luck.' I can easily conceive the anxiety of your mind during your fruitless tour, in a crippled Ship and without a single Frigate ; but as all repining at what is passed is in vain, let us do the best we can under our present circumstances." He then informed Nelson of all they

happy event to all the Courts in Italy, for my head is so indifferent that I can scarcely scrawl this letter. Captain Capel,
who is charged with my Dispatches for England, will give you
every information. Pray put him in the quickest mode of
getting home. You will not send by post any particulars of
this Action, as I should be sorry to have any accounts get
home before my Dispatches. I hope there will be no difficulty in our getting refitted at Naples. Culloden must
be instantly hove down, and Vanguard all new masts, and
bowsprit. Not more than four or five Sail of the Line will
probably come to Naples; the rest will go with the Prizes to
Gibraltar. As this Army never will return, I hope to hear
the Emperor has regained the whole of Italy. With every
good wish, believe me, dear Sir,

Your most obliged and affectionate,
HORATIO NELSON.

had heard at Naples since his departure on the 17th of June; that he had read his
letters to General Acton, "abuse and all;" that the case was then altered, as the
Treaty between the Emperor of Austria and that Court had arrived, so that the Ports
of the Two Sicilies were open to the Ships of England without limitation; and his
Imperial Majesty would defend the King of Naples if attacked on account of his
opening his Ports to the British Fleet: "God bless you, my dear Friend, it is late
at night. . . . May all disappointments be at an end, and every success attend you!"
—*Autograph*, in the Nelson Papers.

In a Letter, also written on the 1st of August, by Sir John Acton to Sir William
Hamilton, he pointed out, in very pathetic terms, the deplorable condition of Naples:
"I have seen with a true concern the contents of Admiral Nelson's letters, from Syracuse. I must condole with all of us the misfortune which has befallen the activity
of our brave Admiral, by miscarrying the French in their course, notwithstanding
the most energetical efforts to meet them, before their sending an Army, God knows
in what a direction, and what is their mischievous project. We must, however, do
as well as we can in this disagreeable but not desperate case. His Sicilian Majesty
has been acquainted immediately of what you have been so good to communicate to
me. Both their Majesties are in the greatest uneasiness for their own situation at
this moment. Admiral Nelson is certainly at present, and every English Squadron,
most heartily welcome to the Ports of the Two Sicilies." He then alluded to the
Treaty with Austria, and added, "We are since yesterday on another footing, but we
are now *open*, exposed to a War directly, on Admiral Nelson's account. You see
fairly our situation. Are we to be left in this position? Will Admiral Nelson run
to the Levant again, without knowing for certain the position of the French, and
leave the Two Sicilies exposed in their movements? Buonaparte has absconded
himself, but in any part he has taken, security is not to be placed. God knows
where he is and whether we shall not see him again in a few days, if we do not hear
of what course he has taken! I present all this to your consideration. The brave
Nelson will certainly have them present. He may defeat the French coming to us
—he expected and we hoped in their passage on our Coasts. I am for ever, &c.,
J. ACTON."—*Autograph*, in the Nelson Papers.

9th August.—I have intercepted all Buonaparte's Dispatches, going to France. This Army is in a scrape, and will not get out of it.

---

## TO THE RIGHT HONOURABLE THE LORD MAYOR OF LONDON.

[From the "Annual Register," vol. x. p. 87.]

Vanguard, Mouth of the Nile, 8th August, 1798.

My Lord,

Having the honour of being a Freeman of the City of London, I take the liberty of sending to your Lordship, the Sword of the Commanding French Admiral, Monsieur Blanquet, who survived after the Battle of the first, off the Nile ; and request, that the City of London will honour me by the acceptance of it, as a remembrance, that Britannia still rules the Waves, which, that She may for ever do, is the fervent prayer of your Lordship's most obedient Servant,

HORATIO NELSON.

---

## TO HIS EXCELLENCY THE GOVERNOR OF BOMBAY.

[Letter Book.]

Vanguard, Mouth of the Nile, 9th August, 1798.

Sir,

Although I hope the Consuls who are, or ought to be resident in Egypt, have sent you an express of the situation of affairs here, yet, as I know Mr. Baldwin has some months left Alexandria, it is possible you may not be regularly informed. I shall, therefore, relate to you, briefly, that a French Army of 40,000 men in 300 Transports, with 13 Sail of the Line, 11 Frigates, Bomb Vessels, Gun-boats, &c. arrived at Alexandria on the 1st of July : on the 7th, they left it for Cairo, where they arrived on the 22nd. During their march they had some actions with the Mamelukes, which the French call great victories. As I have Buonaparte's dispatches before me, (which I took yesterday,) I speak positively : he says, 'I am now going to send off to take Suez and Damietta;' he does not speak very favourably of either the Country or people : but there is so much bombast in his letters, that it is difficult to get near the truth ; but he does not mention India in these dispatches. He is what is called organizing the Country, but you may be assured is master only of what his Army covers.

From all the inquiries which I have been able to make, I cannot learn that any French Vessels are at Suez, to carry any part of this Army to India. Bombay, if they can get there, I know is their first object; but, I trust, Almighty God will in Egypt overthrow these pests of the human race. It has been in my power to prevent 12,000 men from leaving Genoa, and also to take eleven Sail of the Line, and two Frigates; in short, only two Sail of the Line and two Frigates have escaped me. This glorious Battle was fought at the Mouth of the Nile, at anchor: it began at sunset, August the 1st, and was not finished at three the next morning; it has been severe, but God blessed our endeavours with a great victory. I am now at anchor between Alexandria and Rosetta, to prevent their communication by water, and nothing under a Regiment can pass by land. But I should have informed you, that the French have 4000 men posted at Rosetta to keep open the Mouth of the Nile. Alexandria, both Town and Shipping, are so distressed for provisions, which they can only get from the Nile by water, that I cannot guess the good success which may attend my holding our present position, for Buonaparte writes his distress for stores, artillery, things for their hospital, &c. All useful communication is at an end between Alexandria and Cairo: you may be assured I shall remain here as long as possible. Buonaparte had never yet to contend with an English Officer; and I shall endeavour to make him respect us. This is all I have to communicate. I am confident every precaution will be taken to prevent, in future, any Vessels going to Suez, which may be able to carry troops to India. If my letter is not so correct as might be expected, I trust for your excuse, when I tell you that my brain is so shook with the wounds in my head, that I am sensible I am not always so clear as could be wished; but whilst a ray of reason remains, my heart and my head shall ever be exerted for the benefit of our King and Country.

I have the honour to be, &c.

HORATIO NELSON.

The Officer, Lieutenant Duval, who carries this Dispatch voluntarily to you, will, I trust, be immediately sent to England, with such recommendations as his conduct will deserve.

---

## TO LIEUTENANT DUVAL.[9]

[Letter-Book.]

Vanguard, in the Road of Bequier, at the Mouth of the Nile,
9th August, 1798.

You are hereby required, and directed to proceed with the Dispatches you will herewith receive, in the Vessel that will be appointed for you, to Alexandretta, in the Gulf of Scandaroon, and having furnished yourself with every information from the Consul, Vice-Consul, or, in their absence, any British Merchants at that place, you will lose no time in proceeding to Bombay by the shortest and most expeditious route, that may be pointed out by the before-mentioned gentlemen, delivering the said Dispatches to his Excellency the Governor of Bombay, on your arrival there.  You will, on your arrival at Alexandretta, direct Mr.         to proceed with the Vessel under his command, with all possible expedition to Syracuse, but should you think it probable the Vessel will have a difficulty in returning to that place, you will request the Consul or Vice-Consul at Alexandretta, to obtain for the Midshipmen and people a passage to Naples or Messina in any Neutral Vessel bound that way, and sell the Vessel to the best advantage.

HORATIO NELSON.

---

## TO LIEUTENANT DUVAL.

[Letter-Book.]

Vanguard, in the Road of Bequier, at the Mouth of the Nile,
9th August, 1798.

Sir,

You are hereby authorized to draw such Bills as you may find necessary from time to time, to provide you with money sufficient to defray all your expenses, in your route, &c., to

---

[9] Lieutenant Thomas Duval was then fourth Lieutenant of the Zealous: he was made a Commander in the following year, and in 1802 commanded the Fly Sloop in the West Indies.

Bombay, on the East India Company, to whom, I shall write
by the earliest opportunity and acquaint them of these my
instructions to you, that the Bills may be duly honoured.

HORATIO NELSON.

---

TO HIS BRITANNIC MAJESTY'S CONSULS, VICE-CONSULS—AND
MERCHANTS IN THEIR ABSENCE—AT ALEXANDRETTA, AND
ONE OF THE ABOVE AT ALEPPO.

[Letter-Book.]

Vanguard, in the Road of Bequier, at the Mouth of the Nile,
9th August, 1798.

Sir,

Having occasion to forward with the utmost haste to India,
Lieutenant Duval of the Navy, who will deliver you this, he
being charged with Dispatches of the greatest consequence to
our Possessions in that Country, I am to request you will be
pleased to furnish him with everything that may be necessary
to forward him as fast as possible, particularly with money of
the Country, and letters of recommendation on the route;
also, a proper person to go with him as is customary in cases
of Officers and others going overland to India, and he will
give you Bills on the East India Company. In doing this,
you will not only be of infinite service to our Country, particularly the East India Company, but greatly oblige, Sir, &c.

HORATIO NELSON.

---

TO EARL SPENCER.

[Letter Book.]

My Lord,                    Mouth of the Nile, 9th August, 1798.

Was I to die this moment, ' Want of Frigates' would be
found stamped on my heart. , No words of mine can
express what I have, and am suffering for want of them.
Having only the Mutine Brig, I cannot yet send off Captain
Capel, which I am very anxious to do; for as an accident
may happen to Captain Berry,[1] it is of some importance, I

---

[1] The accident thus provided against, did occur, by Captain Berry being taken
prisoner in the Leander, nine days after the date of this Letter.

think, for your Lordship to be informed of our success as speedily as possible. If the King of Naples had joined us, nothing at this moment could prevent the destruction of the Store Ships, and all the Transports, in the Port of Alexandria; four Bomb-vessels would burn the whole in a few hours; but, as I have not means, I can only regret the circumstance.

I send you a pacquet of intercepted Letters, some of them of great importance; in particular, one from Buonaparte to his brother. He writes such a scrawl, no one not used to it can read; but luckily, we have got a man who has wrote in his Office, to decipher it. Buonaparte has differed with his Generals here; and he did want—and if I understand his meaning, does want, and will strive to be, the Washington of France. " *Ma mère*" is evidently meant " my Country." But I beg pardon : all this is, I have no doubt, well known to Administration. I believe our victory will, in its consequence, destroy this Army; at least, my endeavours shall not be wanting. I shall remain here for some time. I have thought it right to send an Officer (by Alexandretta, Aleppo, and Bussarah) over-land to India, with an account of what I have gathered from these Dispatches; which I hope will be approved. I have sent a copy of my Letter to the Board of Control, that they may give the necessary directions for paying the Officer's bills. If it should have gone to the East India Company, I hope that Board will forward it. Ever believe me,

Your Lordship's most obliged, and obedient Servant,

HORATIO NELSON.

---

TO THE RIGHT HONOURABLE HENRY DUNDAS.

[Letter-Book.]

Vanguard, Mouth of the Nile, 9th August, 1798.

Sir,

As President of the Board of Control for India, I have addressed this Letter to you: if I ought to have sent it to the India House, I request you will have the goodness to send it to the Chairman of the Company, and that you will excuse the trouble I have given you. I have thought it right to send an Officer, Lieutenant Duval, (who very handsomely offered his services,) by Alexandretta, Aleppo, and Bussarah, to Bombay,[2] to give all the account I know of the movements of the French Army, and their future intentions. Herewith, I send a copy of my Letter, and of the orders I have given him to draw for money on the East India Company, &c. If I have done wrong, I hope the bills will be paid, and I will repay the Company; for as an Englishman, I shall be proud that it has been in my power to be the means of putting our Settlements on their guard. Mr. Baldwin[3] not having been for some months at Alexandria, has been a great misfortune. I have the honour to be, &c.

HORATIO NELSON.

---

## TO ADMIRAL THE EARL OF ST. VINCENT, K.B.

[From Clarke and M'Arthur, vol. ii. p. 90.]

August 10, 1798.

I send Sir James Saumarez with the Ships and Prizes named in the margin, the others not being yet ready. Although I keep on, yet I feel that I must soon leave my situation up the Mediterranean to Troubridge; than whom, we both know no person is more equal to the task. I should have sunk under the fatigue of refitting the Squadron, but for him, Ball, Hood, and Hallowell: not but that all have done well, but those are my supporters. My head is ready to split, and I am always so sick: in short, if there be no fracture, my head is severely shaken. I shall remain off this Coast as long as circumstances will allow me, and will endeavour to annoy the Enemy to the utmost of my power. God bless you.

HORATIO NELSON.

---

[2] A Narrative of Lieutenant Duval's Journey and Proceedings is printed in James' *Naval History*, vol. ii. Appendix, No. 14.

[3] The British Consul.

TO ADMIRAL THE EARL OF ST. VINCENT, K.B.

[Letter-Book, and "London Gazette Extraordinary," of the 2nd of October, 1798.]

Vanguard, Mouth of the Nile, 11th August, 1798.

My Lord,

The Swiftsure brought in this morning La Fortune, French Corvette of eighteen guns and seventy men. I have the honour to be, &c.,

HORATIO NELSON.

---

TO CAPTAIN SIR JAMES SAUMAREZ, OF H. M. SHIP ORION.

[Order-Book.]

Vanguard, Mouth of the Nile, 12th August, 1798.

You are hereby required and directed to take the Ships named in the margin[4] under your command, their Captains having my orders for that purpose, and proceed with them, with all possible dispatch, down the Mediterranean. On your arrival near Europa Point, you will send a Boat on shore to the Commissioner's Office, to receive any orders which may be lodged there for your farther proceedings. In case you find no orders at Gibraltar, and learn that the Commander-in-Chief is off Cadiz or Lisbon, you will join him at either place, with all possible expedition.

HORATIO NELSON.

---

TO THE RIGHT HONOURABLE SIR WILLIAM HAMILTON, K.B.

[Letter-Book.]

August 12th, 1798.

My dear Sir,

As the greater part of this Squadron is going down the Mediterranean, we shall not want the quantity of wine or bread ordered; therefore, what is not already prepared, had better be put a stop to. I will settle all the matter, if ever I live to see Naples. I have the satisfaction to tell you, the

---

[4] Bellerophon, Minotaur, Defence, Audacious, Theseus, Majestic, Sovereign, Conquerant, Spartiate, Aquilon, Franklin, Tonnant.

French Army have got a complaint amongst them caused by the heat, and nothing but water, which will make Egypt the grave of the greatest part. Ever yours faithfully,

HORATIO NELSON.

---

## TO CAPTAIN MILLER, H. M. SHIP THESEUS.

[Autograph, in the possession of Miss Miller.]

Sunday Morning, [August 12th, 1798.]

My dear Sir,

You was so good as to promise to change six men from the Mutine; pray do it, and you will very much oblige me; Hardy will point out the persons to be sent out of the Brig. With the lark, on Tuesday, all you which are ready are to sail. Hoste⁵ must come to me, chest and bedding, to-morrow.

Ever yours faithfully,

HORATIO NELSON.

---

## TO LIEUTENANT WILLIAM HOSTE.⁵

[Order-Book.]

Most Secret.

Vanguard, 13th August, 1798.

Sir,

Having at Naples procured such articles of provisions as the Mutine may stand in absolute want of, you will receive on board such Dispatches as Sir William Hamilton may send for me, and not hearing of me there, cruize for me eight or ten leagues from the land, between Syracuse and Cape Passaro, frequently sending a Boat into Syracuse. It is my present intention not to sail from hence till the first week in September, and to pass close by the Island of Gozo, and to send a Boat on shore to Syracuse; therefore you will be certain of meeting me. I am, Sir, &c.

HORATIO NELSON.

⁵ Afterwards Captain Sir William Hoste, Bart., K.C.B.

## TO THE HONOURABLE CAPTAIN CAPEL.

[Autograph, in the possession of Lady Hawkes.]

Vanguard, Mouth of the Nile, August 13, 1798.

Sir,

I desire you will proceed with all possible dispatch to some place on the Continent of Europe, in the Neapolitan territories, taking particular care to get pratique in some place in Sicily. You are at liberty (if you think you can get more expeditiously to Naples by land) to quit the Mutine, when you think it right, and resign the command of her to Lieutenant William Hoste, who I send with you, and who has secret orders to open the moment you leave him. Relying on your zeal and judgment, I have only to wish you a good voyage by sea and by land, and believe me, Sir, your most obedient Servant,

HORATIO NELSON.

---

## TO CAPTAIN SIR JAMES SAUMAREZ, H.M.S. ORION.

[Autograph, in the possession of the Dowager Lady de Saumarez.]

August 15th, 1798.

I hope Lady S. and all the little ones are well.

My dear Sir James,

I am not very anxious to receive any persons of the description you mention ; they will all eat our meat and drink. As they chose to serve the French, there let them remain. I have not a line from home—all lost in L'Aigle.[6] You will get off in good time, I dare say. I am sure you will not lose a moment off Cape Brule : the shoal extends six miles. If you favour me with a line, direct it for Naples, where I am going to join the Portuguese Squadron.[7] Zealous, Swiftsure,

---

[6] The L'Aigle Frigate, Captain Charles Tyler (afterwards Admiral Sir Charles Tyler, G.C.B., who commanded the Tonnant at Trafalgar) was totally wrecked on Plane Island, near Tunis, in June or July, 1798.

[7] The Portuguese Government placed its Squadron consisting of the Principe Real of 74 guns, Rear-Admiral the Marquis de Niza, Captain Count de Chestenet Puységur; Rainha de Portugal, of 74 guns, Captain Stone; the St. Sebastian, 74, Captain Mitchell; the Alfonço de Albuquerque, 74, Captain Campbell; the Falcaõ Brig, Captain Duncan, (who, Lord St. Vincent says, was a Master's Mate in our Service in the American war,) under the Orders of the Earl of St. Vincent, who dispatched those Ships, early in July, to reinforce Nelson's Squadron. In a Letter to Nelson, dated on the 2nd of that month, Lord St. Vincent said : "I send this by

and the two Frigates, I leave here as long as possible. Nisbet thanks you for your inquiries. I send you a copy of my Letter intended to be sent to Mr. Nepean : keep it quiet till you get off. Wishing you health, good passage, &c. Believe me ever,

Your obliged,

HORATIO NELSON.

---

TO CAPTAIN HOOD, H. M. SHIP ZEALOUS.

[Order-Book.]

15th August, 1798.

You are hereby required and directed to take under your command the Ships named in the margin,[8] (they having my instructions to follow your orders,) and to cruize off Alexandria, or remain at anchor, as you may judge most proper for the more effectually preventing any supplies being thrown into that Port for the French Fleet, and to endeavour to intercept the French Convoy with provisions, which is expected to arrive there soon ; as also to prevent, as much as possible,

the Marquis de Niza, who will, I hope, soon take you by the hand and support you with a Squadron of four Ships of the Line, well manned, commanded, and ap pointed. The exercise these Ships have had in a cruize off the Azores, has very much improved the seamen in their business, and they are remarkably healthy. The Marquis agrees with me, that it will be best to chequer them in your Line of Battle —two in your Starboard Division, which will be commanded by the Marquis, and two in the Larboard, commanded by Captain Troubridge, which arrangement I have signified to the Lords Commissioners of the Admiralty. In case of a proposition being made by the Court of Naples to give you some Neapolitan Ships, I desire that you will stipulate that no Officer of higher rank than a Post-Captain may be employed in it, to prevent any interference with this system. I send you Captain Retalick's commission enclosed, and I desire you will explain to him that he is entirely subordinate to the Marquis of Niza, and is not to set up his own judgment or opinion against his, unasked. I have given him two able and experienced Signal-Lieutenants, and he will find in the Count de Chestenet Puységur, an intelligent Sea-Officer, and a man of most amiable manners. Captain Retalick has so good a temper and disposition, that I am persuaded he will exert every nerve to give satisfaction to the Marquis, on which, his rank as Post-Captain depends."—*Original*, in the Nelson Papers. Speaking of the Portuguese Squadron, in a Letter to Sir William Hamilton, written on the 15th July, Lord St. Vincent said, " the weak councils and intrigues of that miserable Court have once disappointed me in respect to this auxiliary force ; but by the aid of Don Roderigo de Souza Coutinho, Minister of Marine, and the only ' *man* ' I have found in the Country, I think you may count upon seeing them soon, for the Marquis is instructed to proceed, Coast-wise from Leghorn to Naples, and soon."

[8] Swiftsure, Goliath, Alcmene, Seahorse, Emerald.

all communication between the French Army at Rosetta, and
their Fleet at Alexandria: and you are to continue on this
service until the 30th day of September next.  But should
you receive any intelligence, or anything happen which may
make it necessary for you to remain longer on this service, you
are in that case to remain so long as you may think it proper.
And on your return you are to send a Boat on shore at Syracuse for instructions; not finding any there, you are to proceed with all dispatch to Naples.

HORATIO NELSON.

---

TO EVAN NEPEAN, ESQ., ADMIRALTY.

[Original, in the Admiralty.]

Sir,                    *Vanguard, Mouth of the Nile, August 16th, 1798.*

Six of the Prizes sailed yesterday under Sir James Saumarez.  Three others, viz., Guerrier, Heureux, and Mercure, are in the act of repairing.  In this state I received last
evening Earl St. Vincent's most secret Orders, and most secret
and confidential Letters relative to the important operations
intended to be pursued in the Mediterranean.  Thus situated,
it became an important part of my duty to do justice between
my King and Country, and the brave Officers and Men who
captured those Ships at the Battle of the Nile.  It would have
taken one month, at least, to have fitted those Ships for a
passage to Gibraltar, and not only at a great expense to
Government, but with the loss of the services of at least two Sail
of the Line.  I therefore, confiding that the Lords Commissioners will, under the present circumstances, direct that a
fair value shall be paid for those Ships, ordered them to be
burnt, after saving such stores as would not take too much
time, out of them; and I have further thought it my duty to
tell the Squadron the necessity I am under, for the benefit
of the King's Service, of directing their property to be destroyed; but that I had no doubt but Government would
make them a liberal allowance, all which I hope their Lordships will approve of.  I have the honour to be, &c.,

HORATIO NELSON.[1]

---

[1] The Vanguard's, or rather Nelson's *Journal*, from the 3rd to the 19th of August,
when the Vanguard sailed from Naples, contains the following statements of some

## TO CAPTAIN HOOD, ZEALOUS.

[Letter-Book.]

Vanguard, August 17th, 1798.

Sir,

Should any Frigates or Dispatch-boats arrive off Alexandria in search of me, you will instantly direct them to proceed, without a moment's loss of time, to Naples, where they will be sure to find or hear of me. Captain Hope being appointed to the Thalia, should he not go into her, you will send her to join me at Naples; but should he take command of her, in that case you will keep Thalia with you, and send Alcmene, under Lieutenant Newhouse, to join me at Naples.

I am, &c.

HORATIO NELSON.

---

## MEMORANDUM FOR CAPTAIN HOOD, H.M. SHIP ZEALOUS.

[Order-Book.]

Vanguard, 18th August, 1798.

If the Lion comes, to send Goliath direct to Naples. If Thalia, and Captain Hope does not take her, to be sent direct to Naples. If Terpsichore arrives, to send either Alcmene or

interest:—Saturday 4th, "A.M. came off several French Boats from Alexandria with Flags of Truce for the sick and wounded Prisoners." Sunday 5th, "P.M. at 6, a Gun went off on board the Minotaur which set her on fire, but was extinguished immediately. Fleet employed fitting the Prizes for Sea." Monday 6th, "Sailed hence at 7, P.M. His Majesty's Ship Leander, in whom went Captain Berry of His Majesty's Ship Vanguard with my Dispatches to the Commander-in-Chief, &c." Friday 10th, "½ past 6, A.M. the Swiftsure went in chase of a Sail in the N.E." Saturday 11th, "at 9, A.M. anchored here his Majesty's Ship Swiftsure with a French polacre Corvette, called La Fortune, of 18 guns and 70 men." Tuesday 14th, "supplied La Mutine with provisions and she sailed with my Dispatches; A.M., weighed and sailed hence his Majesty's Ships Orion, Defence, Minotaur, Bellerophon, Theseus, and Audacious, with the French Prize Ships Le Tonnant, Le Franklin, Le Spartiate, L'Aquilon, Le Souverain Peuple, and Le Conquérant." Friday 17, "at ½ past 7, P.M. set the Prize Ship L'Heureux on fire, and at half-past eight she blew up." Saturday 18th, "at ¾ past 2, set the Prize Ship Le Mercure on fire." Sunday 19th, "at 3 P.M. the Guerrier was set on fire: at half-past, she blew up. At 4, the Sérieuse was set on fire to burn her upper works, which were above water. At half-past 8, weighed and [made] sail, in company with H. M. Ships Culloden, Alexander, and Bonne Citoyenne, as did the Seahorse and Emerald, to cruise off Alexandria."

Emerald direct to Naples. Not to keep more than five Sail after the 2nd September. To send one or two Ships before Captain Hope leaves the Station, unless Captain Hood means to leave the Lion and one or two Frigates after the 30th of September. To inquire at Syracuse for orders in their way to Naples, unless under very particular circumstances which may materially delay the passage.

HORATIO NELSON.

---

TO ADMIRAL THE EARL OF ST. VINCENT, K.B.

[From Clarke and M'Arthur, vol. ii. p. 92.]

19th and 26th of August, 1798.

We have just fallen in, off Cape Celadonia, with Sir James and the Prizes, and I hope they will have a good passage to you.[2] If I could have assured myself that Government would have paid a reasonable value for Conquerant and Souverain, I would have ordered them to be burnt; for they will cost more in refitting, and by the loss of Line-of-battle-Ships attending them, than they are worth; but the other four are a treasure to our Navy. You will see what I have written to Mr. Nepean, on my ordering Guerrier, Heureux, and Mercure to be destroyed, and it will, I hope, meet your approbation and support. The case is hard upon poor fellows at a distance, if they do not pay us liberally. I find, by letters from Naples of August 1st, that I am in disgrace for not finding the French Fleet:[3] but such is the chance to which Officers' characters are subject. Whether I shall be able to stay in the Mediterranean is yet a matter of doubt; but if nothing very particular demands my half head, it is my present intention to go to you, and for England: this, however, is to be a secret at Naples. I find Vanguard will not get masted there; they say you stopped all their masts at Gibraltar. I had a plan, if I went home, to put Troubridge into Vanguard with Culloden's masts, yards, &c.,

---

[2] Tuesday 21st, "Sold sundry clothes at the Mast belonging to Officers, &c., killed in Action." Friday 24th, "at 5, A.M. saw thirteen Sail of the Line to the northward, found them to be the Orion with the Squadron and Prizes under her Command. S.E. point of Candia, S. 84-43 W. 250 miles."

[3] Vide Sir William Hamilton's Letter, p. 93, ante.

but as I believe, from more recent examination, the Culloden must be hove down before she can be trusted out of Port, that plan must be laid aside. You may depend on my paying proper attention to the Spanish business of Minorca, &c. My head is so wrong, that I cannot write what I wish in such a manner as to please myself; but I have reason to be thankful.

I am, &c.,

HORATIO NELSON.

TO THE HONOURABLE WILLIAM WYNDHAM,
MINISTER AT FLORENCE.

[Letter Book.]

Vanguard, 21st August, 1798.

My dear Sir,

I received, three days ago, your letter of June 20th, and I beg leave to thank you for it. I send you a paper which will inform you of the extent of our victory. My health, from my wound, is become so indifferent, that I think of going down the Mediterranean, so soon as I arrive at Naples, unless I should find anything very extraordinary to detain me, when my health is of no consequence. The command, in my absence, will devolve on Captain Troubridge, than whom the King has not a better Sea-Officer. Sir James Saumarez is on his way to Gibraltar, with six of our Prizes; the others I burnt, that the Mediterranean might not be left without Ships, for each Prize takes a Ship of the Line to man her, and attend to her wants. This you will believe, when I tell you that only two masts are standing, out of nine Sail of the Line. L'Orient certainly struck her colours,[4] and did not fire a shot for a quarter of an hour before, unfortunately for us, she took fire; but although we suffer, our Country is equally benefited. She had on board near six hundred thousand pounds sterling; so says the Adjutant-General of the Fleet, who was saved out of her, and although he does not say she struck her colours, yet he allows that all resistance on her part was in vain. Admiral Brueys was killed early in the battle, and from the commencement of the fight, declared all was lost. They were moored in a strong posi-

4 Vide p. 65, ante.

tion in a Line of Battle, with Gun-Boats, Bomb-Vessels, Frigates, and a gun and mortar Battery on an Island in their Van, but my band of friends was irresistible. The French Army is in possession of Alexandria, Aboukir, Rosetta, Damietta, and Cairo; and Buonaparte writes that he is sending a detachment to take possession of Suez and Fayoum.

By the intercepted letters from the Army (for we took the Vessel with Buonaparte's courier) they are grievously disappointed, the Country between their Posts completely hostile. I have little doubt but that Army will be destroyed by plague, pestilence, and famine, and battle and murder, which that it may soon be, God grant. The Turks will soon send an Army into Syria, and as for the present, we block them up by sea, they must soon experience great distress. I hope to find, on my arrival at Naples, that the Emperor and many other Powers are at war with the French, for until they are reduced there can be no peace in this world. The Admiral having sent up Mr. Littledale, the victualling of the Fleet does not rest with me.

September 7th.

I feel myself so much recovered, that it is probable I shall not go home at present. The Turks have seized all French Ships in the Levant, in consequence of the taking a Turkish sixty-gun Ship at Alexandria, and seizing all Turkish property. This was done on the 14th of August. I shall always receive pleasure in hearing from you, both as a public and private man; and believe me, dear Sir, &c.

HORATIO NELSON.

---

TO FRANCIS J. JACKSON, ESQ., HIS MAJESTY'S MINISTER AT THE OTTOMAN PORTE.[5]

[Letter-Book.]

Sir,　　　　Vanguard, off the Isle of Rhodes, 27th August, 1798.

I have the honour to acquaint you that I attacked the French Fleet, off the Mouth of the Nile, on the 1st instant,

---

[5] Monday 27th, "South End of the Isle of Rhodes, S.W. B.W., distant six or seven leagues. At 11, dispatched the Bonne Citoyenne to Rhodes with a letter to the British Minister at Constantinople."—*Journal.*

the result of which you will see by the inclosed paper, and
that on the 14th the French took possession of the Turkish
Admiral's Ship at Alexandria, hauled down her colours and
hoisted French colours, and seized upon all the Turkish pro-
perty on shore.  The French are in possession of Alexandria,
Aboukir, Rosetta, and Damietta, on the Coast, and of Grand
Cairo; but all communication is cut off between their Army
and their Transports at Alexandria by sea, by an English
Squadron of three Ships of the Line and four Frigates, which
I have left cruising there; and by land, by the Bedouins: so
that, if the Grand Signior will but send a few Ships of the
Line, and some Bombs, he will destroy all their Transports in
Alexandria; and an Army of ten thousand men may retake
Alexandria immediately, as the French have only four thou-
sand men in it, and the whole French Army very sickly.

I have been informed that the French have put to death
two hundred Turks at Alexandria for rejoicing at our victory,
and that General Buonaparte only wants a communication
opened by sea, to march into Syria, that the Transports with
stores, &c., for the Army may go alongshore with him.

I have the honour to be, &c.

HORATIO NELSON.

TO THE RIGHT HONOURABLE LORD MINTO.

[Autograph, in the Minto Papers.]

Vanguard, off Rhodes, August 29th, 1798.

My dear Lord,

Your affectionate and flattering letter of April 25th, I received
on the 14th August, and I assure you that I feel a great comfort
on your account that I shall not (I fancy) be thought entirely
undeserving of the many handsome things you said of me.[6]
You know, my dear Lord, that I have more than once thought
that the Mediterranean Fleet has been put in our power to
annihilate, therefore I had the advantage of my predecessors.
I regret that one escaped, and I think, if it had pleased God
that I had not been wounded, not a Boat would have escaped
to have told the tale; but do not believe that any individual

---

[6] In his conversation with Earl Spencer, vide p. 25, ante.

in the Fleet is to blame.　In my conscience, I believe greater exertions could not have been, and I only mean to say, that if my experience could (in person) have directed those exertions of individuals, there was every appearance that Almighty God would have continued to bless my endeavours for the honour of our King, the advantage of our Country, and for the peace and happiness (I hope) of all Europe.　It is no small regret that L'Orient is not in being to grace our victory.　She was completely beat, and I am sure had struck her colours before she took fire; for as she had lost her main and mizen-masts, and on her flag-staff, which Hood cut from her wreck, was no flag, it must be true that the flag was hauled down, or it would have been entangled with the rigging, or some remnant remained at the mast-head.[7]　She had on board £600,000 sterling, in ingots of gold and diamonds, for the French brought no coin with them.　I wish you had succeeded in getting Bomb-vessels sent with our Fleet,[8] then, in 48 hours after the victory, every Transport, and all the stores in them, would have been destroyed at Alexandria; for the Port is so very small, and so crowded, that not one shell or carcass could have fell amiss.

The present situation of the French army is briefly this: they have Rosetta and Damietta, the principal entrances of the Nile, for they can get nothing by land to Cairo over the desert; and as we are in possession of the anchorage of Bequier, between Alexandria and Rosetta, the Army can get nothing by water.　Apropos, this being the season of the rising and overflowing of the Nile, it is usual for the different Beys to send their people and open the canals in order to obtain water till the return of this season, and this applies very strongly to Alexandria, where they have no water but what comes by the canal and fills their reservoir.　Now, unless the French are able to buy the Beys and Bedouins, Alexandria must perish for want of water; and I do not think

---

[7] Vide p. 65, ante.

[8] Lord Minto told Nelson, in the Letter referred to in p. 25, ante, that encouraged by the manner in which Lord Spencer had received his communication respecting him, he wrote to his Lordship on the same evening to recommend the employment of two Bomb Ketches in the Squadron.—*Tucker's Memoirs of Earl St. Vincent*, vol. i. p. 350.

it improbable but that the garrison must evacuate it, and an endeavour will be made to get the Ships *armé en flute* with the stores out of the harbour; but, as I have left Hood with three Ships of the Line and three Frigates to annoy Buonaparte, I trust the business will be well attended to. The French Admiral and Officers, who we have on board, were not aware of my leaving a Squadron off Alexandria, and freely declare their opinion that their Army is lost by the measure; for that the Transports are in divisions, with stores, &c., and were to move along the coast as Buonaparte penetrated into Syria. In short, it is hardly possible to calculate what good events may arrive from our victory. I lost not a moment in sending an Officer overland to India: (if you see Mr. Drake, tell him it is his relation, a very clever young man,) for, if Buonaparte should send any troops down the Red Sea, (which now I do not believe he will,) our Settlements will be prepared. And here I would give an opinion on our last Peace with Tippoo, but high respect for the Officers who made it will not allow me.

I have sent an express to Constantinople, and have urged Mr. Jackson to represent to the Grand Signior, that if he will send a few Ships and some Bombs, all the Transports will be destroyed—if 10,000 men, Alexandria may be retaken; and if he will not send anything, he will lose Syria. We have saved Sicily in spite of Neapolitan councils. That Marquis de Gallo is a wretch who minds nothing but fine clothes, his snuff-box, and ring; this is the best I can say of him. I am on my way to Naples, where I hope to put matters in a fair train for the advantage of Italy and ourselves. I am hurried from Egypt by Mr. Dundas's[9] letter to Lord St. Vincent; if you see him, say that what can be done, shall. Now a word for myself. I doubt if I ought to stay here; my brain is in such a state that rest of mind, if that is possible for me, is, the Doctors say, absolutely necessary. The Portuguese are at Naples, but I doubt if they will either go to Egypt, or even cruise (that is, what I call cruising) for ten days. If Naples will give me Bombs, I will either return or send Troubridge to ruin Buonaparte, for his Army may be destroyed if the Grand

---

[9] Secretary of State for the War Department, afterwards created Viscount Melville.

Signior, Naples, and England do but exert themselves for three months; I only wish I had the means in my own power. Now, a word for George.[1] He is well; and Foley tells me that he is one of the most active and best youths he has ever met with. Pray present my most respectful remembrances to Lady Minto, and believe me, my dear Lord, ever your most affectionate and obliged

HORATIO NELSON.

---

TO ADMIRAL THE EARL OF ST. VINCENT, K.B.

[From Clarke and M'Arthur, vol. ii. p. 93.]

Off Candia, September 1st, 1798.

If the Grand Signior will but *trot* an Army into Syria, Buonaparte's career is finished. As for Naples, she is saved in spite of herself: they have evidently broken their treaty with France, and yet are afraid to assist in finishing the vast armament of the French. Four hours, with four Bomb-vessels, would set all in a blaze, and we know what an Army is without stores. Culloden sails dreadfully, but we have not a sick man in the three Ships with me. As to myself, I know I ought to give up for a little while: my head is splitting at this moment, but of this hereafter; you will give me credit for serving as long as I can. My friend Ball is the polite man to entertain the captive Admiral, and the First Captain of the Fleet, who was saved out of L'Orient: the Admiral being wounded, I shall let him go, on his parole, at Naples, and all the rest who are in our Ships. Captain Foote fortunately took the Dispatches away from the Officer who had them, and told him he should seek me where he had seen the French Fleet. I am, &c.

HORATIO NELSON.

---

[1] Lord Minto's second son, now Rear-Admiral the Honourable George Elliot, C.B. He was then a Midshipman in the Goliath, Captain Foley.

### TO CAPTAIN SIR JAMES SAUMAREZ.

[Autograph, in the possession of the Dowager Lady de Saumarez.]

Vanguard, September 1st, 1798.

My dear Sir,

From what I have heard and made up in my own mind, I feel it is absolutely necessary that I should order the Minotaur and Audacious to quit your Squadron when you are in the fair way between Sardinia and Minorca, and join me at Naples, and also with as much salt provisions as can be got out of the Ships victualled for *six* months, reserving only one month's at whole allowance. My Squadron are at two-thirds of salt provisions, making the allowance up with flour: therefore you will direct the same in yours. I have put down the number of casks of beef, pork, and pease, which can be easily spared, if the Commander-in-Chief's orders for victualling have been obeyed. Audacious is, I fancy, short of salt provisions, not knowing of coming so long a voyage. If you can manage to let those Ships have any part of their Officers and men, it will be very useful for the King's Service; but of this you must be the best judge. Retalick will tell you all the news from Rhodes, and I was rejoiced to see you on this side of Candia.

Ever yours most truly,

HORATIO NELSON.

Your Squadron evidently sails better than Culloden. The Bellerophon sails so well that Darby can take very good care of Conquérant, and Aquilon seems to sail remarkably. Remember me kindly to all my good friends with you.

---

### TO EARL SPENCER.

[Original, in the Admiralty.]

Vanguard, 7th September, 1798.

My Lord,

On the 15th August, I received Earl St. Vincent's most secret Orders and Letters. As not a moment was to be lost, I determined to destroy the three Prizes (Guerrier, Heureux, and Mercure,) which had not sailed with Sir James Saumarez, set on fire on the 18th. I rest assured that they will be paid for, and have held out that assurance to the Squadron; for if an Admiral is, after a victory, only to look after the captured Ships, and not distressing the Enemy, very dearly indeed does the Nation pay for the Prizes, and I trust that £60,000 will be deemed a very moderate sum; and I am bold to say, when the services, time, and men, with the expense of fitting those three Ships for a voyage to England is valued, that Government will save nearly as much as they are valued at. I rejoice, in the present instance, that a particular regard for my own interest cannot be supposed to actuate me, for if the moderate sum of £60,000 is paid, my share can only be £625, while if it is not paid, I have defrauded the Commander-in-Chief and the other Classes, of the sums set off against them—

| | | | |
|---|---|---|---|
| Commander-in-Chief . . . | £3750 | 0 | 0 |
| Junior Admirals, each . . . | 625 | 0 | 0 |
| Captains, each . . . . . | 1000 | 0 | 0 |
| Lieutenants' Class, each . . | 75 | 0 | 0 |
| Warrant Officers, each . . . | 50 | 0 | 0 |
| Petty Officers, each . . . . | 11 | 0 | 0 |
| Seamen and Marines, each . | 2 | 4 | 1 |

Your Lordship will do me the justice to say, that pay for Prizes, in many instances, (it is not a new idea of mine,) would be not only an amazing saving to the State, without taking into calculation what the Nation loses by the attention of Admirals to the property of the Captors, an attention absolutely necessary as a recompence for the exertions of the Officers and men. An Admiral may be amply rewarded by his feelings and the approbation of his superiors, but what reward have the inferior Officers and men but the value of the Prizes? If an Admiral takes that from them, on any consideration, he cannot expect to be well supported. However, I trust, as in all other instances, if, to serve the State, any persons or bodies of men suffer losses, it is amply made up to them; and in this I rest confident my brave associates will not be disappointed. I have the honour to be, &c.

HORATIO NELSON.[2]

---

[2] Earl Spencer in his reply to this Letter, on the 24th of December, 1798, said—
"Your Letter of the 7th September, which relates to the Prizes which you burnt off Aboukir, has been under consideration of Government; and though the case is

TO THE CAPTAINS OF SUCH OF HIS MAJESTY'S SHIPS AS MAY BE
IN SEARCH OF ME; WHEN READ, TO BE ENCLOSED AND RE-
TURNED INTO THE HANDS OF THE GOVERNOR OF SYRACUSE.

[Letter-Book.]

Vanguard, September 7th, 1798.

Sir,

I beg leave to tell you that I am on my way to Naples,
where I shall be found for the next fourteen days. I am, &c.

HORATIO NELSON.

---

TO THE RIGHT HONOURABLE SIR WILLIAM HAMILTON, K.B.

[Original, in the State Paper Office.]

Vanguard, September 7th, 1798.

My dear Sir,

The Culloden sails so heavy, by having a sail under her
bottom in order to stop her leak, that it has caused me to be
a much longer time than I can at present spare to make passages. I send the Bonne Citoyenne with this,[4] in order that
everything may be prepared for the reception of the Culloden
at Castel-à-Mare, (which I understand is the place where
large Ships heave down,) and that every necessary order may
be given for her assistance, for I do not wish her to anchor at
Naples. It is, I hope, in preparation for the Court at Naples
to assist in destroying the French Army in Egypt, for if all
their Shipping are destroyed, the Army cannot exist; and if
this opportunity is lost by Naples, such another can never be
expected to offer. Our Squadron quits the Blockade, September 30th, having no provisions, and if I am not furnished
with the means of continuing it, the French will get into

one for which there has never yet been any precedent, and by the strict rules of the
Service could not be admitted as a claim, yet, I believe, I can take upon me to assure
you, that the singular merits of your situation will have such weight as to induce
us to deviate from the usual practice, and an arrangement is making to allow a sum
equivalent to the value of the least valuable of the other Prizes, as it is reasonable
to suppose, that those which you were under the necessity of burning were the
worst-conditioned Ships among those which were captured."

[4] Saturday, 8th September, "Cape Spartivento, N. 61-18 W., distant 38 miles,
dispatched La Bonne Citoyenne with Letters to Syracuse for any of the Squadron
that might touch there."—*Journal.*

Syria, (which at present they cannot do for want of their stores,) and then I am told they can hold out, which in Egypt they cannot do.

I have sent an express to Constantinople, and requested Mr. Jackson to urge the Grand Signior, by every regard for his own preservation, to send an Army into Syria, and his Fleet and Bombs to destroy Alexandria, and all the stores in it. I am writing to the Marquis de Niza, but I fear he will not obey me in going to Egypt; however, I will do my duty in representing the importance of the business, and if our Allies will not assist in completing what has been so gloriously begun, it is not my fault, and too late they will repent it. I am ignorant if the Portuguese are at war with the Grand Signior, therefore I send you my letter to the Marquis de Niza, which you will not deliver if the two Nations are at war. If the letter is delivered, I trust you will (if opportunity offers) say everything which can induce these folks to be ready to sail the moment of my arrival; for myself, I hope not to be more than four or five days at Naples, for these times are not for idleness. With my very best respects to Lady Hamilton, believe me, dear Sir,

Your most affectionate<br>HORATIO NELSON.

---

TO CAPTAIN HOOD, HIS MAJESTY'S SHIP ZEALOUS.

[Letter-Book.]

Vanguard, at Sea, 8th September, 1798.

Sir,

I herewith enclose you a copy of my letter to the Marquis de Niza, who I understand, is gone to Egypt. I sincerely hope his Squadron will stay there, till I can get Ships to continue the blockade of Alexandria, and you will not fail to use every argument to induce him to stay—which, if he does, you are hereby desired to direct the Lion, and one Frigate only, to be left with him. And on your return you are to proceed round the Island of Sicily, in order if any Convoys are on their passage, to intercept them; and on the return of the Cutter, you will order her to call at Rhodes and inquire if they have any news from Constantinople: and if *you* have

any good news to send it to Mr. Jackson, our Minister at
the Porte (the Governor of Rhodes will send an Express);
but if any other Vessel, from a knowledge of the Coast, can
call there better than the Cutter, you will order her. From
the latest intelligence from Malta of the Maltese having re-
possessed themselves of several of the Towns and Forts, you
will call off that Island in your passage round Sicily. I am,
Sir, &c.,

HORATIO NELSON.

---

TO HIS EXCELLENCY THE MARQUIS DE NIZA.

[Letter-Book].

Vanguard, at Sea, 8th September, 1798.

Sir,

It is a matter of regret to me, and, I am sure, it must be to
your Excellency, that your Squadron did not join me before
the 1st of August, when not a single French Ship could have
escaped us; but as that is past remedy, it is necessary to look
forward to the next important service we can render the
Common Cause, which, in my opinion is to prevent the
French Army from getting any supplies of stores by water
from Alexandria. Captain Hood will explain, I am confident, the whole of my ideas on that point: Captain Hood
was directed not to leave Alexandria before the 30th September, longer than which his provisions will not last. I
therefore beg leave to represent to your Excellency what
advantage it will be, if you will take Captain Hood's station
and remain on it till the 20th October, by which time I shall
hope to have the Ships now with Captain H. returned to
Alexandria. This I state as the longest period: I hope to
have Ships there much sooner. Your Excellency will, if you
remain, keep the Lion with you, and I have directed one
Frigate to be left. Having sent an express to Constantinople,
I have reason to hope that the Grand Signior will not only
send an Army into Syria, but also send Ships of War with
Bomb-vessels, Gallies, &c., in order to destroy all the Vessels
in Alexandria. That your Excellency may be a partaker in
these joyful events is the sincere wish of your most obedient
and faithful, humble Servant,

HORATIO NELSON.

### TO ADMIRAL THE EARL OF ST. VINCENT, K.B.

[Letter-Book.]

Vanguard, 9th September, 1798.

My Lord,

I fear you will think me acting wrong, by none of the numerous Frigates, Brigs, Cutters, &c., having returned to you. It was only on the 13th August, the Alcmene, Emerald, and Bonne Citoyenne joined me. On the 17th, the Seahorse joined, and till September 7th, I neither saw or heard of any, when the Earl St. Vincent Cutter joined me, forty leagues from Messina, where I was informed that the Portuguese Squadron, with the Lion and Terpsichore, had passed the Faro, August 28th, on their way to Egypt. I therefore sent the Cutter with a letter to the Marquis of Niza, and to Captain Hood, which I hope you will approve.

September 13th.—On my arrival off Messina, the Thalia came in sight, and got on board me this morning. She brings me accounts from Captain Hood, which I send you. The exertions of the Officers are great and highly to be approved, but I think the two men who saved the Dispatches[5] ought to have a pecuniary reward. You will see by my second letter to the Marquis de Niza, that I have requested him to go off Malta, which may be the means of driving the French out of that Island. Captain Retalick is waiting at Messina to embark on board the Marquis de Niza the moment he makes his appearance. The Flora joined yesterday. I have sent her to Egypt to beg Captain Hood to stay as long as possible. No time shall be lost in my getting Ships to relieve the Squadron, for I am confident by little exertion the French Army will fall a prey to plague, pestilence, famine, and Mamelukes. Sir James Saumarez has my proceedings to the beginning of September; therefore, I have only farther

---

[5] On the 22nd of August, the Alcmene captured La Legére, French Gun-boat, off Alexandria. "We could not," says Captain Hope in his official Letter, "prevent the Dispatches for Buonaparte from being thrown overboard, which was however perceived by John Taylor and James Harding, belonging to the Alcmene, who, at the risk of their lives (the Ship then going between five and six knots) dashed overboard, and saved the whole of them. Both men were most fortunately picked up by the Boat that was sent after them, and I conceive it my duty to make known the very spirited conduct they showed on this occasion for the good of the service."
—*London Gazette* of 23rd of October, 1798.

to say, that Thalia shall sail in twenty-four hours after my arrival at Naples, but as she is in quarantine, taking the men for Alexander and Culloden out of her, would be putting those Ships in quarantine, and prevent, perhaps, their directly going to Castel-à-Mare. I hope your Lordship will excuse this confused letter. I pray give me credit for my earnest endeavours to do what is right, and believe me, &c.,

HORATIO NELSON.

---

TO CAPTAIN HOOD, H. M. SHIP ZEALOUS.

[Autograph, in the possession of Sir Alexander Hood, Bart.]

My dear Hood,                    Off Strombolo, September 13th, 1798.

Not seeing any Papers in your packet, I send you my latest. Our friend Troubridge has lost his wife, and is in much distress. We get on slowly. Malta we shall have, if the Marquis will cruize off there. Nearly all the Forts are in possession of the Islanders, particularly St. Angelo, which commands the entrance of the Port. Généreux lost her mainmast, and is gone to Corfu. The others are off Malta. Naples is idle. I am much better. God bless you, and believe me ever your affectionate

HORATIO NELSON.

Kind remembrances to all with you.

---

TO HIS EXCELLENCY SIR WILLIAM HAMILTON, K.B.

[Original, in the State Paper Office.]

My dear Sir,                          September 13th, 1798.

The Marquis de Niza is returned from Egypt; I have waylaid him to try to get him to cruize off Malta, but I never expect any real service from that Squadron. I am sending the Flora to Egypt, to beg Captain Hood to stay as long as possible. I hope to get the Ships ready to return to him early in October: that Army must be destroyed. I beg my best regards to Lady Hamilton. Captain Nisbet, who you remember a boy, is the bearer of this letter. Ever yours most truly,

HORATIO NELSON.

Pray have the order ready for the Culloden to go to Castel-à-Mare without anchoring.

## TO HIS EXCELLENCY THE MARQUIS DE NIZA.

[Letter-Book.]

Sir,     Vanguard, at Sea, 13th September, 1798.

Captain Retalick will have the honour of delivering to your Excellency my letters, as well as the Dispatches forwarded by the Earl of St. Vincent. Being informed by Captain Hood of your return from Alexandria, I beg to represent to your Excellency the great benefit it would be to the common cause should you proceed off Malta, and to attempt to intercept a French Ship of the Line and two Frigates[6] that made their escape from Alexandria, and which are cruizing there, having been driven out of the Ports of Malta by the Maltese, who are in arms against the French, and have retaken several of their Towns and the Castle of St. Angelo. I send your Excellency two papers with information concerning them; and by your Excellency's cruizing there for a short time, it might be the means of driving the French from the Island, as well as protecting the Colossus, Captain George Murray, and some Victuallers and Storeships sent up by Earl St. Vincent for the use of the Squadron under my command, and ordered to rendezvous between Sicily and Malta, and which I much want to have at Naples. I should have proceeded with the Ships I have with me to that place, had they been in a situation to have kept the seas for ten days. From the intelligence I have received, I think you will find no difficulty in communicating with the inhabitants of Malta or Gozo. Soon after my arrival at Naples I will dispatch a Vessel to your Excellency with any information I may get. Wishing your Excellency every success, I have the honour to be, &c.

HORATIO NELSON.

---

## TO CAPTAIN HOOD, H.M. SHIP ZEALOUS.

[Letter-Book.]

Dear Sir,     Vanguard, 13th September, 1798.

I was in hopes the Marquis de Niza would have stayed off Alexandria till the end of October, but as he is returning, we

---

[6] Le Guillaume Tell of 80 Guns, and La Diane and La Justice Frigates.

have only to trust to ourselves. I am sensible of the great importance of keeping up the blockade, for we must destroy that Army. I have ordered Minotaur and Audacious to Naples. I therefore wish you, my dear Sir, to remain as much longer after the 30th of September as you with propriety can. I will send three Ships as quickly as possible, but I fear it will be late in October. But relying on your zeal and ability, I am sure you will do your best, and believe me, with the greatest respect, &c.

HORATIO NELSON.

P.S.—I have sent this by the Flora Cutter, and request you will dispatch her back again as soon as possible. The Alexander's masts are so bad that they expect them to go by the board; the Culloden so very leaky she cannot keep the sea; so that I have only to trust to this Ship, the Minotaur, and the Audacious. I hope the Lion[7] will be able to stay at Alexandria after I have been able to get two Ships sent to relieve you, and I rely on the exertions of all my gallant friends in the Squadron to complete the destruction of the French Army, &c. I shall not go home until this is effected, and the Islands of Malta, Corfu, &c., retaken.

---

TO CAPTAIN HOOD, H. M. SHIP ZEALOUS.

[Letter-Book.]

Sir,  Vanguard, at Sea, 13th September, 1798.

I have to acknowledge the receipt of your Letter of the 26th August, inclosing one of the 22nd of the same month, from Captain Hope of his Majesty's Ship Alcmene, stating the Capture of La Legere, French Gun-boat, from Toulon, bound to Alexandria, and of having intercepted Buonaparte's Dispatches. I have enclosed his Letter to the Commander-in-Chief, and hope that the men who at the risk of their lives saved the Dispatches, will be rewarded as they deserve.

I have also to acknowledge receipt of your Letter of the same date, enclosing one from Captain Foley, of his Majesty's Ship Goliath, representing the Capture of the French National

---

[7] Captain, afterwards Admiral, Sir Manley Dixon, K.C.B.

Arme        y the Boats of that Ship, and the
very g        Lieutenant William Debusk[8] and the
men under his command, which I shall not fail to communicate to the Commander-in-Chief. I am, &c.

HORATIO NELSON.

DISPOSITION OF THE FLEET UNDER MY COMMAND.

[Letter-Book.]

Vanguard, 13th August, [September] 1798.

Vanguard.—Wants new masts and bowsprit, but shall defer
getting them till I know the situation of

Culloden.—To be careened at Naples.

Alexander.—When her masts are reduced and secured, to be
sent down the Mediterranean, unless particularly wanted
for a month or six weeks.

Goliath.—Ordered to be sent from Alexandria the moment
Lion arrives. Main-mast bad.

Zealous,
Swiftsure,
Emerald,      Ordered to cruize off Alexandria as long as they
Alcmene,         can with propriety.
Seahorse,
La Fortune.

Thalia.—Joined me this morning.

Terpsichore.—Sent by Captain Dixon to Naples, and from
thence to join the Commander-in-Chief. (Parted company 20th May.)

Transfer.—Never joined. Reported to be gone to Cyprus.

Lion.—Joined Captain Hood off Alexandria, the 25th August.

Mutine.—Going down with Dispatches.

Bonne Citoyenne.—Gone to Naples.

Earl St. Vincent.—With Captain Retalick, to join the Portuguese Squadron.

Portuguese Squadron.—Returning from Alexandria, and requested to block up Malta.

Minotaur, ) Ordered, when Sir James Saumarez gets between
Audacious. ⌡      Sardinia and Minorca, to join me at Naples.

---

[8] See *London Gazette* of the 3rd of October, 1798. Lieutenant William Debusk
was slightly wounded. It does not appear that he was rewarded for his gallantry by
promotion, as he was still Lieutenant in 1802, and died before 1809.

Orion,
Defence,
Bellerophon, }On their passage to Gibraltar with the Prizes.
Theseus,
Majestic.
Flora, Cutter.—Gone to Alexandria.

                                        HORATIO NELSON.

_____

TO SIR JOHN ACTON, BART., NAPLES.

[Letter Book.]

Sir,                    Vanguard, at Sea, 15th September,[9] 1798.

I was yesterday honoured with your Excellency's very
handsome and flattering letter of the 9th, conveying to me
their Sicilian Majesties' congratulations on the Victory obtained by my Royal Master's Fleet over the Enemy.[1] I have
to request that your Excellency will have the goodness to
assure their Majesties that I am penetrated with their condescension in noticing this Battle, which I most fervently
pray may add security to their Majesties' Throne, and peace
and happiness to all mankind. The hand of God was visibly
pressed upon the French, and I hope there is not a person in
the British Fleet who does not attribute this great Victory to
the blessing of the Almighty on our exertions in a just cause.
With every sentiment of respect, believe me,
            Your Excellency's most obedient,
                                        HORATIO NELSON.

_____

TO CAPTAIN GAGE, OF H.M. SHIP TERPSICHORE.

[Order-Book.]

                                        15th September, 1798.

Ordered, Captain Gage, in the Terpsichore, to proceed by
the south end of Sardinia, round by the west end of Sicily,

_____

[9] On Saturday the 15th, "Strombolo, W. by S. 8 or 9 leagues, at 7 A.M., came on
a heavy squall of wind and rain which carried away the foremast, head of the main-
topmast, and jib-boom; lost four seamen with the foremast and several wounded, cut
away and cleared the wreck, Thalia took us in tow." Sunday 16th, "rigged a mizen
topmast for a jury foremast, and set a mizen topsail for a foresail."—*Journal.* From
this time until the Vanguard's arrival at Naples she was usually in tow of the
Thalia;—well indeed might Nelson call her the "poor wretched Vanguard!"

[1] Vide p. 72, ante.

and from thence to Malta, to attempt communication with the Maltese in revolt against the French, and having had such communication, to return by the same route, to join me at Naples, keeping a good look-out for the Colossus and Convoy, and acquaint him I am at Naples.

N.B. You will acquaint the Maltese, I shall have great pleasure in coming to their relief, as soon as I have refitted my Squadron.

------

TO LADY NELSON.[2]

[From Clarke and M'Arthur, vol. ii. p. 99.]

At Sea, 16th September, 1798.

The Kingdom of the Two Sicilies is mad with joy; from the throne to the peasant, all are alike. According to Lady Hamilton's letter, the situation of the Queen was truly pitiable: I only hope I shall not have to be witness to a renewal of it. I give you Lady Hamilton's own words: 'How shall I describe the transports of the Queen! 'tis not possible: she cried, kissed her husband, her children, walked frantic about the room, cried, kissed, and embraced every person near her; exclaiming, O brave Nelson! O God bless and protect our brave deliverer? O Nelson, Nelson! what do we not owe you! O Victor! Saviour of Italy! O that my swollen heart could now tell him personally what we owe to him?' You may judge, Fanny, of the rest: but my head will not allow me to tell you half; so much for that. My fag, without success, would have had no effect, but blessed be God for his goodness to me.

Yours, &c.

HORATIO NELSON.

[2] About this time, Nelson must have received the Letter from Lady Nelson, in which she mentioned his Portrait:—" Round Wood, July 23rd, [1798.] My dearest Husband, I am now writing opposite to your portrait. The likeness is great: I am well satisfied with Abbot. I really began to think he had no intention of letting me have my own property, which I am not a little attached to. Indeed, it is more than attachment—it is real affection. It is my company—my sincere friend, in your absence. Our good father was delighted with the likeness. The room is very near eleven feet, therefore, it stands very well, opposite the East window."

TO EARL SPENCER.

[Letter-Book.]

Vanguard, off Strombolo, September 16th, 1798.

My Lord,

Enclosed, I send you General Acton's Letter to me of the
9th. From the present situation of Naples, I am doubtful if
it ought to be sent to Mr. Nepean. If your Lordship thinks
it ought, I have to request you will give it to Mr. Nepean, to
lay before the Board of Admiralty. The Portuguese having
with no small difficulty been got from Naples, have been to
Egypt, but they would neither stay or give our Ships water,
which was all Captain Hood requested. I have waylaid them
off Messina and entreated them to go off Malta, which with
little exertion must be taken from the French, but I hope
your Lordship will not build hope on their exertions.

The moment I can get Ships all aid shall be given to the
Maltese. What would I give for four Bomb-ships! All the
French Armament would long ago have been destroyed.
Pray, if the service will admit of it, let me have them: I
will only say, I shall endeavour to make a proper use of
them. Pray, my Lord, let me know our situation with Genoa.
That she is at war with us is certain, these two years past.
The Judge of the Admiralty has cited me to appear before
him and show cause why I seized a Genoese Ship, (the accounts of which I long since sent to the Board of Admiralty,)
for the sale of her cargo, and which I have long wanted to
be taken out of my hands. The Ship was liberated when
our troops evacuated Porto Ferrajo. The seas are covered
with Genoese Ships, but the Judge[3] of the Admiralty's conduct
has to me so repeatedly militated against my duty, in the
service of my King and Country, that I dare not do my duty.
I have already been half ruined by him, and condemned
without knowing I was before him. The Treasury, it is true,
paid part of the expense, but that does not make the Judge's
conduct the less grievous.

The situation of the French Army in Egypt was this on the

---

[3] Sir John Marriott: he resigned, and was succeeded by Sir William Scott,
(afterwards Lord Stowell,) on the 27th of October, 1798.

27th of August. The garrison of Alexandria, except 1000 men, marched to Rosetta, from whence they are to pass up the Nile. Buonaparte has advanced 15,000 men into a strong Post in Syria, twenty-five leagues from Cairo, which he is fortifying—a proof he expects an attack from that quarter. I pray God he may not be disappointed. The flux still rages in his Army.

I am looking anxiously for the Foudroyant, and also for your Lordship's goodness to my son-in-law: I, of course, wish he had a good Frigate. I beg to offer my respectful compliments to Lady Spencer, and that you will believe me, &c.,

HORATIO NELSON.

---

TO EARL SPENCER.

[Letter-Book.]

Vanguard, at Sea, 19th September, 1798.

My Lord,

Captain Faddy, of the Marines, who was killed on board the Vanguard, has a family of small children: his eldest son is now on board this Ship, only fourteen years of age. I beg to solicit your Lordship for a Commission in the Marines for him. I understand it has been done, and the youth permitted to remain at school, till of a proper age to join the Corps. If, however, this should, in the present instance, be thought wrong, may I request that his name may stand as an *élève* of the Admiralty, and Mrs. Faddy acquainted with it, which must give her some relief under her great misfortune.[4] Ever your Lordship's most obedient Servant,

HORATIO NELSON.

---

[4] To this request, Lord Spencer said, in his Letter of the 24th of December, 1798 :—" In your Letter of the 19th September, you mention the family of the late Captain Faddy of the Marines. I have paid all the attention I could to his Widow ; and though the age of his Son will not allow of his receiving a Marine Commission immediately, he shall be considered as a Candidate for one in due time, when he shall be qualified according to our rules."—*Autograph.*

TO ADMIRAL THE EARL OF ST. VINCENT, K.B.

[From Clarke and M'Arthur, vol. ii. p. 100.]

20th September, 1798.

I detest this voyage to Naples; nothing but absolute necessity could force me to the measure. Syracuse in future, whilst my operations lie on the eastern side of Sicily, is my Port, where every refreshment may be had for a Fleet. I have sent Mr. Littledale to prepare matters at Naples. On the day Hoste left me, I was taken with a fever, which has very near done my business : for eighteen hours, my life was thought to be past hope ; I am now up, but very weak both in body and mind, from my cough and this fever. I never expect, my dear Lord, to see your face again : it may please God, that this will be the finish to that fever of anxiety which I have endured from the middle of June; but be that as it pleases His goodness—I am resigned to his will.

Dear Troubridge and Ball are gone on to Naples, and I hope are there. Murray must be also arrived with the stores, &c. Jackson shall fit us out, and your arrangements, my dear Lord, shall be, and ever are, as punctually attended to by me, as if you were present; for I hold it to be the highest contempt, to alter the mode of discipline and regulations established by the Commander-in Chief. My first order was, to pay the strictest attention to all the orders and regulations of the Commander-in-Chief; and I can truly say, that I have endeavoured to support your orders with all my might. We shall do very well whilst you stay below, but if you should go home, I shall be unfit for this command, where I want so many indulgences. I am, &c.,

HORATIO NELSON.

TO THE RIGHT HON. EARL SPENCER.

[Letter-Book.]

Naples, September 25th, 1798.

My Lord,

Culloden and Alexander arrived here the 16th. The former is at Castel-à-Mare, where every assistance is afforded her. Alexander is fitting for two months' service, when from her battered state she must go down the Mediterranean. Captain Ball is so anxious to get at the Guillaume Tell, that she will soon be ready. He is emulous to give the final blow to the French Navy in the Mediterranean (for I reckon, nor do the Enemy, the Venetian Ships as anything). I wish my friend Ball was fairly alongside of her : our Country need not fear the event. His activity and zeal are eminently conspicuous even amongst the Band of Brothers—each, as I may have occasion to mention them, must call forth my gratitude and admiration. On the 22nd, the wreck of Vanguard arrived in the Bay of Naples. His Sicilian Majesty came out three leagues to meet me, and directly came on board. His Majesty took me by the hand and said such things of our Royal Master, our Country, and myself, that no words I could use would in any degree convey what so apparently came from the Royal heart. From his Majesty, his Ministers, and every class, I am honoured by the appellation of ' Nostro Liberatore.'

You will not, my Lord, I trust, think that one spark of vanity induces me to mention the most distinguished reception that ever, I believe, fell to the lot of a human being, but that it is a measure of justice due to his Sicilian Majesty and the Nation. If God knows my heart, it is amongst the most humble of the creation, full of thankfulness and gratitude! I send your Lordship a correct statement of the loss of the Enemy in the Battle of the Nile. The hand of God was visible from the first to the last. The fate of Généreux and miserable condition of Guillaume Tell are farther proofs of it. All glory be to Him ! Amen![5]

With my sincerest respects to Lady Spencer,[6] the Dowager

[5] Of this Letter, Lord Spencer wrote, on the 24th of December, 1798 : —" If anything could add to the admiration and true regard with which your conduct has inspired every one of us, who have had the opportunity of being correctly acquainted with it, it would be the sentiments which you express in your Letter of the 25th of September, on which I will not enlarge, as I trust you do me the justice to know that I give you all the credit that is due to you; and if your friends in England write you a true state of the Public opinion about you, I think you will have full reason to be satisfied."—*Autograph*, in the Nelson Papers.

[6] Lavinia, Countess Spencer, who died in June, 1831, was the eldest daughter of Charles, first Earl of Lucan, by Margaret, daughter and co-heir of James Smith, Esq. " The Dowager Lady Spencer," was Georgiana, daughter of Stephen Poyntz, Esq.

Lady Spencer, Lady Lucan, and those of your Lordship's
family who have honoured me by their notice, and I beg you
will allow me to assure you with what respect I am,

                    Your most faithful Servant,

                                    HORATIO NELSON.

I have this moment Letters from Mr. Wyndham at Florence,
telling me, that three of the Venetian Ships (64s) with eleven
Transports, are ready to sail from Toulon. I hope Naples is
on the eve of declaring: also, *I hope*—but it is a distant one—
that the Portuguese are off Malta, when all is right.

---

### TO LADY NELSON.

[From Clarke and M'Arthur, vol. ii. p. 101.]

[About 25th September, 1798.]

The poor wretched Vanguard arrived here on the 22nd of
September. I must endeavour to convey to you something
of what passed; but if it were so affecting to those who were
only united to me by bonds of friendship, what must it be to
my dearest wife, my friend, my everything which is most dear
to me in this world?—Sir William and Lady Hamilton came
out to sea, attended by numerous Boats with emblems, &c.
They, my most respectable friends, had really been laid up
and seriously ill; first from anxiety, and then from joy. It
was imprudently told Lady Hamilton in a moment, and the
effect was like a shot; she fell apparently dead, and is not yet
perfectly recovered from severe bruises. Alongside came my
honoured friends: the scene in the boat was terribly affecting;
up flew her Ladyship, and exclaiming, ' O God, is it possible?'
she fell into my arm more dead than alive. Tears, however,
soon set matters to rights; when alongside came the King.
The scene was, in its way, as interesting; he took me by the
hand, calling me his ' Deliverer and Preserver,' with every other
expression of kindness. In short, all Naples calls me ' Nostro
Liberatore;' my greeting from the lower Classes was truly
affecting. I hope some day to have the pleasure of introducing
you to Lady Hamilton, she is one of the very best women in
this world; she is an honour to her sex. Her kindness, with
Sir William's, to me, is more than I can express: I am in their

house, and I may now tell you, it required all the kindness of my friends to set me up. Lady Hamilton intends writing to you.[7] May God Almighty bless you, and give us in due time, a happy meeting.

Yours, &c.,

HORATIO NELSON.

---

TO THE REVEREND MR. NELSON.

[Autograph, in the Nelson Papers.]

My dear Father,　　　　　　　　September 25th, 1798.

I have to thank you for your two affectionate letters from Round-Wood, and if the place and neighbourhood are not so pleasant as could be wished, I trust that my Country will enable me to choose a comfortable resting-place. The Almighty has blessed my exertions for the happiness of mankind, and I am daily receiving the thanks and prayers of Turks and Christians. In short, I am placed by Providence in that situation, that all my caution will be necessary to prevent vanity from showing itself superior to my gratitude and thankfulness. The hand of God was visibly pressed on the French: it was not in the power of man to gain such a Victory. In their Sicilian Majesties' thanks and congratulations, are the following lines:—' History, either ancient or modern, does not record such a Battle. You have saved us, Sir, by this most glorious Action, which, superior to any Battle fought at Sea, has this singular and important consequence—of being to all Europe, I repeat it, of the highest advantage.' The whole Letter being in the same strain, is enough to make me vain. My head is quite healed, and, if it were necessary, I could not at present leave Italy, who looks up to me as, under God, its Protector. May God Almighty bless you, my dear father, is the affectionate wish of your dutiful Son,

HORATIO NELSON.

---

[7] A letter from Lady Hamilton to Lady Nelson, dated on the 2nd of December, is in p. 138.

K 2

TO ADMIRAL THE EARL OF ST. VINCENT, K.B.

[Letter-Book.]

My Lord,                    Vanguard, Naples, 27th September, 1798.

The Vanguard arrived in the Bay of Naples[8] on the 22nd.
Culloden I found at Castel-à-Mare, preparing to heave
down. His first side will be hove out on the 28th. The
whole Ship is very rotten, and nothing but the exertion of a
Troubridge could have kept her afloat. Alexander has a new
main and mizen-mast, (those which were purchased for Vanguard,) but I hope that the Vanguard's two masts, by good
fishing, will hold fast until I can send her to Gibraltar, some
months hence. Her foremast goes in this morning, and
Captain Hardy is using every exertion, I believe, in getting
her ready. Mr. Wyndham writes me, from Florence, that three
Venetian Sixty-fours are ready to sail from Toulon with a
Convoy. I should not be uneasy was any of my brave Companions to meet them ; but two would without difficulty take
the whole. I wish for the arrival of Colossus and Convoy ;
we have occasion for all she brings. I also expect, daily,
Minotaur and Audacious from Sir J. Saumarez, with all the salt
provisions of the Ships going down, except one month ; but I
fear all the Ships did not bring up six months provisions, as
your Lordship directed. Goliath I also expect every moment.
She left Egypt the day after Thalia. I have heard nothing of
the Portuguese. I do not find any person here very anxious
for their return to Naples. The Marquis fired a shot from
his morning-gun into the Town. I wonder at this, when
your Lordship's attention in the Ports of Her Faithful Majesty
is considered. I fire no watch-gun, and I find that the contrast between the whole of my conduct and that of the
Portuguese, is considered as the difference between impudence
and modesty. These are not my words, but the public voice.

I feel it my duty to mention to your Lordship, that when the
Vanguard came in sight of Naples, several leagues off, the King

---

[8] "Saturday, 22nd—At 10 A.M., came on board Sir William Hamilton, the
English Minister: saluted him with thirteen guns. At 11, his Sicilian Majesty
honoured me with a visit: saluted him with twenty-one guns, and the like number
when he left the Ship. At ½ past 11, came to, in Naples Bay. Found here H. M.
Ships Alexander and Bonne Citoyenne—The Culloden over at Castel-à-Mare."—
*Journal.*

of Naples came on board, and, taking me by the hand, thanked me for my conduct. No words of mine can do justice to His Majesty's expressions of regard and gratitude to our King, Country, and myself: they were such as did honour, and evidently came from the Royal heart. His Majesty staid on board near three hours, going all over the Ship, and examining everything; for he prides himself on being a seaman. My reception by every class of people was flattering beyond description. I must beg leave to refer to Captain Newhouse,[1] who, although ready last night for sea, I keep till Sunday morning, in hopes some news may arrive from Vienna. What precious moments the two Courts are losing: three months would liberate Italy; this Court is so enervated that the happy moment will be lost. Even Malta, which is offered by deputation to his Sicilian Majesty, and his colours hoisted on the Forts, yet the Ministry will not step forth; but hope I shall be able to take Malta for them; from which place, incredible as it may appear, they have no news since September 5th. I have sent Terpsichore to communicate with the Island, and I hope she will soon return. I shall send Transfer and Earl St. Vincent as they arrive, with accounts of what is going on in this quarter, and believe me with the greatest truth, &c.,

HORATIO NELSON.

N.B.—The Squadron is in great distress for slops and beds. Alexander and Bonne Citoyenne will, I hope, be ready to sail in twenty-four hours after the arrival of Colossus, for Malta.

---

TO ADMIRAL THE EARL OF ST. VINCENT, K.B.

[From Clarke and M'Arthur, vol. ii. p. 102.]

27th September, 1798.

Dear Troubridge, whom we went to visit yesterday, is better than I expected; the active business, and the scolding he is obliged to be continually at, does him good. I am not surprised that you wish him near you; but I trust you will not take him from me. I well know he is my superior; and

---

[1] Of the Thalia.

I so often want his advice and assistance. A Deputy was here this morning from Cephalonia; but the thing is so in embryo, that I can say no more than that it is probable; when I get the Ships, a Squadron shall try what can be done. May God bless you, my dear Lord! Nothing shall again induce me to send the Squadron to Naples, whilst our operations lie on the eastern side of Sicily; we should be ruined with affection and kindness.

September 28th. We all dined with General Acton yesterday; and he told me that this Country was determined to declare, and not wait for the Emperor; that they well knew the plan of the French against them. After dinner the Queen sent for her son Leopold, to bring me a Letter; the youngster acquitted himself with elegance and affection: I send a copy of Her Majesty's letter. I have been in form to Court, to pay my respects to the King, and am just desired by him to dine on board Caraccioli's Ship at anchor in the bay. I wish it could have been on shore, but until the war that is not possible. A new French Minister, La Combe St. Michel arrives to-day; I hope he will make an impertinent speech, and be instantly turned off.

September 29th. The weather is still dreadfully bad, we can hold no communication with the Ships: I well knew how sad Naples Bay is for Ships to refit in. This being my birth-day, Lady Hamilton gives a fête. The King has directed the Court-mourning to cease for the day; but none of my brave Companions can join the festive scene. I am better, certainly; but truly stand some chance of being killed with kindness. I am, &c.

HORATIO NELSON.

TO LADY NELSON.

[From Clarke and M'Arthur, vol. ii. p. 102.]

28th September, 1798.

The preparations of Lady Hamilton, for celebrating my birthday to-morrow, are enough to fill me with vanity; every ribbon, every button, has ' Nelson,' &c. The whole service is marked ' H. N. Glorious 1st of August!'—Songs and Sonnetti

are numerous beyond what I ever could deserve. I send the
additional[3] verse to God save the King, as I know you will
sing it with pleasure. I cannot move on foot, or in a carriage,
for the kindness of the populace ; but good Lady H. preserves
all the papers as the highest treat for you. The Queen
yesterday, being still ill, sent her favourite son to visit, and
bring me a letter from Her of gratitude and thanks.—Miserable
accounts of Le Guillaume Tell. I trust God Almighty will
yet put her into the hands of our King. His all-powerful
hand has gone with us to the Battle, protected us, and still
continues destroying the unbelievers: All glory be to God!
The more I think, the more I hear, the greater is my astonishment at the extent and good consequences of our Victory.

Yours, &c.<br>HORATIO NELSON.

---

TO HIS EXCELLENCY SIR MORTON EDEN, K.B.[4]

[Letter-Book.]

Naples, September 28th, 1798.

Sir,

As I know Sir William Hamilton has sent to your Excellency every account relative to the Battle of the Nile, I shall
not trouble you on that subject. As the Guillaume Tell is
now the only remaining French-built Ship of the Line, I am
anxious to get some of my Squadron to sea, and am not
without hopes she may yet fall into our hands. The French-
Venetian Ships are good for nothing as Ships of the Line;

---

[3] Said to have been written by a Mr. Davenport, Editor of the " Poetical Mis-
cellany."

> " Join we in great Nelson's name,
> 　First on the rolls of Fame
> 　　Him let us sing.
> Spread we his fame around,
> Honour of British ground,
> Who made Nile's shore's resound,
> 　God save the King."

[4] Minister Plenipotentiary at the Court of Vienna: he was created Baron Henley
in the Peerage of Ireland, in November 1799.

therefore we may consider, with the exception above-mentioned, that there is no longer a French Ship of the Line in the Mediterranean. I have the honour to be, &c.

HORATIO NELSON.

---

### TO CAPTAIN SIR JAMES SAUMAREZ.

[Original, in the possession of the Dowager Lady de Saumarez.]

Vanguard, Naples, 29th September, 1798.

Sir,

I have received your Letter of the 17th from Augusta, as well as your Dispatch of the 27th by Captain Gage. I very much approve of your putting into Augusta to get water, and very highly so of your Officer-like behaviour and conduct relative to Malta, as also of your supplying the Maltese with arms and ammunition. I am, Sir, &c.

HORATIO NELSON.

---

### TO CAPTAIN SIR JAMES SAUMAREZ.

[Autograph, in the possession of the Dowager Lady de Saumarez.]

September 29th, 1798.

My dear Sir James,

Captain Gage is just arrived with your Letters and Papers relative to Malta: I can say with truth that no action of your life, as far as relates to me, but what must be entirely to my approbation. Your summons to Malta[5] is highly proper, and you have done as I wished in sending the arms, &c. The wind here is strong at S.E. I hope you have it, and that it will carry you through the Straits. This is a sad place for re-fitting, the swell sets in so heavy. Never again do we

---

[5] On his passage to Gibraltar with the captured Ships, Sir James Saumarez, while becalmed off Malta, supplied the Maltese with arms and ammunition out of the Prizes, and on the 27th of September, summoned the French Garrison in La Valetta to surrender; but after three hours consideration, Monsieur Varibois, the French General, briefly replied, that the English had forgotten that "they are Frenchmen who are at Malta;" and, "quant à votre sommation, les Francois n'entendent pas ce style."

come to Naples: besides the rest, we are killed with kindness.
Wishing you, my dear Sir James, every felicity in the world,
believe me,

Ever your obliged and affectionate,

HORATIO NELSON.

---

TO EARL SPENCER.

[Letter-Book.]

Private.

Naples, September 29th, 1798.

My Lord,

This Marquis de Gallo I detest. He is ignorant of common
civility. Sir William Hamilton has just found out that a
Messenger sets out for London within an hour, yet I was with
this Minister for an hour last night. He admires his Ribbon,
Ring, and Snuff-box so much, that an excellent Petit-Mâitre
was spoiled when he was made a Minister. The sentiments
of my heart have flown from my pen, and I cannot retract
them. I have letters from Sir James Saumarez, dated the 27th
September, off the west end of Sicily; but this man will
allow me no time to send your Lordship copies of the interesting letter and papers of Sir James Saumarez. The substance
is briefly, that, being becalmed off Malta, he fell in with the
Marquis de Niza, who has obeyed my order and taken post
there. A deputation of the Islanders coming on board, and
stating their belief that a Summons to the French would
induce them to abandon the Island, Sir James Saumarez and
the Marquis sent in a very proper Summons, which was
rejected, after three hours' consideration. Sir James very
properly supplied the Islanders with 1200 stand of arms
from the Prizes, ball-cartridges, cartouche-boxes, &c. I
trust we shall yet get the Guillaume Tell, &c. The Colossus
is arrived, with the Convoy of Victuallers, stores, &c. The
Goliath is in sight from Egypt. We are all right, and as well
situated as heart can wish. Pray excuse this short letter,
and abuse of the Marquis de Gallo. I am, &c.,

HORATIO NELSON.

## TO ADMIRAL THE EARL OF ST. VINCENT, K.B.

[From Clarke and M‘Arthur, vol. ii. p. 103.]

September 30th, 1798.

I trust, my Lord, in a week we shall all be at sea. I am very unwell, and the miserable conduct of this Court is not likely to cool my irritable temper. It is a country of fiddlers and poets, whores and scoundrels. I am, &c.,

HORATIO NELSON.

---

## TO LADY NELSON.

[From Clarke and M‘Arthur, vol. ii. p. 112.]

1st to 6th of October, 1798.

Our time here is actively employed; and between business, and what is called pleasure, I am not my own master for five minutes. The continued kind attention of Sir William and Lady Hamilton[6] must ever make you and I love them, and

---

[6] On the 2nd of December, Lady Hamilton herself wrote to Lady Nelson; and the subsequent history of the writer, perhaps, renders this Letter sufficiently remarkable to justify its insertion; but it is also interesting from containing an account of Nelson's reception at Naples after the Battle of the Nile. Before this Letter was received by Lady Nelson, some suspicious reports seem to have reached her; for Lord Nelson's most intimate friend, Mr. Alexander Davison, writing to him on the 7th of December, said—" I cannot help again repeating my sincere regret at your continuation in the Mediterranean; at the same time, I would be grieved that you should quit a station, if it in the smallest degree affected your own feelings. You certainly are, and must be, the best and only judge. Yet you must allow your best friends to express their sensations. . . . . . Your valuable better-half writes to you. She is in good health, but very uneasy and anxious, which is not to be wondered at. She sets off with the good old man to-morrow for Bath. . . . . Lady Nelson this moment calls, and is with my wife. She bids me say, that unless you return home in a few months, she will join the Standard at Naples. Excuse a woman's tender feelings—they are too acute to be expressed."

"Naples, December, 2nd, 1798.

" I hope your Ladyship received my former Letter, with an account of Lord Nelson's arrival, and his reception from their Sicilian Majesties, and also the congratulations and compliments from this amiable and adorable Queen to your Ladyship, which I was charged with, and wrote a month back, but as the posts were very uncertain, you may not have received that letter. Lord Nelson is gone to Leghorn with the Troops of the King of Naples, and we expect him soon back, as the King is gone to Rome with his Army, and he begged of my Lord Nelson to be as much at

they are deserving the love and admiration of all the world. The Grand Signior has ordered me a valuable diamond; if it were worth a million, my pleasure would be to see it in your possession. My pride is being your husband, the son of my dear father, and in having Sir William and Lady Hamilton for my friends. While these approve of my conduct, I shall not feel or regard the envy of thousands. Could I, my dearest Fanny, tell you half the honours which are shown me here, not a ream of paper would hold it. On my birth-day, eighty people dined at Sir William Hamilton's; one thousand seven hundred and forty came to a ball, where eight hundred supped. A rostral Column is erected under a magnificent canopy, never, Lady H. says, to come down while they remain at Naples. A little circumstance has also happened, which does honour to the King of Naples, and is not unpleasant to me. I went to view the magnificent manufactory of china. After admiring all the fine things, sufficient to seduce the

or about Naples as he could, not only to advise and consult with her Majesty (who is Regent) for the good of the common cause, but, *in case of accident*, to take care of her and her family. Lord Nelson is adored here, and looked on as the deliverer of this Country. He was not well when first he arrived, but by nursing and asses' milk, he went from Naples quite recovered. The King and Queen adore him, and if he had been their brother, they could not have shown him more respect and attentions. I need not tell your Ladyship how happy Sir William and myself are at having an opportunity of seeing our dear, respectable, brave friend return here, with so much honour to himself, and glory for his Country. We only wanted you to be completely happy. Lord Nelson's wound is quite well. Josiah is so much improved in every respect, we are all delighted with him. He is an excellent Officer, and very steady, and one of the best hearts in the world. I love him much, and although we quarrel sometimes, he loves me, and does as I would have him. He is in the way of being rich, for he has taken many prizes. He is indefatigable in his line, never sleeps out of his Ship, and I am sure will make a very great Officer. Lady Knight and her amiable daughter desire to be remembered to your Ladyship. I hope you received the Ode I sent. It is very well written; but Miss K. is very clever in everything she undertakes. Sir William desires his kind compliments to your Ladyship, and to Lord Nelson's dear respected father. The King is having his picture set with diamonds for his Lordship, and the Queen has ordered a fine set of China, with all the battles he has been engaged in, and his picture, painted on china. Josiah desired his duty to your Ladyship, and says he will write as soon as he has time, but he has been very busy for some time past. May God bless you and yours, my dear Madam, and believe me your Ladyship's ever sincere friend and humble servant, EMMA HAMILTON. Sir William is in a rage with Ministers for not having made Lord N. a Viscount; for sure this great Action, greater than any other, ought to have been recompensed more. Hang them, I say!"—*Autograph*, in the Nelson Papers. The Seal bears the words "Nelson, 1st August, 1798."

money from my pocket, I came to some busts in china of all the Royal Family : these I immediately ordered, and, when I wanted to pay for them, I was informed that the King had directed whatever I chose should be delivered free of all cost: it was handsome in the King. Yours, &c.,

HORATIO NELSON.

---

TO LADY HAMILTON.

[Autograph draught, in the Nelson Papers.]

Naples, October 3rd, 1798.

My dear Madam,

The anxiety which you and Sir William Hamilton have always had for the happiness of their Sicilian Majesties, was also planted in me five years past, and I can truly say, that on every occasion which has offered (which have been numerous) I have never failed to manifest my sincere regard for the felicity of these Kingdoms. Under this attachment, I cannot be an indifferent spectator to what has [been] and is passing in the Two Sicilies, nor to the misery which, (without being a politician,) I cannot but see plainly is ready to fall on those Kingdoms, now so loyal, by the worst of all policy—that of procrastination. Since my arrival in these seas in June last, I have seen in the Sicilians the most loyal people to their Sovereign, with the utmost detestation of the French and their principles. Since my arrival at Naples I have found all ranks, from the very highest to the lowest, eager for war with the French, who, all know, are preparing an Army of robbers to plunder these Kingdoms and destroy the Monarchy. I have seen the Minister of the insolent French pass over in silence the manifest breach of the third article of the Treaty between his Sicilian Majesty and the French Republic. Ought not this extraordinary conduct to be seriously noticed? Has not the uniform conduct of the French been to lull Governments into a false security, and then to destroy them? As I have before stated, is it not known to every person that Naples is the next marked object for plunder? With this knowledge, and that his Sicilian Majesty has an Army ready (I am told) to march into a Country anxious to receive them, with the advantage of carrying the War from, instead of waiting for it at, home, I am all astonished that the Army has not marched a month ago.

I trust that the arrival of General Mack will induce the Government not to lose any more of the favourable time which Providence has put in their hands; for if they do, and wait for an attack in this Country, instead of carrying the war out of it, it requires no gift of prophecy to pronounce that these Kingdoms will be ruined, and the Monarchy destroyed. But should, unfortunately, this miserable ruinous system of procrastination be persisted in, I would recommend that all your property and persons are ready to embark at a very short notice. It will be my duty to look and provide for your safety, and with it (I am sorry to think it will be necessary) that of the amiable Queen of these Kingdoms and her Family. I have read with admiration her dignified and incomparable Letter of September, 1796. May the Councils of these Kingdoms ever be guided by such sentiments of dignity, honour, and justice ; and may the words of the great William Pitt, Earl of Chatham, be instilled into the Ministry of this Country—' *The boldest measures are the safest,*' is the sincere wish of your Ladyship's &c.,

HORATIO NELSON.

P.S.—Your Ladyship will, I beg, receive this letter as a preparative for Sir William Hamilton, to whom I am writing, with all respect, the firm and unalterable opinion of a British Admiral, anxious to approve himself a faithful Servant to his Sovereign by doing everything in his power for the happiness and security of their Sicilian Majesties and their Kingdoms.

---

TO CAPTAIN BALL, HIS MAJESTY'S SHIP ALEXANDER.

[Order-Book.]

Vanguard, Naples, 4th October, 1798.

You are hereby required and directed to proceed in his Majesty's Ship Alexander, under your command, off the Island of Malta, taking with you the Ships named in the

margin,[7] whose Captains have my orders to follow your
directions, and to use your endeavour to blockade the Ports
of that Island, so, as to prevent any supplies getting in them
for the French troops, as well as to prevent the escape of the
French Ships now in that place, delivering the dispatch you
will receive herewith to the Marquis de Niza, who is cruizing
off that Island.

Captain Murray, in his Majesty's Ship Colossus, has very
handsomely offered his services to go for a few days with you
off Malta, but will not interfere with the Ships under your
command. On meeting with the Incendiary Fire-Ship, you
will also take her under your command, he having my orders
for that purpose.

HORATIO NELSON.

TO HIS EXCELLENCY THE MARQUIS DE NIZA.

[Letter-Book.]

Vanguard, Naples, 4th October, 1798.

I have to acknowledge the receipt of your Excellency's
letter of the 25th September, and very highly approve of your
meritorious conduct in blockading the Island of Malta, and of
sending the Summons to the French Army; and although not
successful this time, I hope it will soon surrender to the united
efforts of your Excellency and the Ships under my Command.

I have sent Captain Ball in the Alexander, (who will deliver
your Excellency this Letter,) with a Frigate and a Sloop, to
cruize off the Island, and hope to have more Ships there in
a short time. Whenever your Excellency may think it necessary to return into Port with the Ships of her Most Faithful
Majesty, it will have my entire approbation. At the same
time the Blockade ought to be kept up until I can send a
proper Force to relieve you, and it will be of great importance
to prevent the three Venetian Ships now ready for sea at
Toulon from getting into that Island. I have ordered Captain Ball to take the Incendiary Fire-ship under his command,
and have the honour to be, &c.,

HORATIO NELSON.

[7] Terpsichore, Bonne Citoyenne, Incendiary.

TO CAPTAIN MURRAY, H. M. SHIP COLOSSUS.

[Autograph, in the possession of George Murray, Esq.]

Sir,　　　　　　　　　　　　Naples, October 4th, 1798.

I feel most sensibly your kind assistance to the Ships of
my Squadron, and also your very handsome offer of going off
Malta, to assist in the blockade, till some of the Ships under
my orders may be ready. I readily accept your offer for a
few days, longer than which I should be sorry to detain you
from the services you are ordered upon by the Commander-
in-Chief. I have the honour to be, Sir, &c.

HORATIO NELSON.

TO ADMIRAL THE EARL OF ST. VINCENT, K.B.

[From Clarke and M‘Arthur, vol. ii. p. 111. It cannot be unnecessary to state
the views of the Government at that moment, as they appear from a Letter from
the Secretary to the Admiralty to the Earl of St. Vincent, dated on the 3rd of
October, 1798.

"I am commanded by my Lords Commissoners of the Admiralty to acquaint
your Lordship, that in the present state of affairs in the Mediterranean their Lordships conceive that the objects principally to be attended to by the Squadron employed there, are—

1st. The protection of the Coasts of Sicily, Naples, and the Adriatic, and in the
event of War being renewed in Italy, an active co-operation with the Austrian and
Neapolitan Armies.

2ndly. The cutting off all communication between France and Egypt, that
neither Supplies nor Re-inforcements may be sent to the Army at Alexandria.

3rdly. The Blocking-up of Malta, so as to prevent Provisions from being sent
into it.

4thly. The co-operating with the Turkish and Russian Squadrons which are to
be sent into the Archipelago." . . . . " The ninth Article of a Treaty proposed to be
concluded between his Majesty and the Porte (a copy of which is enclosed) will
explain to your Lordship the nature of the engagements likely to be made between
the two contracting Powers; and it is necessary your Lordship should also be
informed that a Treaty has recently been concluded between the Porte and Russia,
by which his Imperial Majesty has engaged to furnish a certain number of Ships
for the purpose of being employed against the common Enemy, part of which has
actually arrived at Constantinople and joined the Turkish Squadron." . . . . . " The
protection of the Coasts of Naples and Sicily, and an active co-operation with the
Austrian and Neapolitan Armies are the objects to which a principal part of the
Squadron should be most particularly directed. If the superiority of the Allied
Forces be such as to admit of their being divided into separate Squadrons, which,

from the great Victory gained by his Majesty's Squadron, under the command of Sir Horatio Nelson, their Lordships conclude will hereafter be the case, many of these objects may be attained by blocking up the Enemy's Ships of War in their own Ports, as in such case few Cruizers, and those of no great force, might then be sufficient to perform most of the other Services." . . . . . " Your Lordship will give such directions to the Officer commanding the Squadron in the Mediterranean as may be necessary for carrying effectually into execution these instructions, in which, however, from the nature of his situation and from the uncertainty of events which may occur, much must of necessity be left to his discretion. But he should be particularly directed in every possible situation, to give the most cordial and unlimited support and protection to his Majesty's Allies, to exert himself to the utmost to preserve a good intelligence between them, and most carefully to avoid giving to any of them the smallest cause for suspicion, jealousy, or offence."—*Original*, in the Nelson Papers.]

4th October, 1798.

My dear Lord,

I cannot, am not able to tell you the quantity I have to communicate. This Country by its system of procrastination will ruin itself: the Queen sees it, and thinks as we do. The Ministry, except Acton, are for putting the evil day off, when it will come with destruction. War at this moment can alone save these Kingdoms. I am decidedly in opposition to Gallo. General Mack is hourly expected here from Vienna, to command the Neapolitan Army: Acton says they are ready to march. I have scolded; anger is necessary. You will not believe I have said or done anything, without the approbation of Sir William Hamilton. His Excellency is too good to them, and the strong language of an English Admiral telling them plain truths of their miserable system may do good. Ball sails, if possible, to-morrow with Terpsichore and Citoyenne. Murray, who gives us everything he has, very handsomely goes off Malta with him for a few days. Vanguard, I hope, will be next, with Audacious, &c. Our wants are great, our means few. I need not tell you we cannot get much from this small Arsenal, but they give us all they have. Culloden is getting forward, Troubridge is indefatigable: none but he could have saved poor Culloden. We all dine this day with the King on board a Ship, he is very attentive; I have been with the Queen, she is truly a daughter of Maria Theresa. I am writing opposite Lady Hamilton, therefore you will not be surprised at the glorious jumble of this letter. Were your Lordship in my place, I much doubt if you could write so well; our hearts and our hands must be all in a flutter: Naples is a dangerous place, and we must keep clear of it. I am, &c.

                                            HORATIO NELSON.[8]

---

### TO CAPTAIN BARKER, INCENDIARY FIRE-SHIP.

[Letter-Book.]

                                    Vanguard, October 5th, 1798.
Dear Sir,

I have directed Captain Ball to take you with him, and I assure you I desire an opportunity of proving how much I respect your character, being Lord St. Vincent's sincere friend.

                                            HORATIO NELSON.

---

### TO J. SPENCER SMITH, ESQ., HIS MAJESTY'S MINISTER TO THE OTTOMAN PORTE.

[Letter-Book.]

Sir,                                Naples, October 7th, 1798.

By the Neapolitan courier, who arrived a few days ago from Constantinople, I am informed of the declaration of War of the Porte against the French, and also that the Battle of the Nile has given satisfaction to the Grand Signior; and I take the opportunity of a courier going from this Court to Constantinople, to tell you that I have directed the Squadron blockading the Transports in Alexandria, to remain on that service as long as possible, or till they are relieved by the Turkish Fleet. Part of my Squadron sailed yesterday to blockade Malta; myself and three Sail of the Line, will also sail in three days. You may assure the Grand Signior that

---

[6] It was apparently in reply to this Letter, that Lord St. Vincent said, in a private Letter, dated on the 28th of October, 1798—

"You're great in the Cabinet as on the Ocean, and your whole conduct fills me with admiration and confidence. I thank God that your health is restored, and that the luscious Neapolitan Dames have not impaired it. As this goes by an American I cannot enter [upon] any military or political subject. . . . . . God bless you, my dear Admiral, and be assured no man loves or values you more highly than your truly affectionate, ST. VINCENT."—*Autograph*, in the Nelson Papers.

I shall be happy in co-operating to destroy the common Enemy, who are the pest of the human race. I think Coron is a good place to get duplicates of letters sent to: I am told a courier can go in four or five days to Constantinople. I do not mean to prevent letters going to Naples for me, but as I may be sometimes in that neighbourhood, I mention the place as convenient for communicating. As Sir William Hamilton will write you, I shall not mention the state of affairs here. Malta, Corfu, and those Islands are my object after Egypt, and therefore I hope that the Russian Fleet will be kept in the East; for if they establish themselves in the Mediterranean, it will be a bad thorn in the side of the Porte. I am, Sir, &c.

HORATIO NELSON.

TO EARL SPENCER.

[Letter-Book.]

Naples, 9th October, 1798.

My Lord,

Vanguard, Minotaur, Audacious, and Goliath, sail on Saturday next; Culloden will get away the week following. I admit three weeks is a long time to refit a Fleet after a Battle, but when it is considered that nearly every mast in the Fleet has taken much more time than if they had been new, that Naples Bay is subject to a heavy swell, of which we have felt the inconvenience; and that we go to sea victualled for six months, and in the highest health and discipline, I trust some allowance will be made for me. Every Transport goes with me to Syracuse.

Naples sees this Squadron no more, except the King calls for our help, and if they go on, and lose the glorious moments, we may be called for to save the persons of their Majesties. I am writing to Sir William Hamilton to have an Article signed, that whenever Malta shall be taken possession of by his Sicilian Majesty, that all the French Ships shall be delivered up to me; and his Excellency will, I fancy, get an Article with their Government, that in the event of getting possession of Malta, that it shall not be ceded to any Power without the consent of his Majesty. I go to Caserta to take leave of the King on Thursday, and shall write you a line on my return. General Mack cannot move without five carriages. I have formed my opinion; I heartily pray, I may be mistaken.[8]

Respecting my movements my intention is to go off Malta, to make myself acquainted with the true state of matters there, to leave a proper Force to blockade the Port; then to proceed to Zante, Cephalonia, and Corfu to see what can be done; if nothing, to fly to Egypt, clap the Turks on the back, and put matters in the best train. This your Lordship will see, is only the outline. What may turn up as we get on, time only can show, but of this be assured, that I will act to the best of my judgment for the honour of my King and Country. With the greatest truth, ever your obliged,

HORATIO NELSON.

---

ADMIRAL NELSON TO THE INHABITANTS OF CORFU, CEPHALONIA, ZANTE, AND CERIGO.

[From a Copy in the Nelson Papers.]

[October 9th, 1798.]

Declares,

That understanding they are heartily tired of the tyrannic conduct of the French, he is coming to offer them the protection of his Britannic Majesty's Fleet. No interested views of his Sovereign actuate the Admiral, as will appear by reading what follows. When the French are drove out of the Islands, by the inhabitants, all the Admiral demands are the French shipping and property, both of war and merchandize. He

---

[8] The disgraceful surrender of Ulm proved the correctness of this opinion of General Mack, though, on meeting him a few days afterwards, Nelson seems to have been more favourably impressed. Harrison states, (and it is repeated by Southey,) that, at a Review of the Neapolitan Army, General Mack made so glaring a mistake in directing the operations of a feigned Battle, as to have his own troops surrounded by those of the supposed Enemy, when Lord Nelson, vexed at the unfortunate and inauspicious blunder, exclaimed—"This fellow does not understand his business !" Harrison also says, that when the Expedition against Leghorn was undertaken, the King of Naples wished Nelson to remain on account of his health ; but he requested Lady Hamilton to inform the Queen, that it was his custom not to say " ' Go,' but 'Let us go.'"—*Life of Lord Nelson*, vol. i. p. 363.

also declares that if the Provisional Government of the Islands
hoist the British Flag, the protection of the Fleet will be given
them. No contribution, or anything like a tax, will be asked
by the Admiral. If the Provisional government of the Islands
request any troops to be landed to assist in garrisoning the
Islands, in that case, if the Admiral has the goodness to
comply with their request, provision must be found gratis for
the troops. Upon the whole, the only wish of Admiral
Nelson is to deliver good men from tyranny and oppression.

---

### TO ADMIRAL THE EARL OF ST. VINCENT, K.B.

[Letter-Book.]

Naples, 13th October, 1798.

My dear Lord,

Although Hoste has arrived with your kind and affectionate
Letter, yet I must begin by telling you my proceedings to this
day, when at noon the Transfer sails to join you. General
Mack arrived at Caserta on Tuesday; on Thursday I went
with Sir William and Lady Hamilton to meet General Mack
at dinner with the King and Queen. Their Majesties introduced us to each other, with every expression of esteem and
regard: the Queen, however, could not help saying, ' General,
be to us by land, what my hero, Nelson, has been by sea.'
I have endeavoured to impress the General with a favourable
impression of me, and I think have succeeded. He is active
and has an intelligent eye, and will do well, I have no doubt.
The Emperor has desired the King of Naples to begin, and
he will support him. Mack says he will march in ten days;
their Majesties have given him their confidence, and I feel I
am in full possession of it. This evening I shall have in
writing the result of last night's Session, the Queen calls it
—not a Council, as in that case *Gallo* must have been at it;
but he is tottering, and the Queen has promised he shall not
be the War Minister. Acton was going down, but we have set
him up again. General M. agrees with me to place our
confidence in him and the Queen alone, the moment War
begins. I shall send the Earl St. Vincent Cutter to you.
We are all ready for sea this evening, except Culloden, who

is only detained for the pintles of her rudder. We sail on Monday morning. When at sea I shall detach Audacious and Goliath to join my dear friend Ball off Malta, who I shall intrust with the blockade. The Government here are very sanguine, expecting to get hold of it in a short time. I am not so sanguine : the French have bread and water. I shall write the French Commander a proper letter, offering my mediation with the injured and plundered Maltese ; but should the French Ships escape, in that case I shall not trouble myself either with their capitulation, or in obtaining mercy for the deluded people who have joined them.

The King of Naples perfectly understands that even in the event of the Island surrendering without communicating with our Ships, all the French Ships are to be given up instantly as my property. The Island is certainly the property of the King of Naples, and I leave all matters to be settled by the Courts. God bless you : your affectionate,

HORATIO NELSON.

---

TO ADMIRAL THE EARL OF ST. VINCENT, K.B.

[From Tucker's " Memoirs of Earl St. Vincent," vol. i. p. 455.]

Begun October 10th, 1798, ended [on the 24th.]

My dear Lord,

Had Leander got to you, perhaps you would have been overwhelmed with my private letters upon numerous subjects, but of which I have no copies. On the subject of our dear friend Troubridge, and on my sending Capel to England and putting Hoste into the [Mutine] I should have been glad you had received my letter : on the former, it was authorizing you to add a paragraph to my Public letter, if you thought it more to the advantage of Troubridge, but I thought it better to make no mention of his disaster; for I consider Captain Troubridge's conduct as fully entitled to praise as any one Officer in the Squadron, and as highly deserving reward. He commanded a Division equally with Sir James Saumarez, by my order of June; and I should feel distressed if any honour is granted to one, that is not granted to the other. This part, I write you, my dear Lord, to make

use of to Lord Spencer, should an⸍                    ⸍.  I
know the Knight has wrote to the f                    inent
services of our friend deserve the ve⸍               ⸍ have
experienced the ability and activit⸍ ⸍                dy :  it
was Troubridge that equipped the Squadron su ⸌⸍    t Syracuse—it was he that exerted himself for me after the Action
—it was Troubridge who saved the Culloden, when none
that I know in the Service would have attempted it—it was
Troubridge whom I left as myself at Naples to watch movements—he is, as a Friend and an Officer, a *nonpareil!*
Off Malta, 24th.—The French are not likely to quit the
Island. The Marquis is going direct for Naples ; he deserves
credit for quitting his Ship and hoisting his Flag in another,
in order to continue the blockade.  God bless you !

HORATIO NELSON.

---

TO ADMIRAL THE EARL OF ST. VINCENT, K.B.

[Letter-Book.]

Vanguard, Marsala, West End of Sicily, 22nd October, 1798.

My Lord,

On Monday the 15th, at 8 o'clock, the King and Prince
Leopold came on board, and did me the honour of breakfast-
ing.[9]  At 10, the Squadron named in the margin[1] weighed
anchor, and at 11, his Majesty left the Ship, expressing himself in the most flattering manner towards me.  His Majesty
had all the respect paid him by the Squadron which our
situation would admit of, and which it was not only our duty,
but so much our inclination to pay him.

The King having desired my return to Naples in the
first week in November, I shall, after having arranged the
blockade of Malta, return to Naples, and endeavour to be
useful in the movements of their Army.  In thus acquiescing
in the desire of the King of Naples, I give up my plan,

---

[9] Monday, 15th of October.  "At 8, A.M., came on board, the English Minister ;
saluted him.  At 9, came on board, His Majesty the King of Naples ; saluted him
with twenty-one guns, and the like number when he left the Ship.  At half-past 10,
weighed and made sail in company with the Minotaur, Audacious, Goliath, and
Mutine Brig."—*Journal.*

[1] Vanguard, Minotaur, Audacious, Goliath, and Mutine.

which was to have gone to Egypt and attended to the destruction of the French Shipping in that quarter : but I hope before Captain Hood quits his Station, that both the Turks and Russian Squadrons will be on that Coast, when all will be right, I hope, although, I own myself not willing to trust any of our Allies to do that which we could do ourselves. I have reason for thinking that a strong wish for our Squadron's being on the Coast of Naples is, that in case of any mishap, that their Majesties' think their persons much safer under the protection of the British Flag than under any other. The Culloden would be ready for sea about this time. I have directed Captain Troubridge to wait my arrival, and also directed the Transports not to sail for Syracuse, as was my intention. On my passage, I met the Emerald from Egypt; left Captain Hood the 19th September—all going on well, and I have sent all Captain Hood's Letters to Sir William Hamilton. He will tell you their contents.

The Emerald is ordered to re-fit, and will be ready to sail on any Service wanted, or wait my arrival. The Earl St. Vincent Cutter is left for the express purpose of sailing the moment the Army marches out of the Kingdom. The Terpsichore I shall direct to be at Naples by the 20th November, and to sail for Gibraltar directly, as she wants, by her Captain's report, much repair. There being no wine to be bought at Naples for the Squadron, I anchored here yesterday evening, and having got 200 pipes of wine, I shall sail in the evening. Except with the black lion, we have not a sick man in the Squadron. I have the honour to be, &c.,

HORATIO NELSON.

---

TO LADY NELSON.

[From Clarke and M'Arthur, vol. ii. p. 119. The Vanguard arrived off Malta on the 24th of October, and joined company with the Portuguese Squadron, and the Alexander, Terpsichore, Incendiary, and Bonne Citoyenne, but the Portuguese Ships sailed the next day for Naples to refit.—*Journal.*]

Off Malta, October 24th, 1798.

I am just arrived off this Island. The French are not yet turned out; but I shall do my best in negotiating. There is

no fighting, I assure you; if there were, it should be settled
before night. Our hearts are in the trim, and God is with
us; ' of whom then shall we be afraid !' Yours, &c.,

HORATIO NELSON.

TO THE RIGHT HONOURABLE SIR WILLIAM HAMILTON, K.B.

[Letter-Book.]

Vanguard, off Malta, 24th October, 1798.

My dear Sir,

I am just arrived off this place, where I found Captain
Ball and the Marquis de Niza: from these Officers I do not
find such an immediate prospect of getting possession of the
Town, as the Ministers at Naples seem to think. All the
Country, it is true, is in possession of the Islanders, and I
believe, the French have not many luxuries in the Town, but
as yet their bullocks are not eat up. The Marquis tells me,
the Islanders want arms, victuals, mortars, and cannon to
annoy the Town. When I get the Elect of the People on
board, I shall desire them to draw up a Memorial for the
King of Naples, stating their wants and desires, which I shall
bring with me. The Marquis sails for Naples to-morrow
morning. Till he is gone I shall not do anything about the
Island, but I will be fully master of that subject before I leave
this place. God bless you, is the sincere prayer of your
affectionate,

HORATIO NELSON.

TO ADMIRAL THE EARL OF ST. VINCENT, K.B.

[Letter-Book.]

[24th October, 1798.]

My Lord,

This day, at noon, I arrived off Malta, and joined the
Marquis de Niza, who very handsomely had shifted his Flag
from the Principe to the Sebastian, in order to continue the
blockade, and to permit Colossus to proceed in the execution
of your orders. The Principe and Rainha being under the
necessity of going to Naples to refit, the Marquis I have
ordered to Naples, as now he is not wanted here, to refit, and

be ready to act as the times may require, and the King of
Naples may wish him. I do not like going back from the
eastward, but I give up my own opinion for this time, as
it is impossible to foresee how the new war may turn out.
Although I have no fears, yet it is good to be on the watch.
I have only time to say, that I will do my best, being ever,
with the greatest respect, &c.,

HORATIO NELSON.

---

### TO THE MARQUIS DE NIZA.

[Order-Book.]

Vanguard, off Malta, 24th October, 1798.

Ordered the Marquis de Niza to proceed to Naples with the
Squadron of Her Most Faithful Majesty, to re-fit with all expedition, and victual to three months, if provisions can be
procured, and to hold himself in readiness to put to sea on
the first notice. And should his Sicilian Majesty request his
services, it is my request that he will pay every attention to
his commands; and have written to Captain Troubridge to·
spare him what salt provisions he can spare, after victualling the Ships of my own Squadron, to the time specified.

HORATIO NELSON.

---

### TO HIS EXCELLENCY THE MARQUIS DE NIZA.

[Letter-Book and Autograph draught, in the Nelson Papers. On the 22nd of
October, the Marquis de Niza wrote to Lord Nelson, representing that, as he was
under Nelson's orders, he ought to be considered as an Admiral commanding an
English Squadron; and that the Officers of an inferior rank to himself ought to
be under his orders, when they were not under Nelson's eye, adding, "I do not
desire to have the power to direct them in the smallest degree contrary to any
commands they may receive from you, or from any Officer who is my senior; I
merely wish that they should have the same deference for me, that they would
show to any Officer of my rank, who has the honour of serving under you. It
is not any personal consideration which has urged me to make this representation;
but it is my duty to preserve the honour of my Nation, as well as my military
rank, and especially, the good of the service, and the support of discipline."—*Copy*,
in the Nelson Papers.

Vanguard, October 24th, 1798.

My Lord,

I am honoured with your Excellency's letter of this evening; and in my public situation I have the honour to acquaint

you, that I consider your Excellency as an Officer serving under my command, and standing precisely in the same situation as an English Rear-Admiral, junior to me ; which is, having no power or authority to give the smallest order to any Ship or Vessel, but those who I may think right to place, by order, under your command. I have the honour to be, &c.,

HORATIO NELSON.

---

TO THE MARQUIS DE NIZA.

[Letter-Book.]

Off Malta, October 24th, 1798.

My Lord,

Having answered your public Letter as my duty called upon me to do, I beg leave to assure you of my very great respect for your character, and that I shall not ever forget your zeal in the blockade of this place. If your Excellency had recollected, I am confident your knowledge of service would not have occasioned you the trouble of writing me a letter. On service with us it is necessary for the Commander-in-Chief, or the Officer Commanding by order from the Commander-in-Chief, to give the superior Officer, when thought right to detach, orders to take such Ships and Captains under his command, and also an order for the Captains of such Ships to obey their superior Officer serving under the Commander-in-Chief or detached Commander. In the present orders to your Excellency, no Ships are placed under your orders but those of Her Most Faithful Majesty. I am, &c.

HORATIO NELSON.

---

TO LADY HAMILTON.

[From " Lord Nelson's Letters to Lady Hamilton," vol. i. p. 3.]

Vanguard, off Malta, October 24, 1798.

My dear Madam,

After a long passage we are arrived, and it is as I suspected—the Ministers at Naples know nothing of the situation of the Island. Not a house or bastion of the Town is in possession of the Islanders, and the Marquis de Niza tells me, they want arms, victuals, and support. He does not know that any Neapolitan Officers are in the Island : perhaps, although, I have their names, none are arrived ; and it is very certain by the Marquis's account, that no supplies have been sent by the Governors of Syracuse or Messina.

However, I shall and will know everything as soon as the Marquis is gone, which will be to-morrow morning. He says, he is very anxious to serve under my command, and by his changing his Ship, it appears as if he was so : however, I understand the trim of our English Ships better. Ball will have the management of the blockade after my departure, as it seems' the Court of Naples thinks my presence may be necessary and useful in the beginning of November. I hope it will prove so, but I feel my duty lays at present in the East, for until I know the Shipping in Egypt are destroyed, I shall never consider the French Army as completely sure of never returning to Europe. However, all my views are to serve and save the Two Sicilies, and to do that which their Majesties may wish me even against my own opinion. When I come to Naples, and that Country is at war, I shall wish to have a meeting with General Acton on this subject.

You will, I am sure, do me justice with the Queen, for I declare to God my whole study is how to best meet her approbation. May God bless you and Sir William, and ever believe me, with the most affectionate regard,

Your obliged and faithful friend,<br>
Horatio Nelson.

I may possibly, but that is not certain, send in the enclosed letter. Show it to Sir William. This must depend on what I hear *and see*, for I believe scarcely anything I hear. Once more God bless you !

-----

TO THE FRENCH GENERAL AND ADMIRAL COMMANDING IN THE TOWN OF VALETTA AND PORT OF MALTA.

[Letter-Book. " 25th October, came on board, the Maltese General and several of the Elect of the Maltese People."—*Journal.*]

His Britannic Majesty's Ship Vanguard,<br>
Off Malta, 25th October, 1798.

Gentlemen,

In addressing to you this letter containing my determination respecting the French now in Malta, I feel confident that

you will not attribute it either to insolence or impertinent
curiosity, but a wish of [having] my sentiments clearly understood.  The present situation of Malta is this : the inhabitants
are in possession of all the Island, except the town of Valetta,
which is in your possession—that the Islanders are in arms
against you—and that the Port is blockaded by a Squadron
belonging to his Britannic Majesty.  My objects are to assist
the good People of Malta in forcing you to abandon the Island,
that it may be delivered into the hands of its lawful Sovereign,
and to get possession of Le Guillaume Tell, Diane, and Justice.
To accomplish these objects as speedily as possible, I offer that
on the delivery of the French Ships to me, that all the troops
and seamen now in Malta and Gozo, shall be landed in France
without the condition of their being prisoners of war; that I
will take care that the lives of all those Maltese who have
joined you shall be spared, and I offer my mediation with
their Sovereign for the restoration of their property.  Should
these offers be rejected, or the French Ships make their
escape, notwithstanding my vigilance, I declare that I will not
enter or join in any capitulation which the General may hereafter be forced to enter into with the Inhabitants of Malta,
much less will I intercede for the forgiveness of those who
have betrayed their duty to their Country.  I beg leave to
assure you this is the determination of a British Admiral; and
I have the honour to be, Gentlemen,

Your most obedient, humble servant,

HORATIO NELSON.

---

MEMORANDUM OF WHAT PASSED WITH THE DEPUTIES OF THE
ISLAND OF MALTA AND MYSELF.

[From a Copy in the Nelson Papers.]

[About 25th October, 1798.]

On Wednesday, October 24th, I arrived off the Islands of
Gozo and Malta.  I saw the French colours flying on the
Castle of Gozo, and in the Town of Malta.  I learned from
Captain Ball that the Islanders were using every endeavour
to force the French to abandon the Island; and I also learned
with astonishment that not the smallest supply of arms or

ammunition had been sent from Sicily by the King of Naples. Sure I am his Ministers told me that the Governor of Syracuse had orders to supply secretly the Inhabitants of Malta with arms and ammunition, and that Officers were gone to Malta to encourage the Maltese in their resistance against the French; and when the Alexander sailed for Malta, I went with Sir William Hamilton to General Acton, to offer that the Alexander should carry to the Island any supplies the King might wish to send. The answer was to this effect, that supplies had been [furnished] and that there was nothing necessary to be [sent] from Naples. Conversations and letters on the subject of Malta, had frequently taken place between Sir William Hamilton, the [Marquis] de Gallo, and myself, and from them, particularly the conversation on Friday evening, the 12th of October, I was led to believe that promises of protection, with supplies of arms, ammunition, and provisions, had been given to the Inhabitants of Malta. What must have been my surprise, when I found that neither promises of protection, nor the smallest supply of arms, ammunition, or provisions, had been sent to the Island; and that so far from supplies of provisions being granted from Sicily, a quarantine had been laid on the Vessels of the good people of Malta, equal to those of the French.

---

TO CAPTAIN BALL, HIS MAJESTY'S SHIP ALEXANDER.

[Order-Book.]

25th October, 1798.

You are hereby required and directed to take under your command the Ships named in the margin,[2] their Captains having my directions to follow your orders, and to undertake the blockade of the Island of Malta, and to prevent as much as in your power any supplies of arms, ammunition, or provisions getting to the French Army or the Port in their possession, and to grant every aid and assistance to the Maltese, and consulting with the Maltese Delegates upon the best methods of distressing the Enemy, using every effort to

[2] Audacious, Goliath, Terpsichore, Incendiary.

cause them to quit the Island or oblige them to capitulate.
And, relying upon your zeal and abilities in the service, in the
event of a capitulation with the Enemy, the Island, Towns, and
Forts to be delivered to the Islanders, to be restored to their
lawful Sovereign, but to insist upon the French Ships, Guillaume Tell, Diane, and Justice, to be delivered up to you, with
all the French property in the place; and you are to dispatch
the Terpsichore to Naples, on the 14th November next, with
an account of your proceedings to that time.

HORATIO NELSON.

---

## TO CAPTAIN BALL.

[Order-Book.]

25th October, 1798.

You will grant Passports for all Vessels which the inhabitants may wish to send to Sicily, and endeavour to establish
a signal by which they may be known; and in case the
French should, after my departure, wish to enter into any
capitulation, you will pay strict attention to my declaration
of this day's date, and not entangle yourself by undertaking to
embark the troops for France.

HORATIO NELSON.

---

## TO JOHN SPENCER SMITH, ESQ., CONSTANTINOPLE.

[Letter-Book.]

Vanguard, off Malta, October 26th, 1798.

Sir,

Having only a left hand, I must trust to your forgiveness
for my making letters wrote by me as brief as possible. I
have received through my friend, Captain Hood, all your
most interesting letters and papers, inclosed from July 29th
to September 1st. Your zeal and ability in the arduous task
of making the Porte think and act right cannot sufficiently be
applauded, and will, I am sure, receive the full approbation of
our gracious King. Captain Hood has told you of his intention
of remaining as long as possible on the Coast of Egypt, and I
was in hopes of having English Ships to relieve him; but the

circumstances of the war just going to begin between Naples and France, in which the Emperor has promised to join, prevent for a few weeks my sending any Ships to Egypt, (where my whole heart is, for I long to see the destruction of Buonaparte and his boasted Armament;) but I hope this is of the less consequence, as doubtless the Turkish and Russian Fleets are, long before this time, off Alexandria. If they have taken Bomb-vessels with them, the Shipping are all destroyed; and if 10,000 men, (or half the number,) as I wrote you off Rhodes, Alexandria has fallen, and the whole Armament destroyed in a moment. Buonaparte, in that case must surrender. I most heartily rejoice that our Victory has given content to the Sublime Porte, and you will have the goodness to say what is proper for me, and when it is proper, for I am so totally ignorant of forms at Constantinople, that I rely on your goodness to act for me. The Neapolitan Minister at Constantinople wrote to his Court that the Grand Signior had ordered a present, as a mark of his approbation. As I have received no official communication of this circumstance, I cannot notice it. My views and instructions are as follow, respecting the disposition of his Majesty's Fleet, which at present consists of nine Sail of the Line, some Frigates, and Sloops.

Three Sail of the Line under Captain Hood off Alexandria, with two Frigates. Three Sail of the Line under Captain Ball, with two Frigates, blockading the Port of Malta, in which are two Ships of the Line, three Frigates, and 4000 French troops in the Town. The rest of the Island is in complete possession of the Islanders. The French are suffering great distress; and time and patience will, I doubt not, put it into our hands for the King of Naples, who is its legitimate Sovereign. One Ship of the Line is repairing at Naples.

With the two others, and two Sloops, I was anxious to go to Egypt from this place, (where I am come to arrange the blockade, and to give assistance to the loyal inhabitants,) but the King of Naples has begged me so earnestly that I would be at Naples in the first week in November, the commencement of the war, that I could not refuse him, especially as my orders are to protect the Kingdom of the Two Sicilies.

However, I hope soon to be able to make my appearance off Zante, Corfu, &c. I send you a Proclamation[3] I have wrote relative to those Islands. The Porte ought to be aware of the great danger at a future day of allowing the Russians to get footing at Corfu, and I hope they will keep them in the East.

It will be pleasant to me to know exactly the movements of at least the Turkish Naval force, and of its intention for the next three months. If I know the wishes of the Porte, and it comes within the possibility of my complying, I shall be happy in doing it. Believe me, dear Sir, with the greatest respect, &c.

HORATIO NELSON.

---

### TO FRANCIS WERRY, ESQ., CONSUL AT SMYRNA.

[Autograph, in the possession of John Werry, Esq., of Smyrna.]

Vanguard, off Malta, 26th October, 1798.

Sir,

I have to acknowledge the receipt of your letters of the 4th and 7th September, and am much obliged to you for the care you have taken in forwarding Mr. Smith's dispatches, as well as for your congratulations on my recent Victory over the French fleet.

I hope soon to hear of the destruction of their whole Armament at Alexandria by the Turkish and Russian Fleets, and of the fall of Buonaparte. Malta is blockaded by a part of the Squadron under my command, and the Maltese who have revolted against the French, are in complete possession of the Island, except the Town of Valetta, and the French are in great distress for the want of provisions, and will, I hope, soon surrender. His Sicilian Majesty is going to head his own troops against the French, and will be assisted by the Emperor, who has sent General Mack to command the Sicilian troops. The French that landed in Ireland have all surrendered to the Marquis Cornwallis, the account of which is published in a Gazette Extraordinary of the 14th September. For any other information, I must refer you to Captain Hoste,[4] and request

---

[3] Vide p. 147.          [4] Of the Mutine Brig, by whom this Letter was sent.

you will furnish me in return with every information in your power, but particularly with the movements of the Turkish and Russian Fleets. I have the honour to be, &c.,

HORATIO NELSON.

---

TO THE RIGHT HONOURABLE SIR WILLIAM HAMILTON, K.B.

[Letter-Book.]

Vanguard, off Malta, 27th October, 1798.

My dear Sir William,

Although I believe I shall be at Naples before the Cutter, yet I should be sorry to omit acknowledging your kind letter of the 20th. When I come to Naples I can have nothing pleasant to say of the conduct of his Sicilian Majesty's Ministers towards the inhabitants of Malta, who wish to be under the dominion of their legitimate Sovereign. The total neglect and indifference with which they have been treated, appears to me *cruel* in the extreme. Had not the English supplied fifteen hundred stand of arms, with bayonets, cartouch boxes, and ammunition, &c., and the Marquis[5] supplied some few, and kept the spirit of these brave Islanders from falling off, they must long ago have bowed to the French yoke. Could you, my dear Sir William, have believed, after what General Acton and the Marquis de Gallo had said in our various conversations relative to this Island, that nothing had been sent by the Governor of Syracuse *secretly*—was the word used to us—or openly, to this Island? And I am further assured that the Governor of Syracuse never had any orders sent him to supply the smallest article. I beg your Excellency will state this in confidence to General Acton. I shall most assuredly tell it to the King. The justice I owe myself, now I feel employed in the service of their Sicilian Majesties, demands it of me, and also the duty I owe our gracious King, in order to show that I am doing my utmost to comply with his Royal commands.

As I have before stated, had it not been for the English, long, long ago, the Maltese must have been overpowered.

5 Of Niza.

Including the fifteen hundred stand of arms, given by us, not more than three thousand are in the Island. I wonder how they have kept on the defensive so long. The Emerald will sail, in twenty-four hours after my arrival, for Malta. At least two thousand of small arms complete, ammunition, &c., should be sent by her. This is wanted to defend themselves: for offence, two or three large mortars, fifteen hundred shells, with all necessaries, and perhaps a few artillery, two 10-inch howitzers, with 1000 shells. The Bormola, and all the left side of the Harbour, with this assistance, will fall. Ten thousand men are required to defend those works, the French can only spare twelve hundred; therefore, a vigorous assault in many parts, some one must succeed. But who have the Government of Naples sent to lead or encourage these people? A very good, and I dare say, brave old man, enervated, and shaking with the palsy. This is the sort of man that they have sent, without any supply, without even a promise of protection, and without his bringing any answer to the repeated respectful memorials of these people to their Sovereign. I know their Majesties must feel hurt when they hear these truths. I may be thought presuming, but I trust General Acton will forgive an honest seaman for telling plain truths. *As for the other Minister,*[7] *I do not understand him.* We are different men. He has been bred in a Court, and I in a rough element, but I believe my heart is as susceptible of the finer feelings as his, and as compassionate for the distress of those who look up to me for protection. The Officer sent here should have brought supplies, promises of protection, and an answer from the King to their Memorials. He should have been a man of judgment, bravery, and *activity*. He should be the first to lead them to glory, and the last, when necessary to retreat: the first to mount the wall of the Bormola, and never to quit it. This is the man to send. Such, many such, are to be found. If he succeeds, promise him rewards: my life for it the business would soon be over.

God bless you! I am anxious to get this matter finished. I have sent Ball this day to summon Gozo: if it resists, I shall send on shore, and batter down the Castle. Three

---

[7] The Marquis di Gallo.

Vessels loaded with bullocks, &c. for the Garrison, were taken yesterday from Tripoli: ten more are coming, but we shall have them.  I had almost forgot to mention that orders should be immediately given that no quarantine should be laid on Boats going to the Coast of Sicily for corn.  At present, as a matter of favour, they have *fourteen* days only.  Yesterday there was only four days' bread in the Island: luckily we got hold of a Vessel loaded with wheat, and sent her into St. Paul's. Once more, God bless you! and ever believe me,

Your obliged and affectionate,

HORATIO NELSON.

This day I have landed twenty barrels of gunpowder, (2800 lbs.) at Malta.

---

TO MR. SIMON LUCAS, CONSUL-GENERAL AT TRIPOLI.

[Letter-Book.]

Sir,                              Vanguard, off Malta, 27th October, 1798.

Out of respect to your situation as Consul-General at Tripoli, I have permitted the Spanish Brig Virgine del Carmen to pass, which Brig brought numerous dispatches for the French Army in Malta, and which (no thanks to you) fortunately fell into my hands.

I am much displeased that you should grant Passes to the Ships of any Power with whom we are at war, and more particularly so to one coming avowedly with dispatches to the French Army, blockaded by the Squadron under my command in Malta; and I must request that you will not give Passes to any Vessels of this description in future, and to announce to the Basha of Tripoli that Malta is blockaded by the British Fleet, and that I look for its surrender in a short time—all the Island, except the Town of Valetta, being in possession of the Islanders who have revolted against the French.              I am, &c.,

HORATIO NELSON.

P. S.—I send you a copy of the orders of the Sublime Porte, which you will not fail to communicate to the Basha, and make my respects to him. He is, I hear, our good friend.

H. N.

## TO ADMIRAL THE EARL OF ST. VINCENT, K.B.

[From a Copy in the Admiralty, and London Gazette of the 25th of December, 1798. " Sunday, 28th October, saw three Sail coming out of Malta, made the signal for a general chase. They proved to be Greeks, took possession of two of them." " Monday 29th, sent a Summons by Captain Ball of H. M. Ship Alexander to the French Garrison of Gozo, and proposed articles of capitulation." " Wednesday 31st, received from the Alexander 115 French prisoners of the garrison of Gozo, which had surrendered, and sent the same number on board the Minotaur. At 6, bore up and made sail in company with the Minotaur for Naples." The prisoners were sent from Naples to Nice.—*Journal.*]

Vanguard, at Sea, 1st November, 1798.

My Lord,

I have the honour to transmit you a letter received from Captain Ball, dated October 30th, together with the Capitulation of the Castle of Gozo, and a list of ordnance, &c., found in it. The prisoners are now embarked in the Vanguard and Minotaur till I can get a Vessel to send them to France. Captain Ball, with three Sail of the Line, a Frigate, and Fire-Ship, is entrusted with the blockade of Malta, in which are two Sail of the Line and three Frigates ready for sea; and from the experience I have had of Captain Ball's zeal, activity, and ability, I have no doubt but that, in due time, I shall have the honour of sending you a good account of the French in the Town of Valetta. I am, &c.,

HORATIO NELSON.

## TO ADMIRAL THE EARL OF ST. VINCENT, K.B.

[Letter-Book.]

Vanguard, at Sea, November 2nd, 1798.

My Lord,

Having left Captain Ball to blockade Malta with the Ships named in the margin,[8] and embarked the French prisoners taken at Gozo in the Vanguard and Minotaur, I left the Island the 30th, at night, and am now on my way to Naples.

On October 25th, the Flora Cutter (who I had sent to Egypt, September 11th, off Strombolo) joined me, with letters from Captain Hood, of September 27th. All were

[8] Alexander, Goliath, Audacious, Terpsichore, Incendiary.

well in his Squadron, and Captain Hood was determined to continue the blockade of Alexandria as long as possible, agreeable to my orders by the Flora, which I rejoice at, as I hope the Turkish and Russian Squadrons will be on that Coast soon after Captain Hood wrote me, for I have letters from Mr. Spencer Smith at Constantinople to the 2nd of September, and he tells me, the Turkish Ships, seven Sail-of-the-Line, &c., were ready to sail, and I know the Russian Squadron, list enclosed, arrived on the 4th. I send you several copies and papers enclosed. His letters had nothing extraordinary in them except a strong recommendation to keep our Ships in discipline. On the 26th, I sent the Mutine to Smyrna, with letters for Mr. Smith at Constantinople— an answer returns in seven days to Smyrna. I urged the immediate necessity, if not already sailed, of sending the Turks and Russians to Egypt, and desired to know the place of the campaign for the next three months, both by land and sea, and that I should readily give every support to them in my power.

It would appear from Captain Hood's advices from Alexandria that Buonaparte's whole force does not exceed 23,000 men, many of whom are in a dysentery. Murat Bey has 20,000 men above Cairo, and Ibrahim Bey has more than that number below Cairo, both on the Syria side of the Nile. Buonaparte has been trying to open a treaty with the Abyssinians on the one side, and preparing the Transports at Alexandria on the other. He must soon move from Cairo— that is very certain. I long to send Ships to Egypt; for I fear to trust any business of importance to any but English. I do not expect the Portuguese will soon be ready to sail from Naples unless for Lisbon, which I learn they are very desirous of doing. They reckon for numbers with me, and I reckon them as nothing to be depended upon.

I have the honour to be, &c.,

HORATIO NELSON.

## TO ADMIRAL THE EARL OF ST. VINCENT, K.B.

[From Clarke and M'Arthur, vol. ii. p. 125. The Vanguard and Minotaur arrived at Naples on the 5th of November, and found there the Culloden and Alliance, and the Portuguese Squadron.]

Naples, 7th November, 1798.

I am, I fear, drawn into a promise that Naples Bay shall never be left without an English Man-of-War. I never intended leaving the Coast of Naples without one; but if I had, who could withstand the request of such a Queen? Leghorn must be speedily attended to : the Grand Duke, I fancy, begins to *see fear*. I hold still sending Troubridge with Minotaur, Emerald, and Flora Cutter to Corfu and those Islands : if nothing can be done there, to go to Egypt, and see and arrange all matters in those Ports, either by victualling Hood's Squadron, staying himself, or, which I have reason to hope, finding the Turks and Russians willing to continue the blockade, to withdraw our Ships from that distant Coast. Your new expedition will, I doubt not, far exceed our most sanguine wishes; for I can say with truth, that you do not mind stripping yourself to take care that the service at a distance should, as far as human prudence can do, secure success. I am a living example of your goodness in that respect, for such a select band, as you gave me, never can, I fear, be equalled; and, I trust, that our Country will not forget that it was principally to you my success has been owing. The King goes to the Army to-morrow; in three days, he hopes to march. His Majesty is determined to conquer or die at the head of his Army, which is composed of 30,000 healthy good-looking troops. I am, &c.

HORATIO NELSON.

---

## TO CAPTAIN LOUIS, H. M. SHIP MINOTAUR.

[From Clarke and M'Arthur, vol. ii. p. 124.]

7th November, 1798.

Sir,

I have this moment received your letter enclosing a Petition from the Ship's company of the Minotaur. In the common course of Service, I ought not to pay attention either to the

Petition of your Ship's company, or to your kind interference in their behalf. I am glad, however, that the prisoners[9] have not presumed to say a syllable on their conduct, which merits the yard-arm.

But, Sir, I can never forget your noble and effectual support to my Flag on the most glorious First of August; and, in remembrance of the gallant conduct of the Minotaur's Ship's company, in obedience to your orders, I do, from these considerations alone, permit you to withdraw your letter for a Court-Martial on the prisoners. I am, &c.

HORATIO NELSON.

---

### TO CAPTAIN LOUIS, H. M. SHIP MINOTAUR.

[From Clarke and M'Arthur, vol. ii. p. 124.]

Private.

7th November, 1798.

I have endeavoured to write such a letter as I wish to be placed in public, and read to your Ship's company. Believe me, I shall never forget your support. ' A friend in need is a friend indeed:' never was it better applied than to the Minotaur. I have written to Troubridge to stop the Court-Martial according to your request. I am, &c.

HORATIO NELSON.

---

### TO ADMIRAL THE EARL OF ST. VINCENT, K.B.

[From Clarke and M'Arthur, vol. ii. p. 128.]

9th November, 1798.

I believe Lady Hamilton has written so fully, and I will answer, so ably, on all subjects, that but little remains for me to say. Your commands respecting the Queen were executed with so much propriety, that if I had never before had cause for admiration, it must then have commenced : her Ladyship's and Sir William's inexpressible goodness to me, is not to be told by words; and it ought to stimulate me to the

---

[9] Two men who had been guilty of mutinous conduct.

noblest actions, and I feel it will.  My mind I know is right, but, alas! my body is weak.  Captain Thompson's action[1] reflected great credit on the Leander.  I am, &c.,

HORATIO NELSON.

TO HIS ROYAL HIGHNESS THE DUKE OF CLARENCE.

[From Clarke and M'Arthur, vol. ii. p. 128.]

[About 10th November, 1798.]

I know my letter to your Royal Highness, by the Leander, was lost by the unfortunate capture of that Ship, and I trust you will forgive my not writing so much as my inclination, in truth, prompts me to do ; but I find my left hand is fully employed, in not only the business of the Squadron, but also in working for the good cause in this Country.  The Army marched on the 23rd of November, into the Roman State, 32,000 men.  Five thousand men embarked yesterday, on board my Squadron, destined to possess Leghorn, if the Grand Duke wishes to preserve his Dominions from plunder and anarchy.  By possessing that Port, any number of troops and stores may be pushed in a few days into Tuscany ; and if the French leave Leghorn on their left, they may be cut off.  But the great difficulty their Sicilian Majesties feel, is the want of money to continue a war, in which they find themselves engaged, from the anger of the French to all Monarchs, and their determination to plunder this fine Kingdom of Tuscany, when all Italy will have had the Fraternal embrace, and be equally miserable.  The King, Queen, Generals Acton and Mack, have all assured me, and I am convinced, that this Country cannot, under its present difficulties, carry on the war without pecuniary assistance from us; and I hope that the King, who is all goodness, will use his influence that assistance in money may be given, to save this Monarchy from the destruction which otherwise awaits it : and, allow me to say, what no English merchant will deny, that our trade to Italy, under its proper Government, is most advantageous to Great Britain.  I hope God will also put it into the heart

---

[1] Defending the Leander against Le Généreux.

of the Emperor, to assist his father-in-law and his brother.—
The wind moderates, and I am going off, to try and sail.
My heart is true to the good cause, and I wish to approve
myself a faithful Servant to the best of Masters. May God
bless your Royal Highness, is the sincere prayer of your attached and affectionate,

HORATIO NELSON.

---

### TO CAPTAIN TROUBRIDGE, H.M. SHIP CULLODEN.

[Autograph draught, in the Nelson Papers. This order was not carried into
effect. See the next Letter.

Vanguard, Naples Bay, November 11th, 1798.

Sir,

Having taken under your command the Ships named in
the margin,[2] you will proceed to sea without a moment's loss
of time, and passing through the Faro of Messina, make the
best of your way to the Island of Zante; and if the Russians
have not taken possession of that Island and Cephalonia, you
will send on shore by the Priest [whom] I shall desire to accompany you, my Declaration.[3] If you can get possession of
those Islands before named, you will send my Declaration
into the Island of Corfu, and use your utmost endeavours to
get possession of it; but in the event of any Capitulation, no
French soldier shall be sent to Ancona, or into any part of
Italy except Nice, (which, as prisoners to be confined.) Should
the Russians have taken possession of these Islands and be
cruizing near with the Turkish Fleet, you will pay a visit to
the Turkish Admiral, and by saluting him (if he consents to
return gun for gun) and every other mark of respect and attention, gain his confidence. You will judge whether he is of
a sufficient rank to hold a confidential conversation with. If
he is, you will request and appear. [?]　I am, &c.

HORATIO NELSON.

[2] No Ships are named in this draught.　　　　[3] Vide p. 147.

TO EARL SPENCER.

[Letter-Book.]

Camp, St. Germaines, 13th November, 1798.

My Lord,

A desire from his Majesty called me here yesterday to concert with General Mack and General Acton the commencement of the War. Thirty thousand of, *Mack says,* " *La plus belle Armeé d'Europe,*" was drawn out for me to see, and as far as my judgment goes in those matters, I agree, that a finer Army cannot be. In the evening we had a Council, and it was settled that four thousand Infantry and six hundred Cavalry should take possession of Leghorn. The Infantry (having stopped Captain Troubridge's Squadron for Corfu) I shall embark in the Vanguard, Culloden, Minotaur, two Portuguese Ships, (if I can get them ready, not that I see they have any wants,) and Alliance Store-ship. A Neapolitan Ship brings the Cavalry in a Convoy after us. The King's order for the destination was to be given to me, and when at sea I was to give it to the General commanding the troops, who was to be totally ignorant that Leghorn was the object and not *Malta,* which, as a secret, was communicated to him. His Majesty approved of this plan, and Mack was to march—I repeat it with pleasure—with thirty thousand of the finest troops in Europe, on Saturday the 17th, to Rome, and keep advancing, trusting to the support of the Emperor. Every hour the French are increasing their Italian Army, and two new Generals are arrived at Rome.

Thus I went to bed last night, and at six this morning came to take leave of their Majesties. I found them in great distress. The Courier who left London on the 4th has not brought any assurance of support from the Emperor. M. Thugut is evasive, and wishes, he says, the French to be the aggressors. It is aggression, if this Court knows, all the World knows, that the French are collecting an Army to over-run Naples; in a week destroy the Monarchy, plunder, and make it a Republic. As this is fully known, surely it is an aggression of the most serious nature. The Emperor's troops have not yet been in the habit of retaking Kingdoms, and it is easier to destroy than restore. I ventured to tell their Majesties directly that one of the following things must happen to the King, and he had his choice,—'Either to advance, trusting to God for his blessing on a just Cause, to die with *l'épée à la main*, or remain quiet and be kicked out of your Kingdoms.' The King replied he would go on, and trust in God, and desired me to stay till noon to consult with Mack on this new face of affairs.

November 15.—I came from the King after dinner, and their Majesties both told me that things stood precisely as they did before the receipt of the dispatches from London and Vienna. There was evidently a great disappointment at not getting money from England. That they want [it] is certain, nor do the Ministers, I believe, know how to get it. Their paper money is at forty per cent. discount. I long ago told the Queen I did not think Mr. Pitt would go to Parliament and ask money of the Country in the present moment; that if England saw every exertion made in this Country to save themselves, John Bull was never backward in supporting his friends in distress. Good God, my Lord, can the Emperor submit to this!

November 18.—Last evening Lady Hamilton received a letter from the Queen, full of the idea that money was indispensable, and desired her Ladyship to show it to me, and that I would say what I saw. That I can do very soon. I see the finest Country in the world full of resources, yet not enough to supply the public wants: all are plundering who can get at Public money or stores. In my own line I can speak. A Neapolitan Ship of the Line would cost more than ten English Ships fitting out. Five Sail of the Line must ruin the Country. Everything else is, I have no doubt, going on in the same system of thieving. I could give your Lordship so many instances of the greatest mal-conduct of persons in Office, and of those very people being rewarded. If money could be placed in the Public chest at this moment, I believe it would be well used; for the sad thing in this Country is, that, although much is raised, yet very little reaches the Public chest. I will give you a fact: when the Order of Jesuits was suppressed in this Country and Sicily, they possessed very large estates. Although these, with every other part of their property, were seized by the Crown, yet to this moment, not one farthing has reached the Public chest. On the contrary, some years the pretended expense of management was more than the produce. Taxes have been sold for sums of money, which now are five times more than when sold. This, it is true, was done by Viceroys to please their distant Masters: but I am tiring your patience. In short, their Majesties look to us for every succour, and without it they are undone.

I have wrote to the Turkish and Russian Admirals, and shall take care to keep on the very best footing with all the Allied Powers. Believe me, &c.

NELSON.[4]

------

TO HIS EXCELLENCY THE MARQUIS DE NIZA.

[Letter-Book.]

Most Secret.

Vanguard, Naples, 15th November, 1798.

My Lord,

As I want all the Ships under my command to be ready for sea by Saturday next, I have to request you will order

------

[4] This is the first Letter that has been found signed by Nelson with his Title of Honour. It appears that the London Gazette, announcing his creation, reached him late on the 17th, or on the 18th of November, as his Letters of the 17th bore his former signature. He did not receive Lord Spencer's official announcement of his elevation to the Peerage until the 7th of December.

Lord Spencer's answer to this Letter was written on the 25th of December, 1798, of which the following are the only material passages:—"I perceive by your subsequent Letters, that the plan laid down in yours of the 9th October, was afterwards altered, and in the present state of the Enemy's force, (or rather weakness,) in the Mediterranean, I think it was altered much for the better; for by dividing yours, you will have carried alarm and activity into many points at once, and as far as we can judge, by the very uncertain information we get through France, you have already done a great deal. I am happy to find that the Culloden was capable of being continued in service, as I well know the value you so deservedly set on Captain Troubridge's assistance. In the strict execution of the King's orders respecting the Medals to be given on occasion of the Battle of the Nile, Captain Troubridge, not having actually been in action, would have been excluded; but I am very happy to tell you, that I have been expressly authorized by his Majesty to present him with a Medal, as well as all the other Captains in the Line on that day, for his services both before and since, and for the great and wonderful exertions he made, at the time of the Action, in saving and getting off his Ship." In another Letter of the same date Lord Spencer said, "I have long since felt very confident that the Battle of the Nile will prove to have as effectually beat the Land part, as it did the Naval part, of the French Armament, with the additional advantage of giving them room enough to rivet the hatred and detestation of a Frenchman in the minds of all the inhabitants of that part of the world, as firmly as it is now fixed in those of Europeans."—*Autograph*, in the Nelson Papers.

every expedition to be used with the Squadron under your command, and that they may be ready by that time, as they are wanted for a short Expedition of great consequence.　If all cannot be got ready I should be glad to be informed by Thursday evening how many Ships can be ready.

I have the honour to be, &c.,<br>HORATIO NELSON.

---

TO HIS EXCELLENCY THE ADMIRAL COMMANDING THE<br>OTTOMAN FLEET.

[Letter-Book.]

Vanguard, Naples, 17th November, 1798.

Sir,

The Grand Signior having condescended to notice my earnest endeavours to serve the cause of humanity against a set of impious men, I should feel sorry to miss an opportunity of expressing to you how anxious I am for the success of the Ottoman Arms, and how happy your Excellency would make me by telling me how I can be most useful to you, for believe me, with the highest respect, your Excellency's most obedient and most humble servant,

NELSON.

---

TO HIS EXCELLENCY THE ADMIRAL COMMANDING THE<br>RUSSIAN FLEET.

[Letter-Book.]

Vanguard, Naples, 17th November, 1798.

Sir,

As I learn that his Excellency the Russian Minister at this Court is going to send off a courier to your Excellency, I greedily embrace the opportunity of paying my respects, and of assuring you how happy I feel that we are so near each other, and working together for the good cause of our Sovereigns.　I shall be proud, when opportunity offers, of paying you my respects in person, and of assuring your Excellency how much I am,

Your most obedient and most humble servant,

NELSON.

TO CAPTAIN GAGE, H. M. SHIP TERPSICHORE.

[Order-Book.]

No. 1.   Secret.

Vanguard, 17th November, 1798.

Ordered, Captain Gage to proceed to Leghorn, to go on shore, and make inquiry for the Marquis de Silva, his Sicilian Majesty's Consul at Leghorn, and deliver him the dispatches sent herewith to his Minister, making sure that he will carry it himself. If he will, you are to get a receipt from him for said dispatch, and a promise to carry it safe. If not, you are to carry it yourself post to Pisa or Florence, but believe the Minister is at Pisa, with the Grand Duke; and, having so done, you are immediately to leave Leghorn and proceed to sea—then to open the Orders No. 2, and proceed to put them in execution.

NELSON.

---

TO CAPTAIN GAGE, H. M. SHIP TERPSICHORE.

[Order-Book.]

Vanguard, 17th November, 1798.

No. 2.   Most Secret, and not to be opened until the Malora bears N.E. 5 leagues.

Ordered Captain Gage to cruize between the Island Caprea and Leghorn, and to stay on this station until you are joined by me, taking particular care not to give the smallest intimation to any of his Officers of this my intention.

NELSON.

---

ORDERS TO THE CAPTAIN OF THE SICILIAN SQUADRON.[5]

[Order-Book.]

17th November, 1798.

Order to Chevalier Naselli, Captain of the Sicilian Frigate Sirena, to put himself under my command.

NELSON.

---

[5] The "Order-Book" contains similar notes to the above, of Orders having been issued by Lord Nelson to Don Carlo Vicuna and to Don Luigi de la Grennelais, Captains of His Sicilian Majesty's Ships Lion and Aretusa, to put themselves under

TO THE RESPECTIVE CAPTAINS.

[From a Copy in the Nelson Papers.]

Vanguard, Naples, 18th November, 1798.

It is the Rear-Admiral Lord Nelson's directions that the Troops be received on board the Squadron to-morrow morning, according to the arrangements made by General Fortiguerra, as under—viz.,

Vanguard—To receive the 1st, 2nd, 3rd, 4th, 5th, and 6th Companies of the Regiment of Terra di Lavoro.

Culloden—To receive the 7th, 8th, 9th, 10th, 11th, and 12th Companies of ditto.

Minotaur—To receive the 13th and 14th Companies of ditto, and the 1st and 2nd Companies of the Battalion of Esterre.

Alliance—To receive the 6th Company of the Battalion of Esterre, and a Detachment of Artillery.

The boats of the Squadron to attend the embarkation at the Mole near the Pratique House.

NELSON.

---

TO EVAN NEPEAN, ESQ., ADMIRALTY.

[Original, in the Admiralty.]

Vanguard, Naples, 18th November, 1798.

Sir,

I have the honour to acknowledge the receipt of your letter of the 3rd of last month, inclosing the copy of a letter to the Earl St. Vincent, and a copy of the 9th Article of the Treaty of the Porte, and am very happy that I had anticipated

---

his command, and of Orders to them to proceed off Malta and put themselves under the command of Captain Ball, dated on the 16th and 17th of November 1798. These Orders are of considerable importance, in relation to a question which it will afterwards be necessary to discuss—namely, the authority vested in Lord Nelson over the Sicilian Navy—as they show that it was of precisely the same description as he possessed over our own Ships, to the Captains of each of which an Order was issued, by Nelson, in the same words, to place himself under his command. It is remarkable that a commission for that purpose from his Sicilian Majesty has not been found in the Nelson Papers. He seems to have had the same authority over the Portuguese Squadron.

their Lordships' wishes. I here enclose the disposition of the Squadron under my command, and have the honour to be, Sir, &c. NELSON.

INCLOSURE.

Genoa, 29th September, 1798.

L'Amiral Nelson est entré dans le Port de Naples avec 4 Vaisseaux et 2 Frégates. On assure qu'il a envoyé le reste de l'Escadre à Gibraltar pour escorter les Vaisseaux pris aux François. On compte renforcer encore de 6 mille hommes la garnison de Corse, ces troupes partiront de Toulon.

---

TO THE REVEREND MR. NELSON. HILBOROUGH.

[Autograph, in the Nelson Papers.]

My dear Brother, Naples, November 20th, 1798.

I have a moment in which I can find time to write you a line to say that I earnestly pray that the Victory of which it has pleased God to make me a principal, may be useful to my Family. As to myself, the probability is that I shall never take my Seat in the House of Peers. My health has declined very much, and nothing keeps me on service but the thought that I am doing good. I am just going to sea, having 5000 troops embarked in my Squadron. Remember me most kindly to Mrs. Nelson, my dear Aunt, who I long to see. Tell her I remember her with the truest affection; to your children do not forget me, and believe me ever,

Your most affectionate brother,
NELSON.

---

TO COMMODORE STONE, HER FAITHFUL MAJESTY'S SHIP RAINHA.

[Order-Book.]

Vanguard, November 22nd, 1798.

Ordered, Commodore Stone to remain at this place, and to keep his Ship complete with provisions and water, to put to sea at a moment's warning; and in case of any unforeseen accident, to follow the directions of Sir William Hamilton, and embark the families and effects of the English and Portuguese, if necessary.

NELSON.

## TO ADMIRAL THE EARL OF ST. VINCENT, K.B.

[From a Copy in the Admiralty, transmitted to Mr. Nepean, in a Letter dated 29th November, 1798. The Vanguard, Culloden, Minotaur, Alliance, Bonne Citoyenne, and Flora Cutter, and the Portuguese Squadron, sailed from Naples on the 22nd of November, and arrived at Leghorn in the afternoon of the 28th, the *Journal* of which day contains the following passage :—" Came on board the British and Neapolitan Ministers, who were saluted. Summoned the Town of Leghorn in concert with the Neapolitan General, Naselli. At 8 P. M., the Governor consented to give up the place. Landed the troops, cannon, baggage, &c., with all expedition, and took possession.—A. M., sent Captains Troubridge and Hardy to take possession of two armed Ligurian polaccas and a Merchant-ship laying in the Roads."]

Vanguard, Leghorn, 28th November, 1798.

My Lord,

It having been considered at a Council held at the Camp at St. Germains, as a proper military measure, to take possession of Leghorn, I offered to embark the troops destined for this service, in the Squadron named in the margin,[6] under my command, and sailed from Naples with them on the 22nd. It blowing a strong gale on that night and the next day, none but the British Ships kept me company, with which I arrived here this day. The Ministers of their Majesties of Great Britain and the Two Sicilies came on board, and they thinking that a Summons in my name, as well as that of the Neapolitan General, would be proper, I submitted to their better judgment, and signed the Paper, No. 1. At 8, P.M. I received the Papers marked No. 2; Duke di Sangro's letter, No. 3; Mr. Wyndham's letter, No. 4. The troops were immediately landed, and possession taken of the Town and Fortress of Leghorn.

I have the honour to be, &c.

NELSON.

|  | Troops. |  | Troops. |
|---|---|---|---|
| [6] Vanguard | 884 | Principe Real | 827 |
| Culloden | 750 | Albuquerque | 823 |
| Minotaur | 811 | St. Sebastian | 758 |
| Alliance | 270 |  | —— |
|  |  |  | 5123 |

### SUMMONS TO THE GOVERNOR OF LEGHORN.

We, the Commanders of the troops of the King of the Two Sicilies, and of the Squadron of His Britannic Majesty, now before Leghorn, demand of the Governor of Leghorn, the free and instant admission of His Sicilian Majesty's troops into the Town and Fortress of Leghorn, and everything thereunto depending.

If you refuse, we have powers to enforce our just demand, which will undoubtedly instantly be done.

NASELLI, General.

NELSON, Rear-Admiral.

Accordata quanto sopra, mediante la Capitolazione firmata questa sera 28 Nov. 1798, alle ore sei e trè quarte, dai Ministri rispittivi delle Corte d'Inghilterra é Napoli.

DE LAVILETTE,

Genl. Govr. Interino.

---

### TO THE HONOURABLE WILLIAM WYNDHAM.

[Letter-Book.]

Vanguard, November 28th, 1798.

My dear Sir,

As far as relates to me, I beg you will assure the Chevalier Seratti, that I would willingly adopt the mode of procedure most agreeable to him for the advantage of the Grand Duke; but the Neapolitan General, it appears, only looks upon me as an agent for transporting him. He sends *his* Summons as he pleases. I shall rejoice to see you afloat—Leghorn does not at this moment receive me on shore. I am anxious to get to the support of the King of Naples.

Ever yours most faithfully,

NELSON.

I had not heard of the capture of Mahon.[7]

---

[7] Port Mahon and the Island of Minorca surrendered to the Combined forces, under Nelson's friend, Lieutenant-General the Honourable Charles Stuart, and Commodore John Thomas Duckworth, on the 15th of November, 1798.

## TO ADMIRAL THE EARL OF ST. VINCENT, K.B.

[From a Copy in the Admiralty.]

Vanguard, Leghorn Roads, 29th November, 1798.

My Lord,

This morning Captains Troubridge and Hardy, with the Boats of the Squadron, captured two (as they call themselves) Ligurian Ships of War, one of which is the Equality, of 22 guns, 170 men; the other named the Tigre, of 18 brass guns, and 110 men : also a large Ship from Palermo, laden with corn. I have the honour to be, &c.

NELSON.

---

## TO CAPTAIN TROUBRIDGE, H. M. SHIP CULLODEN.

[Order-Book.]

Vanguard, Leghorn Roads, 29th November, 1798.

Ordered Captain Troubridge to take under his command the Ships named in the margin,[8] and to cruize off Cape Del Melle, or in such a situation as most effectually to prevent all supplies of every kind from entering the Ports of Genoa, taking some favourable opportunity of looking into Toulon ; and, having signified to the King of the Two Sicilies and the Grand Duke of Tuscany that the Ports of Genoa are in a state of blockade, should any Vessel of either of those Nations presume, after this notice, to attempt entering those Ports, I recommend it to you to sink or burn them with their cargoes. At the same time, I could wish you to keep up a constant communication with Leghorn, where orders will be sent to you, from time to time, for your further proceedings.

NELSON.

---

## TO THE MARQUIS DE NIZA.

[Letter-Book.]

My Lord,        Vanguard, Leghorn Roads, 29th November, 1798.

I have to request that you will order Commodore (Captain) Mitchell of the St. Sebastian, with the Benjamin and Balloon

---

[8] Minotaur, Terpsichore, Bonne Citoyenne.

Brig, to put themselves under the Command of Captain Troubridge, of His Majesty's Ship Culloden, and when you have landed the troops which you have on board at this place, to proceed with the remainder of Her Most Faithful Majesty's Ships under your command, and join me at Naples.

I have the honour to be, &c.,

NELSON.

---

TO EARL SPENCER.

[Letter-Book.]

Vanguard, Leghorn, 29th November, 1798.

I am so much in the habit of writing my mind freely, that I cannot say what I wish in a stiff, formal letter. I am confident your Lordship will not expose me, should I occasionally write too freely of what I see and know. Under this impression, I say that the Portuguese Squadron are totally useless. The Marquis de Niza has certainly every good disposition to act well; but he is completely ignorant of *Sea* affairs. I expect to hear they have all had disasters, and that they are returned to Naples. All their Commanders are Commodores, and it is ridiculous to hear them talk of their rank, and of the impossibility of serving under any of my brave and good Captains, yet these men are English. I say Niza is by far the best amongst them, and I shall keep up a good harmony with him. Your Lordship will read the papers signed by the Ministers of the (at this time) Allied Powers. As to the Porte being neutral, that is impossible; and if the Neapolitan General does not consider it as I do, I will directly have orders sent to him to that effect. General Acton and the Queen will instantly see the propriety of the measure. To-morrow I return in the Vanguard to Naples. Troubridge, with Minotaur, Terpsichore, and Bonne Citoyenne, commands on the Northern Coast, and to the West. Believe me, my Lord, I will be active as long as I can, but my strength fails daily—therefore, pray make allowances for me; and believe me ever your most faithful and obliged,

NELSON.

I beg my kind respects to Lady Spencer.

## TO THE HONOURABLE WILLIAM WYNDHAM.

[Letter-Book.]

Vanguard, 30th November, 1798.

My dear Sir,

I have been thinking all night of the General and Duke of Sangro's saying, that the King of Naples had not declared War against the French. Now, I assert, that he has, and in a much stronger manner than the ablest Minister in Europe could write a Declaration of War. Has not the King received, as a conquest made by him, the Republican Flag taken at Gozo? Is not the King's Flag flying there and at Malta—not only by the King's absolute permission but by his orders? Is not the Flag shot at every day by the French, and returned from batteries bearing the King's Flag? Are not two Frigates and a Corvette placed under my orders? and they would fight the French, meet them where they may. Has not the King sent publicly from Naples, guns, mortars, &c., with Officers and artillery, to fight against the French in Malta? If those acts are not tantamount to any written Paper, I give up all knowledge of what is War. So far, then, I assert, that the General is authorized to seize all French and Ligurian vessels. But that is a small matter to what will happen, if he permits the many hundreds of French which are now in the Mole, to be neutral till they have a fair opportunity of being active. Even the interest of the Great Duke calls loudly that the Neapolitan General should act with vigour, for if all other schemes fail, they have one sure—viz., set one Vessel on fire, and the Port of Leghorn is ruined for twenty years. Pray say this to Seratti. I have, you know, no interest personal to myself in this advice. I wish the Great Duke to have no unnecessary risk, and for the Neapolitan General and myself to take all the odium on ourselves. Pray excuse this letter, but I could not resist writing it.

Ever yours, &c.,

NELSON.

## TO THE RIGHT HONOURABLE SIR WILLIAM HAMILTON, K.B.

[Letter-Book.  At 7 A.M., on the 30th of November, the Vanguard sailed from Leghorn for Naples, and arrived there on the 5th of December.]

Vanguard, [1st December, 1798.]

Sir,

I beg leave to acquaint you that on the troops of his Sicilian Majesty being put in possession of Leghorn, there were laying in the Mole a great number of French privateers, and some of such force as to do the very greatest mischief to our commerce, if permitted to sail from Leghorn.  The Neapolitan General commanding in Leghorn refuses to seize the French vessels, under pretence that the King of Naples is not at War with the French.[9]  I have therefore to request that your Excellency will demand that orders be instantly sent to the General at Leghorn for the seizure of every French vessel.

---

[9] The state of things at Leghorn, will be best understood by a perusal of the following characteristic Letter from Captain Troubridge to Lord Nelson, dated, Culloden, Leghorn Roads, 4th December, 1798:—"My Lord,—As soon as your Lordship was gone, I went on shore, and found a general hurry and movement. On inquiry, I learnt that something was intended to be done by the French and Genoese: of the latter, there were upwards of 3000.  I advised the old General to seize immediately all the French in the Mole, or let me; but he said his orders were very particular, not to make *War with the French*.  I asked him whether taking Rome was to be considered as an hostile transaction of the King of Naples ? If it was, why not act as his King had done ?  After using every argument in my power, offering to send them off myself in the Genoese small-craft, if he would seize them, for the safety of the place, at last he agreed; but took two days, and then wanted the whole of the Genoese vessels in ballast to be let go, and issued a proclamation, stating that they would be permitted.  I represented the matter to Mr. Wyndham as a thing quite contrary to our agreement, and we settled that I should act after the vessels came out for passports, to have no more trouble with the old fool.  In short, the General wanted, in addition, the whole of the French vessels to be liberated, and suffered to sail, which I absolutely refused—telling him I could stay no longer, as we did not get on with our business; and I believe the only thing that at last brought him to take any steps, was my telling him the Mole would be destroyed by fire, and, probably, the Town; and, in the bustle, the French, Genoese, &c., take the place from him.  This staggered him, and he agreed, as I have told you, to a half measure.  In short, your Lordship knows what a poor creature this General is.  I trust your Lordship will approve of my giving passports to the light Genoese tartans, to take away the vagabonds, which otherwise would have found means to commit much mischief.  I sent my miscreants, about 250, in two small boats to Genoa: stowing them close keeps them warm.  I have the honour to be, &c., T. TROUBRIDGE."—*Autograph*, in the Nelson Papers.

I forbear making those observations which the case will allow of, as I am satisfied the General means to do what he considers right for his Sovereign, even at the expense of the British commerce.

I have also to observe that about seventy Sail of Vessels calling themselves belonging to the Ligurian Republic, (before called Genoa,) are ready to sail, loaded with corn, for Genoa and France; and as Genoa is equally at war with Great Britain as the French—for I consider the self-named Ligurian Republic as at present only a Province of France —I submit to your Excellency the propriety of urging the Neapolitan Government not to permit the departure of this corn from Leghorn, which must expedite the entrance into Italy of more French troops. General Naselli has, at my request, laid an embargo on all Vessels, till he receives the orders of his Court. He sees, I believe, the permitting these Vessels to depart in the same light as myself, but there is this difference between us—the General prudently, and certainly safely, waits the orders of his Court, taking no responsibility on himself; I act, from the circumstance of the moment, as I feel it may be most advantageous for the honour of the Cause which I serve, taking all responsibility on myself.

I have the honour to be, &c.

NELSON.

---

TO ADMIRAL THE EARL OF ST. VINCENT, K.B.

[Letter-Book.]

Naples, December 6th, 1798.

My dear Lord,

My letter from Leghorn will tell you of my movements till that time. On my way back, I fell in with the Portuguese Squadron, who had got to my rendezvous, Porto Ferrajo. The Marquis deserves credit for his perseverance, but his Ships cannot do what ours can. Minotaur lost her fore-yard on the Roman coast, but we are got into Mr. Chesa's store-house, and hope to splice it. My arrangements respecting Corfu and Egypt have from necessity been overturned; and a part of my Squadron kept on this Coast of

Italy. Culloden, Minotaur, Terpsichore, and Bonne Citoyenne, with (if the Marquis pleases) two Portuguese Corvettes, are to cruize on the Coast off Cape Del Melle, and to look into Toulon. I expect dear Hood every moment from Egypt; his provisions must be very short; he deserves great credit for his perseverance. I hope the good Turk will have relieved him, but the Russians seem to me to be more intent on taking Ports in the Mediterranean than destroying Buonaparte in Egypt. I hear a Lieutenant from the Russian and Turkish Admirals is in search of me with letters from each. He left this place for Leghorn two days after I sailed. Alliance is missing, but I shall send her down the moment she arrives. The Flora Cutter I should have sent you from Leghorn, but she had parted from me on our passage.

I received yesterday, a private letter from Lord Spencer, of October 7, saying, that the First Lieutenants, of all the Ships engaged, would be promoted.[1] I sincerely hope this is not intended to exclude the First of the Culloden; for Heaven's sake, for my sake, if it is so, get it altered. Our dear friend Troubridge has suffered enough, and no one knows from me, but that Culloden was as much engaged as any Ship in the Squadron. His sufferings were in every respect more than any of us. He deserves every reward which a grateful Country can bestow on the most meritorious Sea-Officer of his standing in the service. I have felt his worth every hour of my command. I have before wrote you, my dear Lord, on this subject, therefore, I place Troubridge in your hands. I have heard nothing lately from Malta. The King has sent mortars to bombard the town, with some artillery.

The state of this Country is briefly this : The Army is at Rome, Città Vecchia taken, but in the Castle of St. Angelo are 500 French troops. The French have 13,000 troops at a strong post in the Roman State, called Castellana. General

---

[1] Lord Spencer, writing to Lord St. Vincent, on the 9th of October, 1798, said, " The exception of the First Lieutenant of the Culloden was necessary, on account of that Ship not having got into action, from the circumstance of being aground : I am, however, so fully convinced of the merit, both of Captain Troubridge and his Officers, on all occasions, that I beg you would be so good as to give the first vacancy of Commander that arises, to the First Lieutenant of the Culloden."

Mack is gone against them with 20,000: the event in my opinion is doubtful, and on it hangs the immediate fate of Naples.  If Mack is defeated, this Country, in fourteen days, is lost; for the Emperor has not yet moved his Army, and if the Emperor will not march, this Country has not the power of resisting the French.  But it was not a case of choice, but necessity, which forced the King of Naples to march out of his Country, and not to wait till the French had collected a force sufficient to drive him, in a week, out of his Kingdom.

I send this by Lieutenant Gregory, of the Swiftsure, and have requested Commodore Duckworth to forward it to your Lordship; and I beg, my dear Lord, you will believe me,

Ever your obliged and faithful,

NELSON.

---

TO ADMIRAL THE EARL OF ST. VINCENT, K.B.

[Letter Book.]

Naples, 6th December, 1798.

My dear Lord,

I send you a Letter I have this day received from Mr. Littledale, relative to the Culloden's vouchers not being signed; Captain Troubridge and Mr. Littledale being so completely different with right and wrong that I cannot undertake to settle it.   Mr. Littledale is not a Contractor or Agent-Victualler, but is to receive $2\frac{1}{2}$ per cent. on all money he lays out.   The point in dispute is, what Mr. Littledale did actually pay?   I wish, my Lord, these gentlemen had some appointment either as Contractors or Agent-Victuallers.   I leave all this matter to your better judgment.

Ever your obliged and faithful,

NELSON.

## TO COMMODORE DUCKWORTH.[2]

[Letter-Book.]

Naples, 6th December, 1798.

My dear Sir,

On my arrival here yesterday, I found Lieutenant Gregory who had been charged with your letters to me, but which were unluckily sent after me, to Leghorn; and as Lieutenant Gregory is very anxious to return to you, it is out of my power to answer such part of your public letter as might require one. However, I most heartily congratulate you on the conquest of Minorca—an acquisition invaluable to Great Britain, and completely in future prevents any movements from Toulon to the westward. My situation in this Country has had doubtless *one* rose, but it has been plucked from a bed of thorns. Nor is my present state that of ease; and my health, at best but indifferent, has not mended lately. Naples is just embarked in a new war: the event, God only knows; but, without the assistance of the Emperor, which is not yet given, this Country cannot resist the power of France. Leghorn is in possession of the King of Naples' troops, as is Cività Vecchia. I have Troubridge, Minotaur, Terpsichore, and Bonne Citoyenne, &c. on the north Coast of Italy. Three Sail of the Line, under Ball, are off Malta; and Hood, with three Sail of the Line and two Frigates, is in Egypt, but I expect his return every moment, and that the Turks and Russian Ships and Flotilla have relieved him. I am here *solus*, for I reckon the Portuguese as nothing. They are all Flag-Officers and cannot serve under any of my brave friends! I wish you may be able to forward my letters to Lord St. Vincent. It is important for him to know our state here. With every good wish, believe me, your most obedient Servant,

NELSON.

---

[2] Afterwards Admiral Sir John Thomas Duckworth. He received the Red Ribbon in June, 1801; commanded in Chief in the Battle of St. Domingo, in 1806; was made a Baronet, in 1813; and died in August, 1817.

TO THE HONOURABLE LIEUTENANT-GENERAL STUART.

[Letter-Book.]

My dear Sir,              Naples, 6th December, 1798.

Allow me to congratulate you on the conquest of Minorca —an acquisition as a Seaport invaluable to our Country. I hurried from Egypt early in August, as, by Earl St. Vincent's orders, I was in expectation of being summoned to attend you. However, I am sure my place was much better filled by Commodore Duckworth. The new war commenced here, is yet impossible to say how it may turn—whether it really hastens the ruin, or saves the Monarchy. At all events, if the King had not begun the war, he would have soon been kicked out of his Kingdom. The King is at Rome, but five hundred French still hold possession of St. Angelo. General Mack is gone to Città Castellana, where thirteen thousand French have taken post. Mack's force with him is twenty thousand fine young men, but with some few exceptions wretchedly officered. If the French are not soon driven from their Post, which is very strong by nature, Mack must fall back to the frontier on the side of Ancona. The French have drove back, to say no worse, the right wing of the King's Army, and taken all their baggage and artillery. The Emperor has not yet moved, and his Minister, Thugut, is not very anxious to begin a new war, but if he does not, Naples and Tuscany will fall in two months. I shall be happy if you will honour me at any time with your commands here or elsewhere, being with the highest respect,

Your most obedient Servant,

NELSON.

Commodore Duckworth's letters have not yet reached me.

---

TO EARL SPENCER.

[Letter-Book.]

My dear Lord,              Naples, 7th December, 1798.

On my arrival here from Leghorn I received your Lordship's letter of October 7, communicating to me the Title his

Majesty had been graciously pleased to confer upon me—an Honour, your Lordship is pleased to say, the highest that has ever been conferred on an Officer of my standing who was not a Commander-in-Chief.[3]

I receive as I ought what the goodness of our Sovereign, and not my deserts, is pleased to bestow; but great and unexampled as this Honour may be to one of my standing, yet I own I feel a higher one in the unbounded confidence of the King, your Lordship, and the whole World, in my exertions. Even at the bitter moment of my return to Syracuse, your Lordship is not insensible of the great difficulties I had to encounter in not being a Commander-in-Chief. The only happy moment I felt was in the view of the French: then I knew that all my sufferings would soon be at an end.

I observe what your Lordship is pleased to say relative to the presenting myself, and the Captains who served under my orders, with Medals, and also that the First Lieutenants of the Ships engaged will also be distinguished by promotions, also the senior Marine Officer. I hope and believe the word ' engaged ' is not intended to exclude the Culloden : the merit of that Ship and her gallant Captain are too well known to benefit by anything I could say. Her misfortune was great in getting aground, while her more fortunate companions were in the full tide of happiness. No : I am confident that my good Lord, Spencer will never add misery to misfortune. Indeed, no person has a right to know that the Culloden was not as warmly engaged as any Ship in the Squadron. Captain Troubridge on shore is superior to Captains afloat. In the midst of his great misfortunes he made those signals which prevented certainly the Alexander and Swiftsure from running on the Shoal. I beg your pardon for writing on a subject which, I verily believe, has never entered your Lordship's head, but my heart, as it ought to be, is warm to my gallant friends.

Ever your Lordship's most faithful and obedient,

NELSON.

[3] Vide p. 75, ante.

PASSPORT FOR THE FRENCH MINISTER ON QUITTING NAPLES.

TO THE CAPTAINS OF HIS MAJESTY'S SHIPS EMPLOYED IN THE
MEDITERRANEAN, AND THE COMMANDERS OF ALL ENGLISH
PRIVATEERS.

[Order-Book.]

By Horatio Lord Nelson, K.B., &c.

The Genoese Pink, La Madonna di Parto Salvo, whereof
Argita Ferraii is Master, having on board La Combe de St.
Michel, the Minister from the French Republic to the Court
of the Two Sicilies, with his suite and baggage, has, by desire of the said Court, my permission to pass in the said Pink
unmolested from the Bay of Naples to the Port of Genoa;
and it is my desire that any of his Majesty's Ships which
may fall in with the said Pink, afford him every assistance
to facilitate his voyage; and should any private Vessel of
War belonging to the English Nation meet with the said
Minister on his voyage, it is my desire that they will pay
attention to my Signature, and facilitate the passage of the
said Combe de St. Michel, with his suite and baggage, to
Genoa.

　　　　Given on board the Vanguard, Naples, 8th De-
　　　　cember, 1798.

　　　　　　　　　　　　　　　　　　NELSON.

---

TO CAPTAIN TROUBRIDGE, H. M. SHIP CULLODEN.

[Letter-Book.]

Naples, December 9th, 1798.

My dear Troubridge,

By Mr. Brodrick, who is going to Leghorn, I write you
this line—not of comfort. It is reported, and, indeed, is
certain, that the Neapolitan Officers, and many of their men,
are run away even at the sight of the Enemy. As must ever
be the case, several brave Officers have fallen. I know not
the extent of the disaster, but I believe it is very bad. Keep
something very often at Leghorn, for I think it very probable
that I may be forced to send for you in a hurry. Everything
you may send here, let them anchor cautiously if my Flag is
not here. What orders have been sent to General Naselli I

know not.   It was determined to order him to seize all French
and Ligurian vessels in the Mole ; but this sad history of the
Army may have driven everything out of their head.   I have
expected the Turkish and Russian Lieutenants for some days,
as also the Marquis.[4]   The Transport is arrived from Corfu,
159 men.[5]   I wish Minotaur had some of them.   Nothing from
dear Hood, or from Malta.   Sir William and Lady Hamilton
desire to be kindly remembered to you and Louis, and all our
friends with you.   God bless you, and believe me ever your
most faithful friend,

NELSON.

Duckworth has a Captain under him.   John Dixon from
England is Post Captain, and Mr. Grey arrived.

P.S.—I have just received Mr. Wyndham's letter of November 30th, and [find] that it is settled that all the cargoes of
the Genoese Ships should be landed, and all the French privateers disarmed, and their crews sent away. So far I am content.
Money is not our object, but to distress the common Enemy.
I hope, if you liked it, you visited the Grand Duke in my
stead : I could not have been better represented.   The Copy
is a d——d deal better than the Original.   Ever yours,

NELSON.

December 10th, 1798.

---

TO THE HONOURABLE WILLIAM WYNDHAM.

[Letter-Book.]

Naples, 10th December, 1798.

**My dear Sir,**
I am truly sensible of the high honour His Royal Highness
the Great Duke has paid me in desiring to see me at Pisa,
and I have to request that your Excellency will present my
most profound acknowledgments to His Royal Highness.   I
was under a sacred promise to return here as expeditiously as
possible, and not to quit the Queen and Royal Family of
Naples without her Majesty's approbation.   This will plead
my excuse for quitting Leghorn so expeditiously.   With
every sentiment of respect, believe me, &c.

NELSON.

[4] Of Niza.            [5] Of the Leander's crew.

## TO HIS EXCELLENCY THE HONOURABLE WILLIAM WYNDHAM.

[Letter-Book.]

My dear Sir,　　　　　　　Naples, 10th December, 1798.

Your several letters of November 30th, came to me this moment. Believe me, no person can set a higher value on your friendship than I do; for I know from experience that you have nothing more at heart than the honour of our King and Country. I rejoice to hear that the cargoes of corn in the Mole of Leghorn will be landed, and the Privateers disarmed, and the scoundrels belonging to them sent away. The Enemy will be distressed, and, thank God, I shall get no money. The world, I know, think that money is our God, and now they will be undeceived as far as relates to us. ‘ Down, down with the French!’ is my constant prayer. I hope that the Emperor is marched to support this Country; for, unused to war, its Officers seem alarmed at a drawn sword, or a gun, if loaded with shot. Many of them, peaceable heroes, are said to have run away when brought near the Enemy. The King and General Acton being at Rome, I know not what orders have been sent to General Naselli; but you may depend I will do nothing which can do away your just demand of retribution to our Merchants robbed by the French at Leghorn. I arrived here on the 5th of December, and found my presence very comfortable for the poor Queen. Ever believe me, &c.

NELSON.

---

## TO CAPTAIN BERRY, AT COOK AND HALFORD’S, BEAUFORT-BUILDINGS, LONDON.

[Autograph, in the possession of Lady Berry.]

Naples, December 10th, 1798.

My dear Berry,

I thank you most sincerely for your several kind letters, the last of November 1st. Your friend, Captain of Généreux,[6]

---

[6] Monsieur Lejoille. The treatment which the Officers and Crew of the Leander received on board Le Généreux was infamous. They were plundered of everything they possessed, Captain Thompson being even robbed of a miniature of his mother. At the very moment the Surgeon of the Leander was performing an

is by this time a prisoner to the Turks, and I dare say
they will off with his head. What a scoundrel he must
have been! I am so much rejoiced at your safety, after
all your perils, that I do not consider at the moment your
great sufferings. I trust that the King will confer the same
honours on you as if you had not been in the Leander:
indeed, your sufferings in her entitle you to more honours. Her
defence was glorious, and does Thompson and you the highest
credit. I have just got 159 of the Leander's from Corfu. I
rejoice that we are now Brother-freemen of London, as we
have before been in serving our Country. I shall never
forget your support for my mind on the 1st of August. I
have not a letter from England since Captain Capel's arrival,
except two private ones from Lord Spencer. Josiah is not
made Post, nor do I see any probability of that event. As to
my stay here, in truth it is uncertain; but if you can get the
Foudroyant out here, if I should go home for all next summer
to rest me, she will be a good Ship for you. My health certainly requires a little rest. We have got Leghorn. Malta
is blockaded by Ball. Hood commands in Egypt, and Troubridge on the north Coast of Italy. We are all united in our
Squadron: not a growler amongst us. I opened your note to
Mr. Campbell, and shall get the fan-mount, and I wish you
had thought of anything else. I should have great pleasure
in doing what you wish me; for believe me, with the greatest
attachment, your affectionate friend,

NELSON.

No charts, or anything of the kind, came to me from the
Spartiate. Galwey gave me the Sword which I presented to
Prince Leopold; but I have the one which you brought me
down the cock-pit,[7] which you shall have.

Best regards to, I *hope*, Lady Berry.

operation, he was robbed of his instruments, and Captain Thompson nearly lost his
life by the attendance of his Surgeon being forcibly withheld. To the remonstrances of the English Officers, Monsieur Lejoille coolly replied—" J'en suis faché,
mais le fait est que les François ne sont bons qu'au pillage."—Memoir of Sir Thomas
Boulden Thompson in the *Naval Chronicle*, vol. xiv. p. 10.

[7] During the Battle of the Nile.

TO THE RIGHT HONOURABLE SIR MORTON EDEN, K.B.,
MINISTER PLENIPOTENTIARY AT VIENNA.

[Letter-Book.]

Naples, December 10th, 1798.
My dear Sir,

Give me leave to thank you for your recollection of me some years back when you was at Copenhagen. I am afraid our friend Captain Payne[8] is in a very declining state of health: he is as good an Officer and man as ever lived.

I have also to thank you for your kindness to Captain Berry.[9] Poor fellow, he has suffered greatly both in body and mind, but I hope his reception in England will perfectly restore him. We have nothing from Egypt. I expect Captain Hood with the Squadron every hour, and hope that the Turks and Russians have long since carried such a body of troops as is necessary to take Alexandria, where all the Transports would be destroyed in half-an-hour. Malta is hard pressed, and in due time must fall, and as it belongs to the King of Naples, I think the Order will never be restored in *Malta*. The inhabitants hate them. With every sentiment of respect, believe me, dear Sir, your most obliged,

NELSON.

---

TO THE RIGHT HONOURABLE SIR MORTON EDEN, K.B.

[Letter-Book.]

Naples, December 10th, 1798.
My dear Sir,

I received with thanks your favour of November 15th, and perfectly agree with you that a delayed war on the part of the Emperor will be the destruction of this Monarchy, and of course, to the new-acquired Dominions of the Emperor in Italy. Had the war commenced in September or October, all Italy would at this moment have been liberated. This month is worse than the last; the next will render the contest doubtful, and in six months, when the Neapolitan *Republic*

---

[8] Apparently Captain Ralph Willett Payne, afterwards a Rear-Admiral.
[9] On passing through Vienna from Trieste to England.

will be organized, armed, and with its numerous resources
called forth, I will suffer to have my head cut off, if the Emperor is not only defeated in Italy, but that he totters on his
Throne at Vienna.    Pray assure the Empress from me, that
notwithstanding the councils which have shook the Throne of
her Father and Mother, I shall remain here, ready to save
the sacred Persons of the King and Queen, and of her Brothers
and Sisters, and that I have also left Ships at Leghorn, to
save the lives of the Great Duke and her Imperial Majesty's
Sister; for all must be a Republic, if the Emperor does not
act with expedition and vigour.    ' *Down, down* with the
French!' ought to be placed in the Council-room of every
Country in the world, and may Almighty God give right
thoughts to every Sovereign, is the constant prayer of your
Excellency's most obliged and obedient servant,

NELSON.

Whenever the Emperor acts with vigour, your Excellency
may say that a proper Naval force shall attend to the safety
of the Adriatic, as far as is in my power.

---

TO LADY NELSON.

[From Clarke and M'Arthur, vol. ii. p. 132.]

Naples, 11th December, 1798.

I have not received a line from England since the 1st of
October.    Lord St. Vincent is in no hurry to oblige me now:[1]
in short, I am the envied man, but better that than to be the
pitied one.    Never mind: it is my present intention to leave
this Country in May.    The poor Queen has again made me
promise not to quit her or her Family, until brighter prospects
appear than do at present.    The King is with the Army, and
she is sole Regent; she is in fact, a great King.    Lady

---

[1] Here is the first indication of that morbid irritability of temper under which
Nelson occasionally laboured during the remainder of his life, and which too often
showed itself in suspicion of the motives and conduct of his best friends.    This
change in his feelings, and which, unhappily, soon after extended towards his wife,
would find a sufficient, even if it were not the real cause, in the severe wound
in the head which he received at the Nile, of the effects of which he so frequently
complained.

Hamilton's goodness forces me out at noon for an hour. What can I say of hers and Sir William's attention to me? They are, in fact, with the exception of you and my good father, the dearest friends I have in this world. I live as Sir William's son in the house, and my glory is as dear to them as their own; in short, I am under such obligations, as I can never repay but with my eternal gratitude. The improvement made in Josiah by Lady Hamilton, is wonderful; your obligations and mine are infinite on that score; not but Josiah's heart is as good and as humane as ever was covered by a human breast. God bless him—I love him dearly, with all his roughness. Yours, &c.

NELSON.

TO EARL SPENCER.

[Letter-Book.

Naples, 11th December, 1798.

My dear Lord,

The Queen has again made me promise not to quit her and her Family till brighter prospects open upon her. She is miserable, we know. None from this house have seen her these three days, but her letters to Lady Hamilton paint the anguish of her soul. However, on inquiry, matters are not so bad as I expected. The Neapolitan Officers have not lost much honour, for God knows they had but little to lose; but they lost all they had. Mack has supplicated the King to sabre every man who ran from Città Castellana to Rome. He has, we hear, torn off the epaulets of some of these scoundrels, and placed them on good serjeants. I will, as briefly as I can, state the position of the Army, and its lost honour, for defeat they have had none. The right wing, of nineteen thousand men, under General St. Philip and Michaux, (who ran away at Toulon,) were to take post between Ancona and Rome, to cut off all supplies and communication. Near Fermi they fell in with the Enemy, about three thousand. After a little distant firing, St. Philip advanced to the French General, and returning to his men, said, ' I no longer command you,' and was going off to the Enemy. A sergeant said, ' You are a traitor: what! have

o 2

you been talking to the Enemy?' St. Philip replied, ' I no
longer command you.' 'Then, you are an Enemy!' and level-
ling his musket, shot St. Philip through the right arm. However, the Enemy advanced ; he was amongst them. Michaux
ran away, as did all the Infantry, and had it not been for
the good conduct of two Regiments of Cavalry, would have
been destroyed. So great was their panic, that cannon, tents,
baggage, and military chest—all were left to the French.
Could you credit, but it is true, that this loss has been sustained with the death of only forty men ? The French
lost many men by the Cavalry, and having got the good
things, did not run after an Army three times their number.
Some ran thirty miles to Pesaro. The peasantry took up
arms—even the women—to defend their Country. However,
the runaways are not only collected, but advanced to Arcoti,
which they took from the French, cutting open the gates with
hatchets. It is said they have got a good General—Cetto, a
Neapolitan Prince, and I hope will be ashamed of their former
conduct. General Michaux is bringing a prisoner to Naples.
    This failure has thrown Mack backward. It is the intention
of the General to surround Città Castellana. Chevalier de
Saxe advanced to Viterbi, General Metch [?] to Fermi, and
Mack, with the main body, finding his communication not open
with Fermi, retreated towards Città Castellana. In his route
he was attacked from an entrenchment of the Enemy, which
it was necessary to carry. Finding his troops backward, he
dismounted, and attempted to rally them, but they left their
General, and basely fled. The natural consequence was, he was
sorely wounded, but saved by some gallant Cavalry, and carried
off by the bravery of a coachman, and is safe, poor fellow, at
Rome, and hopes are entertained of his recovery. The fugitives fled to Rome, fancying the French at their heels, who
never moved from their entrenchment, which was carried
by another party of troops under General Dumas. It is reported that the King has stripped the Prince di Taranto,
Duc di Trani, of his uniform, and disgraced him. He commanded under Saxe, and fled amongst the first to Rome.
'Tis for the traitorous and cowardly conduct of these scoundrels
that the great Queen is miserable, knowing not who to

trust. The French Minister and his Legation went off by sea yesterday.

I have just had letters from the Turkish and Russian Admirals before Corfu, which they hope very soon will fall into their hands. With every sentiment of respect, believe me, your Lordship's most faithful servant,

NELSON.

I beg best respects to Lady Spencer and Lady Lucan.

---

### TO HIS EXCELLENCY THEODORE OUCHAKOFF, VICE-ADMIRAL OF THE RUSSIAN SQUADRON.

[Letter-Book.]

Naples, 12th December, 1798.

Sir,

I was honoured by your Excellency's kind and flattering letter of November 30th, and shall feel proud in cultivating your good and valuable friendship. On my return here a few days ago from Leghorn, I learnt that an Officer from you and his Excellency the Turkish Admiral, had been here and followed me to Leghorn; but as I unluckily missed them on my route, I am deprived of acknowledging the receipt of the letter your Excellency was so good as to write me by that Officer.

I have not yet heard of the junction off Alexandria, of a Turkish and Russian Squadron, with my valuable friend Captain Hood, who I left to command the blockade. I hope soon to hear that all the French shipping in Alexandria are destroyed, as also the whole French army in Egypt. Malta is blockaded by a Squadron of three Sail of the Line, and four Frigates. Mortars and cannon are lately sent from this Arsenal, for the use of the Maltese, who are 15,000 men in arms against the town of La Valetta.

Gozo, some time past, surrendered to his Majesty's arms. I instantly directed the Flag of the King of the Two Sicilies to be hoisted, and the Island delivered into the hands of its legitimate Sovereign, and the same shall be done with Malta, where the Neapolitan Flag is flying, and under which the brave Maltese are fighting. I am just returned from putting his Sicilian Majesty's troops in possession of Leghorn, having left a Squadron to cruize on the northern Coast of Italy. I have the satisfaction also of acquainting your Excellency that the Island of Minorca is taken from the Spaniards by an English Army and Squadron sent from Gibraltar; and I most fervently hope that Corfu will soon surrender to the efforts you are making against it, for believe me that the success of your Royal Master's arms, will be as happy to me as those of my good and gracious King. With every sentiment of respect, believe me,

Your Excellency's most obedient servant,
NELSON.

December 14th.—An English frigate is just arrived from Alexandria, and it is with real sorrow I find that no Squadron had, on the 26th November, arrived to relieve Captain Hood, who has long been in great want of being victualled and re-fitted. A Frigate or two, and ten Gun-boats, are all which have arrived, when certainly not less than three Sail of the Line, four Frigates, with Gun and Mortar vessels, should have been sent. Egypt is the first object—Corfu the second.

---

TO COMMODORE STONE, ON BOARD HER MOST FAITHFUL MAJESTY'S SHIP RAINHA.

[Order-Book.]

Vanguard, Naples Bay, 12th December, 1798.

Whereas I have received information that numbers of the Enemy's privateers are cruizing on the Coast, between Naples and the Island of Elba, and have lately taken several Vessels off Città Vecchia, you are, therefore, hereby required and directed to proceed to sea, without one moment's loss of time, and cruize for the space of twenty days from your getting outside of Ischia, between the Islands of Ponza and the Islands of Monte Christi and Giulio, approaching the Coast of the Continent when the weather will admit, and frequently sending a Boat to Città Vecchia, to inquire if Mr. Bertram, the English Consul, has any letters for you from me, and to gain

information. At the expiration of the above-mentioned time,
you are to join me in this Bay.

NELSON.

N.B.—The above Order was not carried into execution, on
account of the defeat and retreat of the Neapolitan Army.

---

TO CAPTAIN BALL, H.M. SHIP ALEXANDER, OFF MALTA.

[Autograph, in the possession of Sir William Keith Ball, Bart.]

Naples, December 12th, 1798.

My dear Ball,

This will be given to you by a Captain of a Ragusa brig,
who was sent here in the Terpsichore, and Gage either never
had, or has lost his papers. I suppose there is nothing
against the neutral Vessel, only against the cargo. If that
should be the case, I am sure you will instantly liberate her;
but, my dear Sir, I do not pretend to be a judge. You will,
I am sure, do justice.

The moment the Flora arrives from Leghorn she shall
bring you papers, and all our news here, which is not of the
best kind, but I hope will mend. The Neapolitan Officers do
not like fighting, and some are traitors : *so says report.* As I
know not if this will ever reach you, I shall say no more. I
have not had the scrape of a pen from England, except
two private letters from Lord Spencer, since Capel's arrival.
Earl St. Vincent sends me nothing. With every kind
wish to Foley, Gould,[2] and Waller, believe me ever your
affectionate,

NELSON.

Lady Hamilton and Sir William desire to be kindly re-
membered to all their good friends with you : and Lady and
Miss Knight[3] are not indifferent to the welfare of those off
Malta, particularly to an *audacious* and good friend of ours.

[2] Captain of the *Audacious*, now Admiral Sir Davidge Gould, G.C.B.
[3] The widow and daughter of Rear-Admiral Sir Joseph Knight. He was Knighted,
being the senior Captain of the Fleet, at Portsmouth, on the King's Visit in June,
1773, and died in 1775 : his widow, Phillipina, daughter of Anthony Deane, Esq., of
Suffolk, died on the 20th of July, 1799, and a monument was erected to their
memory in the Church of Harwich. Miss Knight, who will be again mentioned,
was afterwards Sub-Governess to H. R. H. the Princess Charlotte of Wales.

TO HIS EXCELLENCY SIR WILLIAM HAMILTON, K.B.

[Letter-Book.]

Naples, 14th December, 1798.

Sir,

As I have been informed that this Kingdom is invaded by a formidable French Army, I think it my duty to acquaint your Excellency, for the information of the English merchants and others residing at Naples, that the three English transports in this Bay have my directions to receive such effects of the English as they can stow, and that the whole Squadron is ready to receive their persons, should such an event be found necessary as for them to embark. I have the honour to be, &c.

NELSON.

N.B.—I need not say that I mean valuable effects, and not household furniture. I also beg leave to recommend that anything sent on board Ship should be done with as little bustle, and as much secrecy as possible.

---

TO LIEUTENANT PHILIP LAMB, AGENT OF TRANSPORTS.

[Order-Book.]

Secret.

Naples, December 14th, 1798.

Whereas, from the exigency of the times, it is necessary to throw all the condemned provisions, and the hoops and staves returned from the different Ships of the Squadron, overboard into the sea. You are hereby required and directed to cause the Masters of the Transports under your directions, to heave the said condemned provisions, with the hoops and staves, overboard into the sea, and to receive on board the said Transports, the effects and persons of such British Families as may be sent on board the said Transports, giving them every assistance in their embarkation, and, at the same time, to keep this as secret as possible.

NELSON.

## TO HIS EXCELLENCY THE MARQUIS DE NIZA.

[Letter-Book. December 14th, "Arrived the Portuguese Ship Alphonso and two polaccas taken by us in Leghorn Roads the 28th November. Arrived also the Marquis de Niza in the Principe Real and the Alcmene, from Egypt, bringing dispatches from Captain Hood of H. M. Ship Zealous, and the Turkish Ambassador and his suite, bringing presents from the Grand Signior."—*Journal.*]

Naples, December 14th, 1798.

Sir,

His Majesty the King of the Two Sicilies having desired that a number of the Portuguese seamen and Officers should be lent to assist in fitting some of his Ships for sea, I have to request that your Excellency will be pleased to direct that such a number of seamen and Officers, as can with propriety be spared from the service of the Ships of her Most Faithful Majesty, may be lent. I have the honour to be, &c.

NELSON.

------

## TO CAPTAIN BALL.

[Autograph, in the possession of Sir William Keith Ball, Bart.]

Most Secret.

Naples, December 15th, 1798.

My dear Ball,

I desire you will send me directly the Goliath, and order Foley to come through the Faro of Messina, that he may get information. He may very possibly see me there and some others. The situation of this Country is very critical—nearly all in it are traitors or cowards. God bless you. Keep this secret, except to caution Foley not to approach Naples but with great caution. I have nothing from England—am here with Alcmene and the Portuguese. All in this house join in best wishes and regards with your faithful friend,

NELSON.

The Flora Cutter is lost, and I have nothing to send to you. Can you spare the Incendiary? Do not send a Neapolitan Ship: there are traitors in the *Marine*. In short, all is corrupt.

### TO CAPTAIN TROUBRIDGE.

[Letter-Book. On the following day, in consequence of the state of Affairs at Naples, the Vanguard "shifted her berth out of gun-shot of the Forts," and got one of the Neapolitan Ships out of the Mole.]

Naples, 15th December, 1798.

Most secret.

Things are in such a critical state here, that I desire you will join me without one moment's loss of time, leaving the Terpsichore in Leghorn Roads to bring off the Great Duke, should such a measure be necessary. Probably, I shall send Commodore Campbell very soon on that service.

The King is returned here, and everything is as bad as possible. For God's sake make haste! Approach the place with caution. Messina, probably, I shall be found at; but you can inquire at the Lipari Islands if we are at Palermo. Caution Gage to act with secrecy, and desire him to write to Wyndham, and give him those instructions which may be necessary at this time for his guarded conduct and secrecy. All here join in love and best regards with your faithful friend,

NELSON.

---

### TO THE GRAND SIGNIOR.

[Autograph Draught in the Nelson Papers.]

Naples, December, 16th, 1798.

Words are entirely inadequate to my feelings for the exalted mark of approbation bestowed on me by the Imperial Grand Signior,[4] which I must ever attribute to his goodness, not to my deserts. As it is my duty, so I shall always pray to the God of Heaven and Earth to pour down his choicest blessings on the Imperial head, to bless his Arms with success against all his Enemies, to grant health and long life to the Grand Signior, and for ever to continue me his grateful and devoted servant,

NELSON.

Requested to be received in hand of the most Sublime Imperial Grand Signior.

---

[4] The Chelengk, &c., *Vide* p. 82.

## TO HIS EXCELLENCY THE GRAND VIZIER.

[Autograph draught, in the Nelson Papers and Letter-Book.]

Naples, December 16th, 1798.

Sir,

I am honoured by your Excellency's letter, delivered to me by Kelim Effendi, for which, and your kind expressions of regard, I sincerely thank you. I beg that your Excellency will lay me at the feet of the Grand Signior, and express what I feel for the great and singular Honour conferred upon me, which I am sensible I owe to his Imperial goodness of heart, and not to my deserts. When I first saw the French Fleet, which, for near three months, I had in vain sought, I prayed that, if our cause was just, I might be the happy instrument of His punishment against unbelievers of the Supreme only True God—that if it was unjust, I might be killed. The Almighty took the Battle into His own hand, and with His power marked the Victory as the most astonishing that ever was gained at sea: All glory be to God! Amen! Amen!

I cannot allow Kelim Effendi to depart without expressing my thanks to him for the very able, dignified, and polite manner in which he has executed his mission, and I beg leave to recommend him to your Excellency's protection, as my dear friend. That your Excellency may long live in health to carry, by your wise councils, the glory of the Ottoman Empire to the highest pitch of grandeur, is the sincere prayer of your Excellency's most faithful servant,

NELSON.

I send my dear son-in-law, Captain Nisbet, to carry Kelim Effendi to Constantinople.

---

## TO ABDUL CADIR BEY, VICE-ADMIRAL OF THE OTTOMAN SQUADRON AT CORFU.

[Letter-Book.]

Sir,　　　　　17th December, 1798.

I feel very highly honoured by your Excellency's letter of November 30th, and at this moment of answering that letter, I received yours by an Officer of your Ship. The glory of the Ottoman Arms is as dear to me as those of my own Country, and I always pray to the God of Heaven and Earth for His blessing on the Grand Signior, and for all his faithful Subjects. I was in hopes, Sir, that a part of the united Turkish and Russian Squadron would have gone to Egypt—the first object of the Ottoman Arms : Corfu is a secondary consideration. I am blockading Toulon and Malta, besides protecting the coast of Italy, and I rested confident that all Countries on the east of Candia would have been attended to by the United Squadron of Ottomans and Russians. I shall always have the greatest pleasure in communicating with your Excellency, and in concerting plans for the destruction of the common Enemy. With every sentiment of respect, believe me,

Your Excellency's most obedient servant,
NELSON.

If it can be done, I wish a Squadron to be sent on the Coast of St. Jean d'Acre, which, if any event drives from the Coast of Egypt, will be attacked by sea. I have Buonaparte's letter before me.

---

TO HIS EXCELLENCY J. SPENCER SMITH, ESQ., CONSTANTINOPLE.

[Letter-Book.]

Naples, 17th December, 1798.

Dear Sir,

I have received your Letters by Mr. Pisani, who accompanied Kelim Effendi to this place. I can assure you that no person could have executed his mission with greater dignity for his Sovereign, nor with greater politeness towards me, than the person selected by the Grand Signior. I send your Excellency copies of my letters to the Grand Signior, the Vizir, and also of those I have wrote to the Turkish and Russian Admirals. I have also had a long and friendly conference with Kelim Effendi on the conduct likely to be pursued by the Russian Court towards the unsuspicious (I fear) and upright Turk. Our ideas have exactly been the same about the Russians. A strong Squadron should have been sent to Egypt, to have relieved my dear friend Captain Hood, but Corfu suited Russia better. Enough Ships were under the Admiral's command for both.

I am now collecting a Squadron to form the blockade of

Toulon, where troops are embarked for Egypt. Surely, my dear Sir, I had a right to expect that the united Fleets of Turks and Russians, would have taken care of the things east of Candia. I never wished to have them west of it. All those Islands would have been ours long ago. Captain Troubridge was absolutely under sail, when I heard, with sorrow, that the Russians were there. I have had the charge of the Two Sicilies intrusted to me, and things are come to that pitch, that I do not know that the whole Royal Family, with 3000 Neapolitan *émigrés*, will not be under the protection of the King's flag this night. I shall keep my letter open, and tell you how affairs look here. Report says my friend, Sir Sidney, is going to join the Turkish Squadron. I had almost forgot to mention, that, notwithstanding the Squadron I am sending to Egypt, at least two Sail of the Line, and four Frigates, should assemble at St. Jean d'Acre, for I know that is the place where Buonaparte has ordered a part of his Fleet to go to, if any accident should happen to our Squadron. The prosperity of the Porte is as dear to me as my own, because it is the pleasure of our Sovereign. You will, my dear Sir, I am confident, say everything which is proper for me, to the Ministers of the Sublime Porte. My time is so fully employed here, that if I do not write so fully as could be wished, consider my one hand, but ever believe me, with the greatest respect, your most obedient servant,

NELSON.

---

TO EARL SPENCER.

[Letter-Book.]

Naples, December 18th, 1798.

My dear Lord,

There is an old saying—that ' when things are at the worst, they must mend.' Now, the mind of man cannot fancy things worse than they are here. But, thank God, my health is better, my mind never firmer, and my heart in the right trim to comfort, relieve, and protect those who it is my duty to afford assistance to. Pray, my Lord, assure our gracious Sovereign that, whilst I live, I will support his glory and

that of our Country, and that if I fall, it shall be in a manner
worthy of your Lordship's faithful and obliged,

NELSON.

I must not write more.   Every word may be a text for a
long letter.

----

TO . . . . .

[Autograph draught, in the Nelson Papers.]

19th December, 1798.

General Fortiguerra came here yesterday and said that he
had been with the King, and was desired by the King to fit
out all his Navy in the Port, and requested that I would allow
some of the Portuguese seamen to be lent, in order to fit them
out, as they understood Italian, and I understood that he was
to prepare for the King's departure, and also, that the King
desired I would not send any of the Ships out of Port.   I
instantly complied with the first part, took no notice of what
was said about the King's departure, and to the last my reply
was, that I could receive no orders from any but the King,
but that his Majesty had not a more faithful subject than
myself in his Dominions.

NELSON.

----

MEMORANDUM RESPECTING THE EVACUATION OF NAPLES.

[Original, in the possession of Captain Hope, R.N.   The words in italics were
added by Lord Nelson in his own hand.]

*Most Secret.*

Naples, December 20th, 1798.

Three barges, and the small cutter of the Alcmena, armed
*half-past seven*
with cutlasses only, to be at the Victoria at ~~eight~~ o'clock precisely.   Only one barge to be at the wharf, the others to lay on
their oars at the outside of the rocks—the small barge of the
Vanguard to be at the wharf.   The above boats to be on board
the Alcmena before seven o'clock, under the direction of
Captain Hope.   *Grapnells to be in the boats.*

All the other boats of the Vanguard and Alcmena to be armed with cutlasses, and the launches with carronades to assemble on board the Vanguard, under the direction of Captain Hardy, and to put off from her at half-past eight o'clock *precisely, to row half way towards the Mola Figlio. These boats to have 4 or 6 soldiers in them.*

*In case assistance is wanted by me, false fires will be burnt.*

*Nelson.*

*The Alcmena to be ready to slip in the night, if necessary.*

---

## TO REAR-ADMIRAL HIS EXCELLENCY THE MARQUIS DE NIZA.

[Letter-Book.]

Naples, 21st December, 1798.

You are hereby required and directed to order the Commodores Stone and Campbell, and the Captain of the Principe Real, to make preparation for burning the Guiscardo, St. Joachim, and Tancredi; and Captain Hope has my orders to prepare the Frigate and Corvettes for the same purpose; and you will be so particular on this service, that on no consideration you will sail until it is accomplished, which when done, you will take all the Vessels under your protection who may wish to keep you company, and come as speedily as possible to Palermo, where you will receive orders for your further proceedings.

Nelson.

---

## TO CAPTAIN HOPE, HIS MAJESTY'S SHIP ALCMENE.

[Order-Book.]

Naples, 21st December, 1798.

You will prepare the Frigate and Corvettes for burning, and, under the orders of the Marquis de Niza, taking care they are burnt before you sail. You will also pay particular attention to the safety of the three English transports, and bring them with you to Palermo, where you will find orders for your further proceedings.

Nelson.

## TO REAR-ADMIRAL THE MARQUIS DE NIZA.

[Letter-Book.]

Vanguard, Naples, 22nd December, 1798.

Notwithstanding my former orders of yesterday's date, you are, in the present circumstances, by the very particular desire of their Sicilian Majesties, to obey the following instructions : to instantly remove Her Most Faithful Majesty's Squadron to as great a distance from the Town as you can, and to remove all the Neapolitan Ships of War without your Ships, and in case [4] *of either the entry of the French troops into Naples, or an insurrection of the People against its legitimate Government,* in that case you are immediately to destroy the Ships : but you are not to consider, under the present circumstances, a refusal to admit *your Boats on shore, as an insurrection against the Government,* as it may arise from fear of the French, in case they unfortunately should get to Naples. And, whereas, General Fortiguerra has received the most positive instructions from the King, to procure and send off to the Ships of his Majesty, such spars and stores as may be necessary to rig them with jury-masts, you are therefore to lend them such stores, from the Ships under your command, as may be necessary to enable them to navigate them to the Mole of Messina; when you are at liberty to take the articles lent, back again, if you want them. When any one Ship, of the Ships of his Majesty, is put in a state to navigate, you will directly order her to sail, and to be manned by part of the crew of the Ship you may order to attend her, if Neapolitan seamen cannot be found to man her. You will, of course, order such men as are wanted to equip them for sea. Herewith you will receive an order for Captain Hope, of His Majesty's Ship Alcmene, to put himself under your command.

HORATIO NELSON.

[4] Clarke and M'Arthur state that the passages in italics were, in the original Order, underlined by Lord Nelson.

## TO COMMODORE DUCKWORTH.

[From a Copy, in the Admiralty.]

Vanguard, Naples Bay, 22nd December, 1798.

Dear Sir,

I have only to tell you that their Sicilian Majesties with their august Family, arrived in safety on board the Vanguard last night at nine o'clock, feeling it a necessary measure in the present moment. You will therefore acquaint all Ships, that may be with you, of this circumstance, that they may approach Naples with caution; and if you have an opportunity, pray tell Lord St. Vincent of this event when you write, for I have no English vessel with me. Ever yours truly,

NELSON.

---

## TO ADMIRAL THE EARL OF ST. VINCENT, K.B.

[Letter-Book. The following notices of the Royal Family, &c. in the *Journal*, are interesting. "December 19th, [18th,] Sailmakers making cots for the Royal Family: Painters painting the wardroom, and offices under the poop; getting ready for sea, and getting off the valuable effects of Her Sicilian Majesty in the night time." Thursday 20th, [19th,] "Smuggling on board the Queen's diamonds, &c." Saturday 22nd, [i. e. Friday 21st,] "At 10, A.M., their Sicilian Majesties and the Royal Family embarked on board, as did the British Ambassador and family, the Imperial Ambassador and suite, several of the Neapolitan nobles and their servants, and most of the English gentlemen and merchants that were at Naples. Saturday 22nd, fresh breezes, unmoored. Sunday 23rd, more moderate, came under the stern and alongside, several Deputations from the City of Naples to His Sicilian Majesty: came on board also, General Mack, who had an audience and returned again to the shore. Weighed and made sail, at 7 P.M., in company with a Neapolitan Ship of the Line, a number of Merchant ships and the English transports." After a very stormy passage, in which the Vanguard split her three topsails, and the driver, though it was brailed up, she anchored in Palermo Mole at two in the morning of Wednesday, the 26th of December. "At 5, His Sicilian Majesty and the Royal Family went on shore *incog.*, and at 9, His Majesty landed; manned ship, and cheered him until on shore; could not salute him by reason of being in the Mole. Found here two Spanish ships of 54 guns each, and a Frigate of 36 guns, and several Merchantships." See Lord Nelson's full and interesting account of the Emigration of the Royal Family in his Letter to the Earl of St. Vincent on the 28th of December, in the next page.

Palermo, December 27th, 1798.

My Lord,

I have just received your orders relative to the taking care of the Coasts of the Sicilies, also for the destruction of the Transports in Egypt, the blockade of Malta and Toulon, and also your letter relative to Captain Sir Sidney Smith. I shall endeavour to comply with them all, by staying myself to take care of this Country, by writing to Commodore Duck-worth to take care of Toulon, placing Captain Ball with a Squadron to blockade Malta, and by sending Captain Trou-bridge to Egypt, to endeavour to destroy the Transports in Alexandria, and directing him to deliver up the Levant Seas to the care of Captain Sir Sidney Smith, all of which I hope your Lordship will approve. I have the honour to be, &c.

NELSON.

TO ADMIRAL THE EARL OF ST. VINCENT, K.B.

[Original, in the Admiralty.]

Palermo, December 28th, 1798.

My Lord,

On the 22nd, I wrote a line to Commodore Duckworth, telling him, that the Royal Family of the Two Sicilies were safely embarked on board the Vanguard, and requested him to take the first opportunity of acquainting your Lordship of this event. For many days previous to the embarkation it was not difficult to foresee that such a thing might happen, I therefore sent for the Goliath from off Malta, and for Captain Troubridge in the Culloden, and his Squadron from the north and west Coast of Italy, the Vanguard being the only Ship in Naples Bay. On the 14th, the Marquis de Niza, with three of the Portuguese Squadron, arrived from Leghorn, as did Captain Hope in the Alcmene from Egypt: from this time, the danger for the personal safety of their Sicilian Majesties was daily increasing, and new treasons were found out, even to the Minister of War. The whole correspondence relative to this important business was carried on with the greatest address by Lady Hamilton and the Queen, who being constantly in the habits of correspondence, no one could suspect. It would have been highly imprudent in either Sir William Hamilton or myself to have gone to Court, as we knew that all our movements were watched, and even an idea by the Jacobins of arresting our persons as a hostage (as they foolishly imagined) against the attack of Naples, should the French get possession of it.

Lady Hamilton, from this time to the 21st, every night received the jewels of the Royal Family, &c. &c., and such clothes as might be necessary for the very large party to embark, to the amount, I am confident, of full two millions five hundred thousand pounds sterling.[5] On the 18th, General Mack wrote that he had no prospect of stopping the progress of the French, and entreated their Majesties to think of retiring from Naples with their august Family as expeditiously as possible. All the Neapolitan Navy were now taken out of the Mole, consisting of three Sail of the Line and three Frigates: the seamen from the two Sail of the Line in the Bay left their Ships and went on shore : a party of English seamen with Officers were sent from the Vanguard to assist in navigating them to a place of safety. From the 18th, various plans were formed for the removal of the Royal Family from the palace to the water-side ; on the 19th, I received a note from General Acton, saying, that the King approved of my plan for their embarkation ; this day, the 20th and 21st, very large assemblies of people were in commotion, and several people were killed, and one dragged by the legs to the palace. The mob by the 20th were very unruly, and insisted the Royal Family should not leave Naples; however, they were pacified by the King and Queen speaking to them.

[5] " Lady Hamilton," says Southey, " arranged everything for the removal of the Royal Family. This was conducted on her part with the greatest address, and without suspicion, because she had been in habits of constant correspondence with the Queen. It was known that the removal could not be effected without danger; for the mob, and especially the Lazzaroni, were attached to the King; and as at this time, they felt a natural presumption in their own numbers and strength, they insisted that he should not leave Naples. Several persons fell victims to their fury ; among others was a Messenger from Vienna, whose body was dragged under the windows of the palace in the King's sight. The King and Queen spoke to the mob, and pacified them ; but it would not have been safe, while they were in this agitated state, to have embarked the effects of the Royal Family openly. Lady Hamilton, like a heroine of modern romance, explored, with no little danger, a subterraneous passage leading from the palace to the sea-side : through this passage the royal treasures, the choicest pieces of painting and sculpture, and other property, to the amount of two millions and a-half, were conveyed to the shore, and stowed safely on board the English ships. On the night of the 21st, at half past eight, Nelson landed, brought out the whole Royal Family, embarked them in three barges, and carried them safely, through a tremendous sea, to the Vanguard. Notice was then immediately given to the British merchants, that they would be received on board any ship in the squadron. Their property had previously been embarked in transports. Two days were passed in the Bay, for the purpose of taking such persons on board as required an asylum ; and on the night of the 23rd, the fleet sailed."

On the 21st, at half-past 8 P. M. three Barges with myself
and Captain Hope, landed at a corner of the Arsenal. I went
into the palace and brought out the whole Royal Family,
put them into the Boats, and at half-past nine they were all
safely on board the Vanguard, when I gave immediate notice
to all British Merchants that their persons would be received
on board every and any Ship in the Squadron, their effects of
value being before embarked in the three English transports
who were partly unloaded, and I had directed that all the
condemned provisions should be thrown overboard, in order
to make room for their effects. Sir William Hamilton had
also directed two Vessels to be hired for the accommodation
of the French emigrants, and provisions were supplied from
our Victuallers; in short, everything had been done for the
comfort of all persons embarked.

I did not forget in these important moments that it was my
duty not to leave the chance of any Ships of War falling into
the hands of the French, therefore, every preparation was made
for burning them before I sailed ; but the reasons given me by
their Sicilian Majesties, induced me not to burn them till the
last moment. I, therefore, directed the Marquis de Niza to
remove all the Neapolitan Ships outside the Squadron under
his command, and if it was possible, to equip some of them
with jury masts and send them to Messina ; and whenever
the French advanced near Naples, or the people revolted
against their legitimate Government, immediately to destroy
the Ships of War, and to join me at Palermo, leaving one or
two Ships to cruize between Capri and Ischia in order to
prevent the entrance of any English Ship into the Bay of
Naples. On the 23rd, at 7 P.M., the Vanguard, Sannite, and
Archimedes, with about twenty sail of Vessels left the Bay of
Naples ; the next day it blew harder than I ever experienced
since I have been at sea. Your Lordship will believe that my
anxiety was not lessened by the great charge that was with
me, but not a word of uneasiness escaped the lips of any of
the Royal Family. On the 25th, at 9 A.M., Prince Albert,
their Majesties' youngest child, having eat a hearty breakfast,
was taken ill, and at 7 P.M. died in the arms of Lady Hamilton ; and here it is my duty to tell your Lordship the obligations which the whole Royal Family as well as myself are

under on this trying occasion to her Ladyship. They necessarily came on board without a bed, nor could the least preparation be made for their reception. Lady Hamilton provided her own beds, linen, &c., and became *their slave*, for except one man, no person belonging to Royalty assisted the Royal Family, nor did her Ladyship enter a bed the whole time they were on board. Good Sir William also made every sacrifice for the comfort of the august Family embarked with him. I must not omit to state the kindness of Captain Hardy and every Officer in the Vanguard, all of whom readily gave their beds for the convenience of the numerous persons attending the Royal Family.

At 3 P.M., being in sight of Palermo, his Sicilian Majesty's Royal Standard was hoisted at the main-top gallant-mast head of the Vanguard, which was kept flying there till his Majesty got into the Vanguard's barge, when it was struck in the Ship and hoisted in the Barge, and every proper honour paid to it from the Ship. As soon as his Majesty set his foot on shore, it was struck from the Barge. The Vanguard anchored at 2 A.M. of the 26th; at 5, I attended her Majesty and all the Princesses on shore; her Majesty being so much affected by the death of Prince Albert that she could not bear to go on shore in a public manner. At 9 A.M., his Majesty went on shore, and was received with the loudest acclamations and apparent joy. I have the honour to be, &c.

NELSON.

----

TO ADMIRAL THE EARL OF ST. VINCENT, K.B.

[Letter-Book.]

My Lord,                              Palermo, 30th December, 1798.

The great anxiety I have undergone during the whole time I have been honoured with this important command, has much impaired a weak constitution. And now, finding that much abler Officers [6] are arrived within the district which I had thought under my command, having arranged a plan of ope-

----

[6] Alluding to the appointment of Captain Sir Sidney Smith in Le Tigre, of 80 guns, in the Levant, which, as will appear from subsequent Letters, gave great offence both to the Earl of St. Vincent and to Lord Nelson, as it seemed to

rations with the Embassy with which I have been honoured
by the Grand Signior, having opened an unreserved correspondence with the Turkish and Russian Admiral, and, I
flatter myself, having made the British Nation and our gracious Sovereign more beloved and respected than heretofore;
under these circumstances I entreat, that if my health and uneasiness of mind should not be mended, that I may have your
Lordship's permission to leave this command to my gallant

interfere with their authority, and because he was to supersede Captain Hood
and the other Captains who were at the Nile, with whose feelings, and the feelings
and interests of his other companions in arms, Nelson always identified himself.
Nothing, however, could be more noble than Nelson's admiration of Sir Sidney
Smith's subsequent actions, or more generous than his expressions of esteem and
regard for him.

In a private and confidential Letter to the Earl of St. Vincent, dated on the 9th
of October, 1798, Earl Spencer thus announced Sir Sidney Smith's appointment
and the views of the Government:—

" The general view of the state of affairs in the Mediterranean, which was transmitted to you before the details of this Action arrived here, is in no respect altered
by that event, as far as relates to its principle; and fortunately only rendered more
easy of execution as to its detail. One great feature of this state of things is the
emotion and sensation which has been excited in Turkey, and the vigorous declarations, at least, which have been drawn from the Porte. Of these, it appears to his
Majesty's Ministers most urgent to make the most, and with a reference to the
former habits of acquaintance which a residence at Constantinople has given him,
as well as his near connexion with our Minister there, it has been judged expedient
to send out Sir Sidney Smith, who will very shortly wait upon your Lordship to
put himself under your orders, and will communicate to you the instructions of which
he is the bearer. His speedy arrival at the Dardanelles with these instructions you
will immediately perceive to be of great consequence; and his Ship having lately
undergone a very thorough repair, will relieve any of those which may be in the
Levant, in a state to render their stay in those seas less advisable. I am well aware
that there may perhaps be some prejudices, derived from certain circumstances
which have attended this Officer's career through life, but from a long acquaintance
with him personally, I think I can venture to assure your Lordship, that added to
his unquestioned character for courage and enterprise, he has a great many very
good points about him, which those who are less acquainted with him are not sufficiently apprised of, and I have no doubt that you will find him a very useful instrument to be employed on any hazardous or difficult service, and that he will be
perfectly under your guidance, as he ought to be. Should the arrangement of the
force to remain for the present in the Levant, to co-operate with the Turks, lead to
there being only one or two Ships of two decks on that service, it may be most
advisable that from the local and personal acquaintance Sir Sidney is possessed of
with the Turkish Officers, he should be the senior Officer; but I have given him
to understand, that if a large force should be thought necessary, his standing on the
List will not admit of it, there being so many Captains of distinguished merit who
are his seniors."—*Copy*, in the Nelson Papers.

and most excellent second in command, Captain Troubridge, or some other of my brave friends who so gloriously fought at the Battle of the Nile.

Captain Ball has the important command of the blockade of Malta, and is as eminently conspicuous for his conciliating manners as he is for his judgment and gallantry. I shall not, if I can help it, quit this command till I receive your approbation; for I am, with every respect, your Lordship's most faithful servant,                              NELSON.

---

### TO ADMIRAL THE EARL OF ST. VINCENT, K.B.

[Letter-Book.]

Palermo, 31st December, 1798.

My dear Lord,

*I do feel, for I am a man*, that it is impossible for me to serve in these seas, with the Squadron under a junior Officer:—could I have thought it!—and from Earl Spencer! Never, never was I so astonished as your letter made me. As soon as I can get hold of Troubridge, I shall send him to Egypt, to endeavour to destroy the Ships in Alexandria. If it can be done, Troubridge will do it. The Swedish Knight[7] writes Sir William Hamilton, that he shall go to Egypt, and take Captain Hood and his Squadron under his command. The Knight forgets the respect due to his superior Officer: he has no orders from you to take my Ships away from my command; but it is all of a piece. Is it to be borne? Pray grant me your permission to retire, and I hope the Vanguard will be allowed to convey me and my friends, Sir William and Lady Hamilton, to England. God bless you, my dear Lord, and believe me your most affectionate friend,

                                      NELSON.[8]

[7] Sir Sidney Smith, was a Knight Grand Cross of the Order of the Sword of Sweden.

[8] In reply to this Letter, Lord St. Vincent wrote to him on the 17th of January, 1799, "I am not surprised at your feelings being outraged, at the bold attempt Sir Sidney Smith is making to wrest a part of your Squadron from you. I have received much the same letter from him, as the one you describe to have been addressed to Sir William Hamilton; a copy of which, with my answer, you have enclosed, and orders for you to take him immediately under your command. I have informed Lord Spencer of all these proceedings, and sent him copies of the letters.

## TO CAPTAIN SIR SIDNEY SMITH, H.M. SHIP TIGRE.

[Letter-Book.]

Palermo, December 31st, 1798.

Sir,

I have been honoured with your letter, from off Malta, with its several inclosures:—viz., An extract of a letter from Lord Grenville to John Spencer Smith, Esq., &c., ' And his Majesty has been graciously pleased to direct that your brother, Sir Sidney Smith, shall proceed to Constantinople, with the 80 gun Ship, Le Tigre. His instructions will enable him to take the command of such of his Majesty's Ships as he may find in those seas, unless, by any unforeseen accident, it should happen that there should be among them any of his Majesty's Officers of superior rank; and he will be directed to act with such Force, in conjunction with the Russian and Ottoman Squadrons, for the defence of the Ottoman Empire, and for the annoyance of the Enemy in that quarter.' Also an extract of another letter from Lord Grenville to yourself and brother. And Earl St. Vincent having sent me an extract of a letter from Earl Spencer to him, saying that, for certain circumstances, you should be the Officer selected for the command of a small Squadron in the Levant Seas; and his Lordship having also informed me that Captain Miller was the Officer of your choice, and desiring me to give you a Frigate, or a Sloop of War, till Captain Miller's arrival, you may rest assured that I shall most strictly comply with the instructions sent by Lord Grenville to your brother: also

The ascendance this gentleman has over all His Majesty's Ministers is to me as_ tonishing, and that they should have sent him out after the strong objection I made to him, in a private letter to Mr. Nepean, passes my understanding. For the sake of your Country, and the existence of its power in the Levant, moderate your feelings, and continue in your command. . . . . The sensations you must have gone through before and since your departure from Naples, must have been very trying; nevertheless, I trust the greatness of your mind will keep up the body, and that you will not think of abandoning the Royal Family you have by your firmness and address preserved from the fate of their late Royal relations in France. Employ Sir Sidney Smith in any manner you think proper: knowing your magnanimity, I am sure you will mortify him as little as possible, consistently with what is due to the great characters senior to him on the List, and his superiors in every sense of the word. God bless you, my dear Lord, be assured no man loves and esteems you more truly than your very affectionate, St. Vincent."—*Original*, in the Nelson Papers.

those of Earl Spencer and Earl St. Vincent. For this purpose I must desire that you will lose no time in proceeding to Alexandria, to take upon you the command of the blockade, &c., which I shall direct to be delivered up to you; and, from my heart, I wish you every success. The united Squadrons of Turks and Russians, and of two Sail of the Line under your command, must be sufficient for the two Ships *armés en flute,* and three Frigates, which, thank God, are all the Enemy have left in those Seas. I have the honour to be, Sir, your most obedient servant,

NELSON.

----

### TO JOHN JULIUS ANGERSTEIN, ESQ., CHAIRMAN OF THE COMMITTEE AT LLOYD'S.

[Letter-Book.]

Vanguard, Palermo, 31st December, 1798.

Sir,

I have had the honour of receiving yours of the 10th October, inclosing a Circular letter addressed to the Commanders in the Squadron under my Command, requesting them to favour the Committee with the Lists of the Killed and Wounded on board their respective Ships at the Battle of the Nile; and I beg leave to acquaint you that I have given the necessary directions to the Captains of the Ships at present under my command to furnish the Committee with Lists, agreeable to their wishes, and will write to the Captains of those Ships that went down the Mediterranean with the Prizes to do the same as soon as possible, in order to forward their charitable intentions. I have the honour to be, &c.

NELSON.

----

### TO THE RIGHT HONOURABLE EARL SPENCER.

[Letter-Book.]

Palermo, 1st January, 1799.

My dear Lord,

I have transmitted to Mr. Nepean, by way of Vienna, a duplicate of my letter to the Commander-in-Chief, which, of course, will also be sent you from him; and it will inform you of all which has passed, from the determination of leaving Naples to our arrival at Palermo. The day after I left Naples, I received a letter from Sir Sidney Smith, with several enclosures. I send you my answer. Everything which the extracts sent me by Sir Sidney Smith point out to him, has been fully talked over, and explained, by Kelim Effendi, a person holding the office similar to our Under-Secretary of State, who had been sent with my Order of Merit; for, by the form of the investiture, that seems to me the properest name to call it.

And now, my Lord, having left the command of the two Sail of the Line in the Levant seas to Sir Sidney Smith, than whom, I dare say, no one could be so proper—Commodore Duckworth will ably, I am sure, watch Toulon, for I shall very soon, I hope, be able to send him one or two Sail of the Line; and Captain Troubridge, or some other of my brave and excellent Commanders, being left to guard the one Sicily and the Coast of Italy, I trust I shall not be thought hasty in asking permission to return to England for a few months, to gather a little of that ease and quiet I have so long been a stranger to.

Captain Troubridge goes directly to Egypt, to deliver up to Sir Sidney Smith the blockade of Alexandria, and the defence of the Ottoman Empire by sea; for I should hope that Sir Sidney Smith will not take any Ship from under my command, without my orders; although Sir Sidney, rather hastily in my opinion, writes Sir William Hamilton, that Captain Hood naturally falls under his orders. I am probably considered as having a great force; but I always desire it to be understood, that I count the Portuguese as nothing but trouble. Ever believe me, my dear Lord, your most obliged,

NELSON.

January 2nd.—General Acton has just wrote me, that the French are within thirty miles of Naples, on the 30th. Marquis de Niza is prepared to burn the Ships when the French get a little nearer. Mack is at Capua with a strong force; numbers not mentioned. Dreadful weather. The great Queen very ill; I fear for her.     N.

DISPOSITION OF THE SQUADRON UNDER MY COMMAND,
JANUARY 1ST, 1799.

Zealous,
Swiftsure,　　⎫
Lion,　　　　⎬ Egypt.
Seahorse.　　⎭

Culloden,　　　⎧ Not yet arrived from the N.W. Coast of Italy,
Minotaur,　　　⎪ but going to Egypt, to relieve Captain
Bomb-Vessels,　⎬ Hood, to attempt the destruction of the
　　　　　　　⎪ Transports, and to give up the command
　　　　　　　⎩ to Sir Sidney Smith.

Alexander,　　⎫
Audacious,　　⎪
Goliath,　　　⎬ Off Malta.
Emerald,　　　⎪
Incendiary,　　⎭

Alcmene　　　⎫ In Naples Bay, ready to burn the Neapolitan
and　　⎬ Ships of War.
Portuguese,　⎭

Bonne Citoyenne.—Going to carry the Turkish Ambassador
to Constantinople.

Mutine—Gone to Smyrna with dispatches.

Terpsichore and Alliance—At Leghorn, to watch events.

Vanguard—At Palermo.

　　　　　　　　　　　　　　　　NELSON.

------

TO THE REVEREND MR. NELSON, HILBOROUGH.

[Autograph, in the Nelson Papers.]

Palermo, January 2nd, 1799.

My dear Brother,

Your kind letter of October 8th, from Round Wood, with
one from Lady Nelson, of the same date, are all which I have
received from England since Captain Capel's arrival. I shall
rejoice if Ministry will do anything kind for my family, but,
believe me, I have no dependence on any of them. You will
have heard of the Royal Family of Naples embarking on
board the Vanguard, and of my bringing them here. All
will, I hope, yet end well, but the Imperial Court acts in
such a way, that it's difficult to foresee what is to happen

six months hence, but by May I hope to be in England, to
rest during the summer; and from my heart I pray that the
French may be crushed, and peace restored to the world.
How is Mrs. Nelson, my Aunt, and your children? Remember
me kindly to them, and to all my friends near you, and ever
believe me,

> Your most affectionate brother,
>                     NELSON.

You must excuse short letters.

---

### TO THE MARQUIS DE NIZA.

[Letter-Book.]

Palermo, 3rd January, 1799.

My Lord,

I have received your several letters up to the 1st January.
Although I can readily conceive the trouble your numerous
passengers give you, yet I cannot but rejoice that you have
not burnt the Neapolitan Ships of War; for until the arrival
or near approach of the French, it was the particular desire
of their Sicilian Majesties that they should not be destroyed,
*and for wise reasons.* If you leave Naples, I rest assured you
will give strict directions that my orders to your Lordship
are obeyed. The Queen is very unwell, as are Sir William
and Lady Hamilton. The weather has been very bad. Pray
make our respects to all your passengers, and believe me, &c.,

> NELSON.

---

### TO REAR-ADMIRAL THE MARQUIS DE NIZA.

[Order-Book.]

Palermo, 5th January, 1799.

You are hereby required and directed to proceed without a
moment's loss of time to Messina, where it is my present intention that all the Ships of Her Most Faithful Majesty
should rendezvous. You will direct that they always hold
themselves in momentary readiness for sea; and, as General
Mack is retreating towards Calabria, your Lordship will en-

deavour to open a correspondence with him ; and, if it is in your power, to afford that brave Officer any assistance, you are hereby directed to give it to the very utmost of your abilities, either by anchoring your Ships to cover his Army, manning any Gun-boats which may be at Messina, and sending them on the Coast of Calabria, by cruising in his vicinity with some of your Ships, or lending him men and cannon, should his Excellency require them. Your Lordship will, from time to time, acquaint me of your proceedings on this service, which you are to remain upon until further orders.

NELSON.

---

TO COMMODORE MITCHELL, COMMANDING THE PORTUGUESE SHIP SAINT SEBASTIAN

[Letter-Book.]

Sir,                                    Palermo, 6th January, 1799.

Although, from the custom of our service, you would of course fall under the orders of every Captain senior to yourself, yet, as I cannot yet comprehend your rank, and this not being a time to enter on that subject, I direct you therefore, if you cannot by the rules of your service, put yourself under the command of a very old and respectable Officer, Captain Louis, that you will co-operate with Captain Louis in the service he is ordered upon on the Coast of Italy towards Leghorn, and you will remain on this service until further orders from me, or Captain Louis's consent for your leaving it. I am, &c.,

NELSON.

---

TO HIS EXCELLENCY GENERAL ACTON.

[Letter Book, and an Autograph draught in the Nelson Papers.]

Sir,                                    Vanguard, 6th January, 1799.

His Sicilian Majesty having directed that all French of whatever description should leave the Island of Sicily, a Ship of 600 tons, an English transport,[9] will be ready by to-morrow

---

[9] It appears, from the Vanguard's Journal, that they did not leave Palermo until the 20th of February, when the Ark transport, on board of which they were embarked, sailed for Minorca under convoy of the Mutine, Captain Hoste.

morning to receive French emigrants, say 200. She will
have put on board her, biscuit, salt provisions, pease, oat-
meal, and the common wine of the Country. As this will
be an additional gratuity on the part of the King of Great
Britain, the *émigrés* will, if they choose it, lay in such stock
of fresh provisions, and other comforts, as they please. All
those pensioned by Great Britain will be received by a note
from            all those pensioned by his
Sicilian Majesty will be receivedby a note from            .
A Neapolitan Corvette to be attached to this Ship to
convoy her to Trieste and back again, and to receive on
board such *émigrés* as the Court shall direct. The Transports and Corvette ought to sail as soon as possible: their
time of departure will depend on the King's order. I am, &c.

NELSON.

TO CAPTAIN TROUBRIDGE, H. M. SHIP CULLODEN.

[Order-Book.]

Palermo, 6th January, 1799.

You will proceed, without a moment's loss of time, to Syracuse, in this Island, which I have ordered for the general
rendezvous of the Squadron under my command; and I expect you will find there three Bomb-ships, with their Ten-
ders, which you are to take under your command, as also all
his Majesty's Ships which you may meet, and fitting them for
sea with all possible expedition. You will direct the Goliath to
proceed and join Captain Ball off Malta, and the Dorothea[1] to
come to me, and such other Ships as you do not want with
you. You will take the Theseus, Alliance, and all the Bomb-
vessels, under your immediate command; and, if the wind
will allow you, I wish you to call off Malta, and render any
assistance, which will not detain you long, to Captain Ball
and his Squadron. You will then, without one moment's loss
of time, proceed to Alexandria, in Egypt, and by a vigorous
attack with the Bomb-vessels, Turkish gun-boats, and such

---

[1] Santa Dorotea, Captain (now Vice-Admiral of the Red) Hugh Downman, of
whom a Memoir is given in the *Naval Chronicle*, vol. xxi. p. 1.

other means as your excellent judgment will point out, endeavour to destroy every Ship in the Ports of Alexandria. Should you succeed in your attack, you will immediately withdraw all the Squadron under Captain Hood, and return with them to Syracuse.

As Captain Sir Sidney Smith is destined to the command in the Levant Seas, you will, therefore, should he not be in Egypt, send a Frigate or Sloop to Constantinople, directing the Captain or Commander to put himself under Sir Sidney Smith's command, and to follow his orders for his further proceedings; but should you unfortunately not be able to succeed in the object of your attack, you are in that case to give up the command of the blockade of Alexandria to Sir Sidney Smith, and the defence of the Ottoman Empire by sea, to which I am directed to consider him as appointed. You will, of course, leave with Sir Sidney Smith one Ship of the Line, until the arrival of Captain Miller, when you will direct Captain Sir Sidney Smith to immediately send that Ship to Syracuse. Should Captain Sir Sidney Smith not arrive at Alexandria before your attack is over, you are at liberty to act in the way you think best for the annoyance of the Enemy, until you can resign the command to Captain Sir Sidney Smith.

If you should succeed in your attack, you will bring Captain Miller, in his Majesty's Ship Theseus, back, to join me; as one Ship of the Line is sufficient in the Levant Seas, and Cruizers are much wanted in the North of Italy.

NELSON.

---

TO FRANCIS WERRY, ESQ., CONSUL AT SMYRNA.

[Letter-Book.]

Palermo, January 7th, 1799.

Sir,

I have been honoured with your letter by the Mutine and should have much pleasure in paying attention to every part of it, but as Sir Sidney Smith is destined for the defence of the Ottoman Empire by sea, I must of necessity refer you to him, and can only, with every good wish, subscribe myself your most obliged humble Servant,

NELSON.

TO J. SPENCER SMITH, ESQ., HIS MAJESTY'S MINISTER AT
CONSTANTINOPLE.

[Letter-Book.]

Palermo, January 7th, 1799.

Dear Sir,

I have to acknowledge the favour of your letter by the
Mutine, which joined me on the 1st of January. The conduct
of the Russians is no more than I always expected, and I
think it not impossible but they may by their conduct force
the Turk to a peace with the French, by a greater fear of the
Russians. As your brother is destined for your Colleague and
for the defence of the Ottoman Empire by sea, our correspondence must necessarily nearly close; but I beg leave from
my heart to thank you for all your kindness to me, and only
wish that all those who you may in future co-operate with,
may be as sensible of your goodness as is, your most obliged,

NELSON.

---

TO THE RIGHT HONOURABLE EARL SPENCER.

[Letter-Book.]

Palermo, January 7th, 1799.

My dear Lord,

The duplicate of my public letter to Earl St. Vincent sent
this day to Mr. Nepean, will detail the particulars of our
leaving Naples, and of our arrival at Palermo. Our news
from Naples has been daily from bad to worse. On the 4th,
the Enemy were not at Naples. There are parties in the
Capital for a Republic; and another for making the Duke of
Parma, who is at Madrid, King; but, I believe, the fighting
party is very small. The events which have taken place in
the Kingdom of Naples have been so rapid and extraordinary,
that it appears a dream. The King, God bless him! is a
philosopher; but the great Queen feels sensibly all which
has happened. She begs me not to quit Palermo; for that
Sir William and Lady Hamilton, and myself, are her only
comforts. I shall, as is my duty, do everything in the best
manner I am able, for the honour of our Country. General
Stuart from Minorca calls for me; Mr. Wyndham from

Florence does the same; and the affairs of Egypt and Malta are endeavouring to be brought to an issue. Captain Ball has done wonders, and I trust will soon succeed. The Bombs from Malta go to Egypt, and are to make a vigorous attack on the Shipping at Alexandria. These two points successful, will set us quite at our ease on the sea. With every sentiment of respect, believe me, your Lordship's most faithful Servant,

NELSON.

---

TO THE EARL OF ST. VINCENT, K.B.

[From a Copy, in the Admiralty.]

Palermo, 7th January, 1799.

My dear Lord,

I wrote you by Captain Galwey,[2] on the 4th, since which, Captain Troùbridge, with Minotaur, Theseus, and Bulldog arrived; the Culloden, Theseus, Bulldog, and Victuallers sailed yesterday for Syracuse, where Captain Troubridge is directed to collect the Bombs, and to proceed with them and the Theseus, to Alexandria, and to make a vigorous attack upon the Shipping in Alexandria; if the thing can be done, Troubridge will do it. Ball is employing the Bombs off Malta, and I hope that place will soon surrender. These two points settled, will place us quite at our ease respecting the sea; I wish I could say the same on the land side. On the 4th, the French were not at Naples, but were only sixteen miles distant, negotiating with the *Nobles* of Naples for the exclusion of the King. The French long to give them the fraternal squeeze, another party is for making the Duke of Parma's *son, married to the King of Spain's daughter*[3] (now at Madrid) King, under French protection, the lower class are the only loyal people; and they, we know, may any moment take a wrong turn. Mack is at Capua, but it was determined should retreat towards Salerno. On the 3rd, at night, the French attempted to force the lines at Capua, they did not

---

[2] Late First Lieutenant of the Vanguard, and promoted for the Battle of the Nile. Vide vol. ii. p. 453.

[3] Louis, (afterwards Duke of Parma and King of Etruria,) son of Ferdinand, Duke of Parma, married in 1795, Maria Louisa, daughter of Charles IV., King of Spain.

succeed; what occasioned their retreat is difficult to guess, although the Neapolitan army is 25,000, and the French not 8000! *Is not this a dream? can it be real?* Minotaur is gone to Leghorn, to endeavour to do good, and Louis will act, I am sure, for the best, as circumstances arise: I want to save thirteen thousand Neapolitan troops, who are in Tuscany. I must refer you, my dear Lord, to Hope,[4] who is very zealous and active. Ever, ever believe me your sincere, obliged, and affectionate,

NELSON.

---

TO COMMODORE DUCKWORTH.

[Letter-Book.]

Palermo, 7th January, 1799.

My dear Sir,
You will have heard by Captain Richardson who left Naples on the 22nd of December, of what had happened, to the astonishment of all Europe. It is incredible, but such things are! I have received the notification of the force expected from Brest; and, if they do get into the Mediterranean, I am confident, they will first go to Toulon, which, when you are apprised of, I submit to your consideration, in concert with his Excellency General Stuart, the propriety of uniting our forces, at what point will be best. I shall be truly happy in coinciding with the General and yourself. I am well aware of the small force of the General and yourself, should an invasion of Minorca take place: but I have a most detestable opinion of the Spanish Officers and troops, and the very highest, from experience, of General Stuart, who, by his abilities, would make a bad Army a good one. From the situation of affairs here, and having now got Bomb-ships, I have determined to bring our matters to issue, both at Alexandria and Malta, as expeditiously as possible; for which purpose, Troubridge goes this day for Egypt, with my orders to make a vigorous attack on the Ships in Alexandria. Captain Ball has, at this moment, I hope, finished with Malta. He was using the Bombs, by the last account, and intended,

---

[4] Captain George Hope, of the Alcmene.

about this time, storming the Bormola, the left side of the
harbour, by which all the Shipping must fall, and the French
be close kept up in the Town of La Valetta. I wish to send
you two Sail of the Line, and to request your look-out upon
Toulon : I am sure it cannot be in better hands. But our
situation respecting Italy every day alters, from *bad* to worse,
[so] that I cannot answer for my present intentions. I have
under my command four Portuguese Ships of the Line : you
are most heartily welcome to them all, if you think they will
be useful. I own I consider them as nothing, except trouble
in writing orders, which are intolerably executed. However,
you may be assured of my ardent desire to do everything
which can render your command pleasant, and for the
security of the valuable acquisition of Minorca.

Ever believe me, dear Sir, your faithful and obliged,

NELSON.

TO THE HON. LIEUTENANT-GENERAL STUART, MINORCA.

[Letter-Book.]

Palermo, 7th January, 1799.

My dear Sir,

Although I could not think the Neapolitans to be a Nation
of warriors, yet it was not possible to believe that a Kingdom
with 50,000 troops, and good-looking young men, could have
been over-run by 12,000 men, without anything which could
be called a battle. Certainly not 100 Neapolitans have been
killed; but such things are, if I am not dreaming. Poor
Mack came on board the Vanguard on the 23rd. My heart
bled for him : he is worn to a shadow. On the 3rd, at night,
8000 French attempted to force Mack's lines at Capua, in which
were 25,000 men. They did not succeed; this is all we know.
I do not flatter myself that all that remains are *good men
and true*. I pray they may be. The Nobles of Naples—I
speak as the Queen tells me—are endeavouring to negotiate
a truce or peace with the French, and that they offered to
exclude the present King from the throne, and to form a
Republic under French protection. There is another party
who wish the Duke of Parma's son, who is married to a Spanish

Princess, should be King under French and Spanish protection. How it will end, God only knows! I keep the Alcmene, to give you the last news from Naples.

The conduct of the Emperor is to me extraordinary: the loss at least of his new Italian Dominions will be the natural consequence. Tuscany must drop from his family; and whether a month sooner or later, is of little importance. You have seen the movements of Austrian armies—so have I; and found, unhappily, all their Generals traders, making the most of their command, by oppressing the poor soldiers. I feel very much, my dear General, for your situation, in the invaluable possession which your excellent judgment placed under the dominion of his Majesty; and, believe me, that I shall have the greatest pleasure in doing everything you can wish me. I am endeavouring to bring matters to a close both in Egypt and Malta. Either one or the other will enable me to give Commodore Duckworth two Sail of the Line from hence. I have nominally a great force, but anybody is heartily welcome to both the Neapolitan and Portuguese Ships. The Vanguard is at Palermo, their Sicilian Majesties desiring me not to leave them; but the moment you want me, I fly to your assistance; for, ever believe me, with the greatest respect, esteem, and regard, your most faithful,

NELSON.

---

TO THOMAS LOUIS, ESQ., CAPTAIN OF H. M. SHIP MINOTAUR.

[Order-Book.]

Palermo, 7th January, 1799.

The present situation of affairs on the Coast of Italy towards Leghorn, requiring the exertion and ability of an Officer of your distinguished character, I desire you will proceed without a moment's loss of time to Orbitello, and make inquiries into the situation of a body of Neapolitan troops retired to that place. Polacres are said to be sent there, and a Neapolitan frigate for their embarkation. You will give every assistance, as circumstances may require, for their safety. If no Transports are there to receive them for a voyage to Sicily, you will endeavour, if Count Damas, the General, wishes it, to get them, for the present, to Longona, in the Island of Elba-You will settle this business in a few hours, when you will get to Leghorn, and act in concert with our Minister, the Hon. William Wyndham, for the safety of Leghorn, the persons of the Great Duke and his family. You will act in this very important crisis, as your judgment will direct, for the benefit and honour of our King and Country; for which purpose you will take the Terpsichore and Portuguese corvette under your command, and I hope Commodore Mitchell will find no difficulty in placing himself under your command. I have wrote him a letter to co-operate with you, and to remain on that service till further orders from me.

In case of the Enemy getting possession of Leghorn, you will, of course, leave either the Terpsichore or the Corvette, to warn any English shipping, or those of our Allies, of the change of affairs in Italy. You will, Sir, I am confident, act in all circumstances which may occasionally arise, in such a way as will do honour to my appointment.

NELSON.

---

TO CAPTAIN NISBET, H. M. SLOOP BONNE CITOYENNE.

[Order-Book.]

Vanguard, Palermo, 7th January, 1799.

You are hereby required and directed to receive on board his Majesty's Sloop, La Bonne Citoyenne, under your command, the Turkish Ambassador, Kelim Effendi, with his dragoman and servants, and proceed, without a moment's loss of time, to Constantinople, showing him every attention and civility in your power during his stay on board; and on your arrival there, you will deliver the dispatches you will receive herewith, to his Excellency Spencer Smith, Esq., his Majesty's Minister, and return immediately, and join me at this place. Should Mr. Smith wish to introduce you to the Grand Signior, or the Vizir, on your arrival, you will comply with his request, and you are to be particularly careful not to permit any irregularities to be committed by any person who may go ashore, but to do the utmost in your power to cause the dignity and discipline of the British Navy to be respected, and you are to bring any dispatches which the Grand Vizir or Mr. Smith may have for me in return.

And I desire you will acquaint all Captains which you may fall in with in your route, senior to you, that it is my desire that they permit you to proceed on your voyage, and not by any other orders, to prolong your passage to join me, which you are to do with all possible expedition. The letters for Smyrna you will leave with Mr. Smith.

NELSON.

TO THE RIGHT HONOURABLE EARL HOWE, K.G.

[Letter-Book.]

Palermo, 8th January, 1799.

My Lord,

It was only this moment that I had the invaluable approbation[5] of the great, the immortal Earl Howe—an honour the most flattering a Sea-officer could receive, as it comes from the first and greatest Sea-officer the world has ever produced. I had the happiness to command a Band of Brothers; therefore, night was to my advantage. Each knew his duty, and I was sure each would feel for a French ship. By attacking the Enemy's van and centre, the wind blowing directly along their Line, I was enabled to throw what force I pleased on a few Ships. This plan my friends readily conceived by the signals, (for which we are principally, if not entirely, indebted to your Lordship,) and we always kept a superior force to the Enemy. At twenty-eight minutes past six, the sun in the horizon, the firing commenced. At five minutes past ten, when L'Orient blew up, having burnt seventy minutes, the six Van ships had surrendered. I then pressed further towards the Rear; and had it pleased God that I had not been wounded and stone blind, there cannot be a doubt but that every Ship would have been in our possession. But here let it not be supposed, that any Officer is to blame. No; on my honour, I am satisfied each did his very best. I have never before, my Lord, detailed the Action to any one; but I should have thought it wrong to have kept it from one who is our great

[5] Vide p. 84, ante.

Master in Naval tactics and bravery. May I presume to present my very best respects to Lady Howe, and to Lady Mary; and to beg that your Lordship will believe me ever your most obliged,

NELSON.

## TO THE MARQUIS DE NIZA.

[Letter-Book.]

Palermo, January 9th, 1799.

My dear Marquis,
You have some Turkish slaves on board. I beg, as a friend, as an English Admiral—as a favour to me, as a favour to my Country—that you will give me the Slaves. In doing this, you will oblige your faithful friend,

NELSON.

## TO THE MARQUIS DE NIZA.

[Letter-Book.]

My Lord,                    Palermo, 11th January, 1799.
Reports are at Court, that although the French are not at Naples, or near it, (for whilst an Army was covering Naples, the Enemy could not be considered as near taking it,) Commodore Campbell has burned all the Neapolitan Ships of War. Now, as this conduct is in positive disobedience of my order to your Lordship, I have to request that you will inform me whether your Lordship has given any orders to Commodore Campbell in contradiction to mine? I only beg that I may not see Commodore Campbell till this very serious matter is explained to my satisfaction.

I have the honour to be, &c.,

NELSON.

## TO CAPTAIN HARDY, H. M. SHIP VANGUARD.

[Order-Book.]

Palermo, 12th January, 1799.

Whereas application has been made to me from her Sicilian Majesty, through her Confessor, for the discharge of one

Patrick Mulligan, a Roman Catholic Priest, who was educated
in a College at Rome, and now serving as a private Marine
on board his Majesty's Ship Vanguard, under your command,
and this request being accompanied by a promise of giving
him promotion to a Living in this Country, you are hereby
required and directed to discharge the said Patrick Mulligan
from the service, complying with the Act of Parliament.

                                                    NELSON.

---

## TO COMMODORE CAMPBELL.

[Letter-Book. The Portuguese Squadron arrived at Palermo from Naples on the
13th of January.]

Sir,                                    Palermo, January 13th, 1799.

General Pignatelli having wrote to the Court, that you had
burned his Sicilian Majesty's Ships at a moment when the
troops of his Majesty were gaining some advantages over the
Enemy, of which the Court has complained to me, I have,
therefore, to request that you will send me your reasons in
writing for destroying the Neapolitan Ships, as it appears,
from the General's letter, that neither of the circumstances
had happened, in which case *only* I had declared the Ships of
his Sicilian Majesty should be destroyed.

        I have the honour to be, &c.,

                                                    NELSON.

---

## TO COMMODORE CAMPBELL.

[Letter-Book.]

                                    Vanguard, Palermo, 14th January, 1799.

Sir,

I am this moment honoured with your letter of yesterday's
date, (in answer to mine), with translations of your letters
to General Pignatelli, and copies of the General's to you.[6]

---

[6] Clarke and M'Arthur (vol. ii. p. 141) have given extracts from Commodore
Donald Campbell's explanation to Lord Nelson, and from his correspondence with
General Pignatelli, whence it appears that he was disgusted with the treachery or
weakness of the Neapolitan General. Those extracts place Commodore Campbell's
conduct in a very favourable light. It will be afterwards seen (p. 271) that the
proceedings instituted against him for destroying the Ships were withdrawn at the
Queen of Sicily's request.

Upon the most mature consideration of all the circumstances you have mentioned, I am sorry to tell you that I entirely disapprove of your destroying the Ships of his Sicilian Majesty, as neither of the cases had arisen, in which alone the Ships of His Majesty were to be destroyed; and the destroying them is in direct disobedience to my orders to the Marquis de Niza, and, as I understand, of his to you. I send a copy of this letter to the Marquis, and have the honour to be, &c.,

NELSON.

---

TO THE MARQUIS DE NIZA.

[Letter-Book.]

Vanguard, Palermo, 14th January, 1799.

My Lord,

I am sorry to send you an entire disapprobation of the conduct of Commodore Campbell in the destroying the Ships of his Sicilian Majesty, in positive disobedience of my order to your Lordship. If Commodore Campbell has not obeyed the instructions you left with him, I submit to your Lordship what, by the custom of your service, is proper to be done.

I have the honour to be, &c.,

NELSON.

---

TO HIS EXCELLENCY SIR JOHN ACTON, BART.

[Letter-Book.]

Palermo, January 15th, 1799.

My dear Sir,

Herewith I have the honour of sending your Excellency my letter to the Marquis de Niza and Commodore Campbell, in which you will see my entire disapprobation of the conduct of the Commodore. I feel that his Sicilian Majesty has great cause for displeasure; and, was Commodore Campbell an English officer, I should instantly order him to be tried by a Court-Martial for the positive breach of my orders to the Marquis de Niza. I am sorry it cannot be done by me to an auxiliary Squadron.

I have the honour to be, &c.,

NELSON.

TO ADMIRAL THE EARL OF ST. VINCENT, K.B.

[From a Copy in the Admiralty, and Letter-Book.]

[About 15th January, 1799.]

My Lord,

General Acton has just sent me notice, that General Pignatelli had signed an armistice with the French, in which the
name of the King is not mentioned, and that his Majesty has
entirely disapproved of this proceeding;[7] and also that the
Ligurian Republic had declared war against his Sicilian
Majesty. What may arise from day to day is perhaps difficult
to say, but unless some great change of measures, in my
opinion, Sicily will soon be in great danger. Commodore
Campbell is just arrived from Naples, (left it the        :)
he has burned the Neapolitan ships, before the time specified
in my orders to the Marquis de Niza, of which the King has
complained to me, and I have entirely disapproved of Commodore Campbell in this matter. The French are in full
possession of Capua, and come to Naples as a friendly place.
If I get a copy of the Articles before Captain Hope sails, I
shall send them. In this new case, I have offered to go to
the Bay of Naples myself, but both the King and Queen have
so seriously pressed me not to move, that I cannot do it;
they have fears, and have confidence in me, for their safety.
Sicily is in this state—*free from Jacobins, hate the French,
love the English, and discontented with their present situation.*

---

[7] See the King of Sicily's spirited Dispatch to his Vicar-General at Naples, Prince
Pignatelli, in Clarke and M'Arthur, vol. ii. p. 143, in which the King called the treaty
" disgraceful," and Pignatelli's instructions to the persons he had appointed to negotiate with the French, " most absurd." " I have been," adds the King, " more
surprised that you have acted in this unwarrantable manner, as you had no powers
from me for such negotiations. The instructions left with you were very different.
In concluding such a treaty, you may either have forgotten you have a Master, or
have remembered it only for the purpose of imposing on him the most scandalous
and disgraceful terms. You may suppose how much I am incensed at finding the
trust I had given you betrayed in such a manner, and how indignant I feel against
your unworthy advisers."

The French entered Naples on the 23rd of January, after much resistance by the
loyal Lazzaroni. On the 27th, General Championnet announced that the Neapolitan Monarchy was at an end, and the Parthenopean Republic established, which
was joined by some of the King's most confidential servants, and by a few of the
highest of the Nobility.

January 16th.—I send you the three last letters of General Acton, as conveying more information than anything I could write. I am very unwell. God bless you. Ever your affectionate,

NELSON.

_____

TO THE REVEREND MR. NELSON, HILBOROUGH.

[Autograph, in the Nelson Papers.]

Palermo, January 18th, 1799.

My dear Brother,

If you get six lines, it is as much as you can expect, for I have more writing than two hands could well get through. I thank you for your congratulations on what the generosity of our Country has done for me. I approve very much of your idea about the Arms, and if you will arrange it at the Heralds' Office, I shall feel very much obliged; it cannot, I know, be in better hands. My situation here is not to be envied, and I hope very soon to be released from it. Remember me in the kindest manner to Mrs. Nelson, our aunt, your children, and to all our friends in your neighbourhood, and ever believe me, your most affectionate brother,

NELSON.

_____

TO THE RIGHT HONOURABLE LORD MINTO.

[Autograph, in the Minto Papers.]

Palermo, January 19th, 1799.

My dear Lord, my honoured Friend, no words of mine can say what I felt on reading your Speech on the motion of thanks to me,[8] and I say it, for that I know will please, that our dear friends, Sir William and Lady Hamilton, express their pleasure in seeing it come from the good, the great Lord Minto. I must try and deserve some part of your praise. I wish here, my dear Lord, that, bad politician as I am, that the councillors of the King were as good, but indeed they are as bad in the cabinet as in the field. Naples is lost, and

_____

[8] Vide p. 77, ante.

Sicily will not be saved but by a total change of system. It is not Council three times a-day, and nothing ever done, but a plan, be it the best or indifferent, well followed up, which can save a Country placed as this is. The state of this Country is this—*Hate the French, love the English, discontented with their present Government, as Neapolitan councillors take the lead,* to the entire exclusion of the Sicilians. These people are proud beyond any I have seen; and, in fairness, I think they ought to be consulted on the defence of their own Country. They may not have the experience of the others, but they cannot act worse than the *foreigners* have done. The Queen is in despair. Acton is on the King's side, or, rather, the King on his. The Parthenopien Republic is forming. I have asked permission to rest a little, for, in truth, I am very unwell, but will never desert my friends or duty, whatever my private feelings may be. With kind remembrances to Lady Minto, believe me ever, my dear Lord, your affectionate,

NELSON.

Goliath, off Malta.—George well.

---

TO CAPTAIN BALL, H. M. SHIP ALEXANDER.

[Autograph, in the possession of Sir William Keith Ball, Bart.]

Palermo, January 21st, 1799.

My dear Ball,

I most heartily pray that your hard fag is over, and that victory has crowned your exertions and perseverance. When Malta is finished, you shall go down when you please. We have a report here that a Russian ship has paid you a visit, with proclamations for the Island. I hate the Russians, and if she came from their Admiral at Corfu, he is a blackguard. Respecting the situation of Malta with the King of Naples, it is this—he is the legitimate Sovereign of the Island: therefore, I am of opinion his Flag should fly. At the same time, a Neapolitan garrison would betray it to the first man who would bribe him. I am sure the King would have no difficulty in giving his Sovereignty to England; and I have lately, with Sir William Hamilton, got a Note that Malta should never be given to any Power without the consent of England.

Now, my dear friend, if, happily, Malta falls, and you like it, the regulation as Governor for the King of Naples and our King shall be placed in you. I know none, without a compliment, so fit for a place where jarring interests are to be consulted; therefore, turn this in your mind, and what you do I am confident I shall approve. I send you the papers, therefore shall not touch on English news. Naples was perfectly quiet on the 18th. The Provisional Government is placed by the people in the hands of three very gallant, and, fame says, loyal Officers. All are turned out and obliged to fly who made the infamous armistice with the French. But, alas! my dear Ball, here is no energy in the Government to profit of favourable moments. The mob to-day loyal, may to-morrow turn the contrary. The Portuguese have, contrary to my orders, destroyed the Neapolitan Navy. This caused much anger, both with the King, and people of all descriptions. I am here, nor will the King or Queen allow me to move. I have offered to go to Naples, and have wished to go off Malta in case the Squadron from Brest should get near you, but neither one or the other can weigh with them. I cannot say I think they will venture a Squadron to certain destruction in the end, even if they get into Malta or Alexandria.

We have all been very unwell; but I can [say] with truth, that Sir William and Lady Hamilton, and myself, have but one opinion about [you], and are equally anxious for your happiness, both as a public man and private friend. Remember me kindly to Gould, Foley, Barker, and Waller. Lady Knight, and the good, the charming Miss Knight, is more amiable than ever, by her kind attention to her mother. Apropos, a very odd thing has happened. By one of the late posts, Lady Knight received a letter from an attorney in England, saying, that one Joseph Knight, a chimney-sweeper of Sherborne in Dorsetshire, had left the family of Sir Joseph Knight a legacy of £2500. This will make Miss K.'s fortune from her father £7500, besides expectations from her mother, who cannot live long. Now all this, if I am not mistaken, Miss K. *longs* to give to one of your Squadron.[9]

Send the Dorothea back, as I am sure she can be of no use

---

[9] Vide p. 199, ante.

to you as a Frigate, and I shall want her. Lord Keith is arrived as Second in Command in the Foudroyant. *Darby* is on his passage up with a Convoy. How will he like this? Not much, but the Earl does not consult his wishes. God bless you, my dear Ball, and believe me ever your most affectionate friend,

NELSON.

P.S.—In case of the Surrender of Malta, I beg you will not do anything which can hurt the feelings of their Majesties. Unite their Flag with England's, if it cannot, from the disposition of the Islanders, fly alone.

---

TO ADMIRAL THE EARL OF ST. VINCENT, K.B.

[Letter-Book.]

Palermo, January 25th [to February 1st], 1799.

My dear Lord,

Since I wrote by the Cutter and Hope, but very little has occurred. We have had nothing direct from Naples since the 19th. On that day Prince Moliterni, who had been chosen General by the people for his loyalty to his King, but who forgot himself the moment of his exaltation, had been, report says, deposed, and a *butcher* elevated to the dignity. But this system cannot go on; a Government that only exists by the caprice of a mob cannot last. Naples must be revolutionized, unless the Emperor acts with vigour and with speed. Mr. Wyndham's letter will show you the state of Tuscany. I am sending to Commodore Duckworth, for, in my opinion, a Convoy arriving and unloading at Leghorn, would be a sufficient plea for the French taking possession of it. General Mack has disappeared, and none can tell us the route he has taken. His conduct, the Court says, is inexplicable. I have nothing since the 6th from Ball. Malta then was half-starving, and the Ships had unrigged.

February 1st.

Since writing the above, the Convoy is arrived. Vanguard[1]

---

[1] Lord Nelson shifted his Flag to the Bellerophon on the 1st of February, on which day the Vanguard and Minerve, Captain Cockburn, sailed for Malta.

and Minerve are gone off Malta, to see if they can be usefu
to Ball. Bellerophon, wanting a little putting in order, has
my Flag till Vanguard returns, when the Bellerophon shall
go and look at Minorca. Minotaur, Terpsichore, and Dorothea, shall go down as soon as I can get hold of them. I
hope our dear Troubridge will soon have done with Egypt;
and if Malta falls, I shall be able to send you several Ships.
As for the great Commodores, their rank is as much a plague
to them as it is to me. Niza is a good-tempered *man*, not
worth ——. We are apparently the very best friends, nor
have I, or will I, do an unkind thing by him. He tore himself from Malta. It was the job I wished for his Squadron.
Now, at the close, the case is altered. Ball has had all the
hard fag, and shall, if in my power, have the merit of driving
the French out. We have nothing official from Naples since
the 19th, but report says the mob are in arms, and going to
houses demanding money to keep the French out, but this
conduct must end in the destruction of the Monarchy.
All in this house have been ill, and are still. Our great
Queen, who truly admires you, our dear invaluable Lady
Hamilton, our good Sir William, and, give me leave to add
myself to this excellent group, have but one opinion about
you, viz.—that you are everything which is great and good.
Let me say so.

About Sir Sidney Smith I thank you most truly.[2] My
health is indeed very indifferent, but whilst I live, if the
Queen desire it, I remain for her security. No consideration of
my own health shall make me abandon my honourable post,
in which you have placed me. A Parliament is called here.
The Queen has her doubts about their temper, and I have
promised under my hand not to leave her, unless by her desire. Let me thank you for your goodness to Captain Nisbet.
I *wish* he may deserve it: the thought half kills me. My
dear Lord, there is no true happiness in this life, and in my
present state I could quit it with a smile. May God Almighty
bless you with health, happiness, and long life, is the fervent
prayer of your affectionate friend,

NELSON.

[2] For supporting his authority against, what Nelson conceived to be, Sir Sidney
Smith's undue assumption.

TO THE HONOURABLE WILLIAM WYNDHAM.

[Letter-Book.]

Palermo, January 28th, 1799.

My dear Sir,

Yesterday the Balloon brig[3] brought me your several letters down to the 19th, for all which I most sincerely thank you. Those for Lord Grenville I shall send to-morrow to Mahon, in order to be forwarded to Lord St. Vincent and England. I am sorry there should have been for a moment a delay in extending the neutrality of Leghorn to its ancient limits and privileges, from the moment the Neapolitan garrison quitted it; but every person must know that a Neapolitan garrison could not protect their Enemies.

*Alas!* the fancied neutrality of Tuscany will be its downfal! You see it, and it cannot fail soon to happen. Tuscany does not, (or cannot,) support its Neutrality for us, or Naples; only to protect the French is this name prostituted. Seratti, who is a man of sound sense, must see it. When the Emperor loses Tuscany and Naples—which, I am bold to say, the conduct of his Ministry conduces to do more than the arms of the French—his newly-acquired Dominions will not keep to him. Active, not passive, actions are the only weapons to meet these scoundrels with. We can, as your Excellency knows, have no desire to distress the Grand Duke by our conduct; on the contrary, it is our duty to support his Royal Highness against the tyranny of the French. Your Excellency will be so good as to say for me to his Royal Highness, that an English Ship of War shall, as long as he pleases, remain at Leghorn, ready to receive his person and family; for, unless the Emperor acts speedily, the British flag will be his only security. Tuscany has the choice, to act like men and take the chance of war, or in a few weeks to become another conquest of the French, and to form a new Republic. I shall send off to-morrow for Mahon, to apprise the Convoy, which I hear is arrived there, of the situation of Leghorn, but merchants will not always follow good advice. From Naples we have heard nothing since the 19th; and from

---

[3] One of the Portuguese Squadron.

those accounts, it is difficult to say what turn the mob will take; at that time, they were certainly loyal, the Nobility, to a man, Jacobins. Mack is disappeared, and no one knows the route he has taken. From Malta we have nothing very lately, but I hope that business is drawing to a close. I have no news direct from Egypt; but Mr. Smith writes Sir William Hamilton, date the 23rd November, that the French are drove out of Cairo, and near 2000 killed, with Berthier.

As to this Island, I cannot take upon me to say much: that they all hate the French is certain; but still they feel themselves an oppressed people. On the 20th, at Augusta, a French vessel, with a hundred and forty Officers and soldiers, arrived from Egypt. The boat-people, and those of the Town, attacked them. Eighty-seven were killed: the remainder escaped on board a Neapolitan frigate, who protected them. Sir William and Lady Hamilton, and I may add myself, are all unwell. The great Queen is far from well. The King is the best of the party. As her Majesty is very anxious to hear of the situation of Tuscany, I shall direct Captain Louis, (who I was sure your Excellency would like,) to send either Terpsichore or this Brig back to Palermo. You may, my dear Sir, depend on my desire to do everything which you can wish, for believe me, with real regard and esteem, your Excellency's most obedient,

NELSON.

If you get the posts regular, a few late newspapers will be acceptable. They have no letters by land.

---

TO CAPTAIN LOUIS, H. M. SHIP MINOTAUR.

[Letter-Book.]

My dear Sir,                    Palermo, 28th January, 1799.

I thank you most truly for your kind letter. I approve entirely that you have considered Leghorn as neutral, and with the same limits as before the Neapolitan troops entered the Town. The circumstances changed with their entry and their departure. You will, I am sure, my dear Sir, act in that way, which will always meet my wishes, and do credit to our Country. Whenever Mr. Wyndham tells you that his Royal Highness the Grand Duke has no occasion for his Majesty's ships, I shall be very glad to see you here; but consult with Mr. Wyndham, and you cannot err, at all events. We are so very anxious for the fate of Tuscany, that I beg you will very soon send us either the Terpsichore or Balloon with information. Here we have neither newspapers or letters by land, nor is there any news from Naples since the 19th instant. As to what turns may take place there, time only can show; but unless the Emperor is active, both Naples and Tuscany must, in the end, be republicanized. I have nothing since you left us, either from Ball or Hood, and our friend Troubridge had not left Syracuse on the 23rd. Our news from Egypt, *via* Constantinople, is, that the French are driven out of Cairo—that Berthier, 60 Officers, and 2000 men have been killed. This part, I believe; but they go much further, and say that General Dessaix, with 5000 men, are killed by Murad Bey, in Upper Egypt. At Augusta, 140 French arrived from Alexandria; 82 were killed by the people on the 20th, the rest were saved by a Neapolitan frigate, (what a fool!) All in this house have been ill, and are now far from well. The air of Palermo is very bad, in my opinion. Sir William and Lady Hamilton desire to be most kindly remembered to you and Gage; and believe me, my dear Sir, with the very greatest regard, your most obliged and faithful friend,

NELSON.

The Foudroyant, Lord Keith, is at Gibraltar.

----

### TO THE RIGHT HONOURABLE LORD LOUGHBOROUGH, LORD CHANCELLOR.

[Letter-Book ]

Vanguard, Palermo, 31st January, 1799.

My Lord,

The high honour conferred upon me by the House of Peers, by its Thanks, demands my most grateful acknowledgments, and I have to request that your Lordship, in words suitable to the occasion, will express my gratitude to the Right Honourable House, and also that of my brave Brethren, to whom I shall, as speedily as possible, convey the Resolutions of their Lordships.

Permit me to thank your Lordship for the very flattering manner in which you have executed the commands of their Lordships, and to assure you that I am, with every sentiment of respect, your much obliged and faithful servant,

NELSON.

---

## TO EARL CLARE, LORD CHANCELLOR OF IRELAND.

[Letter-Book.]

Vanguard, Palermo, 31st January, 1799.

My Lord,

I am this day honoured with your Lordship's very flattering letter of the 6th of October, telling me that you had officially transmitted to Earl St. Vincent the unanimous Resolution of the House of Lords of Ireland, to thank me and the several Officers, &c. who served under my command on the 1st of August. This high honour I have received through the Earl St. Vincent, my Commander-in-Chief, and I beg leave to express my gratitude to the Right Honourable House for this distinguished mark of their favour. I shall not fail to communicate to my gallant Brethren, this most noble of all rewards; and I beg that your Lordship will believe me, with the highest respect, &c.

NELSON.

---

## TO THE RIGHT HON. HENRY ADDINGTON, SPEAKER OF THE HOUSE OF COMMONS.

[Letter-Book.]

Vanguard, Palermo, January 31st, 1799.

Sir,

Believe me, I feel, as I ought, the noble reward which our Country has bestowed on me by its Thanks; and I beg you will, Sir, have the goodness to express to the Honourable House my gratitude. I can answer for that of my brave Brethren who fought with me in the Battle of the Nile. To you, Sir, who have not only so handsomely, but so elegantly

conveyed to me the Resolutions of the House, words are inadequate to express what I feel; but, believe me, Sir, with every
sentiment of respect and esteem, your most obliged and faithful servant,

NELSON.

---

## TO THE HONOURABLE JOHN FORSTER, SPEAKER OF THE HOUSE OF COMMONS OF IRELAND.

[Letter-Book.]

Sir,                          Vanguard, Palermo, 31st January, 1799.

I am this day honoured with your Letter[3] of October the
6th, transmitting the unanimous Resolution of Thanks and
approbation of the House of Commons of Ireland to me, and
the several Captains, Officers, and Men who served under my
command on the 1st of August. This high honour is felt by
myself and my Brethren, as the very greatest reward a Country
can bestow; and I request the favour of you, Sir, to express
to the House our feelings on this most honourable applause of
the Representative body of the loyal and good-hearted people
of Ireland. I beg you will also, Sir, accept my sincere thanks
for the very polite manner in which you have executed the
commands of the Honourable House, and that you will believe
me, Sir, with the highest respect, &c.

NELSON.

---

## TO THOMAS LEYLAND, ESQ., MAYOR OF LIVERPOOL.

[Letter-Book.]

Sir,                          Vanguard, Palermo, 31st January, 1799.

I am this day favoured with your letter, conveying to me
the unanimous Resolution of the Common Council of Liver-
pool, to honour me with their Thanks, and also the Freedom
of their Town. I beg you will assure those whom, from this
moment, I am to call my Brother-Freemen, that my future
exertions shall never be wanting to approve myself worthy of
the high honour conferred upon me by the Representative
body of the second Sea-Port in the Kingdom; and believe
me, with the highest respect, your much obliged and obedient
servant,                                      NELSON.

[3] Vide p. 79, ante.

TO HENRY SMITH, ESQ., CLERK OF THE DRAPERS' COMPANY.

[Letter-Book.]

Vanguard, Palermo, 31st January, 1799.

Sir,

I have this day received your letter, conveying to me the great honour conferred upon me by the Worshipful Company of Drapers of London, by presenting me with the Freedom of their Company. I beg you will, Sir, have the goodness to convey to the Worshipful Company how much I feel honoured by their kind notice of my services, and assure them that it shall be the study of my life to preserve their good opinion. Allow me, also, to thank you for the very flattering manner in which you have executed the orders of the Company. Believe me, Sir, with great respect, your much obliged and most obedient servant,

NELSON.

TO SIR WILLIAM ANDERSON, BART., LATE LORD MAYOR
OF LONDON.

[Letter-Book.]

Vanguard, Palermo, 31st January, 1799.

Sir,

I have only this day received the honour of your letter (when Lord Mayor) of the 16th of October; and I beg that you will convey to the Court of Common Council, my sincere gratitude for all their goodness to me; and assure them, it shall be the business of my life, to act in the manner most conducive to the prosperity of the City of London, on which depends that of our Country.

I am truly sensible of your politeness, in desiring me to say what particular devices I should wish on the Sword which is to be presented to me by the City of London; but I beg to leave that to the better judgment of my Fellow-Citizens. Believe me when I assure you, that I feel myself your most faithful and obliged servant,

NELSON.

## TO VICE-ADMIRAL GOODALL.

[Autograph, in the possession of John Dillon, Esq.]

Palermo, January 31st, 1799.

My dear Friend,

Many thanks for your truly kind and friendly letter[4] of October 3rd. It is the part of a friend to take care of the reputation of an absentee: you have performed that part, and have my gratitude. We have for many years lived in the greatest friendship, both in our public and private stations. The victory of the Nile has not, in Italy, produced those consequences which I, and many others, naturally concluded. Could it be believed that 50,000 men could have vanished in a month, without a battle, before less than 11,000 bad troops; but this I have seen, and with the greatest grief. Palermo is detestable, and we are all unwell and full of sorrow. I will not venture to say this Country will be a Monarchy six months. General Mack has disappeared: a butcher rules at Naples: a French General lives in the palace at        . Where is all this to end? Tuscany is paying money to the scoundrels, but 15,000 French are in the different Towns: Lucca is revolutionized. The Emperor looks on and sees all this. He will repent when too late; for his newly-acquired Venetian dominions will be lost, and he will totter on his throne at Vienna. I have presented your kind respects to Sir William and Lady Hamilton: they are incomparable; therefore, I can only tell you they are as good as ever. Acton, I think, will soon give up his situation and retire to England— that happy Country! Long, very long may it remain so! I have to thank you for your hint of Supporters and Mottoes. Those things I leave to the Herald's Office as unworthy our notice; for soon, very soon, we must all be content with a plantation of six feet by two, and I probably shall possess this estate much sooner than is generally thought; but, whilst I live, I never shall forget the few real friends I have in this world—but amongst [them], I hope, I may rank you; for believe me, I am, with real regard, your most faithful and obliged,

NELSON.

[4] Vide p. 85, ante.

TO CAPTAIN BALL, H.M.S. ALEXANDER.

[Original, in the possession of Sir William Keith Ball, Bart.]

Bellerophon, Palermo, 31st January, 1799.

My[5] dear Ball,

I send you the Minerve and Vanguard if you want them : you may keep the Vanguard, so as not to make her absence from me more than a fortnight : the other if you can spare her, I should also be glad you would send back in a short time afterwards. I am very anxious to hear from you and how you proceed in the blockade. Indeed, I am very anxious to be with you myself, but I am tied so fast here by their Sicilian Majesties that I cannot move.

Sir Sidney Smith, from a letter he wrote Earl St. Vincent, off Malta, has given great offence, having said that he presumed all the Ships in the Levant being junior to him, he had a right to take them under his command. His Lordship has in consequence given him a broad hint, and has taken him down very handsomely ; and, to prevent any further mistakes of this kind, has ordered Sir Sidney to put himself immediately under my command, which I suppose the great Plenipo will not like. However, he has brought this upon himself.

From Minorca, Commodore Duckworth presses hard for a Ship or two of the Line, to re-inforce his Squadron, as they are threatened with an invasion of that Island from the Coast of Spain by a large Army and numerous Gun-boats, besides some Ships of the Line. We have no news from Naples since the 15th instant. From Leghorn our news is very bad. Captain Louis in the Minotaur is laying there for the protection of the Grand Duke and his Family, if they wish to embark, as well as all the British subjects. The French have republicanized Lucca, and have troops in many parts of the Tuscan territories. I have received information of six French Ships of the Line fitting out at Brest to make a push for the Mediterranean, and it is supposed their object is Malta or Egypt. However, should they attempt it, I trust Lord Keith will fall in with them before they get up. For

[5] Added in Nelson's hand, the letter itself having been written by his Secretary.

news, I refer you to Captains Cockburn and Hardy. Sir
William (who has been much indisposed) and Lady Hamilton
join in best wishes and regards with your faithful and obedient
Servant,

NELSON.

[Added, by Lord Nelson.]

Tyson wrote the above. I will send him to you for two
days when I can spare him,—a difficult thing.

---

TO LADY PARKER.[6]

[Autograph, in the possession of Mrs. Ellis.]

Palermo, February 1st, 1799.

My dear Madam,
What shall I say to you and good Sir Peter for all your
goodness to me : you who have known me from my youth
even until now, know that Horatio Nelson is still the same
—affectionate in his disposition and grateful to his friends.
God knows, my dear friend, I have few indeed ! When I go
hence, and am no more seen, I shall have very very few to
regret me. My health is such that without a great alteration,
I will venture to say a very short space of time[7] will send me
to that bourne from whence none return; but God's will be
done. After the Action I had nearly fell into a decline, but
at Naples my invaluable friends Sir William and Lady Hamilton nursed and set me up again. I am worse than ever :
my spirits have received such a shock that I think they cannot recover it. You who remember me always laughing and
gay, would hardly believe the change; but who can see what I
have and be well in health? Kingdoms lost and a Royal
Family in distress; but they are pleased to place confidence in
me, and whilst I live and my services can be useful to them,
I shall never leave this Country, although I know that
nothing but the air of England, and peace and quietness, can
perfectly restore me. I am sorry to hear from Captain Cock-

---

[6] See Lady Parker's letter to Lord Nelson after the Battle of the Nile, p. 83,
ante.

[7] Lord Nelson originally wrote " few weeks."

burn that your health is not so good as your numerous friends
must wish it, and none more ardently than your affectionate,

NELSON.

Say to my dear Sir Peter how much I honour and respect
him ; and to Admiral and Miss Parker [8] present my sincerest
wishes for their health and happiness. I enclose a line for
our friend Macnamara.[9] I am sorry it is not in my power to
do what he wishes me. Darby[1] is at my elbow and desires to
be kindly remembered.

---

TO ADMIRAL THE EARL OF ST. VINCENT, K.B.

[Letter-Book.]

Bellerophon, Palermo, 1st February, 1799.

My Lord,

I have to acknowledge the receipt of your letter of the
16th January,[2] enclosing a copy of one from Sir Sidney Smith,
off Malta, with your answer, as also your Lordship's order to
take him under my command. I consider myself highly
honoured by your Lordship's letter, and flattered by your
attention ; and will order Sir Sidney Smith to put himself
under my command the very first opportunity. I am, with
the highest respect, my Lord, your most obedient and faithful
Servant,

NELSON.

---

TO ADMIRAL THE EARL OF ST. VINCENT, K.B.

[Letter-Book.]

Bellerophon, Palermo, 1st February, 1799.

My Lord,

I have received your Lordship's letter of the 28th December with the several enclosures—viz., Mr. Walpole's letter of
21st December, respecting the French Directory declaring
war against Naples and Sardinia, General Frazer's letter

---

[8] Apparently Anne, their second daughter, who married, in 1800, George Ellis,
Esq. of Sunning Hill.

[9] Captain James Macnamara. Vide vol. i. p. 25.

[1] Captain of the Bellerophon.　　　　[2] Vide p. 214.

and copy of De Souza's letter to General Frazer, respecting the sending the Regiment of Roll from Lisbon to Minorca, and your Lordship wishing me to send any Line-of-Battle Ship that may want repairs to Minorca, as fast as possible.

I beg leave to acquaint your Lordship that the Bellerophon is the only Ship I have here at present, but the moment I can get Minotaur and Terpsichore from Leghorn, I shall order them down, with directions to call at Minorca in their way. With respect to the Merchant-ships bound to Venice, their cargoes being mostly perishable articles, and not the least possibility of selling them here, I have appointed the San Leon to convoy them up to Venice, and from thence to proceed immediately to Trieste, and at the desire of their Sicilian Majesties, to take under her convoy two Neapolitan vessels, laden with small arms, and bring them to Messina or this place. I have the honour to be, &c.

                                                    NELSON.

---

TO HIS EXCELLENCY THE MARQUIS DE NIZA.

[Letter-Book.]

Bellerophon, Palermo, 1st February, 1799.

My Lord,

I have to request your Excellency will order two Ships of the Line of her Most Faithful Majesty, under your command, to join me without loss of time at this place, and I leave it to your choice whether you will come here with the Principe Real, or one of them, or remain at Messina. And I have also to request that your Excellency will send immediately one of your Ships of the Line off Malta, with my positive orders to her Commander to put himself under the command of Captain Ball, of his Majesty's Ship the Alexander, who is appointed to conduct the blockade. I here enclose some dispatches, this day received from Gibraltar, and have the honour to be, &c.

                                                    NELSON.

## TO COMMODORE DUCKWORTH.

[Letter-Book.]

Palermo, 2nd February, 1799.

My dear Sir,

I thank you most truly for your several very interesting letters, and I beg that I may be favoured with your correspondence whenever opportunity offers. You will, I am sure, make allowances for a left-handed man ; but my inclination to write longer letters than I am able to do, is great. I can get but slowly over the paper.

I have sent to make inquiries about the wood, and hope to send you particulars. There is none certainly on this side of Sicily. I have given Lord William Stuart[3] a run to Leghorn, as Lord St. Vincent's order [is] to send there for 1200 pairs of shoes. I return you the Cutter, and I hope you will be able to let her proceed to Gibraltar. El Corso shall return to you the moment she arrives from Leghorn ; and Terpsichore, who I have sent for, shall call at Mahon, for your and the General's dispatches, in her way down. Dorothea will go down in about three weeks, and Minotaur, but they shall all look at you. For ever believe me, &c.

NELSON.

---

## TO ADMIRAL THE EARL OF ST. VINCENT, K.B.

[Letter-Book.]

Bellerophon, Palermo, 2nd February, 1799.

My Lord,

I have to acknowledge the receipt of your Lordship's letter of the 8th January, enclosing one from Mr. Bensamon, his Majesty's Vice-Consul at Algiers, conveying several complaints from the Dey, which your Lordship has requested I would endeavour to redress.

I beg leave to acquaint your Lordship, that I am totally ignorant of the whole of the Dey's complaints, except it be about the thirteen Moors ; but that, on the departure of Kelim Effendi, the Turkish Ambassador, from hence, he observed

---

[3] Captain of the El Corso, brig. He died Captain of the Conquestador in July 1814, on his passage from the Havannah to England.

some Moors call to him from the Principe Real, (which he was passing in a Boat,) then laying in the Mole, and, in consequence sent to me to procure them their liberty.  I immediately made application to the Marquis de Niza[4] for all the Moors and Turks he had on board, and he very handsomely gave them to me, and they were instantly sent to the Ambassador, to the number of twenty-five, and he has taken them along with him to Constantinople.  But whether these are any of the Moors mentioned by Mr. Bensamon I have not been able to learn, but will make inquiries on board the other Portuguese Ships.                    I am, &c.

NELSON.

---

## TO HIS EXCELLENCY SIR JOHN ACTON, BART.

[Letter-Book.]

Palermo, 2nd February, 1799.

Sir,

If six thousand salms of corn are not sent directly to Malta, the inhabitants are in that state of want, that the worst consequences for the interests of his Sicilian Majesty may justly be apprehended.  All these poor people want is, that the King should give them six months' credit, when they could make their payments in money or cotton.  The case is important and demands instant compliance.  Your Excellency will excuse this plain truth for being told, perhaps, too abruptly, and believe me, &c.,

NELSON.

The inhabitants have not seven days' bread.

---

## TO CAPTAIN LOUIS, H. M. SHIP MINOTAUR,

[Letter-Book.]

Bellerophon, Palermo, 2nd February, 1799.

My dear Louis,

I have sent the El Corso for 1200 pairs of shoes left at Leghorn, at the evacuation, belonging to Government, and are already paid for.  Lord William Stuart has all the letters

[4] Vide p. 281, ante.

respecting them, and I must request your assistance to him in getting them off, which, if it cannot be immediately effected, you will receive the letters from him, and dispatch him to me, for he has my orders not to remain at Leghorn more than forty-eight hours.　I have also to request that you will immediately dispatch the Terpsichore to join me at this place, as the Earl St. Vincent has ordered her down the Mediteranean.

We have nothing new since the Balloon sailed, and nothing authentic from Naples.　Sir William and Lady Hamilton desire to be kindly remembered to you, and believe me, &c.

NELSON.

I long to see Minotaur.　Come as soon as you can.

---

### TO H.R.H. THE DUKE OF CLARENCE.

[From Clarke and M'Arthur, vol. ii. p. 149.]

Palermo, 2nd February, 1799.

Sir,

I was yesterday honoured with your Royal Highness's kind letter;[5] and it was with real sorrow that I saw, for one moment, you had been displeased with me.　But, like yourself, it passed away—and your friendship, on which I have and always shall pride myself, remains for one who is attached to your Royal Highness inferior to none in this world.　Indeed, Horatio Nelson is the same as your goodness has ever known him to be—attached, affectionate, and unchangeable; with one hand to a wounded head, and, I may now add, with my heart full, and the business of fifteen Sail of the Line, besides my near connexion with the shore.　I have sent Troubridge and some Bombs to Egypt, to endeavour to do that which could have been done, if I had possessed the means, in forty-eight hours after the Action.　It is now doubtful; but my gallant friend will do what man can do.　I beg your Royal Highness to believe that I am ever your attached

NELSON.

---

[5] Probably the letter in p. 83.　His Royal Highness' displeasure arose from his supposing that Nelson had not written to him after the Battle of the Nile.

## TO ADMIRAL THE EARL OF ST. VINCENT, K.B.

[Letter-Book.]

Palermo, 3rd February, 1799, 3 p.m.

My dear Lord,

The Incendiary is just come from Ball, off Malta, and has brought me information that the attempt of the storming the City of Valetta had failed, from (I am afraid I must call it) cowardice. They were over the first ditch, and retired— *d—n them!* But I trust the zeal, judgment, and bravery of my friend Ball, and his gallant party, will overcome all difficulty. The Cutter[6] just going off, prevents my being more particular. Ever your most faithful,

NELSON.

Naples is declared a Republic, and the French flag flying. We are low in spirits, but all in this house love you.

---

## TO ADMIRAL THE EARL OF ST. VINCENT, K.B.

[Letter-Book.]

Bellerophon, Palermo, 3rd February, 1799.

My Lord,

I have to acknowledge the receipt of your Lordship's letter of the 28th December, conveying the Thanks of the House of Peers of Ireland, to me, the Captains, Officers, Seamen, and Marines of the detached Squadron under my command, at the Battle of the Nile.

I have to request your Lordship will be pleased to communicate to the Lord Chancellor of Ireland, the grateful sense I entertain of the high honour conferred by the House of Peers, and will not fail to make known their Thanks to the Captains, Officers, &c. now under my command as soon as possible. I have the honour to be, &c.

NELSON.

[6] L'Entreprénante.

TO CAPTAIN BALL, H. M. SHIP ALEXANDER.

[Letter-Book.]

Palermo, February 4th, 1799.

My dear Ball,

I have just received your letter with its several enclosures, and although I regret that the *malconduct* of the Maltese has caused the enterprise to fail, yet I trust that at a future day it will succeed. I am satisfied, my dear friend, that you and your brave companions have done all which was possible to do. Respecting the corn wanted for Malta, I wrote yesterday to General Acton, and received the answer, of which I enclose you a copy. This evening I saw the King, and he is exceedingly angry to think that his faithful Maltese subjects should want for any comforts or necessaries which it is in his power to bestow. I would wish you to send over to Girgenti, or Alicati, in order to secure the safe arrival of the corn in Malta. If ever Malta surrenders, the King of Naples is its legitimate Sovereign, and his Flag must fly, and the British Squadron will support it. Should any party hoist the Russian or other flag, the King will not and I will not permit the extraction of corn from Sicily, nor from any other place. I trust you will be able to prevent all French vessels from entering the Port. I well know the difficulty of the task, but I am confident everything which an excellent Officer can do will be done. If I get hold of a Portuguese corvette, she shall come to you. I have ordered a Ship of the Line of that Nation to put herself under your command. If the Commander objects, let it be in writing, and then recommend him to cruize in a particular place, so as not to annoy the Tunis cruizers, who are out against the French. In short, my dear Ball, use the Portuguese in some way or other. As to Gun-boats, or any assistance from this government, it is not [to] be expected, but you shall have every small Vessel I can lay my hands upon. You will, with your usual discretion, tell the Deputies my opinion, about the conduct of the Russians; and should any Russian Ships, or Admiral, arrive off Malta, you will convince him of the very unhandsome manner of treating the legitimate Sovereign of Malta, by wishing to see the Russian flag fly in Malta, and also of me, who command the forces of a Power in

such close alliance with the Russian Emperor, which have
been blockading and attacking Malta for near six months.
The Russians shall never take the lead. Respecting stores
and provisions, I have none here. All are at Syracuse, and
Troubridge authorized to make a distribution of them. Till
the Ships come from Egypt, I cannot change any of your
Ships of the Line, as they are older than yourself. The
Goliath is to carry Sir William and Lady Hamilton to England, whenever they choose to go, but the time is not yet
fixed. Minorca calls for two Sail of the Line; Minotaur goes
directly for Gibraltar; but the Earl tells me he will not send
the Foudroyant till I send him two Sail of the Line. The
exchange of Marine officers will suit Captain Creswell, I
hope; but many Ships will, in my opinion, go down the
Mediterranean before Goliath, as she is kept to attend our
good friends. You will, my dear Ball, always act in such a
manner as to do credit to yourself and Country, and always to
meet the approbation of your sincere and affectionate

NELSON.

I send you the late papers.

---

TO COMMODORE DUCKWORTH.

[Letter-Book.]

Palermo, February 4th, 1799.

My dear Sir,
Lieutenant Atkinson, who came up in the Cutter belongs
to the Theseus, and as two Lieutenants are going down the
Mediterranean, by the time the Cutter gets to Minorca, they
will be used to Cutter sailing, and if you approve, Lieutenant
Swiney can take the Cutter to Gibraltar, and Lieutenant
A. return here to join his Ship. Ever your faithful,

NELSON.

The Vesuvian Republic is formed. Of course all Vessels
belonging to Naples and its Environs ought to be stopped.
At least, I think so.

## TO THE RIGHT HONOURABLE SIR WILLIAM HAMILTON, K.B.

[Letter-Book.]

Bellerophon, Palermo, 5th February, 1799.

My dear Sir,

I find on inquiry into the subject of your Excellency's letter to me, conveying a complaint of the Prince Luigi, Secretary of State, relative to some armed Boats boarding a Vessel in quarantine, that a complete and most gross misrepresentation has been made to your Excellency on this occasion.

In the first place no armed Boats are ever rowed about the Mole of Palermo. The Vessel in quarantine was laying at the Mole-head: every one knows that Vessels in quarantine could not with propriety be placed there—another place being, in all Ports I have seen, appropriated for them: therefore, she could not but be considered as in pratique by any Ship warping into the Mole, and lastly, that the Boat of the Bellerophon was going on board the Vessel to slack her cable, and one man had certainly gone up her side when some soldier called out she was in quarantine; and the man returned to the Boat, and no further communication was made with the Vessel. You will see, sir, that this circumstance of going on board the Vessel was not owing to any fault of the English boat, who was performing an act of kindness in saving the Vessel from being damaged by the large Ship, but a Vessel being in quarantine in such a place, I must say, was highly improper and irregular. I can assure your Excellency that my orders are the very strictest to respect all the regulations of the Pratique-house, on which so much depends the health of all countries. Ever believe me, &c.,

NELSON.

---

## TO THE DEPUTIES OF THE MALTESE PEOPLE.

[Letter-Book.]

Bellerophon, Palermo, 5th February, 1799

Gentlemen,

I here enclose for your information the copy of a letter I have received from General Acton, respecting the supply of corn wanted by the Maltese people. I am happy to have it in my power, and shall always be ready to yield you every assistance.

Captain Ball, who commands the Squadron before Malta, and of whose conduct and abilities I have the highest opinion, will also give you all the assistance in his power to get the corn over to Malta. Wishing you every success against your Enemies and a speedy surrender of the Capital again into your possession, I am, &c.,

NELSON.

---

TO COMMISSIONER COFFIN, PORT MAHON.

[From the " Naval Chronicle," vol. xxiii. p. 388.]

Palermo, February 5th, 1799.

My dear Coffin,

Many thanks for your kind letter, I shall be glad to accept your offers from the arsenal at Minorca, for all my Ships want much repairing. God knows if we shall not all very soon pay you a visit, for if the Vesuvian Republic continues by the permission of the Emperor, the Island must very soon be without a Monarchy. Troubridge is gone to Egypt. We left-handed gentlemen are privileged to write short letters, therefore I shall finish. Believe me, ever your most obliged and faithful friend,

NELSON.

---

TO CAPTAIN BALL.

[Letter-Book.]

Bellerophon, Palermo, 5th February, 1799.

My dear Ball,

I have to request you will send to this place by the first opportunity, Lieutenant Whipple, of His Majesty's Ship under your command, and Lieutenant Jardine of the Go- liath, in order to their going down the Mediterranean to receive their commissions as Captains from the Commander- in-Chief; and in their vacancy, to put Mr. Young of the Vanguard, as one and any other that Captain Hardy may

point out from that Ship, except you have some person
whom you wish to recommend to fill one of them.  Wishing
you every success, believe me your faithful and obedient
servant,

                                          NELSON.

_____

### TO COMMODORE DUCKWORTH.

[Letter-Book.]

8th February, [1799.]

My dear Sir,

As the Vesuvian Republic is formed under the protection
of the French, there can be no doubt that it is at war with
Great Britain : therefore, the property of all those who have not
left this new State, ought to be good and lawful prize.
Gaeta, and the Coast to Naples, and Castel-à-Mare, with
the Islands of Ischia, Procida, and Capri, have flying the new

Flag  | Yellow / Red / Blue |  or | Blue / Red / Yellow | .  Salerno not has yet joined, nor any

of the Coast of Calabria.  I have given orders here to seize
all Vessels belonging to the above-mentioned places.  If the
owners have quit with the King, to have them returned—if
not, they may safely be sold and the money deposited till
they [are] condemned.

Everything is wanting for the defence of this Country and
Calabria ; and a messenger goes off this day for Vienna to point
out their deplorable situation ; but if the Emperor will not act,
both Sicily and Sardinia must belong to the French.  I shall
endeavour to mediate with the Bey of Tunis and Tripoli for
a truce during the war for this Island.  If you have [an] opportunity of sending to Tunis, let us coax the Bey into good-
humour.  At present he is well-disposed to us.  When you
see General Stuart, pray present my very best respects and
to Colonel Graham, and believe me ever your much obliged,

                                          NELSON.

## TO LIEUTENANT-GOVERNOR LOCKER, ROYAL HOSPITAL, GREENWICH.

[Autograph, in the Locker Papers.]

My dear Friend,                    Palermo, February 9th, 1799.

I well know your own goodness of heart will make all due allowances for my present situation, and that truly I have not the time or power to answer all the letters I receive at the moment; but you, my old friend, after twenty-seven years acquaintance know that nothing can alter my attachment and gratitude to you: I have been your scholar; it is you who taught me to board a Frenchman, by your conduct when in the Experiment;[6] it is you who always told [me], "Lay a Frenchman close, and you will beat him," and my only merit in my profession is being a good scholar; our friendship will never end but with my life; but you have always been too partial to me. Pray tell Kingsmill that it was impossible I could attend to his recommendation; indeed I had, not being a Commander-in-Chief, no power to name an Agent; remember me kindly to him. The Vesuvian Republic being formed, I have now to look out for Sicily; but Revolutionary principles are so prevalent in the world, that no Monarchical government is safe, or sure of lasting ten years. I beg you will make my kindest remembrances to Miss Locker and all your good sons, and believe me ever your faithful and affectionate friend,

NELSON.

## TO CAPTAIN BALL, H.M. SHIP ALEXANDER.

[Autograph, in the possession of Sir William Keith Ball, Bart.]

Palermo, February 9th, 1799.

My dear Ball,

I send you the Benjamin,[7] Captain Thompson, but I beg you will endeavour to keep him out of the way of the Tunisian cruizers; for I should be sorry if any action took place,

---

[6] Captain Locker was First Lieutenant of the Experiment of 20 guns and 142 men, commanded by Captain Sir John Strachan, on the 19th of June 1757, when she fell in with Le Telemaque, a large French Ship of 26 guns and 460 men, which was gallantly boarded and carried by the Experiment's crew, led by Mr. Locker.

[7] Portuguese Brig of War. Portugal was then at war with Tunis.

which might lose our friendship with the Bey. We have nothing new here as yet. All is quiet at Naples and its environs: the French flag is flying. They have fitted out the Frigate and Brigs, and I have my fears they will drive off the Mutine. When I get the Minerve, she shall cruize off Naples. God bless you. Sir William and Lady Hamilton desire their regards. You are loved by the fair, and esteemed by the brave ; so says your faithful and obliged friend,

NELSON.

---

### TO MR. JOSEPH LITTLEDALE.

[Letter-Book.]

Bellerophon, Palermo, 11th February, 1799.

Sir,

I have received your letter of the 6th instant, with the vouchers enclosed, and have sent you the certificate you desire, respecting the exchange at Palermo on London, which is this day at fifty-two Taris to the pound sterling. I observe what you say respecting the ruin you apprehend in furnishing the Squadron with provisions, and leave it entirely to your consideration whether you will continue to supply them or not; as if you determine on the contrary, I have no doubt but some other person may be glad to undertake the business. I shall wait your answer, and am, &c.

NELSON.

---

### TO SIR JOHN ACTON, BART.

[Letter Book.]

Palermo, February 11th, 1799.

My dear Sir,

I have to thank your Excellency for the honour of your letter, and for sending for my perusal the report of various Officers on the situation of this Island, and of its means of defence. Respecting an invasion of the French *in propriâ personâ*, I own I have no alarms, for if this Island is true to itself no harm can happen; but I own my fears that Revolutionary principles may be sown here, and the seasons being propitious to the growth, will produce fruit. If the Emperor will not move, and save himself, (for his throne must fall, if the late measures of his councils are persisted in,) the good King, Queen, and Family of Naples, [must be driven out of] the possession of their Kingdoms; we may lament, but what must follow is certain. Having thus openly declared my general opinion, it is perfectly proper, no doubt, to be prepared for defence ; and if Calabria is occupied by the French, the first object is the preservation of Messina, and the Torre del Faro. As to the other parts of the Island, if the inhabitants are loyal, the French may be defied ; they will not venture their carcases. But, indeed, my dear Sir, it is on the fidelity of the Islanders we must depend for its defence. When Captain Troubridge returns from Egypt, I shall have the power of having more Ships on the East Coast ; as to Palermo, it shall never be without a proper defence in Shipping from all attacks by sea, that is, from what the French have at present in the Mediterranean. In other things I beg that your Excellency will have the goodness to assure his Sicilian Majesty that nothing shall be wanting on my part for the defence of his Kingdoms, and whatever can administer to his comforts ; and I beg your Excellency will believe with what great respect I am, &c.

NELSON.

---

TO THE MARQUIS DE NIZA, OR THE COMMANDING OFFICER OF HER MOST FAITHFUL MAJESTY'S SHIPS AT MESSINA.

[Order-Book.]

Bellerophon, Palermo, 11th February, 1799.

**Most Secret.**

Notwithstanding former orders or letters, it is my direction that only the Ship of the Marquis de Niza comes to Palermo, and that the other three Ships of her Most Faithful Majesty remain on the Messina coast of Sicily. And, whereas his Sicilian Majesty will probably send immediate orders to seize all the Boats and Vessels on the Coast of Calabria, it is my positive orders, that you use every means in your power for the effectual execution of the King's orders; and you will consult with the Governor of Messina, and the Officer who is to command the Galliots and Gun-boats, on the best mode of executing these orders. You will, as I have by my

order of the 5th of January, either by manning Gun-boats or
Galliots, or by getting your Ships under sail, or anchoring on
the Coast of Calabria, facilitate his Sicilian Majesty's orders.
On your good and active co-operation and judgment, probably,
depends the prevention of the French getting over to Sicily;
and I expect everything from your rank and ability.

NELSON.

---

### TO LIEUTENANT LAMB, AGENT OF TRANSPORTS, SYRACUSE.

[Letter-Book. On the 12th of February, the Vanguard returned to Palermo, and
Lord Nelson re-hoisted his flag on board of her.]

Bellerophon, Palermo, 12th February, 1799.

Sir,

I very much approve of your keeping the Transports in
constant readiness for sea, and have to request you will continue to do so, as I shall send a Ship very soon to convoy
them all round to this place; and when she appears off the
harbour of Syracuse, and makes the signal, you will get them
all under weigh immediately, to join her. I am, &c.

NELSON.

---

### TO ADMIRAL THE EARL OF ST. VINCENT, K.B.

[From Clarke and M'Arthur, vol. ii. p. 150.]

Palermo, 13th February, 1799.

Our news from Calabria is very bad, as most of the Towns
have planted the Tree of Liberty, and the madness approaches
the coast towards Sicily. In this Island are many discontented
people, who have shown themselves in various places in a
manner contrary to law, and nearly approaching rebellion.
Thus situated, who can say but the chance is, that the Royal
Family will be obliged once more to take refuge under the
British flag? I have letters from Mr. Wyndham at Florence,
who represents the situation of Tuscany as very critical. The
French make no scruple of declaring their intention of revolu-
tionizing the Grand Duchy. Not content with turning the King
of Sardinia out of Piedmont, they intended seizing his person
after he left Leghorn, by some of their privateers, and carry-

ing him to Corsica; for if they could have prevented it, His Majesty would never have got to Sardinia.[8]

Captain Louis had been requested to allow the Terpsichore to go, as if by accident, in company with the Vessel; for to such a state of degradation is this Monarch reduced, that he dared not publicly accept of the offered protection of the British flag. His Holiness the Pope is not expected to live.[9] The French ordered him, although living in Tuscany, to quit that country, and repair to Sardinia; and when he represented his ill state of health, Salicetti was present when the old man's blisters were taken off, to see he did not sham: however, he will soon be at rest from all his cares and troubles. As to myself, I see but gloomy prospects, look which way I will. We have accounts that sixty thousand Russians are arrived at Saltzburg, the German side of the Tyrol; but as the Russians have been marching the whole war, so they will I fear, arrive too late in Italy. At present I see but little prospect of the fall of Malta; several Vessels with provisions are got in. Ball is indefatigable, and has great hopes. In short, my dear Lord, everything makes me sick, to see things go to the Devil, and not to have the means of prevention. I am, &c.

NELSON.

---

TO THE MARQUIS DE NIZA.

[Letter Book. On the 14th of February, 1799, a promotion of Admirals took place, when Lord Nelson became, from Rear of the Blue, a Rear-Admiral of the Red.]

My Lord,                    Vanguard, Palermo, 14th February, 1799.

His Sicilian Majesty wants to send immediately 500 men to Messina, and they must go in the Principe Real as soon as they can be got on board; and I desire your Excellency will give the most energetic orders for the speedy arrival of these troops at Messina, as you know the probable safety of that place depends on a re-inforcement of good troops. Unless your Excellency wishes to go in the Ship, you have my permission to remain at Palermo till her return.

I have the honour to be, &c.,

NELSON.

[8] The King of Sardinia and his family, after taking refuge at Florence, sailed in a Danish frigate for Cagliari, the capital of Sardinia, on the 23rd of February, protected by the Terpsichore, Captain Gage.

[9] Pope Pius the Sixth died at Valence, in France, on the 29th of August 1799, aged eighty-one.

TO JAMES TOUGH, ESQ., CONSUL-GENERAL, PALERMO.

[Letter-Book.]

Vanguard, 14th February, 1799.

Sir,

His Excellency, Sir William Hamilton, having acquainted me by letter of this day's date, that a certain quantity of lead is wanted by his Sicilian Majesty, in order to make musket-balls, and as I think it absolutely necessary that his Majesty should be supplied with that article for the better defence of his Kingdom, I am under the necessity of desiring that you will sell to the Officers of his Sicilian Majesty the lead wanted—say, 100 tons; but in selling this lead you are to be particularly careful to receive in money, or other articles of equal advantage to the owners of the lead, the full value which this or any other market in the Mediterranean would give; and you will take care not to part with the lead until you receive the full value, freight, &c. &c.   I am, &c.,

NELSON.

---

TO HIS EXCELLENCY ABDUL CADIR BEY, VICE-ADMIRAL
COMMANDING THE TURKISH FLEET, OFF CORFU.

[Letter-Book.]

Vanguard, Palermo, 15th February, 1799.

Sir,

Your Excellency, without doubt, has heard of the melancholy news from Naples. The French, not content with having, by perfidy, declared Naples a Republic, but have forced a great part of Calabria to erect the Tree of *Terror*, which those unbelievers call of *Liberty;* and their emissaries are sowing the seeds of anarchy in this Island, and particularly at Messina, which it is of the very greatest consequence to prevent falling into the hands of the French or Jacobins: therefore, as I have in Egypt, for the Grand Signior, the following Ships—viz., Culloden, 74; Zealous, 74; Lion, 64; Tigre, 80: Swiftsure, 74; Theseus, 74; Seahorse, 38; Vesuvius and Etna bombs, I must earnestly request, for the benefit of the common cause, that your Excellency will immediately send such Ships as you can possibly spare to Messina, in order for defending that invaluable place, on which depends the safety of Sicily. I rest also confident that your Excellency will urge any Turkish General who may be near you, to embark as many troops as possible on this very important occasion. I have the honour to send you a copy of a letter wrote by the Russian Minister at Florence to the English Minister. I have, blockading Malta, four Sail of the Line, and four Frigates and Corvettes, and I hope to have a good account of its surrender to the King of Naples, its legitimate Sovereign, in a few days. I have the honour to be, &c.,

NELSON.

-------------------

### TO HIS EXCELLENCY THEODORE OUSCHAKOFF, VICE-ADMIRAL COMMANDING THE RUSSIAN FLEET BEFORE CORFU.

[Letter-Book.]

Vanguard, Palermo, 15th February, 1799.

Sir,

His Sicilian Majesty having sent letters, and a confidential person to talk to your Excellency and the Turkish Admiral on the present situation of affairs in this Country, and requesting that you will direct a part of your Fleet to come to Messina to assist in preserving this Kingdom from falling into the hands of the French, and as your Excellency will receive letters from your Minister on this very important subject, I shall only beg leave to point out to your Excellency the very great service you will render the common cause, and his Sicilian Majesty in particular, by sending as many Ships and troops as possible to Messina. I have at present in Egypt the following Ships—viz., Culloden, 74 ; Zealous, 74 ; Lion, 64 ; Tigre, 80 ; Theseus, 74 ; Swiftsure, 74 ; Seahorse, 38 ; Etna and Vesuvius Bombs ; and blockading Malta, four Sail of the Line and four Frigates and Corvettes ; and I hope, in a short time, to see his Sicilian Majesty's Flag fly in the Town of La Valetta. I have also two Portuguese Ships of the Line at Messina, and two English Ships of the Line at Palermo. With every sentiment of respect, I have the honour to be, &c.,

NELSON.

## TO COMMISSIONER COFFIN, PORT MAHON.

[From the "Naval Chronicle," vol. xxiii. p. 389.]

Palermo, 15th February, 1799.

My dear Coffin,

I send you the Mutine. Pray see if you can patch her up, and give her some stores. I am obliged to send El Corso on her mission, for which Duckworth will scold. How long we shall remain here, you must ask the French; for at present I see nothing to oppose their progress. God bless you.

I am, &c.,

NELSON.

---

## TO COMMISSIONER INGLEFIELD, GIBRALTAR.

[Letter-Book.]

Vanguard, Palermo, 16th February, 1799.

Sir,

I herewith transmit you a demand for slops for his Majesty's Ship Goliath, and beg leave to observe that all the Ships now under my command are equally in want of them, and some of them very much distressed, as slops are not to be purchased here but at an enormous price, and very disadvantageous to the seamen. I am, &c.,

NELSON.

---

## TO LIEUTENANT-GENERAL THE HONOURABLE CHARLES STUART.

[From a Copy, in the Admiralty.]

Palermo, 16th February, 1799.

What a state we are in here!—without troops, and the Enemy at the door; for although there are 4000 Neapolitan regular troops, these are not to be trusted; 13,000 Sicilian troops are raising, and 26,000 Militia; but I fear, before these are got together, the active French will get possession of Messina, the key of Sicily. There is a good Citadel, and might be defended for a long time; but there is such treachery, that probably it will be given without a shot. I know, my dear Sir, your situation at Minorca, and I regret that you cannot, I fear, send here and save us, for 1000 English troops in the citadel of Messina would, I am convinced save Sicily. I dare not hope such a thing; but having ventured to mention this subject, I leave it to your excellent judgment. With every sentiment of respect, believe me, my dear Sir, yours, &c.

NELSON.

I have sent my letter to Lord St. Vincent open, for Duckworth to read, which tells all the news I can learn.

---

### TO CAPTAIN TROUBRIDGE, H. M. SHIP CULLODEN.

[Letter-Book.]

Palermo, February 18th, 1799.

My dear Troubridge,

Whatever has been the result of your expedition to Egypt, I am confident it is such as will do you credit; and if you, and my other brave friends, are well in health, all is well. You will find that I have ordered all our Transports from Syracuse to Palermo; for, in truth, I do not think this Country safe from the *infection* which has spread itself over Calabria, and yet I am certain the Sicilians hate the French. I am anxious for the safety of Messina; for until the tri-coloured Flag fly there, I am in [no] fear for the rest of the Island: therefore, I wish you to go to Messina, approaching it with caution. Look at its state, and if you think that 300 good Marines can be raised from the Ships with you, and that they may be of great use in defence of the Citadel, I would have you land them for the use of the Citadel, under the command of Major Oldfield,[3] or the senior Marine Officer with you, if he is equally good. I would have you remain at Messina till you can hear from me, keeping three Ships with you, and sending the rest, and the Bombs, to this place. Some of the Ships, I presume, want our friend Coffin's help at Mahon. I wish the great Sir Sidney Smith may return with you; for I hope he will not be wanted in the Levant, and we want him here. It had been my intention, provided the Citadel could

---

[3] Vide vol. ii. p. 457.

have been defended by 1200 men, to have put you and some of my brave friends into it with seamen and marines; but as 3000 are necessary for its defence, it is beyond my power. We can only do our best to serve the good cause, and hope the great Powers will not suffer this fine Island to fall to the French. The Russians, we know, are in the Tyrol, and I hope the Germans will join them on their entering Italy, when the French yet may be drove out of the Kingdom of Naples. God bless you, and so say our friends, Sir William and Lady Hamilton; and with the desire to be kindly remembered to all with you, believe me ever your affectionate friend,

NELSON.

---

### TO THE MASTERS OF THE ENGLISH SHIPS NOW AT PALERMO.

[Letter-Book.]

Vanguard, Palermo, 20th February, 1799.

Gentlemen,

I have received your letter of yesterday's date, and in answer, I beg leave to transmit you extracts from his Excellency the Honourable William Wyndham's letters to me ; also one from Captain Louis of the Minotaur, and a letter of the English Factory at Leghorn to Captain Louis.

As you, gentlemen, are now in possession of as much information respecting Leghorn, and the state of Tuscany, as I am, I must necessarily leave you to your own judgment. In the present situation of this Kingdom, I cannot recommend the landing of valuable cargoes here. I am, &c.,

NELSON.

---

### MEMORANDUM.

[Letter-Book.]

Palermo, 22nd February, 1799.

Wrote Commodore Mitchell that I had received his letter, and that I was confident he would do everything in his power for the benefit of the Common Cause, and that with the aid of Captain Troubridge, and the exertions of the Sicilians, that he would be able to save Messina.

## MEMORANDUM.

[Order-Book.]

Palermo, 24th February, 1799.

His Sicilian Majesty having been graciously pleased to order one thousand ounces to be given to the Officers, seamen, and marines of his Majesty's Ship the Vanguard, as a mark of his approbation of their conduct during the time he was on board, one hundred ounces to be given to the two Barges' crews who assisted in bringing off the Royal Family, one hundred ounces to be given to the Admiral's servants, and one hundred ounces to be given to the Barge's crew of the Alcmene,—the Rear-Admiral has thought proper to have the one thousand ounces distributed in the following manner :—

|  | Ounces. |
|---|---|
| Wardroom | 100 |
| 27 Gentlemen of the Quarter-deck and Warrant-officers, 4 each | 108 |
| 579 Seamen and Marines, 1 and ⅓ each | 772 |
| 26 Boys, at half each | 13 |
|  | 993 |
| Remains to be laid out for soup, &c. | 7 |
|  | 1000 |

NELSON.

TO MR. ROBERT ATKINSON, MR. WILLIAM BRITTON, MR. ROBERT DIXON, MR. THOMAS ESART, MR. THOMAS MARSHALL, AND MR. ROBERT SHEPPARD, COMMANDERS OF THE ENGLISH SHIPS IN THE PORT OF PALERMO.

[Letter-Book.]

Palermo, 25th February, 1799.

Gentlemen,

I have received your letter of the 23rd. I can assure you, I have always the greatest pleasure in paying attention to the representations of the Masters of Merchant ships who, at this distance, act for their owners in Great Britain. I can have no difficulty [in granting you] a Convoy to Leghorn; but it is my duty to again point out to you the expressions of Mr. Wyndham's several letters, and the request of the English Factory at Leghorn to Captain Louis; and, at the same time, you must be sensible that an English Man-of-War cannot always lay in the Neutral Port, and I expect the Minotaur is now on her passage to join me. If, under all these circumstances, you still persist in going to Leghorn, I will grant a Convoy to that Port as soon as possible. You cannot, of course expect that, when all the knowledge you have of the situation of Tuscany is known in London, that the underwriters or myself can in the smallest degree be answerable for what may happen to your Ships or cargoes. I can only again assure you of my readiness to afford you all the protection possible, compatible with the other important duties entrusted to me, and that I am, with great respect, your most obedient servant,

NELSON.

---

### TO THE MASTERS OF THE ENGLISH SHIPS AT PALERMO.

[Letter-Book.]

Palermo, 26th February, 1799.

Gentlemen,

I will with pleasure grant you the convoy to Leghorn as soon as possible, and such further protection as is in my power; but still with the reservation for the underwriters and myself as I think the case requires. I am, &c.

NELSON.

---

### TO THE MARQUIS DE NIZA.

[Letter-Book.]

Palermo, February 27th, 1799.

My dear Lord,

The good and amiable Queen has desired that all proceedings against Commodore Campbell may be at an end: therefore I have to request that all proceedings against the Commodore may finish, and that he may hoist his Broad Pendant without any thought of what is passed. I am sure of his good intentions, however they may have differed from my orders to your Lordship. Ever believe me, your most faithful friend,

NELSON.

---

TO ALEXANDER DAVISON, ESQ.

[From Clarke and M'Arthur, vol. ii. p. 171.]

[About the end of February, 1799.]

Thank you most heartily, my dear Davison, for your letter. Believe me, my only wish is to sink with honour into the grave, and when that shall please God, I shall meet death with a smile. Not that I am insensible to the honours and riches my King and Country have heaped upon me, so much more than any Officer could deserve; yet I am ready to quit this world of trouble, and envy none but those of the estate six feet by two. I am, &c.,

NELSON.

---

TO CAPTAIN BALL, HIS MAJESTY'S SHIP ALEXANDER.

[From a Copy, in the Admiralty.]

Palermo, 28th February, 1799.

Whereas, the Deputies from the Maltese People have represented to his Excellency Sir William Hamilton, K.B. and myself, that the distracted state of their Councils, frequently render it necessary to have some person of respectability to preside at their meetings, and that you had by your address, frequently united the jarring interests of different Chiefs, and it being also their wish that you should preside at their meetings, and knowing your conciliatory manners, judgment, activity and zeal, which renders you a fit person to assist and preside at their Councils, and it being also the desire of His Sicilian Majesty, you are, therefore, hereby permitted, whenever it may be necessary for you to be on shore, to preside at the Maltese Councils, to leave your Ship in charge of the First Lieutenant, directing him how to proceed, and you are at full liberty to be on shore, with the Maltese army, or on board your

Ship, whenever you may think it necessary :—and His Sicilian Majesty having desired that the British Flag should be hoisted on all parts of the Island of Malta, as well as the Sicilian Flag, you are therefore, whenever a Flag-staff is erected to hoist the Sicilian Colours, to erect another near it, and hoist the English Colours thereon, in order to mark that the Island is under the special protection of his Britannic Majesty; but whenever the English Colours are hoisted, the Sicilian Colours must also be hoisted, as the said Island is to be considered only as under the protection of His Britannic Majesty, during the war. From the situation you are now placed in, you will naturally incur an additional expense, but it is not in our power to annex any salary to it; but His Majesty's Minister here, the Right Honourable Sir William Hamilton, K.B., as well as myself will represent the same to His Majesty's Ministers in England : you will therefore keep an account of your expenses, that they may be allowed you.

NELSON,

---

### TO PERKIN MAGRA, ESQ., CONSUL AT TUNIS.

[Letter-Book. This letter was not forwarded until the middle of March. Vide p. 294.]

Sir,　　　　　　　　　　　　　　Palermo, February, 1799.

I have been favoured with your several highly interesting letters, which you had the goodness to send off Malta, together with the important papers relative to the situation of the French in the Town of La Valetta; and give me leave to say, that your arduous task in keeping the Bey in good humour, and inducing him to act with vigour against the common Enemy, deserves more praise and approbation than it is in my power to bestow; and I hope it will be properly noticed by our superiors in England.

In the present situation of this Island, it is to be wished that a truce could be made between His Sicilian Majesty and the Bey; and I have offered to send any person, authorized by His Sicilian Majesty, in an English ship. The Bey has been misinformed that I have sent any Ship to either Algiers or Tripoli. You will have the goodness to assure His Highness, that he is the first person that I have sent a Ship to. The Vesuvian Republic being formed, renders the situation of this Island the more dangerous; and, if the French get here, to a certainty they will endeavour to destroy Tunis and Algiers. This, with submission to your better judgment, should be pressed upon the Bey and his Minister.

Mrs. Magra and your family are here; Lady Hamilton is so good to them, that in truth they require nothing from me; but, whenever they think it right to go to Tunis, a Ship of War shall carry them. Respecting the purchasing the cargo of provisions destined for Malta, probably, although it might be bought cheap, yet many of the articles might not suit our Ships' companies. Therefore, however desirable, I cannot ask you to purchase any such cargoes for us. I have very great hopes that our affairs at Malta will soon be brought to a close, by the surrender of the Town; and I have sent two Bomb-ships to Egypt to endeavour to destroy the Transports in Alexandria, and if we succeed in this matter, I shall have a very respectable force in Sicily. As I expect the Marquis de Niza, the Portuguese Admiral, here every day, I hope he will send a person to talk with the Bey relative to a truce during the war with France, equally desirable to both parties.

NELSON.

TO ADMIRAL THE EARL OF ST. VINCENT, K.B.

[Letter-Book.]

Palermo, March 2nd, 1799.

My dear Lord,

Since I wrote you by the Mutine, who I sent to Minorca to get some little re-fit, and to convoy a Ship with French émigrés, who are obliged to quit this Country for Tangier, I have had a letter from Captain Troubridge, of which I send you a copy, and also a letter from Alexandria. You will see, my dear Lord, that although the Turks and Russians have not less than twenty Sail of the Line, and as many Frigates, that Great Britain must keep up the blockade of Alexandria, at a time when I want all the Ships for the service from Malta to Leghorn.

The situation of affairs in Naples and Tuscany is, from what we hear, not better than when I last wrote. At Naples are only as yet six thousand French; but we hear they are forming a new Army of twenty thousand men, and I dare say they will be made to fight. In Calabria and the Provinces the French have not dared to advance; although the Nobles, who have remained at Naples, have wrote to their vassals to erect the Tree of Liberty, which has been done, and cut down again in many places. A Cardinal is the Vicar-general in those Provinces, and, by preaching and money, has collected a number of people. Still nothing can be said, whether all is lost, or may yet be saved; that must depend on the movements of the Emperor. The lower class in Italy are truly loyal and attached to their Sovereign, but the Nobles are infamous. As Captain Louis has not sent the Terpsichore, although so positively ordered—as your Lordship directed me to send her down—and the Minotaur was not to stay one moment after the Grand Duke thought himself safe from falling into the hands of the French, that time is not yet arrived. The English merchant-ships, which came up under convoy of the Bellerophon, have made such repeated applications for a convoy to Leghorn, that I have determined to send the Bellerophon with them, and, after waiting a proper time for Mr. Wyndham's opinion, then to either leave the Merchant-ships or bring them back again. The Minotaur shall come here the instant of Captain Darby's arrival, and she shall go down the Mediterranean the instant I can spare her.

Ball has four Ships of the Line off Malta, and we have a report that the three Venetian ships from Toulon, with a convoy of 10 Sail, passed Trapani on the 20th ult., but as yet I can hear nothing from Malta. In this Island, we are in a state of quiet in every sense of the word, both for defence and offence. God bless you, my dear Lord, and be assured that all my actions are to do as I believe you would wish me. I send you the disposition of the Squadron, and ever believe me, your faithful and obliged,

NELSON.

We shall, if we remain, want shells for the Mortars, therefore, pray send me some. The moment the Emperor moves, I shall go, with all the Ships I can collect, into the Bay of Naples, to create a diversion.

#### DISPOSITION OF THE SQUADRON UNDER THE COMMAND OF REAR-ADMIRAL LORD NELSON, K.B.

[Letter-Book.]

Le Tigre  
Theseus  
Lion } Blockading Alexandria.  
Seahorse

Culloden  
Zealous  
Swiftsure  
Alliance } On their way from Alexandria.  
Perseus  
Bull-dog } Bombs

Alexander  
Audacious  
Goliath  
Emerald } Blockading Malta.  
Incendiary  
Strombolo

Bellerophon, going with Convoy to Leghorn.  
Vanguard, at Palermo.  
Minotaur  
Terpsichore } At Leghorn, hourly expected at Palermo.  
Bonne Citoyenne, gone to Constantinople.  
La Mutine, at Minorca, refitting.  
San Leon, gone with Convoy to Venice.  
Santa Dorotea, with the Convoy for Gibraltar.

#### DISPOSITION OF THE PORTUGUESE SQUADRON.

Il Principe Real, expected at Palermo from carrying troops to Messina.  
Affonço, with Captain Ball, off Malta.  
A Rainha, gone with the French Princesses to Trieste from Brindisi.  
St. Sebastian, at Messina.  
Benjamin, with Captain Ball, off Malta.  
Balloon, with Minotaur at Leghorn.

NELSON.

## TO THE HONOURABLE WILLIAM FREDERICK WYNDHAM.

[Letter-Book.]

My dear Sir,                              Palermo, March 2nd, 1799.

The Masters of the English ships here, notwithstanding the extracts of your letters which have been given them, have so pressed me for a Convoy to Leghorn, that I have thought myself obliged to grant it them. I was in hopes the Minotaur and Terpsichore would before this time have joined me, as the latter has been long ordered down the Mediterranean; and if I had more Ships, the service I have to look after requires them—therefore I have to request that you will acquaint Captain Darby, whether he may with safety leave the Convoy at Leghorn. If your Excellency's answer is, ' Yes ;' he has my orders to return here immediately. If it should be the contrary, the signal for Convoy will be made, and those who choose to quit a place of danger, will be brought back here, with the comfort of having lost the present Convoy for England. However, it is my duty, and it is my inclination to do everything for the protection of our commerce, consistent with the other important duties required of me; but you must be sensible that our Country cannot keep a Guard-ship at Leghorn—that is, if she had the power of guarding, it would be well, but she is to do nothing, not even to take a French privateer, which daily rows in and out of the Port, without adhering to the neutrality *required of us*. I find my dear Sir, although the Turks and Russians have twenty Sail of the Line and as many Frigates, yet I am forced to continue the blockade of Alexandria. However, thank God, the plague has got into both the French Army, and into their Shipping—God send it may finish those miscreants ! We are anxious for accounts of the march of the Germans and Russians into Italy. The moment I can hear this, all the Ships I can collect shall go into the Bay of Naples to create a diversion in favour of the Austrians. Your Excellency's account of the treatment of his Royal Highness the Grand Duke, of the King of Sardinia, and of the poor old Pope, makes my heart bleed ; and I curse, in the bitterness of my grief, all those who might have prevented such cruelties. Adieu, my dear Sir, and believe me, &c.,

NELSON.

## TO CAPTAIN DARBY, H.M. SHIP BELLEROPHON.

[Order-Book.]

Vanguard, Palermo, 4th March, 1799.

On the arrival of her Most Faithful Majesty's Ship, the Principe Real, at this place, you are hereby required and directed to take under your protection such British or other Ships, as may be at this Port, and wish to profit of it, and convoy them to the Port of Leghorn; and on your arrival there, to send the Minotaur and Terpsichore immediately to join me, and write to his Excellency, the Honourable William Wyndham, his Majesty's Minister at Florence, requesting his opinion, whether the British merchant-ships may be left with safety at Leghorn. If his Excellency's opinion be, 'Yes, they may;' then you will rejoin me without loss of time. Should his Excellency's opinion be, that there is danger in their being left at Leghorn, you are then to make the signal for a Convoy, and take such Ships under your protection as choose to quit that Port, and join me at this place. But you are at liberty, should circumstances require it, to wait a reasonable time for such of the Merchant-ships as may have perishable cargoes on board, to enable them to dispose of them: I should suppose eight or ten days would be abundance of time for this purpose. You will always keep in mind how much the service requires active, not passive service.

NELSON.

---

## TO ADMIRAL THE EARL OF ST. VINCENT, K.B.

[Letter-Book.]

Vanguard, Palermo, March 5th, 1799.

My dear Lord,

Since my last, I have been made a Citizen of Palermo.[1] The Court thought it might have a good effect; therefore, I accepted the honour, which I hope may have a good effect of showing the attachment of the English to this Royal Family.

---

[1] Clarke and M'Arthur say that he thereby became a Grandee of Spain; but it is very doubtful if such were the fact.

As Sir William Hamilton sends you his letter to Lord Grenville open, I shall not trouble you with repetitions of what is
so much better told by my friend. We have none of us in
this house been well, and wish for better times, which would
cure all our ills. God bless you! and believe me ever your
faithful and affectionate,

NELSON.

---

### TO CAPTAIN LOUIS, H. M. SHIP MINOTAUR.

[Letter-Book.]

Vanguard, Palermo, 5th March, 1799.

My dear Sir,
　　You will join me here with the Terpsichore as soon as
possible; indeed, Lord St. Vincent has been so pressing for
her departure for Gibraltar, that I wish you had sent her immediately as my letter reached you; for, by various Vessels
from Leghorn, I see no prospect of the King of Sardinia's
departure. We have full employment here for all our Ships;
for I am obliged to keep up the blockade of Alexandria.
Darby will tell you what is *not* passing here, for none can
tell what we *are* doing; ever your faithful,

NELSON.

---

### TO COMMODORE DUCKWORTH, PORT MAHON.

[Letter-Book.]

Vanguard, Palermo, March 5th, 1799.

My dear Sir,
　　I have ordered Captain Downman, unless the wind is particularly unfavourable, to call off Mahon, in case you have
any Vessels to send under his Convoy to Gibraltar. We are
without news of importance, except that Great Britain must
bear all the burden and fatigue of defending these Countries.
I am obliged even to continue the blockade of Alexandria;
for neither Turks or Russians will send a Ship. I have
intercepted letters from Alexandria of February 1st. The
plague is both in their Ships and Army. I fear Troubridge
will not be able to destroy the Shipping; they have, since I

was there, fortified so strongly all the points of the harbour.

If you can send us shells for the mortars, they will be very acceptable; for I fancy Naples will require a few very soon. In that Capital and in the Provinces all the lower orders as yet retain their loyalty; but the Nobles and superior class are infamous. If the Emperor would but move, all would yet be well; if he will not, worse must befal us. It is useless to tell you of our truly uncomfortable state here: I am not indeed just now to be envied; but ever believe me, my dear Sir, your much obliged,

NELSON.

March 6th.—Since writing the above, the Emerald[2] is arrived from off Malta, having been on shore and got so much damage as to require heaving down. I beg you will have the goodness to direct her equipment as fast as possible, as I am in great distress for Frigates and small Craft. I had letters yesterday from Corfu;[3] it was not taken February the 13th. The Squadron there have suffered Le Généreux to escape on the 5th, in a manner not much to their credit. Ever yours faithfully,

NELSON.

---

### TO ADMIRAL THE EARL OF ST. VINCENT, K.B.

[Letter-Book.]

Palermo, 6th March, 1799.

My dear Lord,

I send you a copy of the Turkish Admiral's letter to me, and also (the, I think I may call it, impertinent), one of Sir

---

[2] Captain Thomas Moutray Waller commanded the Emerald in the attack on Teneriffe.

[3] Corfu was then blockaded by the Russian and Turkish Squadron, and surrendered on the 1st of March. The terms of the capitulation were so liberal that they were made the subject of eulogy in the *Annual Register* for 1799, vol. i. p. 80, as "there was nothing of that Asiatic barbarity which the friends of the French Revolution affected to apprehend from the accession to the coalition of Turks and Russians." The Leander which had been captured by Le Généreux in August, 1798, was at Corfu when it surrendered, and she was afterwards restored to Great Britain by the Emperor of Russia.

Sidney Smith,[4] and the very elegant one of the Emperor of Russia.[5]  As good Sir William sends open for your perusal all the letters from Corfu, you will see what have been my plans respecting the Coast of Egypt and Syria.  If Sir Sidney was an object of anger, I would not serve unless he was taken away; but I despise such frippery and nonsense as he is composed of.  God bless you, my dear Lord, and ever believe me your faithful and affectionate,

NELSON.

The Emerald is in sight from *Malta*—I have sent copies of Ball's letters to Lord Spencer, as they principally relate to taking men into British pay—pray read them; I would have written copies for you; but I have no scribes to write for me, therefore pray excuse me.  I have just received the Emperor of Russia's picture in a box magnificently set with diamonds; it has done him honour and me a pleasure to have my conduct approved; ever, my dear Lord, your affectionate

NELSON.

---

[4] Three Letters from Sir Sidney Smith to Lord Nelson, dated on the 24th of January, and 6th and 18th of February, are in the Nelson Papers, and though from his strong feeling against Sir Sidney's appointment, they may not have pleased him, as they are written in an independent and decided tone, neither of them deserves to be called "impertinent." The letter particularly alluded to, seems to have been that of the 6th of February, wherein Sir Sidney Smith communicated the result of his conference with the Reis Effendi respecting the number of Ships which were to be placed under Sir Sidney's orders in the Levant.  "It is easy," Sir Sidney said, "to answer the Reis Effendi's remark on the small number of Line of Battle Ships destined for that service; but I found it impossible not to admit that a proportionate number of Frigates having been promised, the promise ought to be performed, and it was agreed that the number should not be less than those which your Lordship supposed to be that of the Enemy in Alexandria, whereas Captain Hood's list reported them to be eight, (in addition to the two *Flutes*,)" . . . . "I found it difficult to limit the number to those.  However, on the faith of your statement, I insisted that it would be sufficient; I suppose you reckon on the Junon, La Muiron, and la Carriere, which were stated to be fitting for a run to France, being already sailed from Alexandria, by your fixing the number so much lower than Captain Hood.  Be this as it may, I trust to your Lordship's enabling me to keep faith with the Turks, and thereby show ourselves to be more correct and liberal than *those* [the Russians] you allude to so justly in your dispatches to my brother."

[5] Vide p. 82, *ante*.

## TO COMMISSIONER COFFIN, PORT MAHON.

[Letter-Book.]

Vanguard, Palermo, March 6th, 1799.

My dear Sir,

I have to request that you will heave down and refit the Emerald as expeditiously as possible ; for I assure you her services are very much wanted. In doing this public service, you will very much oblige your friend,

NELSON.

---

## TO THE RIGHT HONOURABLE EARL SPENCER.

[Letter-Book.]

Vanguard, Palermo, 6th March, 1799.

My dear Lord,

I send you a copy of the Turkish Admiral's letter to me from Corfu, also a very elegant one from the Emperor of Russia, and one from Sir Sidney Smith—those parts of which that are Ministerial, are, I doubt not, very proper; but indeed, my dear Lord, those parts of Sir Sidney's letter which, as Captain of a Man-of-War to an Admiral commanding the Squadron in the Levant, are not so respectful as the rules of our service demand from the different ranks in it. No man admires Sir Sidney's gallantry and zeal more than myself; but he should recollect how I must feel in seeing him placed in the situation which I thought naturally would fall to me. You may be assured that I shall take care and arrange proper plans with the Porte for the service of Egypt, and shall support Sir Sidney to the utmost of my power. It is matter of regret that no Squadron of Turks and Russians are yet gone to Egypt; for I want all our Ships for the service of Malta, Sicily, Naples, and Leghorn; and my only wish is, that the Turks and Russians would take care of all the French to the east of Malta. Our situation here is quiet; but who can say, if the French get into our neighbourhood, that we shall remain so ? In Calabria the people have cut down the Tree of Liberty; but I shall never consider any part of the Kingdom of Naples safe, or even Sicily, until I hear of the

Emperor's entering Italy, when all my Ships shall go into the
Bay of Naples, and I think we can make a Revolution against
the French—at least, my endeavours shall not be wanting. I
hope to go on the service myself, but I have my doubts if the
King and Queen will consent to my leaving them for a
moment. A few days past, I was presented in due form with
the Freedom of the City of Palermo, in a gold box, and
brought upon a silver salver. I have endeavoured so to conduct
myself as to meet the approbation of all classes in this Country,
and I hope to be equally fortunate in meeting your Lordship's.
A Ship is in sight from Malta. I shall keep this letter open
till her arrival; but I do not expect anything particularly
good. The blockade must continue to the end of the chapter;
for neither Maltese nor Italians will fight by themselves.

　　　　Ever your Lordship's faithful and obedient,

　　　　　　　　　　　　　　　　NELSON.

　　P.S.—I send your Lordship copies of Captain Ball's letters
from Malta. It is not for me to judge the propriety of Captain
Ball's plans; but I can assure you he is a man of great judgment and abilities, and ought to have a recompence for all
his expense and trouble.

———————

TO THEIR EXCELLENCIES SIR W. SIDNEY SMITH AND
J. SPENCER SMITH, ESQ.

[Letter-Book.]

Vanguard, Palermo, March 7th, 1799.

Gentlemen,

　　I have received a letter from Sir Sidney Smith, dated January
23rd, which I consider for the most part as a letter from his
Majesty's Ministers, and as such I beg leave to answer it, as I
shall write to Sir Sidney Smith on the subject proper for me, as
an Admiral, to him as a Captain, now put under my command.
I have, therefore, to request that your Excellency will, upon
all occasions, arrange plans of operations with me, and desire
the Minister of the Sublime Porte to establish Corvettes for
holding a constant communication between me and Constantinople; and I beg you will assure the Porte of my anxious
desire to do everything they can wish me, either by coming, or

sending, under such Officers as I can place confidence in, such a force as the service may require. I therefore again urge that good Corvettes may be immediately sent me, to keep open a constant communication.

Captain Sir Sidney Smith is the Officer at present destined to command the blockade of Alexandria, if that force, as my orders tell me, does not exceed two Ships of the Line. With Captain Sir Sidney Smith's zeal and gallantry you are well acquainted; therefore, it is only necessary for me to say, that I shall give the strictest orders to Sir Sidney Smith to do everything in his power to assist in the destruction of the French in Egypt; and, at the same time, I must desire that your Excellency will urge the Porte to send Turkish and Russian Ships sufficient, with Sir Sidney Smith's own Ship, to attend to the business of Egypt; for the service in these Ports demands all the force I can collect. And I shall direct Sir Sidney Smith not to keep a ship, after the force is four Sail of the Line, and three or four Frigates of Russians and Turks, including his own Ship.

I have this day (March 7th) received letters from Sir Sidney Smith, in his Ministerial capacity I believe. I wish that all Ministerial letters should be wrote in your joint names; for it may be difficult for me to distinguish the Captain of the Man-of-War from the Joint Minister, and the propriety of language in one might be very proper to what it is in the other. I beg of your Excellency to forward my letter to Sir Sidney Smith, Captain of the Tigre. I have the honour to be your Excellency's most obedient Servant,

NELSON.

---

TO CAPTAIN SIR WILLIAM SIDNEY SMITH.

[Letter-Book.]

Sir,                              Vanguard, Palermo, 8th March, 1799.

I have received your letters of January the 23rd, February the 6th, 10th, and 23rd. Your situation as Joint-Minister at the Porte makes it absolutely necessary that I should know who writes to me—therefore, I must direct you, whenever you have Ministerial affairs to communicate, that it is done jointly with your respectable brother, and not mix Naval business with the other, for what may be very proper language for a Representative of Majesty, may be very subversive of that discipline of respect from the different ranks in our service. A Representative may dictate to an Admiral—a Captain of a Man-of-War would be censured for the same thing; therefore you will see the propriety of my steering clear between the two situations. I have sent you my orders, which your abilities as a Sea-officer will lead you to punctually execute. Not a Ship more than the service requires shall be kept on any particular station; and that number must be left to my judgment, as an Admiral commanding the Squadron detached by the Commander-in-chief to the extent of the Black Sea. I shall of course keep up a proper communication with the Turkish and Russian Admirals, which no Captain of a Man of-War under my orders must interfere in. I am, Sir, your very humble Servant,

NELSON.

---

TO ADMIRAL THE EARL OF ST. VINCENT, K.B.

[Letter-Book.]

Private.

Palermo, March 8th, 1799.

My dear Lord,

The arrival of the Bonne Citoyenne enables me to send the Ministers' letters from Constantinople; but, in truth, I am at a loss to guess when Sir Sidney Smith writes to me as Minister or Captain in the Navy; as the latter, they are highly indecent to write to an Officer of my rank. You will agree with me, that the manner of saying the same thing makes it proper or otherwise; but Sir Sidney's dictatorial way of writing is what I never before met with. I shall, my Lord, keep a sufficient force in the Levant for the service required of us, but not a Ship for Captain Smith's parade and nonsense —Commodore Smith—I beg his pardon, for he wears a Broad Pendant—has he any orders for this presumption over the heads of so many good and gallant Officers with me?[6] Whenever Sir Sidney Smith went on board the Tigre in state, as he calls it, the *Royal Standard* was hoisted at the mast-head, and twenty-one guns fired. The Turks, however, who love solid sense and not frippery, see into the Knight, and wonder that some of Sir Sidney's superiors were not sent to Constantinople: but I have done with the Knight. I have letters from dear Ball, off Malta; I send you a copy. The moment the Terpsichore arrives, she shall sail to join you. The Grand Signior has ordered 10,000 Albanese troops to come to Sicily. God bless you, and ever believe me your affectionate,

NELSON.

---

TO CAPTAIN BALL, H. M. SHIP ALEXANDER.

[Letter-Book.]

Palermo, 8th March, 1799.

My dear Ball,

I have received with pleasure all your very interesting letters, and particularly the last, which gives hopes of a speedy end to your long and arduous labours. Money, clothing, &c., is a very difficult matter to be got here, but I yet hope some will be sent you. Whenever the French are driven out, you are certainly fitted for the station of Chief, and I should suppose his Sicilian Majesty could have no objection to give you the proper appointments.

You will receive seven thousand ounces, or 21,000 ducats, which the King confides in you to dispose of to the best advantage. You are sure, I shall do everything that is in my power for your honour and benefit. Having said this, I must finish, for I am tired to death with writing. You must keep Minerve, and if I had more Ships you should have them; for I trust to nothing but your blockade. No news yet of the Emperor's movements, but move he must, and all the lower order in the Kingdom of Naples are ready to take arms against the French. 10,000 Albanese are, I hope, near Messina, and

---

[6] Lord St. Vincent wrote in reply, on the 28th of April, that Sir Sidney Smith had no authority to wear a Distinguishing Pendant, unless Nelson had given it; and he expressed in strong terms his disapprobation of Sir Sidney's letters to Lord Nelson, and of the " bombast" in those to Earl Spencer.

12,000 Russians are out this side Constantinople for the same destination, besides the Russian Army passing the Tyrol. Apropos, the Emperor of Russia has sent me his picture, in a magnificent box; but this shall not prevent my keeping a sharp look-out on his movements against the good Turk. Remember me kindly to all our friends with you.   I am, &c.,

NELSON.

TO CONSTANTINO YPSILANTI.

[Letter-Book.]

Palermo, 8th March, 1799.

Sir,

Your very elegant and friendly letter was delivered to me yesterday by Captain Nisbet; and I return him to Constantinople, to assure the Sublime Porte, that whilst I have the honour of commanding the detached Squadron of his Britannic Majesty's Fleet in the Levant Seas and Coast of Italy, whatever the Sublime Porte wish me to do, it is my duty, and indeed it is my inclination; for I shall, if it is necessary, go myself to serve the Grand Signior.   I have given Captain Sir Sidney Smith orders to do everything in his power to serve the Common Cause.   It will not escape your Excellency's discerning judgment that the joint Minister Sir Sidney Smith is a different person from Captain Sidney Smith of the Tigre. I have directed Captain Nisbet, who is acquainted with my sentiments, to express them to your Excellency.

I have only to beg, through the favour of your Excellency and of the Grand Vizir, to be laid at the feet of the Grand Signior, and that you will ever believe me your most obliged and faithful,

NELSON.

TO ABDEL CADIR BEY, COMMANDER-IN-CHIEF OF THE OTTOMAN FLEET.

[Letter-Book.]

Palermo, 9th March, 1799.

Sir,

I have been honoured by your Excellency's letter of the 13th of February, and from my heart I hope before this time, the Citadel of Corfu has surrendered to the united efforts of your Excellency and the Russian Admiral. You will believe that my anxiety for sending a Squadron to Egypt is, to expedite the destruction of that robber, Buonaparte, with all his gang, and to have the pleasure of seeing the Dominions of the Grand Signior cleared from infidels and murderers; I pray God it may be soon. It is my desire to keep up a constant communication with your Excellency, and to inform you of all my movements.

Malta, I have no doubt, will very soon surrender; four Sail of the Line are there blockading it; six Sail of the Line are now in Egypt; two of the Line at Leghorn to guard the Grand Duke against the French, who wish to plunder Tuscany; and four Sail of the Line are on the Coast of Sicily, towards Naples. Whenever your Excellency can point out to me, how I can best serve the cause of the Grand Signior, you have only to tell me; and I shall fly to execute it. Believe me, with the greatest respect, your Excellency's most obliged and obedient Servant,

NELSON.

Your Excellency will understand that Sir Sidney Smith is Captain of the Tigre; and, although destined for the present to serve with part of the Squadron in the Levant, is under my command, and that all plans of operations are to be concerted by me.

N.

---

TO CAPTAIN GAGE, OF HIS MAJESTY'S SHIP TERPSICHORE.

[Order-Book.]

Vanguard, Palermo, 10th March, 1799.

You are hereby required and directed to receive on board the Ship you command the three Maltese Deputies,[7] with such arms, ammunition, or other stores, and money, as may be sent on board by order of his Sicilian Majesty; and taking under your protection the Severer bomb-tender, convoy her to the Island of Malta; and having landed the Deputies, you

[7] On the 8th, Captain Nisbet was directed to convey the Maltese Deputies to Malta, but that order appears to have been cancelled.

will deliver the ammunition, stores, and money to the
order of Captain Ball, commanding the blockade; and,
putting the Severer under his directions, you are to proceed
from thence, with all dispatch, to Cagliari in Sardinia, and
deliver my letter to his Sardinian Majesty; which, having
done, you are to proceed, with all possible dispatch, down
the Mediterranean, and join the Commander-in-Chief at
Gibraltar, or wherever he may be.

NELSON.

N.B.—Calling in your way at Minorca, to take any dispatches Commodore Duckworth may have for the Earl St.
Vincent.

---

TO ADMIRAL THE EARL OF ST. VINCENT, K.B.

[From Clarke and M'Arthur, vol. ii. p. 153.]

March 10th, 1799.

At nine o'clock I was most agreeably surprised with the
appearance of General Stuart, who has brought with him
1000 English troops.[8] This conduct of the General most
assuredly demands the warmest gratitude from his Sicilian
Majesty, and I have no doubt but Sir Charles[9] will experience
it. This goodness reflects on him the highest honour. He
has probably, by his quick decision, not only saved this
Kingdom, but may be the instrument of driving the French
out of Naples. It will be an electric shock both to good and
bad subjects. Europe may yet be happy, if Austria and
Prussia would exert themselves.

NELSON.

[8] March 19th, "Arrived H. M. Ship Terpsichore from Leghorn, and the Haerlem,
Europa, Dolphin, Pallas, Aurora, and two Transports, with General Stuart and two
Regiments of Foot from Mahon." March 11th, "Sailed the Haerlem, Europa and
Pallas, with troops for Messina, General Stuart going by land."—*Journal.*

[9] Lieutenant-General the Honourable Charles Stuart, was appointed a Knight
of the Bath, on the 8th of January 1799, for the capture of Minorca.

TO CAPTAIN BURLTON,[1] OR THE COMMANDING OFFICER OF HIS MAJESTY'S SHIPS CARRYING TROOPS — VIZ., HAERLEM, EUROPA, AND PALLAS.

[Letter-Book.]

Vanguard, Palermo, March 11th, 1799.

Sir,

I do not know the precise nature of your orders; but I think they were—having carried the troops to their places of destination, to leave them, and obey the other part of your orders. You will therefore, unless His Excellency Sir Charles Stuart desires the contrary, follow the orders you are at present under. I am, Sir, your most obedient Servant,

NELSON.

---

TO THEIR EXCELLENCIES SIR SIDNEY SMITH AND J. SPENCER SMITH, ESQ., HIS MAJESTY'S JOINT MINISTERS AT THE OTTOMAN PORTE.

[Letter-Book.]

Vanguard, Palermo, 12th March, 1799.

Gentlemen,

I have the pleasure to tell you that his Excellency General Sir Charles Stuart, K.B., arrived here on the 10th with a respectable force—about 2000 men; but, as more are expected at Messina, I believe the whole force will be 3000. We are very anxiously waiting the arrival of the promised succour from Russia under General Harman; and from the favourable appearance in the Kingdom of Naples, I shall strongly recommend their going direct to Naples, and taking possession of that Capital—an operation of no difficulty, if 12,000 are the number of troops. All the lower order would immediately join; and all those traitors, who could hope for pardon, would now be glad to get rid of French fraternization; for they, as usual, begun by stripping their friends, upon principles that our ' good friends must have pleasure in giving, —from our enemies we will take.' In short, I can say with truth, that the French and Neapolitans are heartily sick of each other. All Calabria has returned to its loyalty, even to

---

[1] This officer died Rear-Admiral Sir George Burlton, K.C.B., in September, 1815.

within forty miles of Naples. Apulia and Lecce have never admitted the French amongst them. In the Roman State all is insurrection against the French; in Cività Vecchia the Enemy have been beat off. What a moment for the Emperor to march! I hope he will, and it will give me pleasure to communicate our success in Italy, and am most exceedingly anxious to hear of Buonaparte's destruction in the East. I have the honour to be, your Excellencies' most obedient Servant,

NELSON.

---

TO JOHN SPENCER SMITH, ESQ.

[From a Copy, in the Nelson Papers.]

Palermo, 12th March, 1799.

Dear Sir,

I wish very much for two or three very fine India shawls : the price is no object. As I am entirely unacquainted with any person at Constantinople, I take the liberty of requesting the favour of you to ask some of your friends to do me that kindness. The amount I shall pay, with *many, many* thanks, either in London or any other place, when I know it. In doing this favour you will confer a lasting obligation on,

NELSON.

---

TO HIS EXCELLENCY THE HONOURABLE WILLIAM WYNDHAM.

[Letter-Book.]

Palermo, 14th March, 1799.

My dear Sir,

Your Excellency will be pleased to signify to the Government of Tuscany, that a Squadron of his Majesty's Ships is blockading the Port of Naples, and all Ports of that Kingdom in possession of the French troops. Therefore, directions will be given for the destruction of all Neutral ships and cargoes, who may be cleared out after the time your Excellency gives this notification, or who may be found approaching the Bay of Naples, or any place in possession of the French troops. Your Excellency will not fail, I am confident, in representing forcibly this Notice; for I am determined to

U 2

enforce with rigour this just and necessary measure. I have the honour to be, &c.

NELSON.

Will you have the goodness to communicate the measure to Sir Morton Eden, in order that the Imperial vessels from the Adriatic may not plead ignorance.

---

TO HIS EXCELLENCY THE HONOURABLE WILLIAM WYNDHAM.

[Letter-Book.]

Palermo, 14th March, 1799.

My dear Sir,

I have to thank you, which I do sincerely, for all your letters to the 19th February, and for the invaluable present of newspapers. I have had the honour of a letter from his Sardinian Majesty, from the Bay of Cagliari, and shall have pleasure, if it is in my power, of being useful to that unfortunate Monarch. I have great pleasure in telling your Excellency, that Sir Charles Stuart arrived here on the 10th, with the 30th and 89th Regiments, who are gone to Messina; which will not only save that important place from all danger, but has acted like an electrical shock over the whole Island, and will extend its influence to Naples. The Russian army from the Black Sea, under General Harmann, is expected every moment; a plan of operations is marked out for them, which cannot fail of being successful.

As this is a new mode of conveyance, I dare not enter into particulars; we are all loyal in Sicily, and the Country fears not the French scoundrels. Malta will fall the latter end of this month. I hope for good news from Alexandria. I find, by a small Vessel escaped the 19th February, that our Bombs have done much mischief at Malta, although the French, by intercepted letters of February 26th, say that our shells have repeatedly fell into the French ships, but that they have not taken fire. We have nothing so late from England as what you was so good as to send us. Pray consider us poor creatures, shut up in an Island. I have written to Mr. Huddard, respecting my care of the Tuscan trade, which shall never cease to be an object of great attention. But you know, my dear Sir, that although I have sixteen Sail of the Line, my call for them is so great, that if I had ten more, I could employ them with great advantage to the State; at present, I have only one Frigate, and she is in Egypt. Now, my dear Sir, if you can send us news of the march of the Emperor, Italy, I am satisfied, may be speedily released from the band of murderers and robbers which have so long infested it. Adieu, my dear Sir, and believe me ever your obliged and affectionate,

NELSON.

Having the comfort of living with good Sir William and Lady Hamilton, I do not fail communicating everything to them.

---

### TO HIS HIGHNESS THE BEY OF TUNIS.

[Letter-Book.]

Vanguard, Palermo, 15th March, 1799.

Sir,

I have received through the hands of Mr. Magra, his Britannic Majesty's Consul at Tunis, the very interesting letters from the French at Malta; for which I beg leave to thank your Highness, and return them by a Vessel I have fitted out for that express purpose. The infamous conduct of the French during the whole war, which it has wantonly waged against all religion and civil order, has at last called down the vengeance of all true Mussulmen; and your Highness, I am sure, will agree with me that Divine Providence never will permit these Infidels to God to go unpunished. The conduct of your Highness reflects upon you the very highest honour; and, if any State has failed to exert its utmost abilities against the enemies of God and His Holy Prophet, I rely with confidence they will be your enemies, as they will be of all good men.

Your Highness is not, I am sure, insensible, that, although I have a Squadron of Portuguese Ships under my orders, I have during the whole time they have been under my command, prevented their cruizing against the Vessels of War of your Highness; and further, that all the Mussulmen slaves who were in their Ships, have been sent to Constantinople.

For at this moment all wars should cease, and all the world should join in endeavouring to extirpate from off the face of the earth this race of murderers, oppressors, and unbelievers. This necessarily brings to mind the unfortunate situation of His Sicilian Majesty—a Prince, who became an object for plunder in the same manner as the rich Provinces of Egypt, from a belief of their inability to resist this horde of thieves. The perspicuity of your Highness's judgment will point out the necessity of all Powers at war with the French, uniting cordially together for their destruction. I beg leave, therefore, to offer the Victor of the Nile as a mediator for peace or truce during the war, between your Highness and His Sicilian Majesty. If your Highness will favour me with your ideas upon this very important subject, I shall feel happy, and I am confident the great Monarch, whom I have the honour of serving, will have real satisfaction in having his faithful servant the instrument by which peace should be restored between your Highness and His Sicilian Majesty. I have the honour to remain, &c.

NELSON.

TO PERKIN MAGRA, ESQ., CONSUL AT TUNIS.

[Autograph, in the possession of the Reverend Thomas Wilkinson.]

Palermo, March 15th, 1799.

Dear Sir,

I have received with real pleasure all your very interesting and important letters, from the beginning of January to March the 3rd; the great difficulty which I am sure you must have had to keep the Bey always steady to our interest, reflects the highest credit on your judgment and zeal, and will I hope meet with its proper reward from our superiors in England. I send you a letter, written the very beginning of February,[1] the impossibility of sending it by a Ship of War has prevented my finishing it, or your reception of it—I have wrote a letter to the Bey, which I send under a flying seal, the papers are also returned and I cannot be sufficiently thankful for the perusal of them. As I have given notice to your family of this op-

---

[1] Vide p. 273, ante.

portunity, they will tell you all the chit-chat of the place; from the Continent, we know of the very serious insurrection in Flanders, where the French are entirely driven out; in Holland, are likewise insurrections; but I send you the latest papers I have, and Mr. Wyndham's two last letters. The letters you will have the goodness to return by this Vessel. As writing is truly a very serious operation to me, you must excuse the shortness of my letter, but believe me, dear Sir, your most obliged servant,

NELSON.

March 17th.—Our news yesterday from Calabria is of the most comfortable kind; all the provinces, even to Salerno, are in arms against the French, and a Turkish and Russian Army may be hourly expected to land at Manfredonia.

I must request that you will have the goodness to get the Bey's answer, that the Vessel may not be more than three days in the Bay of Tunis, and I wish her not to get into quarantine if that is possible.

---

TO HIS EXCELLENCY SIR JOHN ACTON, BART.

[Letter-Book.]

Palermo, 18th March, 1799.

Sir,

The Agents to the captors of La Grazia polacre, cut out of the Bay of Sorento on the second day of February last, having requested me, by their letter of the 13th instant, which is here enclosed, to apply to His Sicilian Majesty for a confirmation of your note to Sir William Hamilton and myself of the 11th of February last, declaring that His Sicilian Majesty must consider at present those once beloved subjects as rebels, and also requesting an explanation of the same, I have to request that your Excellency will be pleased to explain, whether His Sicilian Majesty considers the said polacre as coming under this declaration, and whether the Agents may proceed in the sales of the Vessel and cargo as a lawful prize? I have the honour to be your Excellency's most obedient Servant,

NELSON.

## TO CAPTAIN SIR WILLIAM SIDNEY SMITH, H.M. SHIP LE TIGRE.

[Letter-Book.]

Sir,                                    Vanguard, Palermo, 18th March, 1799.

Captain Troubridge arrived here last evening,[2] and, as he has delivered to me all the papers he received from you, amongst which I see a form of a passport ;[3] and Captain Troubridge tells me it was your intention to send into Alexandria, that all French ships might pass to France—now, as this is *in direct opposition to my opinion,* which is, *never to suffer any one individual Frenchman to quit Egypt*—I must therefore *strictly charge and command you,* never to give any French ship or man leave to quit Egypt. And I must also desire that you will oppose by every means in your power, any permission which may be attempted to be given by any foreigner, Admiral, General, or other person; and you will acquaint those persons, that I shall not pay the smallest attention to any such passport after your notification; and you are to put my orders in force, not on any pretence to permit a single Frenchman to leave Egypt. Of course, you will give these orders to all the Ships under your command. As I am very anxious for the return of the Emma polacre, I have to request that you will not detain her more than two hours. As I shall hope to have a constant communication with you, through the means of the Turkish or Russian Admirals, all letters for your Squadron I shall direct to be left in the Vanguard. I am, Sir, your very humble servant,

NELSON.

---

## TO CAPTAIN SIR WILLIAM SIDNEY SMITH, H.M. SHIP LE TIGRE.

[Letter-Book.]

Sir,                                    Vanguard, Palermo, 18th March, 1799.

In consequence of advices this moment received from the Earl of St. Vincent[4] desiring a re-inforcement may be sent,

---

[2] On the 17th, Captain Troubridge in the Culloden, with the Seahorse, Zealous, and Perseus bomb, arrived at Palermo from Alexandria, having failed in their attempt to destroy the French transports, for the reasons mentioned in a subsequent letter. Vide p. 298.

[3] Vide p. 335, post.

[4] Lord St. Vincent wrote to Lord Nelson on the 25th of February, stating, that as two Ships of three decks and two seventy-fours were fitting at Carthagena to

from the Squadron under my command, to Minorca, it is my positive directions that the moment the Turks and Russians join you, so as to make up four Sail of the Line with your own Ship, that you dispatch the Lion and Theseus immediately to join me at this place. I am, Sir, your very humble Servant,

NELSON.

TO COMMODORE MITCHEL, COMMANDING THE PORTUGUESE SHIP ST. SEBASTIAN, MESSINA.

[Letter-Book.]

Vanguard, Palermo, 19th March, 1799.

Sir,

On the receipt of this letter, you will immediately use the utmost dispatch in joining me at this place, to go on service of the greatest importance. I am, Sir, your most humble servant,

NELSON.

TO ADMIRAL THE EARL OF ST. VINCENT, K.B.

[Letter-Book.]

Palermo, 20th March, 1799.

My dear Lord,

The arrival of the Bulldog this morning who has so many wants, determines me to send her direct for Gibraltar, especially as her mortars are burst, as are those of the Perseus. The Strombolo is off Malta and her mortars on shore. Pray, my dear Lord, beg General O'Hara to give me mortars and plenty of shells: I really want them. I congratulate you on the capture of Corfu. As I send you all Mr. Consul Foresti's letters on that subject, I shall not repeat it. You will observe what is said respecting the Russians being ordered to Malta. I know this is a favourite object of the Emperor's, and is a prelude to a future war with the good Turk, when Constantinople will change masters. This is so clear, that

cover a descent on Minorca, for which great preparations were making on the Coast of Spain, he was to reinforce Commodore Duckworth's Squadron with two Ships of the Line, as soon as possible, consistently with his operations against Alexandria and Malta.

a man must be blind not to see it. I have ordered Bellerophon from Leghorn to Minorca, and will the Minotaur, very
soon. Troubridge arrived from Egypt the 16th. I am endeavouring to do little matters for his Squadron, but we have
not a store to give him, and I also know your wants. A
Squadron, under Troubridge, goes directly into the Bay of
Naples. I wish first to take the Island of Procida, which will
secure tolerable anchorage, and effectually blockade Naples.
It must, also, have the effect of preventing the French from
detaching any troops from Naples to the Provinces, who are
all loyal. The Court tells me that twelve thousand Russians
and fifteen thousand Turks are ready to cross the Adriatic, to
land in the Kingdom of Naples; *if so*, our Squadron will
create a powerful diversion. Sir William Sidney Smith has
the blockade of Alexandria intrusted to him. I send you
copies of my letters to him; for the Victory of the Nile
would in my opinion be useless, if any Ship or Frenchman
is suffered to return to Europe. I hope you will approve of
my conduct; for as a Captain to an Admiral, either Sir
Sidney Smith or myself must give way. Troubridge could
not destroy the transports by shells, as all the mortars burst
and six Fire-ships were lost in a gale of wind. Besides,
Alexandria is now so well fortified, that it will be a very
difficult matter to take it, unless the plague thin their ranks.
Buonaparte is at Cairo, not more than sixteen thousand
strong. He must and will fall sooner or later, if Sir Sidney
does not allow him to retreat by sea. As to myself, I am
at times ill at my ease, but it is my duty to submit, and you
may be sure I shall not quit my post without absolute necessity. If the Emperor moves, I hope yet to return the Royal
Family to Naples. At present, I cannot move. Would the
Court but let me, I should be better, I believe; for here
I am writing from morn to eve: therefore you must excuse
this jumble of a letter. I send you the disposition of the
Squadron, and be assured that everything you have desired
both public and private shall be complied with, with the
greatest pleasure, by your faithful and affectionate,

NELSON.

## DISPOSITION OF THE SQUADRON, 20TH MARCH, 1799.

[Letter-Book.]

Tigre ⎫
Lion ⎬ Blockading Alexandria.
Theseus ⎭

Alexander ⎫
Audacious ⎪
Goliath ⎪
La Minerve ⎬ Blockading Malta.
La Bonne Citoyenne ⎪
Incendiary ⎪
Strombolo ⎭

Culloden ⎫
Zealous ⎪
Swiftsure ⎪
Seahorse ⎪
Vanguard ⎬ At Palermo.
El Corso ⎪
Perseus ⎪
Bull-Dog ⎭

Bellerophon, gone with Convoy to Leghorn.
Minotaur, hourly expected from Leghorn.
Alliance, on her passage from Egypt.
Emerald, gone to Mahon to repair.
Mutine, daily expected from Mahon.
L'Entreprenant, gone with dispatches to Tunis.
San Leon, gone with Convoy to Venice.

### PORTUGUESE SQUADRON.

Principe Real, going to Leghorn.
Affonço, with Captain Ball, off Malta.
San Sebastian, ordered from Messina to Palermo.
Rainha, gone with the French Princesses from Brindisi to
    Trieste.
Benjamin, with Captain Ball, off Malta.
Balloon, Brig, at Leghorn.

NELSON.

TO HIS HIGHNESS THE BEY OF TRIPOLI.

[Letter-Book.]

Vanguard, Palermo, March 20th, 1799.

Sir,

Reports have reached me from Tunis, and also by intercepted French letters from Malta, that your Highness has renounced the defence of the true Mussulman faith, and joined in a new alliance with the French infidels, who are endeavouring to overthrow the Ottoman Empire, and the Worship of the True Only God and his Holy Prophet. I do not credit one syllable of this report, so injurious to the honour of your Highness. I have, therefore, sent a Ship to receive not only the contradiction of this report from your Highness's own hand, but also an assurance that you will use every exertion for the destruction of that band of robbers, who have so wantonly attacked the Grand Signior in a part of his Dominions where they thought to have found no opposition.

I beg leave also to acquaint your Highness, that the French in Malta pretend that your subjects will supply them with provisions : this I believe to be equally false with the other reports. As the subject of a Sovereign who is in the closest alliance with the Sublime Porte for the defence of the Ottoman Empire, and being also in alliance with your Highness, I shall anxiously wait your Highness's answer ; for, should evil councillors have abused the goodness of your heart, I beg leave, with all respect, to offer the Victor of the Nile as a mediator between your Highness and the Sublime Porte : for it will be my duty to join with the Admiral of the Ottoman Fleet in chastising those enemies of the True Faith and of the Grand Signior, who have so much betrayed the trust your Highness hath reposed in them. For what may be further necessary to be said on this very unpleasant subject, I beg to refer you to Mr. Lucas, his Britannic Majesty's Consul-General to your Highness, who I have written to by this opportunity. Believe me your Highness's truly attached and faithful servant,

NELSON.

## TO SIMON LUCAS, ESQ., CONSUL-GENERAL, TRIPOLI.

[Letter-Book.]

Sir,　　　　　　　　　　　　　　Palermo, March 20th, 1799.

I am this moment favoured with your important letter of the 5th instant. I send the Vanguard[4] directly with my letter to the Bey, which I put under a flying seal for your perusal. If his Highness renounces his evil councillors, and retracts in writing and in due form any treaty he may unthinkingly have entered into against the Grand Signior and the true faith of Mahomet, it will give me sensible pleasure. If his Highness should still determine to adhere to the French, the enemies of all true Mussulmans, it will become my duty to assist the Admiral of the Grand Signior, with all my power to defend the Mahometan faith, against all who assist the French in striving to destroy it. You will urge this point with energy and delicacy, so as to make it appear that it is the cause of the Grand Signior, and the Mahometan religion, that we are called upon to defend as the most faithful Ally of the Porte.

It is a matter of small moment to Great Britain herself; but she is so faithful to her Allies, that every exertion will be made to support them. You will state clearly that orders are given for sinking all Vessels attempting to carry supplies. In short, Sir, you must take care that the Bey must always suppose (what is true) that we are supporting the Grand Signior and the Faith against atheists, assassins, and robbers. I am, Sir, your most obedient servant,

NELSON.

[4] The Vanguard sailed on the 23rd of March, Lord Nelson's Flag being transferred to the Culloden. The arrival of the Vanguard at Tripoli produced an immediate effect on the Bashaw. Mr. Lucas, the Consul, in a letter to Lord Nelson, dated Tripoli, 28th March, 1799, said :—

"It would be difficult to explain to your Lordship the effect the appearance of so formidable a Ship, and your letter, had upon his Excellency the Bashaw. The French who were free before, are now in slavery, and their three Tartans confiscated to his use, as he said it would be inconsistent with his *honour* to deliver them up for destruction to Captain Hardy, who claimed them. In short there is nothing but he would do for the English, whom he now styles the saviours and protectors of the Mahometan faith, and, as a further proof of his good disposition, he intercepted a packet of letters which this French Consul was sending overland to Buonaparte." —*Autograph*, in the Nelson Papers. But no sooner had the Vanguard sailed than the Bashaw released the French and renewed his former proceedings.

## TO ADMIRAL THE EARL OF ST. VINCENT, K.B.

[Original, in the Admiralty.]

My dear Lord,                                     March 21st, 1799.

I send you a letter from Mr. Lucas relative to the bad conduct of the Bey, and I have thought it right to send off this day the Vanguard, being the only Ship fit for sea, with a letter to the Bey,[5] which I hope will have its proper effect.

Ever yours faithfully,<br>NELSON.

---

## TO CAPTAIN HALLOWELL, H. M. SHIP SWIFTSURE.

[Letter-Book.]

Dear Sir,                         Vanguard, Palermo, March 21st, 1799.

In consequence of your letter received yesterday, enclosing one from Captain Charles Allen, of the Marines of his Majesty's Ship under your command, requesting leave of absence for Captain Allen to go to England, his presence there being absolutely necessary, in consequence of the fortune left him, amounting to ten thousand pounds a year, and requesting also to be discharged from the said Ship, I beg leave to acquaint you that it is not in my power either to grant him leave of absence to go to England, or to order his discharge from the Swiftsure; but he has my permission to go down to Gibraltar to join the Commander-in-Chief. I am, Sir, &c.

NELSON.

---

[Letter-Book.]

Culloden, Palermo, 21st March, 1799.

Wrote Mr. Wyndham of the surrender of Corfu, and of sending the Marquis de Niza to take the command at Leghorn; also of sending the Bellerophon and Minotaur to Minorca.

---

[5] Lord St. Vincent, in a letter to Lord Nelson, dated the 30th of April, 1799, expressed his regret that Nelson had had so much trouble about Mr. Lucas and the Bashaw of Tripoli, as Lord St. Vincent said he entertained a very unfavourable opinion of Mr. Lucas, and placed no reliance on his statements about the Bashaw.

## TO HIS EXCELLENCY THE HONOURABLE WILLIAM WYNDHAM.

[Letter-Book.]

Culloden, Palermo, 22nd March, 1799.

My dear Sir,

The Ambassador of Buonaparte being intercepted by my friend Troubridge, on his way to Constantinople, and amongst other articles of his instructions, is a very important one—viz., an offer to enter on terms for his quitting Egypt with his Army. This offer is what I have long expected the glorious Battle of the Nile would produce; but it was my determination from that moment never, if I could help it, to permit a single Frenchman to quit Egypt.

Captain Sir William Sidney Smith, who has the present command of the Squadron off Alexandria, I have reason to believe, thinks differently from me, and will grant passports for the return of that part of the French army which God Almighty permits to remain. I have, therefore, thought it highly proper to send Captain Sir Sidney Smith the order of which I transmit a copy; for I consider it nothing short of madness to permit that band of thieves to return to Europe. *No;* to Egypt they went with their own consent, and there they shall remain whilst Nelson commands the detached Squadron; for never, never, will he consent to the return of one Ship or Frenchman.

I beg your Excellency will take the earliest opportunity of sending this important information, and a copy of my letter to Captain Sir Sidney Smith; to England, and ever believe me, with the greatest respect, your obliged and faithful servant,

NELSON.

---

## TO REAR-ADMIRAL THE MARQUIS DE NIZA.

[Order-Book.]

Culloden, 22nd March, 1799.

You are hereby required and directed to proceed with her Most Faithful Majesty's Ship, Principe Real, under your command, to Leghorn, informing yourself, from the British Vice-Consul there, of the situation of affairs respecting that Port, and opening a correspondence with his Excellency the

Honourable William Wyndham, his Britannic Majesty's Minister at Florence, for your information respecting the affairs of Tuscany in general. And, whereas information has been received, that an Armament is preparing in Corsica for the invasion of some part of the Tuscan or Sardinian Territories, or the Dominions of his Sicilian Majesty in Elba or Orbitello, you will use every means in your power to intercept and destroy the said Armament, and any Convoy of corn, or any other stores which the French may be sending into the Roman State; and, for the purpose of gaining intelligence, you will order the Balloon brig to cruize in the Piombino passage, and towards Orbitello, and to keep a good look-out, and to intercept all French and Genoese vessels that he may fall in with. And, whereas I have information that the French have contracted for 28,000 sacks of corn to be sent into the Roman State, you are to signify at Leghorn, that if any neutral Vessel receive on board any provisions for the use of places in possession of the French troops, that those Vessels will be sunk.

NELSON.

---

TO HIS EXCELLENCY THEODORE OUSCHAKOFF, VICE-ADMIRAL OF THE RUSSIAN FLEE, &c. &c.

[Letter Book.]

Palermo, 23rd March, 1799.

Sir,

Most cordially do I congratulate your Excellency on the capture of Corfu; and I can assure you that the glory of the arms of a faithful Ally, is equally dear to me as those of my own Sovereign. I have the greatest hopes that Malta will very soon surrender to the efforts making against it. The Flag of his Sicilian Majesty, with that of Great Britain, is flying on all parts of the Island, except the Town of Valetta, the inhabitants of which have, with his Sicilian Majesty's consent, put themselves under the protection of Great Britain.

A Squadron sails to-morrow for the blockade of Naples, which will be continued with the greatest vigour, till the arrival of your Excellency, with your Royal Master's troops,

who, I have no doubt, will replace his Sicilian Majesty on
his throne. In doing this good deed, it will be my pleasure
to co-operate most cordially with you, and to assure you in
person how much I feel myself your Excellency's most obedient and faithful servant,

NELSON.

---

## TO HIS EXCELLENCY ABDUL CADIR BEY, VICE-ADMIRAL OF THE OTTOMAN FLEET.

[Letter-Book.]

Palermo, 24th March, 1799.

Sir,

I sincerely thank your Excellency for your letter of
March 9th, and beg leave to offer my cordial congratulations
on the surrender of Corfu to the united efforts of the Ottoman
and Russian arms. This success will set your Excellency at
liberty to render more important service—viz., that of uniting
to place again in their capital, the good King and Queen of
Naples. To say how happy I should be to see your Excellency transporting an Army for this purpose, is impossible;
nor to say what pleasure it would give me to make a personal
acquaintance with you, being your Excellency's most obliged
and faithful servant,

NELSON.

---

## TO CAPTAIN BALL, H.M. SHIP ALEXANDER.

[Letter-Book.]

Palermo, 25th March, 1799.

My dear Ball,

Although Commodore Campbell is going to join his Ship,
yet he is to be considered as under your command, and he
understands that perfectly. You will not hurt his feelings, I
am sure. Tyson[6] writes you all the forms for changes of Ships,
&c. Now, my dear friend, Captain Nisbet is appointed to

---

[6] Lord Nelson's old follower and Secretary. He was afterwards Clerk of the
Survey in Woolwich Dockyard, and died at Southampton, on the 16th of November, 1814.

the Thalia, a very fine frigate, and I wish he may do credit
to himself, and in her. Will you do me the favour of keeping her, and sending me the Minerve, for I want Cockburn,
for service of *head?* As soon as Captain Barker's[7] surveys,
&c. are over, make one of the small craft bring him here. I
have sent Vanguard to Tripoli to scold the Bashaw. Tunis
behaves well. As Corfu has surrendered, I hope Malta will
follow the example very soon. I am pressed for Ships for
other services, but you are sure I shall do everything to make
you comfortable. As the mortars are, I believe, of no use to
you, I wish they could again be put in the Strombolo, and
she sent to me; for I am preparing for Naples, where our
friend Troubridge goes directly. The French have certainly
made war upon the Emperor, and have surprised some of his
troops. Serve him right! why did he not go to war before?
In Tuscany, the French are expected every moment. Here
we are quiet, and in Calabria all goes on well. At Naples
they tell me the French are hated: however, we shall very
soon know all the truth from experience. Bellerophon and
Minotaur are ordered to Minorca. I am not well, but keep
rubbing on, from day to day. God bless you! Finish the
business as soon as you can; and ever believe me, your affectionate

                                                  NELSON.

TO CAPTAIN BALL, H.M. SHIP ALEXANDER.

[Letter-Book.]

Culloden, Palermo, 25th March, 1799.

My dear Ball,

I send you Captain Dunn,[8] with the Thalia for Captain
Nisbet, in which Ship Captain Maling[9] takes his passage to
supersede Captain Nisbet in the Bonne Citoyenne. Captain
Dunn is appointed also to supersede Captain Barker in the
Incendiary. You will, therefore, give the necessary orders
for his survey, and the provisions and stores to be delivered
to Captain Dunn. Captain Barker, being appointed to the

---

[7] Captain George Barker, now a Vice-Admiral of the White.
[8] Captain Richard D. Dunn. He died a Post Captain in 1813.
[9] Captain Thomas James Maling, now a Vice-Admiral of the Blue.

Barfleur, you will send him here by the first opportunity, in order to his going down the Mediterranean.

Lieutenant John Yule,[1] of the Alexander, is appointed Lieutenant of the Thalia, and enclosed is his commission for that Ship, as also one for Captain Nisbet for the Thalia; and Lieutenant Lawrence is on board the Thalia, a passenger, to supersede Mr. Yule. You will, therefore, order these arrangements to take place. I am, wishing you every success, my dear Ball, your faithful and obedient servant,

NELSON.

---

TO SPIRIDION FORESTI, ESQ., BRITISH CONSUL AT CORFU.

[Letter-Book.]

Palermo, 26th March, 1799.

Sir,

I feel very much obliged by your interesting and important letters of March 9th, which I have sent to Lord St. Vincent. Give me leave to say, that throughout my command in the Levant seas, you have done yourself the highest honour, and rendered, as far as was possible, the greatest services to your Country. This public testimony, from a stranger to everything except your good conduct, will, I trust, be not unacceptable. I observe what you tell me of Lord Grenville's orders to obey Sir William Sidney Smith. You will, of course, follow Lord Grenville's orders, as Sir William Sidney Smith is considered as a Minister at Constantinople. I also know him in that capacity, jointly with his worthy brother; but [as] Captain of the Tigre, and in all matters relative to Naval operations, he is under my orders; and this I would have you perfectly understand, and explain when it may be necessary; for an idea seems gone abroad, very injurious to my credit in the world, that although I was intrusted with the command of the detached Squadron, even into the Black Sea, should the French have got there, that although I had the happiness of commanding the Squadron who obtained the glorious victory off the Nile, Captain Sir William Sidney Smith was

---

[1] He was one of the Lieutenants of the Victory at Trafalgar, and was made a Commander on the 24th of December, 1805, in which rank he died a few years ago.

x 2

sent out to command somewhere, in prejudice to me, and four or five Captains now serving with me, in the Levant. Having stated this fully to you, you will be equal to every explanation. Whenever you favour me with your very interesting correspondence, I shall receive it with pleasure. As Sir William Hamilton writes you, I shall not repeat, &c.

NELSON.

---

TO CAPTAIN TROUBRIDGE, HIS MAJESTY'S SHIP CULLODEN.

[Order-Book.]

Palermo, 28th March, 1799.

Whereas it is of the utmost importance that the City and Towns in the Bay of Naples should be immediately blockaded to prevent the French forces in those places from getting any supplies of corn or other articles by sea, and it being expedient that an Officer of your distinguished merit and abilities should command the blockade, in order to render it the more effectual, you are hereby required and directed to take under your command the Ships named in the margin,[2] embarking on board them the Governor of Procida and two hundred troops, as also such Officers as are ordered by his Sicilian Majesty to embark with them, and proceed to the Bay of Naples. And it being necessary that the Squadron employed on this service should have some safe anchorage, the more effectually to carry on the said blockade, and the Island of Procida affording the anchorage desired, you will use your endeavours to seize and get possession of the said Island of Procida, if possible, and reinstate the Governor in the command thereof, and using every means in your power to conciliate the affections of the loyal part of the inhabitants; and also, those of the Islands of Ischia and Capri, and, if possible, bring them to their former allegiance; and also, to communicate with the loyal inhabitants of Naples, as much as is in your power, and by every opportunity; but by no means to fire upon the City without farther orders from me, or circumstances render it necessary to fire on some parts of it, in case of the loyal taking arms against the French. And you will

---

[2] Minotaur, Zealous, Swiftsure, Seahorse, Perseus Bomb, and El Corso Sloop.

use every effort to prevent all supplies of corn, or other articles, from entering the City and Ports in the Bay of Naples; and also of Gaeta and its vicinity, and along the Roman coast to Cività Vecchia; and as it is said, the Ponza Islands continue in their allegiance to his Sicilian Majesty, you will direct that all protection and assistance may be given to them, should they stand in need. And you will consider that every means is to be used, not only by yourself but by all those under your command, to communicate with the inhabitants on all the Northern coast of the Kingdom of Naples and the Islands before mentioned, and as much as in your power to cultivate a good understanding with them and conciliate their affections, in order to induce them to return to their allegiance to his Sicilian Majesty, and to take arms to liberate their Country from French tyranny and oppressive contributions.

NELSON.

---

## TO HIS EXCELLENCY THE GRAND VIZIR.

[Letter-Book.]

Palermo, 29th March, 1799.

Sir,

With the care of a great Empire entrusted to your Excellency, it would be highly improper in me to take up one moment more of your precious time than is necessary; therefore, I only beg leave to transmit a copy of my letter to His Highness the Bey of Tunis and to the Bashaw of Tripoli, together with the extract of a letter from the British Consul at Tripoli. Your Excellency will form your own judgment on them. I have only to entreat that your Excellency will lay me at the feet of the Grand Signior, and to assure him that, as a faithful servant of my gracious Sovereign, it is my duty and not less my inclination to do everything that His Imperial Majesty can order me; and I beg your Excellency to believe that I am with the highest respect your most obliged and faithful,

NELSON.

## TO ADMIRAL THE EARL OF ST. VINCENT, K.B.

[From Clarke and M'Arthur, vol. ii. p. 150.]

March 29th, 1799.

My dear Lord,

Captain Darby arrived here this morning from Leghorn, with all the Ships, both British and American, that chose to leave that place. Mr. Wyndham has thought it right to abide by the fate of the Grand Duke, which I am sure must be very unpleasant; for the French long before this time are in complete possession of all Tuscany. How Thugut and Manfredini can endure the misery they have brought on their respective Masters, I cannot comprehend; their conduct has been infamous. I am, &c.,

NELSON.

---

## TO CAPTAIN TROUBRIDGE, H.M. SHIP CULLODEN.

[Letter-Book.[1]]

Palermo, 30th March, 1799.

Dear Sir,

I herewith enclose you the final instructions of His Sicilian Majesty, and request you will have them copied, and the originals returned to me; and, as far as lies in your power, to carry them into execution, always bearing in mind, that speedy rewards and quick punishments are the foundation of good government. Wishing you every success in your expedition, I am, dear Sir, yours &c.,

NELSON.

---

## TO LIEUT. PHILIP LAMB, AGENT OF TRANSPORTS, PALERMO.

[Order-Book. March 31st, "Sailed H.M. Ships Culloden, Zealous, Minotaur, Swiftsure, Seahorse, Perseus and El Corso for the Bay of Naples—Shifted the Flag to a Transport."—*Journal*. On the Vanguard's arrival from Tunis, on the 2nd of April, Lord Nelson's flag was again hoisted on board of her.]

At Palermo, 30th March, 1799.

You are hereby required and directed to hoist my Flag on board the Transport in which your Pendant is flying, whenever Captain Troubridge sends it on board.

NELSON.

TO FRANCIS WERRY, ESQ., CONSUL AT SMYRNA.

[Autograph, in the possession of — Werry, Esq., of Smyrna.]

Palermo, April 1st, 1799.

Dear Sir,

I have to request you will have the goodness to forward my
letter to Constantinople, and I shall always be obliged if you
have any news from Egypt or the situation of the French and
Turkish Armies in that Country, that you will let me know
it by the many Ships which sail from Smyrna to Messina. The
French took possession of Leghorn on the 24th, and, I have no
doubt, mean to revolutionize Tuscany. This is the natural fruit
of the conduct of the MM. Thugut and Manfredini. By their
delay of the war which *the French* have now waged against
their Masters, they have lost for the present both Naples and
Tuscany. However, I now hope it will have this good effect,
that all the Sovereigns in Europe will see the absolute necessity of a *sincere* coalition against these modern Goths. Naples
has many loyal good people remaining in it, and is now closely
blockaded by a part of my Squadron. We are anxiously
waiting the arrival of the Russian army. Pray God they
may soon come to us. A few thousand good troops to go
forward with the loyal Calabrese, would get to Naples in a
week. I am, dear Sir, your most obliged servant,

NELSON.

---

TO MESSRS. BIRCH AND BROADBENT, MESSINA.

[Letter-Book.]

Palermo, 2nd April, 1799.

Gentlemen,

I have received your letter of the 26th March, and am
exceedingly surprised that the Governor of Messina should
presume to interfere in the captures made by a British Ship
of War. Captain Foley is justifiable in taking the French
tartan, although she was going into the Port, or even in the
Port. You will, therefore, claim from him the materials of
which the Vessel has been plundered; and, at the same time,
demand from him what he has done with the French prisoners
of war taken in the Vessel, as it is highly presumptuous in

him to interfere with British Prisoners of War. As to his demands made against the Vessel, it is my desire that they are not paid, nor has he any right to make them. On the contrary, the captors have a right to demand from him satisfaction for the employment of the Vessel on the Coast of Calabria. I am, Gentlemen, your very humble servant,

NELSON.

---

### TO CAPTAIN BALL, H.M. SHIP ALEXANDER.

[Autograph, in the possession of Sir William Keith Ball, Bart.]

Secret.

Palermo, April 3rd, 1799.

My dear Ball,

I send you a copy of Sir Charles Whitworth's letter to Sir William Hamilton, and also a Secret Article of the Treaty with His Sicilian Majesty. Lord Grenville's letter, and the paper attached to it, will show you his ideas, as will an extract of Lord Spencer's letter. You will now be satisfied I have done perfectly right in keeping the course I have. You will, therefore, whenever these Russians arrive, enter with all apparent pleasure into the closest and most friendly concert for the speedy reduction of the place. As to the Ships, &c., leave all to be settled by the two or three Courts always: it will be certain that very long ago they would have been in the Port of Toulon but for your close blockade. The Vanguard is just come from Tripoli, and the Bashaw promises faithfully that no provisions shall be sent by his subjects to Malta; but interest, we know, is the predominant passion with those gentlemen. I send you two intercepted letters sent me by the Bashaw. Troubridge is in the Bay of Naples, with five Sail of the Line, &c. *Darby* is gone to Minorca. None shall interfere with you; and if it is in my power, you shall be elected a Chevalier of the Order.[1] I find the Russian

---

[1] At the request of the Grand Bailiff and other distinguished members of the Order of Saint John of Jerusalem, commonly called the Order of Malta, assembled at St. Petersburg, in October 1798, the Emperor of Russia accepted the Sovereignty of the Order. He established a Grand Priory in the Capital of his Empire, and endowed it with an annual revenue of 216,000 rubles, and bestowed the decoration on many

Langue has the privilege of admitting married men.  No one ever deserved honours more than you, and I feel what you will suffer in having this child of your own taken out of your hands.  I need not say how very necessary it is to keep all this secret, and when necessary to be told, to be done in its true point of view, that the Order will not be able or inclined to oppress the inhabitants as heretofore.  You must excuse short letters.  God bless you.  All in this house join in kindest regards with your obliged and affectionate,

Nelson.

---

TO HIS EXCELLENCY SIR CHARLES WHITWORTH, K.B., BRITISH MINISTER AT ST. PETERSBURG.

[Letter-Book.  On the 4th of April, Lord Nelson heard of his promotion, which is thus noticed in the *Journal*:—" Received a commission as Rear-Admiral of the Red: shifted the Blue flag, and hoisted the Red one."  The *Journal* states that on the 5th of April, Lord Nelson ordered a salute to be fired by the Ships at Palermo, to celebrate the victories gained by the Austrians over the French Armies.]

Palermo, 5th April, 1799.

Dear Sir,

I have been honoured, *viâ* Constantinople, with your letters of                , and I shall be happy in paying attention to your friend, Mr. Aylmer.  My excellent friend, Sir William Hamilton, has shown me all your letters to January 21st. We certainly have, at an expense of fifteen thousand pounds a month, so closely blockaded the Port of La Valetta, that the appearance of the Russian troops on the Island must insure its fall in a week, if famine does not force its surrender before their arrival.  The Garrison are mutinous, and in dreadful want of provisions.  The scurvy cannot be checked.

I am sure, my dear Sir, you have done me the honour to say so much about me, that you will allow my anxiety to get

of his own subjects, upon the Nuncio from the Pope, and upon the Envoy from the King of the Two Sicilies.  In February, 1799, the Emperor ordered his Ministers at the Courts of Europe to make known that he had accepted the title of " Grand Master of the Sovereign Order of St. John of Jerusalem," and his Ministers were forbidden to receive any letters addressed to his Imperial Majesty, in which that title was omitted.  The Emperor afterwards, at Lord Nelson's instance, gave the Cross of Commander of the Order to Captain Ball, who had certainly well deserved it; and the small Cross to Lady Hamilton!

possession of the Guillaume Tell and the two Frigates, the last remains of an immense Fleet of near 400 Sail, including Transports, which sailed from Toulon on the 20th May last. *How are the mighty fallen!* These Ships, but for our close blockade, would long ago have been in France. This I submit to the gracious judgment of his Imperial Majesty. I have given directions to Captain Ball to co-operate in the most cordial manner with the Russian troops, who so ably has conducted himself, not only as a Sea-officer, but in conciliating the affections of the Maltese, that he is unanimously, by the Islanders, and with the approbation of his Sicilian Majesty, elected their General and Chief. I should hope that when the Order is restored, which I pray God may be soon, that Captain Ball will be a Knight of it, for a more gallant, able Officer does not grace this world. I feel I have said a great deal, but with my honour I pledge myself for the truth of it.

His Imperial Majesty will know that the poor Islanders have often in their distress, and as a mark of their gratitude, offered (as far as they could) themselves for subjects of our King, and made this request to his Sicilian Majesty; but both Sir William Hamilton and myself, knowing that no views of individual aggrandizement actuate the breast of our gracious Sovereign, have invariably refused every offer of that nature; but in the present situation of his Sicilian Majesty, and by his desire, his colours and the British flag fly in this manner [*i.e.*, side by side, that of England being on the right hand,] to mark that Great Britain protects the Flag of his Sicilian Majesty. It is proper in this place to mention, as the heart of the Emperor overflows with justice, that in many instances the Islanders have been grievously oppressed by the Order— probably more by their consummate pride than by a wish to oppress. I know it is only necessary to mention this matter for the consideration of the present illustrious Grand Master to have it remedied, by which a brave and industrious people will be rendered happy.

We wait with impatience the arrival of the Russian troops. If 9 or 10,000 come to us, Naples will be recovered in a week, and his Imperial Majesty have the glory of replacing a good Monarch and an amiable Queen on their throne again: that

this may soon happen is the fervent wish of your Excellency's
most obedient, &c.,

NELSON.

P.S.—I have late letters from the unfortunate King of
Sardinia, at Cagliari, full of gratitude for the protection of the
British flag,[2] in conveying him from Leghorn.

---

TO EARL SPENCER.

[Letter-Book.]

Palermo, 6th April, 1799.

My dear Lord,

I have to thank you for your letters of December 24th and
25th, duplicates of which I also received by sea the same
day. I am happy that everything which I have done respecting Malta, has been exactly what has been wished at hom
To say the truth, the possession of Malta by England, wou..
be an useless and enormous expense ; yet any expense should
be incurred, rather than let it remain in the hands of the
French. Therefore, as I did not trouble myself about the
establishing again the Order of St. John at Malta, Sir William Hamilton has the assurance from his Sicilian Majesty
that he will never cede the Sovereignty of the Island to any
power, without the consent of his Britannic Majesty. The
poor Islanders have been so grievously oppressed by the
Order, that many times have we been pressed to accept of
the Island for Great Britain; and I know if we had, his
Sicilian Majesty would have been contented. But, as I said
before, I attach no value to it for us ;[3] but it is a place of such
consequence to the French, that any expense ought to be
incurred to drive them out.

[2] " AU MILORD, ET AMIRAL NELSON.

"Milord, et cher Amiral, Je viens de recevoir par le Capitaine Gage la lettre
que vous m'avez adressée en date du 10 du courant de Palerme, par laquelle j'ai
appris avec plaisir vos bonnes dispositions pour moi, et pour ma famille. Je me
rapporte donc à ce, que je vous ai écrit dans mes précédentes, et j'y recourerai si
quelque occasion pressante se présente. En attendant je ne manquerai pas d'en in-
former votre Cour, et de vous y rendre la justice duë à votre procédé. Je prie Dieu,
qu'il vous ait dans sa sainte garde. Cagliari le 21 Mars, 1799. C.E."—*Autograph*,
in the Nelson Papers.

[3] Perhaps no opinion expressed by Nelson is more extraordinary than that Malta
is not of value to this Country.

I have this moment letters from Captain Ball, stating the distress of the Island, and his fears that when harvest comes, which will be in three weeks, they may make their peace with the French, in the belief that Sicily will fall into their hands before winter; on the other hand, the garrison is in great distress, and eat up with the scurvy. The Bashaw of Tripoli, having made a treaty with Buonaparte, on February 24th, and received a present of a diamond, I wrote him a letter on the subject, and sent it by the Vanguard; Captain Hardy brought me back a letter of promise of future good conduct.

I can now get to more interesting subjects; being sensible that by a close blockade of Naples with the largest force I could collect, must prevent any French troops from being sent against the Italian Armies (as they are called) in the Provinces, I sent my friend Troubridge, with five Sail of the Line, on this service, and directed him to use every means in his power to take Procida, in order to secure the anchorage: he sailed on the 31st ultimo. Yesterday I had the most satisfactory letters from him, of his complete possession of all the Islands in the Bay of Naples, and of his getting possession of all Jacobin municipality, officers, &c. Some well-timed and speedy punishments will have the happiest effects. The French are not more than 2000 troops in Naples, and about 2000 civic troops; the last are weathercocks, and will always be on the side of the conqueror. We are anxious for the promised succours of Russian troops; 10,000 would possess Naples in twenty-four hours. I am, &c.

NELSON.

---

TO CAPTAIN TROUBRIDGE, H. M. SHIP CULLODEN.

[Letter-Book.]

Palermo, 7th April, 1799.

My dear Troubridge,

Many thanks for your letters by the Perseus, and for the good news you have sent us.[4] May God ever give you that

---

[4] Extract from a Letter from Captain Troubridge to Lord Nelson, dated 3rd April 1799.

"All the Ponza Islands have the Neapolitan flag flying. Your Lordship never beheld such loyalty; the people are perfectly mad with joy, and are asking for their

success which your high merit deserves! We go to the Queen
this evening, where all your letters are already gone, and I
have pressed for flour: everything which the Islanders want,
must and shall be instantly sent. Money, £500, is sent you.
I well know, from experience, that all Ships ought to have
money on board. I have drawn on the Victualling Board,
therefore you will procure proper vouchers, that is, as near
as circumstances will permit, receipt and price paid. The
universal joy over Palermo for this first success (which I really
look upon as the near forerunner of the fate of Naples,) is as
great as can be wished. I shall finish when I return from
the palace.

beloved Monarch. If the Nobility were men of principle and of respectability, how
easy it would be to get the Neapolitan soldiers and militia to declare for their King.
I wish we had a few thousand good English troops, I would have the King of Naples
on his throne in forty-eight hours. I beg your Lordship will particularly recommend Captain Chianchi; he is a fine hardy seaman, a good and loyal subject, desirous of doing everything for the welfare of his Country. If the Navy of the King
of Naples had been composed of such men, the people would never have revolted. I
have a villain, by name Francesco, on board, who commanded the castle at Ischia,
formerly a Neapolitan officer, and of property in that Island. The moment we took
possession of the castle, the mob tore this vagabond's coat with the tricoloured cape
and cap of liberty button to pieces, and he had then the impudence to put on his
Sicilian Majesty's regimentals again; upon which I tore his epaulet off, took his
cockade out, and obliged him to throw them overboard; I then honoured him with
double irons. The mob entirely destroyed the Tree of Liberty, and tore the tri-
coloured Flag into ten thousand pieces, so that I have not been able to procure even
a small remnant to lay at the King's feet. I, however, send two pieces of the Tree
of Liberty for his Majesty's fire, with the names of the people who brought the pieces
to me painted upon them."

April 4th, 1799. "The French troops in Naples amount to about 2000, and are
thus distributed: In St. Elmo 300, Castle Uovo 200, Castle Nuovo 1400, Puzzuoli
100, Baia 30. Their actions at Salerno, &c. have been attended with serious
losses: not one of their men returned from Salerno, out of 1500, except a few who
were wounded; and in Abruzzo, at a place called Andre, it is said that nearly
3000 have been killed. The French and Jacobins have quarrelled, and a great dis-
trust reigns amongst them. It frequently happens in the rounds at night, if, when
challenged *Chi viva?* they answer *La Republica*, they are shot; and the Republicans
do the same if the answer is *Il Rè*, which makes it dangerous to move after dark.
The whole of the chief Jacobins are quarrelling about their honesty. I have just
received an account that a priest, named Albavena, is preaching up revolt in Ischia;
I have sent 60 Swiss and 300 loyal subjects, to hunt him, and shall have him, I
expect, dead or alive, to-day. I pray your Lordship to send an honest Judge here,
to try these miscreants on the spot, that some proper examples may be made. 2, P.M.
Pray press the Court to send the Judge by the return of the Perseus, as it will be
impossible to go on, else; the villains increase so fast on my hands, and the people
are calling for justice; eight or ten of them must be hung."—*Clarke and M'Arthur*,
vol. ii. p. 160.

Just come from the Queen and Acton—every provision asked for will begin to be loaded to-morrow. Minerve shall bring the *troops* and *Judge*. Send me word some proper heads are taken off: this alone will comfort me. With kindness remember me to all with you, and believe me your affectionate

NELSON.

---

## TO HIS EXCELLENCY THE MARQUIS DE NIZA.

[Letter-Book.]

Palermo, 8th April, 1799.

My Lord,

I am happy to inform you of our success in the Bay of Naples, and of having taken the Islands of Ischia, Procida, &c., the inhabitants of which have manifested a spirit of loyalty, by delivering up their Municipal officers, who are all prisoners on board the British Ships of War. We have received information here of the Port of Leghorn being in the hands of the French. If this be the case, your stay there will not be necessary, as it is not possible to blockade the Port with one Ship; you will therefore return, and join me at this place. I have the honour to be, &c.

NELSON.

---

## TO CAPTAIN COCKBURN, H. M. SHIP LA MINERVE.

[Order-Book.]

8th April, 1799.

You are hereby required and directed to receive on board the Ship you command, for a passage to join Capt. Troubridge in the Bay of Naples, two hundred troops of his Sicilian Majesty, also a Judge, and such other Civil officers as may be sent on board, victualling them at two-thirds allowance during their stay on board.

NELSON.

TO CAPTAIN THE COUNT DE THURN, COMMANDING HIS
SICILIAN MAJESTY'S SHIP LA MINERVA.

[Order-Book.]

Vanguard, 8th April, 1799.

Having received on board his Sicilian Majesty's Ship you
command, the troops destined for Procida, you are hereby
required and directed to proceed without loss of time, and
join Captain Troubridge, of his Majesty's Ship Culloden, in
the Bay of Naples, and deliver him the dispatches you will receive herewith.

NELSON.

————————

TO CAPTAIN BALL, H. M. SHIP ALEXANDER.

[Autograph, in the possession of Sir William Keith Ball, Bart.]

April 9th, 1799.

My dear Ball,

You will have received so much of the affairs of Malta, by
the Hyæna, that I need not mention the subject, except to
say that I hope you will not take these arrangements to heart.
You have long deserved to take it, and had the Maltese been
brave and truly good, you would have done it.　But, my
dear friend, your whole conduct reflects upon you the highest
honour.　You will break the new arrangement of the Order
to such of the Maltese as you choose, but this I leave to your
judgment.　Things wear a favourable appearance in the Bay
of Naples; and if the reports are true that the Emperor's
troops are near Bologna, I hope yet we shall soon again see
Naples; then Malta would fall of course.　It has been the
successes of the French which have kept up the spirit of the
garrison of La Valetta.　God bless you, and believe me ever
your affectionate friend,

NELSON.

I told Tyson to write you, but I could not help writing a
line, although I am tired to death.

## TO CAPTAIN SIR EDWARD BERRY, KENSINGTON.

[Autograph, in the possession of Lady Berry.]

My dear Berry,                         Palermo, April 10th, 1799.

I yesterday had the pleasure of receiving your very affectionate and friendly letter of January 1st, the whole of which is so manly and kind, that I can never sufficiently [thank you.] I grieve that you should be ill, but I am far from being surprised at it, knowing the great fatigue and uneasiness you have undergone: quietness will cure you. As to my movements, it was my plan to have gone to England from Naples. Events have multiplied so fast upon me, that the time of my departure still is uncertain; but I fully intend to quit this ·Country, when I can do it with honour to myself. I have not heard a syllable from Captain Capel since he left Naples; but, my dear friend, it has happened to me, the want of common gratitude, so often, that I ought not to be surprised. The Narrative[4] is well drawn up, and I feel highly sensible of the flattering manner in which you have mentioned me. As to both our Honours, it is a proof how much a battle fought near England is prized to one fought at a great distance. The conduct going to be pursued about the Ships I ordered to be burnt, is mean and unjust.[5] All our friends here, think as I do on that subject. Ball, Gould, and Foley, are off Malta; Troubridge, Hood, Louis, and Hallowell, in the Bay of Naples; Smith, Miller, and Dixon, in Egypt. The first of those last batch, has been sent here to lower my importance; at least, by his conduct, he appears to think so. You must excuse a short letter from me, for the truth is, that I am, in addition to my duty as an Admiral, become a Councillor and Secretary of State. God bless you. Remember me most kindly to your Mother, Sister, and Lady Berry, and believe me ever, with the truest affection, your obliged friend,

NELSON.

I am glad you approve of my friend Davison.[6]

[4] Vide p. 40, et seq. ante.

[5] Probably in considering the Ships that were destroyed as of less value than the others. See Lord Spencer's letter, p. 116, ante.

[6] Lord Nelson and the Captain of the Squadron had appointed Alexander Davison, Esq., sole Agent for the sale of the Ships taken at the Nile. As a proof of his grati-

### TO THE REVEREND MR. NELSON, HILBOROUGH.

[Autograph, in the Nelson Papers.]

Palermo, April 10th, 1799.

My dear Brother,

I thank you for your letter of February 5th, enclosing one from Charlotte : those you mentioned to have wrote, and Horace's, came to me in due time by sea, but our communication with Gibraltar and England is not very certain or frequent. You must not, nor any of my friends think, that because my letters are scarce and short that in any way they are forgot : the wonder even to me is, that I am able to write what I do. My public correspondence, besides the business of sixteen Sail of the Line, and all our commerce, is with Petersburg, Constantinople, the Consul at Smyrna, Egypt, the Turkish and Russian Admirals, Trieste, Vienna, Tuscany, Minorca, Earl

---

tude, Mr. Davison struck a Medal to commemorate that event, which he presented to the Admiral, Captains, Officers, Seamen and Marines who were in the Battle, so that the inferior Officers and Seamen owed to the munificence of a private individual, that distinction which ought to have proceeded from their King and Country.  Mr. Davison's letter on the occasion is so honourable to his memory that it ought to find a place in this work :—

"My dear Lord,                    "St. James' Square, 18th March, 1799.

"The very kind and truly flattering manner in which your Lordship, and the Officers under your command, have conferred upon me the sole Agency for the sale of the French Ships of War, taken by you at the ever-memorable Battle of the Nile, commands my warmest acknowledgments.  But being anxious to express these sentiments in the strongest possible degree, it occurred to me that a Medal, to commemorate this unparalleled achievement, would convey in the most durable manner the respect which I entertain for this mark of your confidence, and the admiration which I am impressed with upon this truly glorious event.

"I have therefore thus gratified my inclination, and I hope and trust that your Lordship, and all the Officers and men, who were then under your command, will do me the honour to receive it as a tribute of my respect and admiration.  I have the honour to be, my dear Lord, your Lordship's most faithful and obliged friend, and humble servant,

"ALEXANDER DAVISON.

"P.S. The Medals that I have had struck for your Lordship and the Captains of your Fleet are of gold, those for the Lieutenants and Officers who rank with them are of silver, those for the Warrant and inferior Officers are of copper gilt, and those for the Men are of copper bronzed."

The following Extracts from two letters from Mr. Davison to Lord Nelson respecting the Medals are highly interesting, as they show the regard which the King entertained for his Admiral :—

VOL. III.                    Y

St. Vincent and Lord Spencer. This over, what time can I
have for private correspondence? Consider this and I shall
stand acquitted. Whenever [I can] in ANY way be useful to
you or my nephew and niece, you know me not to be
disinclined. I neither wish to be thought richer or poorer
than I am, but of this be assured, that except my pension I
am much poorer than when I left England a year ago. I
feel that you have cause for complaint that not one relation of
the *Victor of the Nile* has been noticed. I wrote to both Mr.
Pitt and Mr. Wyndham and Lord Spencer: the two first
never answered my letter; the latter has told me he does
not know how he can be useful to my brother Maurice.

So much for *my* interest! However, time must I think
bring matters round, for I can never bring myself to believe
that Nelson's family should be unnoticed by the English
Government. I had not heard of poor Mr. Suckling's death

---

"St. James's Square, 6th April, 1799.
"I waited upon the King early last Sunday morning, at the Queen's House, and
presented him with a gold and a silver Medal. He received them most graciously
and with much joy and pleasure, and paid me many compliments upon the occasion.
I was *alone* with the King a full hour, when much of the conversation was about
you. It is impossible to express how warmly he spoke of you, and asked me a
thousand questions about you. I promised his Majesty a copper-gilt and a bronze
Medal, as soon as I received them, which I shall have also the honour of presenting."

"St. James's Square, 7th May, 1799.
"I have again been at the Queen's House, and have given the King a copy of
your last letter to me, giving an account of your health, which he read twice over,
with great attention, and with apparent emotion of concern. I said a great deal
(but not too much) regarding my idea of your situation. His Majesty speaks of you
with the tenderness of a father. He was much pleased with the portrait I presented to him of you, and said he thought it very like."—*Autographs*, in the Nelson
Papers.

The *Obverse* of the Medal represents the allegorical figure Hope, with the emblem,
standing on a rugged rock, with an olive branch in her right hand, and supporting
by her left arm the profile of Lord Nelson, on a medallion, to which she is pointing
with her fore-finger. Hope is crowned with oak and laurel, and the motto round
the medallion is, EUROPE'S HOPE AND BRITAIN'S GLORY. The legend is REAR-
ADMIRAL LORD NELSON OF THE NILE. The *Reverse* represents the French Fleet
at anchor in the Bay of Aboukir and the British Fleet advancing to the attack.
The fortified Islands in the Enemy's Van, the four Frigates that were moored
within the Line, to cover their flank, and the Gun-boats near the Islands—the
setting sun, the Coast of Egypt, the Mouth of the Nile, and the Castle of Aboukir;
The Legend, ALMIGHTY GOD HAS BLESSED HIS MAJESTY'S ARMS; and on the
exergue, VICTORY OF THE NILE.

till I received your letter.[7] The desires of his children do not
surprise me. I love his memory, and am not sorry that he
has forgot me, except as his executor, [in] which I will be
faithful. I loved my dear Uncle for his own worth, and not
from any views of interest to myself. As to my going to
England, that must depend so much on circumstances that I
cannot form any guess on the subject. I should wish to
carry the King back to Naples, and then I will think of it.

April 11th, 1799.—I cannot write more; my hands are
full: therefore can only say, God bless you all, and believe
me, your affectionate brother,

NELSON.

---

### TO CAPTAIN BALL, ALEXANDER, OFF MALTA.

[Letter-Book.]

Palermo, 10th April, 1799.

My dear Ball,

I have received your letter by La Minerve of the 31st
March; and have sent you a Victualler, to complete your
Squadron with provisions. I have also sent you an anchor
and cable left here by the Minotaur, and request you will
order receipts for them to be forwarded to that Ship. I am
sorry for the sufferings of the Maltese, which you so feelingly
describe; but you will see the arrangements made by the
Allied Courts, sent you in my letter per Hyæna, which puts
it out of my power to alleviate them; and as summer is now
come, they will not feel the want of clothing so much.

I am happy to acquaint you of the success of Captain
Troubridge in the Bay of Naples; Ischia and Procida are
returned to their allegiance; and the whole municipality of
the latter Island are prisoners on board Culloden. Wishing
you every success, I am, my dear Ball, &c.,

NELSON.

---

[7] Mr. William Suckling died at Kentish Town, on the 15th of December, 1798,
aged 69. He left Lord Nelson a legacy of one hundred pounds, and appointed him
one of his executors.

TO H. R. H. THE DUKE OF CLARENCE.

[From Clarke and M'Arthur, vol. ii. p. 159.]

Palermo, 11th April, 1799.

Sir,

Your Royal Highness[8] will, I am sure, from my knowledge
of your goodness, make every fair allowance for not receiving
those letters from me, which I should have the greatest
pleasure in writing, were it possible that I had the power.
But besides the business of sixteen Sail of the Line, I have
the constant correspondence of Petersburg, Constantinople,
Vienna, Venice, Trieste, Smyrna, Florence, Leghorn, Earl
St. Vincent, Minorca, and Lord Spencer: this must plead
my excuse. Being now shut out from all the continent
of Italy, we know nothing of the movements of the Austrian
army: I pray God they may be successful. I have sent a
Squadron of five Sail of the Line, &c. into the Bay of Naples,
and all the Islands are in our possession. The inhabitants
have delivered up the Jacobins. At Naples all of the lower
order are loyal and attached to their Sovereigns, and indeed
so they are in the Provinces; for this war presents the very
extraordinary circumstance of the rich taking the road for the
destruction of property, and the poor protecting it. I long to
hear of the extirpation of the French army in Egypt. I
believe Buonaparte is heartily tired of his expedition, and

---

[8] His Royal Highness wrote to Lord Nelson on the 18th of March, 1799:

"Dear Nelson,

"I am to acknowledge yours of 20th November from Naples, which, from various
causes, did not reach me till a few days ago : sad events have taken place in Italy,
and such indeed as were not to have been expected after your glorious Action. The
Emperor let escape the favourable moment, and consequently, the Kings of Sardinia
and Naples have fallen victims to the Directory. It is astonishing Europe *cannot*,
or *will not*, see that resistance alone can only meet the exigence of the time. The
war is no longer of choice but necessity. I am still in hopes that hostilities being
again commenced in Germany, the Austrians will advance in Italy and allow you,
with the Russians, to reinstate the Neapolitan family, who really deserve a better
fate. You may easily conceive my anxiety, and you will, therefore, I hope, write
frequently, or employ some other person, to relate the events as they arise.

"As you say nothing about your health in your letter, I trust your wound in your
head is quite well; and that the King and the Country may long enjoy your abilities :
in the meantime adieu, and ever believe me to be, dear Nelson, yours sincerely,
WILLIAM."—*Autograph*, in the Nelson Papers.

would readily enter into a negotiation with the Porte to quit Egypt, for which purpose he made a treaty, and sent rich presents to the Bashaw of Tripoli. In this Island we are loyal, and certainly detest the French. I trust the Monarch of Spain means fair to his brother; but ... I hope that Providence will long continue its present good Sovereigns in possession of their rights.

[In continuation.]

10th of May, 1799.—In addition to my want of power to detail events, I am at this moment seriously unwell; and nothing, Sir, but the very peculiar circumstances of the times, with the confidence reposed in me, not only by your Royal Father and my Commander-in-Chief, but also by their Sicilian Majesties and the whole Nation, could induce me to remain. They all know that I have no desire, but of approving myself a most faithful servant to my gracious King; therefore, there is nothing which I propose, that is not, as far as orders go, implicitly complied with. But the execution is dreadful, and almost makes me mad. However, as his Sicilian Majesty has now ordered two Generals to be tried for cowardice and treachery, and, if found guilty, that they shall be shot or hanged; should this be effected, I shall have some hopes that I have done good. I ever preach that rewards and punishments are the foundation of all good Government: unfortunately, neither the one nor the other have been practised here. The French troops have all left the City of Naples, and are encamped at Caserta, sixteen miles distant; preparatory, we think, to their leaving the Kingdom. The Jacobins must now shift for themselves, and I hope they will be severely punished, in person by their King, as they have already been, in pocket, by their Allies. With every sentiment of true attachment, believe me your Royal Highness's faithful servant,　　　　　NELSON.

---

TO ADMIRAL THE EARL OF ST. VINCENT, K.B.

[Letter-Book.]

My dear Lord,　　　　　　　　　Palermo, April 12th, 1799.

By my letter of March 20th, you will know of my intentions of sending a Squadron, under Captain Troubridge, into

the Bay of Naples, to take Procida, &c., and create a diversion
in favour of the (Christian Army) loyal people in the Provinces. The Squadron sailed,—viz., Culloden, Zealous,
Minotaur, Swiftsure, San Sebastian, Seahorse, Perseus, and El
Corso, on the 31st; and on the 7th, I had the pleasure of hearing from Captain Troubridge that he was in complete possession
of Procida, Ischia, and Capri—the inhabitants of which Islands
had joyfully hoisted his Sicilian Majesty's colours, cut down
the Trees of Liberty, and delivered up all the Municipality
and the detested Jacobins, all of whom are confined on board
Ship, and in the Chateau of Ischia. The French in Naples
are not more than 2000—the Civic guards about 20,000;
but as these last will not remain fighting for the French if
there is any risk, I am warranted in saying, that 10,000 troops
would place the King again on his throne in twenty-four
hours; therefore, we are very anxiously looking out for
the promised 9000 Russians coming by way of Zara; 3000
are also destined for Malta, which will fall the moment such
a landing is made; for I am satisfied the garrison only wants
a good pretence for giving up. They have been led to believe
that Sicily would soon be revolutionized; but in this I flatter
myself they are mistaken.

Shut out as we are from the Continent, I can only give
you, as report believed, that the Great Duke and family were
ordered to quit Tuscany, which they have done. Porto
Ferrajo is also given to the French—so much for the counsels
of MM. Thugut and Manfredini. I hope the Austrians
will fight better this war than the last. A Russian General,
Suwarrow, is to command in Italy. We of this house are all
anxious to get home, yet, in the present moment, cannot move.
Indeed, we have been the main-spring, joined with you, that
have kept and are keeping this so much out-of-repair machine
from breaking to pieces. May God bless you! Believe
me ever your obliged and affectionate,

NELSON.

The Europa sails to-morrow for Minorca and Gibraltar; so
shall the Haerlem and Pallas the moment I can get them
from Messina. The Hyæna I was obliged to send with
orders to Malta—the Convoy taking two of my small Craft,
one for Smyrna, the other to Venice. I had almost forgot to

tell you Mr. Stuart cannot find his commission for the Seahorse, nor have I any order what Lieutenant to remove.  I
have this moment letters from Troubridge; all going on
well both in the Islands and Continent.

---

### TO COMMODORE SAMPSON MITCHELL.

[Letter-Book.]

Private.

Palermo, April 13th, 1799.

My dear Sir,

I have received your letter of April 10th, relative to the
Portuguese Commodores serving under Captain Troubridge.
Now, my dear Sir, I have Lord St. Vincent's opinion, which
perfectly agrees with mine, that every Captain under my
command, in a Line-of-Battle Ship, must command the
Chef de Division in the Portuguese service.  You will believe
that I could have no desire to lower your rank, but, on the
contrary to exalt it; but not at the expense of the rank of
those in the English Navy.   There is only one circumstance,
that, if you cannot remain, your Ship must, and the next
Senior Officer must necessarily command her.   The Marquis
de Niza, I apprehend, cannot alter my destination of your
Ship; nor will he, I am sure, encourage disobedience to my
orders for the public good, and in which her Most Faithful
Majesty is as much interested as the King of Great Britain.
I send you Lord St. Vincent's opinion.

Sir William and Lady Hamilton desire particularly to be
remembered, and believe me your faithful humble servant,

NELSON.

---

### TO LADY PARKER.

[Autograph, in the possession of Mrs. Ellis.]

Palermo, April 13th, 1799.

My dear Lady Parker,

I cannot allow Captain Stevenson,[1] who says he has the
happiness of your acquaintance, to return to Portsmouth
without taking a line from me to say what is true, and what I

---

[1] Captain James Stevenson, of the Europa, died a Post-Captain, about 1816.

feel—that every Honour I receive, it had its origin in your
and good Sir Peter's friendship and partiality for me. Believe
me, it is my pride that I never have yet done anything to
bring a blush on the cheeks of my dear friend. I am here
almost become a Secretary of State; but I have my hopes
that his Sicilian Majesty will soon again take a passage in the
Vanguard for Naples. The lower orders are to a man loyal:
the Priests and Nobles all Jacobins. God bless you. Remember me kindly to Sir Peter, Admiral Parker,[9] Miss
Parker, and pray do not forget me to all my friends near you,
and believe me ever your faithful and grateful,

NELSON.

---

TO PERKIN MAGRA, ESQ., CONSUL AT TUNIS.

[Autograph, in the possession of John Bullock, Esq.]

Palermo, April 14th, 1799.

Dear Sir,

This moment I am told that the Chevalier Tr. sends off a
boat for Tunis with letters for you respecting the Vessel
seized with my passport. I did not intend writing to you till
I could have answered satisfactorily the Bey's letter. As
matters are in a train for restoring a peace or truce during
the war, it is time that neither the Bey or myself ought to
cover Enemy's property; but both Sicily, Malta, and Tunis
are at war with those miscreants the French. How cruel,
to take provisions which Sicily sends to succour the Maltese
against French tyranny! Be so good, with your ability, to
urge this point. I can say nothing equal to what you know
in your management of these people. I can almost take upon
me to say that His Sicilian Majesty will, in fourteen days, be
in the Bay of Naples, and, I hope, on his throne: he has
not a hundred men in his Kingdom that does not wish it. I
shall write to you fully very soon, and believe me, dear Sir,
with all respect, your most obedient humble servant,

NELSON.

[9] Vice-Admiral Christopher Parker, eldest son of Sir Peter Parker. He died a
Vice-Admiral of the Red, in his father's lifetime, in May 1804; and was father of
the gallant Captain Sir Peter Parker, who was mortally wounded near Baltimore, in
August, 1814. There are few instances of an Admiral living to see his son attain
the rank of Flag Officer.

The Christian Army is surrounding Naples, in which are only 2500 French, and the English are in full possession of all the Island. I send a letter for the Bey of Tunis. Open it and read if it's proper; also one from Rear-Admiral Duckworth[1] and the Duke of Portland.

------

TO CAPTAIN TROUBRIDGE, H.M. SHIP CULLODEN.

[Letter-Book.]

Palermo, 14th April, 1799.

My dear Troubridge,

Captain Harward arrived this morning, and brought your interesting letters and papers to the 10th.[2] I have been pressing both to the Queen and General Acton the great importance of sending provisions in the greatest abundance, and I hope that very soon you will have no wants. Acton says three Gun-boats shall be ordered to you; but probably the Sicilians will not go such a long voyage. I send you a

[1] Commodore Duckworth obtained his Flag as Rear-Admiral of the White, in the promotion of the 14th of February, 1799.

[2] On the 9th of April, Captain Troubridge wrote: " Since writing to your Lordship by the El Corso, we have accounts that the Islands of Vendutina and Ponza have both submitted, cut down the Tree of Liberty, and hoisted his Majesty's colours. To-morrow the Governor goes in one of our Ships to form a government. The Officer and invalids in garrison at these Islands we must take into his Majesty's pay. Naples is in a devil of a ferment, and M'Donald is much alarmed . . . I have two deserters from their gun and mortar boats, who assure me, if the French force them within gun-shot, they will murder all the French soldiers in them, and bring the boats over to us. The whole of the common people, without exception, are truly loyal; the Jacobins begin to shake . . . . I have a report that the Jacobins begin to talk of trying to make their peace . . . . The Governor of Procida is a truly honest and valuable subject; the King can never do enough for him. Captain Chianchi is also indefatigable in examining the people that came from all quarters. Some came from Sorrento to see the King, having heard he was here. So much loyalty among the common people was never before seen . . . . . Our numbers on the Islands increase fast. The fishermen are forbid to fish: to prevent them starving I give them leave to fish here: in order to man their gun-boats and galleys, they drew the sailors into the arsenal to get their pay. When they had got them in, the gate was shut, and all driven into the gun-boats without a carline. So much for *French honour*. I just learn that *Caraccioli has the honour* to mount guard as a *common soldier*, and was yesterday a sentinel at the palace: he has refused service. I believe, they force every one to do duty as militia. . . . . . Rocca Romana, they say, is now of no consequence. The whole of the great Jacobins are quarrelling about their *honesty*, accusing each other. I hope things will end well, and soon, in his Majesty's favour."—*Original* in the Nelson Papers.

chart of the Interior, and I hope that soon, by your exertions and the loyalty of the people, that I may be able to
carry the King and Queen back to Naples. I shall, my dear
Troubridge, you may be assured, do everything which you can
wish me; and, if Vessels must be hired by you, I will take
upon me to order payment. You will do what is right, and
as time and circumstances arrive. I am, &c.

NELSON.

---

TO ADMIRAL THE EARL OF ST. VINCENT, K.B.

[Letter-Book.]

My dear Lord,                          Palermo, April 17th, 1799.

Since I wrote you by the Europa, the Hyæna is arrived
from Malta, where she went with copies of Sir Charles Whitworth's letters, and of the Treaty between his Sicilian Majesty and the Emperor of Russia. The account that the
Russians are likely in any way to become masters of Malta,
has caused the greatest alarm in that Island; and if they do
not arrive very soon, I have my fears that they may make
their peace with the French: if so, for the next six months
they have plenty of Corn in the Island. The distresses of the
poor people are terrible, and the Islanders are rapidly decreas-
ing by an epidemic fever. I have asked this Court to send
£10,000 to the Island, but I cannot succeed, as General Acton
says they have it not to give. Therefore Malta must take its
chance; the only chance of saving the Island is by my friend
Ball, who is adored, and deservedly, by all ranks. My obligations to him are greater than any words of mine can express. From October 15th, he has never been one moment
off his station, and through such a winter as we all know is
seldom experienced. Mr. Neave[1] has been there, and it is
lamentable to hear his accounts of the distress in Malta.

This day has brought me letters from dear Troubridge;
all his flour he has been obliged to give to keep the Islands
from starving. I have eternally been pressing for supplies,

---

[1] Richard Neave, Esq., third son of Sir Richard Neave, Bart.; now Secretary and
Registrar to the Royal Hospital, Chelsea. He was recommended to Lord Nelson
and Sir William Hamilton by Lord St. Vincent, and received many marks of attention from both.

and have represented that £100,000 given away in provisions just now, might purchase a Kingdom. In short, my dear Lord, my desire to serve, as is my duty, faithfully their Sicilian Majesties, has been such, that I am almost blind and worn out, and cannot, in my present state, hold out much longer. I would, indeed, lay down my life for such good and gracious Monarchs; but I am useless when I am unable to do what, God knows, my heart leads me to. Porto Ferrajo is in the hands of the French; so is Longona by this time. God bless you, my dear Lord, and believe me your obliged and affectionate

NELSON.

---

DISPOSITION OF THE SQUADRON, 17TH APRIL, 1799.

### Sent by Hyæna.

Culloden,
Minotaur,
Zealous,
Swiftsure,  } Blockading Naples and Ports adjacent.
Seahorse,
Perseus,
San Leon,

Alexander,
Audacious,
Goliath,
Thalia,
Stromboli,  } Blockading Malta.
Bonne Citoyenne,
Incendiary,

Le Tigre,
Theseus,  } Blockading Alexandria.
Lion,

Vanguard, at Palermo.

La Minerve carried Troops to Procida, and to go to the northward for information.

Alliance, on her passage from Alexandria.

Emerald, at Mahon, heaving down.

El Corso, convoy to Venice.

Mutine, cruizing with Rear-Admiral Duckworth's Squadron.

L'Entreprenant Cutter, Convoy to Smyrna.

Haerlem,) at Messina, under orders to go down the Mediter-
Pallas,  ) ranean.

Europa, sailed with Convoy for Minorca, the 14th instant.

Hyæna, to see a Convoy of Gun-boats from hence to Procida,
and then to proceed to Mahon.

### PORTUGUESE SQUADRON.

Principe Real, arrived yesterday from Port Longona.

Affonço, arrived two days ago from Malta.

St. Sebastian, with Captain Troubridge, blockading Naples.

Rainha, carried the French Princesses to Trieste. (Not returned.)

Benjamin, with Captain Ball, blockading Malta.

Balloon, with Captain Troubridge, off Naples.

---

### TO CAPTAIN BALL, H.M. SHIP ALEXANDER.

[Autograph, in the possession of Sir William Keith Ball, Bart.]

Palermo, April 21st, 1799.

My dear Ball,

Your late letters, I have no doubt, contain a true, but most
melancholy account, of the state of the unhappy Maltese.
Believe me, I urged by every way in my power, the sending
you at least a small sum of money; but my efforts were useless, till the arrival of the Cutter from England, which brought
this Court such accounts of goodness, that Sir William and
myself again pushed the point about Malta, when the Queen
gave up 7000 ounces; for although the Island has granted
two million of money, yet not one sixpence is yet collected,
therefore they are in distress enough. If any person can
keep the Maltese in good humour, it is, my dear friend, you,
and you only; therefore, for all our sakes, try hard till the
arrival of the Russians, who cannot now be long before they
make their appearance. All goes on as it should on the other
side; the lower order only want a little support from regular
troops, and the business is over. Tuscany being revolutionized, prevents our hearing any of the important events
which have taken place between the two armies, therefore we

can only hope the best. Genoa and Naples are both trying to send provisions to Malta. The moment I can get some more small Vessels, you shall have one or two; at present, I have two in the Adriatic, and one gone to Smyrna. I send you all the papers in the house. Sir Charles Thompson is dead; so is Christian.[3] Send me back Lord St. Vincent's letter, which is full of news. I can only say, what I hope you are convinced [of], that you shall have, in your more than commonly arduous task, every assistance and support from me, for believe me, &c.

NELSON.

I hope Captain Nisbet behaves properly; he is now on his own bottom, and by his conduct must stand or fall. Kind remembrances to Foley, Gould, &c. As this money was put at Naples, Sir William recommends having the barrels or bags opened before witnesses. Mr. Neave is full of thanks for your goodness to him.

---

TO CAPTAIN TROUBRIDGE, H.M. SHIP CULLODEN.

[Letter-Book.]

Palermo, April 25th, 1799.

My dear Troubridge,
I thank you again and again for your letters, and for the ability and exertion you show on all occasions.[4] As to Mr.

---

[3] Vice-Admiral Sir Charles Thompson (vide vol. ii. p. 33,) died on the 17th of March, 1799; and Rear-Admiral Sir Hugh Cloberry Christian, K.B., died in November, 1798, being then Commander-in-Chief at the Cape of Good Hope.

[4] Extracts from Captain Troubridge's letters to Lord Nelson, of the 13th and 18th of April:—

"Culloden, off Procida, 13th April, 1799.

"I am happy my conduct meets your Lordship's approbation. The whole of the Islands are now in our possession. The Governor, with 100 soldiers, is gone with the Seahorse, and two of the Feluccas, to settle the Government of Capri, Vendutina, and Ponza. The latter has a French governor left there by the King—a suspicious character. I have directed Don Curtis to inquire particularly about him: if found to possess a particle of the Jacobin, to appoint a Royalist. The Judge appears to me to be the poorest creature I ever saw—frightened out of his senses, says seventy *families are concerned*, and talks of it being necessary to have a Bishop to degrade the Priests, before he can execute them. I told him to hang them first, and if he did not think the degradation of hanging sufficient, I would——"
. . . . "The Governor, Curtis, will be absent for two or three days. I shall be

Judge, he must hang, or let it alone, as he pleases. It has been that miserable system which has caused much of the present misery in Naples. In respect to the Cardinal,[5] he is a swelled-up priest. If his letter had been directed to you, his answer would have, I am sure, been proper. Such impertinence, in speaking of the assistance of England, deserves reprobation. He makes his Army great or small as it suits his convenience: he is now frightened at a thousand men going against him, which at one time is thirty thousand—at another, not three thousand. In short, my dear friend, without Foreign troops, the stream will sometimes run different ways. Some Russian ships are said to be at Otranto; but we know less than you. If the Austrian armies are beaten, Naples will be lost—if victorious, our exertions, with the constant loyalty of the lower order, will hasten the King's return. More provisions will go to you in two days. I hope your Islands will be well supplied. Three Packet-boats are again ordered to go to you, that we may have a daily communication.

What are your ideas of the King's going into the Bay of Naples, without Foreign troops? If it should cause an insurrection in Naples which did not succeed, would it not be worse? The King, if a rising of loyal people took place, ought to be amongst them; and that he will never consent to. As to news, we have very little. Hoste will tell you that from Minorca. Affonço is going to Tripoli—the Bashaw has taken another twist. Lord Spencer disavows the con-

---

anxious for his return, as he is really an active, diligent, and I think, honest man—perhaps the only one on the Island. . . . . I enclose your Lordship one of Caraccioli's letters, as head of the Marine. I hope he has been forced into this measure. This was intercepted at Capri. I have another from Gaeta to Ponza, sent by that route, as he says he cannot forward it by the Bay of Naples."—"18th April, 1799. Your Lordship will see by the enclosed paper, that the Islands were deemed the property of the French Republic, as belonging to the House of Medicis and Fernase, and not part of the Neapolitan Republic: we have disappointed them. Caraccioli, I am assured by all the sailors, is not a *Jacobin*, but forced to act as he does. They sign his name to printed papers without his authority, as they have, in my opinion, the Archbishop's. The fellow from Toranto, *Sir William's friend*, I believe is a Jacobin."—*Autographs*, in the Nelson Papers.

[5] Cardinal Ruffo, who took so prominent a part in public transactions, as Vicar-General, and Commander of the army of Neapolitan Royalists.

duct of Sir William Sidney Smith, as being in any manner independent of me.[6] What will his Lordship say, when he reads the Passports?[7] Your wants and wishes shall, as far as I am able, be complied with. Your bill for extra expenses, if the Court will not pay, I will answer for. With kind remembrances, &c.,

NELSON.

[6] The "disavowal" was expressed in a letter to Lord Nelson, dated, Admiralty, 12th March, 1799. After acknowledging the receipt of many letters from Lord Nelson, Earl Spencer said:—

"The details contained in these letters are equally distressing, with respect to the unfortunate series of events which they relate to, as affecting the Kingdom of Naples, as they are honourable and glorious for your Lordship, who, by your exertion, your spirit, and your extraordinary resources of every kind, have been enabled to save the Royal Family of that Country, as well as so many other respectable persons, who had no other means of protection, but those they derived from your abilities" . . . . "On the subject of Sir Sidney Smith, there must certainly have been some very great misunderstanding, as it never was our intention here that he should consider himself as a Commander-in-Chief, or that he should be authorized to take a single Gun-boat even from under your command without your orders. He was sent to serve in the Mediterranean fleet, and, of course, under your command, as well as that of every other Officer senior to him under Lord St. Vincent; but from the circumstance of his connexion with the King's Minister at the Ottoman Porte, and his own acquaintance with several of the principal persons at Constantinople, it was judged advisable by Government to join his name in the full powers which had been granted to his brother, to conclude a treaty with that Court, and Lord St. Vincent was accordingly directed to send him up in the first instance to Constantinople, as the very uncertain state of the Continent, at the time he received his orders for sailing, made it not improbable that he might arrive there before the courier overland. He was, however, most specifically and pointedly told by me, before his departure, that he would most probably find senior Officers to him in the Levant, and I had not the most distant idea of his being any otherwise considered than under your Lordship's orders, which I understand from Lord St. Vincent, he has since been more regularly informed of, by an order from him. I am much concerned to perceive that you so often allude to your health being in a bad state. I am aware that you must have undergone very great fatigues and anxieties, but I trust that the brilliant successes which have hitherto attended, and with the protection of Divine Providence, will I hope, ever continue to attend, your exertions in the service of your King and Country will make you ample amends for all your labours; and the reflection of the great advantages derived by the Public from your presence in the Mediterranean, will induce you (unless it should be absolutely necessary for you to return), to postpone the idea of it till matters are in a state a little more settled."—*Autograph*, in the Nelson Papers.

[7] As Sir Sidney Smith's passports gave so much offence to Lord Nelson, a copy of them is inserted. Every part (except what is here printed in italics) is printed; in the upper corner is a seal of Sir Sidney's arms; and under his signature is a Turkish seal:

TO THE CAPTAINS AND COMMANDERS OF HIS MAJESTY'S SHIPS
AND VESSELS OF WAR AND PRIVATEERS, AND THE COM-
MANDERS OF THE RUSSIAN AND OTTOMAN CRUISERS.

[Order-Book.]

Passport.          26th April, 1799.

Whereas I have thought proper to hire into the service of
His Britannic Majesty the Boat, named Gesù Maria e Guiseppe,
whereof Carmalo Gegante, a Trapanese, is Master, and to
establish her as a Packet boat between Palermo and Zara
or Trieste, in the Adriatic Sea, with my orders to the Master
to wear the British flag; it is my direction to all the Commanders of all his Majesty's Ships of War, that they render
every assistance to the said Boat whenever they may fall in
with her. And the Commanders of the Ships of War of the
Allies of his Britannic Majesty, the Russian and Ottoman
cruisers are hereby desired to suffer the said Boat to pass unmolested.

NELSON.

This Pass to be in force for three months. Given the 26th
April, 1799; but not permitted to carry any cargo in trade.

---

TO LIEUT.-GENERAL THE HON. SIR CHARLES STUART, K.B.

[Letter-Book.]

Vanguard, April 28th, 1799.

My dear Sir Charles,

By the Mutine I was favoured by your letters of the 17th,
till when I did not know that the King had intended to make a

---

"De par le Chevalier SIDNEY SMITH, Grand Croix de l'Ordre Royal et Militaire de l'Epée de Suede, Ministre Plénipotentiaire de Sa MAJESTE BRITANNIQUE
près la PORTE OTTOMANE et Chef de son Escadre dans les Mers du Levant.

"Tous Amiraux, Généraux et Officiers, tant Militaires que Civils de SA MAJESTE
BRITANNIQUE, ceux de ses Alliés et des Puissances amies, sont priés de laisser libre-
ment et surement passer le nommé . . . . . agé de . . . . ans, taille de . . . . cheveux
et sourcils . . . . yeux . . . . nez . . . . bouche . . . . visage . . . . allant à . . . . . . et
de lui prêter aide et assistance en cas de besoin, pour poursuivre sa destination. Bon
pour . . . . mois.

"Donné abord du Vaisseau de SA MAJESTE le . . . .

"No. . . . .          ce . . . . .

"Signature du porteur.          "W. SIDNEY SMITH.

. . . . . . . .

"Par ordre,
"John Keith, Secretary."

present of the wood. However, I instantly put all the matter right, and your Commissary shall pay for it. I perfectly agree with you, that no presents should be received; and to this hour I can say that I have never received anything of which proper lists have not been exchanged, in order to their being paid for; and as to myself, I wrote General Acton a letter, which he laid before their Majesties, declining any presents for myself, which I knew was intended.

Our news from the Continent is good, and, I believe, for the most part, true: on the Rhine, the Archduke Charles has forced Jourdan to repass it; the Swiss in revolution on the Adige; General Serrurier has been defeated, and forced to retreat into Mantua. In consequence of these events, nearly all the troops have left Tuscany. All the French troops, except 500, have left Naples for Capua on the 22nd instant, taking with them sick, cannon, &c., &c. Those left keep possession of St. Elmo, which, it is supposed, would be evacuated the 24th. Many of the principal Jacobins are gone off; therefore Troubridge tells me, he thinks his next letter will be from Naples. So far this is good. I sincerely hope it will continue. Captain Edmonds[1] has this moment arrived. The landing of some Russian troops on the Adriatic to[2] join the Cardinal. Believe me, &c.,

NELSON.

---

TO SIMON LUCAS, ESQ., HIS MAJESTY'S CONSUL AT TRIPOLI.

[Letter-Book.]

Palermo, 28th April, 1799.

Sir,

As you have so very handsomely offered to return to Tripoli with Commodore Campbell, in order, if possible, to bring the Bashaw to a proper way of thinking, by representing to him forcibly the numerous evils which bad councillors are sure to bring upon him, should he persist in his present disloyal conduct, I enclose a copy of my letter to the Bashaw, which will be your guidance. The latter Article, relative to the dismissal of the Captain of the Port, although a very desirable

---

[1] Captain Joseph Edmonds of the Pallas, *arme-en-flûte*. He was made a Post Captain in February 1807, and died between 1816 and 1820.　　[2] *Sic.*

thing, is not to be persisted in, so as to occasion the hostilities of Commodore Campbell against his Highness ; for every Master has a right to choose his own servants; but the other Articles are not in any manner to be given up. Therefore, at the end of the two hours, you will acquaint Commodore Campbell of the result of your conference ; but you are to be careful to impress upon the Bashaw, that his Britannic Majesty, our gracious Master, is not at war with him; but that I, having hitherto checked his Highness's enemies from committing much depredation on his Coast, had, from his conduct, interested myself no more for his particular good ; but that, if he returned to a proper way of thinking and acting, I should be equally careful of his interests (as much as the situation of the war between Her Most Faithful Majesty would allow) as I have hitherto been. You will, of course, either remain at Tripoli, or return with Commodore Campbell, as your judgment points out for the interest of his Majesty.

Wishing you a successful negotiation, I remain, your most obedient humble servant,

NELSON.

---

TO HIS HIGHNESS THE BASHAW OF TRIPOLI.

[Letter-Book.]

Vanguard, Palermo, 28th April, 1799.

Sir,

When I received your Highness's letter, by Captain Hardy, of the Vanguard, I was rejoiced to find that you had renounced the treaty you had so imprudently entered into with some emissaries of General Buonaparte—that man of blood, that despoiler of the weak, that enemy of all good Musselmen ; for, like Satan, he only flatters that he may the more easily destroy; and it is true, that since the year 1789, all Frenchmen are exactly of the same disposition. I had sent your letter to the great King, my Master; I had done the same to the Grand Signior ; for I never believed that your Highness would say a word that was not most strictly true : a lie is impossible for a true Musselman to tell—at least, I had always believed so. What, then, must have been my astonishment to have heard from his Britannic Majesty's Consul, Mr.

Lucas, that the moment the Vanguard sailed, the French Consul and all the French, were liberated, and also the French Vessels in the Port allowed to fit for sea, and one, to my knowledge, had sailed for Malta? Why will your Highness be thus led astray by evil councillors, who can have no other object in view but your ruin?

Your Highness knows that although a powerful Squadron of Portuguese Ships has been, since last August, under my command, that by every. means in my power they have been prevented from cruising against the Ships of your Highness, or from approaching your Coast. It is now my duty to speak out, and not to be misunderstood. That Nelson who has hitherto kept your powerful Enemies from destroying you, can, and will, let them loose upon you, unless the following terms are, in two hours, complied with—viz., that the French Consul at Tripoli, Vice-Consul, and every Frenchman, are delivered on board her Most Faithful Majesty's Ship Affonço, to Commodore Campbell, in two hours from Mr. Lucas setting his foot on shore; that hostages are also sent on board, to remain till every Frenchman in the State of Tripoli shall be sent off, which shall not exceed four days. N.B. There shall be no reservation or trick about the French Consul, &c., at Tripoli. He shall be on board in two hours after the demand being made. All French Vessels, or Vessels pretended to be taken from the French, shall be destroyed in two hours. These terms complied with, Commodore Campbell will, as he has done upon the passage, refrain from taking your Vessels, until his arrival at Palermo. If these proper terms are not complied with, I can no longer prevent the Ships of her Most Faithful Majesty from acting with vigour against your Highness.

Your Highness will, without difficulty, write me a letter, the substance of which will be dictated by Mr. Lucas. You will also, as a convincing proof of your detestation of the evil counsels which have been given to you by Hamet Reis, your Captain of the Port, either cause him to be delivered to Commodore Campbell, that I may send him to Constantinople, or *dispose* of him in such a manner, that he may for ever be incapable of giving your Highness any advice; for his heart is so black, that I am informed he can give you no good.

z 2

Your Highness will, I am confident, approve of the open and unreserved manner of this letter, and consider it as a proof of the honest, upright intentions of the Great Monarch who I have the honour of serving, and that it comes from your Highness' most attached and faithful servant,

NELSON.

---

## TO THE RIGHT HONOURABLE EARL SPENCER.

[From a Copy, in the Admiralty.]

Palermo, 20th April, 1799.

My dear Lord,

Since I wrote you last, things have been every day improving in the Kingdom of Naples; and from appearances, I think it very probable that in ten days their Sicilian Majesties may be again in Naples. These happy prospects have been brought about, first, by the war of the Emperor; secondly, by the wonderful loyalty of the lower order of the people; and lastly, I flatter myself I may say, by the conduct of the English. Captain Troubridge has given a portion of that spirit he so eminently possesses, to all who communicate with him. The Great Devil[1] who commands a portion of the Christian army, has been on board the Culloden, and an attempt was to be made to take Gaeta on the 26th, at night. Captain Hood has taken Salerno; his Marines and a party of Royalists garrison it. The distance from Naples twenty-eight miles. Castel-á-Mare is also now with the King's colours flying. I had just sent the Minotaur and Swiftsure to support them. These events have determined the French to evacuate Naples, and I hope the whole of the Neapolitan Dominions. On the 25th, Macdonald left the Town for Capua, with all the troops, except 500 in the Castle of St. Elmo, who were expected to make off on the 27th.

Orders have been given by the *Jacobin* Government, for the batteries *not* to fire on the English ships. In short, the communication with Naples is so open, that a General took a boat from the city, and came on board Troubridge, to consult about surprising St. Elmo. The Civic Guard have individually declared that they assemble to keep peace in the City,

---

[1] The name given to a Calabrese who distinguished himself in the Royal cause.

and not to fight. Many of the principal Jacobins have fled,
and Caracciolo has resigned his situation as Head of the
Marine. This man was fool enough to quit his Master when
he thought his case desperate; yet, in his heart, I believe he
is no Jacobin. The fishermen, a few days ago, told him publicly, ' We believe you are loyal, and sent by the King; but
much as we love you, if we find you disloyal, you shall be
amongst the first to fall.' I am not in person in these busy
scenes, more calculated for me than remaining here giving
advice; but their Majesties think the advice of my incom-
petent judgment valuable at this moment, therefore I submit,
and I can only say that I give it as an honest man, one without hopes or fears; therefore they get at the truth, which
their Majesties have seldom heard.

Malta still holds out; but the moment all hopes of getting
supplies from Naples cease, I am in great hopes the garrison
will surrender to the meritorious and indefatigable Ball, whose
good conduct is equalled by few, exceeded by none. As to
myself, I shall only say what your partiality has always believed, that I shall do my best, and believe me, my dear
Lord, &c.,　　　　　　　　　　　　　　　　NELSON.

P.S. April 30th.—Castel-à-Mare has the King's colours
flying. Our two Ships at anchor there. All the Jacobins
retired to St. Elmo.

May 1st.—Much blood has been shed near Naples since
the 28th. We have lost a few men near Salerno. A very
handsome order of the King is come out, stating the few
exceptions to pardon; and even those, or any one which
Troubridge says *pardon*, it is done by the instrument. I am
this moment sending 1200 infantry and 400 horse,—sail in
two days in the Haerlem and Vanguard.

---

TO COMMODORE CAMPBELL, OF HER MOST FAITHFUL MAJESTY'S
SHIP AFFONÇO DE ALBUQUERQUE.

[Order Book.]

Vanguard, Palermo, 29th April, 1799.

You are hereby required and directed to receive on board
her Most Faithful Majesty's Ship Affonço, under your com-

mand, Simon Lucas, Esq., his Britannic Majesty's Consul at
Tripoli, charged with my letters to the Bashaw, and proceed
with him to Tripoli in Barbary. And as the circumstances of
the war are such as to render it very improper for you to
molest or detain any of the Cruizers belonging either to the
States of Tripoli or Tunis, on your passage to and from thence,
you will refrain from making captures of the Vessels belonging
to either of those States; and, on your arrival at Tripoli, you
will assist Mr. Lucas in his negotiations with the Bashaw,
and in carrying my demands on him into execution. For your
information, I herewith send you a copy of my letter to the
said Bashaw, and to Mr. Lucas, requesting you to give every
assistance to see the terms in it complied with, excepting the
last Article respecting the delivery up of the Captain of the
Port, which is not to be persisted in, so as to occasion the
commencement of hostilities; but in case of the refusal of the
Bashaw to deliver up the French Consul, &c. and the destruction of the French Vessels in the Port, you are then at perfect
liberty to act in such a manner as you think most proper for
the service of her Most Faithful Majesty; and, having finished
this important business, you will return and join me at this
place.

                                                    NELSON.

TO ADMIRAL THE EARL OF ST. VINCENT, K.B.

[Letter-Book.]

                                        Palermo, 30th April, 1799.
My Lord,
    I herewith enclose your Lordship an abstract of the state
and condition of most of the Ships under my command; but,
from their being so much dispersed, I have not been able to
collect them to any given period. I have desired Rear-
Admiral Duckworth to send up stores, as the Squadron in
general is in extreme want, and some of them much distressed. I enclose your Lordship a copy of a Memorandum I
have given out respecting the seizure of Tuscan Vessels, which
I hope your Lordship will approve. I am, my Lord, &c.

                                                    NELSON.

## TO ADMIRAL THE EARL OF ST. VINCENT, K.B.

[Letter-Book.]

Palermo, 30th April, 1799.

My dear Lord,

As I know good Sir William sends his letters for Lord Grenville open for your perusal, it is needless for me to enter into those details which his pen so much more ably recites. The Earl St. Vincent Cutter arrived the 19th, and I have to thank you for your kind letter. As to Lord Spencer, my mind is made up to do by Sir Sidney Smith what is handsome, right, and proper; and whilst you do me the honour in giving me the command of the detached Squadron, *I will be* commander of it, and suffer no, not the smallest, interference of any Captain, however great his interest may be.

On the Continent my friends are doing wonders. Hood has taken Salerno, twenty-eight miles from Naples, and garrisoned the small Castle with his Marines and Royalists. He has caused Sorento, &c., to Castel-a-Mare, to rise and massacre the Jacobins. The Swiftsure and Minotaur are at anchor at the latter place, which is opposite Naples, and, by the round of the Bay, twelve miles distant. These events, so near the Capital, together with the success of the Austrian army both on the Rhine and in Italy, have induced the French to call in all their outposts; and, leave 500 men in the Castle of St. Elmo, to retire from Naples to Capua, taking with them all their sick and plunder; when assembled, they will be about 5000 men. I believe nothing can prevent the people of Naples from rising, and attempting the Castle of St. Elmo, where the Jacobins have retired, and our friend Caraccioli amongst them. I wish they may succeed, but our friend Troubridge wishes they could have stopped a few days. However, he has prepared 800 seamen and marines to garrison one of the Castles. I am preparing the Haerlem, to carry over 800 troops. Three hundred cavalry are also preparing, with provisions, &c. This Court being very poor, and no revenue, makes things slower than they would otherwise be; but we do the best with the slender means we have.

I own, my dear Lord, myself much fitter to be the actor, than the counsellor of proper measures to be pursued, in this very critical situation of public affairs; but, at least, their Sicilian Majesties are satisfied that my poor opinion is an honest one. Their Majesties are ready to cross the water whenever Naples is entirely cleansed. When that happy event arrives, and not till then, a desire will be expressed for the British troops to be removed from Messina into Naples to guard the persons of their Majesties. Whenever your name is mentioned, I can assure you their expressions are the very handsomest that tongue can utter, and, as is my duty, both as my Commander-in-Chief, and my friend, I do not fail ever to speak of you in the only way, if truth is spoken, that you can be represented— as the very ablest Sea-Officer his Majesty has, and as the best and truest friend that can be in this world. My dear Lady Hamilton is always my faithful interpreter on all occasions, and never with so much pleasure. My dear Lord, you will forgive my short sketches of what is going on here; for neither my head or my hand is equal to what is absolutely necessary for me to write; therefore all private correspondence is given up, for I cannot answer a letter. One of Sir William Sidney Smith's ships, with sick Frenchmen, is stopped by Trou-bridge; the poor devils are sent to Corsica. I am very much displeased with this Levant Commodore with a Broad Pen-dant. I send one of his Passports;[8] we are not forced to understand French. Malta is as usual: the moment a land force arrives, it will fall. God bless you, my dear Lord, &c.,

NELSON.

---

TO ADMIRAL THE EARL OF ST. VINCENT, K.B.

[From Clarke and M'Arthur, vol. ii. p. 164.]

3rd May, 1799.

You must forgive, my dear Lord, my short sketches of what is going on; for neither my head nor my hand is equal to anything more. We learn from Lieutenant Parkinson, who joined the Squadron off Malta in the Emma tender, on her way from Egypt to Palermo, that Sir Sidney Smith has given up the blockade of Alexandria, and proceeded off St. Jean d'Acre, where are Buonaparte's head-quarters. I am far from

⁸ See p. 336, ante.

well, and the good news of the success of the Austrian arms
in Italy does not even cheer me. I enclose a detailed account
of their campaign, extracted from the letters of a Mr. Walter
Burn to me, who is now at Genoa. I am, &c.,

NELSON.

---

TO ADMIRAL THE EARL OF ST. VINCENT, K.B.

[Letter-Book.]

Palermo, 3rd May, 1799.

My dear Lord,

I send you the dispatches of the Court for London, through
your Lordship being the only sure way of communicating
with England. Yesterday the Earl St. Vincent Cutter came
from off Malta, where Ball is doing everything a man can do,
to keep all the people in good humour, until the arrival of the
Russian troops, which I hope will not be very long. A small
battery is erected by Captain Ball, at the head of the harbour,
which sweeps the straight harbour to the very entrance, therefore the Ships are obliged to be kept in the coves. In short,
the exertions of Captain Ball and all the Squadron under
him, do them the highest credit. A prize polacre which I
sent to Egypt, was off Malta, a few days ago, on her way here.
Herewith I send you the report sent me by Mr. Sargeant,
who saw the Lieutenant. If half is true, it is very bad.
From Naples no alteration since I wrote last. A small regular
force would instantly do the business; and we wait with the
greatest impatience the arrival of the Russian troops. A
Cartel which I sent to Genoa a month past, is just returned,
and brings details of the glorious success of the Austrian arms
in Italy. The French Army is said to be nearly destroyed,
and they are retreated to Milan and Lodi. Mantua is
blockaded, and the Rampart di S. Giorgina taken. On
April 14, Ferrara was taken: and it appears that Tuscany
and Naples must both, if it is possible for the French to
escape, be evacuated.

I shall write more by the Haerlem, who will sail on Wednesday, at furthest, for Naples, and then down the Mediterranean. I am far from well, and this good news does not
even cheer me. God bless you, and believe me ever your
obliged and affectionate

NELSON.

TO HIS MAJESTY THE KING OF SARDINIA, CAGLIARI.

[Letter-Book.]

Palermo, 4th May, 1799.

Sire,

I have been honoured with your Majesty's letter of
April     ,[9] and I beg you will be assured that in offering
services to your Majesty, I do no more than fulfil the wishes
of my gracious Sovereign; and was I to fail in showing
your Majesty all the attention in my power, I should be
sure of my Royal Master's censure: therefore, I presume to
request you will lay your commands upon me, and consider me only as a faithful servant, devoted to your Majesty,
from the many unhappy events which you have so lately
experienced from a set of infidels, robbers, and murderers;
but the measure of their iniquity is, I believe, full, and that
God, in his wisdom, is in the act of punishing them by the
hand of the Austrians. The successes of the Emperor's arms,
both in Italy and on the Rhine, I shall have the honour of
briefly relating, and I send you such papers as have come to
my hands. The Archduke Charles, after several severe
battles, has forced Jourdan to repass the Rhine with immense
loss. His Royal Highness has taken Kehl, and is before Stras-
burg, where General Massena has retreated. All Switzer-
land has revolted against the French, and the Austrians' head-
quarters in that Country, are at Little Basle and Schaffhausen.
In Italy everything is victorious, and therefore the fairest
prospect presents itself, that before May is over, there will not
be a Frenchman from Milan to the Adriatic. Lodi was the
last quarter-general of the French, and it is since said, and
universally believed, that the French have abandoned Lodi,
and returned across the Po. The State of Genoa is in a
deplorable situation for corn, which makes all the lower
orders desirous of a change in their Government: I therefore
submit to your Majesty's wisdom, to check as much as possible,
corn being sent from Sardinia. It may be effected by orders
for long quarantines, and other means. The messenger you

[9] Query, 21st of March? Vide p. 315, ante.

sent to Leghorn with dispatches for London, and who was forced to come here by the French being in Tuscany, sails tomorrow for London, in a Ship of War.  Upon this, and all other occasions, I shall be happy in obeying your commands, being your Majesty's faithful and obedient

NELSON.

---

TO ADMIRAL THE EARL OF ST. VINCENT, K.B.

[Letter Book.]

My Lord,　　　　　　　Vanguard, Palermo, 6th May, 1799.

I herewith enclose you a detail of the present campaign, extracted from the letters of a Mr. Walter Burn (to me), who is now at Genoa, and reduced to great distress.  He had his Vessel seized by the Genoese, when lading wine for our Fleet at Toulon.  These accounts have been nearly all confirmed by letters received from the Continent by this Court.  I have the honour to be, my Lord, &c.,

NELSON.

Our friend Troubridge had a present made him the other

---

[1] The King of Sardinia replied to this letter on the 8th of May :—

" Mon cher Amiral,

"Vous ne sauriez croire, mon cher Amiral, avec quelle satisfaction j'ai lû votre lettre du 4 du courant, que j'ai reçue hier à 5 heures après midi, et je l'ai tout de suite communiquée à toute la Famille Roiale, ainsi qu'à mes premiers Officiers, lesquels en ont été tous bien charmés.  Sans entrer dans des details, je profite de l'occasion que le Chevalier Balbi, mon premier Ecuier, se propose de faire un tour en Allemagne, et en Russie, pour le charger de passer par Palerme, et vous instruire de mes intentions, et de mes vues dans les circonstances actuelles, lesquelles nous laissent espérer que le bon Dieu veut à la fin que le brigandage cesse, et que la bonne cause soit victorieuse.  Voilà les vœux que nous faisons incessamment au Ciel pour le bien de l' humanité, et le soutien de la Religion.  Vous pourrez donc ajouter foi à tout ce que le Chevalier Balbi vous dira de ma part.  C'est un gentilhomme qui, par ses talents, et ses services, soit dans le militaire, soit à ma Cour, a acquis des droits à ma confiance.  Ainsi je me flatte que vous voudriez bien lui accorder la votre.  Je l'ai chargé de vous assurer combien je suis reconnoissant de votre attention, et combien je compte sur une personne aussi digne, et aussi vertueuse, que vous l'etes, mon cher Amiral.  Je vous remercie des lettres de la Cour de Naples, que vous m'avez adressées, et je vous prie de lui faire passer les reponses ci jointes.  En attendant je prie Dieu de vous avoir sous sa digne et sainte garde, &c. &c.  Cagliari, 8 Mai, 1799, Votre Ami, C. E."—*Autograph*, in the Nelson Papers.

day, of the head of a Jacobin;[2] and makes an apology to me, the weather being very hot, for not sending it here!

---

## TO CAPTAIN TROUBRIDGE, H. M. SHIP CULLODEN.

[Letter-Book.]

Vanguard, Palermo, 8th May, 1799.

My dear Troubridge,

I desire you will express to Captain Hood the true sense I have of his conduct, not only at Salerno, but upon all other occasions; and that I never expect any but the most useful services where he commands; and I beg you will say the same for me to Captains Louis, Hallowell, Foote, and Oswald; not forgetting Captain Harward and Commodore Mitchell, as far as they have been concerned. As to yourself, your conduct is so all of a piece, that I can only say what is true, that the last service seems to eclipse the former ones. You have an arduous task in your present command; and no Officer in his Majesty's service could, I am convinced, perform it with more judgment and advantage for His Majesty's service than yourself, and I beg that you will ever believe me your faithful, affectionate, and obliged friend,

NELSON.

Count Thurn will tell you he takes from hence all the shells and 800 shot, and one month's provisions. I hope he will get off to-day.

---

[2] The following is a translation of the curious letter sent to Captain Troubridge with the head, on which copy Troubridge wrote:—"A jolly fellow.

"T. TROUBRIDGE."

"TO THE COMMANDANT OF THE ENGLISH SHIP.

"Sir,

"As a faithful subject of my King, Ferdinand IV., (whom God preserve,) I have the glory of presenting to your Excellency the head of D.Charles Granozio di Giffoni, who was employed in the Administration directed by the infamous commissary, Ferdinand Ruggi. The said Granozio was killed by me in a place called Li Puggi, district of Ponte Cagnaro, as he was running away. I beg your Excellency would accept the said head, and consider this operation as a proof of my attachment to the Royal Crown, and I am with due respect, the faithful subject of the King,·

"JOSEPH MANUISO VITELLA.

"Salerno, 26th April, 1799."

TO GEORGE BURLTON, ESQ., CAPTAIN OF H. M. SHIP HAERLEM.

[Order-Book.]

Vanguard, Palermo, 8th May, 1799.

Whereas, Guy Head, Esq., an eminent painter and British subject, wishing to return to England with his studies and pictures, books, prints, and other materials necessary for the studying his profession, after an absence of fifteen years, and having been first driven out of Rome and latterly out of Naples, also by the French, and having made application to me for a passage, you are hereby required and directed to receive on board the Ship you command, the said Guy Head, Esq. and his family, with his pictures, books, prints, and other materials; and give them a passage to England, victualling them at two-thirds allowance.

NELSON.

---

TO CAPTAIN TROUBRIDGE, H. M. SHIP CULLODEN.

[Letter-Book.]

My dear Troubridge,　　　　　　Palermo, May 9th, 1799.

Perseus arrived yesterday, after my pacquet was made up for the Minerve; but who is not yet sailed, nor will, I dare say, this day; therefore, I return you Mr. Atkinson. I have wrote strongly to General Acton of the infamous conduct of Yauch.[3] I hope the French are out of Naples; and if the people ever rise, they are as good as the Jacobins; but I would not risk any of our people amongst them. The Lion came yesterday from Egypt, the French Frigates and Corvettes having escaped from Alexandria. Sir William Smith is at St. Jean d'Acre; but that is all Captain Dixon knows; for he, finding the Ships got out, came away here. He is going to Leghorn and Longona. I send you another Gazette to send to Naples. Ever yours faithfully,

NELSON.

[3] See pages 350 and 360. In reply to Lord Nelson's representation of the misconduct of General Yauch, Sir John Acton wrote to him on the 9th May, 1799:— "The conduct of Yauk deserves inquiry, and punishment if found guilty, as I believe his conduct shows it evidently. Orders are given for a Court-Martial. The King begs and hopes that Captain Troubridge will direct some of his Officers to attend to it, with the Officers of this Service, and order accordingly what shall be thought proper at the conclusion of it."—*Autograph*, in the Nelson Papers.

### TO REAR-ADMIRAL DUCKWORTH.

[Letter Book.]

Palermo, 9th May, 1799.

My dear Sir,

Three or four Frigates and as many Corvettes have made their escape from Alexandria. Sir William Sidney Smith having left it on the 7th of March, these Ships escaped between the 5th and 18th of April. I think they are gone to Tripoli; if so, as I have sent Commodore Campbell, I hope to hear a good account of them. A Frigate was said to be seen off Maritimo, she hoisted Algerine colours; it is probable she was one of them. The success of the Austrians in Italy gives us some reason to hope, that the French may soon be entirely driven out; pray God it may be soon! The Transport is lading wood; but not yet arrived; I shall send her alone when she comes to me. Believe me, dear Sir, your obliged, humble servant,

NELSON.

---

### TO ADMIRAL THE EARL OF ST. VINCENT, K.B.

[Letter-Book.]

Palermo, May 9th, 1799.

My dear Lord,

Since I wrote by the Pallas, the French are said to have all evacuated Naples and retired to Caserta and Capua, having robbed all the shops as they passed along. This conduct looks like leaving the Kingdom: the Neapolitan Republic are organizing their troops, and as yet do not seem inclined to give in. Probably, the Royalists wait till the French are out of the Kingdom, before they begin. We hear no tidings of the Russian Troops by the way of Zara. If they would arrive, the business of Naples would be over in a few hours. The conduct of the King's Officer sent to Orbitello and Longono has been so infamous, that Troubridge is almost mad with rage, and I am in a fever. We have reports that the Austrians have entered Tuscany, but it is only report. Last night, the Lion came in from Egypt. I send you Captain Dixon's letter, and Ball's from Malta. Captain Dixon tells me that

Sir William Sidney Smith left him off Alexandria, and went
to St. Jean d'Acre on the 7th of March. Captain Dixon's
water falling short, he went on the 5th April to Cyprus, and
returning the 18th, found some French Ships had escaped
from Alexandria. I had detained the Haerlem to carry troops
to Naples, but as they were not yet ready, I will not detain
her a moment longer. The Lion goes to Leghorn to look out
on the French, and to get information of what is going on
in Tuscany and to the northward. Our Ships are very
healthy, and I have no doubt, from the constant attention
of the Captains, will always be kept so. Believe me ever,
my dear Lord, your affectionate and obliged

NELSON.

---

TO MANLEY DIXON, ESQ., CAPTAIN OF H. M. SHIP LION.

[Order-Book.]

Vanguard, Palermo, 10th May, 1799.

You are hereby required and directed to proceed in his
Majesty's Ship, under your command, to the Port of Longono,
in the Island of Elba, and inquire into the state of the siege
of that fortress, and, if necessary, to give them any assistance
in your power—acquainting the Commandant that they will be
supported, and encouraging them to hold out; but to be careful
in approaching it, lest it should be in the hands of the Enemy.
From Longono, you are to proceed to the north part of the Roads
of Leghorn, and attempt to get what intelligence you are able
from them, either by communicating with the shore, or Neutral
Ships laying in the Roads, of the movements of the Austrian
army; and, if you gain such intelligence as you think of consequence for me to know, you will return to this Port immediately—otherwise, you will cruize in the vicinity of Leghorn;
and, at the expiration of three weeks, you are to return to
the Bay of Naples, where you will find orders for your
further proceedings.

NELSON.

## TO REAR-ADMIRAL DUCKWORTH.

[Letter Book.  On the 12th of May, the Espoir arrived at Palermo with intelligence that the French Fleet from Brest had been seen off Oporto, on their way to the Mediterranean, intending, it was supposed, to join the Spanish Fleet, and to act against Minorca and Sicily.  It was, therefore, necessary to reinforce our Fleet, and Lord Nelson immediately recalled most of the Ships from Naples Bay, and determined to proceed to sea; but in consequence of a gale of wind, his Squadron did not sail until the 20th, when it proceeded off Maritimo.  The Squadron returned to Palermo on the 29th, to complete their provisions.]

Palermo, May 12th, 1799.

My dear Sir,

I am sending you eight, nine, or ten Sail of the Line with all expedition, that they may be ready to either form a junction with our great and excellent Commander-in-Chief, or proceed down the Mediterranean, and join him, as he may direct.  I would venture to offer my opinion, that the Ships had better be under sail off Port Mahon than in the harbour. With my best wishes for success, for I cannot come to you, believe me, your obliged,

NELSON.

---

## TO CAPTAIN TROUBRIDGE, H. M. SHIP CULLODEN.

[Letter-Book.  Captain Troubridge joined Lord Nelson at Palermo, on the 18th of May.]

May 12th, 1799.

My dear Troubridge,

The French Fleet will, before this, have formed their junction with the Spanish Fleet.  What the event of Lord Keith's action may be before they get in, time can only discover.  The Earl comes upwards to join us; therefore you will send me the Minotaur, Swiftsure, and St. Sebastian, and either Culloden or Zealous.  Either you or Hood must remain with the Seahorse, Minerve, &c.  Send a small craft to Leghorn, and order the Lion to join the Ships at Procida directly. Direct the Ships to call off here, but not to anchor, and I shall give them further orders.  The Brig goes directly to Mahon and Gibraltar.  We have a report that a Ship of the Line is frequently seen off Ustica; I do not believe it.  God bless you, &c.,

NELSON.

The Seahorse must take care of Salerno.  Send the Ships as you get hold of them; be as considerate as you can in leaving Marines.

---

TO CAPTAIN BALL, H.M. SHIP ALEXANDER.

[Autograph, in the possession of Sir William Keith Ball, Bart.]

Palermo, May 12th, 1799.

My dear Ball,

The French Fleet, of nineteen Sail of the Line, have before this joined the Spanish Fleet, of twenty-five Sail of the Line, at Cadiz.  What the event of the action has been off Cadiz, time only can discover.  When the junction is effected, Lord St. Vincent comes up the Mediterranean to join his detached Squadrons.  You will, therefore, if the Russian Squadron is before Malta, proceed with all the Line-of-Battle Ships, and the Thalia frigate, off Port Mahon, and deliver my letter to Rear-Admiral Duckworth, and follow his orders for your further proceedings.  Should, unfortunately, the Russian Squadron not be with you, you must send the Audacious and Goliath to Mahon, and the Cutter direct with my letter to Earl St. Vincent at Gibraltar.  If Vice-Admiral Ouschakoff is with you, you will lay my letter before him, and the Ottoman Admiral if with him, and submit it to their consideration, to send as many Ships as possible to Minorca, in order to reinforce Earl St. Vincent.  Ever yours faithfully,

NELSON.

No time must be lost.  If any of your Ships meet Commodore Campbell, tell him to go to Mahon.

TO ADMIRAL THE EARL OF ST. VINCENT, K.B.

[Letter-Book.]

Palermo, 12th May, 1799.

My dear Lord,

Eight, nine, or ten Sail of the Line shall, in a few days, be off Mahon, ready to obey your orders, (not in the Port.) I hope the Russians are off Malta. If so, I have wrote to the Admiral to send some of his Ships to Minorca. In short, you may depend upon my exertion, and I am only sorry that I cannot move to your help; but this Island appears to hang on my stay. Nothing could console the Queen this night, but my promise not to leave them unless the battle was to be fought off Sardinia. May God Almighty bless and prosper you, is the fervent prayer of your obliged and affectionate,

NELSON.

---

TO CAPTAIN BALL, HIS MAJESTY'S SHIP ALEXANDER.

[Order-Book.]

Vanguard, 13th May, 1799.

Notwithstanding my former orders of yesterday, you are hereby required and directed, immediately on the receipt hereof, to collect the Squadron with you, and stand with them over to the Coast of this Island, coming down the shore for Maritimo, and sending on shore at Marsala, to know whether I am still at Palermo, and continue your course within Maritimo, and not finding me cruising near that Island, you will proceed alongshore towards Palermo, keeping a good look out for me. And should the Russian and Turkish Admirals be arrived off Malta, you are forcibly to represent to them the immediate necessity of forming a junction with me for his security, and informing him where I am to be found.

NELSON.

## TO ADMIRAL THE EARL OF ST. VINCENT, K.B.

[Autograph in the Nelson Papers.]

My dear Lord,　　　　　　　　Palermo, 13th May, 1799.

Should you come upwards without a battle, I hope in that case you will afford me an opportunity of joining you ; for my heart would break to be near my Commander-in-Chief, and not assisting him in such a time. What a state I am in ! If I go, I risk, and more than risk, Sicily, and what is now safe on the Continent; for we know, from experience, that more depends on *opinion* than on acts themselves. As I stay, my heart is breaking ; and, to mend the matter, I am seriously unwell. God bless you. Depend on my utmost zeal to do as I think my dear friend would wish me ; for believe me with real affection your faithful friend,

NELSON.

## TO SIR JOHN ACTON.

[Autograph, written on a Letter from Captain Troubridge, in the Nelson Papers.]

May 13th, 1799.

How terrible is this conduct! Whoever has refused these Boats supplies, deserves to be hanged. Pray let a general order be given. I fear *all* the Islands will be lost by improper conduct.

NELSON.

## TO CAPTAIN TROUBRIDGE, HIS MAJESTY'S SHIP CULLODEN.

[Order Book, and "Captain Foote's Vindication of his Conduct," p. 108.]

Vanguard, Palermo, 13th May, 1799.

As the French Fleets have passed the Straits of Gibraltar, and have been seen near Minorca, you are immediately, on the receipt hereof, to join me, with all the Ships of the Line under your orders, at this place, and if you could spare a Frigate, so much the better—disposing of the small Vessels to the best advantage, and leaving whom you think proper in the command.

NELSON.

A A 2

## TO ADMIRAL THE EARL OF ST. VINCENT, K.B.

[Letter-Book.]

Palermo, 14th May, 1799.

My dear Lord,

In consequence of the very important intelligence brought me last night, of the French Fleet having passed the Straits' Mouth, I shall alter my plan of sending such Ships as I can collect, which I hope will be ten Sail of the Line, off Mahon, and rendezvous with the whole of them off the Island of Maritimo, hoping that Rear-Admiral Duckworth will send his Squadron to reinforce me, which will enable me to look the Enemy in the face; but should any of the Russians and Turks be off Malta, I hope to get a Force of different Nations equal to the Enemy, when not a moment shall be lost in bringing them to battle. I have directed the Peterel, so soon as she has delivered my letter to Captain Ball, to proceed to Minorca, and to join your Lordship. Believe me ever,

Your most faithful Servant,

NELSON.

To be read by Admiral Duckworth.

---

## TO THE RESPECTIVE CAPTAINS AND COMMANDERS OF HIS MAJESTY'S SHIPS, AND ALSO OF THE SHIPS OF WAR OF HER MOST FAITHFUL MAJESTY, THAT MAY TOUCH AT PALERMO.

[Order-Book.]

Vanguard, Palermo, 16th May, 1799.

You are hereby required and directed to join me in the Ship you command, as soon as possible, off Maritimo, without anchoring in the Bay of Palermo, and to desire the Captains of all Ships of War which you may fall in with, to join me immediately at the above rendezvous, sending on shore at Maritimo or Favigniano for information.

NELSON.

## TO CAPTAIN TROUBRIDGE, OR COMMANDING OFFICER, PROCIDA.[4]

[Letter-Book.]

Palermo, 17th May, 1799.

Dear Troubridge,

If the Line-of-Battle Ships have not all sailed, I desire you will bring them all with you immediately, and make the utmost dispatch in joining me at this place. The Vanguard is under weigh, and I only wait for you to join. I am all impatience until you join me. Believe me ever your faithful

NELSON.

Leave the Frigate in care of the Islands.

---

[4] Extracts from Captain Troubridge's letters to Lord Nelson, from the 16th of April to the 11th of May:—

"April 16th.—Our situation now becomes more serious than ever. I pledged myself to the people, in consequence of her Majesty's promise, that they should want neither grain nor flour. I know Trabia, and feel much hurt that I am made the tool of his deception. In short, my Lord, these Islands must return under the French yoke, as I see the King's Ministers are not to be relied on for supplies. I trust your Lordship will pardon my stating the case so plainly: but I think I should be highly culpable, if from delicacy I were to sacrifice the lives of 50,000 inhabitants.

"April 18th.—The Judge made an offer, two days since, if I wished it, to pass sentence; but hinted that it would not be regular on some. I declined having anything to do with it. By his conversation I found his instructions were to go through it in a summary manner, *and under me*. I told him the latter must be a mistake, as they were not British subjects. The trials are curious; frequently the culprit is not present: however, he assures me he shall soon have done with them all. I doubt it much. The odium I find is intended to be thrown on us. I will outmanœuvre him there, and push him hard, too.

"25th of April, 1799.—Oh, how I long to have a dash at the thieves! Your Lordship will see that the Cardinal is quite frightened; he appears to me to be very low and dejected. I have three good field-pieces, which I could mount, if they have any field carriages at Palermo. Hood is mounting some howitzers (which we got from the French) on cart-wheels. A person, just from Naples, tells me the Jacobins are pressing hard the French to remain; they begin to shake in their shoes. Those of the lower order now speak freely. The rascally nobles, tired of standing as common sentinels, and going the rounds, say, if they had known as much as they do now, they would have acted differently.

"April 27th.—I have had a long talk with the Judge about the villanous Priests. I am completely stupid. I have been all day since four o'clock this morning examining vagabonds of different descriptions; and as no one ever gives a direct answer, and not being possessed of much patience, I am quite fagged out. The horrid treatment of the French has made all classes mad. The work we have to do

## MEMORANDUM.

[Autograph, in the Nelson Papers.]

### Boats sent from Lord Nelson.

**Sunday Night, May 19th, [1799.]**—A Boat with Captain Hallowell's note.

**Monday.**—With Admiral Duckworth's letters.

**Tuesday.**—With a copy of Lord St. Vincent's, and that sent to Maritimo.

**Wednesday.**—

is nothing; but the villany we must combat is great indeed, and wears us all out. I shall weather all yet, I trust. I have just flogged a rascal for loading his bread with sand; the loaf hung round his neck all the time, and when he was taken on shore afterwards, to be shown to the people. The governor of Procida is the most diligent, active man I ever met with in this country; and, what will surprise you, is an honest man, and deserving of his Majesty's favour. He studies his Sovereign's interest in everything, without the little dirty policy of making money himself.

"May 1.—Caraccioli, I am now satisfied, is a Jacobin. I enclose you one of his letters. He came in the gun-boats to Castel-à-Mare himself, and spirited up the Jacobins.

"About May 7th.—I am in such a rage at the cowardly and treacherous conduct of the General who was sent to Longono and Orbitello, that I am really unable to tell the story, and therefore sent Captain Oswald to relate all. Orbitello is sold, and I fear Longono will be the same. I desired the General, and all his cowardly gang, to get out of a British Man-of-War. We want people to fight; he does not come under that description. I told him plainly that his King would never do well until he hanged half his Officers. I hope the King will order this General to give an account of himself, and not leave him here as a nuisance. The French are going off fast, robbing and plundering every person and shop as they go. Sorrento Castel-à-Mare, &c., &c., have all been plundered. I hear that Caraccioli saved the two former from being burnt. Pray, my dear Lord, hear Oswald, and urge the King to make an example of this General. I am really very ill. I must go to bed. This treachery fairly does me up.

"May 7th, 1799.—My Lord: I have just had a long conversation with the Judge. He tells me he shall finish his business next week; and that the custom with his profession is, to return home the moment they have condemned. He says he must be embarked immediately, and hinted at *a Man-of-War*. I found also from his conversation, that the priests must be sent to Palermo, to be disgraced by the King's order, and then to be returned for execution to this place. *An English Man-of-War to perform all this!* at the same time making application to me for a hangman, which I positively refused. If none could be found here, I desired he would send for one from Palermo. I see their drift: they want to make us the principals, and to throw all the odium upon us. I cannot form the least idea of their law-process, as carried on against the prisoners, for the culprits are seldom present while the trial is proceeding. By the Judge's account, he is making a rapid progress: some of the villains are very rich. I am fairly worn out with fretting for

Thursday Night.—The Boat which was sent to Maritimo sent at a quarter past 11, the moment she returned.

Friday.—No boat sent me from Palermo; that is, none came to me.

Saturday.—Three Boats came from Palermo in a quarter of an hour—after 3 o'clock. One sent to Palermo at a quarter past 4, and second sent at a quarter past 10.

Sunday.—A Boat sent at 2 o'clock. No Boat with me.

the breach of my word given to the Inhabitants, in consequence of her Majesty's promise to me. The distress for bread in Ischia is so great, that it would move even a Frenchman to pity. Cannot a subscription be opened? I beg to put my name down for twenty ducats; I cannot afford more, or I would give it. I feed all I can from a large private stock I had, but that will not last long. No fault shall attach to us. Palermo is full of grain, as is the neighbourhood: the French, I fear, have more interest there than the King. I have put the palace in this Island into a good state of defence, and got six guns up, with plenty of grape and canister. If the Enemy attempt it, we shall certainly break some of their shins. To strengthen the whole, I have landed fifty marines and twelve gunners, dug a ditch on the road to the gate, and levelled all the ground about, and broke part of the steps, and fixed a ladder to be drawn up at sun-set. I hope your Lordship, when you come this road, will approve of our engineering. The expense is nothing worth mentioning. Hood is at Salerno. The Enemy have ordered 100 gun-boats to be built to drive us away; before they are finished, I hope we shall be in Naples. The examples of villains and cowards which the Archduke has made, has driven away my melancholy fever. I send the General from Longono and Orbitello, for the King of Naples to follow such an example. He has desired to speak to me, but I have declined having anything to do with him until he clears up his dastardly conduct to his King.

"May 11th, 1799.—My Lord: The moment I received your Lordship's letter I wrote to Captain Oswald, on service, a copy of which I have the honour to enclose with his answer. Much *matter* will come out to prove he would not *land*. When the Court-Martial is ordered, which, by General Acton's letter, we may expect immediately—as he is in the service of another Sovereign, I submit to your Lordship if we had not better leave them to themselves. Oswald and the Russian will give evidence to his refusing to land. If this Colonel, who at present commands here, is President, he will be s—t. If that should be the case, shall I confirm the sentence? My hand will not shake signing my name. Without some examples, nothing can go well. I beg your Lordship's answer. I have the honour to be, &c. T. TROUBRIDGE."—*Autograph*, in the Nelson Papers.

"11th of May, 1799.—It is with deep concern I inform your Lordship, that a spirit of sedition has begun to show itself amongst the Swiss. I have great reason to think it arose from the price of meat being much higher here than at Palermo, and the King's not allowing more pay a day. . . . . Your Lordship will see, by the sentence of death which was passed, that we do not mean to suffer the smallest relaxation of discipline; but in consequence of their good conduct before, and nothing more than murmurs being proved, I took upon myself to remit the sentence of death, and send them to Palermo as subjects for the galleys. The men were all drawn up in a square formed by the Troops and Marines, with their eyes bound, and all the

### TO CAPTAIN FOOTE.

[From " Captain Foote's Vindication," p. 115.]

Palermo, May 19th, 1799.

My dear Sir,

As the command of the Ships in the Bay of Naples will devolve upon you, I need not pretend to point out what your local situation enables you so much better to judge of than myself.[5] You will address your letters to me. Sir William

ceremony was gone through, except firing, when I directed the pardon to be read : one of them was almost gone, before it was finished. I trust it will have a good effect. I have communicated your Lordship's handsome compliment to the Captains of the Squadron, which they most sensibly feel, and are only sorry that the nature of the service they are employed on, will not admit of their distinguishing themselves more particularly. For my own part, I feel so much indebted to your Lordship for your constant attention to me, that I am satisfied I can never do enough : I wish my powers, or ability, would permit my acting more vigorously against the horrid, plundering, and treacherous Enemy. His Majesty will, I hope, the moment he regains Naples, make some great examples of his villanous nobles. Pignatelli has loaded my man with irons for carrying the letter sent by her Majesty for him, through Lady Hamilton : I trust, before long, I shall have a pull at his nose for it. I have two or three to settle with, if we get in. I hope the King will not employ Micheroux : he will only disgrace any corps he may be intrusted with. I am glad that his Majesty has promoted the Swiss Lieutenant, who was wounded, poor fellow, at the head of his men.

" 12th of May. Cockburn has just joined, and brings such famous news, that I am half mad with joy. The scoundrels will and must be annihilated.

" 14th of May. You will see, my Lord, by the enclosed translation of Prince Trabia's letter, that his Majesty has ordered a Court-Martial to try Marshal Yauch ; but as there are only four Officers here of the rank qualified to sit, according to the Neapolitan laws, I think he cannot legally be tried, until his Majesty sends over three more Officers. I should have been happy to have sat on it, and to have directed some of our Captains to have accompanied me : but as we are not in his Sicilian Majesty's service, it would have caused some noise at home, and certainly would not have been legal : I submit to your Lordship's better judgment. Officers can be sent here in a few days. In the meantime, I have directed the General to be put under arrest, and the depositions to be taken, that the trial may be short when it begins. This mode is perfectly regular in their service. All that is to be done, when a witness is to be called after this, is to ask, whether the written paper read be his evidence ; and a few other questions may arise. I trust your Lordship will explain to his Majesty, that we have every inclination to comply with his orders : in this instance, I think it is impossible."—*Clarke and M'Arthur.*

⁵ Captain Foote wrote to Lord Nelson from off Procida, on the 28th May, 1799 :— " Caraccioli threatens a second attack, with a considerable addition of force. I have put two of the Seahorse's 32-pound carronades into the Bombard, brought off from Castel-a-Mare, and we are, in every respect, prepared to receive the Enemy. . . . . That your Lordship may know that I have done my utmost to recover the brave

Hamilton will open them, and do everything which he can to meliorate the condition of the poor Islanders, for I know that your letters must be of complaint. I know nothing more of the French. Not a Boat from either Minorca, or the Earl. I hope to get ten Sail of the Line together, and shall keep off Maritimo, to either receive reinforcements, if they are bound upwards, or to fly to Minorca, if that is their destination.

I wish very much to have had you with me, but that is impossible at present. Believe me, dear Sir, with real regard, your affectionate servant,

NELSON.

---

TO LADY HAMILTON.

[From " Letters of Lord Nelson to Lady Hamilton," p. 9.]

Vanguard, May 19th, 1799, Eight o'Clock.　Calm.

My dear Lady Hamilton,

Lieutenant Swiney coming on board, enables me to send some blank passports for Vessels going to Procida with corn, &c., and also one for the Courier boat. To tell you how dreary and uncomfortable the Vanguard appears, is only telling you what it is to go from the pleasantest society to a solitary cell; or, from the dearest friends to no friends. I am now perfectly the *great man*—not a creature near me. From my heart, I wish myself the little man again! You, and good Sir William, have spoiled me for any place but with you. I love Mrs. Cadogan.[6] You cannot conceive what I feel, when I call you all to my remembrance. Even to Mira, do not forget your faithful and affectionate

NELSON.

Marines of the Zealous, I enclose the letters which I have written to the French Commanding Officer about them, with his answers; and I have resolved in consequence of his breach of faith, and infamous expressions, neither to send or receive a Flag of Truce from the French."—*Autograph*, in the Nelson Papers.

[6] Lady Hamilton's mother.

### TO LADY HAMILTON.

[From " Letters of Lord Nelson to Lady Hamilton," p. 11.]

My dear Lady Hamilton,                    May 20th, 1799.

Many thanks to you and Sir William for your kind notes. You will believe I did not sleep much, with all my letters to read, &c. My letters from Lord St. Vincent are May 6th. He says: ' We saw the Brest Squadron pass us yesterday, under an easy sail. I am making every effort to get information to Lord Keith; who I have ordered here, to complete their water and provisions. I conjecture, the French Squadron is bound for Malta and Alexandria, and the Spanish Fleet for the attack of Minorca.' I must leave you to judge whether the Earl will come to us. I think he will: but, *entre nous*, Mr. Duckworth[7] means to leave me to my fate. I send you (*under all circumstances*) his letter. Never mind; if I can get my eleven Sail together, they shall not hurt me.

God bless you, Sir William, and all our joint friends in your house; Noble, Gibbs, &c., and believe me ever, for ever, your affectionate friend,

NELSON.

---

### ORDER OF BATTLE AND SAILING.

[Order-Book.]

| No. | Ships. | Captains. | Guns. | Men. | |
|-----|--------|-----------|-------|------|---|
| 1 | Culloden | T. Troubridge | 74 | 590 | |
| 2 | Zealous | S. Hood | 74 | 590 | |
| 3 | | | | | { Rear-Admiral Lord Nelson. |
| 4 | Alexander | A. J. Ball | 74 | 590 | |
| 5 | Vanguard | T. M. Hardy | 74 | 595 | |
| 6 | Swiftsure | B. Hallowell | 74 | 590 | |
| 7 | Affonço | Comm^rc. Campbell | 70 | 625 | |
| 8 | Principe Real | { Comm^r. Conde de Puységur } | 92 | 788 | { Rear-Admiral Marquis de Niza. |
| 9 | St. Sebastian | Comm^r. Mitchell | 64 | 600 | |
| 10 | Goliath | T. Foley | 74 | 590 | |
| 11 | Lion | M. Dixon | 64 | 500 | |
| 12 | Audacious | D. Gould | 74 | 590 | |
| 13 | Minotaur | T. Louis | 74 | 640 | |
| 14 | | | | | |
| 15 | | | | | |
| 16 | | | | | |
| 17 | | | | | |

*Vanguard 2 Points: Order of Sailing.*

*Haarlem.*

*Starboard, or Weather Division.*

*Larboard or Lee Division.*

*All Frigates to repeat.*

Given on board the Vanguard, at Sea, 20th May, 1799.

NELSON.

---

[7] He had requested Rear-Admiral Duckworth, to send some Ships to increase his Squadron. Vide p. 355.

DIRECTIONS FOR CAPTAIN COCKBURN, AND ALL HIS MAJESTY'S
SHIPS WHO MAY SPEAK HIM, TO GET THE COPY LANDED AT
MARITIMO.

[Letter-Book.]

Vanguard, foul Wind, May 21st, 1799.

Circular.

I am proceeding with the Ships under my command,
named in the margin,[8] with all possible expedition off Maritimo, where I hope to join Captain Ball, with the Alexander,
Audacious, and Goliath. The Alfonso has been at Tripoli,
but I have been expecting her this week past with this force.
I am under no apprehension for the safety of his Majesty's
Squadron; on the contrary, from the very high state of discipline of the Ships, I am confident, should the Enemy force
us to battle, that we shall cut a very respectable figure; and
if Admiral Duckworth joins, not one moment shall be lost in
my attacking the Enemy.

N.B. All Ships of the Line to join me as expeditiously as
possible; smaller Vessels to stand to the southward, westward,
and northward, to endeavour to get information of the French
Fleet. A copy of this to be left at Maritimo; Captain Cockburn to remain in that neighbourhood, and to use his judgment
in getting information, sending copies on shore to the Governor of Maritimo. The Thalia is cruising off Lampedosa.

NELSON.

---

TO LADY HAMILTON.

[From " Letters of Lord Nelson to Lady Hamilton," p. 7.]

[About May 21st, 1799.][9]

My dear Lady Hamilton,

Accept my sincere thanks for your kind letter. Nobody
writes so well: therefore, pray, say not you write ill; for, if
you do, I will say—what your goodness sometimes told me—
" You l—e !" I can read, and perfectly understand, every
word you write. We drank your and Sir William's health.

---

[8] Vanguard, Culloden, Minotaur, Zealous, Swiftsure, Principe Real, St. Sebastian, Haerlem, Minerve, Pallas, Incendiary, L'Entreprenant Cutter.

[9] The date assigned to this letter is the *twelfth* of May, but Captain Troubridge
did not join Lord Nelson until the 18th of May.

Troubridge, Louis, Hallowell, and the new Portuguese Captain, dined here. I shall soon be at Palermo ; for this business must very soon be settled. No one, believe me, is more sensible of your regard, than your obliged and grateful,

NELSON.

I am pleased with little Mary; kiss her for me. I thank all the house for their regard. God bless you all! I shall send on shore, if fine, to-morrow; for the Feluccas are going to leave us, and I am sea-sick. I have got the piece of wood for the tea-chest; it shall soon be sent. Pray, present my humble duty and gratitude to the Queen, for all her marks of regard; and assure her, it is not thrown away on an ungrateful soil.

---

TO ADMIRAL THE EARL OF ST. VINCENT, K.B.

[From a Copy, in the Admiralty. It was on the day this letter was written, that Lord Nelson received his coffin from Captain Hallowell, of the Swiftsure, which Ship formed one of his Squadron.]

Vanguard, off Maritimo, 23rd May, 1799.

My dear Lord,

L'Espoir arrived at Palermo, with information of the French Fleet being seen off Oporto, at 6 P.M., May 12th, and sailed at midnight for Procida and Minorca, with orders for Troubridge's Squadron (except one Ship of the Line and the Frigates, &c.) to call off Palermo, it being my intention to send them directly off Port Mahon, to be ready to follow your orders for their further proceedings: the Principe Real was also ordered to the same place. At the same time L'Espoir sailed for Procida, the Penelope Cutter sailed for Malta, with orders for Captain Ball to detach the Goliath and Audacious off Port Mahon, and with a letter to the Russian Admiral, who I then thought was there, to request he would detach a part of his Squadron off Mahon. Expresses were also sent to different parts of the Island, in case any Russian or Turkish Ships were arrived.

At 9 o'clock, on the evening of the 13th, the Lieutenant of the Peterel arrived by land, the Sloop not being able to get up, owing to strong east winds. Captain Austen[1] very properly sent the Lieutenant on shore; on the 14th, at noon, the Sloop came in sight; water was sent to her, and I went alongside, and gave my orders to Captain Austen to proceed to Malta, and directed Captain Ball to quit Malta, and join me off Maritimo, and there I was in hopes Rear-Admiral Duckworth would have joined me, when my force would have been sufficient to have fought the French Fleet; I sent off for the remaining Ship of the Line from Naples Bay, and for the Lion from Leghorn; this force united, I reckoned to be fifteen or sixteen Ships of the Line, the greater part of them the best ordered Ships that ever went to sea.

On the 17th, the Culloden, Minotaur, Swiftsure, and St. Sebastian, arrived off Palermo, but it blew so hard from the E.S.E. that the Ships were obliged to strike yards and topmasts : this gale continued to the 20th, when I put to sea ; the Haerlem, in the meantime, having taken in eight 24-pounders, with shot, &c., lent us by His Sicilian Majesty ; the Zealous joined at daylight of the 21st, as did the Swallow Portuguese Corvette, with your Lordship's letter of May 6th, and with a letter from Rear Admiral Duckworth, saying he was waiting your Lordship's arrival. 23rd. This morning I arrived off Maritimo, and was sorry to find neither Captain Ball's Squadron or any account from him; I can only have two queries about him—either that he has gone round to Messina, imagining that the French Fleet were close to him, or he is taken. Thus situated, I have only to remain on the north side of Maritimo, to keep covering Palermo, which shall be protected to the last, and to wait intelligence or orders for regulating my further proceedings.

Your Lordship may depend that the Squadron under my command shall never fall into the hands of the Enemy; and before we are destroyed, I have little doubt but the Enemy will have their wings so completely clipped that they may be easily overtaken. I am, ever, with the greatest respect,

     Your Lordship's faithful and obedient servant,

                            NELSON.

---

[1] Now Vice-Admiral Sir Francis William Austen, K.C.B.

Vanguard
Culloden
Minotaur
Zealous
Swiftsure
Principe Real ⎫ Off Maritimo.
St. Sebastian
Haerlem
La Minerve
Incendiary F. S.
L'Entreprenant Cutter ⎭

No doubt by this time the Austrians are at Leghorn; and if this event had not happened, we should have been in Naples.

---

## TO CAPTAIN DIXON, H. M. SHIP LION.

[Letter-Book.]

Vanguard, at Sea, 25th May, 1799.

Sir,

I desire that you (if at Palermo) will go directly to Procida, and protect those Islands till further orders; or, if this finds you at Procida, to remain there till further orders. I am, &c.
NELSON.

---

## TO ADMIRAL THE EARL OF ST. VINCENT, K.B.

[Letter-Book.]

Vanguard, off Trapano, 28th May, 1799.

My dear Lord,

I am this moment favoured with your letters of 21st and 22nd. Your Lordship is acquainted with my intentions of raising the blockade of Malta and of uniting my whole force off Maritimo. I have not yet heard from Captain Ball, what he has done, in consequence of my orders. He was apprised, by the Cameleon, of the French Fleet being in the Straits, and she passed on for St. Jean d'Acre on the 17th—therefore we are completely on our guard. Your Lordship having informed me of your intentions also, with what was, at that time, the situation of the two Fleets, French and Spaniards, and leaving me to act as I thought best from the situation of affairs, I have determined to carry the Ships named at the bottom, to the Bay of Palermo, to complete their provisions to six months, and as much wine as they stow, and to hold them in momentary readiness to act as you may order or the circumstances call for.  My reason for remaining in Sicily is the covering the blockade of Naples, and the certainty of preserving Sicily in case of an attack, for if we were to withdraw our Ships, it would throw such a damp on the people that I am sure there would be no resistance.  But from the favourable aspect of affairs in Italy, I am sure no attack will be made here, whilst the French know we have such a force to act against them.  If Captain Ball has not entirely given up the blockade of Malta, and the poor Islanders have not given up to the French, I intend to continue the blockade with two Ships of the Line, a Frigate, two Sloops and a Cutter; for as the danger from your happy arrival is not so great, I will run the risk of the Ships for a short time.  The Russians will, I am told, be off there in a week or fortnight.  In all this plan I am subject to your Lordship's more able judgment.  I shall send a Frigate off Cape Corse, in case the French Fleet should come to the eastward of Corsica, and if I can find a small craft, one shall be on the west side of Sardinia, but the Bay of Naples draws me dry.  With the most ardent desire to do everything your Lordship would wish me, and praying for a glorious termination of your great zeal and ability, believe me with the highest regard and affection, your obliged and faithful servant,

NELSON.

---

TO CAPTAIN BALL, H. M. SHIP, ALEXANDER.

[Letter-Book.]

Vanguard, at Sea, 28th May, 1799.

My dear Ball,

Should you have already given up the blockade of Malta, in pursuance of my order to you of the 13th instant, you will again re-commence it with the Ships named in the margin,[2] as it is of the greatest importance that as many Ships

---

[2] Alexander, Audacious or Goliath, Bonne Citoyenne, Strombolo, Benjamin.

as possible should be sent to me.  You will send either the
Audacious or Goliath, the Thalia, and Earl St. Vincent
Cutter with all speed to join me at Palermo.  And to use
your endeavours to prevent the escape of the French Ships
out of Malta, and to keep up the spirits of the Islanders to hold
out, until the Russian forces arrive, taking care that the Ships
never anchor, and to keep a particular good look-out not to
be surprised by the Enemy.

The moment the Russian Admiral arrives, you will detach
the Line of Battle Ship and the Bonne Citoyenne to me at
Palermo, staying yourself to co-operate with him in the
blockade, and to give him that information which you are so
capable of doing.  I am, my dear Ball, your most obedient
Servant,

NELSON.

---

TO ADMIRAL THE EARL OF ST. VINCENT, K.B.

[From Clarke and M'Arthur, vol. ii. p. 172.]

Palermo, 30th May, 1799.

The Vanguard anchored here yesterday; but it has been so
calm, that, except the Emerald, none have yet got in.  After
two days, I hope they will all be as ready for service as our
means allow of.  I have our dear Troubridge for my assistant;
in everything we are brothers.  Hood and Hallowell are as
active and good as ever : not that I mean to say any are
otherwise; but you know these are men of resources.  Hardy
was bred in the old school, and I can assure you, that I never
have been better satisfied with the real good discipline of a Ship
than the Vanguard's.  I hope from my heart that you will
meet the Dons alone : if the two Fleets join, I am ready, and
with some of my Ships in as high order as ever went to sea.
The Russian Ships are blocking up Ancona; but again the
Généreux has escaped them.  As to politics, they are my
abomination : the Ministers of Kings and Princes are as great
scoundrels as ever lived.  The brother of the Emperor is just
going to marry the great something of Russia; and it is more
than expected that a Kingdom is to be found for him in Italy,
and that the King of Naples will be sacrificed.  I am, &c.,

NELSON.

TO PERKIN MAGRA, ESQ., HIS MAJESTY'S AGENT AND CONSUL-
GENERAL AT TUNIS.

[Letter-Book.]

Vanguard, Palermo, 31st May, 1799.

Dear Sir,

I only wish for these circumstances, that I was Commander-
in-Chief for one day in the Mediterranean; first, that I might
more forcibly represent the very high opinion I have of your
proper and manly conduct with his Highness the Bey of
Tunis; and secondly, that I might settle our business with
the Bey in one conference; for as my conduct to His Highness
has been marked by kindness and a sincere regard to his real
interests, I have a fair right to expect the same.

My granting passports has not been to cover Merchants or
Vessels of War from any attack of the Bey's cruizers; all
my passports have been a solemn assurance, that the Vessel
carrying it was, *bonâ fide*, carrying provisions and dispatches,
for the support of those who were fighting the enemies of
*His Highness*, as well as those of our Most Gracious Sovereign
and His Sicilian Majesty. Have any of His Highness's
Vessels been taken either by Portuguese, or His Sicilian
Majesty's Vessels of War, in the act of carrying provisions to
the support of those fighting the common enemy? His
Highness's Vessels of War have been taken on the Coast of
His Sicilian Majesty, and *not* on the Coast of the common
enemy. All my conduct is *firm, open,* and *generous.* Has a
single Cruizer of His Highness' Enemies, under my orders,
been employed on the Coast of Africa? *Not one,* although I
have long known that was the track pursued by the French
both to Malta and Egypt.

On the contrary, I have employed them as much with the
English as possible, and not a Vessel of His Highness's has
been taken, but what, from the common war in which Her
Most Faithful Majesty, His Sicilian Majesty, Great Britain,
and the Sublime Porte, ought to have been in very different
places to where they were found. Tell His Highness that
I have checked, as much as possible, the Ships under my
orders, from annoying him. It was not in my power to prevent captures in their passages, when separated from the
English; it was not more in my power to stop His Highness's

Enemies from taking His Ships, than it would be allowed by His Highness that I should stop His Ships from taking his enemies. I will be instrumental in making a fair and honourable truce or peace with both His Highness and Portugal. I can, and without the smallest breach of good faith, on the part of Great Britain, take off this check, which I have studiously given to please His Highness, and mark the goodness of His Majesty; and then it will soon be seen what Great Britain has done for him.

I *will* have my passports respected; given only to serve the cause in which His Highness ought to be as much interested as I am. I would, with as much pleasure, grant passports to his Vessels when actually carrying provisions to brave men, fighting against the infamous infidel French. This you will state clearly and forcibly to the Bey, that, as I will do no wrong, I will suffer none: this is the firm determination of a British Admiral; this is the determination of, my dear Sir, your faithful humble servant,

NELSON.

No presents of any kind have been sent from this Squadron to the Bashaw of Tripoli—His Highness has been advised by me to think right, and to hate the French.

---

TO CAPTAIN BALL, H. M. SHIP ALEXANDER, OFF MALTA.

[Autograph, in the possession of Sir William Keith Ball, Bart.]

My dear Ball,                              June 1st, 1799.

I will give you a Frigate as soon as I can get one liberated from other very important services, which the present moment calls for. I will not lose sight of the Maltese, and I sincerely pray that you may soon be able to see the inside of La Valetta and the Ships. No one man in this world deserves success so much as yourself, and believe me no one is more truly sensible of your great merits than your affectionate friend,                              NELSON.[3]

---

[3] To this letter two additions were made: the following was by Lady Hamilton; "If you could but have come for five minutes, my dear Sir, how happy I should have been to see you. How I pitied you when you were called from Malta, knowing your energy and attachment to these unfortunate people; but I hope all will

## TO CAPTAIN FOOTE, H. M. SHIP SEAHORSE.

[From Captain Foote's " Vindication," p. 121.]

Palermo, June 1st, 1799.

Dear Sir,

I have scolded about the provisions, and I hope you will have plenty in future. I thank you for your letters, which I received on my return here. The French fleet were seen in the Gulf of Lyons, steering for Toulon—the Spanish fleet off Cape de Gatte—Lord St. Vincent off Barcelona. The man has only just called to say he is going off this moment. I am ever, dear Sir, your faithful servant,

NELSON.

---

## TO HIS HIGHNESS THE BEY OF TUNIS.

[Letter-Book.]

Palermo, June 2nd, 1799.

Sir,

As I have wrote so fully to Mr. Magra on the subject of his conference with your Highness, I have only to assure you, that I have granted no passports to any Vessels which your Highness, and every good man, will not highly approve of. And those who would or *dare* counsel your Highness to prevent food from being given to those who are fighting in the cause of God against vile Infidels, the French, are no better than Frenchmen. I have offered before to your Highness my mediation for a truce or peace with his Sicilian Majesty. As the Court sends over a proper person to settle this business, it would be improper in me to say more on the subject.

yet go well, and that you will have the pleasure of soon driving the monsters out. I have not been well: can any body, with a little sensibility, be well in these moments of anxiety? But at all times, and in all circumstances, I shall ever be, my dear Sir, your attached, and obliged, and grateful—EMMA HAMILTON." The other addition was by Sir William Hamilton:—"June 1st, 1799. My dear Sir, I received your letter from off Marsala this day at noon, from a handsome man, with a monstrous deal of hair under his chin and on his throat, and communicated it directly to Lord Nelson. I rejoice in your going back to Malta, for my heart already bled for the consequences that might arise from your being obliged to quit that station. God bless, and give you the success your assiduity so well deserves. General Acton has assured me that Cordoni shall have the rank he wishes for, as it is Captain Ball that intercedes for him."

His Excellency the Marquis de Niza, the Admiral and
Commander-in-Chief of the Portuguese Squadron under my
orders, has requested me to tell your Highness that, if you
wish it, he is ready to send a Ship, and negotiate a truce, or
peace, between her Most Faithful Majesty and your Highness.

Most sincerely praying to God for your Highness's health
and happiness, I am, with great respect, your most faithful
and obedient servant,

NELSON.

---

TO ALL TO WHOM THESE PRESENTS MAY COME, GREETING.

[Order-Book.]

Vanguard, Palermo, 3rd June, 1799.

Whereas I have employed the English Brig Susannah,
whereof William Rand is Master, as a Cartel to carry prisoners
of war from the British Squadron under my command, and
the Port of Palermo in Sicily, to the Port of Genoa, to land
them there, and to proceed from thence to the Port of Leghorn for English prisoners of war, and to return to Palermo,
it is my request that the said Brig be considered and respected
as a Cartel carrying prisoners of war, according to the laws
of Nations, and that she may be permitted to proceed on her
intended voyage as a Cartel without interruption.

NELSON.

---

TO MR. ANDREW TULLOCH, HEREBY APPOINTED TO CONDUCT
PRISONERS OF WAR, IN THE SUSANNAH CARTEL, TO GENOA.

[Order-Book.]

Vanguard, Palermo, 3rd June, 1799.

You are hereby required and directed to receive on board
the Susannah Transport, the persons named in the list sent
herewith, who are not to be considered as prisoners of war
—they having been sent from Tripoli, in Barbary, for political
reasons—; and you are also to receive on board the Susannah
all such prisoners of war as may be sent to you from the
Ships of the Squadron under my command, victualling them
at two-thirds allowance, as is usual, and proceed with them

to the Port of Genoa, and land them there, making application to the French Commissary or Consul at that place for receipts for the number of prisoners you land, and for all English prisoners of war that may be at Genoa, which you are to receive on board, and give proper receipts for them. And you will also make application to the French Consul at Genoa for letters to the French Consul at Leghorn, to request the delivery of all English prisoners of war that may be at that place, where you will proceed with the Susannah, and make the necessary application, and give receipts to the French Consul at Leghorn for the number you may receive from him, and from thence you will return with all expedition, and join me at this place.

NELSON.

---

### TO J. SPENCER SMITH, ESQ. CONSTANTINOPLE.

[From a copy, in the Nelson Papers.]

**Private.**

Palermo, 5th June, 1799.

**Dear Sir,**

I feel very sensibly your goodness about the shawls, and with *many, many* grateful thanks, have directed my agent in London to pay the amount to the house of Herries and Co.

I can assure you that I have [been], and am fully sensible of the benefit derived to our Country from your indefatigable and able management of our affairs with the Porte; and no one Officer in the service more fully appreciates the value of your brother, as a Sea-officer, on every occasion, which have been very numerous. I do not believe any Officer in Europe stands higher in his profession. Having said this, it may readily be conceived that I could not like to have any *Junior* in some measure placed, if not over my head, at least as taking from my consequence. I did not think that it was necessary for any Sea-officer to be joined in signing a treaty which you had brought to such a happy issue; but if it was, I shall ever think that Sea-officer should have been *Nelson*. We have all here been on the alert, as the Combined fleets are in the Mediterranean. Briefly—on April the 26th, the French fleet sailed from Brest—nineteen of the Line, Frigates, &c.; and from

Corunna and Ferrol five Spanish ships joined. They passed
the Gut on May 5th. On the 12th they were seen past
Minorca, with their heads pointed for Toulon. Lord St
Vincent left Gibraltar on the 8th : his force, twenty Sail of
the Line. On the 15th, I have letters from the last off
Minorca, to say he was going to endeavour to prevent the
junction. This is the whole I know. I had for two days
called the Ships from off Malta, but they are returned to it
again. Naples is also completely cut off from all communication by sea. I have been for many months expecting the
3000 Russian troops for Malta, where I know the French
General intended to try to make off with the Ships, and for
[the] garrison to capitulate. Could I know how to be useful
to you here, I should truly be happy in executing your commands. The speedy departure of the Turkish messenger, who
is come from Tripoli, prevents my getting Captain Hood's
answer to your question [for] Sir Sidney Smith. I have just
seen Captain Hood, and he desires me to say, that your
brother being in Egypt when your letter came, it was given to
him to answer. With every sentiment of respect, believe me
your obliged humble servant,

                                                NELSON.

The Neapolitan corvette does not return to you : therefore
any other conveyance will I doubt not be safe for the other
two shawls—for getting me which, I again sincerely thank you.

---

TO ADMIRAL THE EARL OF ST. VINCENT, K.B.

[Letter-Book.]

                                      Palermo, June 5th, 1799.

My dear Lord,

We are so on the tip-toe of expectation, that, in truth, we
can think nor talk of anything but you, and I am almost
unable, from that account, to detail my operations. Alexander, Goliath, Bonne Citoyenne, Benjamin, and El Corso,
are sent again off Malta. Thalia saw the French Ships ready
for sea on the 27th. Captain Ball was round Maritimo on
the 1st June ; therefore, I hope he will get in time to stop
them, either inside or out of the harbour. As to trusting
to Russians, I never will believe any more. Thalia goes

between Cape Corse and Del Melle to look out; therefore, if your Lordship wants her, you know where to find her. I hope her Captain will improve,[4] and do everything that we wish him. You will hear, if ready by to-morrow, (but I doubt it,) of all my history with Tripoli. The Consul is exactly as you describe him;[5] but as I am not apt to be led by such gentry, he could do me little harm, and when put upon my guard, by your just description of him, I troubled not my head about him. However, we are better friends with the Bashaw than ever. Commodore Campbell, who I selected for this service, in the first place, because he was fit for the business; and, secondly, to mark, that although I could *censure* when wrong,[6] yet, that I bore no resentment for the past, having done on that occasion what I thought right;—the Commodore has on this occasion conducted himself with proper spirit and judgment, and he has by it made a very advantageous peace for Portugal. The Bey of Tunis has stopped, and pretends to justify it, some Vessels with my passports, carrying provisions for me, fighting in the same cause with himself. The Earl St. Vincent Cutter sailed this morning, with my letter to the Consul and the Bey. I shall send you copies of them, and I hope to bring the gentleman to reason. My time has been so much occupied, that I have not been able to pay that attention to the Barbary States I could have wished: but I know these folks must be talked to with honesty and firmness. At present we seem at a stand for news, as if waiting the event of what is to happen with you. May every success attend you; may health and long life be granted you, and may you ever be the friend of your affectionate,

NELSON.

A number of Officers are invalided: they are in a dreadful state. The Surgeon[7] of the Goliath, who was ill on shore, died last night.

---

[4] The conduct of Captain Nisbet, which had been made the subject of a strong but friendly representation by Lord St. Vincent, occasioned great uneasiness to Nelson.

[5] Vide p. 231, ante.                    [6] Vide p. 302, ante.

[7] Dr. Wood.

## TO CAPTAIN FOOTE, H.M. SHIP SEAHORSE.

[From Captain Foote's "Vindication," p. 126.]

Palermo, June 6th, 1799.

My dear Sir,

Your letters of June 1st, 31st May, and those of the dates prior, I have received, and thank you for them. I send all your letters to General Acton; it is perfectly right they should know all the truth. The corn destined first for Lisbon, was, on the return of the Convoy, purchased by the King, from his private purse. I agree with you that all has not been right in the management of sending corn for the Islands. Your news of the hanging of thirteen Jacobins gave us great pleasure; and the three Priests, I hope, return in the Aurora, to dangle on the tree best adapted to their weight of sins.[8] The news from all parts of the Continent is excellent. Turin was taken on the 7th May, and the King's government re-established. We know nothing of the Fleet, and are, as you will believe, all anxiety. Could we move, I fancy we should all pay you a visit, and it is I hope not far distant that we shall. With every kind wish from all of this house, believe me, your obliged, humble servant,

NELSON.

---

## TO CAPTAIN FOOTE, H.M. SHIP SEAHORSE.

[Letter-Book.]

Vanguard, Palermo, 7th June, 1799.

Dear Sir,

On the receipt hereof, you will immediately order Lieutenant Millbank of the Royal Artillery, with all the Artillerymen, out of the Bulldog, on board the Seahorse, and to hold themselves in constant readiness to go on the service they are wanted for. Yours most truly,

NELSON.

[8] Captain Foote's correspondence with Lord Nelson, while he was Senior Officer off Naples, is printed in the Appendix to the "Vindication of his Conduct." On the 28th of May, he informed Nelson that " Caraccioli threatens a second attack with a considerable addition of force;" and in his letter of the 2nd of June, he said, "Thirteen Jacobins were hanged at Procida yesterday afternoon, and the bearer of this has charge of three condemned Priests, who are to be degraded at Palermo, and then sent back to be executed."

## TO CAPTAIN FOOTE, H.M. SHIP SEAHORSE.

[From Captain Foote's "Vindication," p. 126.]

Palermo, June 8th, 1799.

Dear Sir,

I agree in all the sentiments you express in your letters relative to the affairs of Naples; a few regular troops would do the business in better order, but not more effectually, than the Royalists. I do not believe that the French have gained any such victory as they pretend; the battle upon the Rhine carries *lie* upon the face of it. It is not possible they could tell the number of the killed, much less the number of the wounded. As to a few thousands being killed, it is naturally to be expected, victories cannot be obtained without blood; but as the Russians were obstinate, I dare say the French lost some few, although they do not tell us of *one* this time.

The Governor of Ischia,[9] General Acton tells me, shall be superseded; his conduct is infamous. I have not a Frigate or Sloop; all are gone from hence to the Earl.[1] If you can spare the Mutine, which I hope you can, as the Neapolitan frigates have joined, pray send her directly. Ever your obliged

NELSON.

---

## TO ADMIRAL THE EARL OF ST. VINCENT, K.B.

[From Tucker's Memoirs of Earl St. Vincent, vol. i. p. 481.—Lord Nelson shifted his Flag from the Vanguard to the Foudroyant, on the 8th of June, and removed into that Ship, from the Vanguard, Captain Hardy, five Lieutenants, the Surgeon, Chaplain, and many Mates and Midshipmen.]

Palermo, 10th June, 1799.

My dear Lord,

We have a report that you are going home.[2] This distresses us most exceedingly, and myself in particular; so much so, that I have serious thoughts of returning, if that event should

---

[9] Captain Foote afterwards informed Lord Nelson that the Governor of Ischia had in a great measure justified his conduct.—*Vindication*, p. 131.

[1] On the 6th of June, Lord Nelson's Squadron was strengthened by the arrival at Palermo of the Foudroyant, of 80 guns, intended for his Flag ship; and the Leviathan, bearing the Flag of Rear-Admiral Duckworth, Majestic, and Northumberland, from the Earl of St. Vincent's fleet.

[2] In consequence of the ill state of his health, Lord St. Vincent resigned the Mediterranean command to Vice-Admiral Lord Keith, on the 16th of June, and

take place. But for the sake of our Country, do not quit us at this serious moment. I wish not to detract from the merit of whoever may be your successor; but it must take a length of time, which I hope the war will not give, to be in any manner a St. Vincent. We look up to you, as we have always found you, as to our Father, under whose fostering care we have been led to fame. If, my dear Lord, I have any weight in your friendship, let me entreat you to rouse the sleeping lion. Give not up a particle of your authority to any one; be again our St. Vincent, and we shall be happy. Your affectionate

NELSON.

---

### TO CAPTAIN FOOTE, H.M. SHIP SEAHORSE.

[From Captain Foote's "Vindication," p. 129.]

June 12th, 1799.

Most Secret,

Dear Sir,

The bearer, Prossidio Amante, is charged on a business of great importance, and the Queen desires me to recommend him to your notice. Keep your Vessels ready to join me at a moment's notice. Yours truly,

NELSON.

sailed from Mahon for England on the 23rd of that month. On the 11th of June he wrote to Nelson:—

"My dear Lord,—It is a most fortunate circumstance that you withheld the orders for the return of the Portuguese Squadron to Lisbon, as you will perceive by the enclosed, that the Prince of Brazil has directed the Marquis of Niza to continue to act with us until the fate of the Brest Fleet is decided, which I hope soon to hear of, much lamenting that the rapid decline of my health has totally deprived me of the possibility of sharing in the glorious event, for I am literally incapable of any service. I have transferred the command to Lord Keith, not deeming it for the public good, or just to his Lordship, to hold a trust which I cannot exercise in person. I shall, however, continue here until the arrival of the detachment from Lord Bridport. Have the goodness to make my apologies to Sir William and Lady Hamilton, for not answering their very kind letters, not being able to do more than assure them, and your Lordship, of my sincere regard and affection. Yours most truly,—ST. VINCENT." *Tucker's Memoirs,* vol. i. p. 482.

### TO ADMIRAL THE EARL OF ST. VINCENT, K.B.

[From Tucker's " Memoirs of Earl St. Vincent," vol. i. p. 481.]

June 12th, 1799.　Nine o'clock at night.

My dear Lord, our St. Vincent!

What have we suffered in hearing of your illness, and of your return to Mahon! Let me entreat you to come to us with a force fit to fight. We will search the French out, and if either in Leghorn, Espezia, or Naples, we will have at them. We shall have so much pleasure in fighting under the eye of our ever great and good Earl. If you are sick, I will fag for you; and our dear Lady Hamilton will nurse you with the most affectionate attention. Good Sir William will make you laugh with his wit and inexhaustible pleasantry. We all love you. Come, then, to your sincere friends. Let us get you well; it will be such a happiness to us all, amongst the foremost to your attached, faithful, and affectionate

NELSON.

---

### TO VICE-ADMIRAL LORD KEITH, K.B.

[On the 10th of June, the King of Naples wrote to Lord Nelson, describing the state of his Neapolitan dominions, and entreating him to proceed to Naples with the Squadron. His Majesty said he had placed the Hereditary Prince at the head of his Generals; that his Royal Highness would act under his advice; and that he relied fully and entirely on Nelson's zeal for his service, and attachment to his person and family, of which he had afforded him so many proofs. This measure was strongly urged by Lady Hamilton, in a letter written after an interview with the Queen, on the 12th;[2] and Lord Nelson determined on complying with their Majesties' wishes. On the 13th, the Hereditary Prince came on board, and the Foudroyant, with the Squadron, weighed, and made sail for Naples. The next day, however, Lord Nelson received intelligence from Lord Keith respecting the French fleet, which caused him to return to Palermo, land the Prince, troops, &c., and proceed on the 16th with the Squadron, consisting of sixteen Sail of the Line, a Fire-ship, a Brig, and a Cutter, off Maritimo.]

My Lord,　　　　　　　　Foudroyant, at Sea, 16th June, 1799.

I was honoured with your letter of June 6th, by the Belle-rophon and Powerful,[3] on the 13th—being then on my way to

---

[2] See these Letters in the APPENDIX.

[3] " My Lord,　　　　　　" Barfleur, off Monaco, 6th June, 1799.

" Soon after I dispatched the Telegraph last night, the wind came fresh from the East, which is of course a fair wind for the Enemy, if bound towards you, and a foul wind for me to follow them, which is unfortunate; for if my information was just, I had no doubt of overtaking them before they had left the Coast of Italy; or

Naples with troops, &c., in order to finish all matters in that Kingdom, and again place his Majesty on his throne. But considering the force of the French fleet on the Coast of Italy, twenty-two Sail of the Line, four of which are First-rates, and that probably the Ships left at Toulon would have joined them by the time I was reading the letters, (the force with me being only sixteen Sail of the Line, not one of which was of three decks, three being Portugese, and one of the English a sixty-four, very short of men,) I had no choice left, but to return to Palermo, and land the troops, ammunition, &c.; which having done, I am now at sea proceeding off Maritimo, where I hope to be joined by the Alexander and Goliath, who I have, ten days [since] ordered their Captains to raise the blockade of Malta, and come to me. My force will then be eighteen Sail of the Line, with the notations as above mentioned. I shall wait off Maritimo, anxiously expecting such a reinforcement as may enable me to go in search of the Enemy's fleet, when not one moment shall be lost in bringing them to battle; for I consider the best defence for his Sicilian Majesty's Dominions, is to place myself alongside the French. That I may be very soon enabled to have that honour, is the fervent prayer of your Lordship's most obedient servant,

NELSON.

---

TO ADMIRAL THE EARL OF ST. VINCENT, K.B.

[Letter-Book.]

Foudroyant, at Sea, 16th June, 1799.

My dear Lord,

I send your Lordship a copy of my letter to Lord Keith, and I have only stated my regret that his Lordship could not have sent me a force fit to face the Enemy: but, as we are, I shall not get out of their way; although, as I am, I cannot think myself justified in exposing the world (I may almost

shutting them up in some harbour, so as rendering them harmless; but the defence-less state of Minorca, without a Fleet, the great force prepared to attack it, added to my having so far exceeded my orders already, will oblige me to relinquish the pursuit, and return to the protection of that Island. But I have detached to your Lordship the two Ships [Bellerophon, Powerful] mentioned in the margin, which I hope will arrive in time, and be useful, as I am confident the French are not thirty leagues hence at this moment. My Squadron is spread over the sea, without being able to see a Vessel which might give me information. I have the honour to be, &c.,

" KEITH."

say), to be plundered by those miscreants. I trust your Lordship will not think me wrong in the painful determination I conceived myself forced to make, for agonized indeed was the mind of your Lordship's faithful and affectionate servant,

NELSON.

---

TO ADMIRAL THE EARL OF ST. VINCENT, K.B.

[Letter-Book.]

Foudroyant, at Sea, 16th June, 1799.

My Lord,

I herewith enclose, for your Lordship's information, the papers and correspondence respecting the dispute with the Bashaw of Tripoli; and in consequence of Commodore Campbell's acting up to the spirit of my orders, the Bashaw delivered up all the French that were at Tripoli—near forty in number, who were not considered by me as prisoners of war; but were sent in a Cartel carrying prisoners to Genoa, which sailed the 6th instant. I have the honour to be, &c.,

NELSON.

P.S.—I also send you a copy of Mr. Consul Magra's letter from Tunis.

---

TO CAPTAIN FOOTE, H.M. SHIP SEAHORSE.

[Letter-Book; and Captain Foote's "Vindication," p. 136, where this note occurs to it:—" N.B. This letter was not received till the 24th of June, at eight o'clock in the morning.—E. J. F."]

Foudroyant, at Sea, off Maritimo, June 18th, 1799.

Dear Sir,

I am very much obliged to you for all your interesting letters; and should the Cardinal, or Russians, be in possession of Naples, and it should be subdued for its lawful Sovereign, and you think that the Neapolitan ships, with the Bulldog and San Leon, are sufficient to guard the Islands and the Bay of Naples, you will join me without loss of time off Maritimo, with the Ship you command, the Mutine and Perseus bomb, as I have not one Frigate with me; but, if you think otherwise, I must leave it entirely to your judgment to act for the good of His Majesty's service. Send me, if possible, the Perseus bomb and Mutine brig, directing them

to join me at the above rendezvous : but not finding me there,
to send a Boat on shore to the Castle at Maritimo for information where I am to be found. I am, &c.,

NELSON.

---

TO CAPTAIN BROUGHTON,[1] HIS MAJESTY'S BOMB-VESSEL
STROMBOLO.

[Order-Book.]

Foudroyant, at Sea, 20th June, 1799.

You are hereby required and directed to receive on board
the Strombolo bomb-vessel under your command, the Portuguese Officer sent to you by the Marquis de Niza, and proceed, without loss of time, with him to Tunis, and on your
arrival, you will deliver the letter you will receive herewith to
Perkin Magra, Esq., His Majesty's Agent and Consul at that
place, waiting five days for his answers; and if the Portuguese
Officer completes his mission in that time, you will give him
and the Sicilian Ambassador a passage back to join me, but at
all events not to exceed the five days, when you will return to
this rendezvous. Not meeting me here, you will proceed to
Palermo, and inquire where I am to be found.

NELSON.

---

TO PERKIN MAGRA, ESQ., CONSUL AT TUNIS.

[Letter Book.]

Most Secret.

Foudroyant, at Sea, 20th June, 1799.

Dear Sir,

I have been favoured with your letter by the Earl St.
Vincent Cutter, and also of the 15th, sent me from
Palermo. Having ever found the conduct of these Italians,
weak and indecisive, I am not, in the least, surprised at the
conduct of a Sicilian lawyer; however, I am sure you will
make the best of him. Sir John Acton sends a letter for
him, which I suppose are his final instructions; and I hope a
good truce or peace will be concluded for His Sicilian
Majesty.

[1] Captain John Broughton; he died a Rear-Admiral of the White in October
1837.

Prince Paterno's conduct, I agree with the Bey, is infamous; but I cannot think the Sicilian Government has anything to do in it. The Bey had him, and let him go, believing his word or his bond; the fault of being without the money or the Prince's company, lay with His Highness. The Marquis de Niza sends his first Captain, Don Something Pinto, to negotiate a truce or peace for Portugal. This man detests the *English*. I earnestly beg you will contrive and keep back the business of his mission, till that of the King of Naples is settled. Try and prevent, by all possible means, the peace with Portugal; hold out to the Bey that both peaces or truces must go together. I need not say more to a gentleman of your penetration and judgment, than that I am sure our gracious Master takes the interest of His Sicilian Majesty as much to heart as his own. I have the pleasure to tell you, that His Sicilian Majesty's colours were hoisted in Naples on the 14th, and on the 15th, all the Castles were put in the hands of the Royalists; and that there is not a Frenchman in the Kingdom, but as a prisoner.

Ancona has been taken by storm, and every Jew put to the sword for their infamous conduct. In Tuscany, the French, under General Victor, have been defeated at Pistoja, and Leghorn alone remains in the hands of the French. To this place I think the French fleet is bound, and will carry off the army and plunder, and return to Toulon. I am here anxiously waiting reinforcements to enable me to go in search of them; they are four First-rates and twenty-one Sail of Two-decked Ships, twenty-five of the Line. In the whole, mine is one 80, thirteen 74, one 64, and three Portuguese, but, if I can only get two Three-deckers, I will search them out, and bring them to battle.

To say one word on our affairs: I hope Lord St. Vincent, who arrived at Mahon the day after the Tunis convoy, and the Governor will seize the Vessel so shamefully condemned by the Bey's orders; for, I most perfectly agree with you, we must never suffer an insult to pass unpunished. With every sentiment of respect, believe me, dear Sir, your most obedient servant,

NELSON.

The Ship is ordered to wait five days.

## TO REAR-ADMIRAL DUCKWORTH.

[From Clarke and M'Arthur, vol. ii. p. 179.—Lord Nelson having on the 16th of June proceeded with the Squadron off Maritimo, to watch for the French fleet, he was, on the 18th, joined by the Alexander and Goliath from off Malta. On the 20th he received a dispatch from Lord Keith, which induced him to return to Palermo, and propose to the King that the Squadron should go to Naples, where he supposed the French fleet was bound. (Vide p. 391, post.) The Foudroyant arrived in Palermo Bay on the 21st, but did not anchor. Lord Nelson went on shore and saw the King, and after remaining three hours, the Hereditary Prince, and Sir William and Lady Hamilton accompanied Nelson to the Foudroyant, and having rejoined the Squadron, they made sail for Naples.]

21st June, 1799.

On the return of our Squadron, which the Jacobins gave out was for fear of the French fleet, all is undone again, although they had in some measure agreed to terms : therefore his Majesty has requested my immediate presence in the Bay of Naples, which I shall execute this afternoon.

I am, &c.,

NELSON.

## OBSERVATIONS ON THE ARMISTICE CONCLUDED BETWEEN THE CARDINAL AND THE FRENCH AND REBELS, 24TH JUNE, 1799.

[From a Copy, in the State Paper Office, and Order Book. The Squadron entered the Bay of Naples on the 24th of June ; and having on his passage, received letters informing him that Captain Foote of the Seahorse, had signed a treaty for the surrender of the Castles of Uovo and Nuovo, wherein the principal Neapolitan rebels had taken refuge, the conditions of which treaty Nelson considered "infamous," and finding a Flag of Truce still flying on the Castles, as well as on board the Seahorse, he instantly annulled the Truce, by signal. A copy of the Treaty, and of many other documents, together with some observations on the subject, will be found at the end of the volume.]

Opinion delivered before I saw the treaty of Armistice, &c., only from reports met at sea.[6]
The Armistice I take for granted is, that if the French and Rebels are not relieved by their friends in twenty-one days from the signing the Armistice, then that they shall evacuate Naples, in this infamous manner, to His Sicilian Majesty and triumphant to them, as stated in the Article.

[6] This paragraph is in Lord Nelson's hand.

All Armistices signify that either party may renew hostilities, giving a certain notice fixed upon by the contracting parties. In the present instance, I suppose the Cardinal thought that in twenty-one days he had not the power of driving the French from the Castle of St. Elmo, or the Rebels from the lower Castles of Uovo and Nuovo. The French and Rebels thought that if they could not be relieved in twenty-one days, they could, when unable to remain any longer, covenant to be removed to a place where they may be in a situation to renew their diabolical schemes against His Sicilian Majesty and the peace and happiness of his faithful Subjects, and their removal to be at the expense of His Majesty; and those Enemies and Rebels to be protected by the Fleet of His Sicilian Majesty's faithful Ally, the King of Great Britain. Therefore evidently this agreement implies that both parties are supposed to remain in *statu quo;* but if either party receive relief from their situation, then the compact of course falls to the ground, and is of no effect; for if one party can be liberated from the agreement, it naturally implies the other is in the same state. And I fancy the question need not be asked whether, if the French fleet arrived this day in the Bay of Naples, whether the French and Rebels would adhere one moment to the Armistice? 'No!' the French Admiral would say, ' I am not come here to look on, but to act.' And so says the British Admiral; and declares on his honour that the arrival of either Fleet, British or French, destroys the compact, for neither can lay idle.

Therefore, the British Admiral proposes to the Cardinal to send, in their joint names, to the French and Rebels, that the arrival of the British fleet has completely destroyed the compact, as would that of the French if they had had the power (which, thank God, they have not) to come to Naples.

Therefore, that it shall be fixed that in two hours the French shall give possession of the Castle of St. Elmo to His Sicilian Majesty's faithful subjects, and the troops of his Allies; on which condition alone, they shall be sent to France without the stipulation of their being prisoners of war.

That as to Rebels and Traitors, no power on earth has a right to stand between their gracious King and them: they must instantly throw themselves on the clemency of their

Sovereign, for no other terms will be allowed them; nor will the French be allowed even to name them in any capitulation. If these terms are not complied with, in the time above mentioned—viz., two hours for the French, and instant submission on the part of the Rebels—such very favourable conditions will never be again offered.

NELSON.

Foudroyant, Naples Bay, 24th June, 1799.

[Added, in Lord Nelson's own hand.]

Read and explained, and rejected by the Cardinal.

---

## "DECLARATION SENT TO THE NEAPOLITAN JACOBINS IN THE CASTLE OF UOVO AND NUOVO."

[From a Copy, in the State Paper Office.]

His Britannic Majesty's Ship Foudroyant,<br>Naples Bay, 25th June, 1799.

Rear Admiral Lord Nelson, K.B., Commander of his Britannic Majesty's Fleet in the Bay of Naples, acquaints the Rebellious Subjects of His Sicilian Majesty in the Castles of Uovo and Nuovo, that he will not permit them to embark or quit those places. They must surrender themselves to His Majesty's Royal mercy.

NELSON.

---

## SUMMONS SENT TO THE CASTLE ST. ELMO.

[Order-Book, and Copy in the State Paper Office.]

His Britannic Majesty's Ship Foudroyant,<br>Naples Bay, 25th June, 1799.

Sir,

His Eminence the Cardinal de Ruffo and the Commanding Officer of the Russian Army having sent you a Summons to surrender, I acquaint you, that unless the terms are acceded to within two hours, you must take the consequences, as I shall not agree to any other. I am, Sir, your most obedient servant,

NELSON.

## TO REAR-ADMIRAL DUCKWORTH, H.M. SHIP LEVIATHAN.

[From Clarke and M'Arthur, vol. ii. p. 180.]

My dear Admiral,　　　　　　　　　25th June, 1799.

As you will believe, the Cardinal and myself have begun our career by a complete difference of opinion. He will send the Rebels to Toulon,—I say they shall not go. He thinks one house in Naples more to be prized than his Sovereign's honour. Troubridge and Ball are gone to the Cardinal, for him to read my declaration to the French and Rebels, whom he persists in calling patriots—what a prostitution of the word! I shall send Foote to get the Gun-boats from Procida. I wish the Fleet not to be more than two-thirds of a cable from each other. I shall send you a sketch of the anchorage, in forty fathom water. The Foudroyant to be the Van-ship. If the French fleet should favour us with a visit, I can easily take my station in the centre. I am, &c.,

NELSON.

## TO CAPTAIN DRUMMOND,⁵ HIS MAJESTY'S SLOOP BULLDOG.

[Order-Book.]

Foudroyant, Naples Bay, 25th June, 1799.

You are hereby required and directed forthwith to proceed in the Sloop you command, and cruize about five leagues west, off the Island of Ischia, keeping a very good look out for the French fleet, and gaining all the intelligence in your power from the Vessels you may fall in with; and at the expiration of a week to return, and join me at this place.

NELSON.

## TO CAPTAIN HOSTE, HIS MAJESTY'S SHIP LA MUTINE.

[Order-Book.]

Foudroyant, Naples Bay, 25th June, 1799.

You are hereby required and directed to take under your direction His Majesty's Brig San Leon, whose commander has my orders to follow your instructions, and proceed with-

---

⁵ Now Vice-Admiral Sir Adam Drummond, K.C.H.

out delay to Gaeta, co-operating as much as possible with
the Grand Diable, and using your endeavours to reduce that
Fortress, in conjunction with him, to obedience to its lawful
Sovereign, returning in one week for further orders.

NELSON.

N.B.—You are not to subscribe to any terms with Rebels,
but unconditional submission to their Sovereign.

------

### LORD NELSON'S OPINION, DELIVERED IN WRITING TO THE CARDINAL.

[Order-Book. On the 25th or 26th of June, Cardinal Ruffo came on board the
Foudroyant, and was saluted with thirteen guns. A discussion of several hours'
duration took place between him and Lord Nelson, in the presence of Sir William and
Lady Hamilton, who acted as interpreters; but all Nelson's arguments failed to convince the Cardinal that the treaty was, *ipso facto*, terminated by the arrival of the
English fleet, and that as its conditions had not been executed, it required the ratification of his Sicilian Majesty. Nelson, therefore, expressed his own opinion to
that effect in the annexed Memorandum, and proceeded to act according to his own
views, by taking possession of the Castles, and making prisoners of all the Neapolitans in them; and he then invested St. Elmo, with the Seamen and Marines of
his Ships, under the Command of Captain Troubridge.]

Foudroyant, 26th June, 1799.

Rear Admiral Lord Nelson arrived with the British fleet
the 24th June in the Bay of Naples, and found a treaty
entered into with the Rebels, which, in his opinion, cannot be
carried into execution, without the approbation of his Sicilian
Majesty.

------

### TO CAPTAIN THOMAS TROUBRIDGE, HEREBY APPOINTED TO COMMAND ALL THE MARINE FORCES, SEAMEN, ETC. LANDED FROM THE SQUADRON UNDER MY COMMAND AT NAPLES.

[Order-Book.]

Foudroyant, Naples Bay, 26th June, 1799.

You are hereby required to take upon you the charge
and command of all His Majesty's Marine forces landed
from the Squadron under my command in the Castles and
City of Naples, as well as all artillerymen, seamen, and
others that may be landed, to assist in attacking the Citadel
of St. Elmo, and proceed to invest and besiege the said

Citadel, and use every means in your power to reduce the French garrison therein, to surrender the said Castle to its lawful Sovereign. And you are to take to your assistance Captain Ball, of His Majesty's Ship Alexander, as second in command of the said Marine forces, seamen, &c., who has my directions to follow your orders, and to assist you in all matters and things relative to the said siege of St. Elmo, and all other things necessary for the good of His Majesty's service. NELSON.

---

TO CAPTAIN DIXON, H. M. SHIP LION.

[Order-Book.]

Foudroyant, Naples Bay, 26th June, 1799.

You are hereby required and directed to proceed in the Ship you command, without loss of time, to the Island of Malta, taking under your command the Sloops named in the margin,[1] which are cruizing off that Island, and to prevent as much as in [your] power, any supplies getting into the Port of La Valetta, for the relief of that garrison ; and to be careful to keep a very good look out, to prevent a surprise, either from the westward, or by the Ships out of that Port, and to give any advice or assistance in your power to the Maltese people. NELSON.

---

TO EVAN NEPEAN, ESQ., SECRETARY TO THE ADMIRALTY.

[Autograph, in the State Paper Office.]

Sir,                                    Bay of Naples, June 27th, 1799.

I am this morning honoured with your letter of May 4th, with its several inclosures relative to the French fleet. I am happy in being able to congratulate their Lordships on the possession of the City of Naples. St. Elmo is yet in the hands of the French, but the Castles of Uovo and Nuovo I took possession of last evening, and his Sicilian Majesty's colours are now flying on them.[6] This morning I am going

---

[1] La Bonne Citoyenne, El Corso, and Benjamin.

[6] The paragraph commencing " I am happy," and ending with the words " flying ' on them," was published in the " London Gazette" of the 17th of August, 1799.

to send a detachment under Captain Troubridge, to cut down the dangerous Tree of Anarchy, and to burn it before the King's palace. The moment I can find the City a little quieted, guns shall be got against St. Elmo, when, I am sure, the French will be glad to surrender. I transmit a copy of my letter to Lord St. Vincent, which will inform their Lordships more particularly of my situation. In my present position, I have not the smallest alarm should the Enemy favour us with a visit, inferior as my force is to oppose them. I have the honour to be, with great respect, your most obedient servant,

NELSON.

***

## TO REAR-ADMIRAL THE MARQUIS DE NIZA.

[Letter Book.]

Foudroyant, Naples Bay, 27th June, 1799.

My Lord,

You will be pleased to give directions that the troops on board Her Most Faithful Majesty's Ships of the Line under your command, be ready to land to-morrow morning, at six o'clock, at the Castle Uovo, with provisions for two days, and sixty rounds of ammunition, with a sufficient quantity of gunners, so as to make up the number of one hundred men from each Ship. I have the honour to be, &c.,

NELSON.

***

## TO VICE-ADMIRAL LORD KEITH, K.B.[7]

[Autograph, in the Admiralty, and Copy in the Letter-Book.]

Bay of Naples, June 27th, 1799.

My dear Lord,

Having detailed my proceedings to the 16th of June, by the Telegraph brig, I have now to go on with my movements.

On the 17th the Alexander and Goliath joined me from off Malta; leaving to look out in that quarter, three Sloops of War;—the force with me was now fifteen Sail of two-decked Ships, English, and three Portuguese, with a Fire-ship and

---

[7] Lord Nelson wrote this letter to Lord St. Vincent, but seems to have changed the address, on hearing of the Earl's having resigned the command to Lord Keith.

Cutter. On the 20th, the Swallow, Portuguese corvette, brought me your Lordship's dispatch of the 17th, acquainting me of the near approach of the Squadron under Sir Alan Gardner,[8] and that Lord Keith was going in search of the French fleet. As I had now no prospect of being in a situation to go in search of the Enemy's fleet, which at least is twenty-five Sail of the Line, and might be reinforced with two Venetian ships, although I was firmly resolved they should not pass me without a battle, which would so cripple them that they might be unable to proceed on any distant service, I determined to offer myself for the service of Naples, where I knew the French fleet intended going. With this determination I pushed for Palermo, and on the 21st I went on shore for two hours, saw their Majesties and General Acton, who repeated to me what the General had wrote, (but which I had not received,[9]) to request that I would instantly

---

[8] Early in June, Lord Bridport detached Vice-Admiral Sir Alan Gardner, with sixteen Sail of the Line, to reinforce the fleet off Cadiz, and in the Mediterranean.

[9] There are two important letters in the Nelson Papers, from Sir John Acton to Sir William Hamilton, one dated on the 19th, and the other on the 20th June, 1799; but there is no letter about that time from Sir John Acton to Nelson himself. From the first of these letters an extract only is necessary:

"I have read to their Majesties in the Council your paragraph of Lord Nelson being fretting that he cannot directly go and come at the French fleet; but his declarations of the French not getting neither to this Island nor Naples but through his heart's blood, has produced, as you may imagine, the highest feelings in their Majesties, and every one of their faithful servants then present. I beg of you, my dear Sir, to present their Majesties' most sensible gratitude for this repeated comforting declaration. All their trust is in Lord Nelson certainly, and the safety of both the Kingdoms. Naples is in our hands excepting St. Elmo, with the French in it. Castel Nuovo and Dell' Uovo in the hands of the felons. In those two places consists at present the Neapolitan Republic."—*Autograph*, in the Nelson Papers.

The other Letter, dated on the 20th of June, it is desirable to insert at length :—
"My dear Sir,

"I went to the King this afternoon in order to present you with his Majesty's answer to Lord Nelson's letter. I am therefore authorized to tell you that upon the Cardinal's letter of the 17th, arrived to-day, and those of Procida of the 18th, we find that the news being spread amongst the Republicans of the French Fleet being at sea, they broke the truce granted at their desire, for a capitulation of the Castles *Uovo* and *Nuovo*, and of *St. Elmo*, by the French. These last, however, seem willing still to hear of terms, but the Republicans are making continual *sorties* from the Castles and St. Martino. The Cardinal seems in a disagreeable position. His Majesty, on this circumstance especially, accepts of the kind offer of Lord Nelson, to present himself before Naples, and procure the intimation for surrendering, to be supported by the English fleet. Its appearance, and the certainty of the French being distant, would certainly produce the desired effect. I hurry

go into the Bay of Naples to endeavour to bring His Sicilian Majesty's affairs in that City to a happy conclusion.

I lost not one moment in complying with the request, and arrived in the Bay of Naples on the 24th, where I saw a Flag of Truce flying on board His Majesty's Ship Seahorse, Captain Foote, and also on the Castles of Uovo and Nuovo. Having on the passage received letters informing [me] that an infamous Armistice was entered into with the Rebels in those Castles, to which Captain Foote had put his name, I instantly made the signal to annul the Truce, being determined never to give my approbation to any terms with Rebels, but that of unconditional submission. The Fleet was anchored in a close line of battle, N.W. by N. and S.E. by S., from the Mole head one and a-half mile distant, flanked by twenty-two Gun and Mortar boats, which I recalled from Procida. I sent Captains Troubridge and Ball instantly to the Cardinal Vicar-General, to represent to his Eminence my opinion of the infamous terms entered into with the Rebels, and also two papers which I enclose.[1] His Eminence said he would send no papers, that if I pleased I might break the Armistice, for that he was tired of his situation. Captain Troubridge then asked his Eminence this plain question: ' If Lord Nelson breaks the Armistice, will your Eminence assist him in his attack on the Castles?' His answer was clear, ' I will neither assist him with men or guns.' After much communication, his Eminence desired to come on board to speak with me on his situation. I used every argu-

this answer, my dear Sir, for the expedition to Lord Nelson. I shall acquaint the Cardinal and De Curtis to-night, of the probability that the English fleet will be a few hours after the arrival of my letter, before Naples. "I return to you Captain Foote's letters, of which I have taken copy. I do not know whether he has granted the demands of the Rebel Officers to go free to their families. His intimation was for surrendering as prisoners of war. If Captain Foote has kept to his declaration, then these prisoners might come to Sicily, when they shall be ordered to Africa till further orders. I am constantly, my dear Sir, your most obedient and most faithful servant, J. Acton."—Autograph, in the Nelson Papers.

On forwarding this letter, on the 20th of June, to Lord Nelson, Sir William Hamilton wrote him:—

"The offer your Lordship made in your letter, was to take place when you had a certainty of the French fleet's being disposed of somehow; and General Acton has had your letter to me, and I have not seen him, so you may decide your own way; for we are under no kind of engagement."—Autograph, in the Nelson Papers.

[1] Vide p. 386, ante.

ment in my power to convince him that the Treaty and Armistice was at an end by the arrival of the Fleet; but an Admiral is no match in talking with a Cardinal. I therefore gave him my opinion in writing—viz., 'Rear-Admiral Lord Nelson, who arrived in the Bay of Naples on the 24th June with the British Fleet, found a Treaty entered into with the Rebels, which he is of opinion ought not to be carried into execution without the approbation of His Sicilian Majesty, Earl St. Vincent,—Lord Keith.'

Under this opinion the Rebels came out of the Castles, which was instantly occupied by the Marines of the Squadron. On the 27th Captains Troubridge and Ball, with 1300 men, landed from the Ships, united with 500 Russians and a body of Royalists, half of whose *Officers* are, I have every reason to believe, *Rebels,*—cowards they have already proved themselves. Our batteries are open on St. Elmo, and a few days will, I hope, reduce it. The Alexander and another are just going to resume their station off Malta, which I am confident will very soon surrender, now all hopes of relief are cut off. I shall not fail to keep up a constant communication with your Lordship, and have the honour to be, with the greatest respect, your most obedient faithful Servant,        NELSON.

Carracciolo was executed on board H. S. Majesty's Ship Minerva, on the 29th June.

---

TO THOMAS TROUBRIDGE, ESQ., CAPTAIN OF HIS MAJESTY'S SHIP CULLODEN, HEREBY APPOINTED TO COMMAND THE BRITISH AND PORTUGUESE MARINES, ETC. LANDED AT NAPLES.

[Order-Book.]

Foudroyant, Naples Bay, 28th June, 1799.

Whereas the reduction of the Castle of St. Elmo and City of Cupua is of the utmost importance to the restoration of the peace and security of His Sicilian Majesty's Dominions; and whereas the French in those posts are superior to the united force of the troops in His Sicilian Majesty's service now in arms against them, I have judged it expedient, for the good of His Majesty's service and that of his Allies, that a body of troops formed of the effective marines and seamen, and artillery of the English and Portuguese Ships in the Squadron under my command, should be landed to besiege and reduce the said places, You are, therefore, hereby required and directed to take upon you the charge and command of all the said troops, and other persons sent to aid and assist you, and proceed with them to perform the said services, acknowledging and taking the assistance of such superior Officers as His Sicilian Majesty shall appoint, for providing artillery, ammunition, and other matters necessary in such cases. And having appointed Mr. Daniel Butler Dawes, Purser of His Majesty's Ship under your command, to act as Commissary to the said troops while serving on shore, you are to furnish him with proper instructions for providing provisions at such times and places and in such proportions, as you may think convenient and necessary, for the maintenance of the said forces, and give such directions for the payment thereof, as may appear to be most advantageous for His Majesty's service; informing me, from time to time, by a regular correspondence, with the success of the undertaking; for which this shall be your warrant.                                              NELSON.

### TO THE OFFICERS COMMANDING THE CASTLES UOVO AND NUOVO.

[Order-Book.]

Foudroyant, Naples Bay, 28th June, 1799.

It is my directions [that] the Officers commanding the Forts Uovo and Nuovo, do permit Brigadier-General Minichini, and such people as he may bring with him, to inspect the works and fortifications, for the purpose of repairing the damages of the same.                                              NELSON.

### TO HIS EMINENCY CARDINAL RUFFO.

[Letter-Book.]

Foudroyant, Naples Bay. [No date, but apparently 28th June, 1799.]

Sir,

I am just honoured with Your Eminency's letter; and as His Excellency Sir William Hamilton has wrote you

this morning, that I will not on any consideration break
the Armistice entered into by you, I hope Your Eminency
will be satisfied that I am supporting your ideas. I send once
more Captains Troubridge and Ball, to arrange with Your
Eminency everything relative to an attack on St. Elmo: whenever your army and cannon are ready to proceed against it,
I will land 1200 men to go with them, under the present
Armistice. I have only to rejoice that His Britannic Majesty's fleet is here, to secure the City of Naples from all
attacks by sea,—I am, &c.,

                                              NELSON.

---

### TO LIEUTENANT SARGEANT, COMMANDING THE CUTTER EARL ST. VINCENT.

[Order-Book.]

Foudroyant, Naples Bay, 28th June, 1799.

You are hereby required and directed to proceed in the
Cutter you command (without a moment's loss of time) to
Palermo, with my dispatches, and deliver them to his Excellency Sir John Acton; and having received an answer, you
are to return, without a moment's loss of time.

                                              NELSON.

N.B.—These dispatches being of so great importance, you
are not on any account to chase anything in your passage.

---

### TO CAPTAIN FOOTE, H. M. SHIP SEAHORSE.

[Order-Book, and Captain Foote's " Vindication," p. 142.]

Secret.

Foudroyant, Naples Bay, 28th June, 1799.

You are hereby required and directed to proceed in His
Majesty's Ship Seahorse, under your command, with all expedition to Palermo, and attend the orders of their Sicilian Majesties, who may in all probability embark on board for this
place; and, on your arrival there, to call on General Acton,
who will inform their Majesties thereof.

                                              NELSON.

## PROCLAMATION ISSUED AT NAPLES.[2]

[Order-Book.]

Foudroyant, Naples Bay, 29th June, 1799.

Horatio Lord Nelson, Admiral of the British Fleet, in the Bay of Naples, gives notice to all those who have served as Officers Civil or Military, in the service of the infamous Neapolitan Republic, that, if, in the space of twenty-four hours for those who are in the City of Naples, and forty-eight hours for those who are within five miles of it, they do not give themselves up to the clemency of the King, to the Officer commanding the Castles Uovo and Nuovo, that Lord Nelson will consider them still as in rebellion, and enemies of His Sicilian Majesty.

NELSON.

———————

## TO THE COMMANDING OFFICERS OF THE CASTLES UOVO AND NUOVO, AND AT THE KING'S PALACE.

[Order-Book.]

Foudroyant, Naples Bay, 29th June, 1799.

Whereas the Office of the Secretary at War, and the Printing Office, are situated in the King's Palace, and which Offices are both wanted for the better carrying on of the

---

[2] This Proclamation was translated into Italian, and printed: the following copy of it is taken from one of those papers in the State Paper Office:

"Abordo il Fulminante, 29 Giugno, 1799.

" Orazio, Lord Nelson, Ammiraglio della Flotta Britannica nella Rada di Napoli, da notizia a tutti quelli che hanno servito da officiali nel Militare, e nelle cariche civili l'infame sedicente Repubblica Napoletana, che se si ritrovano nel circuito della Città di Napoli, debbano in termine di 24 ore, presentarsi ai Comandanti del Castello Nuovo, o del Castello dell' Ovo, fiandosi alla clemenza di S. M. Siciliana, e se si ritrovano nelle vicinanze di detta Città fino alla distanza di cinque miglia, debbano egualmente presentarsi ai detti Comandanti, ma in termine di 48 ore; altrimenti saranno considerati dal sudetto Ammiraglio Lord Nelson come ribelli, ed inimici della prefata M. S. Siciliana."

In consequence of this Proclamation, General Minichini wrote to Lord Nelson on the 30th of June, asking whether certain persons, whose names he enclosed, who had been promoted in the service of the Republic against their will, and had never exercised the duties of the Offices conferred upon them, were included in his demand ; and a similar inquiry was made of his Lordship on the same day, by the Commander Ruffo, respecting the Cavaliere Ottavio Caracciolo, but the answers have not been found.

Executive Government, you are hereby required and directed to permit the Secretary at War, with his Officers and attendants, to take possession of the said Office and the Printing Office, as also to permit proper persons to take inventories of such things as may be found in the Palace, and the Castles Uovo and Nuovo.

NELSON.

---

TO CAPTAIN WILSH, COMMANDING HER MOST FAITHFUL MAJESTY'S SLOOP BALLOON.

[Order-Book.]

Foudroyant, Naples Bay, 29th June, 1799.

You are hereby required and directed to proceed, in Her Most Faithful Majesty's Sloop Balloon, under your command, with all expedition to Palermo, and deliver the dispatches you will receive herewith to Her Sicilian Majesty in person, waiting at that place for Her orders, and to return with Her Majesty's answers to me at this place, and by no means to chase anything you may fall in with, either in your passage or on your return.

NELSON.

---

TO CAPTAIN BALL, HIS MAJESTY'S SHIP ALEXANDER.

[Order-Book.]

Foudroyant, Naples Bay, 29th June, 1799.

You are hereby required and directed to put yourself under the command of Captain Thomas Troubridge, of His Majesty's Ship Culloden, and act as Commander, under him, of all His Majesty's Marine forces, artillerymen, seamen, and others, that are or may be landed from the Squadron under my command, in the Castles and City of Naples, and for the investing and besieging the Citadel of St. Elmo, giving every assistance in your power in carrying on the said Siege, and willing and requiring all Officers and men to obey you as their second in command, in carrying on the said service.

NELSON.

### TO COUNT THURN, COMMODORE AND COMMANDER OF HIS SICILIAN MAJESTY'S FRIGATE LA MINERVA.

[From a Copy, in the Nelson Papers. Some observations on the trial and execution of Caraccioli will be found at the end of the volume.]

By Horatio Lord Nelson, &c. &c. &c.

Whereas Francisco Caracciolo, a Commodore in the service of his Sicilian Majesty, has been taken, and stands accused of rebellion against his lawful Sovereign, and for firing at his colours hoisted on board His Frigate the Minerva, under your command,

You are, therefore, hereby required and directed to assemble five of the senior Officers under your command, yourself presiding, and proceed to inquire whether the crime with which the said Francisco Caracciolo stands charged, can be proved against him ; and if the charge is proved, you are to report to me what punishment he ought to suffer.

Given on board the Foudroyant, Naples Bay, the 29th June, 1799.

NELSON.

---

### TO COMMODORE COUNT THURN, COMMANDER OF HIS SICILIAN MAJESTY'S FRIGATE LA MINERVA.

[Order-Book.]

By Horatio Lord Nelson, &c. &c. &c.

Whereas a Board of Naval Officers of his Sicilian Majesty hath been assembled to try Francisco Caracciolo for rebellion against his lawful Sovereign, and for firing at His Sicilian Majesty's Frigate La Minerva ;

And whereas the said Board of Naval Officers have found the charge of rebellion fully proved against him, and have sentenced the said Caracciolo to suffer death ;

You are hereby required and directed to cause the said sentence of death to be carried into execution upon the said Francisco Caracciolo accordingly, by hanging him at the fore yard-arm of His Sicilian Majesty's Frigate La Minerva, under your command, at five o'clock this evening ; and to cause him to hang there until sunset, when you will have his body cut down, and thrown into the sea.

Given on board the Foudroyant, Naples Bay, the 29th of June, 1799.

NELSON.[3]

---

TO CAPTAIN TROUBRIDGE, H.M. SHIP CULLODEN.

[Letter-Book.]

Foudroyant, June 30th, 1799.

Sir,

In answer to your letter of this date, requesting, for the reasons therein given, that Mr. James Harriman may have my authority to assist you in the capacity of Secretary and Interpreter, at the Sieges of St. Elmo and Capua, I am to inform you that I have authorized and appointed the said Mr. Harriman to render you the assistance you may require, with an assurance of such reward for the performance of services, as may hereafter be deemed adequate. I am, &c.

NELSON.

---

TO COMMODORE CAMPBELL, HER FAITHFUL MAJESTY'S SHIP ST. SEBASTIAN.

[Letter-Book.]

My dear Sir,                               Foudroyant, 3rd July, 1799.

I send you an order to put yourself under the command of Captain Ball, for I am determined to bring the point of your rank to issue ; and therefore I begin with you, who, I am told, is the senior. It is a public matter of great consequence, and therefore, must be settled. Yours truly,

NELSON.

---

[3] Count Thurn's official Report of having obeyed this Order, is in the Nelson Papers :—

"L'Ammiraglio Lord Nelson Rapporto, a S.E.

"Si da parte a S.E. l'Ammiraglio Lord Nelson, d'essere stata eseguita la sentenza di Francesco Caracciolo, nella maniera da lui ordinata.

"Bordo della Fregata di S.M. la Minerva, 29 Giugno, 1799.

"H. CTE. DI THURN, Brig.re"

The trial and execution are thus summarily noticed in the *Journal :—*

"Saturday, 29th June. Moderate and cloudy. Arrived Her most faithful Majesty's Ship Rainha and Balloon Brig. A Court Martial assembled. Tried, condemned, and hung, Francesco Caraccioli, on board the Neapolitan Frigate La Minerva. See also Extracts from the Foudroyant's *Log* in the APPENDIX.

TO SIR STEPHEN LUSHINGTON, BART., CHAIRMAN OF THE COURT
OF DIRECTORS OF THE HONOURABLE EAST INDIA COMPANY.

[Original, in the East India House.]

Foudroyant, Bay of Naples, July 3rd, 1799.

Sir,

I was this day honoured with your letter of May 1st, conveying to me the Resolutions of the Honourable East India
Company.⁴ It is true, Sir, that I am incapable of finding
words to convey my feelings for the unprecedented honour
done me by the Company; [but] having in my younger days
served in the East Indies, I am no stranger to the munificence
of the Honourable Company; but this generous act of theirs
to me so much surpasses all calculation of gratitude, that I
have only the power of saying that I receive it with all respect.
Give me leave, Sir, to thank you for your very elegant and
flattering letter; and I am, with the greatest respect, your
most obliged and obedient servant,

NELSON.

---

TO CAPTAIN HOOD, OF HIS MAJESTY'S SHIP ZEALOUS, HEREBY
APPOINTED TO COMMAND THE CASTLE OF NUOVO.

[Order-Book.]

Foudroyant, Naples Bay, 4th July, 1799.

You are hereby required and directed to repair to the
Castle Nuovo, in the Bay of Naples, and there take upon
you the command of the said Castle, requiring all persons
therein to obey you as their Commander; and you also to
obey all such orders and directions, as you may, from time to
time, receive from Captain Troubridge, Commander-in-Chief
of the British forces landed at Naples.

NELSON.

⁴ At a Court of Directors held on Wednesday, the 24th April, 1799.
"Resolved unanimously—That the thanks of this Court be given to the Right
Hon. Rear-Admiral Lord Nelson, for the very great and important Services he has
rendered the East India Company, by the ever-memorable Victory obtained over the
French Fleet, near the Mouth of the Nile, on the 1st, 2nd, and 3rd of August,
1798. Resolved unanimously—That in further testimony of the high sense this
Court entertain of the very great and important benefits arising to the East India
Company from his Lordship's magnanimous conduct on that glorious occasion, this
Court request his Lordship's acceptance of the sum of ten thousand pounds."

## TO THOMAS TROUBRIDGE, ESQ., CAPTAIN OF H.M. SHIP CUL-
LODEN, AND COMMANDER-IN-CHIEF OF THE BRITISH FORCES
LANDED AT NAPLES.

[Order-Book.]

Foudroyant, Naples Bay, 6th July, 1799.

Whereas John Jolly, Private Marine, belonging to his
Majesty's Ship Alexander, hath this day been tried by a
Court-Martial, on charges exhibited against him by Lieutenant Pearce, Second Lieutenant of Marines, for having
struck the said Lieutenant Pearce while in the execution of
his duty, and threatening to shoot him as soon as he should
be released; and the Court finding him guilty of the said
crimes, have adjudged the said John Jolly to suffer death, in
the manner, and at such time and place, as I might think fit;
and, whereas I think it proper, in pursuance of the said
sentence, and to mark the heinousness of the crime he hath
committed, that the said John Jolly should suffer death accordingly, you are here hereby required and directed to cause all
the Marine forces that can properly be spared to be assembled
at the most convenient place near your Camp on shore, and
carry the said sentence into execution upon the said John
Jolly on Monday morning next, the 8th instant, by causing
him to be shot to death at the head of the said Marine forces,
and in the usual manner;—a copy of which sentence you
will receive herewith.                                    NELSON.

---

### TO CAPTAIN FOOTE, H.M. SHIP SEAHORSE.

[From Captain Foote's " Vindication," p. 144. On the 8th of July, the Seahorse
arrived from Palermo, accompanied by La Sirena, on board of which Frigate His
Sicilian Majesty had preferred to embark. When Lord Nelson says in p. 408 post,
that the King arrived in Naples Bay on the 10th, he must have meant the day on
which His Majesty came to that part of the Bay in which the English Squadron
was at anchor. The *Journal* has only the following notice of the King:—" 11th
July, [i. e. P.M. of the 10th,] the King of Naples and suite came on board; the
Squadron saluted him twenty-one guns each."]

My dear Sir,                                    July 8th, 10 P.M.

When you have seen the Convoy safe into Procida, I wish
the Seahorse not to anchor, but for you to wait upon his
Majesty, and to say, if he has no commands for you, I desire
you will join me here, as I want to send you and the Thalia

directly on service. I hope you will not think it an unpleasant one ; for believe me, with real regard, your faithful and obe-dient servant,

NELSON.

---

## TO CAPTAIN TROUBRIDGE, COMMANDING ALL THE BRITISH AND PORTUGUESE TROOPS LANDED FROM THE SQUADRON.

[Letter-Book.]

Sir,                                    Foudroyant, July 9th, 1799.

You will, in obedience to my orders, prepare everything for the execution of the sentence of the Court-Martial held on John Jolly ; but when all the forms, except the last, are gone through, you will acquaint the prisoner, that, although there has been no circumstance to mitigate the severity of the law, yet that I have reason to hope that the sparing of his life will have as beneficial an effect for the discipline of the Service, as if he had suffered death. You will, therefore, respite the prisoner from the sentence of death, till his Majesty's pleasure is known. I hope that this extraordinary mark of lenity will have its full effect on the mind of those under your command, and be a beacon to them to avoid the crime of drunkenness, which brings with it even the punishment of death. And here I pledge myself to them that, if any similar circumstance happens in future, that I will most assuredly order the sentence to be immediately carried into execution. I am, Sir, yours, &c.,

NELSON.

---

## RETURN OF KILLED AND WOUNDED AT THE SIEGE OF THE CASTLE ST. ELMO, WHICH SURRENDERED 12TH JULY, 1799.

[From a Copy in the Admiralty.]

Foudroyant, Naples Bay, 13th July, 1799.

Marine Forces landed from the Squadron:

John Hickson, private, Vanguard . . . . . Killed.

Daniel Elliot
Christopher Calonie } Vanguard, privates,
Serjeant Morgan
Thomas Jones, private } Foudroyant,          } Wounded.
Benjamin Cole, do.

Royal Artillery :

Lieutenant Milbanke . . . . . . . . . Killed.

(Signed,)

T. STRICKLAND, Lieutenant-Colonel Marine Forces.

Swiss Regiment :

2 Officers, 7 Rank and File . . . . . . . Killed.

9 Rank and File . . . . . . . Wounded.

Albanese Volunteers :

4 Rank and File . . . . . . . Wounded.

Russians :

1 Officer, 3 Rank and File . . . . . . . Killed.

1 Officer, 3 Rank and File . . . . . . Wounded.

Calabrese Regiment :

1 Officer, 21 Rank and File . . . . . . . Killed.

4 Officers, 62 Rank and File . . . . . . . Wounded.

TOTAL, 5 Officers, 32 Rank and File . . Killed.

5 Officers, 79 Rank and File . . Wounded.

NELSON.

---

TO VICE-ADMIRAL LORD KEITH, K.B.

[From a Copy in the Admiralty, and the "London Gazette" of the 17th of August, 1799.]

Foudroyant, Bay of Naples, 13th July, 1799.

My Lord,

I have the pleasure to inform you of the surrender of Fort St. Elmo, (on the terms of the enclosed Capitulation,) after open batteries of eight days, during which time our heavy batteries were advanced within 180 yards of the ditch. The very great strength of St. Elmo and its more formidable position, will mark with what fortitude, perseverance, and activity the combined Forces must have acted. Captain Troubridge was the Officer selected for the command of all the forces landed from the Squadron; Captain Ball assisted him for seven days till his services were wanted at Malta, when his place was ably supplied by Captain Hallowell, an Officer of the most distinguished merit, and to whom Captain

Troubridge expresses the highest obligation.   Captain Hood, with a garrison for the Castle Nuovo, and to keep good order in the Capital, an arduous task at that time, was also landed from the Squadron; and I have the pleasure to tell you that no Capital is more quiet than Naples.   I transmit you Captain Troubridge's letter to me, with returns of killed and wounded.[5]

I have now to state to your Lordship, that although the ability and resources of my brave friend Troubridge are well known to all the world, yet even he had difficulties to struggle with in every way, which the state of the Capital will easily bring to your idea, that has raised his great character even higher than it was before![6] and it is my earnest request that your Lordship will mention him in that way to the Board of Admiralty, that His Majesty may be graciously pleased to bestow some mark of his Royal Favour on Captain Troubridge,[7] which will give real happiness to your Lordship's most obedient and faithful servant.

                                                            NELSON.

---

### TO VICE-ADMIRAL LORD KEITH, K.B.

[From a Copy, in the Admiralty.]

                                    Foudroyant, Naples Bay, 13th July, 1799.

My Lord,

Captains Troubridge and Hallowell, with one thousand of the best men, landed from the Squadron, united with four thousand other troops of various denominations, march against Capua to-morrow morning.   I have desired the Commander at Capua to be informed that, if he chooses to evacuate the City and Gaeta, laying down their arms, that they shall be sent to France without any condition, but that if he refuses, and my advice is followed, he shall have no terms but such as I am allowed by His Sicilian Majesty to dictate.   I have the honour to be, &c.

                                                            NELSON.

[5] Published in the " London Gazette," of the 17th of August, 1799.

[6] The following paragraph was not published in the " London Gazette."

[7] Captain Troubridge's gallantry and zeal were rewarded by his being created a Baronet, on the 30th of November, 1799.   It is only from a perusal of his letters to Lord Nelson, that an adequate idea can be formed of the energy and ability displayed by that distinguished Officer.

### GENERAL ORDERS.

[From a Copy, in the Admiralty.]

Lord Nelson most cordially congratulates Captain Troubridge and the Officers and Men employed under him, on the
happy termination of their labours by the surrender of Fort
St. Elmo, which has entirely liberated the Capital of the
Kingdom of Naples from anarchy and misery. Lord Nelson
begs they will accept his feeble tribute of thanks for their
meritorious conduct, which is all he can presume to offer, after
the high honour done them by His Sicilian Majesty. Captain
Troubridge may rest assured, that he will not fail to represent
his conduct in the very extraordinary manner it merits; nor
will Lord Nelson be unmindful of the gallant behaviour of
Captain Hallowell, who unites with the firmest bravery the
most able conduct; and Lord Nelson also begs Colonel
Strickland will accept of his thanks for the very great attention paid to the discipline of the Marines. The Artillery have
conducted themselves with their usual judgment, and he will
not fail to represent the whole party in the way they appear to
merit. Captain da Gama, of the troops landed from the
Portuguese Squadron, is entitled to great merit, and Lord
Nelson will mention his good conduct to the Marquis de
Niza; and Lord Nelson has to request that Captain Troubridge will state to Captain Baillie how sensible he is of the
steady and loyal co-operation with him, and that Lord Nelson
will not fail to represent his truly meritorious conduct in the
way it deserves.

Lord Nelson further requests that Colonel Tschudy will
also accept his acknowledgments for the cordial harmony
with which he has united with Captains Troubridge and Hallowell, and that Colonel Tschudy will express to his troops
the very high approbation entertained of their discipline and
bravery. And the extraordinary good conduct of Mr. James
Harriman having been represented to Lord Nelson, (who had
served as a Volunteer on this occasion) he begs that Mr. Harriman will accept of his sincere thanks; and also begs they
may be made acceptable to Monsieur Monfrese for his able
conduct as an Engineer; and Lord Nelson will be happy in

an opportunity of being useful to him. And finally Lord
Nelson begs that the Duke Salandro will accept his cordial
congratulations on this happy event, and his sincere thanks
for the kindness and attention he has invariably shown to the
forces landed from the Fleet.

NELSON.

---

TO THE RIGHT HONOURABLE EARL SPENCER, K.G.

[Letter-Book].

13th July, 1799.

My dear Lord,

I have much to say, but am unable to write or speak half
so much as my duty would make it right, therefore I must
be brief.    On my fortunate arrival here I found a most
infamous treaty entered into with the Rebels, in direct disobedience of His Sicilian Majesty's orders.    I had the happiness of saving His Majesty's honour, rejecting with disdain
any terms but unconditional submission, to Rebels.    Your
Lordship will observe my Note (No. 1), and opinion to the
Cardinal (No. 2).[8]    The Rebels came out of the Castles with
this knowledge, without any honours, and the principal
Rebels were seized and conducted on board the Ships of the
Squadron.    The others, embarked in fourteen polacres, were
anchored under the care of our Ships.    His Majesty has
entirely approved of my conduct in this matter.    I presume
to recommend Captain Troubridge for some mark of his
Majesty's favour : it would be supposing you, my dear Lord,
was ignorant of his merit, was I to say more, than that he is a
first-rate General.    The King holds his Levées on the quarter-
deck of the Foudroyant, at the same hours as he did when in
his palace.    His Majesty's health is perfect, and he is in the
highest spirits and good-humour.

May I offer my kindest respects to Lady Spencer, and
believe me, I am sensible of her goodness.    Lieutenant Parkinson[9] will, I am sure, meet with your kind protection : he is

---

[8] Vide pp. 386, 388, ante.

[9] Lieutenant William Standway Parkinson was sent to England with dispatches,
on the 16th of July, and on his arrival was promoted to the rank of Commander.
He was made a Post-Captain in February, 1808, and died a few years ago.

an Officer of great merit. Lord Keith writes me, if certain events take place, it may be necessary to draw down this Squadron for the protection of Minorca. Should such an order come at this moment, it would be a cause for some consideration whether Minorca is to be risked, or the two Kingdoms of Naples and Sicily? I rather think my decision would be to risk the former. I am told the alteration of the Government is begun in the Capital, by the abolition of the Feudal system, and it is meant to be continued through the Country. Sir John Acton is with his Majesty : I need not say more than he has the wisest and most honest head in this Kingdom. Sir William and Lady Hamilton are, to my great comfort, with me ; for without them it would have been impossible I could have rendered half the service to his Majesty which I have now done : their heads and their hearts are equally great and good. With every sentiment of respect and attachment, believe me, my dear Lord, your obliged and faithful,

NELSON.

---

TO VICE-ADMIRAL LORD KEITH, K.B.

[Original, in the Admiralty, and " London Gazette," of the 17th August, 1799.]

Foudroyant, Naples Bay, July 13th, 1799.

My Lord,

His Sicilian Majesty arrived in this Bay on the 10th, and immediately hoisted his standard on board the Foudroyant, where his Majesty still remains with all his Ministers.[1] It has been and is my study to treat his Majesty with all the respect due to so great a personage, and I have the pleasure to believe that my humble endeavours have met with the Royal approbation. I have the honour to be, your Lordship's obedient servant, NELSON.

The effusions of loyalty from the lower order of the people to their *Father*—for by no other name do they address the King—is truly moving : with some *few* exceptions the conduct of the Nobles has been infamous ; and it delights me to see that His Majesty remarks the difference in the most proper manner.

[1] Neither the following paragraph nor the postscript, is in the London Gazette.

## TO VICE-ADMIRAL LORD KEITH, K.B.

[Original, in the Admiralty.]

My Lord,                          Foudroyant, Naples Bay, 13th July, 1799.

I have to acknowledge the receipt of your Lordship's orders[2] of June 27th, and as soon as the safety of His Sicilian Majesty's Kingdoms is secured, I shall not lose one moment in making the detachment you are pleased to order. At present, under God's Providence, the safety of His Sicilian Majesty, and his speedy restoration to his Kingdom, depends on this Fleet, and the confidence inspired even by the appearance of our Ships before the City is beyond all belief; and I have no scruple in declaring my opinion that should any event draw us from the Kingdom, that if the French remain in any part of it, disturbances will again arise, for all order having been completely overturned, it must take a thorough cleansing, and some little time, to restore tranquillity. I have the honour to be with great respect, your Lordship's obedient servant,

NELSON.

---

## TO EARL SPENCER, K.G.

[Letter-Book.]

My dear Lord,                        Foudroyant, Naples Bay, 13th July, 1799.

You will easily conceive my feelings at the order this day received here [from] Lord Keith; but my mind, your Lordship will know by my letter sent by Lieutenant Parkinson

---

[2] The following are the Orders alluded to; and it would appear, from the letter to Lord Spencer, (p. 407,) that they arrived late in the day on the 13th, after that letter, and his letter to Lord Keith, in the same page, were written:—

"Queen Charlotte, at Sea, 27th June, 1799.

"Events which have recently occurred render it necessary that as great a force as can be collected should be assembled near the Island of Minorca; therefore, if your Lordship has no detachment of the French Squadron in the neighbourhood of Sicily, nor information of their having sent any force towards Egypt or Syria, you are hereby required and directed to send such Ships as you can possibly spare off the Island of Minorca to wait my orders; and I will take care, so soon as the Enemy's intentions shall be frustrated in that quarter, to strengthen your Lordship as soon as possible. KEITH."—Original, in the Nelson Papers.

and Mr. Silvester, was perfectly prepared for this order;[3] and
more than ever is my mind made up, that, at this moment, I
will not part with a single Ship, as I cannot do that without
drawing a hundred and twenty men from each Ship now at
the Siege of Capua, where an Army is gone this day. I am
fully aware of the act I have committed; but, sensible of my
loyal intentions, I am prepared for any fate which may await
my disobedience. Capua and Gaeta will soon fall; and the
moment the scoundrels of French are out of this Kingdom, I
shall send eight or nine Ships of the Line to Minorca. I have
done what I thought right; others may think differently; but
it will be my consolation that I have gained a Kingdom,
seated a faithful Ally of his Majesty firmly on his throne, and
restored happiness to millions. Do not think, my dear Lord,
that my opinion is formed from the arrangements of any one.
*No;* be it good, or be it bad, it is all my own. It is natural I
should wish the decision of the Admiralty and my Commander-
in-Chief as speedily as possible. To obtain the former, I beg
your Lordship's interest with the Board;[4] and, in all events, I
shall consider myself your Lordship's, &c.

NELSON.

[3] Vide p. 407, ante.

[4] On the 20th of August, Mr. Nepean, the Secretary to the Admiralty communi-
cated to Lord Nelson their Lordships' disapproval of his conduct in not having obeyed
Lord Keith's order. After acknowledging his dispatches of the 14th, by Lieutenant
Parkinson, and of the 27th of July, Mr. Nepean said :—

"In answer to those letters, I have their Lordships' commands to acquaint your
Lordship, that they approve of your having proceeded to the Bay of Naples, for the
purpose of endeavouring to bring the affairs of his Sicilian Majesty in that City to
a happy conclusion, and of your having ordered Captains Troubridge and Ball to
land, with a large body of men from the Squadron, to reduce the Castle of St. Elmo,
and I have their Lordships' commands to express their high approbation of the zeal,
ability, and exertions of Captains Troubridge, Ball, and Hallowell, and of the conduct of all the Officers and Men employed under their orders in the reduction of
that Fortress.

"With respect to that part of your Lordship's letter to the Commander-in-Chief, in
which you mention that one thousand of the best men were landed from the
Squadron, to march, under the command of Captains Troubridge and Hallowell,
against Capua, their Lordships have desired me to observe to you, that although in
operations on the sea-coast, it may frequently be highly expedient to land a part of
the Seamen of the Squadron, to co-operate with and to assist the Army, when the
situation will admit of their being immediately re-embarked, if the Squadron should
be called away to act elsewhere, or if information of the approach of an Enemy's Fleet
should be received—yet their Lordships by no means approve of the Seamen being
landed to form a part of an Army to be employed in operations at a distance from the

## TO HIS ROYAL HIGHNESS THE DUKE OF CLARENCE.[5]

[From Clarke and M'Arthur, vol. ii. p. 197.]

[About 13th July, 1799.]

You will have heard, Sir, and conversation will naturally
arise upon it, that I have disobeyed Lord Keith's orders in not
sending or going down with the Squadron under my command; but, by not doing it, I have been, with God's blessing,
the principal means of placing a good Man and faithful Ally

coast, where, if they should have the misfortune to be defeated, they might be prevented from returning to the Ships, and the Squadron be thereby rendered so de-
fective, as to be no longer capable of performing the services required of it; and I
have their Lordships' commands to signify their directions to your Lordship not to
employ the Seamen in like manner in future.

"I have also to acknowledge the receipt of your Lordship's letter of the 19th July,
delivered to me on the          instant, by the Marquis di Circello, inclosing the
copy of an order you had received from Vice-Admiral Lord Keith, directing you to
proceed with the whole, or to detach a part of the Squadron under your command
to Minorca, and also the copy of your letter to his Lordship in answer thereto, and
I have their Lordships' commands to acquaint you, that although the co-operation
of a British Naval Force with the Army of his Sicilian Majesty might be, and it
appears to have been necessary, yet, as from the information your Lordship had
received from Lord Keith, you must have been satisfied that nothing was to be
apprehended from the Enemy's Fleet, it does not appear to their Lordships to
have been necessary that the whole of the Squadron under your command should
have been kept for such co-operation, but that a part of it would have been sufficient, not only to have inspired that confidence, which your Lordship states to have
been the result of its appearance, but also to have afforded effectual assistance to his
Sicilian Majesty; and that their Lordships do not, therefore, from any information
now before them, see sufficient reason to justify your having disobeyed the orders
you had received from your Commanding-Officer, or having left Minorca exposed to
the risk of being attacked, without having any Naval force to protect it.

"I have their Lordships' further commands to acquaint you, that they have been
pleased to promote Lieutenant Parkinson to the rank of Commander; and I have the
honour to be, &c.—EVAN NEPEAN."—*Original*, in the Nelson Papers.

    5 The following letter from the Duke of Clarence is in the Nelson Papers:
    "Dear Nelson,                    "Bushy House, April 9th, 1799.
"I am to acknowledge yours of 2nd February, from Palermo, which arrived a
few days ago, and can easily conceive your time must be fully occupied. I feel
exceedingly for the King and Queen, and shall wait with anxiety the event of the
Parliament in Sicily. The events on the Continent must be sooner known to you
than to us here. By this time, therefore, you will be able to form an opinion relative to the Kingdom of Naples. I hope, however, victory will side with the
Austrians, both in Italy and Germany. Your next letters will, I trust, convey the
success of your gallant friend Troubridge.

"I shall wait with impatience till I hear from you again: in the meantime
adieu, and ever believe me yours most sincerely,

"WILLIAM."

of your Royal Father on his throne, and securing peace to these two Kingdoms. I am well aware of the consequences of disobeying my orders; but, as I have often before risked my life for the good Cause, so I with cheerfulness did my commission: for although a Military tribunal may think me criminal, the world will approve of my conduct. I regard not my own safety, when the honour of my gracious King is at stake. The Almighty has in this war blessed my endeavours beyond my most sanguine expectations, and never more than in the entire expulsion of the French thieves from the Kingdom of Naples. I am, &c.,

NELSON.

TO VICE-ADMIRAL LORD KEITH, K.B.

[Original, in the Admiralty.]

July 14th, 1799.

My dear Lord,

I am truly so very unwell that I have not the power of writing so much of our situation here as I could wish, but thank God all goes on well, and I hope this country will be happier than ever; I am sure it is their Majesties' desire to make it so. The feudal system is fast breaking up, the entire change is already made in the Capital. To all your wishes, depend on it, I shall pay the very strictest attention. Hope and a large part of this Squadron shall go to you when they can be spared, but at present the safety of this Kingdom depends on us. Captain Foote, says Mr. Moncton, is not intended to remain at sea, therefore does not recommend his promotion at present; he has very bad health, but a modest well-behaved young man. Ever, my dear Lord, believe me, your obliged,

NELSON.

TO LADY NELSON.

[From Clarke and M'Arthur, vol. ii. p. 192.]

Naples, 14th July, 1799.

My dear Fanny,

I have to thank you sincerely for your letters. I rejoice that you gave Mr. Bolton the money, and I wish it made up

£500. I never regarded money, nor wanted it for my own use; therefore, as the East India Company have made me so magnificent a present, I beg that £2000 of it may be disposed of in the following manner;—five hundred pounds to my father; five hundred to be made up to Mr. Bolton, and let it be a *God-send*, without any restriction; five hundred to Maurice, and five hundred to William. And if you think my sister Matcham would be gratified by it, do the same for her. If I were rich I would do more; but it will very soon be known how poor I am, except my yearly income. I am not surprised at my brother's death;[6] three are now dead, younger than myself, having grown to man's age. My situation here is not to be described, but suffice it to say, I am endeavouring to work for good. To my father say everything which is kind. I love, honour, and respect him as a father and as a man, and as the very best man I ever saw. May God Almighty bless you, my dear father, and all my brothers and sisters, is the fervent prayer of your affectionate

NELSON.

TO EVAN NEPEAN, ESQ., SECRETARY TO THE ADMIRALTY.

[Original, in the Admiralty.]

Foudroyant, Bay of Naples, July 14th, 1799.

Sir,

Herewith I have the honour of sending you copies of my letters to the Commander-in-Chief, and the Capitulation granted to the French in St. Elmo. All the chief Rebels are now on board His Majesty's fleet; Capua and Gaeta will very soon be in our possession, when the Kingdom will be liberated from anarchy and misery.[7] I beg leave to recommend Lieutenant Parkinson to their Lordships' notice. He goes home by His Sicilian Majesty's desire, to mark his approbation of my conduct. I trust their Lordships will excuse the brevity of this letter when I have so much to communicate, but I am writing in a fever, and barely possible to keep out of bed: but

---

[6] The Reverend Suckling Nelson: he died in April, 1799.

[7] This paragraph only was published in the "London Gazette," of the 17th of August, 1799.

to the last, I beg you will assure the Board that every exertion shall be used for the honour of my King and Country; and believe me, with real respect, Sir, &c.

NELSON.

---

### TO LIEUTENANT-GOVERNOR LOCKER, ROYAL HOSPITAL, GREENWICH.

[Autograph in the Locker Papers. This is the last Letter in that collection.]

Naples, July 15th, 1799.

My dear Friend,

Although I am so ill that I can scarcely sit up, yet I will not let the courier go off without assuring you that all your kindnesses to me are fresh in my memory. I remember all my friends. I forgive from my heart my envious enemies. May God Almighty grant you, my revered friend, that health and happiness which has never yet been attained by your affectionate grateful friend,

NELSON.

My friend Troubridge is a General Officer.

---

### TO COMMODORE TROUBRIDGE, COMMANDER OF ALL THE FORCES LANDED FROM THE SQUADRON UNDER MY COMMAND.

[Letter-Book.]

17th July, 1799.

My dear Troubridge,

When you send in a Summons to the Commander of the French troops in Capua, His Sicilian Majesty approves that, on condition the Commander immediately gives up *Capua* and *Gaeta*, that after laying down their arms, colours, &c., the French garrison shall be permitted to go to France without any restrictions. If this is not complied with, prisoners of war, and as degrading terms as it is in your power to give them—no covered wagons, no protection to Rebels—in short, the Allies must dictate the terms. You will as often as possible, but at least once a day, make some person send me a Journal of your proceedings. His Majesty places the firmest

reliance on you, and is confident of your exertions in the
glorious Cause. That rapid success may crown your labours,
and that you may receive those honours so justly your due,
is the fervent prayer of your affectionate and faithful Friend,

NELSON.

There is a person who has been a NOTORIOUS *Rebel,* but now
PRETENDS to serve his King faithfully; if he should attempt to
come even into your presence, I earnestly request you will
never voluntarily admit him to your sight, much less speak to
him; for [the] honour and loyalty which you possess, never
ought to be contaminated with infamy and rebellion. His
name is said to be *Rocca Romana.*

NELSON.

---

### TO VICE-ADMIRAL LORD KEITH, K.B.

[Original, in the Admiralty.]

Foudroyant, Naples, July 19th, 1799.

My Lord,

I am this moment honoured with your order of the 9th,
directing me to detach from the Island of Sicily, the whole,
or such part of the force, as might not be necessary in that
Island.[8] Your Lordship, at the time of sending me the order,

[8] The following is a copy of Lord Keith's Order:—

"Queen Charlotte, Port Mahon, 9th July, 1799.

"Having reason to believe, from the repeated information I have received, (the
latest of which is herewith enclosed), that the Enemy have no intention of attempting an impression on the Island of Sicily, or of re-inforcing their army in Egypt
and Syria, but, on the contrary, being inclined to think that their efforts are likely
to be directed against Ireland, and that they are bent towards the ocean, I judge it
necessary that all, or the greatest part of the force under your Lordship's orders,
should quit the Island of Sicily, and repair to Minorca, for the purpose of protecting that Island during the necessary absence of His Majesty's Squadron under
my command, or for the purpose of co-operating with me against the combined
force of the Enemy, wherever it may be requisite. Your Lordship is therefore
hereby required and directed to quit the Island of Sicily with the whole of your
force, or to detach the next Senior Officer for the time being, with the greatest part
thereof, should you deem it absolutely necessary, for the good of His Majesty's
service, and the interest of his Allies, that some part of it should continue there,
under your Lordship's or any other Officer's direction. Your Lordship, with the whole
force, or such part of it as you may bring with you, or such Senior Officer, with
that part to be detached under his direction, in the event of your Lordship's judg-

was not informed of the change of affairs in the Kingdom of Naples, and that all our Marines and a body of Seamen are landed, in order to drive the French scoundrels out of the Kingdom, which, with God's blessing will very soon be effected, when a part of this Squadron shall be immediately sent to Minorca; but unless the French are at least drove from Capua, I think it right not to obey your Lordship's order for sending down any part of the Squadron under my orders. I am perfectly aware of the consequences of disobeying the orders of my Commander-in-Chief; but, as I believe the safety of the Kingdom of Naples depends at the present moment on my detaining the Squadron, I have no scruple in deciding that it is better to save the Kingdom of Naples and risk Minorca, than to risk the Kingdom of Naples to save Minorca. Your Lordship will, I hope, approve of my decision, and believe me, with the greatest respect,

Your Lordship's faithful and obedient servant,

NELSON.

---

TO VICE-ADMIRAL LORD KEITH, K.B.

[Autograph, in the Admiralty.]

Naples, July 19th, 1799.

My dear Lord,
I grieve most exceedingly that you had not the good fortune to fall in with the French fleet before they formed their junc-

ing it absolutely necessary to leave some part of it at Sicily, as above mentioned,—is to proceed to join me at this place, and in case of my absence, to follow the orders and directions which will be left in charge of the Commanding-Officer of His Majesty's Ships and Vessels at this Port, for your Lordship's, or such Senior Officer's, future guidance.—KEITH."

This Order was accompanied by the following private letter:—

"Dear Nelson,　　　　　"Queen Charlotte, Mahon, July 9th, 1799.

"I came in here yesterday to get some water, and had not anchored an hour, when I heard the Combined Fleets had left Carthagena, and steered to the West. I am now unmooring, with very little water in the Ships; for this Island does not afford much more than we drink. If this Island is left without Ships, it will fall. The Spaniards will send their Armament, with two Ships of the Line, Frigates, and Gun-Boats— a great many of which are at the different Ports opposite, to convoy and cover the landing. You must, therefore, either come, or send Duckworth, to govern himself as circumstances offer, until I can determine to a certainty the intentions of the Enemy. With every good wish, I am ever sincerely, &c. KEITH."
—Autograph, in the Nelson Papers.

tion with the Dons, although I am sure, when you are united
with the Channel Fleet, that you will send them to the Devil.
My answer to your order is of such a nature that I deem it
improper in a private letter to give a reason, therefore I decline
touching on the subject.   My health is but indifferent.   Our
dear Sir William and Lady Hamilton are in good health.   His
Majesty is in the highest health and spirits.   We have a
courier from England of June 12th, but I have not the scrap
of a pen from thence.   That every success may attend you, is
the earnest wish of your obliged and faithful servant,

NELSON.

The Purser of the Stromboli is invalided, and will soon be
out of the world: therefore a Purser is wanted for her.   Our
troops reached Caserta this evening, and will be before Capua
to-morrow or next day.

---

TO EVAN NEPEAN, ESQ., ADMIRALTY.

[Autograph, in the Admiralty.]

Foudroyant, Naples, July 19th, 1799.

Sir,
I send you copy of Lord Keith's Order to me, (No. 1,)
my answer, (No. 2,) and a copy of a letter I have received
since my determination was made (not at this moment to
send a single man from this Squadron.)   I feel the importance of the decision I have taken, and know I subject myself
to a trial for my conduct: but I am so confident of the
uprightness of my intentions for his Majesty's service, and for
that of his Sicilian Majesty, which I consider as the same,
that, with all respect, I submit myself to the judgment of my
superiors.   I have the honour to be, &c.

NELSON.

---

TO CAPTAIN SIR WILLIAM SIDNEY SMITH.

[Letter-Book.]

Foudroyant, Naples Bay, July 20th, 1799.

Dear Sir,
Your letters, sent by the Mary Ann, I read with a mixture
of pleasure and sorrow.   I earnestly trust that your exertions

will be crowned with success, and that Buonaparte is gone to
the Devil. As Lord Keith writes to you, I shall not say
much of what is passing to the West, except that the French
Fleet, united to the Spanish (43 Sail of the Line) sailed from
Carthagena on the 29th of June, and Lord Keith was in
Mahon on the 9th of July. My belief is, that the whole
force will push into the Tagus, and carry Lisbon, and of
course Portugal, by a *coup*. Others think Ireland will be
their object; time, and a short time, must discover their
plans to us. In the meantime, we can only sincerely lament
that the scoundrels have escaped the vigilance of Lord Keith.
Minorca is menaced; but I think will not be attacked. Our
news from France is excellent; four of the Directory are
arrested; Abbé Sieyes is the only remaining one. The Councils have decreed the Constitution suspended; Bernadotte
resigned the commissions of more than 500 principal Officers:
in short, (in my opinion,) Monarchy is on the eve of being
established again. In Italy, all goes on well; I hope, in fourteen days, there will not be a Frenchman in the Kingdom.
Tuscany will, I believe, from Mr. Wyndham's letters, be
liberated in as short a time.

July 24th. Yesterday brought us letters from your worthy
brother; and we had the great pleasure of hearing that your
truly meritorious and wonderful exertions were in a fair train for
the extirpation of that horde of thieves who went to Egypt
with that arch-thief, Buonaparte. I beg you will express to
good Captain Miller,[8] and to all the brave Officers and men who
have fought so nobly under your orders, the sense I entertain
of your and their great merit. I am sorry at present it is
not in my power to send you even a Sloop of War; for Lord
Keith has ordered every Ship, not absolutely necessary for
Sicily, to repair to Minorca, which is menaced with an attack.
I think Lord Keith will follow to the Channel; if so, and
when I see what is left me, (for at present everything from
Sicily to Gibraltar has passed the Straits,) I shall have pleasure in giving you a small but active Squadron; for, while
the French remain in any part of Egypt, I see Great Britain
must do everything. Could it have been thought that the

---

[8] Captain Miller was unfortunately killed on the 14th of May.

Turks would never have sent reinforcements to save Egypt?
As for the Russians, they have, I am sure, an object in view.
Lord Keith writes me to send you stores; there is not, and
his Lordship knows it, a bit of canvas, twine, board, nails,
or rope in all the store-rooms in the Squadron. The Siege
of Capua is begun; and I am sure my friends Troubridge
and Hallowell will finish it as soon as possible. The garrison is 1500 French, and a few hundred rebels. I have had
letters from Lord William Bentinck,[9] who is with the Austrian
and Russian Army, detailing their successes. Turin is in
their hands, Florence, &c.: in short, all goes on as well as
heart can wish. Ever believe me, with the greatest esteem,
your faithful, humble servant,

NELSON.

---

## TO REAR-ADMIRAL DUCKWORTH.

[Order-Book.[1]]

Foudroyant, 22nd July, 1799.

You are hereby required and directed to take under your
command the Ships named in the margin,[2] whose Captains have
my directions to follow your orders, and proceed with them to
Mahon, in the Island of Minorca, and on your arrival there

---

[9] Afterwards a General and a Knight Grand Cross of the Bath: he died in June,
1839. In a letter from Lord William Bentinck to Nelson, dated Alexandria, 29th
June, 1799, he said: "Field-Marshal Suwarrow desired I would carry him my
letter to your Lordship, to which he has added, what I can assure you are the real
feelings of his heart:—'My lord Nelson, Baron du Nil, tachéz de devenir Duc de
la rivière Levante Ponente, et de Geres avec Malte. Je vous embrasse tendrement
Excellence, Grand Nelson! Votre ami, frere, et adorateur, COMT. ALEXANDRE
SUWARROW-RYMNIKSKI.'"

[1] On the 22nd of July, the Thetis Lugger arrived from Naples with the following
dispatches from Lord Keith, which caused Lord Nelson to issue the above order to
Rear Admiral Duckworth :

"Queen Charlotte, off Formentera, 14th July, 1799.

"Your Lordship is hereby required and directed to repair to Minorca, with the
whole, or the greater part, of the Force under your Lordship's command, for the
protection of that Island, as I shall, in all probability, have left the Mediterranean
before your Lordship will receive this.

"KEITH."

---

[2] Powerful, Majestic, Vanguard, Swallow Corvette.

to take also under your orders such of his Majesty's Ships as
you may find in that Port, leaving it entirely to your well-
known abilities and judgment to act with them in the best
manner for the protection of that Island and the good of His
Majesty's service.

NELSON.

To which is added, in Lord Keith's own hand:—
"The French Fleet are off Cape Tres Forcas. The wind is East. Yours,
"KEITH."

"Queen Charlotte, off Palma, 14th July, 1799.
"My Lord,

"Having proceeded thus far without seeing anything of the Enemy, or meeting
with any of my Frigates sent out for the purpose of getting intelligence, I find myself obliged to proceed off Carthagena, and even to Ireland, if they should return
towards Brest, as there are so few Ships in England. I therefore trust the defence
of Minorca to your Lordship, and repeat my directions that the Ships be sent for its
protection. I have the honour to be, &c.,
"KEITH."

By the same conveyance, or by the Gun-boat which arrived at Naples on the 23rd
of July, Lord Nelson received the following private letter, dated two days before
the preceding:—
"Off Minorca, 12th July, [1799].
"My dear Lord,

"I have the honour to congratulate your Lordship on the happy turn of the
affairs in Naples, and I trust they will be general and permanent. Any Ship here
will be at your orders if her magnitude will suit the service you are on, and any arrangement you can incline for Troubridge will be most agreeable to me. I thank
you for your attention to Mr. Monckton, and am sorry he is ill. It is very hard I cannot find these vagabonds in some spot or other, and that I am so shackled with this
defenceless Island. Now we have a positive Port in Italy, I shall feel more at ease,
and perhaps a few British regiments may soon appear in that country. I give you
many thanks for your kind expressions towards me, and I have much comfort in
reflecting I have one of such a description so near me. Parker you know goes, as I
can part with the Prince George: she is in bad condition. I have no letter from
Hamilton: tell him how much I respect him, and advise those Neapolitans not to
be too sanguinary. Cowards are always cruel, and apostates the most violent against
their former friends, and too often the least sincere. Give them fair words and little
confidence. I keep this open, in hopes of telling your Lordship something of the
French. On the 17th, off Cape de Gatte, I heard they were gone through the
Straits. On the 19th, I heard they were in Cadiz Bay. The truth I cannot yet
tell, but that I am much, yours, &c.,
"KEITH."

## TO CHARLES LOCK, ESQ., CONSUL-GENERAL, NAPLES.

[Autograph in the Nelson Papers.—An explanation of this Note is afforded by Lord Nelson himself:—"Mr. Lock, having for several days been soliciting me for the exclusive privilege of supplying the Squadron with fresh beef, upon a due consideration I wrote the following Note, and left it with my Secretary. Mr. Lock came to me and said that he could point out to me that Government had been grossly imposed upon in the purchase of fresh beef—that he knew, or had seen, one account, which was only £700, but which bills had been drawn upon Government was £850. The exact sums may not be correct, but I am sure that £150 was the difference mentioned by the Consul. On my saying that if it was so I was obliged to him for the information, but that I doubted it, as all vouchers, before they were brought to the Captains for signature, were testified as to the price by two respectable merchants—his answer was, that the signature of merchants was nothing, they could be got to sign anything. I then asked Mr. Lock who this notorious fraud had been committed by, which he refused to tell me; on which I called Captain Hardy, and told him as he, with all the Captains and Pursers of the Fleet, were accused by Mr. Lock of being thieves, I should leave him to settle the business, and that I should give out an Order for inquiry in the morning. This Order Mr. Lock begged me not to give out, and, through Sir William Hamilton, saying it was only a private communication. My answer to this application was, that the Consul having on His Majesty's quarter-deck, under my Flag, made such an accusation, nothing could be more public; and that if I attempted to conceal it, the next thing he would do would be to accuse me of being the cheat—therefore, nothing should prevent my giving out a Public Order. Mr. Lock's next request was, that I would not mention his name, which I complied with; but, as the conversation was heard by hundreds, it could not be kept a secret. The manner and language of Mr. Lock was highly insulting to my rank and situation, under my Flag,. and in the presence of His Sicilian Majesty, his Court, and His Majesty's Representative. I desire that Captain Hardy may be called upon for his account of this very extraordinary conduct of the Consul."—*Autograph*, in the Nelson Papers.]

Foudroyant, Naples Bay, 23rd July, 1799.

In my situation I never have or ever will interfere in the victualling His Majesty's Ships under my command. Each Captain is at liberty to purchase the provisions and wine, when it can be had of the best quality, and at the cheapest rate.

NELSON.

---

## MEMORANDUM TO THE RESPECTIVE CAPTAINS.

[Autograph draught, in the Nelson Papers.]

Naples Bay, July 24th, 1799.

Whereas I have received information that most gross abuses have been practised in the purchase of fresh beef for the use of the Squadron under my command, to the great detriment of Government, it is my positive direction that in future the Vouchers are strictly examined, and the prices of every article purchased be properly ascertained by the signing Officers, and attested by two respectable merchants on shore before the Vouchers are signed.[3]

NELSON.

---

### TO CAPTAIN HOSTE, H. M. SLOOP MUTINE.

[Order-Book.]

Foudroyant, Naples Bay, 24th July, 1799.

You are hereby required and directed to proceed in the Sloop you command, to Cagliari, in the Island of Sardinia, and deliver my letter you will receive herewith, to His Sardinian Majesty, making inquiry of his Minister whether it is His Majesty's intention to send his Royal Brothers to the Continent by you. If it is his intention to send them, you will wait three days for them, but not more, and give them a passage to St. Stefano, or Orbitello, which are the only places at present you can land them on the Coast; and in case of your landing them at St. Stefano, you will inquire of Signor Luigi Corci, at that place, for any letters he may have for me from the Honourable William Wyndham, and return and join me immediately at this place. But should His Sardinian Majesty not think it proper to send over his Brothers to the Continent by you, you will immediately proceed without loss of time and join Rear-Admiral Duckworth at Mahon, following his orders for your further proceedings.

NELSON.

---

[3] In consequence of this Order, Captains Martin of the Northumberland, Hood of the Zealous, Darby of the Bellerophon, Foley of the Goliath, and Hardy of the Foudroyant, wrote to Lord Nelson a few days afterwards, stating that the fresh beef and wine supplied to their Ships had been of the best quality, and, as they believed, had been purchased at the market prices. The Pursers of the Squadron, whose characters were implicated in Mr. Lock's charges, wrote him a very indignant letter on the occasion. Further correspondence took place on the subject towards the end of the year, and produced one of the most remarkable letters Lord Nelson ever wrote. *Vide* the next Volume.

TO HIS EXCELLENCY JOHN SPENCER SMITH, ESQ.

[Letter-Book.]

My dear Sir,                    Naples, July 25th, 1799.

I thank you truly for your letter of June 9th, containing an extract of one from your brother, who has done so much at Acre. It is like his former conduct; and I can assure you, no one admires his gallantry and judgment more than myself. But if I know myself, as I never have encroached on the command of others, so I will not suffer even my friend Sir Sidney to encroach upon mine. I dare say he thought he was to have a separate command in the Levant. I find upon inquiry it never was intended to have any one in the Levant separate from me. Your goodness, my dear Sir, in procuring the shawls, I feel most sensibly, and if I can be useful to you in any manner here, I beg you will command me ; being with real respect, &c.,

NELSON.

TO HIS EXCELLENCY THE GRAND VIZIR.

[Letter-Book.]

Sir,                    Foudroyant, Naples, July 25th, 1799.

Yesterday I received, through the hands of His Majesty's Minister, the approbation of the Sublime Porte for my conduct at Tripoli and Tunis. I beg leave to assure your Excellency, that I have no object in view, but to fulfil the orders of the great King, my master, which is, to prove himself a most faithful Ally, and that I am a most faithful Servant.

With every sentiment of respect, believe me your Excellency's obedient and obliged servant,

NELSON.

TO SPIRIDION FORESTI, ESQ, BRITISH CONSUL, ZANTE.

[Letter-Book.]

Dear Sir,                    Foudroyant, Naples, July 25th, 1799.

I have to thank you most sincerely for your several letters from May 9th to July 3rd ; and I can only assure you, that both His Excellency Sir William Hamilton and myself are so much pleased with your conduct, that we have wrote a joint letter to Lord Grenville in your favour.[4]

I have to beg that you will, if yours is considered as the proper channel of communicating the information to me, express to the Inhabitants of Zante, how much I feel flattered by their goodness in remembering me.[5] I must believe with them, that the Battle of the Nile enabled the Russian and Turkish Squadron to come to the Islands, and to drive the French out of them. And ever believe me, dear Sir, your obliged and faithful servant,

NELSON.

---

### TO HIS EXCELLENCY JOHN SPENCER SMITH, ESQ.

[Autograph, in the possession of Dawson Turner, Esq., F.R.S.]

Sir,　　　　　　　　　　　Foudroyant, Naples, July 25th, 1799.

I am honoured with your Excellency's letter of June 9th, by way of Zante, and observe what you are pleased to say relative to the various councils held on the situation of affairs. I cannot do otherwise than think it extraordinary that the Ministers of the Sublime Porte do not enforce that a proper force be sent to Egypt; although I hope from subsequent information that the French have raised the Siege of Acre, chiefly owing to the gallantry of English Sea and Artillery Officers, commanded by Captain Sir William Sidney Smith, who I have wrote to this day, to express the satisfaction I truly feel for his meritorious conduct. Lord Keith having directed me to send all the force possible from the Island of Sicily, it is not in my power to reinforce Sir Sidney Smith. Lord Keith naturally thinks with me, that, as there is no maritime force fit to oppose Sir Sidney Smith, that two Sail of the Line would not be necessary, for who could have thought that the Ship's

---

[4] This representation, if previously made, was renewed on the 16th of the following month, when Sir William Hamilton wrote to Lord Grenville, pointing out Mr. Foresti's "indefatigable zeal during the war," and the losses he had incurred "when the French took possession of Zante, and sent him a prisoner to Corfu;" and in his own name, as well as in that of Lord Nelson, Sir William recommended him to Lord Grenville's "kind protection and notice." To this letter, Nelson added, in his own hand, this paragraph: "I cannot say enough in praise of Mr. Foresti. NELSON."—Original, in the State Paper Office.

[5] The inhabitants of Zante presented him with a Sword and Cane, in October following. Vide postea.

company of two seventy-fours could have been wanted on shore? It has turned out fortunate; but when this service is over, I shall expect the Theseus to join me. It will be my business to take care that no French fleet pass into the Levant; and I beg you will assure the Porte, that, if they do, I shall follow them. I do not recollect how I may have sent letters to the Grand Vizir, but I suppose it must have been through the same channel which conveyed the letter to me. I know the character of representative of Majesty too well to omit paying it all proper respect. The Porte not having sent me one Corvette, has prevented my sending your Excellency as frequent communication as I could wish, of all the extraordinary events which are passing here. The letter from Lord William Bentinck will show you the state of the Austrian and Russian Army, as Mr. Wyndham's will that of Tuscany. I am sending a post, taken in Egypt, to Constantinople, if he cannot conveniently be landed short of that place [*illegible.*] I beg of your Excellency [to believe] my desire of fulfilling the order of the Great King, our Master, and believe me, with real respect, your faithful, humble servant,

NELSON.

---

TO CAPTAIN BALL, H. M. SHIP ALEXANDER.

[Letter-Book.]

My dear Ball,                              Naples, July 27th, 1799.

I have the pleasure to tell you, that all Tuscany is liberated;[5] and that Field Marshal Suwarrow was expected to enter Genoa on the 20th. Macdonald has set off by sea; and I wish any of our Cruizers may pick him up. Troubridge is before Capua, which, from its distance from us, is a very tedious job. I hope our Maltese affairs are drawing to a close, and that your labours, my dear friend, may have an end. As to myself, I have been long sick and tired out. Captain Ricketts[6] will, of course,

---

[5] " June 27th. Saluted with seventeen guns, on account of the capture of Leghorn. Sunday, 28th. At 4, P.M. a courier arrived from Captain Troubridge at Capua, with news of the capture of that place. Captain Oswald arrived with the French and Republican colours from Capua. Saluted his Majesty with nineteen guns on the occasion."—*Journal.*

[6] Captain William Ricketts, of El Corso: he was made a Post-Captain in 1802, and died a retired Rear-Admiral in May 1840.

tell you of the escape of the French fleet. They passed the Straits on the 8th or 9th. I have a letter from Lord Keith, relative to Lieutenant Soane's leaving the Bonne Citoyenne. With every good wish, believe me, dear Ball, your most obliged and affectionate friend,

NELSON.

You will send either El Corso, or Transfer to Mahon, as you choose, with Lord William Stuart.

---

### TO CAPTAIN LOUIS, H. M. SHIP MINOTAUR.

[Order-Book.]

Foudroyant, Naples Bay, 30th July, 1799.

You are hereby required and directed to receive on board the Ship you command, such Marines as may be sent to you from the different Ships of the Squadron, and proceed with them to Gaeta; and, on your arrival there, to send to the French Governor of that Fortress the terms of Capitulation entered into between me and the Commandant of Capua for the surrender of Gaeta; which Articles are enclosed herewith, and with which you will comply on your part, and you will embark the French garrison therein on board Polacres, which will be immediately sent you to put them on board; but should the Polacres not arrive in time, you will embark them on board such craft as you may be able to procure there, to convey them round to this place, in order for their embarkation for Toulon.

NELSON.

---

### TO EVAN NEPEAN, ESQ., ADMIRALTY.

[From the " London Gazette Extraordinary," of the 3rd of September, 1799.]

Sir,                    Foudroyant, Naples Bay, 1st August,[7] 1799.

I have the honour to transmit you copies of my letter to the Commander-in-Chief, with its several inclosures, and most sincerely congratulate their Lordships on the entire

---

[7] August 1st. At 1, P.M. saluted with twenty-one guns each, in commemoration of the glorious battle of the Nile."—*Journal.* On that day the Royal Family sent Lord Nelson a very gracious letter, styling him, " Defenseur des Deux Siciles," in which

liberation of the Kingdom of Naples from the French robbers; for by no other name can they be called for their conduct in this Kingdom. This happy event will not, I am sure, be the less acceptable from being principally brought about by part of the crews of His Majesty's Ships under my orders, under the command of Captain Troubridge. His merits speak for themselves. His own modesty makes it my duty to state, that to him alone is the chief merit due. The commendation bestowed on the brave and excellent Captain Hallowell will not escape their Lordships' notice, any more than the exceeding good conduct of Captain Oswald, Colonel Strickland and Captain Cresswell, to whom I ordered the temporary rank of Major, and all the Officers and men of the Marine Corps—also, the party of Artillery and the Officers and men landed from the Portuguese Squadron.

I must not omit to state that Captain Hood, with a garrison of seamen in Castle Nuovo, has for these five weeks very much contributed to the peace of the Capital; and Naples, I am told, was never more quiet than under his directions. I send Captain Oswald,[8] of the Perseus Bomb, with this letter, and I have put Lieutenant[9] Henry Compton (who has served with me ever since January 1796, as a Lieutenant) into the Perseus; and I beg leave to recommend these two Officers as highly meriting promotion. I have the honour to be, &c.,

NELSON.

they said, " Receive, most gallant and deserving Admiral, on this for ever memorable day, when by your glorious battle you saved Italy, the sincerest thanks of a grateful Family, attached to you beyond all expression. We shall enjoy this immortal day in the midst of our Family, and shall offer up vows for your prosperity and happiness. Remember us to your brave Officers, who by following your example have contributed to your fame ; and remain assured, that all the infinite obligations we are under towards you in the course of the present year, will never be erased from our remembrance."—*Clarke and M'Arthur.*

[8] Captain James Oswald, third son of George Oswald, Esq. of Scotstoun and Anchintruive, was made a Post Captain on the 3rd of September, 1799, and died in 1822.—*Burke's Commoners.*

[9] Lieutenant Henry Compton was promoted to the rank of Commander on the 3rd of September, 1799, and is now a retired Post Captain, which rank he obtained by seniority in 1840.

TO THE RIGHT HONOURABLE EARL SPENCER, K.G.

[Letter-Book.]

Naples, August 1st, 1799.

My dear Lord,

I certainly, from only having a left hand, cannot enter into details which may explain the motives which actuate my conduct, and which may be necessary for a Commanding officer, who may wish to have every subject of duty detailed by those under his command. My principle, my dear Lord, is, to assist in driving the French to the Devil, and in restoring peace and happiness to mankind. I feel I am fitter to do the action than to describe it; therefore, briefly, all the French being forced to quit this Kingdom, and some order restored, two more Ships of the Line are to sail this evening for Minorca, which I will take care of. 500 Marines, united with 600 excellent Swiss, are going to attack Città Vecchia, and to encourage the insurrection in the Roman State. The sea part of this business will be commanded by Captain Louis of the Minotaur, and the land part under Captain Hallowell of the Swiftsure, assisted by an excellent Officer, Captain Cresswell of the Marines, to whom it has been necessary for me to give the temporary rank of Major, which I wish the Board would confirm. I trust to your Lordship's goodness to promote Lieutenant Compton, who has been long with me.

The Northumberland, Captain Martin, with some Frigates, if they can be found—but I am stripped to the skin—goes on the Coast of Genoa, to co-operate with Field Marshal Suwarrow. The importance of an active Squadron on that Coast no one is better acquainted with than myself. I wish to send the Portuguese Squadron to Lord Keith, as his Lordship seems to consider them as [of] some consequence. I cordially congratulate you on the happy arrival of the combined Fleets at Cadiz; for having escaped the vigilance of Lord Keith, I was fearful they would get to Brest. His Sicilian Majesty having settled a certain degree of order, returns to Palermo on the 7th.

I send you a letter of Sir John Acton to me, which gives reasons for the continuing the Cardinal at the head of affairs in this Country.   My opinion of him has never altered, but, as he is now, only Lieutenant-General of the Kingdom, with a Council of eight, without whose consent no act is valid—but we know the head of every Board must have great weight— this man must soon be removed ; for all about him have been and are so corrupt, that there is nothing which may not be bought.   Acton and Belmonte seem to me the only un-corrupted men in the Kingdom.   Lord Keith has told me of Russian and Turkish fleets taking care of the Coast of Italy. I hear [of] them, but not even a Corvette have I yet seen.   I have only to say that with your every indulgence give me credit for my inclination to do what is right, and believe me, your faithful and obliged,

Nelson.

August 4th.

---

### TO VICE-ADMIRAL LORD KEITH, K.B.

[From the " London Gazette Extraordinary," of September the 3rd, 1799, and Letter-Book.]

Foudroyant, Bay of Naples, 1st August, 1799.

My Lord,

I have the honour to transmit you a copy of Captain Troubridge's letter to me,[9] and the capitulation of Capua and

---

[9] Captain Troubridge's letter was published in the "London Gazette" of the 3rd September, 1799.   As Lord Nelson signed the Articles for the capitulation of Gaeta, a copy of them is annexed :—

### " ARTICLES FOR THE SURRENDER OF THE TOWN OF GAETA.

"Art. I.—Considering that the Garrison of Gaeta has not been regularly besieged, but only blockaded, his Majesty the King of the Two Sicilies will allow the Troops of the said Garrison to march out of the place with the Honours of War, taking with them their firelocks, bayonets, swords, and cartouche-boxes, without deeming them Prisoners of War on their being sent to France.

"Art. II.—In virtue of the preceding Article, the place shall be delivered up free of all pillage, and without any part of the effects being removed or injured, to the Officer who shall be appointed to take possession thereof.

"Art. III.—The French Garrison shall be allowed to remove all their effects, being personal or private property; but all public property shall be given up with the place.

"Art. IV.—No Subject of his Sicilian Majesty shall be sent to France with the French Garrison, but the whole, without exception, given up to the Officer appointed to take possession of the place.

"Art. V.—The Sick belonging to the Garrison shall be taken care of by their own Surgeons at the expense of the French Republic, and shall be sent to France as soon after their cure as possible.

" Art. VI.—A detachment of his Sicilian Majesty's Troops, or of his Allies, shall

Gaeta, &c. Too much praise cannot be given to Captain
Troubridge, for his wonderful exertion in bringing about
these happy events, and in so short a space of time. Captain
Hallowell has also the greatest merit. Captain Oswald, whom
I send to England with a copy of my letter, is an Officer most
highly deserving promotion. I have put Lieutenant Henry
Compton, who has served as a Lieutenant with me from
January 1796, into the Perseus bomb in his room, and whom
I recommend to your Lordship.

I sincerely congratulate your Lordship on the entire liberation of the Kingdom of Naples from a band of robbers,
and am, with the greatest respect, my Lord, your, &c.,

NELSON.

---

### TO REAR-ADMIRAL DUCKWORTH.

[Letter-Book.]

Naples Bay, 1st August, 1799.

My dear Sir,

You will rejoice with me on the entire liberation of the
Kingdom of Naples from French robbers. I send you a copy
of the capitulation of Capua—that for Gaeta is not yet finished.
The Bellerophon and Zealous sail to-morrow to join you,
with all your Marines. The garrison of Capua being 2817
regular troops, will mark the propriety of my keeping the
Marines of the Ships detached. As the Lugger goes by the
way of Leghorn, to bring you the latest news from the Armies
in the north of Italy, it is probable the Ships will join you
before the Lugger. Sir William and Lady Hamilton join me
in truest regards and affectionate remembrance, and believe
me, ever your obliged,

NELSON.

---

take possession of the place two hours after this capitulation shall have been
delivered; and the embarkation of the Garrison shall have effect twenty-four hours
after the gates are given up, according as may be agreed upon and settled between
the respective Commanding-Officers.

"Done at Naples, the 12th Thermidor, 7th Year, (July 31, 1799.)

"GENERAL ACTON.

"NELSON.

"GIRARDON, General of Brigade."

TO HIS EXCELLENCY THE HONOURABLE WILLIAM WYNDHAM.

[Autograph, in the possession of his relict, the Honourable Mrs. Wyndham.]

My dear Sir,                                    August 2nd, 1799.

I have received all your very interesting letters, to the 27th, and I thank your Excellency for all the trouble you have taken; I am more than sorry that you should think it necessary to call upon me for an explanation of a part of my letter to you, which I thought required none. I, as a junior Officer in the fleet, can have no right to put Government to any expense for couriers, except for business relative to the fleet, for Government would not pay ten pounds for me for any news, however interesting. I am anxious to hear of the movements of the Armies; they are most interesting, but I could [not] pay sixpence for the news of the greatest victory from the public purse. I am forced to confess that our Government keep us seamen from putting our hand in the public chest. The Incendiary goes off this day to Palermo, in order to convoy the Transport with your baggage; and I have ordered Captain Dunn to take on board your son,[1] and I hope he will be landed in safety. A Squadron is ordered for the Gulf of Genoa, which I hope will be useful; all is quiet in this Kingdom; to our surprise, not less than 600 regular French troops were in the three garrisons of St. Elmo, Capua, and Gaeta. I beg of your Excellency to forward my letter to Field Marshall Suwarrow; Sir William Hamilton, and General Acton, see all your letters. The King returns to Palermo on the 7th. I sent off last night the Officer from Suwarrow to the King of Sardinia. Pray tell General Klenau that I have received his letter, and thank him for it. The Russian Admiral has doubtless very good reasons for raising the blockade of Ancona, no less than to unite with me for to destroy the French fleet. Your Excellency must excuse the brevity of my letter, for my left hand is tired, but ever believe me, your Excellency's faithful Servant,

NELSON.

[1] George Francis Wyndham, born in August, 1785, who entered the Navy, and became a Post Captain in 1812. In November, 1837, he succeeded his uncle as third Earl of Egremont; and dying without issue in April last, the Titles of that ancient family became extinct.

## TO CAPTAIN DARBY, H. M. SHIP BELLEROPHON.

[Letter-Book.]

Foudroyant, 3rd August, 1799.

My dear Sir,

You will stay at Gaeta till the garrison is embarked, either for Naples or France. The greatest care is to be taken that no property which they did not bring with them into the country, can be theirs, or is suffered to be carried away. We are to send them to France, and will, properly—but not as they dictate. As to horses, it is nonsense; as well might they say, ' we will carry a house!' If the fellow[2] is a scoundrel, he must be thrashed. And I have sent Troubridge to command the Marines and Seamen landed from the Ships, and it is my positive directions, that every assistance is given to Captain Troubridge in the execution of my orders. I am, dear Sir, yours &c.,

NELSON.

## TO CAPTAIN GEORGE MARTIN, H.M. SHIP NORTHUMBERLAND.

[Order-Book.]

Foudroyant, Naples Bay, 3rd August, 1799.

You are hereby required and directed to proceed in His Majesty's Ship Northumberland to Gaeta, and take under your command His Majesty's brig San Leon, whose Commander has my directions to follow your orders, and proceed off Città Vecchia, looking out for His Majesty's Ship Thalia, cruizing off that place, whom you will take under your command. Captain Nisbet having also my orders to follow your directions, you will then proceed to Leghorn, and either go through the Roads yourself, or send a boat on shore for intelligence respecting the affairs of the North of Italy, and of the situation of the Allied Armies; and should you fall in with the Seahorse in your route, you will also take Captain Foote under your orders. From Leghorn you will proceed to the Gulf of Genoa, and make what inquiries you are able respecting the

---

[2] Apparently General Girardon, commander of the French garrison at Gaeta.

Army of Field Marshal Suwarrow, with whom you will, as soon as possible, open a correspondence, acquainting him of your arrival on the Coast, and of your readiness to co-operate with him, to the utmost of your power, in annoying the Enemy, and for the good of the common Cause. And should you fall in with La Minerva, or any Frigates cruizing under Lord Keith's orders, you will also take them under your command, except the time be elapsed for which they were to cruize; in that case, you will give their Captains orders to join me at Palermo. And should you gain any intelligence of importance for me to know, you will send either the San Leon or a Frigate with it to me at Palermo. Relying on your well-known abilities and judgment, you will act in the execution of those orders as circumstances may arise, giving what assistance and support you are able to the Allied Armies, and remaining upon this station until further orders.

NELSON.

---

TO CAPTAIN NISBET, H. M. SHIP THALIA.

[Letter-Book.]

Foudroyant, Naples Bay, 3rd August, 1799.

My dear Sir,

I herewith enclose you a letter received some days ago, and on the receipt of this, you will keep a good look-out for the Northumberland, who is coming your way, and join her as soon as you can, Captain Martin having letters for you. I am sorry to find you have been cruizing off Cività Vecchia. I was in hopes of your being on the North Coast of Italy, but I am persuaded it was done for the best. I here enclose you the copy of a letter sent open to me from Mr. Smith, at Constantinople, respecting some supplies furnished the Bonne Citoyenne, at the Dardanelles, and request that you will give the necessary directions to have it settled, or explain it to me that it may be settled. Mr. Tyson has written the Purser, Mr. Isaacson, to desire he will draw out bills for the amount, and fresh vouchers for your signature, and the settlement of his account.

I am, wishing you every success, yours very affectionately,

NELSON.

### TO CAPTAIN LOUIS, H. M. SHIP MINOTAUR.

[Letter-Book.]

Naples Bay, August 3rd, 1799.

Sir,

You carried with you the treaty, and, in two hours after your arrival, and the Capitulation was presented, you was to take possession of the gates, and in twenty-four hours the garrison were to be embarked. I am hurt and surprised that the Capitulation has not been complied with. It shall be, and the Commander has agreed to it. I have not read your paper enclosed. You will execute my orders, or attack it. The fellow ought to be kicked for his impudence. You will instantly take possession of the gates and the fortress. I had reason to expect it had been done long ago. I am very much hurt that it has not. Tell Captain Darby, who (I taking for granted that the business had been long settled) was directed to take the Marines, that the Marines must not be taken away until we have possession of the place, and that he must assist in doing it.

I am, dear Sir, your faithful servant,

NELSON.

---

### TO CAPTAIN LOUIS, H. M. SHIP MINOTAUR.

[Letter-Book.]

Foudroyant, Naples Bay, 4th August, 1799.

Dear Sir,

I have received your letter of yesterday, and am happy to find that all matters are settled. I was sorry that you had entered into any altercation with the scoundrel. The Capitulation once signed, there could be no room for dispute. The enclosed order will point out to you how you are to proceed, and believe me, dear Sir, your most obedient

NELSON.

There is no way of dealing with a Frenchman but to knock him down. To be civil to them is only to be laughed at, when they are enemies.

TO LADY NELSON.

[From Clarke and M'Arthur, vol. ii. p. 208.]

Naples, 4th August, 1799.

Thank God all goes on well in Italy, and the Kingdom of Naples is liberated from thieves and murderers. But still, it has so overthrown the fabric of a regular Government, that much time and great care are necessary to keep the Country quiet. The 1st of August was celebrated here with as much respect as our situation would admit. The King dined with me; and, when His Majesty drank my health, a Royal salute of twenty-one guns was fired from all his Sicilian Majesty's Ships of War, and from all the Castles. In the evening there was a general illumination. Amongst other representations, a large Vessel was fitted out like a Roman galley; on its oars were fixed lamps, and in the centre was erected a rostral column with my name: at the stern were elevated two angels supporting my picture. In short, my dear Fanny, the beauty of the whole is beyond my powers of description. More than 2000 variegated lamps were suspended round the Vessel. An orchestra was fitted up, and filled with the very best musicians and singers. The piece of music was in a great measure to celebrate my praise, describing their previous distress, "but Nelson came, the invincible Nelson, and they were preserved, and again made happy." This must not make you think me vain; no, far, very far from it, I relate it more from gratitude than vanity. I return to Palermo with the King to-morrow. May God bless you all. Pray say, what is true, that I really steal time to write this letter, and my hand is ready to drop. My dear father must forgive my not writing so often as I ought, and so must my brothers, sisters, and friends. But ever believe me your affectionate

NELSON.

## TO CAPTAIN, NOW COMMODORE TROUBRIDGE, H. M. SHIP CULLODEN.

[Order-Book.]

Foudroyant, Naples Bay, 5th August, 1799.

Whereas it is necessary for the good of his Majesty's Service, that an Officer above the rank of Post-Captain should command the Squadron in Naples Bay, and along the Coast, especially as a number of Foreign Ships of War are expected; you are, therefore, hereby required and directed to hoist a Broad Red Pendant at the main-top gallant mast-head of the Ship you command, and to wear the same during the continuance of your services on this Coast, or until further orders.　　　　　　　　　　　　　　　　NELSON.

---

## TO EVAN NEPEAN, ESQ., ADMIRALTY.

[Original, in the Admiralty. On the 5th of August the Foudroyant sailed from Naples with the King on board, and accompanied by the Principe Real, with the flag of the Marquis de Niza, for Palermo, where they arrived on the 8th; on which day, "at 1 P.M., her Sicilian Majesty and Royal Family came on board the Foudroyant: saluted with twenty-one guns. At 5, his Sicilian Majesty, the Queen, and all the Royal Family, attended by the Admiral, went on shore: saluted them with twenty-one guns, which was answered from all the forts."—*Journal.*

Foudroyant, Naples Bay, 5th August, 1799.

Sir,

As I am proceeding in his Majesty's Ship Foudroyant, with his Sicilian Majesty on board for Palermo, and it being necessary, for the good of his Majesty's service, that the command of this Squadron should be left with an Officer above the rank of Captain, especially as the Russian and Turkish Squadrons are very soon expected in this Bay; I have, therefore, thought it right to give Captain Troubridge an order to wear a Broad Pendant, he being an Officer highly deserving their Lordships' attention, and which I hope they will approve.[5]

I have the honour to be, &c.,

NELSON.

---

[5] It appears that, under the peculiar circumstances in which Captain Troubridge had been serving, the Admiralty did not disapprove of the orders Lord Nelson had given; but their Lordships took it for granted, that when the cause for it should no longer exist, he would order the distinguishing Pendant to be struck.—*Nelson Papers.*

## TO EARL SPENCER, K.G.

[Letter-Book.]

Naples, August 5th, 1799.

My dear Lord,

It is absolutely necessary for the safety of this Capital, that a respectable Squadron of Ships should be left in the Bay, and that an Officer apparently beyond the rank of Captain should command it. The Marquis de Niza would, on every account, be improper to command here, therefore I take him with me to Palermo ; for I am obliged to continue to keep commands from devolving on the Portuguese : I have once suffered by it.[6] I shall very soon send them to Lord Keith, on the first call for more of this Squadron.

I trust to your Lordship's goodness, that Troubridge may wear the distinguishing Pendant, whilst he is employed on this service. He merits every mark of honour which can be shown him. Ever, my dear Lord, your obliged,

NELSON.

---

## TO COMMODORE TROUBRIDGE, H. M. SHIP CULLODEN.

[Order-Book.]

Foudroyant, Naples Bay, 5th August, 1799.

You are hereby required and directed to take under your command the Ships named in the margin,[7] whose Captains have my directions to follow your orders, and to co-operate with Cardinal Ruffo, the Lieutenant-General of the Kingdom of Naples, in all things necessary for its safety, and the peace and quiet of the Capital ; and, should you find it necessary, you are at liberty to detach a part of the Squadron along the Roman coast to the northward, and as far as Leghorn, in order to prevent the French from carrying off the plunder of Rome ; informing me of every circumstance that may arise necessary for me to know.

NELSON

---

[6] Apparently by Commodore Campbell's having burnt the Neapolitan Ships
[7] Audacious, Goliath, Swiftsure, St. Sebastian, Rainha, Perseus.

### TO THE RIGHT HONOURABLE LORD KEITH, K.B.

[Letter-Book.]

Palermo, August 10th, 1799.

My dear Lord,

I have the pleasure to tell you that his Sicilian Majesty arrived here on the 8th, and was received with that joy which a loyal people must always pay to a beloved Sovereign.

As it is your Lordship's orders not to keep more Ships on the service here than is absolutely required, I have directed the Portuguese Squadron to be in momentary readiness to join your Lordship, or, not meeting you, to proceed to Lisbon to refit. When it is possible to get more Ships from the Bay of Naples, I want to have more Ships off Malta, which I am sure would then surrender. As events turn up, I beg you will be assured, that I shall act to the best of my judgment. I am ever, with the greatest respect, &c.

NELSON.

---

### TO CAPTAIN BALL, H.M. SHIP ALEXANDER.

[Letter-Book.]

August 12th, 1799.

My dear Ball,

I have directed the Queen of Portugal[8] and St. Sebastian to join you off Malta, and will spare you the Foudroyant for a few days; and I hope the sight of such a force will finish your hard labours. I am sorry to tell you the Seahorse has been on shore and greatly damaged.[9] The weather is intolerable. Cordone will, I hope, get the money this evening. Send Lieutenant      , the Agent for Transports, here as soon as you can, as Mr. Lamb is gone to Mahon. All quiet in Naples, by letters of the 11th. Lady Hamilton, I know, intends to write you a line; therefore, I will only say, God bless you! and believe me ever your obliged friend,

NELSON.

Mr. Macaulay is determined to pay you a visit, and has taken

---

[8] The Ship which Lord Nelson always before called " Rainha."

[9] Captain Foote's letter, describing the accident to the Seahorse, by getting on shore at Leghorn, on the 29th of July, is printed in his " Vindication," p. 144.

the trouble to collect the Gazettes. You may send in an Officer to talk to Vaubois; but I would not have you regularly summons him. The Garrison may be sent to France, leaving *their Arms, and every Colour of the place,* and *Regimentals,* without being prisoners of war. But this is ONLY to be granted if it will save fourteen days' labour; for the garrison never can be succoured.

NELSON.

---

### TO HIS MAJESTY THE KING OF THE TWO SICILIES.[1]

[From a Copy in the Admiralty.]

Palermo, 13th August, 1799.

Sire,

The bounty of your Majesty has so overwhelmed me that I am unable to find words adequate to express my gratitude; but it shall be my study to continue in the same line of conduct which your Majesty has been pleased to approve, and to mark with such very extraordinary proofs of your Royal

---

[1] A copy of the King's letter is in the Nelson Papers, and the following is Clarke and M'Arthur's (vol. ii. p. 213) translation of it:—

"My dear Lord,

"The expressions that are generally used to denote real gratitude, by no means correspond with or satisfy the exclusive sense which I feel, of how much ought to be, and I know is, engraven on my mind. The service which you have doubly rendered to me and the Two Sicilies, can never be equalled. In the month of August you were, last year, their sole preserver, as also, during the present one, by organizing a most judicious defence for those Kingdoms, with an active and imposing force; preserving for me and my family, after so many disasters, the possession of both countries: your powerful co-operation having rendered the force of my faithful soldiers efficacious, as well as that of my Allies who are united with them.

"In thus repeating to you those services, of which at this moment I feel so sensible, permit that some lasting marks of my gratitude may be presented to your Lordship in my name, which cannot hurt your elevated and just delicacy; but on that subject I will be silent. When my August Father took leave of me, he gave me with these Kingdoms a Sword, as a symbol to preserve what he had intrusted to me. To you, my Lord, I send it, in memory of the obligation I then contracted, and which you have given me an opportunity of fulfilling; since it was you, and your brave followers, who have liberated Naples and its Coasts from the Enemy who had gained possession of them, and who have supported my steps by the establishment of quiet and order. To your magnanimous Sovereign, my best Ally, to your generous nation, I owe an avowal of my immense gratitude; and rest assured, my lord, that this gratitude will never cease, but with your affectionate, FERDINANDO."

favour, and which has also gained me the approbation of my own most gracious Sovereign, your Majesty's faithful Ally.

That the Almighty may pour down his choicest blessings on your sacred person, and on those of the Queen and the whole Royal Family, and preserve your Kingdom in peace and happiness, shall ever be the fervent prayer of your Majesty's faithful servant,

BRONTE NELSON.

---

## TO HIS EXCELLENCY PRINCE DE LUZZI.[2]

[From a Copy in the Admiralty.]

Sir,                                          Palermo, 13th August, 1799.

I have this moment received the honour of your Excellency's letter, conveying to me his Sicilian Majesty's most gracious approbation of my conduct, and also, that his Majesty had been pleased to confer upon me the title of Duke of Bronté,

---

[2] On the second day after the King's return to Palermo, Lord Nelson was informed by Lady Hamilton, that His Majesty intended to create him DUKE OF BRONTE, and to grant him the Feudal estate to which that Title was annexed. It is said, that some time before, when Ferdinand himself acquainted him with his intention, Nelson begged leave to decline the gift, upon which the King observed—" Lord Nelson, do you wish that your name alone should pass with glory to posterity, and that I, Ferdinand de Bourbon, should appear ungrateful?"—*Clarke and M'Arthur*, vol. ii. p. 213. The following translation of the Prince di Luzzi's letter is given by Clarke and M'Arthur (vol. ii. p. 484):

"TO THE MOST EXCELLENT ADMIRAL LORD NELSON.

" Palace, August 13th, 1799.

" The glorious enterprises of your Excellency, which gained the admiration and applause of the greatest and wisest part of Europe, more particularly excited in the mind of the King, my Master, the most lively sentiments of approbation, gratitude, and esteem, towards your illustrious person; but the constant vigilance employed by your Excellency in defending these Kingdoms of the Sicilies, in freeing them in the parts where they were invaded, and in repelling from the same a barbarous and insatiable Enemy, by the means of a powerful and victorious Squadron destined for this purpose, under your command, by his Britannic Majesty; and the unwearied assistance given by your Excellency to the Sacred Person of his Majesty, and to the Royal Family, while they have drawn still tighter the happy bonds of friendship and faithful alliance between his Sicilian and his Britannic Majesty, have awakened, in a singular manner, the sincere gratitude of the King my Master. Hence, his Majesty, desirous of giving your Excellency a public and lasting proof of these sentiments, and of transmitting to future generations the illustrious remembrance of your merits and of your glory, has resolved and ordained, that the ancient and famous Town of Bronte, on the skirts of the Etna, with its territory and dependencies, shall be constituted a feudal tenure, and shall be raised to the Dignity and Title of

together with the estate attached to it. I request that your Excellency will lay me with all humility, and full of gratitude at his Majesty's feet; express to him my attachment to his Sacred Person, the Queen, and Royal Family, and that it shall be the study of my life, by following the same conduct which has gained me his Royal favours, to merit the continuance of them.

I sincerely thank your Excellency for the very handsome manner in which you have executed the Royal Commands, and believe me, with the highest respect, your Excellency's most obliged servant,

BRONTE NELSON.

---

TO CAPTAIN BALL, H. M. SHIP ALEXANDER.

[Letter-Book. The Foudroyant sailed from Palermo, for Malta, on the 14th, and Lord Nelson's flag was on the preceding day transferred to the Samuel and Jane Transport, there not being a Ship of War at Palermo to receive it.

Palermo, August 14th, 1799.

My dear Ball,

I send you the Foudroyant for ten days; and for *that* time you may land her Marines, and also those from all the other Ships of the Squadron, which I hope will be of use in the advanced posts, as I understand the Maltese suffer many

a Duchy, with full and mixed authority—that is, the right of absolute jurisdiction, both civil and criminal; and, that the said Duchy and Title, with its revenues and jurisdiction, shall be conferred on your Excellency, and on the heirs of your body, in a right line, according to the laws of this Kingdom; and in default of the same, to any one of your relatives, in whatever degree, whom your Excellency may think proper to appoint, to whom His Majesty will grant a new investiture and testamentary power, according to the laws of this Kingdom, enlarging from the present moment the limits of the Feudal succession, to demonstrate more fully the sentiments of his royal mind with respect to your Excellency.

"Your Excellency will receive the Royal Patent which is making out for the solemn investiture, and the actual concession of the before-mentioned Duchy; and in the meanwhile, it is with the truest and most heartfelt pleasure that I obey his Majesty's order in sending you this intelligence for your information, and that you may assume the Title.

"PRINCE DI LUZZI."

A copy of the Patent will be found in the APPENDIX. Lord Nelson immediately assumed the Title; but he did not sign by it, except in his letters to Foreigners, for some time. The licence granting him his own Sovereign's permission to accept the Dignity, was not issued until the 9th of January, 1801.

articles to be carried into the Town. Four sail of Russians are in sight; they will, I hope, go on the coast of Genoa. I send you various letters and papers; the letters return to me, the papers you can send to Vaubois. I am, &c.

NELSON.

---

### TO THE REVEREND EDMUND NELSON.

[From a Fac-simile in the possession of James Young, Esq., of Wells, in Norfolk.]

Palermo, August 15th, 1799.

My dear Father,

His Sicilian Majesty having created me a Duke, by the title of Bronté, to which he has attached a Feud of, it is said, about £3000 a year, to be at my disposal, I shall certainly not omit this opportunity of being useful to my family, always reserving a right to the possessor, of leaving one third of the income for the payment of legacies. It shall first go to you, my dear father, and in succession to my elder brother and children male, William the same, Mrs. Bolton's boys, Mrs. Matcham's, and my nearest relations. For your natural life, the estate shall be taxed with £500 a year, but this is not to be drawn into a precedent, that the next heir may expect it. No, my honoured father, receive this small tribute as a mark of gratitude to the best of parents from his most dutiful son,

NELSON.

---

### TO ALEXANDER DAVISON, ESQ.

[From Clarke and M'Arthur, vol. ii. p. 213.]

[About 15th August, 1799.]

You will observe in a part of the King's letter, an observation is made, that this present could not hurt my delicate feelings; that is, I might have before received money and jewels, but I rejected them, as became me, and never received one farthing for all the expenses of the Royal Family on board the Vanguard and Foudroyant. This I expect from the Board of Admiralty, and that they will order me a suitable sum. It has been honour, and not money which I have sought, nor sought in vain. I am, &c.,

NELSON.

TO HIS EXCELLENCY COUNT CHILEMBERT CAGLIARI, PRIME
MINISTER OF THE KING OF SARDINIA.

[Letter-Book.]

Palermo, 16th August, 1799.

Sir,

I was yesterday honoured with your Excellency's letter[3] of
August 11th. The situation of the poor people taken by the
Bey of Tunis is shocking to humanity, and must sensibly
touch the Royal heart; but I will not attempt to cherish a
hope that the Bey will abate one sequin of the sum fixed in
the Convention of June the 21st, and I very much doubt if a
longer time than that fixed by the Convention, and witnessed
by six friendly Consuls, will be granted. However, I have,
I can assure your Excellency, no difficulty in sending a
letter to Mr. Magra, his Britannic Majesty's Consul, covering
one for the Bey, to say that I am confident such a mark of
his goodness will be highly acceptable to the great King, my
Master.

The Chevalier Marechal is gone towards Malta after the
Foudroyant, and I hope she will be at Cagliari in three days
after this letter; and I have only to entreat that everything
for the service of His Majesty may be ready to put on
board the moment she anchors. I send the Foudroyant, as she

---

[3] On the 6th of August, Count Chilembert wrote to Lord Nelson, stating, that as
soon as the Piedmontese Dominions had been reconquered by the combined Austrian
and Russian armies, his Sardinian Majesty had resolved to send some eminent
persons belonging to his Court, to his Continental Dominions, who would be commissioned to restore the former order of things, and to re-organize the Royal
government of his House; and for this purpose, his Majesty requested Lord Nelson
to detach two Frigates to Cagliari, for the safe conveyance of the Commissioners.

On the 11th of August, the King himself wrote to Lord Nelson on the subject:—
    "Dear Admiral Nelson,
    "I have felt great pleasure from your letter of the first of this month; and I
acknowledge myself much obliged to you for your polite attention in offering me a
sufficient number of Ships for the conveyance of the Royal Family to my Continental Dominions. I shall send one of my Ministers to concert with you; and
I shall be ready to embark as soon as the Ships arrive. My brother, the Duke of
Agosta, has been obliged to hasten from this Island, owing to the loss of Prince
Charles, his only son; which has overwhelmed us and the whole Kingdom with
sorrow. You also, my dear Admiral, will sympathize with me on this unfortunate
event. With an assurance of my esteem and gratitude, I am your true friend—
CHARLES EMMANUEL."—Translation in *Clarke and M'Arthur*, vol. ii. p. 206.

is my own Flag-Ship, and the first two-decked Ship in the
world. I would send more Ships, but the service of the
civilized world requires every exertion; therefore I have not
the power to send another Ship of War. A very fine Brig I
have directed from Naples to assist in carrying his Majesty's
attendants, and as a much less Ship has carried a much more
numerous Royal Family, I trust their Majesties will not be
pressed for room. I beg that your Excellency will lay me at
their Majesties' feet, and assure them of my sincere desire to be
useful for their service, and believe me, with the greatest
respect, your Excellency's most obedient servant,

BRONTE NELSON.

There is a Russian Squadron in this Bay, but they are not
in the smallest degree under my orders.

---

## TO CAPTAIN HARDY, HIS MAJESTY'S SHIP FOUDROYANT.

[Order-Book.]

The Samuel and Jane Transport, Palermo, 16th August, 1799.

Immediately on the receipt hereof, you are required and
directed to embark the Marines of the Foudroyant, (should
they be landed,) and proceed without one moment's loss of
time to Cagliari, in Sardinia, and embark on board His
Sardinian Majesty and such other of the Royal Family, Ministers, &c. as His Majesty may think proper to take with him,
and take them to Leghorn and land them there, except you
hear of the capture of Genoa by the Allied Armies. In that
case, should his Majesty wish to be landed at Genoa, you will
proceed with him to that Port. On your arrival at Cagliari,
you will urge, in the most delicate manner, the speedy embarkation of the King, &c., and also on his landing, to get the
Ship cleared again immediately, not waiting more than
twenty-four hours at the Port the King may choose to land
at, when you will return without delay, and join me at this
place.

NELSON.

## TO CAPTAIN BALL, H. M. SHIP ALEXANDER.

[Letter-Book.]

Samuel and Jane Transport, Palermo, 16th August, 1799.

My dear Ball,

I am sorry to be under the necessity of taking the Foudroyant from you, but his Sardinian Majesty having requested a Ship to carry him and his family to the Continent, I have no other to send. I have ordered a Ship from Naples to supply her place. Wishing you speedily in possession of Valetta, believe me your faithful friend,

NELSON.

---

## TO CAPTAIN HARDY, H. M. SHIP FOUDROYANT.

[Letter-Book.]

August 16th, 1799.

My dear Hardy,

It is now told me that his Sardinian Majesty does not intend to leave Cagliari until the middle of September; if so, I would have you fix the exact time, and proper Ships shall be arranged to carry him to Leghorn, and do you join me as soon as possible. Yours truly,

NELSON.

4 P.M.—The King of Sardinia's letter and the Queen's are at complete variance: the former says, ' Hurry;' the latter, ' Next month.' Settle the exact time, and return to MALTA for ten days, and then join me.

NELSON.

---

## TO PERKIN MAGRA, ESQ., CONSUL-GENERAL AT TUNIS.

[Letter-Book.]

Samuel and Jane Transport, Palermo, 16th August, 1799.

My dear Sir,

I yesterday received a letter from His Sardinian Majesty's Minister, of which I send you a copy. I own I do not see how it can be expected that any alteration of the Convention of last June can be effected. If a little delay could be managed, it might be represented as a thing which would be very grateful to the King; but even this must be touched with a delicate hand. I send you a line for the Bey.

I may have appeared neglectful; but believe me, I have had my hands full of business for restoring, as far as my powers go, tranquillity to the world. I most truly congratulate you on the surrender of Mantua. The French now only possess Ancona and the Castle of St. Angelo in this part of Italy, and Genoa and Riviera in the North, all which will fall before August finishes. As this goes a round-about way, probably you will not hear from your family. Ever, with great respect, believe me, dear Sir, your most obedient servant,

NELSON, DUKE OF BRONTE, IN SICILY.

---

TO HIS HIGHNESS THE BEY OF TUNIS.

[Letter-Book.]

Sir,                          Foudroyant, Palermo, August 16th, 1799.

The French villains who have robbed half the world, but who are at this moment, thank God, receiving the punishment due to their manifold crimes! The King of Sardinia and all his faithful subjects in Piedmont, have been cruelly treated, your Highness has heard, by those thieves and murderers, a race of men void of all honour and good faith. Therefore, as the Island of Sardinia is not rich, there may be some little difficulty in raising such a very large sum of money, more especially in the time specified. If, therefore, your Highness could have the goodness of heart to moderate the sum fixed by the Convention of June last, or at least extend the time of payment, I am sure it would be received as an act of kindness to the Great King, my Master, who is the faithful friend of your Highness and his Sardinian Majesty.

I sincerely congratulate your Highness on the almost total destruction of the French Army in Egypt, on the restoration of the King of Naples, the Great Duke of Tuscany, and the King of Sardinia, and on the happy prospect of this race of monsters being annihilated from the face of the world. I assure your Highness of my desire to pay you a visit, and beg you to believe that I am, with real respect, your faithful servant,

NELSON.

## TO H. R. H. THE DUKE OF CLARENCE.

[From Clarke and M'Arthur, vol. ii. p. 216.]

[About 16th August, 1799.]

Thus our King, Sir, will have the comfort that his Ships afford an asylum and protection to other Monarchs besides the King of Naples ; and will have the satisfaction of knowing, that his Sardinian Majesty is likewise returned, under the sanction of the British flag. I am, &c.,

NELSON.

## TO LORD WILLIAM BENTINCK.

[Letter-Book.]

Palermo, 16th August, 1799.

My Lord,

I thank you for all your letters, and felicitate with you on the happy success of the Allied Arms. A Russian Squadron is here from the Baltic, under Rear-Admiral Kartzow ; but as they are not under my orders or influence, I cannot send them to assist the brave and excellent Suwarrow. I am increasing the Squadron under Captain Martin, by every means in my power ; and his Sicilian Majesty has promised to send four Galliots to join our Ships, &c. I know nothing of the Russian and Turkish Levant fleets. The combined Fleets are reported to be in Cadiz the 22nd ultimo. With every sentiment of respect, &c.

NELSON.

## TO REAR-ADMIRAL DUCKWORTH.

[Letter-Book.]

Palermo, 16th August, 1799.

My dear Admiral,

Send us cables and ropes. The Seahorse has been drove on shore for want of both, and half the Squadron will be in the same state. The Audacious has not a sail to her yards, and both she and Goliath must soon go down, to be entirely refitted. Alexander and Lion are also in a terrible state. The former must go to England the moment Malta is taken. The

Russian Squadron of three Sail of the Line, under Rear-Admiral Kartzow, arrived yesterday; but having 520 sick to land, are for the present, unfit for service. The united Squadrons from Corfu are the Lord knows where, therefore I must desire, if it is possible, that you send at least one Frigate, the Minerva, or, if possible, one equally as good, with a good Corvette, to join Captain Martin on the Coast of Genoa; for I must have a respectable Squadron on the Coast, to support Field-Marshal Suwarrow. The Seahorse, I hope, got off on the 4th, but this news is not certain; but I rely on Captain Foote's exertion. The Swiftsure is gone to her assistance. My Flag is in a Transport—the Foudroyant being gone to Malta, where I want to make an exertion to possess it. The Gulf of Spezzia is said to be taken by the Austrians. In Naples everything is quiet; but the Cardinal appears to be working mischief against the King, and in support of the Nobles: he must, sooner or later, be removed for his bad conduct.

We are dying with heat, and the feast of Santa Rosalia begins this day: how shall we get through it? The King sent me a diamond-hilted sword with a most affectionate letter, and also, I received a dispatch that he had created me Duke of Bronte, and attached an estate to it. The Title, of course, I cannot assume, without the approbation of our King, which I now hear has been some time desired. Darby and Hood, I hope, have long joined you. Pray be so good as to deliver to them the Medals, with my best regards. Our dear Lady has been very unwell, and if this fête to-night do not kill her, I dare say she will write you to-morrow, for there is none she respects more than yourself. Good Sir William is much better for his trip. I send the Aurora to get everything, and if you cannot supply her she must go to Gibraltar. Our distress for stores is, you know, very great, and we must hold out another winter. Make my best regards acceptable to Sir James St. Clair. I really have not the power of writing, and I am nearly blind; but whilst I have life, believe me, my dear Admiral, your obliged and affectionate,

NELSON.

### TO FIELD-MARSHAL SUWARROW.

[Letter-Book.]

Palermo, 16th August, 1799.

My dear Field Marshal,

Yesterday brought me your Excellency's letter of July 30th, and four Galliots are ordered by his Sicilian Majesty to protect provisions, &c., for the use of your Army, to be under the orders of my friend, Captain Martin. I have ordered another Frigate and Brig to join the Squadron on the Riviere of Genoa; I wish I could come to you myself: I shall truly have a pleasure in embracing a person of your exalted character, but as that cannot be at present, I only regret I cannot send you*more Ships. Rear-Admiral Kartzow is here with three Sail of the Line and a Frigate, but they are not under my orders or INFLUENCE. May God bless you, my honoured friend, and believe me for ever your attached friend,

BRONTE NELSON.

---

### TO VICE-ADMIRAL OUSCHAKOFF, COMMANDING THE RUSSIAN SQUADRON.

[From a Copy in the Admiralty.]

Palermo, 18th August, 1799.

Sir,

I enclose your Excellency the copy of a letter from the Right Honourable Lord Keith, the Commander-in-Chief of his Majesty's Fleet in the Mediterranean, respecting the restoration of the Leander, taken by the Squadron under your Excellency's command at Corfu, which mentions a copy of an order from the Admiralty of England to be enclosed, but which was not sent up to me. I must, therefore, beg leave to apologize to your Excellency for not being able to present you with a copy of it. I presume the Courts of Petersburg and London have decided the matter respecting the restoration of the Leander, otherwise the Admiralty would not have sent such order to the Commander-in-Chief, and appointed Officers to that Ship. Captain Drummond, who is appointed to the command of the Leander for the present, will wait upon your Excellency with this letter, and I have to request you will be

pleased to give directions to the Officer commanding at Corfu
to give Captain Drummond what assistance he may want in
fitting out the said Ship, and also to assist him with seamen
to proceed with her to Mahon.

I beg leave to congratulate you on your happy arrival at
Messina, and have the honour to be your Excellency's

Most obedient and faithful servant,

NELSON.

---

### TO CAPTAIN DRUMMOND, H. M. SHIP LEANDER.

[From a Copy in the Admiralty.]

Samuel and Jane Transport, at Palermo, 19th August, 1799.

You are hereby required and directed to proceed in the
Bulldog to Messina, and deliver the letter you will receive
herewith to the Russian Admiral, and request his assistance
to fit out the Leander, by giving directions to the Commander
at Corfu to furnish you with the articles necessary for that
purpose, and also for men to navigate her down to Mahon. I
have directed Captain Dacres to stay with you a fortnight or
three weeks, to give you what assistance he is able, at the
expiration of which time you will dispatch him to me, report-
ing by him the progress you have made, and what further
assistance will be wanted to bring the Leander from thence ;
but I am in hopes you will be able to sail with the Bulldog,
and, in that case, she will see you down to Mahon.

NELSON.

---

### TO CAPTAIN DACRES,[4] COMMANDING H. M. SLOOP BULLDOG.

[From a Copy in the Admiralty.]

The Samuel and Jane Transport, at Palermo, 19th August, 1799.

You are hereby required and directed to proceed in his
Majesty's Sloop under your command, with Captain Drummond and the Officers of the Leander to Messina, waiting
there until Captain Drummond has arranged his business
with the Russian Admiral, and from thence you will proceed

---

[4] Captain Barrington Dacres was made a Post-Captain in 1802, and died before 1809.

with them to Corfu, and give every assistance you are able to fit out the Leander for sea, for a fortnight or three weeks, if she can be got ready in that time; if not, after the expiration of three weeks from your arrival at Corfu, you will return and join me at this place; but if the Leander be ready in that time, you will proceed with her to Mahon.

NELSON.

---

### TO CAPTAIN SIR WILLIAM SIDNEY SMITH, H.M. SHIP TIGRE.

[Letter-Book.]

Sir,       Samuel and Jane Transport, Palermo, 19th August, 1799.

I here enclose an acting order for Captain Stiles[5] to command the Theseus in the room of my much-lamented friend, Captain Miller; and also an acting order for Mr. Canes[6] to command the Cameleon, in the room of Captain Stiles, until further orders; and which orders I hope the Lords Commissioners of the Admiralty will confirm, for Mr. Canes' bravery and good conduct in the arduous and memorable Siege of Acre. I have the honour to be, Sir, yours, &c.,

NELSON.

---

### TO COMMODORE TROUBRIDGE.

[Letter-Book.]

Most Secret.

My dear Troubridge,       Palermo, August 19th, 1799.

Notwithstanding my former orders, I have now such a letter from Lord Keith, he having left the Mediterranean for to pursue the combined Fleets,[7] who were off Cape St. Vincent, the 24th. The British Fleet passed the Straits, the

---

[5] Captain John Stiles became a Flag Officer in July, 1830, and died a Rear-Admiral of the White, in December, 1830.

[6] Captain Edward Jekyll Canes was afterwards appointed to L'Utile of 18 Guns, which upset in gale of wind on her passage from Gibraltar to Minorca, in November, 1801, when every man perished.—Vide "Naval Chronicle," vol. vii. p. 172.

[7] On the 21st July, the combined French and Spanish Fleets sailed from Cadiz for Brest, and on the 30th, Lord Keith, with thirty-one Sail of the Line, left Gibraltar in pursuit of them. The Enemy arrived in safety at Brest on the 13th of August, and Lord Keith returned to his command in the Mediterranean towards the end of the year.

30th; Lord St. Vincent sailed for England, the 31st, in the Argo. I must, therefore, take care of the four or five Ships left at Cadiz, and to keep the Straits open—therefore, you will receive orders to proceed to Gibraltar, *viâ* Palermo. If the business of Cività Vecchia cannot instantly be accomplished, and if the English Ship destined for Malta is not sailed, bring her with you. In short, the moment the Russians arrive, bring or order everything before Naples. I send to Martin, to proceed to Minorca with all the English Ships, Frigates, Sloops, &c., from whence a proper force will go on to Gibraltar; but keep all this secret, that the Russians may not even suspect that we are going to leave the Coast of Italy for one moment. We have great news from Egypt. The Siege of Acre was raised May 21st—Buonaparte leaving all his cannon and sick behind. The vagabond has got again to Cairo, where I am sure he will terminate his career. Communication is cut off between the Coast and Cairo. Damietta, Rosetta and Aboukir being taken by the Turks. Alexandria is besieged, and will soon fall. *Adieu, Mr. Buonaparte!*

Our news from India, from Blanket,[8] is good. Sir Sidney Smith had a letter from him at Mocha. Tippoo has been completely defeated. The La Forte, French frigate, has been taken by the Sybille;[9] but poor Captain Cooke has been killed. And here we must shed a tear for dear Miller.[1] By an explosion of shells which he was preparing on board the Theseus, he and twenty-five others were killed, nine drowned by jumping overboard, and forty-three wounded; but you shall see all when you arrive. Again I repeat, that if the orders for the embarkation of Tschudy's corps, with field-pieces, howitzers, &c., can be instantly done—I mean in two or even three days —then go to work on Cività Vecchia, affording all assistance in your power. The whole country is said to be our friends; but if you find the expedition cannot go on, then collect your Ships, and the moment the Russians make their appearance join me.

---

[8] Commodore Blanket obtained his Flag, and died, second in command in the East Indies, in 1801.

[9] La Forte was captured by the Sibylle in the East Indies, in the morning of the 1st March, 1799, after a gallant resistance. Captain Cooke, who served with Nelson at Calvi, (vide vol. i. p. 409) died at Calcutta of his wounds, on the 25th of May, following.

[1] Vide vol. ii.

2 P.M.—Your letter of the 13th is just arrived. The Neapolitans must manage their own Jacobins. We have, thank God, done with them. Ever, for ever, your affectionate friend,

NELSON.

August 22nd.—We are so slow in movements here, that I must give you precise orders to send me all but English Ships from the Bay of Naples. Direct the Peterel to order Swiftsure to join me, and the moment either Turks or Russians get in sight, weigh and join me, when some provisions shall be given you; for I am doing wrong not to use every expedition in getting Ships to Gibraltar.

---

## TO THE RIGHT HONOURABLE LORD MINTO.

[Autograph, in the Minto Papers.]

Palermo, August 20th, 1799.

My dear Lord,

Reports say you are at Vienna, therefore I send a letter, hoping it is so, to assure you of my unalterable regard. Under you, I have before worked for the public good, for the sake of the civilized world let us again work together, and as the *best* acts of our lives, manage to hang Thugut, Cardinal Ruffo and Manfredini. As you are with Thugut your penetrating mind will discover the villain in all his actions; there is nothing of an honest man about him: if he was in this room, where I have told Manfredini as much, I would tell him the same. Their councils have been equally destructive to their Sovereign and to Europe; try them before that great Court, and they will be found *friends* of the French, and *traitors* to Europe. Pardon this, but it comes from a seaman who speaks truth and shames the Devil. My dear Lord, that Thugut is caballing against our English King of Naples and his Family; pray keep an eye upon this rascal, and you will, soon find what I say is true. I am living with Sir William and Lady Hamilton, therefore I need not to say, in private life, I am happy, and nothing vexes me but the storms of State; but let us hang these three miscreants and all will go on smooth. Sir William and Lady Hamilton desire their kind regards, and believe me as ever your truly affectionate friend,

NELSON.

## TO REAR-ADMIRAL DUCKWORTH,

[Order-Book.]

The Samuel and Jane Transport, at Palermo, 20th August, 1799.

Whereas the Commander-in-Chief hath informed me, that he was proceeding with the Fleet into the Western Ocean, and perhaps, off Brest,—you are therefore hereby required and directed to proceed, or send two Ships of the Line, (the Zealous to be one of them) to Gibraltar, and render every assistance in your power to General O'Hara and the garrison there, and by keeping the Ports of the Barbary States and the Gut of Gibraltar open, to protect the trade until the arrival of three Sail of the Line more, which will be sent you with Frigates, Sloops, &c. When they have joined, you will then proceed off Cadiz and watch that Port, keeping the Straits open, and also, as far as you are able, to watch over and protect the trade of Lisbon and Oporto to the utmost of your power, acquainting the Lords Commissioners of the Admiralty and me, with any events that may happen, necessary for them or me to know. And in the event of the return of the Spanish Fleet to Cadiz, or such a number of them as you may not be able to cope with, you will be particularly careful to guard against surprise, and prevent them getting up the Mediterranean before you, so as to surprise the Squadron off Minorca; and send a Frigate or other Vessel off Cape St. Vincent or to Lisbon, with the news, to prevent any of our trade falling into their hands, and you to make the best of your way up to join the Squadron off Minorca, sending also some Vessel to apprise me of such event, that all the force may be collected as soon as possible. Relying on your well known judgment and abilities to act as circumstances may require for the good of His Majesty's Service, it is not necessary for me to be more particular.

NELSON.

---

## TO REAR-ADMIRAL DUCKWORTH.

[From a Copy in the Admiralty.]

Palermo, 20th August, 1799.

My dear Admiral,

Many thanks for your kind letter by the Bulldog, and sincerely hope that both your Leviathan and Zealous are perfectly recovered. No one, my dear Admiral, be assured, estimates your worth as an Officer and a friend more than *we* of this house : you must consider a line from me as a side of paper from any one else. Lord Keith is gone, and all my superior Officers, therefore I must now watch from Cape St. Vincent to Constantinople. Thank God our affairs in Italy are in that prosperous state that our Ships can be spared, therefore I have fixed to have five Sail of the Line to watch Cadiz, with a proportion of Frigates and Sloops, and to keep open the Straits; and four Sail of the Line at Minorca, with an assortment. Troubridge shall be at one—you at the other; the choice shall be with yourself; therefore as Troubridge will, I hope, in a fortnight be off Mahon, I wish you, if you like the station off Cadiz better, to proceed directly with two Sail of the Line to Gibraltar, Zealous one of them, as she is destined for England when we can spare her. The St. Vincent Cutter shall be a runner between us, as she sails very fast.

O'Hara may depend on my attention, and you or Troubridge will keep an eye to the trade of Lisbon and Oporto : and you are directed to represent home if you want more Small-craft : and to say what is true, that if I have not given you enough, it is because I have them not to give ; in short, to act in the best manner for His Majesty's Service. In giving this command I know who I trust to, and that it is not necessary to enter into the detail of what is to be done. As to myself, although thirteen Sail of the Line, Frigates, &c. are in Sicily, they insure no confidence ; it is England alone these Countries look to, and even favourable as affairs, was I to move, although my Flag is only in a Transport, they would be miserable. The Marquis de Niza goes off Malta, and I hope that place will very soon surrender ; Ball will then be a Governor, and all our Small-craft shall travel westward : what a relief that will be to my mind ! I have urged letters to be wrote to Admiral Ouschakoff, at Messina, to send a Squadron into the Gulf of Genoa, and orders go to-morrow to Martin, to bring all the Ships on that coast to Mahon. Minerve and Thalia shall go to the station off Cadiz, and also Seahorse if she can be spared : as to Minorca being attacked whilst we have Naval force in hand, I do not credit such an idea. Niza

goes down when Malta is finished.   The wind being easterly
prevents the Alceste from arriving.   God bless you! believe
me, &c.,

NELSON.

---

TO CAPTAIN SIR WILLIAM SIDNEY SMITH, H.M. SHIP TIGRE.

[Letter-Book.]

Palermo, 20th August, 1799.

My dear Sir,

I have received with the truest satisfaction all your very
interesting letters to July 16th.   The immense fatigue you
have had in defending Acre against such a chosen army of
French villains, headed by that arch-villain Buonaparte, has
never been exceeded, and the bravery shown by you and
your brave companions is such as to merit every encomium
which all the civilized world can bestow.   As an individual,
and as an Admiral, will you accept of my feeble tribute of
praise and admiration, and make them acceptable to all those
under your command.   I have returned the Cameleon, that
your First-lieutenant might have a good Sloop, which I hope
Lord Keith will approve, and in everything, in my junior
situation in the Fleet, you may be assured of my readiness to
do what you can wish me.   I hope Alexandria is long before
this in your possession, and the final blow given to Buonaparte ; but I hope no terms will ever be granted for his individual return to Europe.   Captain Stiles will tell you all
our news here, and good Sir William Hamilton tells me he
thinks he has told you the heads of all.   In short, all is well,
if Lord Keith falls in with the Combined fleet.   I think you
had better order the Theseus to Mahon, and I will endeavour
to send you either a good Sloop or small Frigate.   The
Factory at Smyrna, in my opinion, have wrote a very improper
letter to you.   I do not like the general style of Mr. Werry's
letters : they too much talk of Government affairs.   It is our
duty to take care of the Smyrna trade, as well as all other, and
it never has yet been neglected; but Great Britain, extensive
as her Navy is, cannot afford to have one Ship lay idle.

Be assured, my dear Sir Sidney, of my perfect esteem and
regard, and do not let any one persuade you to the contrary.

But my character is, that I will not suffer the smallest tittle of my command to be taken from me; but with pleasure I give way to my friends, among whom I beg you will allow me to consider you, and that I am, with the truest esteem and affection, your faithful humble servant,

NELSON.

---

### TO CAPTAIN BALL, MALTA.

[Letter-Book.]

Private and secret.

Palermo, August 21st, 1799.

My dear Ball,

Being now forced to send six Sail of the Line to Gibraltar, and to keep four or five at Mahon, I am obliged to send Niza to co-operate with you in the reduction of Malta. He is a good young man, and will afford you every assistance. From Malta, his Squadron proceeds to Lisbon, if it is not taken by the French; but I have still some hopes that Lord Keith will get hold of them. General Acton tells me you will have His Sicilian Majesty's letter, to act as Chief of the Maltese for the present, or until the Order is re-established.

I pray fervently for your success, and then you must do the best you can for a garrison. The Alexander shall remain with you; and every comfort which I can give, you may be assured of from your faithful and affectionate

NELSON.

---

### TO THE REVEREND MR. NELSON, HILBOROUGH.

[Autograph, in the Nelson Papers.]

Palermo, August 21st, 1799.

My dear Brother,

I am truly sorry that Administration have neither done that for me or my family which might have been expected. Lords St. Vincent and Duncan have £1000 a-year from Ireland: I have heard of no such thing for *Nelson*. You may be assured that I never have [forgotten] or will forget my family: I think that would be a crime, and if you will tell me to whom and what I am to ask for, for the descent of the Title and the pension goes with it, I will do it. My father, Maurice, yourself and children, Mrs. Bolton's, and Mrs. Matcham's, this is the way I have fixed the Bronté estate, as I have wrote our dear father; that letter you will see. You may be assured, that when a year comes round, and I really know my income, no brother will be more ready to assist than myself. How is Aunt Mary? Assure her she shall want for nothing, and if she does, pray write Lady Nelson, and she will send her anything she desires. Give my kind love to Mrs. Nelson, and when you write, to the children. Kind regards to all our friends at Swaffham, and don't expect a ' turnover the leaf,' for that I cannot ever accomplish; but believe me ever your most affectionate brother,

NELSON.

I do not assume the name of ' Bronté,' except in Sicily, till the King's approbation.

---

TO CAPTAIN BALL, H. M. SHIP ALEXANDER.

[Order-Book.]

The Samuel and Jane Transport, at Palermo, 21st August, 1799.

You are hereby required and directed to put the Ship you command, with all the English Ships under your orders off Malta, under the command of the Marquis de Niza, and follow his orders for your further proceedings. And you are at liberty to repair on shore yourself, leaving the Ship you command in charge of the First Lieutenant, and act and consider yourself as Commander-in-Chief of all the Maltese people, and of all such Seamen, Marines, or others landed from the Squadron on the Island of Malta. And you will co-operate with the Marquis de Niza in all matters and things for the good of his Majesty's service, and in everything tending to the reduction of the French garrison in that Island, for which this shall be your order.

NELSON.

TO MRS. SUCKLING.[1]

[Autograph, in the possession of Captain Montagu Montagu, R.N.]

Palermo, August 22nd, 1799.

My dear Madam,

It was only yesterday that your letter of May 27th reached me. I can easily conceive the great affliction you must have suffered in losing two friends so justly dear to you. My dear Uncle, God only knows with what disinterested affection I loved him, and if I can in any manner be useful to those he has left behind, they may command [me]. I rejoice that my dear friend has done what satisfies you; rest assured I shall do what you wish me respecting the estate, and if you and Mr. Hume[2] will sign a power of attorney, and send it out to me, I shall sign it; but to say the truth, the trust is in such very good hands, that I see no occasion for my acting; but in this and all other matters, which can add to your comfort, I am at your disposal, for believe me with the sincerest esteem, your obliged and affectionate friend,

NELSON.

Excuse this short letter, for my time is more than employed in writing. I know it will give you pleasure to hear, that his Sicilian Majesty has created me Duke of Bronté, and has annexed an estate of £3000 sterling a year, both Title and Estate at my disposal, together with a magnificent diamond-hilted Sword. Make my regards acceptable to all the family; and I must not forget Price and Hickman.

NELSON.

---

TO COMMODORE TROUBRIDGE, H. M. SHIP CULLODEN.

[Order-Book.]

The Samuel and Jane Transport, at Palermo, 22nd August, 1799.

Notwithstanding any former orders, you are hereby required and directed to send me immediately all the English Ships from the Bay of Naples, to join me at this place, except two Sail of the Line; and direct Captain Austen of the Peterel

---

[1] Widow of his uncle, Mr. William Suckling.
[2] James Hume, Esq., Secretary to the Commissioners of the Customs, who was Mr. Suckling's co-executor with Lord Nelson.

to call off Cività Vecchia with your orders to the Swiftsure
to join me also, without a moment's loss of time, and whenever
a Turkish or Russian Squadron come within sight of Naples,
you will immediately weigh with your Ship and join me at
this place.

NELSON.

---

TO CAPTAIN MARTIN, H. M. SHIP NORTHUMBERLAND.

[Letter-Book.]

August 22nd, 1799.

My dear Martin,

The moment either a Turkish or Russian Squadron comes
as far as Leghorn, you must instantly proceed, with every
Ship under your orders, off Mahon; and if Admiral Duckworth is there, follow his orders for your further proceedings.
If he is gone to Gibraltar, you must instantly follow him,
taking with you the Minerva and Thalia. I hope Captain
Nisbet[3] will go on board ; if not able, leave her at Leghorn, to
take him on board, with orders to proceed to Gibraltar, and
follow the orders of his superior Officer. Peterel and Vincejo
will remain at Minorca. I have sent orders to Duckworth. I
am become hard pushed. Ever, my dear Martin, believe me,
your obliged friend,

NELSON.

If Minerve can be spared before the arrival of the Russians,
send her directly to Gibraltar.

---

TO REAR-ADMIRAL DUCKWORTH.

[Letter-Book.]

Palermo, August 23rd, 1799.

My dear Admiral,

The Alceste is this moment arrived, and goes to Messina
for the Convoy this evening. By the report from Gibraltar,
I think there can be no doubt but Lord Keith will have a
battle with those miscreants : the event cannot be doubted.
I am anxiety itself. We are none of us well since our return
—the heat is so excessive. You will go to Gibraltar, or stay

---

[3] He was then ill on shore at Leghorn.

on your present station, as you please.  All the Turkish and
Russian Squadrons are coming here, except those destined for
Genoa, who, I hope, are sailed; and Martin will soon join
you.  Two Ships are ordered, even under present circumstances, from Naples; but the Nobles are caballing against
the power of the King, and as yet, none of them are hanged.
God bless you! and believe me ever, your obliged and affectionate friend,

NELSON.

------

TO LADY NELSON.

[From Clarke and M'Arthur, vol. ii. p. 218.]

August 23rd, 1799.

The last letter from the King's Minister here, Sir John
Acton, is as follows, ' My formal demand is, however, to beg
of your Lordship to protect the Two Sicilies, with your name
and presence, until at last, all Italy is perfectly quiet; therefore,
whatever my state of health may be, I cannot move.  I have
written fully to my father about Bronté, and send you a little
history of it; the present was magnificent, and worthy of a
King.  Yours, &c.,

NELSON.

------

TO ALEXANDER DAVISON, ESQ.

[From Clarke and M'Arthur, vol. ii. p. 219.]

[About 23rd August, 1799.]

The estate[4] is said to be about £3000 a year; I am determined on one thing, that the inhabitants shall be the happiest
in all his Sicilian Majesty's dominions.  I have to thank you
for the interest you have taken in the business of the India
House; their present has been magnificent; but my friend,
these presents, rich as they are, do not elevate me; my pride
is, that at Constantinople, from the Grand Signior to the
lowest Turk, the name of Nelson is familiar in their mouths;
and in this Country, I am everything which a grateful Monarch
and people can call me.  Poor dear Miller is dead, and so will

4 Of Bronté.

be your friend Nelson; but until death, he will wear your Medal⁵ that was intended for Miller. I have the full tide of honour, but little real comfort; could I have that, with a morsel of bread and cheese, it would be all I have to ask of kind Heaven. If the war goes on, I shall be knocked off by a ball, or killed with chagrin. My conduct is measured by the Admiralty by the narrow rule of law, when I think it should have been done by that of common sense. I restored a faithful Ally by breach of orders—Lord Keith lost a Fleet by obedience, against his own sense, yet as one is censured, the other must be approved. I am, &c.,

NELSON.

---

### TO EVAN NEPEAN, ESQ., ADMIRALTY.

[Original, in the Admiralty.]

Palermo, 23rd August, 1799.

Sir,

I herewith enclose you, for the information of their Lordships, the copy of Sir Sidney Smith's letters to me, detailing the Siege of St. Jean d'Acre, with an account of the killed and wounded in the several attacks. And it is with extreme concern I have to mention the death of Captain Miller of his Majesty's Ship Theseus, who was killed on board that Ship on the 14th May last, by the explosion of some shells on the quarter-deck, which killed twenty-six men, wounded forty-five, and nine were drowned by jumping overboard. The Ship is much damaged, but has been in part repaired. The Commander-in-Chief having left the Mediterranean, I have appointed Captain John Stiles from the Cameleon to act as Captain of the Theseus, and Lieutenant Canes, First Lieutenant of the Tigre, to act as Captain of the Cameleon, which I hope their Lordships will approve. I have the honour to be, &c.

NELSON.

⁵ Vide p. 321, ante.

### TO EVAN NEPEAN, ESQ., ADMIRALTY.

[Autograph, in the Admiralty.]

Palermo, August 24th, 1799.

Sir,

His Sicilian Majesty arrived here on the 8th, and was received with the very greatest joy by his Sicilian subjects. On the 13th, I received a letter from his Majesty, with a Sword magnificently ornamented with diamonds; also a dispatch from Prince di Luzzi, Secretary of State. I send copies of the letters. The Russian and Turkish Squadrons are arrived at Messina; but I do not find they inspire much consolation to the inhabitants, whose whole and only hopes are in the English. I have ordered five Sail of the Line to proceed to Gibraltar with a proportion of Frigates. Four Sail of the Line will also be at Minorca; only two Sail of the Line will remain at Naples till the arrival of the Turks and Russians: Portuguese Squadron is gone off to Malta, and I hope to bring this long and tedious business to a close. Their Lordships may be assured that I shall use my utmost endeavours to give security to every part of the Mediterranean during the absence of the Commander-in-Chief. I have the honour, &c.,

NELSON.

---

DISPOSITION OF THE SQUADRON, ENCLOSED IN THE FOREGOING LETTER.

Culloden,
Minotaur,
Goliath,
Audacious,
} Bay of Naples, under Commodore Troubridge.

Swiftsure, at Leghorn, assisting in getting off the Seahorse.
Seahorse, on shore at Leghorn.

Northumberland, 74,
Thalia, 36,
San Leon, 16,
Vincejo, 18,
} On the Coast of Genoa, to assist Field Marshal Suwarrow.

Alexander, 74,
Lion, 64,
Success, 32,
El Corso, 18,
Bonne Citoyenne, 20,
} Off Malta, under Captain Ball.

Foudroyant, 80, gone for the King of Sardinia, to carry him to Leghorn.

Portuguese.—Principe Real, 92, Palermo.

Alfonso, 74, off Malta.

Rainha, 74, on her passage to Malta.

St. Sebastian, 64, ditto, ditto.

Benjamin, 20, off Malta.

Balloon, 14, off Cività Vecchia.

The Portuguese all under orders to proceed down the Mediterranean, as soon as Malta is taken.

Incendiary, Fire-Ship, gone to Leghorn with a Convoy.

Mutine, gone to carry the King of Sardinia's Brothers.

Leviathan, 74,
Majestic, 74,
Vanguard, 74,
Powerful, 74,
Bellerophon, 74,
Zealous, 74,
Aurora, 28,
Swallow, 18,
Portuguese,

Sent by me to Minorca, and there to remain under the orders of Rear-Admiral Duckworth, besides the Frigate, &c. &c., left there by Lord Keith, for the Naval defence of that Island.

Strombolo, Bomb, Bay of Naples.

Perseus, ditto, gone to Sardinia.

St. Vincent, Cutter, cruising after some French privateers.

---

TO HIS EXCELLENCY THE MARQUIS DE NIZA.

[Letter-Book.]

Palermo, August 25th, 1799.

My dear Marquis,

I was most exceedingly sorry to hear that your First Captain, Don Rodrigo de Pinto, was ordered by the Minister of Marine to Lisbon, and as it appeared, on an idea that his conduct had not met with my approbation. If this is the case, I can assure you that I never had the smallest cause of complaint against this gentleman. It is true I have heard that Don Rodrigo did not love the English; but from the account of Captain Retalick, and many other English officers, I am satisfied this is a calumny. I must, therefore, request that your Lordship will do me the favour not to remove Don Rodrigo de Pinto from his situation, until further orders from Lisbon, especially at this moment, when the whole of your Squadron is employed together on a very important service. Believe me, with the truest regard and esteem, my dear Marquis, your obliged and affectionate servant,

NELSON.

TO HIS EXCELLENCY REAR ADMIRAL, THE MARQUIS DE NIZA.

[Order-Book.]

The Samuel and Jane Transport, at Palermo, 25th August, 1799.

You are hereby required and directed to proceed to the Island of Malta, and take under your command all the Combined Squadron that are cruizing there for the blockade of that Island, and use your endeavours to prevent supplies of every kind from getting into the French garrison, by blockading closely the Port of La Valetta, and to co-operate with Captain Ball, who is appointed by His Sicilian Majesty and myself as Chief of the Maltese people, and to command on shore all the Marines, Soldiers, &c., which it may be necessary to land from the Squadron under your command, on the said Island, rendering to him what assistance you are able for the good of the Common Cause, and the reduction of the French garrison, informing me of any events that may happen, necessary for me to know.

NELSON.

TO HIS EXCELLENCY DON R. SOUZA COUTINHO.

[Letter-Book.]

Palermo, August 27th, 1799.

Sir,

Yesterday his Excellency the Marquis de Niza showed me your order for the removal of Don Rodrigo de Pinto from his situation of First Captain. It certainly is not for me to know the reasons which may have induced her Most Faithful Majesty to give this order; but it is justice in me to state to your Excellency that, if it has arose from a belief that any part of the Major's conduct has been disapproved by me, I beg leave to assure you that I never had the smallest reason for displeasure against him; on the contrary, I have always heard Don Rodrigo Pinto spoken of as an excellent Officer. I have therefore presumed to request the Marquis to suspend the execution of your order, as I am convinced it has arose from some mistake.

I feel it also my duty to inform your Excellency, that the Marquis de Niza's conduct has, during the whole time he has been under my command, been such as to entitle him to the appellation of an excellent Officer, and in private life I love him with the affection of a brother; and I beg your Excellency to be assured that I am, with every sentiment of respect, yours, &c.

BRONTE NELSON.

---

### TO CAPTAIN GEORGE HOPE, H. M. SHIP MAJESTIC.

[Autograph, in the possession of his son, Captain James Hope, R.N.]

Palermo, August 28th, 1799.

My dear Hope,

I have his Sicilian Majesty's orders to present you in his name a Diamond Ring, as the dispatch states it, ' To Captain Hope, who embarked his Majesty and the Prince Royal in his barge, on the night of December 21st, 1798,' and which his Majesty desires may be accepted by Captain Hope, as a mark of his Royal gratitude. Ever yours, my dear Hope, faithfully and affectionately,

NELSON.

You will have heard that his Majesty has presented me with a Sword richly adorned with diamonds, also a Dukedom and Estate of £3000 a year.

---

### TO REAR-ADMIRAL DUCKWORTH.

[Letter-Book.]

Palermo, August 28th, 1799.

My dear Admiral,

As the Russian Squadron is sailed for the Gulf of Genoa, I hope the Northumberland and Frigates will soon be with you; for I am exceedingly anxious to keep the Straits free. If you go down, and find that Ships can be spared by the inferiority of the Enemy at Cadiz, I think it for the benefit of the service, that the Zealous, who is so much in need of repair, should go as soon as possible to England; after her, the Majestic, and then Goliath.

You will, if nothing is arranged from England, cause those who go to England, to take the trade from Gibraltar; or, if they sail without a Convoy from Gibraltar, then, if you think a Convoy may be wanted from Lisbon or Oporto, arrange that matter. I am venturing out of my line of duty; but, as the Commander-in-Chief may not even be on the station, I must do the best which my judgment tells me during his temporary absence; and with the greatest [confidence,] my dear Admiral, do I consign the arrangements, from Gibraltar to the limits of the station to you or Troubridge, if you rather choose to stay at Minorca, which I never felt in danger of being attacked. I shall write to Sir James St. Clair,[5] and I hope he will be induced to lend his Sicilian Majesty, for one or two months, an English regiment, if not two—the Regiment of Rolle. As for Russians, or Turkish Ships, this Country has no confidence in anything but English, and are this day writing to England, that a permanent English Squadron may remain on the Coast of Italy. If Sir James could have allowed the troops from Lisbon to have proceeded to Malta, I would forfeit my life, if, in three days, it did not surrender.

The air here is very heavy, and cannot be wholesome. We of this house feel it severely. Mrs. Cadogan has been very ill, and still keeps her bed. Lady Hamilton exceedingly unwell, and I am far from good health; and the infamous politics of the Austrian Minister, Thugut, (who ought to be hanged, if half of what is said is true,) does not serve to give me comfort. If the Commander-in-Chief is with you, or within your reach, I am sure you will communicate all this to him. I expect Incendiary every moment, when Captain Dunn shall join you. I am, &c.,

NELSON.

---

[5] Major-General Sir James St. Clair Erskine, Bart., Commander of the Forces at Minorca, afterwards Earl of Rosslyn, G.C.B.

TO THE CHEVALIER ITALINSKY, RUSSIAN MINISTER AT THE
COURT OF NAPLES.

[Letter-Book.]

Palermo, August 28th, 1799.

My dear Sir,

Herewith I have the honour of sending you a copy of my
letter to Admiral Ouschakoff, and of his answer, in order that
you may transmit them to your Court. Whenever the
Admiral chooses to send the Leander to Mahon, she will be
received, but after even my word not being taken by his
Excellency, I cannot again subject myself to a refusal of
giving up the Leander, agreeable to the intentions of the
Emperor, although the form of order on this occasion is not
arrived. I have the honour to be, &c.,

NELSON.

---

TO CAPTAIN HOOD, H. M. SHIP ZEALOUS.

[Letter Book.]

Palermo, 28th August, 1799.

My dear Hood,

I never had greater pleasure than in executing his Sicilian
Majesty's orders, in sending you a Box from his Majesty,
and as the dispatch expresses it—'To Captain Hood, for
services in the Gulf of Naples and Salerno ; for his operations
on shore, and his care of the Castles of Naples.'

Sir John Acton takes the same opportunity of sending his
Excellency Sir William Hamilton a Box containing sundry Boxes
and Rings, requesting his Excellency will have the goodness to
present them to the Duke of Bronté, that he may distribute
them according to the note enclosed, and in the name of his
Majesty, as a small mark of his Royal gratitude to the several
English commanders.

You will see, my dear Hood, that the Zealous is ordered to
Gibraltar, and whenever the service will admit of it, the
Zealous, Majestic, and Goliath shall go to England. You may
depend my regard is unalterable, and that I am ever, &c.,

NELSON.

TO THE RIGHT HONOURABLE LORD KEITH, K.B.

[Letter-Book.]

Palermo, 28th August, 1799.

My Lord,

Upon Captain Drummond's arrival, I immediately sent the Bulldog with him to Messina, with a letter to the Russian Admiral. Herewith, I send a copy, and also of the Admiral's answer. Captain Drummond will explain to you what passed between the Russian Admiral and himself on the subject. I shall not wait until the Russian Admiral sends the Leander to Mahon. I have the honour to be, &c.,

NELSON.

---

TO CAPTAIN ADAM DRUMMOND.

[From a Copy in the Admiralty.]

Samuel and Jane Transport, Palermo, 29th August, 1799.

Sir,

As Admiral Ouschakoff, commanding the Russian Fleet in these seas, has refused to deliver up the Leander without orders to that effect from his Court, you will proceed in the Bulldog, with the Officers and men appointed to that Ship down to Mahon, and leave them at that place to assist in fitting out any Ships that may want such assistance, proceeding yourself with my letter in the Bulldog, to join Rear-Admiral Duckworth or down to Gibraltar; and from Gibraltar you must take the opportunity of the first Ship to join the Right Honourable Lord Keith, the Commander-in-Chief, and deliver him my letter, and, at the same time, give him the information of the Russian Admiral's refusal to deliver up the Leander; but in failure of meeting with the Commander-in-Chief, you must proceed on to England, and deliver my letter for the Commander-in-Chief unto the Secretary of the Admiralty, and acquaint him with the cause of your arrival. I have the honour to be, &c.,

NELSON.

TO MAJOR-GENERAL SIR JAMES ST. CLAIR ERSKINE, BART.,
MAHON.

[Letter-Book.]

Palermo, 29th August, 1799.

My dear Sir James,

Although, thank God, things are in the fairest way possible of the French being drove not only entirely out of Italy, but of Field-Marshal Suwarrow fixing himself in the southern Provinces of France during the winter, yet, as all, or nearly so, of the force is at present in the northern part of Italy, the Roman State, with insurrections and daily murders, is still under the French flag, with not more than 1500 regulars in the whole State except Ancona. In Città Vecchia are about 1000 Regulars, with the whole Country against them; but such mobs are going about plundering, that they (that alone being their object) are sometimes good Republicans and sometimes their bitter enemies.

This mobbing system has also its desire of getting also into the Neapolitan Dominions, which would thus be in nearly as bad a state as when in possession of the French. This is, my dear Sir James, a true statement of the Roman State; therefore we can only look to you for help to deliver us from anarchy and confusion, by freeing the Roman State from the French. The answer given to Captain Hallowell on his sending to Città Vecchia was, that they certainly knew the situation of Italy; but that such a place could not be given up without the appearance of a regular force. If you can spare from the garrison of Minorca 1200 good men for two months, I am sure that, as Sir Charles Stuart by his timely exertion saved this Kingdom from anarchy and confusion, and perhaps from rebellion, so it is now, my dear Sir, I trust, in your power (and I have assured both the King and Queen of your readiness to serve them and the good Cause as much as Sir Charles) to send [them] for the taking possession of Città Vecchia and Rome; this done, and with my life, I will answer for the success of the expedition. All would be quiet and happy; and their Sicilian Majesties might return to their throne without any alarms from mobs. It is to our King and Country, that these good Sovereigns owe their present state of comfort, and which you will have the power to increase to perfect happiness. I know it is not probable that you would like to send all British troops; but one good Regiment, and Rolls' Regiment would do the business. I am sure I need not venture to say more on this subject. Your Excellency's judgment and heart will point out the necessity of the measure, if it can be accomplished. When I know your determination, I will take care to have every part of my Naval force off Cività Vecchia, ready to co-operate in the good work. Believe me, dear Sir James, your obliged and faithful servant,

NELSON.

---

TO HIS EXCELLENCY J. SPENCER SMITH, ESQ., CONSTANTINOPLE.

[From a Copy in the Nelson Papers.]

Palermo, 31st August, 1799.

My dear Sir,

I received by the Charon your letter of the 10th July, and am sorry I could not succeed with Captain Mackellar for the discharge of Mr. Miles. First, as the Ship had not *pratica;* and a stronger reason of Captain Mackellar was a letter from the young man's friends, saying that his wife, a very improper connexion, was going to join him at Constantinople, and begging Captain Mackellar not to discharge him. No one rejoices more than myself at the rewards your brother is receiving for his indefatigable labours, and no one has done more ample justice to his merits. A Turkish Messenger, who yesterday brought me your letter of 26th July, is this moment come to say he shall wait an hour for my answer. As, most probably, he will not be so soon with you as many other conveyances, I shall only say that we have no news whatever of the two Fleets, except that they were both to the north of Lisbon on 8th August. Field-Marshal Suwarrow is still successful, having taken the *Bocchetta,* and is, probably, at this moment in possession of Genoa. In France there are also great insurrections, and I have little doubt but Suwarrow will establish his winter-quarters in the south of France.

I am glad to see the Grand Vizir's letter to your worthy brother, and it is reported here, that the Grand Sultan has sent him an *Aigrette*. As the Egyptian campaign is, I hope, finished by the death of every Frenchman, (for I own it is against my principles to suffer one man of that Army to return to France,) perhaps Sir Sidney may be with you, if so, pray remember me most kindly to him ; and believe me, my dear Sir, your much obliged humble servant,

NELSON.

P.S.—I have communicated your letters to our good friend Sir William Hamilton, and he would write, but he does not think that the messenger will soon get to you; but he desires his kindest regards to you and Sir Sidney.

---

TO HIS EXCELLENCY SIR JOHN ACTON, BART.

[Letter-Book.]

Palermo, 31st August, 1799.

My dear Sir,

I send your Excellency a letter from Captain Ball of his Majesty's Ship Alexander, with two papers enclosed. I cannot bear the thought of what the papers convey ; but it is my duty, as a British Admiral, to ask of your Excellency an explanation of this very extraordinary business, (which, I trust in God, is entirely false, as far as relates to his Sicilian Majesty and Prince Luzzi.) If this man is an unauthorized person, his Majesty will have no difficulty in approving of my condemning him as a spy, and as such, ordering him to be hanged. But what shall I say if Prince Luzzi has authorized this man to enter La Valetta, and to communicate with the Enemy ? I must say, that the Minister has betrayed his trust; for I never will believe that their Sicilian Majesties could treat in such a —— manner his Britannic Majesty, my Royal Master. On your Excellency's communication of his Sicilian Majesty's pleasure, depends the line of conduct which my duty will call upon me to perform. I have the honour to be, &c.

BRONTE NELSON.

## TO COMMODORE TROUBRIDGE.

[Letter-Book: an Extract only.]

31st August, 1799.

Our joint exertions have been used to get the King to go to Naples, but of no avail: the Austrians will be there before him. I do not expect any of the Russian troops this some time to come. I am indeed sick and tired of this want of energy, and when I find the impossibility of being longer useful, I will retire from this inactive service.

You send the report that there are no Spaniards at Cartha-gena—Cockburn that there are no French at Toulon; Duck-worth tells me the contrary, but I trust he is mistaken: Lord Keith that there are seven Sail at Cadiz. I do not believe it, but I must take care and keep the Straits open. If Duck-worth is not gone to Gibraltar I shall not keep you here four hours; and if he is, I shall send you to arrange a proper Naval defence for Minorca. Hood, Foley, and Hope go home before the winter. I owe it to the two former if they wish it. I have wrote before that we must pay for the Portuguese people landed at Naples, when the accounts come here, but you must draw for the whole at Naples.

# APPENDIX

# APPENDIX.

## A.

### BATTLE OF THE NILE.

THE following Letter ought to have been added to those in pages 73—76 :—

TO REAR-ADMIRAL LORD NELSON.

[Autograph, in the Nelson Papers.]

"Admiralty, 9th January, 1799.

" My Lord,

" The King having been pleased to order a certain number of Gold Medals to be struck, in commemoration of the Victory obtained by His Majesty's Fleet under your Lordship's command, over that of the French, on the 1st and 2nd of August last, off the Coast of Egypt, I am commanded by His Majesty to present to your Lordship one of the Medals above mentioned, and to signify His Majesty's pleasure that you should wear it when in your Uniform, in the manner described by the directions which (together with the Medal and Riband belonging to it) I have the honour to transmit to your Lordship.

" I am also commanded to communicate to you the King's pleasure, that your Lordship shall be presented to His Majesty the first time you appear at St. James's, with this Decoration.

" Allow me to express the great satisfaction I feel in being made the channel of communicating to you so distinguished a mark of His Majesty's approbation. I have the honour to be, &c.            " SPENCER."

#### DIRECTIONS FOR WEARING THE MEDAL.

In the same manner as the Medal which Lord Nelson received on the occasion of the Victory obtained by his Majesty's Fleet under Lord St. Vincent's command is worn ; hanging it a little higher or lower than that, as may be most convenient, so that both the Medals may be distinctly seen.

A spare parcel of Riband is sent herewith, and more may be had (if wanted) at Potter's, Haberdasher, Charing-Cross.

---

It is proper to state, in corroboration of the claim made on behalf of the late ADMIRAL SIR THOMAS FOLEY, to the merit of having acted upon his own responsibility in leading *inside* the Enemy's line at the Battle of the Nile, that the Editor has been favoured with a Note from REAR-ADMIRAL BROWNE, who was for some

months First-Lieutenant of the Elephant, in 1800, when commanded by Captain
Foley, which proves that Sir Thomas Foley himself said that he adopted that proceeding without any previous order or arrangement.

                                              "Bath, April 27th, 1845.

"Having had the honour of being First Lieutenant of the Elephant for some
months, when commanded by Captain Foley, and in the constant habit of conversing
with him on that Engagement, I can speak positively to the fact of his having
stated, that he led the British Fleet inside *without* any previous order or arrangement, except (I believe) that each Ship should have her cables arranged so as to
anchor by the stern, if necessary." . . . . "Captain Foley also told me, that he
had a conviction, on observing the Enemy's position so near the shore, that a
feeling of security would make them less attentive to their preparation for battle on
that side than on the other, by which a great advantage would be gained by attacking
on the weak side, which was the fact, as much confusion was occasioned by not
having made such preparation.   I believe this is all you wished to be informed of,
and as Captain Foley's character as a man of honour, as well as one of the bravest
and most zealous Officers in his Majesty's Navy, and so great a favourite with Lord
Nelson that he chose the Elephant as his Flag-Ship at Copenhagen, you may
suppose no consideration whatever would have induced him to state what was not
the fact, and to his having thus stated, I bear witness.   I am, dear Sir, your very
obedient servant,

                    " THOMAS BROWNE, Rear-Admiral of the Red."

                         ———————

It has been stated, in p. 199, that MISS KNIGHT, the daughter of Rear-Admiral
Sir Joseph Knight, was the friend of Lord Nelson, and of many of the Captains of
his Squadron.   That intelligent Lady was at Naples in 1798, and removed to
Palermo with the Court, in December of that year, where she remained until she
accompanied the Queen, Sir William and Lady Hamilton, and Lord Nelson to
Leghorn, and thence to Vienna and England, in June 1800.   Miss Knight kept a regular *Journal* of her life, from the age of fifteen to within a few days of her decease in
1837, and the original MS. is now in the possession of Lady Egerton, the daughter
of Rear-Admiral Sir Thomas Troubridge, Bart., and wife of Lieutenant-General Sir
Charles Bulkeley Egerton, G.C.M.G.

Lady Egerton most obligingly permitted the Editor to make such extracts from
Miss Knight's Journal, as he might think desirable for this work; and they will be
read with great interest.

The following relate to the BATTLE OF THE NILE :—

" Naples, 3rd September, 1798.—"The joy expressed by the Neapolitans is very
great.   The King, when he heard it, was at table; he rose and kissed the Queen
and children, and said, 'Now, Children, you are safe.'   It happened to be a Gala
for the birth of a Princess of Tuscany: the Queen told all the ladies, &c., that
Sicily was safe."

" 21st September.—This evening two balls gave signal of Ships being in sight.
22nd.—In the evening, went out with Sir William and Lady Hamilton, music, &c.,
to meet Admiral Nelson, who in the Vanguard, with the Thalia Frigate (Captain
Newhouse) was seen coming in.   We went on board, about a league out at sea, and
sailed in with him : soon after us, the King came on board, and staid till the
anchor was dropped.   He embraced the Admiral with the greatest warmth, and said
he wished he could have been in the engagement, and served under his orders; and
that he likewise wished he could have been in England, when the news of the

victory arrived there. He went down to see the Ship, and was delighted to perceive the care taken of a wounded man, who had two to serve him, and one reading to him. He asked to see the hat which saved the Admiral's life, when he was wounded in the head with a splinter. The Queen was taken with a fit of the ague when she was coming on board with the Princesses. Commodore Caraccioli came soon after the King, and many of the Neapolitan nobility, bands of music, &c. It happened to be the anniversary of our King's coronation. The Admiral came on shore with us, and said, it was the first time he had been out of his Ship for six months, except once on board Lord St. Vincent. The Russian Ambassador and all the Legation came out to meet him. When we landed at the Health Office, the applauses and the crowd of people were beyond description. Admiral Nelson is little, and not remarkable in his person either way; but he has great animation of countenance, and activity in his appearance : his manners are unaffectedly simple and modest. He lodges at Sir William Hamilton's, who has given him the upper apartment. The whole City is mad with joy. . . . . In the evening, went to visit the Admiral, at Sir William Hamilton's, where there was a grand illumination. The Neapolitans have written up *Vittoria* and *Viva Nelson* at every corner of the streets."

The circumstances noticed in the next Extracts, are mentioned in Lord Nelson's letters.

" 5th November, 1798.—Appeared in sight Admiral Nelson, in the Vanguard, with the Minotaur, Captain Louis, from Malta, and they were all day coming in ; but the Admiral came on shore at four o'clock, and went immediately to Caserta, where he was scarce arrived when the Hereditary Princess was brought to bed of a daughter, and the bells were ringing, guns firing, &c. Next morning, the 6th, the Admiral presented to the King the French Colours taken at Gozo, telling his Majesty that he had sixteen thousand subjects more than before." (*Vide* p. 164, ante.)

" 15th December, 1798.—The night before last, came in two Portuguese Ships, and the Alcmene (Captain Hope) with a Turkish Ambassador, interpreters, &c., bringing the diamond Aigrette, &c., for Lord Nelson. This Court is in the greatest consternation, and does not trust any of its subjects. We were desired by Lord Nelson and the Hamiltons to pack up our things, previous to an embarkation, which seems inevitable. The Queen and Princesses are to go with Lord Nelson." (*Vide* p. 202, ante.)

In her communications with Lord Nelson and his Officers, Miss Knight collected several anecdotes of him, of which the following are new:

" He says, that when he was seventeen years of age, he won £300 at a gaming-table ; but he was so shocked at reflecting that, had he lost them, he should not have known how to pay them, that from that time to this he has never played again."

" When Admiral Nelson's arm was cut off, the Surgeon asked, if he should not embalm it, to send it to England to be buried; but he said, ' throw it into the hammock, with the brave fellow that was killed beside me'—a common seaman."

" As we were going in the Admiral's barge, the other day, looking at the Ships and talking of the victory, Sir William Hamilton could not be pacified for the French calling it a drawn battle. ' Nay, it was a drawn battle,' said the Admiral, ' for they drew the blanks, and we the prizes.' "

" The Queen has desired to have a portrait of the Admiral. Little Prince Leopold says, he will get a copy, and stand continually opposite to it, saying, ' Dear Nelson, teach me to become like you.' "

To these may be added a very characteristic circumstance respecting the gallant Troubridge, whose Ship ran aground before the Battle of the Nile.

" Captain Troubridge wrote to condole with Captain Darby, of the Bellerophon, for his wounds, and the number of people killed in his Ship; but added, that had his sufferings been fifty times as much, *he* had rather have been in his place, than have borne the anguish he felt from running aground, and being kept out of the Action— that he had found great difficulty in keeping from shooting himself, and that he even then frequently shed tears. Captain Darby, and Captain Gould who was present when he received the letter, both wept."

---

## B.

[From the Enrolment, referred to in p. 74, ante.]

Sir Horatio Nelson, K.B., Creation of Baron.

GEORGE THE THIRD, by the Grace of God, &c., to all Archbishops, Dukes, Marquesses, Earls, Viscounts, Bishops, Barons, Knights, Provosts, Freemen, and all other our Officers, Ministers, and Subjects whatsoever, to whom these presents shall come, greeting, Know ye, that We, of our especial grace, certain knowledge, and mere motion, have advanced, preferred, and created Our trusty and well-beloved SIR HORATIO NELSON, Knight of the Most Honourable Order of the Bath, Rear-Admiral of the Blue Squadron of our Fleet, to the State, Degree, Dignity, and Honour of BARON NELSON OF THE NILE, and of BURNHAM THORPE, in Our County of Norfolk; and him, the said Sir Horatio Nelson, Baron Nelson of the Nile and of Burnham Thorpe aforesaid, do by these presents create, advance, and prefer, and We have appointed, given, and granted, and by these presents for Us and Our heirs and successors do appoint, give, and grant, unto him, the said Sir Horatio Nelson, the Name, State, Degree, Style, Dignity, Title, and Honour of BARON NELSON of the Nile and of Burnham Thorpe aforesaid, to have and to hold the said Name, State, Degree, Style, Dignity, Title, and Honour of BARON NELSON of the Nile and of Burnham Thorpe aforesaid, unto him the said Sir Horatio Nelson, and the heirs male of his body lawfully begotten, and to be begotten. Willing, and by these presents, granting for Us, Our heirs and successors, that the said Sir Horatio Nelson and his heirs male aforesaid, and every of them successively, may bear and have the Name, State, Degree, Style, Dignity, Title, and Honour of BARON NELSON of the Nile and of Burnham Thorpe aforesaid; and that they and every of them successively may be called and styled by the name of BARON NELSON of the Nile, and of Burnham Thorpe, in Our County of Norfolk; and that the said Sir Horatio Nelson and his heirs male aforesaid, and every of them successively, may in all things be held and deemed BARONS NELSON of the Nile and of Burnham Thorpe aforesaid, and be treated and reputed as Barons; and that they, and every of them successively and respectively, may have, hold, and possess a seat, place, and voice in the Parliaments and Public Assemblies and Councils of Us, Our heirs and successors within Our Kingdom of Great Britain, amongst other Barons, as Barons of Parliament and Public Assemblies and Councils. And also, that he, the said Sir Horatio Nelson and his heirs male aforesaid, may enjoy and use, and every of them may enjoy and use, by the name of BARON NELSON of the Nile and of Burnham Thorpe aforesaid, all and singular the rights, privileges, pre-eminences, immunities, and advantages to the degree of a Baron in all things duly and of right belonging, which other Barons of this Our Kingdom of Great Britain have heretofore honourably and quietly used and enjoyed, or as they do at present use and enjoy. Lastly, we will, and by these presents for Us, Our heirs and successors, do grant to the said Sir Horatio Nelson, that these Our Letters Patent, or the enrolment thereof, shall be sufficient and effectual in the law for the dignifying, investing, and really ennobling him, the said Sir Horatio Nelson, and his heirs male aforesaid, with the Title, State, Dignity, and Honour of BARON NELSON of the Nile and of Burnham Thorpe aforesaid, and this without any investiture, rites, ornaments, or ceremonies whatsoever, in this behalf due and accustomed, which, for some certain reasons best known to Us, We could not in due manner do and perform, any ordinance, use, custom, rite, ceremony, prescription, or provision due, or used to be had done or performed, in conferring Honours of this kind or any other matter or thing to the contrary thereof notwithstanding. We will also, and without Fine in the Hanaper, &c. In witness, &c., witness, &c., the sixth day of November, in the thirty-ninth year of Our Reign. By Writ of Privy Seal."

---

# C.

## SURRENDER OF THE CASTLES OF UOVO AND NUOVO, AND TRIAL AND EXECUTION OF COMMODORE CARACCIOLI.

[Referred to in page 384.]

The importance of these Transactions in relation to Lord Nelson's character and fame, makes it necessary to insert *every document*, and to state *every fact* which has been discovered, so that the world may be enabled to form a just opinion on the subject.

A perusal of the Letters in this Volume for the months of April and May, and until the middle of June, 1799, will shew the state of the Kingdom of Naples, and the success which had attended the Royalists, aided by the English Squadron and some Russian and Turkish troops, in expelling the French army, subduing the Rebels, or, as they called themselves, Patriots, and re-establishing the Monarchy. Early in May, the French troops withdrew from Naples, and encamped at Caserta, leaving a strong garrison in the Castles of St. Elmo, Uovo, and Nuovo. Cardinal Ruffo, who had placed himself at the head of the Royalists, and whom the King had appointed Vicar-General, advanced upon Naples ; and after obtaining possession of Caprea and Castel-a-Mare, proceeded to invest the Castles of Uovo and Nuovo, where the principal Neapolitans who had joined the new Republic and borne arms against their Sovereign, had taken refuge.

The English Squadron had been under the orders of Captain Troubridge, in the Culloden, but about the 15th of May, Lord Nelson recalled him, in consequence of the Enemy's Fleet being at Sea, when the command of the few English Ships which were left there devolved upon Captain Edward James Foote, of the Seahorse Frigate, who had under his orders the Perseus Bomb, Captain Oswald, and the Sicilian Squadron, under Commodore Count de Thurn. With these Vessels, after the surrender of the Forts Revigliano and Castel-a-Mare on the 15th of June, Captain Foote proceeded against the Castles of Uovo and Nuovo; and his subsequent measures will be best understood from his own Statement and Dispatches :— [6]

---

[6] All these dispatches and other letters are taken from Captain Foote's "Vindication."

"A COPY OF THE STATEMENT GIVEN BY CAPTAIN FOOTE TO LORD NELSON, AT HIS LORDSHIP'S DESIRE; IN WHICH ARE INCLUDED THE TERMS OF THE CAPITULATION WITH THE FORTS REVIGLIANO AND CASTEL-A-MARE, AND THE LETTER WHICH CAPTAIN FOOTE SENT TO THE GARRISON OF CASTEL DEL UOVO, WITH THE COMMANDANT'S ANSWER.

"I shall not take any notice of the various Letters which I received from the Cardinal; they will prove, if investigated, how very little he knew about the force that was under my orders, or what was possible to be done by a few small Ships of War; and that he kept advancing, without any fixed plan or project, trusting entirely to the chapter of accidents.

"On the 9th of June, I received a letter from the Cardinal, in which he mentioned, that, on the 13th or 14th, he should be at the Tour del Greco; and he gave me some signals, by which I was to know when the Royal Army reached that place; at which time, I was to give him all the assistance that lay in my power, by sea. Accordingly, on the 13th, I stood into the Bay, and it appeared to me, that the Coast, from Portici to Castel-à-Mare, was in a state of insurrection; but I saw no signals. Innumerable requests were made to me, for assistance, but no one could tell me for certain, where the Cardinal was. I supplied the Chief of the Tour del Greco with powder, musket-ball, and canister, and seeing the French and Neapolitan colours flying on the Fort of Granatelli, I immediately stood for it, having the Neapolitan Frigate Sirena and two Gun-boats with me. This Fort was garrisoned by upwards of 200 men, who kept up a constant fire on a party of Royalists, who were in the King's palace at Portici, and just outside of it, which they returned with musketry, and from one piece of artillery: when close in with Granatelli, I fired a few shot at it, and the Republican colours were hauled down, and the Royalists rushed in, putting the whole of the garrison to the sword. Shortly after, a certain D. Constantine di Felippi came onboard, and acquainted me, that he commanded about 4,000 Royalists, that he meant to attack Villema the next day, when I promised to assist him as much as I possibly could.

"The Cardinal, as I have since learnt, instead of being at his rendezvous, the Tour del Greco, at the appointed time, was at Nola; but as to any direct information, I had none, not receiving any letter from him between the 9th and 17th of this month. Some country people informed me that the Republicans had a camp of 800 infantry and 120 cavalry, near the Tour del Annunziato, which was protected on the sea-side by ten Gun-boats and two Mortar-boats. I had written to the Count de Thurn for three Galleys, which were then not much wanted at Procida; but, instead of their coming, I only received excuses about the weather (which, no doubt, was at one time threatening, but it afterwards cleared up). This caused me to write a positive order, and the galleys were sent; but the Count de Thurn at the same time informed me, that his instructions were quite independent of my orders, and that he could not receive any but from his Sovereign, or those who were his superiors. Reference may be had to my letters on this subject, but I do not wish it to be renewed, as I am on very good terms with the Count de Thurn, and am perfectly satisfied that the evil originated in his having secret orders—which, if I had not acted cautiously, might, in consequence of those left with me, have been attended with very fatal consequences. On the evening of the 13th, the Cardinal, (or rather Russians) took the Fort of Villema, and the bridge of Madalena; Caraccioli's Gun-boats annoyed them a good deal, the weather preventing my approaching sufficiently close with the Frigates; but if the Galleys had been with me, I should certainly have taken some of the Gun-boats, or caused them to retreat. On the 14th the weather was bad; and it was not until the 15th, the day the Galleys joined me, that I could venture so deep into the Bay as the Castles of Revigliano and Castel-à-Mare, which capitulated on terms mentioned in my Letter-book, (and which I will also insert at the end of this statement,) which circumstance I considered of the utmost consequence—for if their garrisons, or friends, amounting to about 1000 men, had availed themselves of the opportunity to concert with the Republicans at Annunziato, and make an attack on the rear of the Cardinal's army, his enterprise must inevitably have failed.

" On the 17th, I informed the Cardinal, that I should immediately join the Gunboats and Mortar-boats at the Pie di Grotta, with a view of attacking Castel Uovo ; and, on the 18th, I sent Captain Oswald, of the Perseus, with a letter to the Commandant of that Fort, in the hope of its opening the way to a negotiation,[7] (a copy of which I shall also insert at the end of this). On the night of the 17th, I had sent an Officer to the Cardinal, who told him that the Rebels and the French, particularly the latter, had refused to capitulate to an Ecclesiastic ; that his means were scarcely sufficient to reduce determined and obstinate people ; and that he wished me to try what I could do, by offering to hearken to the terms they might have to propose. I received a very insolent verbal answer from the Commandant of Castel Uovo, which I made the Cardinal acquainted with, and that it was my intention to attack it by every means in my power ; to which his Eminence replied, ' that it was no longer time to hearken to Capitulations, and that it became necessary to think seriously of attacking Fort St. Elmo.'

" The next day (the 19th) to my great surprise, I received a letter from the Cardinal, requesting me to cease hostilities, and not to re-commence them whilst the Flag of Truce was flying, as a negotiation had taken place. The same night I sent an Officer to the Cardinal, to acquaint him, that the British were not accustomed to grant so long a suspension of arms ; and that, as my Sovereign was a principal Ally of the King of the Two Sicilies, I claimed a right to be made acquainted with what was going on. The Cardinal sent word back, that the Chevalier de Micheroux conducted the Treaty, and that he had sent my letter to him, that he might inform me what steps were taken. Not receiving a line from the Chevalier de Micheroux, I informed the Cardinal that I thought nothing could be more prejudicial to the interest of his Sicilian Majesty than the having such a multiplicity of Chiefs, and that I knew of no other than his Eminence, who was specially charged with the interests of the King of Naples, and that I could act with no other person. The Cardinal told the Officer whom I sent, that he knew nothing of what was going on ; that he stood in great need of the aid of the Russians ; that he would not give them the least ground for complaint ; and that it was the Russians who conducted the Treaty. On the 19th, I received a plan of a Capitulation, already signed by the Cardinal, and the Chief of the Russians, with a request that I would put my name to it. In answer, I informed the Cardinal, that I had done so, because I considered him as the confidential Agent of His Sicilian Majesty, and that some advantage would result from the Capitulation, otherwise he would not have signed it ; but I could not say I approved of such a manner of treating, and that I could not be answerable for its consequences. I also made some observations relative to St. Elmo's capitulating, which may be seen in my Letter-book.

---

[7] Extract from the Seahorse's *Log*, in the Admiralty:—" Monday, *June* 17, 1799. Standing towards Naples ; at 3, anchored off Pausilippi ; at 9, made the signal for a Flag of Truce. Captain Oswald went with terms of Capitulation to the Castle del Uovo, which immediately refused.

" 18. Our Gun and Mortar Boats bombarding Castle Uovo. Made the signal for a Flag of Truce."

"At length, on the 22nd, I received a letter from the Chevalier de Micheroux, with the Capitulation in form, already signed by the Cardinal and the Chief of the Russians. I replied to the Chevalier de Micheroux, that I had signed where he pointed out; but that I protested against everything that could be in the least contrary to the honour and rights of my Sovereign and the British Nation. I signed this Capitulation—lest, on a reverse of fortune, or the arrival of the Enemy's fleet, it might have been asserted, that my refusal was the cause of such misfortunes as might occur, and because I considered that the Cardinal was acquainted with the will and intention of his Sovereign; and the Count de Thurn had told me, that the Chevalier de Micheroux was authorized to act in a diplomatic character.

"The result of all this is, that, with a very small force, I have had to conquer difficulties, which were only got the better of by that terror which the British flag inspires; that I never was consulted by the Cardinal relative to the Capitulation; and that I had neither instructions, or any document, to assist or guide me."

COPY OF THE CORRESPONDENCE BETWEEN CARDINAL RUFFO AND CAPTAIN FOOTE, WITH CAPTAIN FOOTE'S LETTERS TO LORD NELSON, FROM THE 16TH TO THE 24th OF JUNE, 1799.

TO CAPTAIN FOOTE.

"Excellency, [June 16th or 17th, 1799.]
"As the Castle Nuovo is treating, I have to request you will cease hostilities for the present; to recommence them, however, the moment that the Treaty shall be at an end, without the desired effect. Your Excellency's most devoted and faithful servant, "F. CARD. RUFFO, V.G.

"It may be proper, however, to continue hostilities against the Castle Uovo, if a Flag of Truce is not constantly kept flying on it."

TO CARDINAL RUFFO.

"Eminence, "On board the Seahorse, June 17th, 1799.
"I have the honour to receive your Eminence's letter, informing me that the Castle of Nuovo was treating. Whenever a Flag of Truce is hoisted on the Castle of Uovo, I shall direct all hostilities against it to cease, but it is now ten o'clock, and I see no such Flag flying on it. I shall therefore order the Bombards and Gun-boats to continue firing; and it is with pleasure I inform your Eminence, that a considerable number of bombs were thrown yesterday with great effect. I have the honour to be, your Eminence's most devoted and obedient servant,
"EDWARD JAMES FOOTE.

"P.S.—A letter and some orders have this minute been delivered to me from the Chevalier Micheroux; I have laid them aside, and sent him word, that I can receive no other orders than those of your Eminence."

TO CAPTAIN FOOTE.

"Excellency, "Head-quarters, near Naples, June 17th, 1799.
"All goes on very well, and I have reason to hope that the Castel Nuovo, and also the Castel dell Uovo, will surrender: because they show reluctance to surrender to an Ecclesiastic, let your Excellency's flags be displayed, and I believe they will yield at the sight of them.

"Send your orders on shore, that hostilities may cease as the Treaty commences. The conditions are simple and plain enough. It is granted to the French to be carried back by sea to France, with their effects and property, at his Majesty's expense; and those who are not French are allowed the liberty of following them, and to embark with their effects, but at their own expense. There is the whole of the matter. I enclose you two Proclamations, which however concern only the interior of the City. I remain, with all respect, your Excellency's most devoted servant,

"F. CARD. RUFFO, V.G.

"P.S.—I must add, that should you approach and summon them to surrender, we may hope that they would surrender to the English forces, previous to the attack of the Bombards and Gun-boats.

"2 P.S.—In the Capitulation offered to those in the Castles above-mentioned, are also to be comprised those Republicans who are actually encamped under the Fort of St. Elmo.

"F. CARD. RUFFO, V.G."

TO CAPTAIN FOOTE.

"Excellency, "Head-quarters, near Naples, June 18th, 1799.

"It is useless to think of Capitulations, instead of which we must now think seriously of attacking the Castle of St. Elmo. Those mortars therefore that we may have occasion for, should be landed at the bridge of Maddalena, to be drawn up from thence to St. Elmo. We have got one here, which shall be added to the two you will send; even those with platforms, with much care and management, may be used. In the mean time let us have the two above-mentioned, that are not with platforms, and the bombs that belong to them. Send also some guns of large calibre, with the corresponding ammunition.

" I have sent 200 of the Foreign troops, and now send 500 more of our Fusiliers to Chiaja; but the fright has been great, and they go reluctantly. They must be placed in the houses, where they will make a better stand, than when uncovered and unsheltered. I speak of the irregular troops. We will send more troops if necessary. I remain, with great respect, your Excellency's most devoted Servant,

"F. CARD. RUFFO, V.G."

TO CAPTAIN FOOTE.

"Excellency, "Head-quarters, June 19th, 1799.

"At present it is necessary to cease firing, because a Flag of Truce is just come, even from the Castel Uovo. Let this regulate your Excellency's conduct for the present; keeping at the same time everything ready to renew the attack as soon as I request you to do so, or that hostilities shall have recommenced against the Castles on the sea. I return your Excellency my best thanks for your attention and politeness towards me. If you think proper to send a person to treat on the part of the British Nation, it will be very well; it being my intention that all the coalesced Powers should join in the Treaty. I am, with distinguished regard, your Excellency's most devoted and faithful Servant,

"F. CARD. RUFFO, V.G."

TO REAR-ADMIRAL LORD NELSON, K.B.

" Seahorse, off Naples, June 18th, 1799, at Noon, and continued to the 20th.

" My Lord,

" I got under weigh from Castel-à-Mare yesterday morning, with the Seahorse and Perseus, leaving the Neapolitan frigate Sirena at that place to get the Bombs and Gun-vessels out, and to forward them to the anchorage opposite Sir William

Hamilton's Casino, where I anchored at 3 P. M. with the intention of countenancing a small battery in the Tuilleries, that had greatly damaged the Castel del Uovo; but during the night the Enemy spiked the guns, and in the morning I got under weigh, and stood into the Bay. In consequence of the very interesting news which the Count de Thurn, and the Governor of Procida, sent me yesterday evening, relative *to the change in the destination of the Squadron* under your command, I sent Captain Oswald to the Cardinal, to represent the absolute necessity of getting possession of the Castles, even by granting favourable terms; and his Eminence having sent me the enclosed answer, I this morning sent Captain Oswald with a letter to the Castles of Uovo and Nuovo, a copy of which, and the Commandant of Uovo's verbal answer, I herewith transmit : Captain Oswald thought it unnecessary to go to the Castle Nuovo.

"June 18th, P. M.—I am just returned from a conference with the Cardinal, to whom I spoke my mind very freely. I told his Eminence, I feared he would be betrayed by the Officers who were sent from Palermo, as they were unworthy to serve His Sicilian Majesty, and yet were now not only employed, but placed in high situations. I observed that the regular Troops were disgusted at being commanded by the numerous Chiefs at the head of the Calabrese, and other undisciplined armed men; and I also recommended uniting the Regulars, and then making some considerable effort. The Cardinal then told me St. Elmo was his object, and that he wished me to send for the mortars which I had told him were at Castel-à-Mare; this I instantly did, and at the same time remarked there could be no doubt, but if St. Elmo could be brought to surrender, the Castles of Uovo and Nuovo must fall of course; yet it was necessary to consider whether there was a sufficient number of Regular troops to put such a plan in execution; to which his Eminence replied, that the French had so few men they could not make a successful sortie. The Mortar-boats, and Gun boats, arrived this evening from Castel-à-Mare; they are all in good order, and far superior to those sent from Palermo.

"June 19th.—During the whole of last night and this morning, the Castel-à-Mare mortar-boats have been throwing shells at Castel del Uovo, under the direction of Captain Oswald of the Perseus, (who is uneasy if any duty is performed without him,) and Lieutenant Milbanke, of the Royal Artillery, with his party and those belonging to the Perseus; and I have great pleasure in saying the service was remarkably well executed. I have sent the whole of the late garrison of Castel-à-Mare, on board the Xebeck at Procida, giving the Corporal, who has charge of them, an order, of which I have the honour to send your Lordship a copy. 5 P. M.—I have just sent a letter to the Cardinal, of which I have the honour to send you a copy, with his Eminence's answer.

"20th, 4 P. M.—The Armistice still continuing, I have again sent to the Cardinal to beg to be acquainted with what is going on, and to recommend expedition. 8 P. M.—From the answer I have just received from the Cardinal, it appears that a Capitulation is likely to take place with the Castles Uovo and Nuovo, which I make no doubt will be favourable to the Rebels, as the regular force employed against them is so small, and the destination of the French fleet is as yet unknown to us. I was informed yesterday that the Commandant of Castel del Uovo had been dismissed for his insolent behaviour to Captain Oswald, when he went with a Flag of Truce to that Fortress on the 18th instant, and that the letter I sent on that day had greatly accelerated the present treaty. I have recalled the Bulldog, and she is now cruizing in the Bay. The Mutine is stationed off the Western part of Ischia, and the Perseus remains with the Seahorse off Pausilippi. I have the honour to be, my Lord, your Lordship's most obedient, humble servant, "EDWARD JAMES FOOTE."

### COPY OF THE LETTER SENT TO THE CASTEL OF UOVO.

" I, Edward James Foote, Commanding the united Naval force of his Britannic Majesty, and that of the Two Sicilies, being grieved at the misfortunes which naturally afflict a Nation immersed in all the horrors of civil war, and earnestly wishing to restore peace and tranquillity to your unhappy Country, I am willing, previous to having recourse to arms, to observe to you, that your situation is truly dangerous, and to offer you an asylum under the Flag of my Sovereign. I shall wait for your answer with the impatience of a man, whose object is to prevent the effusion of blood; and I assure you, that your submission may enable me to meliorate your situation exceedingly; and that a rash and obstinate resistance will not only be the cause of your own misery, but that of all who belong to you.

" Given under my hand, on board His Britannic Majesty's Ship Seahorse, off Pausilippi, this 18th day of June, 1799.

"EDWARD J. FOOTE."

### " THE COMMANDANT OF THE CASTEL UOVO'S VERBAL ANSWER.

" Nous voulons la République, une et indivisible, nous mourons pour elle; voilà notre réponse. Eloignez vous, Citoyen—vite, vite!"

" N.B.—The rest of the garrison of Castel Uovo were so much displeased with the Commandant, that they complained of him, and he was displaced."

### TO CARDINAL RUFFO.

" Eminence,               " Seahorse, June 19th, 1799.

" I consider it my duty to inform your Eminence, that so long an Armistice may prove very prejudicial to the interest of His Sicilian Majesty; the only way to reduce these Rebels is, to fatigue them with our energy, and, by constantly attacking them, not to allow them time to breathe; for while we remain inactive, they form their mischievous schemes; and we have but too good reason to expect everything from their treachery, which may show itself when we least expect it.

" As my Sovereign is a principal Ally of the King of the Two Sicilies, I claim a right to be made acquainted with the subject of the present Treaty, as I am extremely anxious to learn, before night, how I am to conduct myself; since, if the Rebels are not seriously treating for a Capitulation, I see no reason why the firing on them should not re-commence at sun-set. I must also inform your Eminence, that, after the answer I received yesterday morning, I shall not treat with those gentlemen, until they beg of me to do so. I have the honour to be, your Eminence's most devoted and obedient Servant,

"EDWARD J. FOOTE."

### TO CAPTAIN FOOTE.

" Excellency,           " Head-quarters, near Naples, June 19th, 1799.

" The Commandant of Fort St. Elmo, in his answer, requested that hostilities should cease during the time necessary to send you his answer, and to receive your Excellency's reply. You see by that, that the duration of the Armistice is not precisely determined on.

" Your Excellency seems to think that in the meantime the delay may be dangerous: I rather believe that in the present situation of affairs it cannot be otherwise than favourable to us. Ever since this morning, from the moment they began to treat of a Capitulation, a great many began to desert from the two Castles, and among them forty Frenchmen at least, besides a great many Italians; and the number of the fugitives will increase more and more under the favour of the night. We have placed some Officers round the Castle Nuovo to receive these voluntary prisoners, and to assure them they shall be forgiven; and this seems to succeed very well; and should those who have not yet fled, find the same reception and asylum on the water, I do believe that the French, in case of their being disposed to re-commence hostilities, would find the two Castles empty. We are rather afraid that the Treaty may be interrupted by the Castle being stormed by the people, as the Castle is all open, and the Calabrese have already penetrated it. It does not appear to me therefore that they can entertain any reasonable hopes of rendering our position less favourable by delay. As however the Treaty is principally carried on in the name of the Russians, I send your letter to Micheroux, that he may reply as he thinks proper to your Excellency.

"In the course of last night the besieged lost, in a sortie, more than sixty men from St. Elmo. I do not think they will be desirous of making another attempt very soon. I am, with distinguished regard, your Excellency's most devoted Servant,

"F. CARD. RUFFO."

TO CARDINAL RUFFO.

"Seahorse, at anchor, off Pieda Grotta,
"Eminence,                               June 20th, 1799.

"You were good enough to write to me last night, that General Micheroux, who was treating about the Capitulations, should make me acquainted with the circumstances. Six-and-thirty hours have now passed since I was first made acquainted with the Armistice, without being informed of anything further. I consider it a duty incumbent on me to represent to your Eminence, that it is far from improbable, that the Enemy's fleet may appear, which would certainly frustrate our operations; I therefore think the affair should be expedited, to prevent as much as possible the reverses that would consequently follow.

"Your Eminence must be aware that I am too much interested in the success of the Treaty, not to be extremely anxious to know how it goes on, which is the true motive of my impatience. I have the honour to be, your Eminence's most devoted and obedient servant,

"EDWARD JAMES FOOTE."

TO CAPTAIN FOOTE.

"Excellency,                               "June 20th, 1799, 6½ hour.

"I have nothing satisfactory to say in answer to the very polite letter of your Excellency; and that you may get some satisfactory answer, I have sent your Officers to the Minister Micheroux, who manages this affair with the Russian Commander, to whom, without proving myself an ungrateful man, I cannot offer the least displeasure. Do therefore excuse me, if I do not give your Excellency a satisfactory answer; and believe me, with all esteem and respect, your Excellency's most devoted Servant,                               "F. CARD. RUFFO, V.G.

"P.S.—I thank you for your very clever manœuvres on the sea; and beseech you to continue them this evening, in case the Truce should continue."

TO CAPTAIN FOOTE.

"Excellency,                               "June 20th, hour 10.

"Enclosed are the Capitulations, which have been settled and agreed to, with the Commandant of St. Elmo, and which I send in order that you may be pleased to sign them; as well as that you may deign to take proper measures to have the prisoners conveyed as far as Toulon, as it has been stipulated in the Capitulation. The King, my Master, will bear the expense of the passage, and the necessary Transports we may get with the greatest solicitude from this Port, in which I see abundance of shipping. I do not think, after all, that the conditions are very bad. They afford us leisure and opportunity to re-establish our batteries, and of placing our Gun boats for our defence, in case of any misfortune, (which, God forbid) that the English fleet may meet with, or, if some remnant of the French squadron should make its appearance. I beseech you to take under your protection those of our Ships, that are coming out of the Port, forced out by our seamen, to restore them to his Majesty. Such vessels might be expeditiously armed by the Count di Thurn, to whom I beg my respects, in case he is with you. I am, with the greatest esteem and respect, your Excellency's most devoted and faithful Servant,

"F. CARD. RUFFO, V.G."

TO CARDINAL RUFFO.

"Eminence, "Seahorse, 20th June, 1799, at midnight.

"I am happy to see your object thus far advanced; and although I find the terms of the Capitulation very favourable to the Republicans, yet I have lost no time in signing it, to avoid throwing the least impediment in the way of the interests of his Sicilian Majesty, which are more particularly in the hands of your Eminence. I think it right, however, to observe, that, in the 8th article, mention should be made of the dangers of the seas, to guarantee the hostages.

"I will take care to have a British Vessel of War ready to act as Convoy at half an hour's notice; and I have written to the Count di Thurn, to prepare, immediately, the Polacres that are to serve as Transports. It also appears to me, that, by the said 8th article, the French are too long secured in the possession of St. Elmo, as that fortress cannot, with propriety, be attacked until advice is received of the arrival of the Republicans at Toulon. All the Vessels at anchor in the Port shall be considered as under the protection of the Squadron. I have the honour to be, your Eminence's most devoted and obedient Servant,

"EDWARD JAMES FOOTE."

TO CAPTAIN FOOTE.

"Excellence, "Naples, June 21st, 1799.

"The terms are already settled, and we only wait for the Commandant of St. Elmo's signature. I shall write to the Chevalier Micheroux a short account of the news that has arrived, that, if possible, he may take advantage of it. An Armistice is requested for St. Elmo, and it is right to grant it, for many reasons which are too long to enumerate, but which I will communicate in the best manner I am able, to the Officer who acts as an interpreter. In case of an attack on that Fort, we should wish to preserve that part of it which looks towards the City, and make the attack on the other side. I am, with the highest respect, your Excellency's most devoted and faithful Servant,

"F. CARD. RUFFO, V.G."

"N.B.—My sentiments were written in Italian, by the gentleman who assisted me in the French language. E. J. F.

TO CAPTAIN FOOTE.

"Sir, "Naples, June 22nd, 1799.

"I have the honour to send you the Capitulation, reduced to the accustomed forms. I beg you will have the goodness to sign it on the following page, and to affix your seal to it.

"As there are no Polacres in the Mole, I have caused three to be freighted at Soriento. I beg, Sir, that you will inform the Captains of Procida, that some more

Polacres will still be wanted, in order that they may be kept ready. I am every moment expecting the list of the miserable people who wish to go away ; then you will know the number of polacres that will be required. I have the honour to be, with sentiments of the most distinguished consideration, Sir, your very humble and most obedient Servant,

"LE CHEV. DE MICHEROUX."

### TO THE CHEVALIER MICHEROUX.

" Sir,   " On board the Seahorse, off Pausilippi, June 23rd, 1799.

"Your letter, enclosing the Capitulation of the Forts, did not reach me till near midnight; you will receive it with this, signed by me in the manner you have pointed out.

" I think it right, however, to inform you, that being but little acquainted with the customs, and prerogatives of Nations relative to Treaties, and Signatures, I protest against everything that can in any way be contrary to the rights of His Britannic Majesty, or those of the English Nation.[2] I shall send your letter to the Count de Thurn, who will attend to the Polacres; it is to him therefore you will have to address yourself with respect to the number necessary: as to the escort which I am to furnish, it will be ready in a quarter of an hour. I have the honour to be, with the most distinguished sentiments, Sir, your very humble and most obedient Servant,

" EDWARD JAMES FOOTE."

### TO REAR-ADMIRAL LORD NELSON.

" Seahorse, at anchor off Pausilippi, June 23rd, 1799.

" My Lord,

" The enclosed is a copy of the Capitulation which was signed yesterday, and I believe an Armistice is for the present to take place with the French at St. Elmo.

" I shall direct Captain Drummond of His Majesty's Sloop Bulldog, to take under his protection the Polacres destined to carry the Neapolitan Republicans to Toulon, where he is to get a proper receipt for them, and then to return with the Vessels to this Bay, considering the Sloop he commands as a Cartel during her passage to and from Toulon. I have the honour to be, my Lord, your Lordship's most obedient humble servant,

" EDWARD JAMES FOOTE."

### PLAN OF THE CAPITULATION FOR THE FORTS NUOVO AND UOVO.

[From Captain Foote's " Vindication."]

"Article 1.—The Forts Nuovo and Uovo shall be delivered into the hands of the Commanders of the Troops of the King of the Two Sicilies, and those of his Allies, the King of England, the Emperor of all the Russias, and the Ottoman Porte, with

---

[2] In a letter to Dr. Clarke, dated on the 2nd of May, 1809, printed in the " Vindication," p. 59, Captain Foote said:—"As you seem to think that these words referred to the substance of the Capitulation, and gave some colour to a breach of that sacred agreement, I beg to inform you that these words were inserted by me *solely* because I had signed my name under those of the Russian and Turkish Commanders, which might not be proper, as I was at that time acting as the immediate representative of my King, whose dignity with Foreign States I had no right to infringe. This, Sir, was my only reason for inserting the words quoted in your work, which you seem to imagine was done for a very different purpose."

all warlike stores, provisions, artillery, and effects of every kind now in the magazines, of which an inventory shall be made by Commissaries on both sides, after the
present Capitulation is signed.

" Article 2.—The Troops composing the Garrisons, shall keep possession of their
Forts until the Vessels which shall be spoken of hereafter, destined to convey such
as are desirous of going to Toulon, are ready to sail.

" The Evacuation shall not take place until the moment of embarkation.

" Article 3.—The Garrisons shall march out with the honours of war, arms, and
baggage, drums beating, colours flying, and lighted match, with each two pieces of
artillery; they shall lay down their arms on the beach.

" Article 4.—Persons and Property, both moveable and immoveable, of every
individual of the two Garrisons, shall be respected and guaranteed.

" Article 5.—All the said individuals shall have their choice of embarking on board
of Cartels, which shall be furnished them to go to Toulon, or of remaining at Naples,
without being molested either in their persons or families.

" Article 6.—The conditions contained in the present Capitulation are common
to every person of both sexes now in the Forts.

" Article 7.—The same conditions shall take place with respect to the Prisoners
which the Troops of His Majesty the King of the Two Sicilies, and those of his
Allies, may have made of the Republican troops, in the different engagements which
took place before the blockade of the Forts.

" Article 8.—Messieurs the Archbishop of Salerno, Micheroux, Dillon, and the
Bishop of Avelino, detained in the Forts, shall be put into the hands of the Commandant of the Fort St. Elmo, where they shall remain as Hostages until the arrival
of the individuals, sent to Toulon, be ascertained.

" Article 9.—All the other Hostages, or State prisoners, confined in the two Forts,
shall be set at liberty, immediately after the present Capitulation is signed.

" Article 10.—All the Articles of the said Capitulation must be fully approved of
by the Commandant of Fort St. Elmo before they can be executed.

(Signed)      " F. Card Ruffo, V.G.

" Kerandy Neut Prescaje.[3]

" Bonieu Kubuffuterre.[3]

" Edward James Foote,

" Commanding the Ships and Vessels of His
Britannic Majesty in the Bay of Naples."

The following literal copy of the Capitulation, which is more complete in form,
and contains the dates and ratification by the Commandant of St. Elmo, is from the
Nelson Papers:—

" Libertà.                    " Eguaglianza.

" Republica Napolitana.

" Dal Castel Nuovo, li 2 Messidoro, Anno 7º della Libertà.

" Il Cittadino Massa, Generale d' Artiglieria, e Commandante del Castel Nuovo.
Essendosi dal Commandante Foote della flotta Inglese intimata la resa del Castel
dell 'Ovo; ed indi dal Cardinale Ruffo, Vicario Generale del Regno di Napoli, dal
Cavalier Micheroux, Ministro Plenipotenziario di S. M. il Re delle due Sicilie presso
la flotta Russo-Ottomana, e dal Commandante in Capite delle Truppe Ottomane a

---

³ " I could not decipher the signatures of the Russian and Turkish Commanders
and I am therefore by no means certain that they are correctly spelled.—E. J. F."

questo Castello Nuovo : il Consiglio di Guerra del Castel Nuovo si è adunato, ed avendo deliberato sulla sud<sup>a</sup> intimazione, ha risoluto che i due Forti saranno rimessi ai Commandanti delle truppe di sopra enunciate per mezzo di una onorevole Capitolazione, e dopo aver fatto conoscere al Commandante del forte S. Elmo i motivi di questa resa, in conseguenza il Sud<sup>o</sup> consiglio ha ridotto gli Articoli della seguente Capitolazione senza l' accettazione de'quali la resa de' Forti non può aver luogo.

" 1. Li Castelli Nuovo e dell, Ovo saranno rimessi al Commandante delle truppe di S. M. il Ré delle due Sicilie, e di quelle de' suoi alleati, il Re d' Inghilterra, l' Imperatore di tutte le Russie, Accordato e la Porta Ottomana, con tutte le munizioni di guerra, e di bocca, artiglieria ed effetti di ogni specie esistenti nei magazini di cui si formerà inventario dai Commissarj rispettivi, dopo la firma della presente Capitolazione.

" 2. Le truppe componenti le guarnigioni conserveranno i loro Forti, Accordato fino che i bastimenti di cui si parlerà qui appresso, a trasportar gl' individui, che vorranno andar a Tolone, saran pronti a far vela.

" 3. Le guarnigioni usciranno con gli onori di guerra, arme, e bagagli, Accordato tamburo battente, bandiere spiegate, micia accesa, e ciascun con due pezzi d' artiglieria ; essi deporranno le arme sul lido.

Accordato " 4. Le persone, le proprietà mobili ed immobili di tutti gl' individui componenti, le due guarnigioni, saranno rispettate, e garantite.

" 5. Tutti i sud<sup>i</sup> individui potran scegliere d' imbarcarsi sopra i bastimenti parlamentari, che saran loro preparati per condurli a Accordato Tolone, o di restar in Napoli senz' esser inquietati, essi, ne le loro famiglie.

Accordato " 6. Le condizioni contenute nella presente Capitolazione son communi a tutte le persone de' due sessi rinchiuse ne' forti.

" 7. Le stesse condizioni avran luogo riguardo a tutti i prigionieri fatti sulle truppe Republicane dalle truppe di S. M. il Re delle due Accordato Sicilie, e quelle de' suoi alleati, ne' diversi combattimenti che hanno avuto luogo, prima del blocco de' forti.

" 8. I sig<sup>i</sup> arch<sup>o</sup> di Salerno, e di Micheroux, di Dillon, e 'l Vescovo di Avellino, detenuti, saranno rimessi al Commandante del Forte di Accordato S. Elmo, ove resteranno in ostaggio, fino a che sia assicurato l' arrivo a Tolone degl' individui che vi si mandano.

" 9. Tutti gli altri ostaggi prigionieri di Stato rinchiusi ne' due Forti Accordato saranno rimessi in libertà subito dopo la firma della presente Capitolazione.

" 10. Tutti gli articoli della sud<sup>a</sup> Capitolazione non potranno eseguirsi Accordato se non dopo che saranno stati intieramente approvati dal Commandante del Forte di S. Elmo.

" IL GENERALE MASSA Commandante del Castel Nuovo."

"En vertu de la délibération prise par le Conseil de Guerre du Fort St. Elme le 3 de Messidor, sur la lettre du Général Massa Commandant le Fort Neuf en date du

1ᵉʳ du dit mois, le Commandant du fort S. Elme approuve les Articles de la Capitulation ci-dessus.

"Au Fort S. Elme le 3 Messidor, an 7ᵉ de la Rep. Franc.

"Le Chef de Brig. Comᵗ. le Fort S. Elme.
"Jʜ. Mejan.
"F. Card. Ruffo.
"Ko Maugrouse Syeninoue Dourieu.
"Kuburi Puffere.¹
"E. I. Foote, Commanding the Ships and Vessels of His Britannic Majesty in the Bay of Naples."

TO REAR-ADMIRAL LORD NELSON, K.B.

"Seahorse, off Pausilippi, June 24th, 1799,
at 7 o'clock in the morning.

"My Lord,

"I had the honour of receiving your Lordship's letter⁴ of the 18th instant, about an hour ago. The not being able to join you with His Majesty's Ship under my command, gives me more uneasiness than I can possibly describe ; it is what I wish to do beyond anything; it would be putting myself in a truly enviable situation; whereas I am sure I may with great truth assert, I am far from enjoying any comfort at present, or having scarce a moment's ease : however, after mature reflection, I consider that my leaving Naples at present might be attended with very serious consequences. I shall therefore immediately direct the Perseus and Mutine, to join your Lordship; and by Captain Oswald you will be informed of every circumstance that has passed, and is passing here, in which he has always taken a very useful and active part.

"I sent the San Leon away on the 16th, with the Castel-à-Mare Capitulation, being in great hopes she would meet your Lordship at least half way between Palermo and Naples. She has not yet returned, and I am obliged to send the Bulldog to convoy the Polacres, on board of which the Republicans are about to embark for Toulon, as it was particularly stated they should have a British ship of war to escort them. When the Capitulation⁵ is put into effect, and the Troops of His Sicilian Majesty, or those of his Allies, have taken possession of the Forts, Arsenal, &c., I shall be better able to judge what is to be done. I shall not be easy until I see His Sicilian Majesty's Colours flying on St. Elmo.

"I cannot close this letter without again assuring your Lordship that a sense of duty keeps me here, and that if I followed my private feelings and wishes, the Seahorse would ere this have been under weigh to join you. I have the honour to be, my Lord, your Lordship's most obedient, humble servant,

"Edward James Foote."

---

Such was the state of affairs at Naples on the 24th of June. But although the Capitulation was signed by Captain Foote, the last of the contracting parties, early in the morning of the 23rd, little, if anything, had been done towards carrying it into execution before Lord Nelson's arrival, in consequence of the Vessels not being ready which were intended to convey to Toulon, the garrisons of Uovo and Nuovo, and the Neapolitans who had taken refuge in those Castles.

---

¹ These signatures are almost illegible.
⁴ Vide p. 381, ante.      ⁵ Of Uovo and Nuovo.

In the afternoon of the 24th, Lord Nelson appeared in the Bay of Naples with a large Squadron; and it is of great importance to ascertain the authority and powers which were at that moment vested in him. Though he did not hold a Commission as Commander-in-Chief of the British Fleet, and was immediately responsible to Lord Keith for his proceedings, he had full power to assemble Courts-Martial, and to carry sentences of capital punishment into effect, without reference to any superior Officer.[6] It is, however, with relation to the special authority granted to him by the King of the Two Sicilies, that his measures at Naples are to be judged. He had long been Commander-in-Chief of the Sicilian Navy, and exercised over its Ships and Officers, in most cases, if not in all, the same authority as over those of England.[7] To what extent he could at that time interfere with the internal discipline of the Sicilian Squadron is not known, because no Commission to him to command it has been found; and it has not been ascertained whether those Ships were placed on a different footing from the Portuguese Squadron, in which he said he had no power to order a Court-Martial, because it was an " auxiliary Squadron."[8] His admission of that inability, when highly displeased with a Portuguese Officer commanding a Ship under his orders, shows that Lord Nelson was perfectly aware of the limits of his authority, and was careful not to exceed them. There are, however, good reasons for thinking that the Sicilian Squadron was differently situated from the Portuguese, and that it had always been, for all purposes, and in all respects, as much under his command as the English.

Whatever may have been Lord Nelson's authority over the Sicilian Navy before the month of June 1799, it is unquestionable that when he yielded to the entreaties of the King of the Two Sicilies, by proceeding to Naples, he was armed with extraordinary, if not unlimited, powers.[9] It is remarkable that no Commission or other instrument for that purpose, should have been discovered, but the fact itself is established by the implicit obedience which all the functionaries at Naples, civil, naval, and military, paid to his commands. Cardinal Ruffo, the King's Vicar-General, though he dissented from his opinion, and refused to co-operate with him, did not dispute his authority; and the style of his Proclamation, his Declaration to the Neapolitans in the Castles of Uovo and Nuovo, his Summons to the Castle of St. Elmo, his Orders to the King's Officers,[1] and, indeed, every Document issued by him after he came to Naples, between the 24th of June and the 10th of July, when the King arrived, prove that, as he himself expressly asserted, " *The whole affairs of the Kingdom of Naples were at the time absolutely placed in his hands.*"[2] It is impossible to imagine that Lord Nelson would have assumed such authority over

---

[6] For proof of this fact, vide p. 401, ante.

[7] Vide p. 174, ante.                [8] Vide p. 233, ante.

[9] Much light is thrown on the nature and extent of Lord Nelson's authority, by showing that which Captain Troubridge possessed when he was sent to Naples in April 1799, as it is impossible to suppose that, when Nelson proceeded there in June, he had *less* powers than had been granted to one of his Captains. It appears that Captain Troubridge received Instructions from his Sicilian Majesty; that under them, he could place a Sicilian Officer in arrest, and, (even if he could not have directed a Court Martial to try him,) still, that he could desire the evidence to be prepared; and though he did not think it right for English Officers to sit on such Courts-Martial, yet that he was fully authorized to order a sentence of death to be carried into effect. Vide pp. 310, 359, 360, ante.

[1] Vide p. 386, 388, and 396, ante.

[2] Vide his letter to Mr. Davison, p. 510, postea.

the Subjects of a Foreign Monarch, unless it had been actually and formally granted to him; more especially when that authority was exercised in the presence of many of that Sovereign's most confidential Officers, and of the British Minister to his Court. Though no Commission is known to exist, there is a Letter, hitherto unpublished, from King Ferdinand to Lord Nelson, written on the 10th of June, shortly before he first sailed for Naples, which fully confirms the opinion that great powers were entrusted to him.[3] Of that Letter, it is desirable to insert a translation:

"Very worthy Lord Nelson,

" The various accounts which reach me from Naples, requiring a speedy resolution,
" and the present circumstances of this Kingdom and of my Family preventing me
" from leaving them, that I may take care of their safety and defence in any event, I
" place all my hopes of the wished-for recovery of that Capital in the powerful
" assistance of the English forces under your command. The good and loyal among
" the inhabitants desire to shake off the yoke which treachery imposed upon them. A
" great number of the people here cannot tranquilly see the approach of the troops of
" Cardinal Ruffo, and the successes in the Provinces, of many Chiefs rising in favour

---

[3] The expedition to Naples in June 1799, is thus noticed in Miss Knight's *Journal*, which tends to confirm the opinion that a regular Commission had been issued by the King. That Lady was then at Palermo:

" 16th June, 1799.—Dined at Sir William Hamilton's. In the afternoon, went
" with them, and Lord Nelson, on board the Foudroyant, where Lord Nelson has
" hoisted his Flag—a fine new eighty-gun Ship. Went on board the Serapis, Captain
" Duncan—a forty-four gun Ship; and afterwards dined at Sir William Hamilton's.
" The Fleet is to sail to-morrow morning early, for Naples, and the Hereditary Prince,
" with Duke Gravina, and General Acton, goes on board the Admiral's Ship, as do Sir
" William and Lady Hamilton, with a Commission from the King. Cardinal Ruffo,
" with his Army, will be at Naples by the time the Fleet arrives, and it appears
" certain that the Castle St. Elmo will capitulate, as soon as the Fleet is seen."

" 21st.—Lord Nelson came in, in his barge, the Foudroyant and Earl St. Vincent
" Cutter laying off. Brought the account of Sir Alan Gardner, with 16 sail of the
" Line, coming into the Mediterranean, that the French Fleet was seen off the Gulf
" della Spezzia, and Lord Keith following them. Met Lord Nelson and Sir William
" and Lady Hamilton at dinner on board the Serapis, Captain Duncan; and at
" five, they all embarked for Naples, whither the Fleet goes."

The following Letter from Lady Hamilton to Lord Nelson, shows the anxiety of their Sicilian Majesties that he should go to Naples:

" TO THE RIGHT HON. LORD NELSON.

[*Autograph* in the possession of the Right Hon. John Wilson Croker.]

" Thursday evening, June 12th.

" I have been with the Queen this evening. She is very miserable, and says,
" that although the people of Naples are for them in general, *yet* things will not be
" brought to that state of quietness and subordination till the Fleet of Lord Nelson
" appears off Naples. She therefore begs, entreats, and conjures you, my dear Lord,
" if it is possible, to arrange matters so as to be able to go to Naples. Sir William
" is writing for General Acton's *answer*. For God's sake consider it, and do. We
" will go with you, if you will come and fetch us. Sir William is ill—I am ill: it
" will do us good. God bless you. Ever, ever yours sincerely.—E. HAMILTON."

" of Religion and the Crown, without burning with a like spirit and desire to unite
" their efforts for the same end with those of the Provinces. The efforts of my Officers
" are not sufficient to restrain their (perhaps) premature ardour, so that the Neapo-
" litans should await the arrival of the troops of the Line, which I am preparing, and
" the succours which, as you know, I am expecting from my good Allies, in order
" that they might labour together with greater certainty and the greatest energy, to
" free the Kingdom of Naples from oppression. Under these circumstances, an insur-
" rection already breaking out in the Capital, I must avoid the evident misfortune
" which the fury of the rebels might bring upon so many faithful subjects. I have
" thought, therefore, of assembling such troops of the Line as, without weakening
" this Kingdom too much, may unite with the body already existing in the Islands of
" the Cratere, in seconding the disposition of those good people, in expectation always
" of the Foreign forces, which will co-operate with them for the entire restoration
" of order. This measure, however, without your valuable assistance and direction,
" cannot produce the necessary result. I have recourse, therefore, to you, my Lord,
" to obtain both the one and the other, so that (if God will bless your efforts and
" ours,) this Kingdom being speedily delivered from the scourge it has experienced,
" I may henceforward be in a condition to perform the engagements contracted,
" which duty and reason prescribe. I send, therefore, a copy of the instructions I
" give to the superior Generals, and which I forward to those on the Continent. At
" the head of these, I have placed my Son,[3] whom I trust to your friendly assistance,
" so that his first steps in the present critical career which he will have to run,
" may be guided by your wise advice, requesting you not only to help him with
" your powerful aid, but that you will always act principally, as your forces are the
" true means and support on which I rest my future hopes, as they have hitherto
" been my safety. The intention, as you will observe, of restoring quiet and order
" (in Naples) by the possession of the Capital by means of its own inhabitants
" devoted to the good cause, would not be with that expectation embraced by me at
" this moment, if I were not obliged to encourage and profit by the good will of the
" people, with cautious steps, lest their disposition should either cool or they become
" the victim of their devotion. The powerful and distinguished Fleet with which
" you will support the expedition, leads me to flatter myself with that happy result
" which will especially depend upon it, and to trust that, without doing injury to
" the greater operations which you have constantly in view for the common good,
" my safety, and that of Sicily, you will proceed, as I request, to add this essential
" service to those other most important ones, which with so much zeal, and my most
" lively gratitude, you have rendered me. I flatter myself, also, that, without injury
" to the Capital, the Rebels will yield, as well as the Enemy, who still occupy St.
" Elmo, to the measures which will be taken. When, therefore, (after weighing
" every proper consideration relating to your Squadron, and the destination for which
" it may, for the general good, be required, as well as my own circumstances,) you
" shall judge necessary to employ actual and powerful force to bring effectually to
" their duty the obstinate oppressors of my (Neapolitan) people, and to extirpate,
" as is urgent, that nest of malefactors, you will be obliged to put into execution
" every means which may best tend to obtain that necessary end. I confide, my
" Lord, (and I repeat it with pleasure and particular satisfaction,) fully and entirely

---

[3] The Hereditary Prince, accordingly, embarked on board the Foudroyant on the
13th of June, but was landed after the sudden return of the Squadron on the 15th;
and His Royal Highness did not (as has been erroneously said in p. 384) re-embark
with Sir William and Lady Hamilton on the 21st.

" on the great zeal for my service, and the attachment to my Person and Family,
" which you have so loyally shown me by deeds, for which I am infinitely grateful
" and obliged. In the meanwhile, I pray that the Omnipotent God may have and
" preserve you, my Lord, in his holy keeping.

" Palermo, 10th June, 1799." " FERDINANDO.[4]

It is, therefore, evident that the King contemplated the employment of " actual
force" by Lord Nelson at Naples; that even though it was intended to send there
the Hereditary Prince, Nelson was " always to act principally;" and that his
Majesty considered that he might " use every means which could best tend" to effect
the objects entrusted to him. There is, moreover, this other and conclusive evidence
that Lord Nelson acted with the King's authority, and that he did not exceed his
powers—namely, that his Majesty not only ratified and approved of all he had done,[5]
but that he rewarded Nelson with the highest honour in his power to bestow.[6]

Very shortly before the British Squadron entered Naples Bay, Lord Nelson
received a letter informing him that an Armistice had been agreed to with the
Castles of Uovo and Nuovo, to which Captain Foote of the Seahorse was a party,
and that favourable terms had been granted to the Rebels in those fortresses. As
Lord Nelson knew that Cardinal Ruffo had been expressly ordered by the King
not to treat with the Rebels,[7] he felt indignant at the measure, which he at once
denounced as " infamous." It is remarkable, that Lord Nelson's first information
respecting the transaction was *erroneous*, and that he immediately acted upon such
erroneous impression. As soon as he heard of the Capitulation, he wrote his

---

[4] *Autograph*, in the possession of the Right Honourable John Wilson Croker. A
copy of the *original* will be found in p. 522, post.

[5] Lord Nelson said, in his letter to Earl Spencer on the 13th of July:—" His
" Majesty has entirely approved of my conduct in this matter." Vide p. 406, and
Prince de Luzzi's letter to Nelson, in p. 439.

[6] He was created DUKE OF BRONTE, on the 13th of August following.

[7] This stands on the authority of Lord Nelson himself, (*vide* p. 406, ante, and
pp. 510—520, infra,) and of Clarke and M'Arthur, (vol. ii. p. 175.) Those
writers state that the Cardinal had received from his Royal Master orders which
" peremptorily commanded him not to treat with Rebels;" and they add, in a
note—" A private letter from the King to Cardinal Ruffo, found amongst the
" Nelson Papers, amply supports this assertion, which might have been expressed in
" stronger terms." In a letter to Captain Foote, in March 1809, Dr. Clarke said—
" There is a letter from the King to Ruffo, in which his Majesty upbraids him for
" daring to treat with Rebels, *directly contrary to his orders.*" And in another letter,
dated on the 20th of April, 1809, Dr. Clarke wrote:—" My being inclined (from
" the conversation I had with Admiral Foley and with Hardy, and from seeing the
" King of Sicily's private letter, *in his own hand,* to Ruffo) to think more favourably
" of Lord Nelson's subsequent conduct surely cannot, in any way, prove that I wished
" to attach blame to you."—Captain Foote's *Vindication*, pp. 50—56. The letter
alluded to has not *now* been discovered in the Nelson Papers: assuredly, those
Editors ought to have printed it in their Work, and thus have prevented the doubt
expressed by Captain Foote of its existence, when he asked, and not without reason,
" If such a letter be among the Nelson Papers, why was not the whole, or an extract
" of this letter published? for it does not appear that the authors incline to withhold
" letters, as the whole work may show; and how came such a letter to be among
" those Papers?"—*Vindication*, p. 75.

"Opinion"[8] of it, which needed not the addition he afterwards made, in his own hand, to the copy sent to the Admiralty—namely, "Opinion delivered *before I saw* " *the Treaty of Armistice*, &c., only from reports met at sea"—to prove that at the time of writing it he was *wholly misinformed of the precise nature of the transaction.* It is manifest, from that paper, that Lord Nelson had been told that an *Armistice* was granted, of which the principal condition was, that if the French garrisons and rebels were not relieved within twenty-one days, they should then evacuate the fortresses in safety. Now, the Capitulation, which had been actually signed on the 22nd and 23rd, instead of being only conditional, was absolute and conclusive, so far as the powers of the contracting parties extended; and it contained not one word about the garrisons being "relieved in twenty-one days," &c. Thus Lord Nelson, misled by the imperfect information he had received, *confounded an Armistice with a Capitulation.* The misconception pervades the whole of that paper, which without this explanation is, indeed, scarcely intelligible. His impression was confirmed as soon as the Seahorse and the Castles were seen from the Foudroyant; for a *Flag of Truce* was flying on board the Frigate, and on both the Castles[9], thus indicating the *suspension*, and *not the termination* of hostilities—that a *Capitulation* was in *progress, not* that it was *actually concluded.* The instant the Flags of Truce were discovered from the Foudroyant, Lord Nelson signalled the Seahorse to haul down the Truce flag,[1] when (conformably with his imperfect knowledge of what had taken place, and with his opinion of the nature of an *Armistice*) he supposed that the garrisons returned to their original condition, and that the party which had been reinforced, had a right to renew hostilities, and to impose any terms it thought proper.

It is not necessary to inquire how far this view of the subject is consistent with the Law of Nations, for the transaction was of a different character; and instead of being a mere *Armistice*, or, as it has sometimes been considered, the *project* or *plan* of a Capitulation—it was, in fact, a *formal Capitulation*, signed by all the Contracting Parties, and ratified by the only authority, whose approbation was stipulated for, in the instrument.

At four o'clock in the afternoon of the 24th, immediately after the Squadron arrived, Captain Foote[2] waited upon Lord Nelson, when he learnt *for the first time* the true nature of the transaction. Lord Nelson then told Captain Foote, that "he was " aware he had been placed in an arduous and unpleasant situation, that he gave him " all possible credit for zeal, assiduity, and good intentions, but that he had been im- " posed upon by that worthless fellow,[3] Cardinal Ruffo, who was endeavouring to form " a party hostile to the interests of his Sovereign; and he requested Captain Foote

---

[8] Vide p. 384.   [9] Vide p. 392, ante.   [1] Ibid.

[2] Extracts from the Seahorse's Log:—

"June 24th.—Saw several large Ships in the offing. At 2, weighed. At 3, " Captain Harward of the San Leon, came on board, and informed me the strange " Fleet were Lord Nelson's. At 4, I went on board of the Foudroyant to wait on " Lord Nelson. At ... (*sic*) she anchored in Naples Bay. A.M., the Fleet stood " in and anchored in line-of-battle.

" 26th.—At sunset, saw the King's colours flying off the Forts of Uovo and " Nuovo.

"28th.—Answered the signal to prepare to weigh. At 7, weighed and made sail " out of the Bay. A.M., fine weather."

[3] See Lord Nelson's opinion of Cardinal Ruffo, p. 334, ante.

" to give him a Statement in the form of a Narrative,[4] of the heads of his proceedings,
" from the time the Cardinal approached near to Naples." Captain Foote justified
himself by saying, that " he had, indeed, been placed in a most anxious situation,
" having had more reason, among many disagreeable and trying circumstances, to
" expect the Enemy's Fleet, rather than that under his Lordship's command, in
" Naples Bay; that he could not be supposed to know, or even imagine, that the
" Cardinal was acting contrary to his Sovereign's interest, when he saw him retained
" in his *very high* and *confidential* situation, and his instructions directed him to
" co-operate, to the utmost of his power, with the Royalists, at whose head Cardinal
" Ruffo was known to be placed, even before the Squadron under Sir Thomas Trou-
" bridge had sailed from Palermo." [5]

With this knowledge of the real character of the Capitulation, the questions which
properly arose, were of a peculiarly technical nature :—

I. As Cardinal Ruffo, one of the contracting Parties, *disobeyed his instructions*, did such disobedience justify the suspension of the Capitulation by an authority superior to him?

II. Did the fact, that the Capitulation *was not even begun to be carried into effect
before the arrival*[6] (with a large force) *of an Officer, superior* to one (Captain Foote)

---

4 Printed in pp. 478—480, ante.

5 Captain Foote's "Vindication," pp. 22, 23.

6 This important fact is admitted in the Petition to Lord Nelson, of Dominico Forges
D'Avanzati and Amadeus Ricciardi, on the part of the Neapolitans who had been in
the Castles, printed in Miss Helen Maria Williams' " Sketches," on which she so
much relies, as evidence of the injustice of Lord Nelson's conduct. After mentioning
a Proclamation issued on the 15th of June by Cardinal Ruffo, and the Capitulation
of Uovo and Nuovo, the Petitioners state that *after the arrival, in this road, of the
British Fleet, they began to put the Capitulation into execution,* [après l'arrivée dans
cette Rade de la Flotte Brittannique commandée par V. E. on commença à mettre en
exécution la Capitulation,] the garrisons on the one part, by setting the state prisoners
and ten English prisoners of war at liberty, and by giving up to the British troops the
gate of the Palace, which led to Castle Nuovo, and the Russian troops on the other
part allowed the garrison to depart, with the honours of war, laying down their arms
on the side of the Marine Arsenal, where they embarked in Vessels to be taken to
Toulon. By these Acts, they contended that the Articles of the Capitulation were
ratified by Russia and England, which received the prisoners and the gate of the
Castle. Upon this Petition Lord Nelson wrote—" I have shown your Paper to your
" gracious King, who must be the best and only judge of the merits and demerits
" of his subjects, NELSON."—*Sketches of Manners and Opinions in the French
Republic,* vol. ii. p. 319. The fact that Lord Nelson arrived *before* the surrender
of the Forts, &c., is also shown by Captain Foote's letter to Lord Nelson, of the
24th of June, (vide p. 487,) ante, in which he speaks of the Republicans " *being about*
" to embark for Toulon," and says, " *when* the Capitulation is put into effect, and
" the Troops of His Sicilian Majesty's Arsenal, or those of his Allies, have taken
" possession of the Forts, &c., I shall be better able to judge what is to be done."
Upon the copy of the Capitulation printed in Miss Williams's *Sketches,* Lord Nelson
wrote, " *Never executed, and therefore no Capitulation.*"—Clarke and M'Arthur,
vol. ii. p. 182. Lord Nelson drew a distinction between the present Capitulation,
and the Capitulation concluded by Captain Foote with the Garrisons of Revigliano
and Castel-à-Mare on the 15th of June, which having been so far carried into exe-

and apparently to another (Cardinal Ruffo) of the Contracting Parties, entitle such superior Officer to suspend or annul the Capitulation?

Lord Nelson, as representative of His Sicilian Majesty, decided that the Capitulation should not be carried into effect without the sanction of that Sovereign, because Cardinal Ruffo had exceeded his powers, and disobeyed his instructions in granting terms to the Rebels, and as the Cardinal had not that power, no representative of any other Sovereign could possess it;[7] and, both as an English Admiral and as the representative of the King of the Two Sicilies, because he, with the English Squadron, arrived *before* the Capitulation was even begun to be carried into effect.

That a superior authority may justly refuse to allow a Capitulation to be carried into effect, if a Contracting Party exceeds his authority, and still more if he disobeys his instructions, is a principle admitted by all writers on Public Law, and has been often acted upon.[8]

---

cution that the Garrison and Rebels were embarked for Toulon, though they had not sailed, he held it sacred, and it was strictly fulfilled. (Vide p. 510, infra.)

[7] Vide p. 385, ante.

[8] *Vattel* says, " Si une personne publique, un Ambassadeur ou un Général " d' Armée, fait un Traité, ou une Convention sans ordre du Souverain, *ou sans y* " *être autorisé* par le pouvoir de sa charge, et *on sortant des bornes de sa com-* " *mission le Traité est nul, comme fait sans pouvoir suffisant ; il ne peut prendre* " *force que par la ratification du Souverain expresse ou tacite.*"—(Chap. xiv. § 207.) *Martens*, in his " Précis du Droit des Gens," says, " D'autres Conven- " tions sont particulières, et les circonstances individuelles, où se trouve l'ennemi, " les font naître. De ce genre sont les *Capitulations* par lesquelles une forteresse, " une province, un corps de troupes se rendent conditionellement à l'ennemi. Elles " ont pour objèt tant le sort des troupes qui se rendent, quant à leurs personnes, " leurs armes, munitions de guerre, &c., que le sort de la place ou province, quant " à son gouvernement, ses domaines, les propriétés, la religion, etc. Ces Capitula- " tions diffèrent des Traités solennels tant par la forme, qu'en ce qu'elles sont " obligatoires sans une ratification expresse des Souverains, à moins qu'on ne " l'ait expressement reservée, *ou que celui qui les a signées passait les bornes du* " *pouvoir qui lui etait confié.*"—Ed. Gottingen, 1821, p. 500.

*Klüber*, in his " Droit des Gens moderne de l'Europe," states, that "Capitulations " sont obligatoires sans être acceptées ou ratifiées par les Souverains respectifs, " pourvû que les Officiers commandans qui les ont signées, aient été de bonne foi, " *et qu'ils n'aient point passé les limites de leurs attributions ou agi hors de leurs* " *pouvoirs.*"—Paris, 1831, Tome ii. p. 75.

This principle was acted upon in the following recent instances, and no writer of any authority has questioned the justice of the proceedings :—

" Bonaparte avait confié au Maréchal Gouvion-Saint Cyr 27,000 hommes, pour se " maintenir à Dresde. Après la bataille de Leipzig, ce Général fût bloqué par le " Comte de Klenau ; le defaut de vivres l'engagea à faire, le 6 Novembre, une " tentative pour se frayer un chemin à travers les troupes qui le cernaient ; le " mauvais succès de cet acte de desespoir le força à signer le 11 Novembre, à " Herzogswalde, une Capitulation par laquelle la garnison Française de Dresde, " après avoir déposé ses armes, se mit en route pour s'en retourner en France, à " condition de ne pas servir pendant six mois contre les Alliés. Arrivé à Altenbourg

Lord Nelson having determined that the Capitulation should not be carried into execution without the approbation of His Sicilian Majesty, he intimated that resolution to Cardinal Ruffo, on the following morning; and at the same time, (the 25th of June,) he sent a formal Declaration to the Neapolitan Jacobins in the Castles of Uovo and Nuovo, that he would not permit them to embark or to quit those places, but that they must surrender themselves to the Royal mercy.[1] His communication not having satisfied Cardinal Ruffo, he came on board the Foudroyant in the afternoon of the same day (the 25th), when a stormy discussion of long duration occurred between His Eminence and Lord Nelson, Sir William and Lady Hamilton acting as interpreters;[2] but the Cardinal's opinion that the Capitulation ought to be observed, remained unshaken, and he appears to have refused to be a party to its suspension.[3] Nelson therefore gave him his sentiments in writing, in the words above stated, and proceeded to act in conformity with his own conviction. On the 25th, he also wrote to the Commandant of St. Elmo, that unless he complied with the terms of the Summons which he had received from Cardinal Ruffo and the Commanding Officer of the Russian Army, within two hours, he must take the consequences, for he (Nelson) would not agree to any other.

Lord Nelson took possession of the Castles of Uovo and Nuovo on the 26th, the garrisons and other persons quitting them with the full knowledge that the terms of the Capitulation would not be carried into execution. They were embarked in Polaccas, which were brought out of the Mole to the English Fleet, and some of the principal Officers were placed in confinement on board of our Ships, where they remained until after the arrival of the King of Naples, on the 10th of July, when all the prisoners were given up to the Neapolitan authorities. The prisoners appear to have suffered many privations while on board

---

" le Maréchal Gouvion Saint-Cyr reçut la nouvelle que le Prince de Schwarzenberg
" avait refusé de ratifier la Capitulation, *parceque le Général Klenau n'avait pas*
" *été autorisé à accorder des conditions si défavorables à la cause des Alliés.* En
" pareil cas, le droit des Gens veut que tout soit replacé dans l'état où les choses
" étaient au moment de la signature de la Capitulation. En conséquence on offrit
" au Maréchal de le ramener avec sa garnison à Dresde, et de lui rendre ses armes et
" les munitions qu'on avait trouvées ; mais convaincu sans doute que la place de
" Dresde ne pouvait pas être défendue plus long tems, le Maréchal aima mieux
" accepter des conditions moins avantageuses, que d'exposer inutilement sa troupe
" et les malheureux habitans de la ville aux horreurs de la famine. Il consentit
" donc à être prisonnier de guerre avec son armée. Ainsi 27,000 hommes et 6000
" malades qui etaient dans les hôpitaux de Dresde, avec un Maréchal de France,
" 12 Généraux de Division, et 20 Généraux de Brigade, tombèrent au pouvoir des
" Alliés.
"Dantzig bloqué depuis le 16 Janvier, 1813, etait défendu par le Général Rapp.
" Aprés avoir successivement délogé les Français des ouvrages extérieurs, le Duc
" Alexandre de Wurtemburg commenca le siège le 3 Novembre. Le Général Rapp se
" soutint près d'un mois ; mais le 30 Novembre il signa une Capitulation *qui eut le*
" *même sort que celle de Dresde ; l'Empéreur Alexandre ne voulut pas la ratifier.*
" En conséquence le Général Rapp consentit le 24 Decembre à ce que les troupes
" qui etaient sous ses ordres se rendissent prisonnières de guerre."—Histoire abrégée des Traités de Paix, par Köch, tom. ix. p. 319. See also "Memoires du Général Rapp," pp. 337, 409—439.

[1] Vide p. 368, ante.  [2] Harrison's Life of Nelson, vol. ii. p. 100.
[3] Vide pp. 386, 387, 388, 393, ante, and p. 507, infra.

the Polaccas, and numerous petitions for relief were sent to Lord Nelson,[4] some of the petitioners throwing themselves entirely upon his clemency, while a few, (like those whose Memorial Miss Williams has printed,) insisted upon being considered as prisoners of war, and entitled to be sent to Toulon, under the Capitulation. Whether their sufferings were greater than was unavoidable from so many individuals being confined on board of small Vessels, or whether Lord Nelson made an effort to ameliorate their situation, does not appear from any papers now extant. But there is nothing to justify the supposition that they were treated with unnecessary harshness, and it is not pretended that he subjected any one of them to trial or punishment; they were simply detained as prisoners until the King's arrival, when Lord Nelson's interference with them entirely ceased.

That Lord Nelson should have felt it his duty to suspend the Capitulation, must be deeply regretted on account of the consequences which ensued after the Rebels were handed over to the Neapolitan authorities; but it is surely not too much to infer that (to use Lord Spencer's words to him on the subject) his "*motives and inten-* "*tions were pure and good.*" It was not only his opinion, at the time, that he acted correctly, but he retained it to the end of his life; and if (notwithstanding the authorities and instances above referred to) it be now thought that he was mistaken, and that he had no right to suspend the Capitulation, either on the ground that he arrived before its conditions were executed, or because Cardinal Ruffo had disobeyed the King's orders, yet assuredly the error might have been committed without the slightest departure from those principles of duty, patriotism, humanity, and honour, which distinguished his whole previous career. It is, no doubt, desirable that on that, as on many other occasions, feelings of humanity should have prevailed over those of justice, or of what now wears too much the appearance of vengeance; but the conduct of men can only be fairly judged by the circumstances in which they were placed; and though the necessity for severe and prompt measures may be denied, after events have long passed away, and when from political feelings strong sympathy prevails for the sufferers, yet it would be uncandid to insist that the transaction ought to have borne the same aspect to the chief actors in them, who were answerable for whatever failure might have attended their measures, as they now bear to our unprejudiced and irresponsible judgment.

A motive has been found by various writers for what they consider Nelson's misconduct at Naples, in the influence of Lady Hamilton, who, with her husband, was on board the Foudroyant. But, for the proceedings at Naples previous to the King's arrival, however much they may be lamented, Nelson alone was responsible; and if his judgment was in any degree perverted, there were ample causes for it in the character and events of the time, as well as in the peculiar feelings of his own mind. The French Revolution and its effects, especially in Italy, had inspired him with horror and disgust. Loyalty was his predominant passion. He detested those who entertained democratic opinions: a Rebel or a Traitor was, in his opinion, the impersonation of every crime that. disgraces human nature; and "no terms with Rebels," was with him as sacred a principle as that he ought to destroy the Enemies of his Country. Such a mind needed no inducement to deceive itself into the belief that, where men who had fought against their King were concerned, severity was an imperative duty; and that as the Nation was to a great extent imbued with seditious principles, and as the principal Fortress of Naples was still in the hands of the Enemy, there was a strong necessity for prompt and exemplary punishment. Under such circumstances, other men besides Nelson have disregarded the suggestions of mercy, in the performance of

---

[4] Many of these Petitions are now in the Nelson Papers.

what they believed to be their duty; nor is he the only Chief whose conduct, on a similar occasion, has been visited with severe censure.

Before pointing out the misstatements of writers on these transactions, it is proper to notice the affair which, more than any other, has been used to load Nelson's memory with obloquy—*the trial and execution of* CARACCIOLI, the facts of which have been generally misunderstood.

FRANCESCO CARACCIOLI, a cadet of an ancient and noble family, was a Commodore in the Neapolitan Navy, and had served with distinction against the French, especially with Nelson, in command of the Tancredi of 74 guns, in Lord Hotham's Action of March, 1795.[5] When the Royal Family were driven from Naples in December, 1798, Caraccioli accompanied them to Palermo, where he remained until the new Parthenopœan Republic declared that the estates of such persons as did not return to Naples, would be forfeited. He consequently obtained the King's permission to go back to Naples, to prevent the confiscation of his property. According to some authorities,[6] the King warned Caraccioli to "beware of intermeddling with French politics;" adding, "Avoid the snares of Republicans. I know I shall recover the Kingdom of Naples."

Soon after Caraccioli arrived at Naples, he was found serving under the new Republic; but it was at first thought that he had been compelled against his inclination to do so, and that he remained at heart a faithful subject of his King. These doubts, however, soon vanished;[7] *and besides other overt acts of treason, he commanded the Republican Gun-boats that fired upon the Neapolitan Frigate, La Minerva.*[8] Though the King had gone to another part of his Dominions, yet, so far from having abandoned his right to the throne of Naples, he had never ceased to take active measures for its recovery, as well by empowering Cardinal Ruffo to land in Calabria, head the Calabrese, and administer the functions of Government in his name, as by sending his own Ships to aid those of England before Naples, by which united Squadrons almost daily attacks were made on the French and Republicans. It is therefore indisputable that Caraccioli and the other Neapolitans who fought against those forces, had, according to the Law of every Nation in Europe, committed *high treason* of a flagrant description, and that they were, consequently, *Rebels.*

When the King's troops advanced upon Naples, Caraccioli took refuge either in Castle Uovo or Nuovo, but he quitted it on or before the 23rd of June; so that, even if he was there on the morning of the 23rd, when the Capitulation was signed by Captain Foote, he had left the Castle of his own accord, before any part of the Capitulation was carried into execution, and one, if not two, days before Lord Nelson arrived. The time when he quitted the Castle is material, if, as has been supposed, his safety was guaranteed by that Capitulation; but no other information has been found than the statement of Clarke and M'Arthur, that he fled to Cal-

---

[5] Vide vol. ii. p. 8.       [6] Southey.

[7] Vide pp. 329, 334, 341, 358, 360, 376, ante. So late as the end of April 1799, Lord Nelson thought Caraccioli was not a Jacobin. Vide p. 341, ante.

[8] Vide Captain Foote's Letters to Lord Nelson, printed in his "Vindication." On the 26th of May he says, "Caraccioli threatens a second attack, with a consi- "derable addition of force" (p. 119); and on the 11th of June he said, "Caraccioli's "gun-boats have for some days past been firing at the town of Annunciata and the "adjacent houses," (p. 128). Yet, in 1810, Caraccioli was, in Captain Foote's opi- nion, only an "unhappy victim of French perfidy!" (ibid., p. 94). Captain Trou- bridge wrote to Lord Nelson, on the 1st of May, "Caraccioli, I am now satisfied, "is a Jacobin: I enclose you one of his letters. He came in the gun-boats to "Castle-a-Mare himself, and spirited up the Jacobins." Vide p. 359, ante.

viranno, and from that place wrote a letter, on the *twenty-third* of June, to the Duke of Calviranno, at Portici, in which he implored the countenance of the Duke and his application to Cardinal Ruffo for protection : he also " expressed " in it his apprehensions, under the unfortunate circumstances of his situation, that " violence might be committed on his life by the brigands. He confessed that he " was bound to account for his actions to those who should be legally authorized " by His Sicilian Majesty, and he trusted that the few days during which he had been " forced to obey the French Republic, would not obliterate forty years of most faithful " service; but that it would be duly weighed and valued in the scale of justice."[7] This letter has not been found; and it is to be regretted that those writers did not give a literal copy of it, because it tends to shew that Caraccioli did not consider himself protected by the Capitulation. Failing to obtain a favourable answer from the Duke de Calviranno or Cardinal Ruffo, he fled to the mountains, and a reward was offered for his apprehension; or, to use Clarke and M'Arthur's words, " a price was set upon his head." Five days after Lord Nelson arrived at Naples —namely, on Saturday, the 29th of June—Caraccioli was brought on board the Foudroyant disguised as a peasant, his arms bound, and in a state of much wretchedness. His fetters were immediately removed by order of Captain Hardy; refreshments were offered him, but which he declined, and he was placed, in charge of Lieutenant Parkinson, in a cabin, with two sentinels at the door. The apprehension of so celebrated a person, whose treasonable conduct was notorious, produced, it is said, great excitement. " Captain Hardy, who was on deck at the time, had his attention sud- " denly attracted to a clamour that prevailed, and it was some time before he could " gain information from the Italians who were on board, *that the traitor Carac-* " *cioli was taken.* It was with the utmost difficulty that this humane Officer " could restrain the insults and violence of the Neapolitan Royalists towards this " unhappy victim of French perfidy; who, with his hands bound behind him, and " wretchedly attired, displayed a painful instance of the uncertainty of all worldly " grandeur. When last on board, this Prince had been received with all the respect " and deference that were then due to his rank and character."[7]

As soon as Lord Nelson was informed of Caraccioli's apprehension, measures were adopted for bringing him to trial. He immediately issued a Warrant to Count Thurn, the Commander of the Sicilian Squadron, which recited, that Francesco Caraccioli, a Commodore in the service of his Sicilian Majesty, had been taken, and stood accused of rebellion against his lawful Sovereign, and for firing at his Colours hoisted on board the Minerva, under Count Thurn's command. He was therefore directed to assemble five of the senior Officers under his command, he himself presiding, and proceed to inquire whether the crime with which Caraccioli stood charged could be proved, and if the charge was proved, to report to Lord Nelson what punishment he ought to suffer.[8]

Upon this Warrant many observations have been made : it has been asked, What authority had Lord Nelson to order Sicilian Officers to form a Court Martial for the Trial of an Officer of that service ? Secondly, Whatever might have been the conduct of Caraccioli, was he not protected by the Capitulation of Uovo and Nuovo from any process, civil or military ?

These are important questions, and upon them the legality of the subsequent proceedings against Caraccioli entirely depends. The first question has been already partly discussed.[9] Caraccioli was a Naval Officer, accused of the highest Military offence, and for which he was amenable to a Naval Court Martial. Whether in order-

---

[7] Clarke and M'Arthur, vol. ii. p. 184.   [8] Vide p. 398.

[9] Vide pp. 490—493, ante.

ing that Court Martial Lord Nelson was acting as Commander-in-Chief of the Sicilian Squadron, or under the general powers granted to him by the King on leaving Palermo, has not been ascertained, but he probably acted in the former capacity. It is indisputable that he himself, as well as those who were responsible for obeying his orders—namely, Count Thurn and the other Sicilian Officers—knew that he had full authority for his proceedings; and it is equally certain that he exercised no other authority over Sicilian Officers than he could have exercised over British Officers, situated like Count Thurn and his colleagues, or like Caraccioli himself.

The Warrant, which did not specify where the Court Martial was to be held, was immediately obeyed; and the Members assembled on board the Foudroyant, where the prisoner was, instead of his being removed for Trial on board one of the Sicilian Ships.

It has been objected that it was unfair to the prisoner to select Count Thurn to preside at the Trial, because he was the personal enemy of Caraccioli, and entertained a vindictive feeling against him, for having fired into his Ship. The personal enmity is mere assertion, while the integrity of Count Thurn's character has been vouched for;[1] and few men—certainly no Naval Officer—will contend that the duty which properly belonged to Count Thurn, as the senior Sicilian Officer present, ought to have been transferred to a junior Officer, whereby an unworthy suspicion would have been cast upon his honour, because it happened to be his own Ship into which Caraccioli's gun-boats had fired some weeks before, when she formed part of a Squadron which was equally exposed, and in which most, if not all, the other Sicilian Naval Officers, then at Naples, were employed. It has also been said that the Trial ought not to have taken place on board a British Ship. The real value of this objection depends mainly upon the effect which the locality had on the fate of the prisoner; and unless the absurd idea be entertained that if he had been tried on board a Sicilian Ship, the crew would have risen to release and protect him,[2] which (if a refutation can be necessary) is refuted by the fact that they did nothing of the kind at his execution—his Trial on board the Foudroyant was, for every other reason, an advantage to Caraccioli, inasmuch as if any injustice or irregularity had been desired, it could scarcely have been perpetrated in the presence of numerous British Officers, on board a British Ship of War; and no one has ever shown that there was any *unfairness* in the proceedings. There is, however, a generous feeling in Englishmen, that their Officers and Ships shall not be concerned in any way with the punishment of Foreigners, and as this was entirely a Sicilian transaction, it may be wished that the scene had begun as it ended, in a Sicilian Vessel, or on the Sicilian Territories.

The next and most important question is, whether Caraccioli was or was not comprehended in the Capitulation of Uovo and Nuovo?

It is plain that neither Caraccioli himself, nor any of his fellow Rebels, or Patriots, thought that he was included in the Capitulation. Without attaching undue weight to the facts that the Capitulation was not signed by Captain Foote until early in the morning of the 23rd; and that, as on that day, Caraccioli was at Calviranno, a few miles from Naples, he probably was not in the Castle when the Capitulation was signed, it is apparent from other circumstances that he knew he could derive no benefit from it. His plea for mercy to the Duke of Calviranno rested entirely on his former services, without any allusion to the Capitulation;— he fled from the Castle before there was the least idea of suspending its execution; and neither on his Trial, nor in his subsequent appeal to Lord Nelson for pardon, is he anywhere stated to have claimed the benefit of the Capitulation.

This silence, when his life was at stake, can only be attributed to *his conviction*

---

[1] Vide p. 521, post.      [2] Clarke and M'Arthur.

*that he had no right whatever to claim protection from the Capitulation*, and that his case was entirely distinct from that of those who were in the Castles on the 26th of June, when they were taken possession of by the English. In all circumstances, men are likely to be competent judges of what may best conduce to their own safety; and it is perfectly incredible that if Caraccioli thought himself entitled to the benefit of the Capitulation, he would not have referred to it. Is it likely that a man on trial for his life, before a Military tribunal, would have confined his defence to such doubtful grounds as his having been forced into the crime of commanding a Flotilla against his Sovereign's Ships, when he could have said—"Guilty or not guilty, my safety is guaranteed by a Capitulation executed " only one week ago ?" From the beginning to the end, however, of every statement that has appeared respecting Caraccioli, and bitterly as Lord Nelson has been reproached on the subject, it is nowhere suggested that Caraccioli ever claimed to have been protected by the Capitulation.

This opinion of Caraccioli's position with reference to the Capitulation is strongly supported by the admission of the very writer whose statements were the original source of most of the injustice that has been done to Lord Nelson. Miss Helen Maria Williams, a lady deeply imbued with Republican principles, published, in 1801, her " Sketches of the state of Manners and Opinions in the French " Republic." To that work it will be again necessary to refer; and though, as will afterwards be shown, her ignorance and prejudices render the book generally unworthy of credit, yet on the point for which it is now cited, it is of the highest authority, because there can be no doubt that she faithfully stated the opinions of the Neapolitan Jacobins on what took place ; and she is well known to have represented the conduct pursued towards them by Lord Nelson and the King of Sicily in the most unfavourable colours.

After mentioning the Capitulation of Uovo and Nuovo, its suspension, the arrival of the King, and the measures afterwards adopted against the Rebels, Miss Williams says :—

" The executions began with the Patriots who were NOT included in the Capitu- " lation, and one of the first victims was the Prince Caraccioli."[3]

No particulars can be added to the following account of the Trial and Execution of Caraccioli, given by Clarke and M'Arthur, which has never been contradicted:—

" The Admiral had now a most painful and severe duty to perform. Every one who " had known Caraccioli had regarded him; but justice was to have its course, and " the only man who could secure it, had been and was the affectionate friend of the " unhappy prisoner. Lord Nelson, who was much agitated, felt it all most keenly; " but he also knew that he must perform his duty, not only to his own Sovereign, " but to that Monarch whose cause Caraccioli had neglected, and who looked alone " to a British Admiral for that redress which the treacherous Neapolitan had shown " no disposition to secure. Sir William and Lady Hamilton were both on board ; but " Lord Nelson, during the whole of Caraccioli's confinement, would see no one " except his own Officers. The step which he immediately took was certainly a " bold and unprecedented one ; as it would have been extremely dangerous to have " ordered a Court Martial to assemble on board a Neapolitan ship, from the love " which the Sicilian seamen bore to Caraccioli, and as the Foudroyant was consi- " dered as the seat of Government of the King of Naples, his Lordship issued the " following Order[4] to Commodore Count Thurn, Commander of the Sicilian Frigate " La Minerva, to assemble a Court Martial of Neapolitan Officers on board his " Britannic Majesty's Ship.

---

[3] " Sketches," vol. i. p. 210, 211.          [4] Vide p. 398, ante.

"During the Trial, which commenced the same morning, and lasted from ten
" o'clock to twelve, the wardroom of the Foudroyant was open, as is customary, to
" every one who chose to enter. Some account of what passed has therefore been
" preserved. Everything appeared to be fairly and honourably conducted, to such of
" the English Officers as understood Italian. Caraccioli was repeatedly asked
" questions best calculated to enable him to clear those aspersions that had been
" attached to his character; and these he answered by endeavouring to prove that
" he had been forced into the Republican service, had been compelled to perform
" the duty of a common soldier for a considerable time, when he was offered the
" command of the Republican Neapolitan Navy, which necessity alone had at length
" compelled him to accept. This necessity the prisoner repeatedly attempted to
" substantiate; but it certainly was not proved to the satisfaction of the Court,
" nor of our own Officers who were present. On the contrary, it was clearly de-
" monstrated that the prisoner had enjoyed opportunities of escaping; and on being
" frequently asked why he had not embraced those opportunities, no satisfactory
" reply was made. Caraccioli, nevertheless, answered firmly and collectedly, and
" the manner in which he conducted himself gained the commiseration of the
" British Officers who were present. He appeared to be about seventy, of a com-
" manding figure, and with a dark expressive countenance. The Court, afterwards,
" particularly directed its attention to the two following points. First, the pri-
" soner's having been actively present on board the Republican vessel that had
" attacked the Sicilian frigate La Minerva, the Gun-boats, and the English Ships
" on that service, in which some of his Britannic Majesty's subjects had been
" killed, and others wounded. Secondly, his not endeavouring to escape previous
" to that attack, when it evidently appeared he had possessed opportunities to do
" so. Caraccioli in vain attempted to prove his innocence; his answers were vague,
" and supported by no evidence whatever—the last efforts of a man striving to
" save his life. The Court was then cleared, and sentence of death passed on the
" prisoner. On its being transmitted by the President to Lord Nelson, his Lord-
" ship immediately issued the following Order[5] for its being carried into execution
" on the same evening.

"During the awful interval that ensued from the close of his Trial to the execution
" of his sentence, Caraccioli twice requested Lieutenant Parkinson to go and inter-
" cede with Lord Nelson; at first for a second trial, and afterwards that he might
" be shot. 'I am an old man, Sir,' said Caraccioli, 'I leave no family to lament
" my death—I therefore cannot be supposed to be very anxious about prolonging
" my life; but the disgrace of being hanged is dreadful to me.' Lord Nelson
" replied, 'Caraccioli has been fairly tried by the Officers of his own Country; I
" cannot interfere.' 'Forgetting," says Dr. Southey, 'that if he felt himself justified
" in ordering the trial and the execution, no human being could ever have questioned
" the propriety of his interfering on the side of mercy.' On being urged the second
" time by Lieutenant Parkinson, he exclaimed with much agitation, 'Go, Sir, and
" attend to your duty.' Caraccioli, then, as a last hope, asked Lieutenant Parkinson
" whether he thought an application to Lady Hamilton would prove beneficial?
" Upon which that Officer went to the quarter-deck, but not being able to meet with
" her, he returned; she was, however, present at the execution. At five o'clock
" Caraccioli was removed from the Foudroyant, and hanged at the fore yard-arm of
" the Neapolitan Frigate La Minerva. His body was afterwards carried out to a
" considerable distance, and sunk in the Bay of Naples.

---

[5] Vide p. 398, ante.

"It has been objected to the fairness of the whole proceedings against Caraccioli,
"and to the justice of Lord Nelson in sanctioning their execution, that Count Thurn,
"who presided at the trial, was an inveterate enemy of the Sicilian Commodore, and
"was not generally considered as possessing sufficient magnanimity to cause his
"private feelings to give way to his public duty. But if it could even be made ap-
"pear that Lord Nelson was aware of the private and secret politics of the Sicilian
"Navy, they who urge this objection should recollect, that he who was incapable of
"possessing the feelings imputed to Count Thurn, would be the last man to suspect
"another, particularly a loyal Officer, of dishonourable conduct in the discharge of
"public duty; and that he had sent Caraccioli to the only competent tribunal to
"which he could be committed, to whose authority the Commodore had felt amen-
"able, as appears from his letter on the 23rd of June to the Duke of Calviranno.
"The judgment of Lord Nelson, in this cruel transaction, was influenced and
"warped by the artful influence of Lady Hamilton, whose devotion to the Royal
"family of Naples made her the immitigable enemy of all rebels to their authority.
"The trial and execution of Caraccioli were indecently and unjustly accelerated by
"this wicked siren."[6]

Lord Nelson's motive for ordering the immediate execution of Caraccioli is unknown; but the magnitude and notoriety of his crime, and the supposed necessity,
from the state of Naples, of an immediate example, seem the most probable cause.

Before the misstatements of the writers who have alluded to the transactions at
Naples in June 1799, are pointed out, and Lord Nelson's proceedings on the subject are stated, it is desirable to insert two more extracts from Clarke and M'Arthur's
work :—

"On the 28th of June, 1799, the day previous to this Trial and Execution of
"Caraccioli, Captain Foote had sailed in the Seahorse, by Lord Nelson's order, for
"the purpose of conveying the King and his family to Naples. On his arrival in
"the Bay of Palermo, he informed the Prime Minister, Sir John Acton, that the
"Seahorse was ready to receive the Royal family, or to execute their commands. Sir
"John Acton then informed Captain Foote of the intention of their Sicilian Majes-
"ties to proceed to Naples in their own Frigate, the Sirena, lest they might hurt
"the feelings of their Naval Officers who had remained faithful; but that their
"Majesties wished him to convoy them and the Transports with troops on board,
"and also to embark their treasure and staff in the Seahorse. This Minister
"also assured Captain Foote that both the King and Queen were very sensible of
"the service he had rendered them in the Bay of Naples. Upon which Captain
"Foote availed himself of what appeared a favourable opportunity to perform his
"promise to the Republican garrisons of Revigliano and Castel-à-Mare; and, at
"the Minister's request, explained to him the terms of the Capitulation which
"had been granted; frequently observing, that the reliance which those Garrisons
"had placed in Captain Foote's intercession, had principally induced them to
"submit without the effusion of blood, which Sir John Acton, who well knew
"the immense strength of Castel-à-Mare, must be aware would have been very
"great, if they had made a determined resistance. On that Minister's appearing
"exasperated at the black ingratitude of some of the Officers to their King, who
"had composed the Garrison of Castel-à-Mare, Captain Foote begged, as a per-
"sonal favour, since their Sicilian Majesties were pleased to think he had rendered
"them some service, that the Capitulation which he had made with those Garrisons
"might be regarded as sacred. This honourable conduct of Captain Foote, after the

---

[6] Clarke and M'Arthur's "Life of Lord Nelson," vol. ii. p. 187.

" insults and duplicity he had experienced, was also supported by Lord Nelson. As
" no Neapolitan intrigues had been employed to deceive his Officers in forming their
" Capitulation, he with Captain Foote, considered the honour of the English Nation
" as being implicated in its perfect observance. In consequence of which, the Articles
" were strictly executed, and considered as inviolable by the King of Naples. On the
" 3rd of July, 1799, their Sicilian Majesties embarked on board the Sirena, and
" sailing for the Bay of Naples, under the protection of Captain Foote, arrived
" again in their Capital on the 8th of the same month.

" As the castles of Uovo and Nuovo had surrendered to Lord Nelson fourteen days
" before the return of the King, it had been found difficult, in the critical situation
" of Naples, to provide for the security of those traitors who had been thus taken in
" their own net; and in consequence, many of them were exposed to great privations
" and hardships, the whole odium of which was most industriously cast on Lord
" Nelson. The King, on his arrival, publicly disavowed any authority having been
" delegated to Ruffo to treat with subjects in rebellion. The trials of these traitors
" then commenced according to the Neapolitan laws, and were conducted with as
" much regularity as could well be expected, before one of their Judges, and chiefly
" in the presence of the Cardinal. Lord Nelson throughout determined in no
" respect whatever to interfere with the course of the Neapolitan law; in which
" opinion he was supported by Captain Troubridge. They both were well aware
" that it was the determination of the traitors and disaffected to implicate the
" English, if possible, in the odium of everything that ensued on the King's arrival.
" His Lordship was therefore compelled to reply to the numerous petitions that
" were presented to him from these unfortunate persons, " *I have shown your paper*
" *to your gracious King, who must be the best and only judge of the merits and*
" *demerits of his subjects.*"[7] The number of traitors, who in consequence suffered
" at different times, after being regularly tried and condemned by the laws of their
" Country, amounted to about seventy persons: of these Lord Nelson, in one of
" his private Notes, declared, that ' Eleonora Fonseca had been a great rebel; and
" that Dominico Cirillo, who had been the King's physician, might have been
" saved, but that he chose to play the fool, and lie; denying that he had ever made
" any speeches against the Government, and that he only took care of the poor in
" the hospitals.' The Queen of Naples, on her knees, begged of his Majesty the
" life of Cirillo,[8] but in vain."

" On his return to Naples,[9] 8th of July, 1799, his Sicilian Majesty again held his
" Court and resided on board Lord Nelson's Ship, under the secure protection of the
" British Flag; where he enjoyed the constant loyalty, more particularly of the
" lower classes of his subjects, and renewed that courtesy and condescension to all
" ranks, which had retained so powerful an ascendancy over the artifices and
" calumnies of the French. About a week afterwards, a Neapolitan, who had been

---

[7] Helen Maria Williams's " Sketches," vol. i. page 189, and vol. ii. page 328.

[8] A Petition from Cirillo to Lady Hamilton to that effect, and imploring her to
intercede for him with the King, is in the Nelson Papers. If the statement about
the Queen's intercession be true, he must have been executed after the King's
return to Palermo, because her Majesty was not then at Naples.

[9] The discrepancy, noticed in page 401, in the date of the arrival of the King at
Naples, is explained by the Seahorse's Log:—

" July 1.—At 3, Thalia showed her pendants coming out of Palermo. At 7,
" came to in Palermo Bay.

" 3rd.—At 6, unmoored. 9, weighed and made sail. The Sirena, (N[eapolitan]

" fishing in the Bay, came one morning to the Foudroyant, and assured the Officers
" that Caraccioli had been seen, who had risen from the bottom of the sea, and
" was coming as fast as he could to Naples, swimming half out of the water. The
" story of the Neapolitan was slightly mentioned to his Majesty. The day being
" favourable, Lord Nelson, as usual, indulged the King by standing out to sea: the
" Foudroyant, however, had not advanced far, before the Officers of the watch beheld
" a body upright in the water, whose course was directed towards them. Captain
" Hardy soon discovered that it was actually the body of Caraccioli, notwithstand-
" ing the great weight which had been attached to it; and it became extremely
" difficult to decide in what manner the extraordinary circumstance should be com-
" municated to the King. This was performed with much address by Sir William
" Hamilton;[1] and with his Majesty's permission the body was taken on shore by a
" Neapolitan boat, and consigned to Christian burial. The Coxswain of the boat
" brought back the double-headed Neapolitan shot, with a portion of the skin still
" adhering to the rope by which they had been fixed. They were weighed by
" Captain Hardy, who ascertained that the body had risen and floated with the
" immense weight of 250 lbs. attached to it."[2]

As the Queen of Naples is said by some writers to have taken an active part in
the proceedings against the Rebels, Captain Foote having stated that " their Sici-
" lian Majesties embarked on board the Sirena, and sailed from Palermo under the
" protection of the Seahorse,"[3] it is proper to correct an error into which it is extra-

---

" F[rigate],) Strombolo, Balloon, and thirty-seven sail of Merchantmen in com-
" pany.
" 6th.—At 1, saw Capri.
" 7th.—At daylight, found the Minerva (N[eapolitan] F[rigate]) in the Convoy.
" 8th.—Under sail in the Bay of Naples. A.M. At 9, I went on board the
" Sirena, to wait on his Sicilian Majesty." [In a letter to Lord Nelson, dated on
this day at 2 P.M., in the Capri passage, Captain Foote informed him that the
King had directed the Convoy under his charge to anchor off Procida:—"I do
" not," he said, " expect to reach Procida until to-morrow," and he begged to be informed whether the Seahorse was to join his Lordship or to remain at Procida.—
Autograph, in the Nelson Papers.]
" 9th, A.M.—At 10, made the signal, 'Shall I anchor?' Answered in the affir-
" mative; came close to Naples.
" 10th.—Answered the signal to salute with 21 guns. At 4, the Sirena anchored;
" and on his Sicilian Majesty's going on board the Foudroyant, the standard was
" hoisted, and the whole Fleet saluted with 21 guns. At ½ past 9, weighed. Thalia
" in company."

[1] He told the King that Caraccioli could not rest until he had come and implored pardon of his Majesty himself, for his crimes against him!

[2] Clarke and M'Arthur, vol. ii. p. 187—189. Dr. Clarke, in a Letter to Captain
Foote, in January 1809, said, " Hardy told me that Caraccioli floated, notwithstand-
" ing three double-headed shot had been tied to his legs, and that these shot, on
" being weighed, were 250 pounds! How can three double shot weigh so much?
" I have made it 150. I will write to Hardy, and if wrong, mark it in the Ap-
" pendix." Captain Foote replied—" The weight of double-headed shot, of course,
" depends on the bore of the gun, and it is probable that three belonging to a 32-
" pounder weigh 250 lbs."—Vindication, p. 44.

[3] " Vindication," p. 28.

ordinary that Captain Foote should have fallen. *The Queen did not go to Naples,*[4] but remained at Palermo, with the Prince Royal and the rest of the Royal Family, where they were joined by the King, in the Foudroyant, on the 8th of August.[5]

No public notice seems to have been taken of the events at Naples, until February in the following year. It has been shown that the King of Naples entirely approved of Lord Nelson's conduct; and there is no trace whatever, (except for dis-

---

[4] Vide the Foudroyant's Log, p. 508, post. Miss Knight, writing at Palermo, says:—

"June 27th. Arrived a Frigate (Cav. Naselli) from Naples. Lord Nelson, with " the Fleet, anchored there in the evening of the 24th, and broke the Truce, which " Cardinal Ruffo had improperly concluded for twenty days. It is said that very " favourable conditions would have been granted to the French and their party, by " the Cardinal, had not our Fleet arrived.

"July 8th. Nine of our Ships, with some Gun-Boats, are gone to Gaeta. Frà " Diavolo attacks it by land. Cav. Caracciolo was hanged on board the Minerva, " Neapolitan Frigate, commanded by Count Thurn, on the 30th, at Naples.

"July 15th. A Cutter arrived this morning from Lord Nelson, with the Rebel " standards, which were dragged through the streets, and afterwards burned by the " hangman before the Castle. The Queen went to Church yesterday, to return " thanks for the deliverance of Naples."—*Journal.*

[5] Some authentic information on the transactions in the Bay of Naples, is afforded by the following extracts from the Log Book of His Majesty's Ship Foudroyant, from the 8th of June to the 15th of July 1799. These Extracts contain *every fact* of the slightest interest. All similar Extracts from the *Journal* in the Nelson Papers, within the same period, have been given in Notes to the Text. It must be remembered, that the Nautical day *begins* at Noon, so that whatever occurred after Noon is entered as part of the proceedings of the *following day.* Thus, the Fleet is said to have anchored in Naples Bay at 9 P.M. on *Tuesday* the 25th, instead of on *Monday* the 24th; thus also Caraccioli's trial is stated to have occurred on Saturday the 29th, which was the fact, and his execution on Sunday the 30th, whereas it took place in the afternoon of the 29th:

"Moored in Palermo Road.
- SATURDAY, 8th *June.* Hoisted Lord Nelson's Flag. Captain Brown went on board H. M. Ship Vanguard.
- SUNDAY, 9th. Arrived a Vessel from Genoa, with dispatches.
- MONDAY, 10th. Arrived dispatches from Naples.
- TUESDAY, 11th.

"Single Anchor, Palermo Road.
- WEDNESDAY, 12th. Employed taking in and stowing away baggage, &c., for the Prince of Naples. Unmoored Ship.

Mount Pelegrino, W.S.W. 3 or 4 Leagues.
- THURSDAY, 13th. At 3 A.M., made the signal to weigh. At 8, outside of the Bay. At 10, the Prince of Naples, with his *suite*, came on board; also, the King, Queen, and most of the Royal Family. Hoisted the Royal Standard: each Ship in the Fleet saluted with 21 guns. At Noon, the King, Queen, and Royal Family went on shore. The Prince and suite remained on board.

Single Anchor, Palermo Road.
- FRIDAY, 14th. At 4, joined company H. M. Ships Powerful and Bellerophon. Tacked and stood for Palermo. A.M. At 8, made the signal for the Fleet to anchor. Several boats came from the shore. The Prince and *suite* went on shore: landed all the baggage, &c. Joined company, Telegraph brig. Anchored:
- SATURDAY, 15th.

obeying Lord Keith's order to go to the protection of Minorca,) of his having been in the slightest degree censured by his own Government. On the contrary, the Board of Admiralty approved of his having gone to Naples, and in the only other communication from the Admiralty which has fallen under the Editor's observation, *all* Lord Nelson's proceedings there seem to have been fully approved of. On the 7th of October 1799, Lord Spencer wrote a long letter to Nelson, which began with this sentence :—

---

Mount Pelegrino, S.W. 7 or 8 Leagues. { SUNDAY, 16th. At 9, weighed and stood out of the Bay. Joined company the St. Vincent Cutter from Tunis. 16 sail of the Line, 1 Fire-ship, 1 Brig, and a Cutter, in company.

MONDAY, 17th. Fleet in company.

TUESDAY, 18th. A.M. Joined company the Alexander and Goliath. Fleet in company.

Maritimo, W.S.W. 7 or 8 Leagues. } WEDNESDAY, 19th. At 10, came on board a boat from Palermo. Fleet in company.

Maritimo, S.W. by W. ½ W., 7 Leagues. } THURSDAY, 20th. Fleet in company.

FRIDAY, 21st. At 7, parted company with the Fleet. At Noon, working into Palermo Bay.

SATURDAY, 22nd. At 3, brought to in Palermo Bay. At ½ past 5, filled and made sail. A.M. joined the Fleet.

Capri, N.E. by N., 10 or 12 Leagues. } SUNDAY, 23rd.

MONDAY, 24th. Spoke a Neapolitan Sloop of War, and supplied her with water. Fleet in company. A.M., joined company H.M. Brig Mutine.

TUESDAY, 25th. At 4, Naples Town N.E. 3 or 4 leagues. Answered a salute from the shore with 13 guns. At 9, anchored abreast of Naples. A.M., at daylight, weighed and stood further in. Moored Ship. Fleet moored in a line S.S.E. and N.N.W., consisting of 18 Sail of the Line, 1 Frigate, and 2 Fire-ships.

WEDNESDAY, 26th. Saluted a Cardinal who came on board, with 13 Guns. A.M., employed occasionally.

THURSDAY, 27th. At 4, P.M. landed 500 Marines from different Ships : Captain Troubridge went on shore to take command. Arrived, a King's messenger from England.

FRIDAY, 28th. A.M. A Boat, manned and armed, from each Ship, went into the Mole, and attended some Vessels coming out, having Prisoners on board.

SATURDAY, 29th. Several of the principal Officers of the Rebels were put in confinement in different Ships. A.M. At 9, a Court-Martial assembled on board, to try for rebellion Cavaliere Francisco Caracciolo.

SUNDAY, 30th. At 5 P.M., landed the remainder of the Marines from each Ship. The sentence of the Court-Martial of yesterday was put in execution, on board a Neapolitan Frigate, on Cavaliere Francisco Caracciolo, and he was hanged accordingly. A.M. Mustered Ship's company at quarters.

MONDAY, 1st *July*. A.M. Several of the Rebel party were brought on board. Saw several shot and shell fired at and from Castle St. Elmo.

TUESDAY, 2nd. A.M. Arrived, a Courier from Sicily. Several of the Rebel party were brought on board for examination.

WEDNESDAY, 3rd. Sailed, Alexander and Alphonso, (a Portuguese.)

" My dear Lord,—In answer to your letter of the 23rd of July,[6] which did not
" reach me till the 26th of last month, I can only now repeat what I believe I have
" before said on the subject—namely, that the intentions and motives by which all
" your measures have been governed, have been as pure and good, as their success
" has been complete."[7]

On the 3rd of February, 1800, on the motion for the Address thanking his
Majesty for refusing to negotiate with the French Republic, Mr. Fox said—
" I wish the atrocities of which we hear so much, and which I abhor as much as
" any man, were indeed unexampled. I fear that they do not belong exclusively to
" the French. When the Right Honourable Gentleman speaks of the extraordinary
" successes of the last campaign, he does not mention the horrors, by which some of
" these successes were accompanied. Naples, for instance, has been, among others,

THURSDAY, 4th. A.M. Sent a Lieutenant, with 20 Seamen, to assist at the Forts.

FRIDAY, 5th. A.M. Several of the Rebels were brought on board: sent them to
the Prison-ships. Supplied them with provisions.

SATURDAY, 6th. Arrived, H. M. Ship Thalia. Leviathan made the signal for a
Court-Martial.

SUNDAY, 7th. John Jolly, Marine, was brought on board, the Court-Martial
having sentenced him to suffer death.

MONDAY, 8th. At 5, A.M. sent on shore to the Marine Camp, John Jolly,
prisoner.

TUESDAY, 9th. Came in here, the Strombolo and Balloon.

WEDNESDAY, 10th. Saw two Neapolitan Frigates to S.W., also H.M. Ship
Seahorse and a convoy. A.M. Leviathan made the signal for a Court-Martial.

THURSDAY, 11th. At 4 P.M., his Sicilian Majesty and suite came on board this
Ship; each Ship in the Fleet saluted with 21 guns. A.M. Sailed, the Seahorse and
Thalia.

FRIDAY, 12th. The French hoisted a Flag of Truce on the Castle of St. Elmo.
At 9 A.M., the Neapolitan Colours were hoisted at the Castle of St. Elmo; each
Ship saluted with 21 guns. Sent a Launch to assist to embark the French pri-
soners. At Meridian, Captain Troubridge brought on board the keys of the Castle
St. Elmo, also the French colours, which were delivered to His Sicilian Majesty.

MONDAY, 15th. Arrived, a Neapolitan frigate, which saluted with 21 guns, which
we returned with 17. A.M., Sailed, the Balloon, with the Cartel Vessels, with French
prisoners for Toulon.

TUESDAY, 16th. At 3, P.M. Lieut. Parkinson, with the King's Messenger, went
on shore to proceed to England."

The annexed Extracts prove that the Queen of Naples remained at Palermo:—

" August 8th. Noon, standing in for Palermo.

" 9th. At 1, P.M. came on board the Queen, Prince, and most of the Royal
" Family; saluted with 21 guns. At 3, anchored. At 6, the King and Royal
" Family, suite, and servants, went ashore; saluted with 21 guns."

---

[6] No letter to Lord Spencer, of the 23rd of July, has been found, nor is there
any trace of such a letter in his " Letter-Book;" it may have been a mistake for
the 13th, on which day Lord Nelson wrote an important letter to him. *Vide*
p. 406, ante.

[7] *Autograph*, lately in the possession of Mr. Evans, of Maddox Street, Hanover
Square. This letter, of which the remaining part related to other matters, will
be found in the fourth Volume.

" what is called *delivered;* and yet, if I am rightly informed, it has been stained and
" polluted by murders so ferocious, and by cruelties of every kind so abhorrent, that
" the heart shudders at the recital. It has been said, not only that the miserable
" victims of the rage and brutality of the fanatics were savagely murdered, but that,
" in many instances, their flesh was eaten and devoured by the cannibals, who are
" the advocates and the instruments of social order. Nay, England is not totally
" exempt from reproach, if the rumours which are circulated be true. I will mention
" a fact, to give Ministers the opportunity, if it be false, to wipe away the stain that
" must otherwise affix on the British name. It is said, that a party of the Republican
" inhabitants at Naples took shelter in the fortress of Castel del Uovo. They were
" besieged by a detachment from the Royal Army, to whom they refused to surrender,
" but demanded that a British officer should be brought forward, and to him they
" capitulated. They made terms with him under the sanction of the British name.
" It was agreed that their persons and property should be safe, and that they should
" be conveyed to Toulon. They were accordingly put on board a Vessel; but before
" they sailed, their property was confiscated, numbers of them taken out, thrown into
" dungeons, and some of them, I understand, notwithstanding the British guarantee,
" absolutely executed."

As a division on the Motion took place immediately on the conclusion of Mr.
Fox's speech, (which, as is manifest, contained numerous errors,) no reply was
made to any part of it; but as soon as it reached Lord Nelson, he wrote the following indignant letter to his friend Mr. Davison:—

" My dear Sir,                                   " Malta, May 9th, 1800.
" Mr. Fox having, in the House of Commons, in February, made an accusation
" against somebody, for what he calls a breach of a Treaty with Rebels, which had
" been entered into with a British Officer, and having used language unbecoming
" either the wisdom of a Senator, or the politeness of a Gentleman, or an Englishman,
" who ought ever to suppose that His Majesty's Officers would always act with
" honour and openness in all their transactions; and as the whole affairs of the
" Kingdom of Naples were at the time alluded to absolutely placed in my hands, it is
" *I* who am called upon to explain my conduct, and therefore send you my Obser-
" vations on the infamous Armistice entered into by the Cardinal; and on his refusal
" to send in a joint declaration to the French and Rebels, I sent in my Note, and
" on which the Rebels came out of the Castles *as they ought,* and as I hope all those
" who are false to their King and Country will, *to be hanged,* or otherwise disposed
" of, as their Sovereign thought proper. The terms granted by Captain Foote, of
" the Seahorse, at Castel-à-Mare, were all strictly complied with—the Rebels having
" surrendered before my arrival. There has been nothing promised by a British
" Officer, that His Sicilian Majesty has not complied with, even in disobedience to
" his orders to the Cardinal. I am, &c.
                                   " BRONTE, NELSON OF THE NILE.

" Show these Papers to Mr. Rose, or some other, and, if thought right, you will
" put them in the papers."[8]

In 1801, Miss Helen Maria Williams published her " Sketches;" in which, after
describing the Capitulation of Uovo and Nuovo, she says:—

" While the two garrisons, to the number of about fifteen hundred, who had
" declared their intention of emigrating, were waiting for the preparing and provi-

---

[8] Letter-Book, and Clarke and M'Arthur, vol. ii. p. 181. The Papers alluded to
were, no doubt, those printed in pp. 384, 386, 388, ante. Clarke and M'Arthur say
that they had searched for them in vain.

" sioning of the Vessels which were to convey them to France, Lord Nelson arrived
" with his whole Fleet in the Road of Naples, having on board his ship Sir William
" Hamilton and his Lady.   On the evening of the twenty-sixth of June, the patriots
" evacuated their forts, and embarked on board the Transports prepared for their
" conveyance to France.   The next day, the Transports were moored, under the direc-
" tion of English Officers, alongside the English fleet, which was stretched across
" the Bay as it were in a line of battle, where they remained at anchor, each under
" the cannon of an English vessel.   On the day following, the Members of the Exe-
" cutive Commission, a great part of those of the Legislative Commission, the
" whole of the Officers who had occupied the first ranks in the Republic, and others
" who had been marked by the Court of Sicily, were hauled out of the Transports
" on board the British Admiral's Ship.   Among these was the celebrated Dominico
" Cirilli, Member of the Legislative Commission, and who had been thirty years the
" friend and physician of the English Ambassador."[9]  . . . The authoress then com-
ments, in an inflated strain, upon their meeting, and upon the presence of Lady
" Hamilton on the occasion, and proceeds :—" Some amongst the sufferers, from
" the menacing parade with which they were surrounded, believed that their last
" moment was arrived; but Admiral Caraccioli, who was better acquainted with
" Naval etiquette, whispered his fellow sufferers, that this threatening aspect of
" their guards was only meant for mockery and terror."[1]  . . . Some severe com-
ments are then made upon Lady Hamilton's having been present :—" After this
" review on board the Admiral's Ship, these illustrious victims were momentarily
" (sic) distributed in the other Ships of the Fleet.   If the Capitulation was thus
" fulfilled with respect to the persons on board the Transports, it may easily be
" imagined what was the fate of those who remained in the Forts, and who, on the
" faith of the Treaty, were confident of returning to their homes.   On the entrance
" of the English troops, who were the first to take possession, they were all made
" prisoners, and shut up in the dungeons of the respective Castles.   A few days
" after, the King of Sicily, accompanied by his Minister, Acton, arrived from
" Palermo, on board an English frigate in the Bay.   He immediately declared by
" an Edict, that it never was his intention to capitulate with Rebels, and that, con-
" sequently, the fate of those who were in the Transports, or in the Forts, was to
" depend entirely on his justice and clemency.   While the patriots who had capi-
" tulated were waiting the effects of this justice and clemency with respect to their
" persons, the King published another Edict, ordering all their property to be put
" under sequestration.   These Edicts were too humiliating for the Commanders of the
" coalesced Powers, who had assisted in the reduction of Naples, to pass by without
" remonstrances; but remonstrances had no effect against the mandate of the King,
" and the Turk, the Russian, and Cardinal Ruffo, were compelled to remain passive
" spectators of the infraction of the Treaty which they had solemnly signed, and
" which they imagined it behoved their own honour, and that of the Powers they
" represented, to see carried into strict execution."[2]
In these statements there is no allusion to the important fact which occurs in
the Petition she has herself printed—viz., that the English Fleet arrived *before* the
Capitulation was begun to be carried into execution; nor to Lord Nelson's notification
to the Rebels in the Castles on the *twenty-fifth* of June, that if they surrendered, it
must be to the King's mercy, for the Capitulation would not be observed without his
Majesty's ratification; nor to the fact that the Rebels came out with that knowledge.
Her ignorance on other points was no less extraordinary.   Among the patriots who

---

[9] " Sketches," vol. i. 181.    [1] Ibid., p. 183.    [2] " Sketches," vol. i. p. 186.

were " hauled out of the Transports on board the English Ships," " bound hand and
" foot like the vilest criminals," on the *twenty-eighth* of June, was, she says, *Admiral
Caraccioli*, who " whispered his fellow-sufferers that this threatening aspect of their
" guards was only meant for mockery and terror."[3] Now, it is notorious that Caraccioli
was, at the moment when he is said to have been " whispering" on board the Fou
droyant, a fugitive in the mountains, where he was arrested on the *next day*, the
29th, and when, for the first time for many months, he appeared on board an
English Ship of War.   But so ill informed was Miss Williams, that instead
of fixing Caraccioli's execution to the 29th of June, twelve days *before* the arrival
of the King, she represents him to have been executed *after* his Majesty's return
to Naples.[4]   Another of her statements calls for observation.   It must be inferred
from the passage which has been above extracted, that the Commanders of the
coalesced Powers who had signed the Capitulation, especially Cardinal Ruffo and
the Turkish and the Russian Officer, remonstrated with the King against its infraction.   That Cardinal Ruffo did so to Lord Nelson is true ; but there is no evidence
whatever of his having remonstrated with the King, or that either the Russian or the
Turkish Commander made any such representation to his Majesty, or to Lord
Nelson.   The conduct of Captain Foote on this subject requires particular observation, since he came forward after Lord Nelson's death, not only to justify his own
proceedings in signing the Capitulation, but to cast severe reflections upon those
of Nelson in suspending it.

The position of the Russian and Turkish Officers who had signed the Treaty,
when they knew it was not to be carried into effect, suggest this question :—
If a Capitulation be fully concluded (whether carried into effect or not) by five
parties—the Sicilian, the English, the Russian, and Turkish, on the one side, and
the French on the other—and the superior Officer to the Sicilian or English party,
or to both, disavows the Capitulation, what ought to be the conduct of the other
parties on the same side—viz., the Turkish and the Russian ?   This question is
material; for if the Turkish and the Russian Officer who signed the Capitulation,
had a right to insist upon its observance, their acquiescence in its infraction tends
to show that they had no doubt of Lord Nelson's right to suspend, or of the King of
Sicily's power to annul, the Capitulation.

No other statement respecting the transactions in the Bay of Naples has been
found, until after the publication of Mr. Harrison's " Life of Lord Nelson," in 1806.
In that work[5] appeared, for the first time, a copy of Lord Nelson's letter to Earl
Spencer, dated on the 13th of July, 1799,[6] in which he described the Capitulation
of Uovo and Nuovo as " a most infamous Treaty."   In speaking of it, Mr.
Harrison said :—" On the 24th, they arrived in the Bay of Naples, where Lord
" Nelson saw a flag of truce flying on board the Seahorse, Captain Foote, and also
" on the Castles of Uovo and Nuovo.  Having, on the passage, received information
" that an infamous Armistice was entered into with the Rebels of those Castles, to
" which Captain Foote had put his name, his Lordship instantly made the signal
" to annul the Truce, being determined, as he said, never to give his approbation to
" any terms with rebels, but unconditional submission."[7]  This publication naturally
excited the displeasure of Captain Foote, and he wrote to Lord Spencer, who in-

---

[3] " Sketches," pp. 181—183.          [4] Ibid. p. 210.
[5] Vol. ii. p. 120.   Harrison found the letter in Lord Nelson's " Letter-Book."
His work first appeared in that year, under the title of " Genuine Memoirs of Lord
Nelson."
[6] Vide p. 408, ante.        [7] Harrison's " Life of Lord Nelson," vol. i. p. 99.

formed him that he had never authorized the publication of Lord Nelson's private letter. Captain Foote then wrote to Mr. Harrison on the 27th of February 1807, stating that if, in a second edition of his work, the same words were repeated respecting his conduct in the Bay of Naples, he "should be under the very painful " necessity to publish papers and facts which will demonstrate that no such epithets " as you have stated, in the thirteenth part of your first edition, are in any manner " applicable to my conduct on that occasion. This task I am compelled to perform, " notwithstanding my respect for Lord Nelson's memory; and I have considerable " satisfaction in being able to appeal to Sir John Duckworth, and the Captains who " served under his Lordship, for the truth of what I am thus obliged to publish " in defence of my own character."[5]

Not obtaining any satisfaction from Mr. Harrison, who repeated the objectionable words in the second edition of his book, Captain Foote published a Pamphlet, in 1807, entitled, " Captain Foote's Vindication of his conduct, when Cap- " tain of his Majesty's Ship Seahorse, and Senior Officer in the Bay of Naples, in the " summer of 1799," which was reprinted in 1810. That Pamphlet also contained the documents and correspondence relating to Uovo and Nuovo, &c., which have been now reprinted.

It is not necessary for this discussion to inquire whether the Capitulation of Uovo and Nuovo was in itself proper or improper, still less to show that Lord Nelson's opinion of it was correct. There is no doubt that he strongly disapproved of it from the instant he heard of its conditions; and when Captain Foote found that Nelson had applied to it the epithet " infamous," he was fully justified in vindicating his own conduct on the occasion. Here, however, Captain Foote ought to have stopped; and when he,—who had been honoured with the good opinion of Lord Nelson, and had experienced his kindness in generously imputing his mistake in signing the Capitulation, to his having been imposed upon and misled by Cardinal Ruffo, giving him ample credit for the best intentions, and admitting that he had been placed in a difficult and arduous position,—came forward, after Lord Nelson's death, to load his conduct with reproaches, insinuating even more than he ventured to express,—such conduct is not only objectionable on the ground of propriety, but also provokes the inquiry whether his own conduct, after he knew that the Capitulation was to be disregarded, was such as became a British Officer, or was consistent with the strong opinions which he expressed on the subject eight years after the event?

Captain Foote says—

" On my return to England, in the year 1800, I found the transactions in the " Bay of Naples had become a common topic of conversation, and, from rumours " that some blame might possibly be attached to my conduct, I was inclined to request " that a public inquiry should take place, upon what concerned my signing the Capi- " tulations. But before taking this step, I understood from a Naval member of the " Admiralty, and many other respectable friends, that by urging a public investiga- " tion, I should act injuriously to my Country, and in some measure attach my- " self to a party, for which idea there seemed to me to be good ground, in conse- " quence of the speech which the late Honourable Charles James Fox made on " the 3rd day of February, 1800."[6]

He censures Lord Nelson for having acted, respecting the Capitulation, without consulting the two senior Flag Officers, Lord St. Vincent and Lord Keith, forgetting that both were then many hundred miles distant.[7] He endeavours to show that Lord

---

[5] " Vindication," p. 11.  [6] Ibid., p. 8.  [7] Ibid., p. 15.

Nelson's reasons for having suspended the Capitulation were insufficient, and insists, in the strongest manner, that it ought not to have been suspended. He asserts that the "Italians relied with confidence on the National character before the un-"fortunate moment in which a wretched infatuation produced this breach of sacred "engagements."[8] Instead of imitating the consideration shown for him by Lord Nelson, by giving his Lordship credit, at least, for good intentions, or calling his resolution an error in judgment, Captain Foote more than once attributes it to the influence of Lady Hamilton, by saying he was "infatuated";[9] and then proceeds to intimate that he could have said much worse :—" My regard for the memory of a person so "much and so justly valued as that of Lord Nelson, arrests the observations which "it is natural to make on the whole of this transaction ; and that regard will also "prevent my detailing circumstances by no means favourable to the characters con-"cerned in the unfortunate affair."[1]

Captain Foote adverts, and justly, to the fact of Lord Nelson's having chosen him, on the 28th of June, to bring their Sicilian Majesties to Naples ;[2] to his order of the 8th of July to proceed with the Thalia, Captain Nisbet, on a particular service ;[3] and to his Letter of the 14th of September 1799,[4] as proofs that Nelson did not think any infamy attached to his character; yet he afterwards insinuated that his being detached on that special service on the 8th of July, arose from Lord Nelson's desire to send him *to some distance from Naples*,[5] and which has been considered by many subsequent writers as evidence that Nelson stood in such awe of Captain Foote, when measures were likely to be adopted against the Rebels inconsistent with the Capitulation, as to induce him to order him and Captain Nisbet, (who, *they say*, equally disapproved of his proceedings,) away from the scene of those transactions.

In Captain Foote's correspondence with Dr. Clarke, when the latter was writing the Life of Nelson, a few other statements occur which it is proper to notice. It seems that Captain Foote sent a copy of the first edition of his pamphlet to Dr. Clarke, in February 1807, in reply to which communication, Dr. Clarke wrote a very obliging letter on the 23rd of that month, wherein he expressed a desire to submit to Captain Foote all he intended to say respecting the affairs in the Bay of Naples, and gave him an outline of his opinions on the subject; observing, at the same time, that Sir Thomas Hardy, "who is my intimate friend, has with "his usual nobleness of conduct, put me on my guard respecting the Castles "Uovo and Nuovo."[6] In a subsequent letter, Dr. Clarke said—"You afterwards, "if you remember, sent me to Admiral Foley, and urged me repeatedly, and "very kindly, to see him, as a person well acquainted with the whole transac-"tion; I did see him, and it was from seeing and conversing with him and "Hardy, that I found it absolutely necessary to change the opinion I had

---

        [8] "Vindication," p. 17.     [9] Ibid., pp. 17, 66, 90.     [1] Ibid., p. 18.

  [2] Vide p. 395, ante.     [3] Vide p. 401, ante.     [4] Vide the next volume.

  [5] Captain Foote says, their Sicilian Majesties embarked on board their own Frigate, (the Sirena,) on the 3rd of July, to proceed to Naples Bay ; "accordingly, "their Majesties sailed from Palermo, under the protection of the Seahorse, and "reached that Bay on the 8th of the same month ; and on that very day Lord Nelson "was pleased to put the Thalia frigate, (commanded by his son-in law, Captain "Nisbet,) under my orders, and to send me on immediate service *at some* "*distance from Naples.*" Captain Foote's "Vindication," p. 28 and 517, postea.— The significant *italics* are Captain Foote's own.

  [6] "Vindication," p. 31.

" previously formed of *Lord Nelson's conduct*, but not *of yours;* from the first
" to the last I have ever thought you acted in a manner that reflected on you the
" greatest credit, and I have said as much in the Life." [7] These passages would
admit of a construction unfavourable to Lord Nelson, were they not explained in
another part of the last mentioned letter : " My being inclined (from the conversa-
" tion I had with Admiral Foley and with Hardy, and from seeing the King of
" Sicily's private letter *in his own hand* to Ruffo) to think more favourably of Lord
" Nelson's subsequent conduct, surely cannot in any way prove that I wished to
" attach blame to you, or that I was become unmindful of that regard for your
" professional character, which I had shown when I first became known to you." [8]
In that correspondence, Dr. Clarke in vain endeavoured to convince Captain Foote
that full justice could be done to him without suspecting Lord Nelson's motives, or
adopting Captain Foote's opinion that his Lordship was wholly unjustified in suspending the Capitulation. Dr. Clarke was quite ready to say that Captain Foote acted
correctly and properly in signing the Capitulation, and to represent his professional merits, zeal, and ability in the most favourable light : he even offered to
permit him to alter what he intended to print : he sent him the proofs of the first
two sheets, in which the affair was noticed, and did everything in his power,
and much more than was just to Nelson from his biographer, to soothe and
conciliate him. But nothing would satisfy Captain Foote short of entire con-
demnation of Lord Nelson, and the adoption of his own views and statements
respecting the suspension of the Capitulation. Having quarrelled with Dr. Clarke,
he reprinted his pamphlet with a criticism on Drs. Clarke and M'Arthur's account
of the affairs at Naples, and he added to it the Correspondence which had passed
between him and Dr. Clarke. A perusal of Captain Foote's letters will show the
unreasonableness of his demands, and leave little doubt that *resentment* against
Lord Nelson for having used the epithet "*infamous*," was almost as strong a
motive for writing them, as the vindication of his own character, which, it must
be repeated, was in no way affected by the suspension of the Capitulation, nor by
anything that took place after Lord Nelson arrived.

Though Captain Foote's own letter of the 24th of June [9] shows that no part of the
Capitulation was executed before Lord Nelson arrived, and though he could not
possibly have been ignorant of his Lordship's declaration to the Garrisons on the
25th of June, and though he knew [1] that possession was taken of the Castles on
the *next day*, he has asserted, in a letter to Dr. Clarke, " As I finally left Naples
" Bay on the 11th of July, I was not a witness of the disgraceful scenes that passed,
" though I have been made acquainted with most of them by those who were. I be-
" lieve it is but too true that the Garrisons of Uovo and Nuovo were taken out of those
" Castles under the *pretence* of putting the Capitulation, I had signed, into exe-
" cution," (which after having annulled the Treaty must appear truly singular,) and
" that some of those unfortunate people were treated with very great severity : none
" of them suffered death on board of the British Ships, *but Caraccioli was tried on
" board the Foudroyant, bearing Lord Nelson's flag, by Neapolitan officers !*" [2] In
another letter Captain Foote said—"Although nothing had been done" [before Lord
Nelson's arrival] " in the execution of the terms agreed upon, it was equally binding

---

[7] " Vindication," p. 54.          [8] Ibid., p. 56.          [9] Vide p. 489.
[1] See the Seahorse Log, in p. 494, ante. The Log of the Foudroyant (p. 507, 508)
also proves that the Garrisons were embarked before the 28th of June, on which day
Captain Foote sailed for Palermo.
[2] " Vindication," p. 39. The *italics* are those of Captain Foote.

" on all the contracting parties : the truth, however is, that some parts of the agree-
" ment had been performed, and actual advantage was afterwards taken of those parts
" of the Capitulation that had been executed, to seize the unhappy men who were
" thus deceived by the sacred pledge of a Capitulation, into a surrender of everything
" that can affect a human being, in the most critical moments of his existence." [6]

Captain Foote asks :—" Was he [Nelson] insensible of the powers and attrac-
" tions of female beauty and female accomplishments ? Was he proof against delu-
" sions so attractive ? none of those who knew him can say that such perfection
" made part of his character : he was unfortunately involved in such a delusion ; the
" balance of his mind was lost at a critical moment, and produced certain public
" measures which must be deemed unjustifiable, and even criminal, in the eyes of
" all mankind, not blinded by the important services which he performed for his
" Country. But had Providence been pleased to continue his existence until this
" fatal delusion had vanished, he would have been ready to do justice to the pro-
" priety of the step I took to serve His Sicilian Majesty, and would have
" regretted the unhappy moments that had induced him to hazard the reputation of
" his Country upon so unwarrantable and so despicable a plea as female vengeance,
" aided by female insinuation.[7]

" It is thus that my Vindication is confined to some harsh terms used by Mr.
" Harrison, instead of a complete refutation of everything that can be said in de-
" fence, or in extenuation, of measures directly contrary to common justice and
" the universal law of Nations, admitted and practised by the most barbarous and
" uncivilized communities. What I demand in that Vindication is, not only that
" opprobrious epithets should not be applied to the Capitulation which I had signed,
" but that the blame of a breach of the National faith and honour should attach to
" the person who broke the Treaty, and not to the man who sanctioned it as his
" positive duty required."[8]

Because Lord Nelson had said, in a letter to Lady Nelson, in August, 1799, " that
" much time and great care was necessary to keep the Country quiet," Captain Foote
unreasonably inferred, that " these words, *great care*, demonstrate that it was *now*
" his Lordship's opinion that the violence and injustice with which he had acted in
" respect to the Capitulation of the Castles of Uovo and Nuovo, and Commodore
" Caraccioli, were measures radically wrong." [9]

Of Dr. Clarke and M'Arthur's account of Caraccioli's trial and execution, Captain
Foote said, it was necessary for him to " copy at full length that trial, to show how
" far professional integrity was preserved, either in that trial, or in the execution
" which immediately followed ; and those who recollect that the King of Naples
" was in Sicily at the time of this trial and execution, may observe the unhappy
" infatuation which prompted an English Admiral to a conduct, which, if his biogra
" phers had not been pleased to insert the real orders, which they state as Lord
" Nelson's, the whole account would have appeared incredible."[1]

" Was the Captain of a Ship whose life had been endangered by Caraccioli, a
" proper judge of that man's conduct ? Is it possible that he could be divested of
" prejudice ? Because Lord Nelson was incapable of dishonourable feeling, does it
" therefore follow that he was insensible to the natural propensities of mankind ?
" Even if these questions could be satisfactorily answered, how shall we account for
" the rapidity of the trial and execution ? Does the reasoning of the Authors reach
" the power which Lord Nelson exercised ? If he was invested with the full au-

---

[6] " Vindication," p. 48.  [7] Ibid., p. 66.  [8] Ibid., p. 69.
[9] Ibid., p. 82.  [1] Ibid., p. 92.

" thority of His Sicilian Majesty, that authority ought to have appeared. Shocking
" is this omission, if it could have been produced!  The state necessity for im-
" mediate trial, and still less for immediate execution, cannot be admitted, when the
" King was at Palermo, the Admiral in Naples Bay *with his Fleet*, and the Enemy's
" force in rapid decay.  The special power of pardoning, which is vested in Majesty,
" was superseded, and precluded by the order for execution, issued by the British
" Admiral."[2]

These remarks upon Lord Nelson—the severest that had then appeared, and which
have more or less influenced Southey and all subsequent writers—are in strong
and discreditable contrast with the very last letters from Captain Foote to Lord
Nelson, in the Nelson Papers, (not printed in his "Vindication,")[3] and prevent
the least regret from being felt at the inquiry which must be made into Captain
Foote's own conduct after he knew of Lord Nelson's determination to suspend the
Capitulation.

That Captain Foote acted indiscreetly in his discussions with Cardinal Ruffo—
that he took no measures for informing himself of the terms of the proposed Capitulation, though he was asked to send a person to negotiate on behalf of the British
Nation, but at once assented to whatever the Cardinal and Micheroux proposed—is
manifest from the Correspondence he has printed.  But the grave question, so far
as Captain Foote is concerned, is—*If, in the afternoon of the 24th of June, when
he was told by Lord Nelson that the Capitulation would not then be carried into
effect, or between the 24th and the 28th of that month, when he was a daily witness
of its infraction, he entertained the same opinion of that proceeding as he subse-
quently expressed in 1807 and 1810—did he act as he ought to have done, and as
he might have done ?*

If he did *not* then entertain that opinion, what words would be strong enough to
describe the manner in which he has spoken on the subject in his Pamphlets?
If he *did* then entertain such an opinion, who can doubt the course it was
his duty to have pursued ?  He ought to have represented in firm language to
his Admiral, the obligations he had entered into—that he considered the honour
of the Country, and every principle of good faith, as well as the lives and interests
of many human beings, to depend upon the fulfilment of the engagement; and
he ought to have used every argument, and every entreaty to induce Lord Nelson
to maintain the integrity of the Capitulation.  Should such representations have
failed, it was incumbent upon him to have delivered to Lord Nelson a written

---

[2] "Vindication," pp. 102, 103.
[3] On the 13th of August, 1799, Captain Foote wrote to Lord Nelson from Leghorn :—" The polite and, permit me to take the liberty of saying, friendly treatment
" with which your Lordship has ever honoured me, induces me to tell you in con-
" fidence, that I should be heartily glad if the Seahorse is ordered home, as my
" wife's very precarious state of health," &c.
From off Port Mahon, on the 26th of September following, Captain Foote
acknowledged Lord Nelson's "most kind and obliging letter of the 14th," and begged
his Lordship to thank the King of Naples.  He then said—" I have no other merit
" than the endeavouring to act agreeable to your Lordship's orders and the wish of
" my Sovereign.  I am truly grateful for your Lordship's late directions relative to
" the Seahorse, and your polite conduct to me on all occasions." . . . . I request
" your Lordship will do me the honour to accept my most sincere wishes for your
" health and happiness, and that you will believe me your obliged and faithful
" servant,  EDWARD JAMES FOOTE."—*Autographs*, in the Nelson Papers.

Protest against the violation of the Capitulation; and when everything else proved ineffectual, he ought to have signified his resolution of resigning his Commission, if his name and honour were to be thus compromised. Had he done so, who can say what effect such vigorous acts might have had on Nelson's mind in preventing what Captain Foote afterwards so severely condemned? Such firmness in showing Lord Nelson his supposed error, might have led, indeed, to Captain Foote's arrest, and perhaps to a Court-Martial; but in that case all the facts must have been discussed, and the opinion of thirteen of the oldest Captains in the Squadron obtained. The result, or even the preliminary proceedings, if any formal remonstrance had been made by Captain Foote, would have obliged Lord Nelson to reflect—probably to have consulted Troubridge, Hallowell, Foley, or Ball—and the proceedings which Captain Foote discovered, eight years after, to be disgraceful, might never have occurred.

If Captain Foote made no such representations, must it not be inferred that his opinion at the time was not materially different from Lord Nelson's? while his silence, if not acquiescence, naturally tended to confirm his Lordship in his idea that the Capitulation was open to the objections he had taken to it, and could justly be suspended or rejected.

Captain Foote's conduct respecting the Capitulation is so fully related by himself, that fortunately there is no possibility of misrepresenting it. He saw Lord Nelson in the afternoon of the 24th of June, and was then made acquainted with his Lordship's determination to suspend the Capitulation. What Captain Foote said in the interview, he has himself stated in his " Vindication,"[4] and it consisted only of a justification of his having signed the Capitulation; *but he does not pretend to have uttered one word against its suspension.* On the 26th of June, the day on which possession of the Castles was taken, Captain Foote sent Lord Nelson " a list " of such Officers and men, belonging to the late Republican garrisons of Castel-à- " Mare and Revigliano, who wished to go to Toulon," and said that "the remainder " were still on board a Xebeck, off Procida, those first alluded to being in the Castel " del Nuovo :"[5] he again wrote to Lord Nelson on the 27th,[6] and again on the 28th;[7] but in none of these letters is there a word of dissatisfaction or regret at the infractions of the Capitulation which were taking place under his eyes; nor does he assert that he offered any remonstrance, or took any measure whatever to maintain it.

There is, moreover, another remarkable fact, which it is difficult to reconcile with the indignation expressed on this subject by Captain Foote in 1807 and 1810. It will be remembered that he concluded a Capitulation with the garrisons of Revigliano and Castel-à-Mare on the 15th of June, the terms of which were very similar to those of Uovo and Nuovo, and which having been partly carried into execution before Lord Nelson's arrival, he rigidly observed.

Captain Foote says that, when he came to Palermo on the 1st of July, " The Minister " [Sir John Acton] assured me, that their Sicilian Majesties were very sensible of " the service I had done them in the Bay of Naples. I immediately availed myself " of what appeared to me a favourable opportunity to perform my promise to the " Republican garrisons of Revigliano and Castel-a-Mare, and, at the Minister's

---

[4] Vide p. 494, ante.

[5] " Vindication," p. 142, and *Autograph* in the Nelson Papers.

[6] Recommending and praising Lieutenant Milbanke, of the Artillery, and saying he should have waited upon Lord Nelson, instead of writing, were he not extremely unwell. *Autograph* in the Nelson Papers.

[7] " Vindication," p. 142, and *Autograph* in the Nelson papers.

" request, explained to him the terms of the Capitulation which I had granted;
" frequently observing that the reliance those garrisons had placed in my inter-
" cession, had principally induced them to submit, without the effusion of blood;
" which his Excellence, who well knew the immense strength of Castel-a-Mare,
" must be aware would have been very great, if they had made a determined resist-
" ance. The Minister seemed much exasperated with some of the Officers who had
" composed the garrison of Castel-à-Mare, remarking that they had acted with the
" blackest ingratitude, as they owed even their education to his Sicilian Majesty's
" bounty. I expressed myself very sorry for the circumstance, but observed, that
" when endeavouring to recover a Kingdom, relieve it from anarchy, and the
" dominion of Foreigners, violent measures and personal animosities should be
" avoided; and as their Sicilian Majesties were pleased to think I had rendered
" them some service, I begged, as a *personal favour*, that the Capitulation which I
" had made with these Garrisons might be regarded as sacred. The Minister con-
" cluded by assuring me that on my account the most obnoxious should only be con-
" fined during the then very unsettled state of the Neapolitan dominions. This con-
" versation with the Prime Minister being finished, and every effort in my power having
" been made to fulfil my promise to the garrisons of Revigliano and Castel-à-Mare,
" I only delayed putting to sea, until their Sicilian Majesties had embarked on board
" their own Frigate, the Sirena, which they did on the 3rd of July, to proceed to
" Naples Bay. Accordingly their Majesties sailed from Palermo, under the protec-
" tion of the Seahorse, and reached that Bay on the 8th of the same month, and on
" that very day Lord Nelson was pleased to put the Thalia frigate (commanded by
" his son-in-law, Captain Nisbet,) under my orders, and to send me on immediate
" service, *at some distance from Naples*."[8]

No one can read this statement without asking, why did not Captain Foote make a
similar exertion in favour of the garrisons of Uovo and Nuovo, as he did with respect
to those of Revigliano and Castel-à-Mare ? Captain Foote must have known that
nothing except the King's ratification of the Capitulation with Uovo and Nuovo could
ensure its observance; and that if not ratified, it was only his Sicilian Majesty's
clemency which could save the numerous persons who were in the Castles from
proscription or death. Captain Foote does not, however, pretend to have mentioned the subject to the King, or to his Minister, but he left those Garrisons to
their fate.

To what is this fact to be attributed, and how is it to be reconciled with the
opinions so strongly expressed in the " Vindication ?" One way only presents
itself of accounting for Captain Foote's silence respecting his Capitulation with the
Castles of Uovo and Nuovo, when compared with his strenuous efforts in favour
of his Capitulation with Castel-à-Mare and Revigliano, which is consistent with
his own honour—namely, that he was *then* of Lord Nelson's opinion that the circumstances attending the Capitulation of Uovo and Nuovo were totally different
from those relating to the Capitulation with Revigliano and Castel-à-Mare, and
that his Lordship was fully justified in suspending it. But this does not explain
why the same feeling of humanity which was shown in the one case, did not
equally induce Captain Foote to use his influence with the Sicilian Government on
behalf of the other prisoners, whose lives entirely depended upon its clemency.

These remarks are made with pain, because the subject of them is no more. But
as Captain Foote's observations have influenced every historian, and greatly injured
Lord Nelson's fame, it became necessary to ascertain the true character of Captain

---

[8] " Vindication," pp. 27, 28.

Foote's pamphlet; and to prove that his accuser had little right, after Lord Nelson's death, to censure measures, which, when it was in his power, and when, if he thought them wrong, it was his bounden duty, he made no effort to prevent.

The only other paper written by Lord Nelson on this subject which has been found, is a copy of a letter to Mr. Alexander Stephens, Author of the History of the Wars of the French Revolution, (2 vols. 4to, 1803,) in reply to his application for information :—

TO ALEXANDER STEPHENS, ESQ.

"Sir,                                "23, Piccadilly, February 10th, 1803.

" By your letter, I believe that you wish to be correct in your history, and there-
" fore wish to be informed of a transaction relative to Naples.  I cannot enter at
" large into the subject to which you allude.  I shall briefly say, that neither Cardinal
" Ruffo, or Captain Foote, or any other person, had any power to enter into any
" Treaty with the Rebels—that even the paper which they signed was not *acted* upon,
" as I very happily arrived at Naples, and prevented such an infamous transaction
" from taking place : therefore, when the rebels surrendered, they came out of the
" castles as they ought, without any honours of war, and trusting to the judgment of
" their Sovereign.  *I put aside, and sent them notice of it, the infamous* Treaty, and
" the rebels surrendered, as I have before said.  If you attend to that Mrs. Williams'
" book, I can assure you that nearly all relative to Naples is either destitute of founda-
" tion, or falsely represented.  I am, Sir, &c.,                                "NELSON.

" I must beg leave to warn you to be careful how you mention the characters of
" such excellent Sovereigns as the King and Queen of Naples.  If you wish to have
" any conversation with me on the subject, I shall be at home any morning at 10
" o'clock."[9]

It was the Editor's original intention to have reprinted the accounts given by Southey, James,[1] Captain Brenton,[2] Mr. Alison,[3] Reynault,[4] and Colletta,[5] and other writers, of Lord Nelson's proceedings in the Bay of Naples—to have pointed out the gross errors which pervade their statements, and to have commented upon the spirit in which those authors, and the Naval ones[6] especially, have discussed the subject; but it is hoped that the preceding documents and remarks render it unnecessary to do so.

---

[9] *Copy*, in the possession of the Right Honourable John Wilson Croker.

[1] " Naval History," vol. ii. p. 276—279.        [2] " Naval History," vol. i. p. 480.

[3] " History of Europe," vol. iv. p. 86.

[4] " Criminal History of the English Government."        [5] " History of Naples."

[6] A very creditable effort was, however, made by the late Commander Jeafferson Miles, in 1843, to justify Lord Nelson, by the publication of a little tract, entitled " Vindication of Admiral Lord Nelson's Proceedings in the Bay of Naples," in which he exposed most of the errors of the writers who have been alluded to, with much ability; but having misunderstood the true character of the Capitulation of Uovo and Nuovo, and being necessarily ignorant of what has since been discovered, his defence of its infraction is more zealous than successful.  It is remarkable that the gallant Commander who, with true professional impetuosity, defended Nelson against all his assailants, including Captain Foote, should have missed the most vulnerable part of that Officer's conduct.  Commander Miles' book did him the more honour, as it was the *first*, and then the *only* attempt to stem the torrent of abuse against Lord Nelson, by endeavouring to place the transactions at Naples in a favourable point of view.

One of Captain Brenton's innumerable and inexcusable mis-statements requires however a special notice. He says, speaking of Caraccioli :

"Lady Hamilton, from whose former acquaintance he hoped to gain this favour, "was not to be found, being concealed in her cabin during the interval between the "trial and execution. At the last fatal scene she was present, and seems to have "enjoyed the sight. While the body was yet hanging at the yard-arm of the Frigate, "'Come,' said she; 'come, Bronté, and let us have another look at poor Caraccioli!' "The barge was manned, and they rowed round the Frigate, and satiated their eyes "with the appalling spectacle. I have heard that Lady Hamilton, in her last mo- "ments, uttered the most agonizing screams of repentance for this act of cruelty. "The Prince was ever before her eyes; she could not endure to be in the dark; and "left the world a sad, but useful, example of the fatal effects of revenge and of un- "bridled licentiousness." [7]

Captain Brenton adds to these statements, the exclamation—"May she have "found that mercy which she denied to her enemy!" and observes, "I was "informed, by a person well acquainted with the *dramatis personæ* of this sad "tragedy, that Count Thurn, the President of the Court-Martial, was a Genoese, "and a man of unimpeachable integrity. This I am willing to believe, but who were "the other members of the Court, and what right had that Court to sit on board a "British Ship of War? Why should the British Flag have been made the pall of execu- "tion, but merely to gratify the revenge of a modern Astarte? Soon after the publi- "cation of the first edition of this work, a person signing his name 'John Mitford, "R.N.,' and giving his address, wrote a letter in the *Morning Post*, in which he had "the impudence to declare, ' by Him that liveth for ever and ever' (such were his "words) that the scene of rowing round the Minerva never took place. I called "on this man, but never could find him. I discovered that he lodged over a "coal-shed, in some obscure street, near Leicester square, and that he was *not* an "Officer in the Navy. After this, a friend of mine applied to two other Officers "who were actually present, and are both now living. One of them, whose letter "is by me, says, 'No one believes the absurd story about rowing round the "Minerva, &c.;' but this evasion was flatly contradicted by the other, who admitted "the whole to be true. Would to Heaven, for the honour of my Country, it "was all false! I have been also credibly informed that the Queen of Naples never "quitted Palermo, from December 1798, till June 1800, when she embarked on "board the Foudroyant for Leghorn, and went from thence to Vienna: she was, "therefore, not at Naples with the King, in the summer of 1799. 'It is also a "fact,' says the same authority, 'that she interceded for many of the Rebels, and "saved the lives of some of her personal enemies. Sir William and Lady Hamilton, "and Lord Nelson, also saved many.' I give the above as in duty bound, having "the highest opinion of the integrity of the Lady from whom I received it, and "willing at all times to excuse the faults of frail human nature; but how came the "Foudroyant's cabin to be the scene of the Trial, and how came the British flag "and British cannon to sanction the deed?" [8]

Thus, although, on Captain Brenton's own showing, two out of the three persons to whom he refers denied that such a circumstance ever occurred, and though there was evidence in the speech imputed to Lady Hamilton,—"*Bronté*, let us have another look at poor Caraccioli,"—that it could not be true, inasmuch as Lord Nelson did not

[7] Brenton's "Naval History," vol. i. p. 484.
[8] Ibid., vol. i. pp. 483, 484.

# 522 APPENDIX.

obtain that Title until the middle of August following,[9] yet Captain Brenton persisted in retaining the statement. It is therefore satisfactory to be able to assert, not, like Captain Brenton, on anonymous authority, but on that of one of the most distinguished Officers in the Naval Service, who was then on board the Foudroyant, Commodore Sir Francis Augustus Collier, and in his own emphatic words, that the whole story is " *an arrant falsehood.*"[1]

Upon the authority of a Lady who lived many years with Lady Hamilton, and who scarcely ever quitted her room during the last few weeks of her life, it is now declared, that Lady Hamilton's "screams" and "remorse" about Caraccioli existed only in the imagination of the writer who described them, as she was never known to have mentioned his name !

Even writers of such eminence as Southey, Alison, and Lord Brougham,[2] have

---

[9] So, on coming into Naples on the 29th of June, when Captain Brenton says, " our favourite hero disgraced his Country," and " the high character of England " was blasted by the foul breath of a revengeful woman," he makes Lady Hamilton exclaim, on the quarter-deck of the Foudroyant, "Haul down the flag of truce, " *Bronté*, no truce with Rebels."—Ibid. vol. i. p. 482.

[1] In a letter to the Editor, dated Woolwich, 16th May, 1845.

[2] "Historical Sketches of Statesmen who flourished in the time of George the Third." Second series, p. 70.

It has been thought desirable to insert a

COPY OF THE ORIGINAL LETTER FROM THE KING OF THE TWO SICILIES TO LORD NELSON.

[Autograph, in the possession of the Right Hon. John Wilson Croker. See the Translation in p. 491—493.]

" Ben degno Milord Nelson. Le varie notizie che mi pervengano da Napoli, richidendo una pronta risoluzione e le attuali circostanze di questo Regno, e della mia Famiglia, imponendomi la legge di non allontanarmene per accendere, in qualunque evento alla sua sicurezza e difesa. Vengo a riporre nella valida assistenza delle forze Inglesi sotto il Vostro Comando, tutte le mie speranzi, per il sollecito riacquisto di quella Capitale.

" Bramano i buoni, ed affezzionati, tra quegl' abbitanti, di scuotere il giogo, che loro impose il tradimento : un numero ben grande di questi, non può vedere tranquillamente l'avvicinamento delle forze del Cardinal Ruffo, ed i successi nelle Province, di più Capi insorgenti in favore della Religione, e della Corona, senza accendersi di ugual spirito, e desiderio, di unire i proprij sforzi per lo stesso fine, a quelli dei Provinciali. Non bastano a moderare, il forse prematuro, loro ardore le premure dei miei Uffiziali, perche aspettino i Napolitani l'arrivo delle forze di Linea, che preparo, ed i Soccorsi, che attendo, come vi è noto, dai miei buoni alleati. Affine, di operar d'accordo, maggior accerto, e la massima energia, a libberar il Regno di Napoli dall' oppressione. Sui tali circostanze manifestandosi già l'insur rezzione nella Capitale, devo io evitare il danno evidente, che puol produrre contro tanti fedeli sudditi, il furore dei ribelli. Ho creduto perciò di radunare una forza di Linea, che senza troppo sguarnire questo Regno possa unirsi al Corpo già esistente nelle Isole del Cratere, e secondare la disposizioni, di quel buon popolo, in aspettativa sempre, delle forze estere, che coopereranno all' intiera ripristinazione dell'ordine. Questa misura però, senza l'efficace vostro concorso, e la vostra direzzione non puol conseguire il necessario intento.

' Ricorro perciò a voi Milord, per ottenere l'uno e l' atro, affin che riparato spedita-

not only implicitly believed the statements of Miss Williams and Captain Foote, but they have entirely excluded from their consideration the possibility that Nelson could have acted conscientiously, however erroneously, and they have not hesitated to apply to a man as highly distinguished for humanity, as for his unparalleled services and steady devotion to his Country, the most opprobrious expressions. In their opinion, Nelson's conduct was wrong, and the error was attended with lamentable consequences—*therefore*, he could not have been actuated by a sense of duty but by revenge—he did not obey the dictates of his own mind, or merely err in judgment, but committed a great crime in compliance with the suggestions of a vindictive woman. A more accurate knowledge than has hitherto prevailed of all the circumstances connected with Lord Nelson's conduct at Naples, the fact that he had full authority to suspend the execution of the Capitulation of Uovo and Nuovo, and that he felt it his duty to do so, must prove that he has been unjustly and unfairly treated.

---

mente, se Dio vorra benedire le vostre, e nostre cure, al flagello, che ha provato quel Regno, io possa vedermi in grado, di soddisfare ulteriomente, agl' impegni contratti che mi dettano il dovere, ed ogni raggione. Vi accludo pertanto copia delle instruzzioni, che do ai superiori Generali, e che spedisco, a quelli che nel Continente si rattrovano. Alla testa di questi ho collocato mio figlio, che affido all'amichevole vostra assistenza, perchè i primi di lui passi nella entica attual carriera, che dovrà egli percorrere vengano guidati dai savj Vostri consigli, richiedendovi, di volerlo secondare non solo col potente vostro ajuto, ma di agire principalmente, per essere le vostre forze il vero mezzo ed appoggio in cui io riponga le future mie speranze, come lo sono fin quì state per la mia sicurezza. La mira come osservarete, di riacquistare la quiete, e l'ordine in quel Regno col possesso della Capitale, per mezzo degli stessi suoi abitanti, dediti alla buona causa, non si sarebbe con quell' eventualità, da me in quésto momento abbracciata, se non mi vedessi necessitato ad incoraggire, ed approfittarmi della buona volontà del popolo, con un passo, sollecito, perchè non si raffreddi la di lui disposizione, ne resti vittima del suo attaccamento. La potente e cospicua flotta, con la quale vorrete appoggiare la spedizione, m' induce a lusingarmi di un felice esito, che da essa specialmente dipenderà, ed a credere, che senza frastornare l'operazione maggiore, che avete in costante veduta per l'utilità comune, e per la difesa mia, e della Sicilia, vi parterete come ve lo chiedo, ad unire questo essenziale servizio a quegl' altri importantissimi, che con tanto zelo, e la mia più viva gratitudine, mi avete reso. Mi lusingo pure, che senza danno della Capitale, cederanno i ribbelli, cederà il nemico, che tuttaria vi occupa St. Elmo, alle misure, che si prenderranno. Quando poi, bilanciato, ogni giusto riflesso relativo alla vostra Squadra, ed ai destini, ai quali può per commun bene esser riservata come alle proprie mie circostanze giudicherete necessità, di adoprare la viva, ed estesa forza, per costringere al dovere, e con effetto gl' ostinati oppressori di quel mio popolo, ed estirpare come è urgente, il nido di quei malfattori, vi sarà tenuto, di porre in uso ogni mezzo che meglio tenderà a conseguire quel necessario fine.

"Confido Milord, e ve lo ripeto con piacere, e particolar mia soddisfazione, pienamente, ed intieramente nel sommo zelo, per il mio servizio, e nell' attaccamento alla mia persona, e famiglia, che cosi lealmente mi avete dimostrato con i fatti, per cui vi sono infinitamente grato, e riconoscente. Prego intanto Iddio onnipotente, che vi tenga Milord, e conservi nella santa sua custodia.

"FERDINANDO

"Palermo, 10 Giugnio, 1799."

# D.

## PATENTS, ETC. RELATING TO THE DUKEDOM OF BRONTE.

### Referred to, p. 440.

"FERDINANDUS, Deigratiâ utriusque Siciliæ et Hierusalem Rex, Infans His-paniarum, Dux Parmæ, Placentiæ, Castri, &c., Magnus Princeps Hæreditarius Etruriæ, &c.

" Regiam Majestatem populis Divino munere datam nihil adeò decet, quàm ut summorum hominum præclara facinora, præsertim quæ in humanitatis bonum aus-picatò suscepta, e sententiâ cesserunt, laudibus, honore, præmio, atque omni ho-nestatis officio prosequatur. Id quod, si alio unquam tempore post hominum memo-riam æquum fuit religiosè servari, eo præsertim concilio ut quæ cæteras omnes præcellit auctoritas, miro quodam justitiæ, et liberalitatis lumine præfulgeret; evasit profectò iniquâ hâc tempestate necessarium, in quâ scelestissimi et perditissimi homines Divina humanaque omnia, atque ipsam civilem societatem delere conati sunt.

" Itaque, quùm clarissimi HORATII NELSON, Lord, seu Domini Nili, classis Bri-tanicæ et totius Mediterranei Præfecti, nunquam sine laude nominandi, nautica gesta et gloriam quæ per Universum Orbem increbuerunt maxima, et existimatione simul et admiratione prosequeremur, tum ex illius singulari erga Nos fide, ac vigi-lantiâ, quibus duo hæc Regna ab infestissimo hoste vel defendit vel expurgavit, in eos grati animi et benevolentiæ sensu adducti sumus, cum Serenissimo Bri-tanniæ Rege (cujus ille nutu, et validâ classe è littoribus nostris hostem eliminavit) amicitiam et æquissima pacis fœdera impensiùs obstrinximus, et Illustri Nelson ipsi eximium ac perenne grati animi documentum præbere cupiamus. Ea propter ut tanti Viri meritum decus et gloriam, quæ præclarum illi nomen pepererunt non huic solùm ætati, sed posterorum quoque memoriæ commendemus; Brontes oppi-dum, sive Terra ad Etnæ Montis radices, quod Abbatiæ Sanctæ Mariæ de Mania-chio à nostris Prædecessoribus donatum, ex fundatione et dotatione Regum Siciliæ, Nostro regio juri Patronatûs subjectæ, quodque ex aggregatione præfatæ Abbatiæ per Ferdinandum Regem Catholicum, à magno Panormitano Nosocomio detine-batur (cui peræquivalens excambium providimus) quùm nuper ad manus nostras pervenerit, prædicto Illustri Horatio Nelson pro se suisque Hæredibus de suo cor-pore legitimè descendentibus in perpetuum concedimus terram et oppidum ipsum Brontes, tamquam rem Nostram propriam in hoc Nostro Regno ulterioris Siciliæ, et in Valle nemorum positum, cum omnibus et singulis suis tenementis, et districtu, ac cum feudis, mercatis, fortilitiis, hominibus, vassallis, vassalorumque redditibus, censibus agrariis, decimis, laudimiis, foriscapiis, servitiis, servitutibus, gabellis, do-mibus, et possessionibus, eidem terræ sive oppido adnexis et pertinentibus, et quo-cunque modo, jure, nomine, vel causâ spectantibus, ac cum omnibus juribus, rationibus, justitiis, territoriis, montibus, collibus, vallibus, planis, plateis, silvis, salinis, campis, divisis, pasculis, olivetis, terragiis, vineis, nemoribus, terris cultis et incultis, lapi-cidinis, viridariis, et molendinis, aquis, aquarum decursibus, et saltibus, venationibus, piscationibus, mineriis, et pertimentiis universis, ac usibus, et requisitionibus ad prædictam terram, sive oppidum debitis, et consuetis, seu de jure spectantibus, aliis juribus, immunitatibus, exemptionibus, et gratiis, cum quibus prædictus Præde-cessor Noster Ferdinandus Catholicus concessit et dedit eidem magno Nosocomio oppidum, sive terram ipsam ac cum omni jurisdictione, tam civili quàm criminali

usque ad ultimum supplicium inclusivè, et cum facultate creandi et statuendi Offi-
ciales, prout à cæteris Baronibus feuda populata possidentibus, mos est creari et
deputari. Quam quidem jurisdictionem Nostro motu proprio, ac deliberatè ac con-
sultò, quatenus opus est, confirmamus, et de novo concedimus.

" Quinimò ipsum clarissimum Virum Horatium Nelson, speciali gratiâ prosequi
volentes, merum et mixtum imperium, ac jus gladii in incolas, et indigenas terræ,
et oppidi Brontes antedicti eidem concedimus, et elargimur pro se suisque hæredibus
de suo corpore legitimé descendentibus in perpetuum. Quamobrem terram sive
oppidum prædictum Brontes ac omnem ejus districtum ab omni jurisdictione,
præter quam a Nostrâ Supremâ Potestate segregamus ac penitus eximimus ; appella-
tionem tamen causarum omnium, tam civilium quàm criminalium, ad Nostram
Curiam reservamus juxta usus, leges, et consuetudines Nostri Siciliæ Regni.

" Insuper, ad beneficentiæ Nostræ cumulum, volentes personam prædicti Illustris
Horatii Nelson, sicuti cupimus, honorare, et ad majorem dignitatem et gloriam
evehere et promovere, oppidum sive terram ipsam Brontes, cum juribus et pertinentiis suis, ex certâ Nostrâ scientiâ et plenitudine potestatis, in Ducatum erigimus,
ac de novo de eâdem terrâ, sive oppido, Ducatum creamus, constituimus, et ordi-
namus cum omnibus dignitatibus, privilegiis, præeminentiis, prærogativis, juribus,
et jurisdictionibus, quibus ipsa Ducatûs dignitas gaudet et potiri potest, et debet
dictamque terram, sive oppidum, sic per Nos Ducatum factam, in Feudum honorifi-
cum eidem praclaro Viro Horatio Nelson, damus, et concedimus gratiosè, adeò ut tam
ipse quàm Hæredes, de suo corpore legitimè descendentes, aut ab eo quem ut infra
nominaverit, in perpetuum dicti oppidi, sive terræ Brontes Duces intitulentur, sive
nominentur, ac ab omnibus tractentur et reputentur ; et tam in Comitiis Regni hujus,
quàm in quibuscunque aliis Sessionibus tamquam Duces oppidi Brontes locum obtineat
sive obtineant. Ita quod in eodem Ducatu, oppido, et terrâ sic per Nos, ut ante-
fertur, concessis, Hæredes sui vivant jure Francorum nimirum, ut in successione,
major natu minoribus fratribus, ac masculus fæminis præferatur. Et ad majus
Gratiæ Nostræ testimonium, tam existentibus quàm deficientibus hæredibus de
corpore suo legitimè descendentibus, de certâ Nostrâ scientiâ ac de Nostræ Regiæ
Potestatis plenitudine, facultatem sibi concedimus et impertimur, ut quem voluerit,
etiam extra suam agnationem, vel cognationem, tam directam quàm transversalem
nominare possit, et valeat, cui a Nobis solemnis paritur Investitura concedetur juxta
leges, et capitula hujus Siciliæ Regni, et servatâ, quoad successionem, ejusdem juris
Francorum formâ.

" Præterea volumus, et expressè præcipimus, quoòd ipse Dux Horatius Nelson, et
Hæredes, et Successores sui, ut præmittitur, prædictum Ducatum Brontes in feudum
in Capite à Nostrâ Regiâ Curiâ recognoscant, atque debito nostro militari servitio
teneantur, et sint adstricti secundùm redditus et proventus Ducatûs, ejusdem
juxta usum et consuetudinem hujus Regni Nostri Siciliæ. Quod servitium ipse
Illustris Dux Horatius Nelson in Nostri præsentiâ constitutus, per se, hæredesque
suos et successores, Nobis, Hæredibus, et Successoribus Nostris sponte obtulis
præstiturum, præstito tamen priùs per se Nobis fidelitatis et homagii debito jura-
mento, manibus, et ore commendato juxta formam Sacrarum Constitutionum Impe-
rialium ac Capitulorum hujus Nostri Siciliæ Regni. Remanentibus semper salvis,
et illæsis hujus Regni constitutionibus, ac Capitulis, et præsertim Capitulis Serenis-
simi Regis Jacobi aliorumque Regum Prædecessorum Nostrorum reservatis quoque ;
quæ à præsenti concessione omninò excludimus juribus lignaminum, si quæ sint
in pertinentiis dicti feudi, mineriis novis solatiis, forestis, ac defensis antiquis, quæ
sunt de Nostro Regii Demanio, et ea velut ex antiquo ipsi Demanio spectantia,
eidem Demanio volumus reservari.

"Ad hujus autem Nostra concessionis et gratiæ futuram memoriam, et robur perpetuò valiturum, præsens privilegium fieri jussimus Nostro solito Signo signatum Nostrique Magni pendentis Sigilli munimine roboratum, ac per Illustrem Virum Thomam Jirrao, Lutiorum Principem, Nostri Statûs Consiliarium et Secretarium recognitum.

" Datum Panormi, die $X^o$ Mensis Octobris, Anno à Nativate Domini millesimo septicentesimo nonagesimo nono, Regni verò Nostri anno quadragesimo.

" FERDINANDUS.

" THOMAS JIRRAO."

" COPY OF A LETTER FROM HIS MAJESTY, FERDINAND, KING OF THE TWO SICILIES, TO THE RIGHT HONOURABLE WILLIAM, EARL NELSON.

" Milord,

" Ho veduto la inchiesta che mi avete fatto pervenire per prender possesso del feudo e titolo di Duca di Bronte. Nel tempo che passo gl' ordini per eseguirsi quanto richiedete non posso trattenermi dallo spiegarvi il senso che provo nelrammentarmi i gloriosi servizii che mi ha reso l'Eroico defunto Lord Nelson degno vostro fratello : Vengo di nuovo a parlarvi come suo Germano, ed Erede, della viva riconoscenza, che non cessarò di professargli ed alla di lui memoria. I celebri fatti dal medesimo adempiti dopo il riacquisto del mio Regno di Napoli muovono l'ammirazione, ma l'ultimo gloriosissimo che gli tolse la vita nel deplorare con Voi Milord la di lui perdita, mi rammenta ben anche, la continuazione dei servizii veri che anche l'ultimo singolare e distinta di lui Vittoria rese alla Sicilia particolarmente, come ad altre parti del Continente mentre confermava la gloria del Paviglinone Brittanico alla quale ha egli tanto contribuito.

" Ricevete queste dichiarazioni che v'invio nell, atto, che fo passare tutte le providenze, che mi avete richieste, e con sensibile mio piacere, mentre prego Iddio, Milord Nelson Duca di Bronte che vi abbia nella santa e degna sua guardia.

" FERDINANDO."

"Palermo, 9 Giugno, 1806.

COPIE D'UNE NOTE OFFICIELLE DU PRINCE DE CASTELCICALA A SON EXCELLENCE MILORD VICOMTE HOWICK, SECRETAIRE D'ETAT POUR LES AFFAIRES ETRANGERES.

Wimpole street, ce 11 Octobre, 1806.

" Milord,

" Guillaume Comte Nelson et Vicomte Merton de Trafalgar, en exposant qu'en vertu du Testament de feu Milord Horace Nelson son Frère (d'immortelle mémoire) il vient à succèder au Duché de Bronté dans le Royaume de Sicile, dont Sa Majesté le Roi, mon Maitre, avoit fait concession au dit feu Lord, a demandé à Sa Majesté Sicilienne par une requête presentée en son nom, d'être admis à la jouissance du dit Duché, et qu'on m'authorise à intercéder avec lui près cet auguste Souverain la permission de pouvoir à lui et ses Héritiers prendre le Titre de Duc de Bronté, et jouir de tous les honneurs qui y sont attachés. Sa Majesté Sicilienne, en même tems qu'il a donné ses Ordres de procéder à ce qu'il convient en justice pour la dite succession, m'a ordonné, qu'à la demande du dit Lord je fasse connoitre au Gouvernement de Sa Majesté Britannique ses dispositions favorables pour le dit Guillaume Comte Nelson, et de déclarer que Sa Majesté Sicilienne verra avec plaisir l'acquiescence de Sa Majesté Britannique à ce que le dit Lord désire, relativement à la susdite Concession. Sa Seigneurie m'ayant à present requis de passer les Offices convenables, je m'en acquitte avec beaucoup de plaisir et d'empressement, en ayant l'honneur de m'addresser à cet effèt à votre Excellence, et en la suppliant d'avoir la bonté de prendre les ordres de Sa Majesté pour Sa gracieuse permission.

" J'ai l'honneur d'être, avec les sentimens de la plus haute considération, &c.

" CASTELCICALA."

END OF VOL. III.